The Cambridge Handbook of Workplace Training and Employee Development

With comprehensive coverage of topics related to learning, training, and development, this volume is a must-have resource for industrial-organizational psychologists, human resource management scholars, and adult education specialists. Brown provides a forward-looking exploration of the current research on workplace training, employee development, and organizational learning from the primary point of view of industrial-organizational psychology. Each chapter discusses current practices, recent research, and, importantly, the gaps between the two. In analyzing these aspects of the topic, contributing authors present both the valuable knowledge available and show the opportunities for further study and practice.

KENNETH G. BROWN is Ralph L. Sheets Professor of Management and Associate Dean of the Tippie College of Business at The University of Iowa. He is a fellow at the Society of Industrial and Organizational Psychology, the Association of Psychological Science, and the American Psychological Association. He is also a former Fulbright Fellow at Seoul National University in South Korea and former editor of *Academy of Management Learning and Education.*

The Cambridge Handbook of Workplace Training and Employee Development

Edited by

Kenneth G. Brown

University of Iowa

CAMBRIDGE
UNIVERSITY PRESS

University Printing House, Cambridge CB2 8BS, United Kingdom

One Liberty Plaza, 20th Floor, New York, NY 10006, USA

477 Williamstown Road, Port Melbourne, VIC 3207, Australia

314-321, 3rd Floor, Plot 3, Splendor Forum, Jasola District Centre, New Delhi - 110025, India

79 Anson Road, #06-04/06, Singapore 079906

Cambridge University Press is part of the University of Cambridge.

It furthers the University's mission by disseminating knowledge in the pursuit of education, learning and research at the highest international levels of excellence.

www.cambridge.org
Information on this title: www.cambridge.org/9781107085985
DOI: 10.1017/9781316091067

First published 2018

A catalogue record for this publication is available from the British Library

ISBN 978-1-107-08598-5 Hardback
ISBN 978-1-107-45049-3 Paperback

This volume is dedicated to the life and work of Irv Goldstein who helped so many of us on our academic journeys.

Contents

Figures

Tables

Contributors

Editor

KENNETH G. BROWN is Ralph L. Sheets Professor of Management, Associate Dean of the Tippie College of Business, and professor by courtesy appointment of Educational Policy and Leadership Studies, College of Education, University of Iowa. He is a former Fulbright Specialist at Seoul National University, and has been a visiting professor at Deakin and Monash Universities in Australia.

The Contributors

MARGARET E. BEIER is Associate Professor of Industrial-Organizational Psychology at Rice University.

DAVID B. BILLS is Professor, Emma E. Holmes Faculty Research Fellow, Chair of the Department of Educational Policy and Leadership Studies, professor by courtesy appointment of Sociology, and Faculty Affiliate of the Public Policy Center, University of Iowa.

BRIAN D. BLUME is Professor of Organizational Behavior and HR Management and Interim Associate Director of the Hagerman Center for Entrepreneurship and Innovation, University of Michigan-Flint.

LISA A. BURKE-SMALLEY is Guerry Professor of Management at the University of Tennessee Chattanooga College of Business.

MELISSA S. CARDON is Distinguished Professor of Management and Co-Director of the Faculty Center for Innovative Teaching and Professional Development at Pace University.

SAUL CARLINER is Professor and Interim Chair in the Department of Education at Concordia University in Montreal.

ARNE CARLSEN is Professor in the Department of Leadership and Organizational Behavior at BI Norwegian Business School.

ERICH C. DIERDORFF is Associate Professor of Management in the Driehaus College of Business, DePaul University in Chicago.

JOHN J. DONOVAN is Associate Professor and Director of the Executive MBA Program at Rider University.

ANDERS DYSVIK is Professor in the Department of Leadership and Organizational Behavior at BI Norwegian Business School

J. KEMP ELLINGTON is Assistant Professor of Management in the Walker College of Business at Appalachian State University.

STEPHEN M. FIORE is Professor of Cognitive Sciences, faculty member in the Institute for Simulation and Training, and Director of the Cognitive Sciences Laboratory at the University of Central Florida.

SANDRA L. FISHER is Associate Professor of Consumer and Organizational Studies at Clarkson University.

J. KEVIN FORD is Professor and Associate Chairperson of the Department of Psychology, Michigan State University.

SCOTT E. GRASMAN is Professor and Department Head of Industrial and Systems Engineering, Rochester Institute of Technology. He has been a visiting scholar at University of Navarre and Universitat Oberta de Catalunya, Spain.

JAMIE A. GRUMAN is Associate Professor and Graduate Coordinator of the Organizational Leadership Stream, University of Guelph.

PETER A. HESLIN is an Associate Professor of Management at the University of New South Wales Australia Business School, Academic Fellow of Warrane College and PCI Media Impact, and former Chair of the Academy of Management Careers Division.

MIKE HEWITT is Associate Professor in the Quinlan School of Business, Loyola University Chicago.

GARETT N. HOWARDSON is Founder, CEO, and Principle Work Scientist of Tuple Work Science, Limited. He also serves as an adjunct professor for both George Washington University and Hofstra University.

JASON L. HUANG is Assistant Professor in the School of Human Resources and Labor Relations, Michigan State University.

LAUREN A. KEATING is a doctoral student at the University of New South Wales Australia Business School.

JOSEPH R. KEEBLER is Assistant Professor of Human Factors, Embry-Riddle Aeronautical University.

EDEN B. KING is Associate Professor of Industrial/Organizational Psychology, George Mason University.

KURT KRAIGER is Professor of Industrial/Organizational Psychology, Colorado State University. He is the former president of the Society of Industrial and Organizational Psychology.

CHRISTINA N. LACERENZA is a doctoral candidate in Industrial/Organizational Psychology at Rice University.

ALENA D. MARAND is an Education Analyst for the Vermont Agency of Education and a Research Assistant at the University of Maryland College Park.

SHANNON L. MARLOW is a doctoral candidate in Industrial/Organizational Psychology at Rice University.

VICTORIA P. MATTINGLY is a doctoral candidate in psychology at Colorado State University. She also serves as a talent assessment intern at Amazon.

TRACY C. MCCAUSLAND is Associate Behavioral Scientist at RAND Corporation. Previously, she worked at Booz Allen Hamilton and the Office of Personnel Management.

LYNN A. MCFARLAND is Clinical Associate Professor at the Darla Moore School of Business, University of South Carolina. She is also president and cofounder of Human Capital Solutions, Inc.

GEOFF MORTIMORE is Visiting Fellow, Centre for Higher Education, Learning and Teaching, Australian National University and a Course Leader and Instructor at the Australian Graduate School of Management, University of New South Wales.

JESSICA M. NICKLIN is Associate Professor, Associate Dean of Student Services, and Director of the Online Master's Program in Organizational Psychology, University of Hartford.

RAYMOND A. NOE is the Robert and Anne Hoyt Designated Professor of Management and Human Resources at the Ohio State University.

KARIN A. ORVIS is the Director, Transition to Veterans Program Office within the Department of Defense.

SHARON K. PARKER an ARC Laureate Fellow, a Professor of Organisational Behaviour at the UWA Business School, University of Western Australia and an honorary professor at the University of Sheffield where she was previously Director at the Institute of Work Psychology.

BRADY S. PATZER is a doctoral student in Human Factors at the Wichita State University Department of Psychology.

ROBERT E. PLOYHART is the Bank of America Professor of Business Administration and a Moore Research Fellow in the Management Department of the Darla Moore School of Business at the University of South Carolina.

MIGUEL A. QUIÑONES is Department Chair and O. Paul Corley Chair in Organizational Behavior at the Cox School of Business, Southern Methodist University. He served as a Fulbright scholar and visiting professor at Pontifica Universidad Catolica in Chile, Singapore Management University, and the IE Business School in Spain.

SHAN RAN is a doctoral student in Industrial/Organizational Psychology, Wayne State University.

JASON G. RANDALL is Assistant Professor of Psychology, University at SUNY, Albany.

JANA L. RAVER is Associate Professor and E. Marie Shantz Fellow in Organizational Behavior at the Stephen J. R. Smith School of Business. She is also appointed in the Department of Psychology at Queen's University in Canada.

DENISE REYES is a doctoral student in Industrial/Organizational Psychology at Rice University.

ALAN M. SAKS is Professor of Organizational Behavior and HR Management, Center for Industrial Relations and Human Resources, University of Toronto.

EDUARDO SALAS is Professor and Allyn R. and Gladys M. Cline Chair of Psychology at Rice University. He is a former president of the Society of Industrial and Organizational Psychology and former chairman of the Human Factors and Ergonomics Society.

JESSICA M. WEBB is a doctoral student in Psychology, Michigan State University.

MORGAN SHOWLER is a doctoral student in Psychology, Michigan State University.

MIHA ŠKERLAVAJ is Professor in the Department of Leadership and Organizational Behaviour, at BI Norwegian Business School. He is also Adjunct Associate Professor of Management at Ljubljana, Faculty of Economics in Slovenia.

MICHAEL J. TEWS is Associate Professor of Hospitality Management in the College of Health and Human Development, Penn State.

BARRETT W. THOMAS is Associate Professor and Gary C. Fethke Research Fellow in the Tippie College of Business, University of Iowa. He is currently President of the INFORMS Transportation and Logistics Society.

J. BRUCE TRACEY is Professor and Associate Dean for Academic Affairs in the School of Hotel Administration, Cornell University.

HERMAN VAN DE WERFHORST is Professor of Sociology and Director of the Amsterdam Centre for Inequality Studies, University of Amsterdam.

LINN VAN DYNE is Professor of Management, Eli Broad Graduate School of Management, Michigan State University.

STEPHEN D. VALENTIN is the Assistant Director of Lubin Programs and Services for Career Services at Pace University.

ANTON J. VILLADO is the Chief People Officer of RestaurantOwner.com. Formally, he served as Assistant Professor of Industrial and Organizational Psychology at Rice University

MICHAEL E. WASSERMAN is Associate Professor of Consumer and Organizational Studies, Clarkson University.

JON M. WERNER is Professor of Management at University of Wisconsin-Whitewater.

TRAVIS J. WILTSHIRE is a postdoctoral fellow at the University of Southern Denmark.

GILLIAN B. YEO is Associate Professor of Management and Organizations in the University of Western Australia Business School, and Honorary Associate Professor of Psychology in the University of Queensland.

Grant Wood, Spring In Town, oil on panel, Collection of the Swope Art Museum, Terre Haute, Indiana; 1941.30.

Preface

The cover of this volume was selected purposefully to depict the contrast between an image of rural life in the United States in the early 1900s, captured by Grant Wood in his landscape paintings, and the world we live in today. Wood was an Iowa-born artist inspired by the Iowa farms where he grew up. He was also a critic of cities, publishing *Revolt against the City* in 1935, and a man known for wearing overalls and speaking with a Midwest nonaccent (although he was far more complicated, see Evans, 2010). Best known for his painting *American Gothic*, Grant's art shown here is entitled *Spring in Town*. It was his last painting.

Spring in Town captures a time in the United States when many small rural communities thrived: life centered around church, people worked the land as part of day-to-day life, individualism was celebrated, and technologies in common use were clothespins, pitchforks, and push mowers as well as metal wagons and ladders. Although Wood finished the painting in 1942, the lifestyle immortalized in this painting (and many of his other works) is a mixture of romantic myth and turn-of-the-century reality.

The world today is quite different. Increases in urbanization, technology, work and career specialization (demanding continual collaboration), and demographic and cultural diversity have created lifestyles that intersect more with Ridley Scott's vision than Grant Wood's. In the movie *Blade Runner* (an adoption of Philip K. Dick's *Do Androids Dream of Electric Sheep*), Scott portrays futuristic Los Angeles as simultaneously decaying and technologically advancing. Particularly interesting was the city language portrayed, which was a mix of Japanese, Spanish, German, and English. In the film, Chinese, French, and Korean words were also used (http://bladerunner.wikia.com/wiki/cityspeak). It is not hard to imagine a future where increased globalization results in the blending not just of language but also of cultural traditions and social mores. As a result, the world we live in today is socially and technologically complicated. And it is hard to imagine that the pace of change will slow in the years to come.

The ultimate focus of this book is learning – how people do it, how they could do it with greater effectiveness and efficiency, how organizations benefit from investing in learning, and so on. To me, learning is among the most critical topics for modern society to address. We must wrestle with how to help kids and adults adapt successfully to a complex world that, at times, we may not even fully understand. There is so much we don't know about the future except this one certainly – it will demand that we adapt to ever-changing social and technical landscapes.

Another thing that is clear to me is that no one can tackle this complex world alone; the romantic notion of the rugged individualist is fading even further into historical myth. To be successful, we require help from governments, companies, nonprofit organizations, technological resources, and other people including coworkers, managers, and teachers. And given this multilevel landscape, we will not keep pace without looking beyond one level, one perspective, or one field.

In the design of this book, I deliberately sought contributions from scholars with backgrounds in engineering, education, sociology, and economics as well as psychology. Although in the end I failed to obtain a chapter by a labor economist, the economic point of view nevertheless emerges in a few chapters. And I challenged authors to consider the increasingly complex, global landscape of learning as well as the many levels on which learning operates, beginning with the neurological. The authors took up these challenges, and the chapters offer many different views into the complex world of employee training and development. It is my hope that the chapters, taken together, are worthy of the challenges we face heading into the future.

References

Evans, R. T. 2010. *Grant Wood: A Life*. New York: Knopf.

1 Introduction and Overview

Now More Than Ever

Kenneth G. Brown

Learning is an imperative for individuals, organizations, and societies. And while learning is fundamental to human nature, it is also perplexingly sticky. Lessons learned at one point in time, or in one place by one group of people, do not automatically come to mind or move across individuals and teams (see, e.g., Szulanski, 2003). Added to this stickiness is the increased need for learning and transfer of knowledge. The pace of change, and the profound nature of those changes, will render many jobs and even industries obsolete in the years to come. Technological automation and artificial intelligence, in particular, will completely eliminate some jobs and radically transform others. As just one example, what will transportation and shipping look like 20 years from now? What new jobs must forklift drivers, sorters, and truckers learn when their jobs disappear? The answer is, in part, more complex jobs that require displaced workers to gain knowledge of automation and technology (Cassidy, 2016).

The changes that we face will also be social. With increased immigration and political backlashes to it, organizations will have to be able to adjust to swings in the depth, capacity, and diversity of the labor supply. What miscommunications and conflicts will managers deal with 20 years from now, in an organization staffed with people who grew up in different countries, speaking different languages? In short, the capability for people and organizations to adopt is essential for them to thrive.

Viewed against this backdrop, workplace learning and development is a topic of critical importance. How do employees and the teams they comprise learn? What can organizations do to support and guide them? The chapters in this volume address these questions, and more, from a variety of perspectives. The text is organized into four major sections, as described in the following paragraphs.

Fundamentals Issues in Learning and Transfer

The first section covers fundamentals of learning, beginning with neurological and cognitive foundations. The chapters continue to address fundamental concerns about learning and transfer, at both individual and organizational levels of analysis.

The Kraiger and Mattingly chapter begins this section by reviewing cognitive principles that support learning. They go on to discuss how more recent neurological research fits with what is already known. Research on the brain offers some opportunity to confirm or refute what is already known about learning, but we should recognize that neurological research is heavily dependent on new technologies and new data analytic techniques that are not yet mature. So while there are benefits of studying neurological activity, we should recognize that it is but another perspective and another set of research tools that we should employ.

In the next chapter, Marand and Noe offer a multilevel model of expertise, depicting how expertise, cognition, and other phenomena at lower levels aggregate to create organizational expertise. Because training is often deployed to boost individual-level knowledge, it is critical to understand if, when, and how changes at that level make a difference for organizations. The model offered in this chapter is a great start along that journey.

The chapter by Huang, Ran, and Blume categorizes studies of transfer of training based on whether the changes that occur to the task are anticipated or unforeseen. This review helps connect research on training transfer to an emerging literature on adaptive performance. They conclude with specific suggestions for future research based on this connection.

Howardson, Orvis, Fisher, and Wasserman address the fundamental phenomena of control with learning environments. They develop a multilevel model that details dimensions or components of learner control. Drawing on the distinction between individual and situational forces, the model examines use of control, reactions, learning, and transfer.

Understanding the Learner

The second section is the most psychological in orientation because it focuses on individual differences. Individual difference effects on learning and training outcomes are one of the most studied topics within the training subfield in industrial-organizational psychology since the publication of Noe (1986). Consequently, each of the chapters in this section offers a substantial literature reviews.

Beier, Villado, and Randall's chapter begins this section by discussing cognitive abilities. Although some may consider the central role of abilities in training settled and uninteresting, Beier and her colleagues reveal that the issues on this topic are far from settled. They discuss domain knowledge alongside general and specific abilities, and consider the implications for training design. In addition, this chapter raises the concept of team ability and connects it with research on team skills and performance.

The next chapter, Donovan and Nicklin, addresses the topic of motivation through the perspective of self-regulation. Through a series of figures, the chapter reviews key concepts in this domain, and continues to recommend several directions for future research.

Given the increased diversity of most organizations, the McCausland and King chapter is an important contribution to this volume. This chapter notes that both actual and perceived demographic differences are important constructs to study. Their review discusses diversity along several dimensions, including gender, race, age, disability, religion, parental status, and obesity. The influence of stereotypes is also reviewed, and then three specific research programs are proposed.

Designing the Intervention

In this section, we move to thinking about how trainers and organizations design and deliver effective programs. Included in this section are discussion of formal job-focused training programs, new training methods and media, and leadership development programs.

Tews and Burke-Smalley offer a theoretically based yet practical look at how to maximize transfer under different conditions. The chapter uses a stakeholder accountability matrix that depicts what trainers, trainees, and supervisors should do to create the best possible conditions for transfer.

Ford, Webb, and Showler examine two different types of expertise – routine and adaptive – and examine both training and work experiences that foster their development. This chapter builds on the same foundational literature as Huang, Ran, and Blume, but offers a different set of directions for future research.

Marlow, Lacarenza, Reyes, and Salas discuss theory and practice of simulation-based training. As technology becomes less expensive and more portable, technology-based training is becoming mainstream. No longer just the domain of the airline pilot, simulations are being deployed in health care and management education settings. The chapter offers best practices for building simulation-based training along with suggestions for future research.

The Keebler, Patzer, Wiltshire, and Fiore chapter explores an exciting new technological development – the integration of real and simulated worldviews, which we call *augmented reality*. Although the technology has many possible applications, the chapter reviews research and practice in medicine. The technology has a great deal of promise, and suggestions for future research are presented.

Continuing the technology theme, Wasserman and Fisher's chapter looks at mobile learning. These scholars begin by examining definitional challenges and end with suggestions for future research. Key concerns across phases of the instructional design cycle are noted in ways that are at once thought provoking and useful for those designing mobile learning interventions.

Yeo and Parker examine multiple thinking processes that are facilitated by the availability of free or slack time. The pressure for efficiency is ubiquitous, and it is important to recognize that there are real financial and psychological costs to constantly working. One of these costs, as noted by the authors, is reductions in creative thinking, mind wandering, mindfulness, self-reflection, and perspective taking that benefit personal growth and learning. This chapter suggests that one way to design learning environments is to design work environments that allow for free time.

The Quiñones chapter addresses two major issues at the same time – the need to serve a growing but still underserved demographic population in the United States (Latinos) and the need to create theoretically grounded leadership development programs. Quiñones provides details of a program at the Cox School of Business, and provides preliminary results.

Special Topics

The fourth section addresses an array of important topics including different skill sets that can be trained or different contexts within which such training might occur.

As Cardon and Valentin note, the majority of businesses around the world are small and medium-sized enterprises, rather than the large corporations that so often occupy our attention. Their chapter examines training practices based on the size of the firm and the type of ownership (family firms often show different patterns of practices than other small firms). Although there is both U.S. and international research on the type and effectiveness of training in these firms, which is reviewed in detail, more research is needed.

Dierdorff and Ellington review research on team training. This type of training has been the focus of considerable research over the last two decades, resulting in several meta-analyses. The chapter presents examples of team training outcomes and an extensive set of future research directions in three categories: linking different training tactics to different team outcomes, working beyond the intervention environment, and meeting the new reality of teams.

Raver and Van Dyne present an analysis of empirical studies on the development of cultural intelligence. Cultural intelligence (CQ), the capability to function effectively in intercultural contexts, becomes increasingly central in a world of global trade and diverse labor forces. This chapter reviews in detail 28 empirical studies on the development of CQ, and concludes with the statement that "positive changes in CQ occur as a function of systematic interventions."

Saks and Gruman provide insight into another construct that has emerged in the organizational sciences recently – Psychological Capital or PsyCap. PsyCap is a constellation of individual differences that support positive psychological development. Saks and Gruman both review prior research and provide concrete suggestions for intervention strategies to increase PsyCap; strategies that could be used in stand-alone interventions or in combination with another training program.

The Dysvik, Carlsen, and Škerlavaj chapter examines the concept of systems thinking, and explores how training can have impact along three dimensions – beneficiary, business, and society. The authors extend prior discussion of the systems-wide impact of training by providing this three-part conceptualization. They conclude both that it is possible for training to have broad impacts beyond just on the training participant, and that organizations can and should be thinking about addressing systems thinking in training programs.

Most of the chapters in this section deal with the training of particular content. Heslin, Mortimore, and Keating expose another issue that is important in all training programs – the beliefs and actions of the instructor! Their chapter focuses specifically on two possible roles that instructors may take teaching management in business schools, but the ideas presented are relevant to the work of any trainer or instructor. It is our collective hope that this chapter inspires further research on trainer characteristics and behavior, which we believe to be central to training effectiveness but still understudied.

Workplace Learning from Other Lenses

The final section includes contributions from people who do not constrain themselves to psychological literature, and in fact many would not even describe their work in psychological terms. Authors in this section draw from educational, economic, operations, and sociological perspectives.

Werner examines the field of training across industrial-organizational psychology and human resource development, the latter of which is a field more commonly situated in education. He notes similarities and differences and, in that vein, points to ways in which the psychological study of training might expand and grow.

McFarland and Ployhart adopt a strategic human resource management lens, drawing on strategic management and economic theories to describe the ways by which training programs create competitive advantage. To anyone who has not read economic or strategic management literature, there will be many new terms presented. Understanding this language and the concepts that underlie them are critical for interfacing with strategic decision makers in organizations that determine what is and is not worth paying for.

Tracey is a distinguished scholar in a hospitality school. A parallel human resource literature has developed in these schools, and many large sample studies have appeared in that literature. Tracey summarizes these studies and discusses the connection the industrial-organizational psychology literature.

Like Werner, Carliner writes from an educational perspective. In Carliner's case, the topic is informal learning. The vast majority of what is learned in organizations is learned not through formal programs but through various resources, relationships, and experiences on the job. Carliner provides frameworks and reviews research in this area, and offers insight into yet another way of thinking about learning in organizational settings.

Thomas, Hewitt, and Grasman summarize the operations management perspective on training, which focuses on the connections among people, skills, and production. The mathematical orientation of their perspective, strengthened by their backgrounds in industrial engineering, is what makes this perspective so distinct from the industrial-organizational psychology tradition. As more psychologists embrace mathematical modeling, training researchers may find that the optimization approach of operations scholars, noted in this chapter, is a useful approach.

The final chapter is by Bills and van de Werfhorst, sociologists who examine training-related trends both in the United States and rest of the world, with an emphasis on Europe. These authors help us understand organizational and country-level differences in training practices, putting an exclamation point on the multilevel nature of this volume.

Concluding Thoughts

The chapters work together to provide a broad snapshot of research. I also hope they offer several paths forward, avenues that future research could take to further advance our understanding of learning, training, and employee development.

To the future research directions noted in the chapters, I'd like to add a few meta-themes in the form of recommendation for training scholars: (1) increase interdisciplinary collaborations, (2) adopt explicitly multilevel framework, and (3) conduct research that matters to practitioners.

As these chapters reveal, the study of training is not limited to industrial-organizational psychology. Because scholars from other disciplines have studied who is trained, who learns, and to what effect, research in psychology can be strengthened by drawing on their insights. As just one example, the operations management perspective, explained by Thomas and his colleagues in Chapter 26, suggests that optimization equations may be helpful in making decisions about who to train and when. Many studies in industrial-organizational psychology reveal who learns and whether people learn more from one type of training than another, but do not connect the associated management decision, and other related decisions such as staffing, to profit. When profit is considered in the training field, it is typically done with return-on-investment calculations that indicate whether an investment was worthwhile after costs and benefits are known. Optimization methods provide a concrete tool for modeling what might happen under different circumstances and, in that way, the results could be used to help guide training decisions and integrate more traditional human resource management approaches with the world of operations management.

The world is inherently multilevel. Employees are influenced every day by the organization and teams in which they work, and yet at times we excise those entities from thinking or scholarship because it makes our work easier. I have done this in my own work. Certainly it is not necessary for every study to be explicitly multilevel, but it is important to acknowledge contextual effects in our studies, and to have theoretical models that allow us to understand when and how those effects are likely to occur. Considerable progress has been made in this domain, thanks in part to reviews such as Aguinis and Kraiger (2009) and edited books including Kozlowski and Klein (2000), and we should continue to build on what is known to ensure that our models capture that inherent interconnectedness among levels.

I asked each chapter author to consider the practical implications of the literature reviewed, and where applicable the conceptual model proposed, for decisions made by trainers and managers. The connection between research and practice is not always obvious, and it is certainly not simple. Nevertheless, in an applied discipline like ours, it is incumbent on scholars to consider the practical implications of their work. And, looking at the volume in its entirety, there are many specific recommendations that could be adopted by professionals involved in designing and managing training and employee development programs. So, while the book is not explicitly designed for practitioners, our field is working to create knowledge that is useful, and we should continue to do so.

References

Aguinis, H., and Kraiger, K. 2009. Benefits of training and development for individuals and teams, organizations, and society. *Annual Review of Psychology* 60: 451–474.

Cassidy, W. B. 2016. Automated trucks, warehouses seen transforming distribution. JOC.com, September 14. http://www.joc.com/trucking-logistics/trucking-equipment/automated-trucks-warehouses-seen-transforming-distribution_20160914.html (accessed March 14, 2017).

Kozlowski, S. W J., and Klein, K. J., eds. 2000. *Multilevel theory, research and methods in organizations: Foundations, extensions, and new directions.* San Francisco: Jossey-Bass.

Noe, R. A. 1986. Trainees' attributes and attitudes: Neglected influences on training effectiveness. *Academy of Management Review* 11(4): 736–749.

Szulanski, G. 2003. *Sticky knowledge: Barriers to knowing in the firm.* London: Sage Publications.

PART I

Fundamental Issues in Learning and Transfer

2 Cognitive and Neural Foundations of Learning

Kurt Kraiger and Victoria P. Mattingly

In this chapter, we review both well-established effects and emerging trends in disciplines such as cognitive and instructional psychology, as well as neuroscience, and discuss the implications of these findings for the design of effective learning environments. As such, we draw from the science of learning to inform training researchers and practitioners and thus affect training practice. For convenience, in this chapter we will use the term *cognitive science* to include diverse disciplines outside of industrial/organizational psychology such as experimental psychology, cognitive psychology, instructional design and instructional psychology, and cognitive neuroscience.

We thus differentiate the science of learning from the science of training, a term coined by Salas and colleagues (Salas & Cannon-Bowers, 2001; Salas et al., 2012). The science of training, which is rooted in I/O psychology, refers to best practices and guidelines for designing, implementing, and embedding training (in organizations) based on strong empirical support (Salas & Cannon-Bowers, 2001). The science of training builds on sound training theories and research and advocates guidelines such as the importance of *a priori* needs assessment, boosting trainee motivation to learn, providing opportunities for practice and feedback, removing obstacles from transfer, and conducting purpose-based training evaluation (Salas et al., 2012).

How does the science of learning (which is rooted in cognitive science) differ from the science of training? It is important to note that there is overlap. As one example, both recommend the use of practice, and both recognize the importance of trainee motivation and engagement in the instructional process. However, the science of training is built from the study of what works in training, for example, do training programs that promote self-regulation or encourage learners to make errors result in better outcomes than programs that don't? In contrast, the science of learning is built more on a learner-centric approach, for instance, what is the difference between trainees who learn (effectively) and ones who don't, and how can instruction be designed to foster more effective learning? The science of training embeds the training program in a broader organizational system, and considers the impact on learning of factors before, during, and after training.

Because of our broader systems perspective, which we used when researching this chapter, we ended up focusing more on training principles and less on learner characteristics. Subtopics of learner characteristics are well-covered within this volume, for example, cognitive ability (Beier, Villado, & Randall, Chapter 6), demographic differences (McCausland & King, Chapter 8), and goal orientation (Donovan & Nicklin, Chapter 7), as well as more generally by Wilson, Huang, and Kraiger (2013: 543–564). We do not overlook learner characteristics because they are unimportant, but rather because we believe training researchers and practitioners are best served by understanding the fundamental ways in which most learners are alike, rather than how they may differ based on observable or measurable characteristics. Thus, we primarily focus on cognitive processes involved in learning and, primarily, the translation of research from applied cognitive and instructional psychology theory to principles for the effective design and delivery of training.

Specifically, in this chapter we draw on a broad array of cognitive science research to understand how to better the conditions under which trainees learn, and thus guide practice and research toward the design of more effective instructional environments. To narrow this endeavor, we address three primary questions: how to make training more engaging, how to make training more meaningful, and how to training more effortful (with the understanding that each general strategy results in more effective training). Finally, we discuss emerging trends in cognitive neuroscience that we believe have interesting and important implications for training design and delivery.

Training the Human Information Processor

The Human Information Processor refers to an influential 1989 chapter of the same name by Bill Howell and Nancy Cooke. Howell and Cooke (1989: 121–182) ushered in the modern era of training theories by introducing training scholars to basic research on both human cognition and artificial intelligence and their relationship to learning and transfer. Howell and Cooke's chapter served as an inspiration to Kraiger, Ford, and Salas's (1993) transformative monograph, which emphasized the importance of cognitive and affective outcomes beyond merely behavioral ones as the intended results of training. This in turn has given rise to more than two decades of research on topics such as enhancing trainee self-efficacy, mental models, and self-regulation during instruction.

Due largely to the influence of behaviorists such as B. F. Skinner, instruction and training was dominated for more than four decades by a conceptualization of learning as changes in overt behavior. For example, Gagné (1965) explicitly claimed that there must be a change in performance to conclude that learning occurred. While behavioral change is a pillar of modern training models (e.g., Kraiger et al., 1993), an overreliance on observable behavior is deleterious for several reasons. First, adhering to behavioral instructional objectives sometimes creates disconnects between the stated learning outcomes and what is the true goal of instruction. For example, the Sunday school teacher who states that "Given a list of the 10 commandments, the student will correctly identify the 7th one" has created a measurable, behavioral objective, but what he or she really wants is for her charges to know that stealing is morally wrong. Second, the goal of many training programs is for trainees to do (or know) the right thing at the right time whether or not they can behaviorally reproduce skills immediately after training (e.g., preflight instruction on an airliner). Third, and most importantly for present purposes, a focus on behavioral reproduction as a training criterion ignores many important mental events that we know are necessary for learning (of any form) to occur.

Learning as a Cognitive Process

Given what we know from cognitive science about learning processes, what then is learning? Most definitions within I/O psychology frame learning in terms of the attainment of learning outcomes. For example, Salas et al. (2012: 77) stated that "Learning is a desired outcome of training when one acquires new knowledge or behavior through practice, study, or experience." Similarly, Kraiger et al. (1993) defined learning as a relatively permanent change in affect, behavior, or cognition. Such definitions describe the outcomes of learning but not learning itself. Further, they are not particularly helpful for defining training or instruction; those would be simply anything that facilitates progress toward defined outcomes.

We prefer a definition of learning that more clearly articulates what is happening as the learner transitions from "not knowing something" and "knowing something." (Here, we focus on "knowing" while acknowledging a broad array of possible learning outcomes including noncognitive ones.) Alexander, Schallert, and Reynolds (2009) defined learning as a multidimensional, dynamic process that produces an enduring change as a result of the relationship "between the nature of the learner and the object of the learning as ecologically situated in a given time and place as well as over time" (186). Another definition that incorporates both end states and transitional processes is offered by Mayer (2008), who defined learning as: "a change in the learner's knowledge that is attributable to experience … [and] depends on … cognitive processing during learning and includes (a) selecting – attending to the relevant material; (b) organizing – organizing the material into a coherent mental representation; and (c) integrating – relating the incoming material with existing knowledge from long-term memory" (761).

What does Mayer's (2008) definition gain us? Foremost, we have insight into the mental processes that are necessary for change (in knowledge, affect, or skill) to occur. Learners must first be aware of or attend to training stimuli. We want them to pay attention to the same content we deem important, and not be distracted by less important information (e.g., incoming texts, thoughts about tomorrow's workload). Next, they must manipulate that information to facilitate transfer to more permanent memory. This involves at a minimum simply holding information in working memory long enough for consolidation to occur (as opposed to "in one ear ... ") but ideally they actively process the information so that it becomes meaningful to them and more easily stored and later retrieved. Finally, they must integrate new information with what they already know, thereby facilitating transition to long-term memory. This can be done both cognitively (e.g., relate one new fact to an existing knowledge structure) and behaviorally through practice in situations like those to be encountered on the job.

In addition, this definition of learning specifies more precisely what is effective training. Effective training is anything that facilitates learning by helping trainees select, organize, and integrate new knowledge, skills, and affect to improve later job performance. In subsequent sections, we review cognitive science research relating to making training engaging, meaningful, and effortful. These three goals roughly map onto the instructional intent of helping trainees select, organize, and integrate new information.

Also, this definition of learning helps us identify what can go wrong in a training environment. Training fails when the conditions are such that learners fail to select, organize, and integrate the correct information. For example, research summarized by Dunlosky et al. (2013) made the case that learners generally are very bad at managing learning environments. For example, they tend to pay attention to the wrong cues and overestimate their ability to focus on instructional content while multitasking (selecting). Advanced organizers are one strategy by which training can help learners select and organize critical information (Mayer, 1979). In a classic study by Bransford and Johnson (1972), learners who received information about the relevant context (for the training content) *before* reading the content learned better than did a control group or who received no pretraining guidance at all. Finally, conditions of practice are often such that information is learned in a way that it is difficult to recall appropriate skills at a later time. For example, Schmidt and Bjork (1992) reviewed multiple studies in which the absence of stimulus variability during practice (which would most likely occur on the job) accelerates initial skill acquisition, but retards performance in transfer environments.

While a full review of ineffective learner (and trainer) practices is beyond the scope of this chapter, the preceding paragraph makes the point that if training is not properly designed and managed, learning is likely to be suboptimal. In subsequent sections, we discuss empirically supported practices for optimizing learning during training. Specifically, how can we make training more engaging, meaningful, and effortful to maximize learning outcomes? Table 2.1 provides a summary of the points to follow.

Make Training Engaging

Mayer (2008) argued that the first step in the learning process is for learners to "select" or attend to relevant learning information. From a pedagogical perspective, manipulating the instructional environment so that the learner

Table 2.1 *Designing effective learning environments by applying cognitive and neural science to training design and delivery*

Category	Actions	Outcome
Make training engaging	Ensure that learners "select" or attend to relevant learning information	Learners are cognitively, physically, and emotionally immersed in both training content and learning processes
Replicate the transfer domain	Incorporate the physical and psychological context into the training environment	Transfer is more likely to occur because the content was learned in a similar context to the working environment
Capitalize on the spacing effect	Distribute the training program over multiple sessions; segment training content	Training content will be better encoded and retrieved if presented across multiple sessions compared to one session
Provide feedback	Offer ongoing, elaborate, and future-oriented feedback	Learners are provided with a clear direction to improve later performance, which in turn enhances learner motivation
Make training meaningful	Organize incoming information to build upon appropriate cognitive structures	Training content is more likely to transfer to long-term memory because it builds upon previously known information
Reduce cognitive load	Lessen the amount of resources required by learners to consume training content	Learners can focus more on the most relevant training content as opposed to being distracted by unimportant stimuli
Provide meaningful examples	Provide relevant examples to demonstrate the necessary steps to execute a task or problem solve	Learners will be more likely to compare examples and understand commonalities across multiple contexts
Enhance coherence	Limit the amount of unnecessary material included within training content (e.g., cartoons)	Extraneous processing will be reduced to enhance immediate learning by enhancing short-term memory retention
Offer signaling cues	Highlight essential material to make it distinct from less relevant material	Learners are more likely to deeply process the most important training content
Utilize temporal contiguity	Present corresponding words and graphics simultaneously, not in succession	Less effort is required for learners to integrate the text with the graphics, so more processing can be devoted to the content

(*cont.*)

Table 2.1 (*cont.*)

Category	Actions	Outcome
Provide pretraining guidance	Provide the names, locations, and functions of key elements in advance of more complex training	Learners will use more cognitive energy on understanding systems and procedures
Personalize content	Use collaborative learning platforms, first- and second-person narratives and personable language	Learners will relate to personalized content in a more meaningful way compared to how they would process lists of facts and procedures
Incorporate visuals	Integrate simple yet informative graphics to convey relevant information	Reduce germane load and provides the learner with relevance of the material to tasks to be performed
Make training effortful	Encourage learners to make effortful cognitive and behavioral connections between training content to prior knowledge and future applications	Ensure that long-term learning occurs by helping the learners retain and access information in future applied settings
Provide opportunity for practice	Provide opportunities for learners to apply training content to well-designed practice activities	Promote both recall and application of the learned knowledge and skills to real-world tasks, thus enhancing long-term retention
Interleave training content	Intersperse practice activities from previously learned topics throughout training modules	Learners will have to retrieve prior information from long-term memory, thus increasing the likelihood of deeply encoding content
Use practice variability	Require learners to engage in a variety of iterations of a practice activity, varying conditions across trials	Learners will be more likely to transfer training content to novel contexts
Test learners' knowledge of content	Have trainees answer test and quiz questions to assess what they learned in training	Testing learners will increase their retention and retrieval of the training content, thus improving overall learning
Apply established neuroscientific findings	Although in its infancy, some neural underpinnings of learning have been identified (e.g., sleep)	Learning can be enhanced by integrating best practices from neuroscience to capitalize on how our brains best function
Allow for sleep consolidation	Allow consolidation effects using sleep to occur by spreading out training over multiple days	Newly learned information will be better stored and retrieved after being reactivated and reorganized into new representations

Table 2.1 (*cont.*)

Category	Actions	Outcome
Encourage trainees to get adequate sleep	Structure the work and training environment to support good sleeping habits	Getting sufficient sleep can enhance motor skill performance, language acquisition, and learning declarative knowledge
Use breaks to increase attention of trainees	Strategically implement breaks or low cognitive load activities to allow for a resetting of attention	Voluntary attention reflects direct control of cognitive resources to attend to stimuli long enough to aid in transfer to long-term memory
Reduce the occurrence of distracting stimuli	Minimize irrelevant stimuli unless it is to provide cognitive breaks for learners' retention and retrieval of the content	The brain can focus its energy on learning and remembering the most relevant content to the training, thus reducing unnecessary cognitive load

engages in the relevant content is thus critical to facilitating learning. Both theory and research suggest that learners should be engaged in the learning process to maximize their learning (Bell & Kozlowski, 2008). Borrowing from the organizational psychology literature, engagement can be defined as a personal investment or absorption of the self into work-related tasks (Kahn, 1990). Extending this to the training domain, we define learner engagement as the extent to which learners are cognitively, physically, and emotionally immersed in both training content and learning processes.

Learner engagement matters because considerable research shows that deeper processing of training content facilitates later recall and/or application (Craik & Lockhart, 1972). Dunlosky et al. (2013) speculated that "intentionality" on the part of learners promotes deeper processing that in turn enables learners to extract more meaning from materials. Learner engagement also promotes self-regulation (Schunk & Zimmerman, 2012). Self-regulated learners are able to monitor learning activity and adjust proximal goals, effort, and behavior to accomplish more distal learning goals.

The importance of capturing and maintaining the interest and the energy of learners has been long recognized. For example, one of the founders of modern instructional design theory, Robert Gagné (1965), referred to the "first event of instruction" as gaining learner attention. That is, Gagné recognized that instruction cannot occur unless the trainer first has the attention of the learner, who then becomes engaged in the process. Additionally, Herb Simon (1998), one of the first psychologists to study learning from a cognitive perspective, reflected on nearly 50 years of research and concluded that making the learner an active partner is the single most important act of instruction.

Clark and Mayer (2008) distinguished between two types of engagement – behavioral and cognitive engagement – and argued that learning is optimized when both are high (although they also argue for the relative importance of cognitive engagement over behavioral). Behavioral engagement simply refers to acting upon training content – reading text and practicing skills are two forms of behavioral engagement. Cognitive engagement refers to mental activities that promote understanding, organization, and integration. Including learner-focused activities (e.g., questioning, elaborating, and explaining the training content) can enhance behavioral and/or cognitive engagement (Clarke, 2014). For example, learners who ask themselves questions such as "Why is this important for me to know?" or "How is this related to the training objectives?" are more likely to master training content than learners who don't. Thus, trainers should build in time to encourage learner reflection.

The combination of behaviorally and cognitively active learning environments works best when engagement activities share four properties: (1) they do not impose undo cognitive load; (2) they require behavioral responses similar to those required in the transfer domain; (3) they include spaced practice (see following text); and (4) they include explanatory feedback (Clark & Mayer, 2008). We talk about the importance of reducing cognitive load within the subsequent section on making training meaningful, so we will instead focus on how the transfer domain, spaced practice, and feedback can be used to increase engagement in the following text.

Replicate the Transfer Domain

Behavioral engagement can be enhanced by incorporating the physical and psychological context of the transfer environment into the training experience (Clark & Mayer, 2008). In other words, the training context should replicate the transfer context (i.e., the working environment in which what was learned during training will be applied) as closely as possible.

Capitalize on the Spacing Effect

Spacing out training activities over time, as opposed to massing all training into one session, increases trainee engagement by enhancing long-term retention (Clark & Mayer, 2008). Also known as distributed practice, the spacing effect occurs when learning is spread out over multiple intervals, resulting in better memory and retrieval in comparison to learning in one massed session. Evidence demonstrating the benefit of segmenting studying over multiple sessions dates back to 1885 and has been since reliably demonstrated in hundreds of studies (see Cepeda et al., 2006). The spacing effect has been found to be one of the most "dependable and replicable phenomena in experimental psychology" (Dempster, 1988: 67).

Spaced learning works because it capitalizes on the fundamental memory mechanisms of encoding and retrieval. Multiple exposures to the same learning material increases the number of retrieval pathways created (Glenberg, 1979). The same material is encoded not only more often, but also can be linked with multiple cues due to the variations in temporal, physical, or mental contexts (Estes, 1955). Sisti, Glass, and Shors (2007) found that spaced-trial trainings resulted in newer cells being more likely to survive in the hippocampus, which resulted in more persistent memories of spaced versus massed training materials. The spaced training allowed for brain cells to regenerate between study sessions, which resulted in more permanent neural connections and stronger memories, resulting in increased learning. As resources do not often allow for training to be broken down into multiple sessions, trainers can capitalize on the spacing effect by integrating practice activities throughout a training session, as opposed to administering all practice activities at the end. Whenever possible, training should occur over multiple sessions to not only increase engagement but also overall performance, as research shows that when learning is spaced, performance is better when compared to learning in one massed session (Baddeley & Longman, 1978).

Provide Feedback

Trainees should be provided with thorough and ongoing feedback as another means to enhance engagement with training content. The general effectiveness of feedback on performance has been confirmed through several meta-analyses both in terms of work performance (Kluger & DeNisi, 1996) and computer-based training (Azevedo & Bernard, 1995). Applied cognitive and instructional psychology research reveals specific ways in which feedback during practice can be optimized. Responses to practice should be provided in such a way that facilitates better performance in the future – it should be more feed "forward" rather than feed "back" (Clark, 2014). Research also shows that elaborative feedback, as opposed to only being informed that one's work is merely correct or incorrect, results in better learning outcomes (Azevedo & Bernard, 1995; Moreno, 2004). Feedback should also be provided after each step when learners are engaged in complex practice activities. Compared to providing feedback only at the end of the activity, step-by-step feedback can result in better learning and more trainee motivation (Corbalan, Paas, & Cuypers, 2010). Therefore, learners should be provided with detailed feedback as they complete their practice activities.

Summary

Training programs should be designed to maximize trainee engagement with the content. Engagement results in deeper processing during training and, by consequence, facilitates later recall and greater likelihood of posttraining applications.

There are several strategies that can be applied to enhance the cognitive, physical, and emotional immersion of trainees. First, the transfer domain should be replicated as closely as possible to the working environment where the training content will be applied. Second, training programs should be spaced out over time instead of being lumped into one singular session as a way to increase long-term retention of the training material. Lastly, trainees will be more engaged with the learning process if provided with clear and timely feedback throughout training. We will now discuss the significance of meaning on learning outcomes, as well as present explicit strategies that can be applied to make training more meaningful for participants.

Make Training Meaningful

The second phase of learning is organizing incoming information in way that builds appropriate cognitive structures to facilitate transfer to long-term memory (Mayer, 2008). The role of instruction then is to prime the appropriate cognitive processing in learners, helping them to form coherent cognitive representations and integrate new representations with what is already known, including how the new knowledge or skills will be applied back on the job. This is also referred to as generative processing, in which the learner imposes structure on part based on what is already known (Sweller, 1999). The more training content is meaningful to learners, the more likely they are to organize new information in meaningful ways.

Reduce Cognitive Load

Empirical and theoretical reasons for the importance of making training meaningful rest largely on reducing cognitive load during instruction. Cognitive load can be thought of as the sum of total press on a learner, given the cognitive resources of that learner (Chandler & Sweller, 1991). There are three types of cognitive load: intrinsic, extrinsic, and germane. Intrinsic load is related to the difficulty of the material, and while difficult content can sometimes be broken down into smaller chunks, intrinsic load is primarily a function of the tasks to be trained, not instructional design.

In contrasts, extraneous and germane load are directly related to training design. Germane load is related to the level of (useful) mental effort devoted to processing, constructing, and automating cognitive structure or schema in working memory. As a simple example, germane load for a difficult learning task can be reduced by highlighting key words, the use of graphics, or providing learning heuristics (e.g., "Every Good Boy Does Fine"). Conversely, germane load for a simple task can be increased by reducing presented content and making learners generate their own definitions or examples. Extraneous load is created by the way in which material is presented to learners, requiring superfluous processing on the part of the learner. Training segments that run too long, or training slides that contain irrelevant or misleading information are examples of extraneous load. In general, instructional design that reduces extraneous load and optimizes germane load is more effective than training that does not (Merriënboer & Sweller, 2005).

When the training in meaningful to learners, extraneous load is reduced. For example, if the equipment used to train a new skill is identical to that used on the job, then learners can focus on skill acquisition, and devote fewer cognitive resources to processing the differences between equipment in training and equipment used in the job. The use of unfamiliar jargon and acronyms can also create extraneous load, and when trainers cannot avoid the use of jargon, having an easily accessible glossary is one strategy for minimizing deleterious effects.

Provide Meaningful Examples

One well-supported strategy for reducing cognitive load is the worked example (Renkl, 2005: 229–245), in which the trainer demonstrates solving a problem step by step to complete a task or solve a problem. Worked examples reduce extraneous load by the use of scaffolding earlier steps – learners are presented with only the information they need to solve the next step. Germane load can be managed by prompting learners for self-explanations of actions at key steps, focusing their attention (through prompts) of what they did right and what led to errors in execution.

As suggested in the preceding text, examples are an effective way to make training meaningful. Examples should not only be relevant to the tasks performed on the job, but should demonstrate the steps necessary to execute a task or solve a work-related problem. Clark (2014) listed other characteristics of effective examples: (1) for strategic tasks, the examples should be set in a variety of contexts; (2) use more worked examples for novice learners and practice assignments for experience learners; and (3) increase learner engagement related to the examples by using faded examples (gradually reducing the number of steps described), adding self-explanation questions required of learners, and require learners to compare examples to understand commonalities and differences across contexts.

Enhance Coherence, Offer Signaling, and Use Temporal Contiguity

Mayer (2008) summarized several evidence-based and theoretically grounded principles for reducing extraneous processing and increasing essential processing by learners during training. While several of these apply more to the design of computer-based learning environments, others apply to any form of instruction. Three key principles for reducing extraneous processing are coherence, signaling, and temporal contiguity. The coherence principle states that extraneous material should be reduced in training content; a common example of extraneous material is a cartoon or humorous graphic on a presentation slide. While humor can help with long-term learner engagement, in the short term, it can create extraneous processing and reduce immediate learning. The signaling principle states that essential material should be highlighted to separate it visually or orally from less essential material. A common signaling technique used by effective speakers (and parents!) is to lower one's voice in advance of the most important information. Finally, the temporal contiguity principle states that corresponding words and graphics should be presented at the same time, not in succession. For example, in a web-based statistics course, the formula for the slope of a line-of-best-fit should be given on the same slide that illustrates that line.

Provide Pretraining Guidance

Two key empirically supported principles for encouraging essential processing are segmenting and pretraining guidance. Segmenting is simply breaking up larger presentations into shorter, learner-paced segments. While segmenting can be difficult in classroom training, it is more readily accomplished in either online, one-on-one, or on-the-job training. Segmenting is one form of guidance. Another form, pretraining guidance, presents learners the names, locations, and functions of key elements in advance of more complex training. We would suggest that pretraining guidance can take the form of a training prerequisite, training prework, refresher training within training, or sequencing content within training so that fundamental declarative knowledge precedes advanced procedural knowledge.

Personalize Content

Finally, Clark (2014) advocated for two additional techniques to promote meaningful learning. The first is to personalize content. While we think of personalized learning as being primarily related to one's job, personalized learning is also accomplished through the use of simple techniques such as use of first- and second-person language, collaborative learning platforms including discussion boards (see following text), an engaging or personable voice by the trainer, and training content that takes the form of a narrative or story more than a listing of facts and procedures (Ginns, Martin, & Marsh, 2013). While many successful trainers intuitively understand the importance of being personable, it is useful to note that such a style is also empirically supported.

Incorporate Visuals

The second of Clark's (2014) additional techniques to promote meaningful learning is the use of effective visuals. Visuals can reduce germane load and also provide the learner with relevance of the material to tasks to be performed (Butcher, 2006). The importance of visuals is reinforced by considering the number of home do-it-your-selfers who ignore text-based assembly instructions to instead watch narrations online. Consistent with the goal of reducing extraneous load, visuals should generally be as simple as possible to convey relevant information. The most obvious form of a useful visual or graphic is one that illustrates stimuli to be acted on, or actions to be taken. For example, in a word-processing class, a screenshot can be shown with key menu functions highlighted. A second useful form is an explanatory visual. Explanatory visuals are relatively simple graphics that show static or dynamic relationships among elements. One type of an explanatory visual is an organizational one, for example, including an organization chart during socialization to help newcomers understand their position within the organization. A relational visual summarizes quantitative information in a meaningful way; for example, a pie chart of the amount of the earth's surface covered by land versus water creates a clear understanding of how vast are our oceans. Transitional visuals can either be animated or simply a series of steps, for example, a flow diagram showing the steps a researcher must follow to get internal review board approval.

Summary

In sum, once learners are engaged and attending to the relevant training content, the goal of training is to increase the processing of essential content, and minimize processing of extraneous content. Principles of cognitive load, increasing the perceived relevance of training, the personalization of training delivery, and the use of effective visuals all support these objectives.

Make Training Effortful

The goal of training is not to simply present engaging, meaningful material to a trainee, but to also employ methods that help the trainee retain and access information later on in an applied setting. This relates back to the integrative step of Mayer's (2008) definition of learning. Learners should make cognitive and behavioral connections between the training material to prior knowledge and future applications. In other words, training should be effortful to ensure that long-term learning occurs. Learning activities should consist of "desirable difficulties" that require the learner to actually *work* toward mastery over material (Bjork, 1994: 185–205). By rigorously using the knowledge and skills presented in a training program, stronger encoding and retrieval pathways will be created when compared to engaging in more passive learning activities (e.g., listening and reading). One way to increase learner effort is through carefully designed practice conditions.

Provide Opportunity for Practice

To make training material stick, learners should be provided with ample opportunities for practice (Salas et al., 2012). Practice is defined as a well-designed activity assigned to promote both recall of the training content and, more importantly, application of the learned knowledge and skills to real-world tasks (Clark, 2014). Drawing from cognitive-neuroscience, practice aids in mastery over training material due to long-term potentiation. Long-term potentiation is the repetitive activation of synapses caused by activity- and experience-dependent learning. The increased synaptic strength that results restructures neural circuitry, which explains how memories are created and stored at the molecular level (Bear, Cooper, & Ebner, 1989: 156–160). In other words, the more often one engages with the training stimuli, the more likely it will be stored in long-term memory.

Practice activities should replicate how the training material will be used on the job (Baldwin & Ford, 1988). According to transfer appropriate processing theory, content is most likely to be remembered when encoding and retrieval processes are as similar as possible (Morris, Bransford, & Franks, 1977). Greater similarity between training conditions and performance conditions is also referred to as near (rather than far) transfer (Clark & Voogel, 1985). Therefore, it is important to make practice activities as realistic as possible. Several recommendations for improving near transfer include increased specificity about where and how the training will be used on the job, overlearning of the task, and emphasizing procedural knowledge and skills to be utilized on the job throughout training (Clark & Voogel, 1985).

Beyond ensuring near transfer, the extent to which practice in training results in successful transfer can depend on training design factors (Hesketh, 1997). The science of learning has informed us of several empirically supported methods we can apply to make practice activities as effective as possible. These techniques include interleaving learning, practice variability, and providing feedback.

Interleave Training Content

Practice activities covering all previously learned topics should be interspersed throughout training modules. As opposed to covering the material related to one topic in a blocked practice session before moving onto another topic (which we know is not effective, as discussed in the Capitalize on the Spacing Effect section), interleaving is a method that exposes learners to a variety of material by switching between topics throughout the session. Interleaving works because it requires information to be retrieved from long-term memory, whereas blocked practice allows information to remain in working memory with the risk of never being encoded into long-term memory in the first place (Rohrer & Taylor, 2007). Empirical support for interleaving was found when students in an interleaved-practice group had substantially better accuracy compared to those in a blocked-practice group (Taylor & Rohrer, 2010). It is important to note that accuracy was assessed by a criterion test administered one day after the practice took place (the blocked practice group performed better during the practice), demonstrating the positive effect of interleaving on long-term memory.

Moreover, interleaving can help promote transfer of the training material as it is more likely that the trainee will have to switch between a variety of tasks on the job as opposed to tackling a problem by applying only one skillset at a time. Therefore, when designing practice activities, exercises covering a variety of topics should be delivered throughout the training, as opposed to only providing module-specific practice activities.

Use Practice Variability

One way to create engagement and aid retention is through low stakes quizzes or testing. Trainees should be tested on training material, and tested often. Learners have been found to have better retention of learned material after being tested on that material as opposed to simply restudying it, otherwise known as the testing effect (Roediger & Karpicke, 2006). The testing effect works because it capitalizes on the retrieval process of memory (Rohrer, Taylor, & Sholar, 2010). Retrieval plays a dynamic role in learning insofar that the more often information is retrieved from long-term memory, the easier that information will be remembered at a later time (Bjork, Dunlosky, & Kornell, 2013).

Another way in which trainees are exposed to different types of stimuli is through practice variability. Practice variability occurs when the conditions of practice vary substantively across trials. For example, a novice tennis player who is learning a backhand experiences practice variability if, instead of receiving 100 consecutive shots in the exact same place and requiring the exact same motion, instead must move in and out, side to side, and practice multiple versions of the same motion in response to different stimuli. It has been well-established that practice variability slows initial skill acquisition, but promotes effective transfer to novel tasks (Schmidt & Bjork, 1992), which is often the objective for training. It appears that with reduced variability, there are insufficient processing (effort) demands on learners to properly facilitate long-term learning (Wulf & Shea, 2002).

Test Learners' Knowledge

Dunlosky et al. (2013) reviewed several empirically supported techniques for increasing learner engagement, including quizzes, tests, and clickers. Dunlosky et al. distinguish practice tests from more formal periodic assessments of learner mastery (e.g., end of training exams). Practice tests and quizzes show relatively strong effects on subsequent learning, although the mechanisms by which they work are not completely clear. Practice tests seem to result in both direct and mediating effects. Direct effects suggest that the act of taking the test enhances subsequent retrieval processes, for example, triggering more elaborative retrieval. Mediating effects suggest that testing may trigger better organization and storage of tested material, which in turn facilitates later retrieval (see Dunlosky et al. for an overview). Regardless of the mechanism, practice tests increase active engagement by learners which improves retention and retrieval. Multiple studies have shown that learners who respond to questions during training using clickers demonstrate better learning outcomes than learners who do not respond, or do not have access to clicker technology (e.g., Mayer et al., 2009).

Summary

Training should be designed is such a way that learners should take an active approach to their learning. The more trainees work at applying the knowledge and skills taught during the training, the better they will remember this material and use it for better performance on the job. Trainers can incorporate these desirable difficulties which capitalize on encoding and retrieval processes by building practice and testing activities into training programs. Practice and testing allows learners to spend more time on the output side of learning, rather than the input side (Bjork & Bjork, 2011: 56–64), resulting in better memory and transfer of the training material.

Emerging Trends from Neuroscience

We title this section "emerging trends from neuroscience" because while cognitive neuroscientists are making great progress in identifying the ways in which brain activity (broadly defined) is related to learning, this research is not nearly as mature as that of cognitive science (Bruer, 2006). As such, the implications from cognitive neuroscience research for best practices in training are not as clear. Nevertheless, we believe it is important for training researchers to be aware of emerging neuroscience research for several reasons. First, understanding brain activity in response to learning stimuli may change the way we study learning, if not the questions we ask and the way we design training programs. Additionally, as neurological underpinnings of learning become better understood, greater collaboration between training researchers and neuroscientists will be necessary to interpret and apply these findings.

Implications for Measurement

First it is important to understand the predominant experimental paradigm and measurement techniques to understand the neuroscientific implications for the science of learning. Recognize though that this is an oversimplification of the research on both the stimulus and response side. Typically, neuroscientists use some form of functional technique, in which several variations of a learning or memory task are given and direct or indirect measures of brain activation is assessed (Bunge & Kahn, 2009). The former refers to methods of directly measuring electrical activity resulting from neuronal firing; the most common such method is electroencephalography (EEG). The latter methods include functional magnetic resonance imaging (fMRI) in which MRI scanners detect the presence of elevated levels of oxygen in certain areas of the brain, symptomatic of greater neural activity.

Insights from neuroimaging can be seen by considering research on error management training. We know from training research that error-management training works – under the right conditions, encouraging trainees to make errors is associated with greater learning by trainees (Keith & Frese, 2008). Further error-management research has begun to identify training conditions that moderate the effectiveness of specific training conditions related to the promotion of errors (e.g., Carter & Beier, 2010). Less is known about individual differences as moderators, or precisely *how* exposure to errors promotes learning. Klein et al. (2007) used fMRI data to study the role of dopamine in reactions to negative feedback on a learning task. The researchers found that learning from errors requires dopaminergic signaling; additionally, learners with reduced dopamine D2 receptor densities responded less to negative feedback than did "normal" learners. While applications of such research are still well in the future, we can speculate that neuroimaging screens one day could be used to assign learners to optimal training conditions.

In the end, training is effective when it is well-designed and trainees "learn." One could argue that given evidence of increased recognition, recall, transfer, and so forth, that what is occurring in the brain is less critical to observe and quantify; that is, the neurological activity that underlies learning is a set of mediating processes that we don't need to study directly to improve training. However, the preceding example highlights one benefit of understanding the neurological underpinnings of learning processes. A second benefit is that evidence of increased brain activation confirms that learning was, if not intentional, replicable. That is, we have increased confidence that the same training intervention would work in future applications. Thus, neural imaging has great potential as a dependent variable in training research. Finally, neuroimaging has potential for studying internal processes (or confirming a construct) like meta-cognition or self-regulation (Willingham, 2012). It is well-accepted in the science of learning that meta-cognition (thinking about thinking) not only occurs, but is important to learning over time. Yet, *measuring* meta-cognition in the moment is challenging – simply asking participants what they are monitoring disrupts the act of monitoring. However, interventions that encourage meta-cognitive activity can be evaluated using neuroimaging techniques. Thus, it is easy to understand why Poldrack (2000) concluded that the "neuroimaging of learning and development is one of the most exciting and quickly growing areas of cognitive neuroscience, and will no doubt continue to grow as new techniques ... are added to the quiver of neuroimaging methods" (p. 10).

How Applicable Is Neuroscience Research?

That said, there is currently a strong debate on the extent to which neuroscience-based findings can be readily translated into the design and delivery of training and education (Bruer, 2006; De Bruyckere, Kirschner, &

Hulshof, 2015; Hruby, 2012; Tokuhama-Espinosa, 2014). On the one hand, Tokuhama-Espinosa calls for a completely new instructional paradigm based on an integration of mind (psychology), brain (neuroscience), and education science, assuming that research is sufficiently advanced in all three domains inform practice. On the other hand, De Bruyckere et al. cautioned that the state of neuroscience relevant to learning is as yet too immature to readily translate it into instructional principles, concluding, "For the time being, we do not really understand all that much about the brain. More importantly, it is difficult to generalize what we do know into a set of concrete precepts of behavior, never mind devise methods for influencing that behavior" (p. 94; see also Bruer, 2006 and Hruby, 2012).

As Willingham (2009) noted, the application of neuroscience to instructional principles faces both a vertical and horizontal problem. The vertical problem is one of levels analysis. The neuroscientist studies phenomena somewhere between the level of the neuron and brain structures, and attempts to study cognitive functions (e.g., recall) in isolation. Thus, we cannot assume that findings at this level generalize to the learner in the training context, in which the lowest level of analysis is the learner and cognitive functioning occurs in a rich milieu. The horizontal problem refers to the mapping of stimuli to brain activity *and back*. Even if we are able to map human cognitive processes and representations in response to certain stimuli, that doesn't necessarily inform how instructional methods on how to trigger that activity in a learning context. For a well-rounded perspective on the promise and shortcomings of applying neuroscience to learning contexts, see Devonshire and Dommett (2010). For present purposes, we reiterate that the primary value to training researchers of neuroscience is its role as unique (and perhaps necessary) measures of mediating and dependent variables. For training practitioners, we encourage caution in the application of neuroscience findings to instructional practices unless there is a relatively mature set of findings that address both the horizontal and vertical problems. We illustrate two such applications in the following text.

Allow for Sleep Consolidation and Adequate Sleep

Research over the past several decades has accumulated evidence of the relationship between sleep and cognitive performance, including learning. It is well-established that workers worldwide suffer from a lack of sleep (Killgore, 2010). According to a 2008 poll by the National Sleep Foundation, 44% of survey respondents reported receiving less than seven hours of sleep during the work week, and 29% reported becoming very sleepy or falling asleep at work in the prior month.

The quantity and quality of sleep effects learning performance in two broad ways. First, there is considerable support for the proposition that sleep has been shown to enable consolidation of new information into memory (Diekelmann & Born, 2010), with consolidation being an active process in which new knowledge is reactivated and reorganized into new representations (Born, Rasch, & Gais,

2006). Born et al. provided an overview of the specific mechanisms by which sleep types (e.g., slow-wave v. REM sleep) facilitate consolidation depending on where in the brain memories are formed. The benefits of sleep on learning (Curcio, Ferrar, & De Gennaro, 2006) has been documented for a number of outcomes including motor skill performance (Walker et al., 2002), language learning (Fenn, Nusbaum, & Margoliash, 2003), and declarative knowledge (Stickgold, 2005). Consistent with our earlier discussion, note though that Stickgold pointed out that there is insufficient data as of yet to suggest sleep aids in more complex forms of human learning.

When coupled with earlier cited behavioral research, findings on the relationship between sleep and learning help explain the benefits of distributed practice or spacing over multiple days. Neuroscientific research indicates that these benefits accrue in part from the opportunity to sleep between learning trials. Stickgold (2005) quoted the first century AD, Roman rhetorician Quintilian who in turn noted that "what could not be repeated at first is readily put together on the following day; and the very time which is generally thought to cause forgetfulness is found to strengthen the memory" (1272). Though the benefits are documented more for declarative knowledge and simpler skills, our recommendation is that, when feasible, training be spread over multiple days. Sleep prepares the brain for learning.

The second impact of sleep on training performance is when learners have not slept enough. There is considerable research that documents the deleterious effects of lack of sleep on cognitive performance. Killgore (2010) noted that there is a "broad consensus" that a lack of sleep results in slower response speeds and increased variability (primarily negative) in alertness, attention, and vigilance, though there is less agreement regarding the effects of sleep deprivation on certain higher level cognitive capacities including memory. Sleep deprivation has also been shown to have negative effects on integrating information in novel or creative ways (Payne, 2011), divergent thinking, and self-regulation (Harrison & Horne, 2000), processes each important in training performance.

While research originally focused on sleep deprivation, more recent research has also focused on chronic sleep restriction. The former is defined as the result of at least one night with no sleep, the former refers to continually restricting sleep below one's optimal time in bed (TIB) (Banks & Dinges, 2007). For example, Van Dongen et al. (2003) compared participants receiving four or six hours of TIB over 14 consecutive days to participants who went three nights without sleep. We suggest that empirical evidence of chronic sleep restriction is considerably more relevant to most of the workforce than are studies of sleep deprivation. Somewhat surprising then are the conclusions that the neurobehavioral effects and cognitive performance effects due to chronic sleep restriction are very similar to those found for multiple days of total sleep loss (Balkin et al., 2008; Banks & Dinges, 2007; Curcioa, Ferraraa, & Gennaroa, 2006). With respect to neuropsychological functioning, Banks and Dinges concluded: "Recent experiments reveal that following days of chronic restriction of sleep duration below 7 hours per night, significant daytime cognitive dysfunction accumulates to levels comparable to that found after severe acute total sleep deprivation" (519). Further, Curcioa et al. reported strong correlational evidence between sleep loss and academic performance among adolescents.

In sum, emerging research suggests that chronic sleep restriction can negatively affect cognitive performance, which in turn negatively affects learning in training. There are many determinants of sleep restriction, but undoubtedly one is work, for example, shift work, stress, and high workloads (Åkerstedt, 2006; Harrison & Horne, 2000). Training can exasperate the strain caused by work, either because workers are held responsible for fulfilling their work roles or, in the case of online training, workers are expected to complete training on their own time (which is often late at night after family responsibilities are met). Accordingly, we recommend that in preparing workers for training, organizations ensure they have adequate time to fulfill their work roles without the need for less sleep time.

Use Breaks and Reduce Distractions

Attention is critical to learning; attention is the primary means by which we hold sight and sound in sensory memory long enough for it to transfer to working memory. Attention also explains why two learners can attend the same training course and come out with very different memories of what was covered and what should be applied. Physiologically, attention consists of top-down signals throughout the cortex, with frontoparietal areas regulating activity in sensory cortex and the thalamus. Importantly, while neural activity is activating by perceptual processing (attending to external stimuli), it can also be increased simply by directing attention to a location (i.e., focusing).

Because attention requires focused effort, and because our brains were not designed for sustained attention, there are multiple implications both for learners and for instructional design. As should be intuitive, the brain needs rest and recovery to optimize focus and attention. In the short term, this means planned breaks in the learning process (e.g., Ariga & Lleras, 2011). Trainers frequently (and smartly) use learning games or insert simpler material to enable recovery time. Research also suggests that physical activities such as walking or even looking out a window (Kaplan & Berman, 2010) are restorative as is practicing mindfulness (Evans, Baer, & Segerstrom, 2009; Vago & David, 2012).

Assisting the learner in returning to attention assumes we have it in the first place. Researchers distinguish between voluntary and involuntary attention (Posner & Rothbart, 2007). Involuntary attention lasts several milliseconds and is the process involved, for example when we are startled by a sneeze behind us. Voluntary attention reflects direct control of cognitive resources to attend to stimuli sufficiently long enough to aid in transfer to long-term memory, and thus is a key to effective instruction.

To oversimplify, effective instruction requires capturing and maintaining learner attention, although, as we've seen, maintaining attention is largely taking short breaks and coming back to voluntary attention. As effective trainers know, one way to increase effortful attention is to signal that upcoming information is significant and/or relevant. The first author once observed a half-day training program that culminated in trainees breaking a board with their hand in front of their peers. Although the training content consisted largely of having goals and believing in oneself, the trainers held high levels of attention for four hours by continually assuring, "The next thing we tell you will be critical to breaking the board."

Neurologically, evidence exists for partially separated areas of the brain that hold responsibility for attentional functions (Corbetta & Shulman, 2002) or networks of brain areas that carry out different attentional functions. These areas are triggered primarily by stimulus novelty, as well as by relevance of stimuli to individual goals and to the defensive and appetitive motivational systems (Bradley, 2009). In short, we notice external stimuli that are novel and relevant to our fundamental needs. While it is a stretch to suggest that trainers can make training more relevant by appealing to (on-the-job) survival, neuropsychological evidence supports traditional training practices such as providing advanced organizers that both signal what is coming up in training content and how training is relevant to work-related goals (Mayer, 1979).

Neuroscience research suggests that even as we try to attend to relevant stimuli, task and environmental characteristics distract us. Salient-signal suppression theories of attentional control (e.g., Sawaki & Luck, 2010) propose that salient content in our visual field compete for control of our visual perception systems and that the visual system (not the mind) influences whether or not to focus on the most salient features. Further, attention can be influenced by the context, priming, or the individual's attentional control settings. Neuropsychological evidence suggests that our attention is fleeting and that visual distractors are, well, distracting, and thus, instruction should be designed in a way that minimizes irrelevant stimuli unless it is to provide cognitive breaks for learners (Sitzmann & Johnson, 2014). A challenge for future research is to determine in more detail what distinguishes a dysfunctional distraction from a functional one.

Finally, as too many trainers and college instructors know, focusing attention is becoming an increasingly difficult task, particularly for learners who choose to multitask by texting or checking social media from the classroom (Carrier et al., 2009). While both our abilities to selectively attend to priority information and hold it in working memory declines with normal aging beginning in the early twenties (Gazzaley et al., 2005), attention dysfunction seems more prevalent among young learners. It appears that it is not only the distraction of multitasking but the expectations formed by digital media that affect young learners (Richtel, 2010). These same learners may also place lower priority *on* paying attention, believing that the knowledge can be obtained later by other means. In several interesting recent studies, Sparrow, Liu, and Wegner (2011) reported that learners are less likely to remember new information if they believed that they could access that information later online. Further, learners seemed to prioritize remembering where the information could be found over the information itself. While it is tempting to think that the Internet, social media, video gaming, and so forth are creating negative effects on our long-term learning capabilities, it is also the case that technology has positive effects on cognitive development and our ability to learn and to imagine (Greenfield, 2009). And if useful information changes, such as with regularly updated software or company policies, then it may be appropriate for learners to know where to get that information rather than memorize it in the form first encountered.

Summary

In summary, research in cognitive neuroscience has increasingly identified both structures of the brain and neurological response patterns related to learning. We believe that by incorporating psycho-neurological responses into existing research on instructional processes, we can better examine the effectiveness of and mediating processes related to training interventions.

We also offer a cautioned against overinterpreting the results of cognitive neuroscience research as it relates to training, given the maturity and sophistication of the research to date.

That said, we reviewed research on cognitive-neurological responses related to both sleep and attention and offered a number of recommendations for training practice including, when possible, spreading training over multiple days to allow consolidation effects through sleep, structuring the work and training environment to encourage trainees to get sufficient sleep during the course of training, building in breaks to help learners maintain voluntary attentional control, and reducing the number of distracting stimuli in the learning environment.

Conclusion

The implications we have discussed from human cognition and emerging neuroscience should be integrated into the science of training as strategies to increase learning and transfer by preparing learners and developing training programs that are engaging, meaningful, and effortful. We encourage the direct application of our recommendations to improve training as well as more research on connecting basic research on human learning to training.

References

Åkerstedt, T. 2006. Psychosocial stress and impaired sleep. *Scandinavian Journal of Work, Environment & Health* 32: 493–501.

Alexander, P. A., Schallert, D. L., and Reynolds, R. E. 2009. What is learning anyway? A topographical perspective considered. *Educational Psychologist* 44: 176–192.

Ariga, A., and Lleras, A. 2011. Brief and rare mental "breaks" keep you focused: Deactivation and reactivation of task goals preempt vigilance decrements. *Cognition* 118: 439–443.

Azevedo, R., and Bernard, R. M. 1995. A meta-analysis of the effects of feedback in computer-based instruction. *Journal of Educational Computing Research* 13: 111–127.

Baddeley, A. D., and Longman, D. J. A. 1978. The influence of length and frequency of training session on the rate of learning to type. *Ergonomics* 21: 627–635.

Baldwin, T. T., and Ford, J. K. 1988. Transfer of training: A review and directions for future research. *Personnel Psychology* 41: 63–105.

Balkin, T. J., Rupp, T., Picchioni, D., and Wesensten, N. J, 2008. Sleep loss and sleepiness: Current issues. *Chest* 134: 653-660.

Banks, S., and Dinges, D. 2007. Behavioral and physiological consequences of sleep restriction. *Journal of Clinical Sleep Medicine* 3: 519–528.

Bear, M. F., Cooper, L. M., and Ebner, F. F. 1989. Synaptic modification model of memory and learning. In B. Inkhauser, ed., *Encyclopedia of Neuroscience, Supplement One*, 156–160. Amsterdam: Elsevier.

Bell, B. S., and Kozlowski, S. W. J. 2008. Active learning: Effects of core training design elements on self-regulatory processes, learning, and adaptability. *Journal of Applied Psychology* 93: 296–316.

Bjork, E. L., and Bjork, R. A. 2011. Making things hard on yourself, but in a good way: Creating desirable difficulties to enhance learning. In M. A. Gernsbacher, R. W. Pew, L. M. Hough, and J. R. Pomerantz, eds., *Psychology and the Real World: Essays Illustrating Fundamental Contributions to Society*, 56–64. New York: Worth.

Bjork, R. A. 1994. Memory and meta-memory considerations in the training of human beings. In J. Metcalfe and A. Shimamura, eds., *Metacognition: Knowing about Knowing*, 185–205. Cambridge, MA: MIT Press.

Bjork, R. A., Dunlosky, J., and Kornell, N. 2013. Self-regulated learning: Beliefs, techniques, and illusions. *Annual Review of Psychology* 64: 417–444.

Born, J., Rasch, B., and Gais, S. 2006. Sleep to remember. *The Neuroscientist* 12: 410–424.

Bradley, M. M. 2009. Natural selective attention: Orienting and emotion. *Psychophysiology* 46: 1–11.

Bransford, J. D., and Johnson, M. K. 1972. Contextual prerequisites for understanding: Some investigations of comprehension and recall. *Journal of Verbal Learning and Verbal Behavior* 11: 717–726.

Bruer, J. T. 2006. Points of view: On the implications of neuroscience research for science of teaching and learning: Are there any? *CBE Life Sciences Education* 5: 104–110.

Bunge, S. A., and Kahn, I. 2009. Cognition: An overview of neuroimaging techniques. *Encyclopedia of Neuroscience* 2: 1063–1067.

Butcher, K. R. 2006. Learning from text with diagrams: Promoting mental model development and inference generation. *Journal of Educational Psychology* 98: 182–197.

Carrier, L. M., Cheever, N. A., Rosen, L. D., Benitez, S., and Chang, J. 2009. Multitasking across generations: Multitasking choices and difficulty ratings in three generations of Americans. *Computers in Human Behavior* 25: 483–489.

Carter, M., and Beier, M. E. 2010. The effectiveness of error management training with working-aged adults. *Personnel Psychology* 63: 641–675.

Cepeda, N. J., Pashler, H., Vul, E., Wixted, J. T., and Rohrer, D. 2006. Distributed practice in verbal recall tasks: A review and quantitative synthesis. *Psychological Bulletin* 132: 354–380.

Chandler, P., and Sweller, J. 1991. Cognitive load theory and the format of instruction. *Cognition and Instruction* 8: 293–332.

Clark, R. C. 2014. *Evidence-Based Training Methods: A Guide for Training Professionals*. Arlington, VA: American Society for Training and Development.

Clark, R. C., and Mayer, R. E. 2008. Learning by viewing versus learning by doing: Evidence-based guidelines for principled learning environments. *Performance Improvement* 47 (9): 5–13.

Clark, R. E., and Voogel, A. 1985. Transfer of training principles for instructional design. *Education Communication and Technology Journal* 33: 113–123.

Corbalan, G., Paas, F., and Cuypers, H. 2010. Computer-based feedback in linear algebra: Effects on transfer performance and motivation. *Computers and Education* 55: 692–703.

Corbetta, M., and Shulman, G. L. 2002. Control of goal-directed and stimulus-driven attention in the brain. *Nature Reviews: Neuroscience* 3: 201–215.

Craik, F. I., and Lockhart, R. S. 1972. Levels of processing: A framework for memory research. *Journal of Verbal Learning and Verbal Behavior* 11: 671–684.

Curcio, G., Ferrara, M., and De Gennaro, L. 2006. Sleep loss, learning capacity and academic performance. *Sleep Medicine Reviews* 10: 323–337.

De Bruyckere, P., Kirschner, P. A., and Hulshof, C. D. 2015. *Urban Myths about Learning and Education*. New York: Academic Press.

Dempster, F. N. 1988. The spacing effect: A case study in the failure to apply the results of psychological research. *American Psychologist* 43: 627–634.

Devonshire, I. M., and Dommett, E. J. 2010. Neuroscience: Viable applications in education? *Neuroscientist* 16: 349–356.

Diekelmann, S., and Born, J. 2010. The memory function of sleep. *Nature Reviews Neuroscience* 11: 114–126.

Dunlosky, J., Rawson, K. A., Marsh, E. J., Nathan, M. J., and Willingham, D. T. 2013. Improving students' learning with effective learning techniques promising directions from cognitive and educational psychology. *Psychological Science in the Public Interest* 141: 4–58.

Estes, W. K. 1955. Statistical theory of distributional phenomena in learning. *Psychological Review* 62: 369–377.

Evans, D. R., Baer, R. A., and Segerstrom, S. C. 2009. The effects of mindfulness and self-consciousness on persistence. *Personality and Individual Differences* 47: 379–382.

Fenn, K. M., Nusbaum, H. C., and Margoliash, D. 2003. Consolidation during sleep of perceptual learning of spoken language. *Nature* 42 (5): 614–616.

Gagné, R. M. 1965. *The Conditions of Learning*. New York: Holt, Rinehart and Winston.

Gazzaley, A., Cooney, J. W., Rissman, J., and D'Esposito, M. 2005. Top-down suppression deficit underlies working memory impairment in normal aging. *Nature Neuroscience* 8: 1298–1300.

Ginns, P., Martin, A. J., and Marsh, H. W. 2013. Designing instructional text in a conversational style: A meta-analysis. *Educational Psychology Review* 25: 445–472.

Glenberg, A. M. 1979. Component-levels theory of the effects of spacing of repetitions on recall and recognition. *Memory and Cognition* 7: 95–112.

Greenfield, P. M. 2009. Technology and informal education: What is taught, what is learned. *Science* 323 (5910): 69–71.

Halls, J. 2014. Memory and cognition in learning. *Infoline; Tips, Tools, and Intelligence for Training* 31 (May): Issue 1405.

Harrison, Y., and Horne, J. A. 2000. The impact of sleep deprivation on decision-making: A review. *Journal of Experimental Psychology: Applied* 6: 236–249.

Hesketh, B. 1997. Dilemmas in training for transfer and retention. *Applied Psychology: An International Review* 46: 317–339.

Howell, W. C., and Cooke, N. J. 1989. Training the human information processor: A look at cognitive models. In I. Goldstein, ed., *Training and Development in Work Organizations*, 121–182. New York: Jossey-Bass,

Hruby, G. G. 2012. Three requirements for justifying an educational neuroscience. *British Journal of Educational Psychology* 82: 1–23.

Kahn, W. A. 1990. Psychological conditions of personal engagement and disengagement at work. *Academy of Management Journal* 33: 692–724.

Kaplan, S., and Berman, M. G. 2010. Directed attention as a common resource for executive functioning and self-regulation. *Perspectives on Psychological Science* 5: 43–57.

Keith, N., and Frese, M. 2008. Effectiveness of error management training: A meta-analysis. *Journal of Applied Psychology* 93: 59–69.

Killgore, W.D.S. 2010. Effects of sleep deprivation on cognition. *Progress in Brain Research* 185: 105–129.

Klein, T. A., Neumann, J., Reuter, M., Hennig, J., Von Cramon, D. Y., and Ullsperger, M. 2014. Genetically determined differences in learning from errors. *Science* 318: 1642–1645.

Kluger, A. N., and DeNisi, A. 1996. The effects of feedback interventions on performance: A historical review, a meta-analysis, and a preliminary feedback intervention theory. *Psychological Bulletin* 119: 254–284.

Kraiger, K., Ford, J. K., and Salas, E. 1993. Application of cognitive, skill-based, and affective theories of learning outcomes to new methods of training evaluation. *Journal of Applied Psychology* 78: 311–328.

Mayer, R. E. 1979. Can advance organizers influence meaningful learning? *Review of Educational Research* 49: 371–383.

Mayer, R. E. 2008. Applying the science of learning: Evidence-based principles for the design of multimedia instruction. *American Psychologist* 63: 760–769.

Merriënboer, J. J., and Sweller, J. 2005. Cognitive load theory and complex learning: Recent developments and future directions. *Educational Psychology Review* 17: 147–177.

Moreno, R. 2004. Decreasing cognitive load for novice students: Effects of explanatory versus corrective feedback in discovery-based multimedia. *Instructional science* 32 (1–2): 99–113.

Morris, C. D., Bransford, J. D., and Franks, J. J. 1977. Levels of processing versus transfer appropriate processing. *Journal of Verbal Learning and Verbal Behavior* 16: 519–533.

Payne, J. D. 2011. Learning, memory and sleep in humans. *Sleep Medicine Clinics* 6: 15–30.

Poldrack, R. A. 2000. Imaging brain plasticity: conceptual and methodological issues – A theoretical review. *Neuroimage* 12: 1–13.

Posner, M. I., and Rothbart, M. K. 2007. Research on attention networks as a model for the integration of psychological science. *Annual Review of Psychology* 58: 1–23.

Renkl, A. 2005. The worked-out examples principle in multimedia learning. In R. E. Mayer, ed., *Handbook of Multimedia Learning*, 229–245. New York: Cambridge University Press.

Rey, G. D. 2012. A review of research and a meta-analysis of the seductive detail effect. *Educational Research Review* 7: 216–237.

Richtel, M. 2010. Growing up digital, wired for distraction. *New York Times*, Available from: http://www.nytimes.com/2010/11/21/technology/21brain.html? pagewanted=all&_r=0 (accessed April 23, 2017).

Roediger, H. L., and Karpicke, J. D. 2006. The power of testing memory: Basic research and implications for educational practice. *Perspectives on Psychological Science* 13: 181–210.

Rohrer, D., and Taylor, K. 2007. The shuffling of mathematics problems improves learning. *Instructional Science* 35: 481–498

Rohrer, D., Taylor, K., and Sholar, B. 2010. Tests enhance the transfer of learning. *Journal of Experimental Psychology: Learning, Memory, and Cognition* 36: 233–239.

Salas, E., and Cannon-Bowers, J. A. 2001. The science of training: A decade of progress. *Annual review of psychology* 52: 471–499.

Salas, E., Tannenbaum, S. I., Kraiger, K., and Smith-Jentsch, K. A. 2012. The science of training and development in organizations: What matters in practice. *Psychological Science in the Public Interest* 132: 74–101.

Sawaki, R., and Luck, S. J. 2010. Capture versus suppression of attention by salient singletons: Electrophysiological evidence for an automatic attend-to-me signal. *Attention, Perception, and Psychophysics* 72: 1455–1470.

Schmidt, R. A., and Bjork, R. A. 1992. New conceptualizations of practice: Common principles in three paradigms suggest new concepts for training. *Psychological Science* 3: 207–217.

Schunk, D. H., and Zimmerman, B. J., eds. 2012. *Motivation and Self-regulated Learning: Theory, Research, and Applications*. New York: Routledge.

Simon, H. A. 1998. What do we know about learning? *Journal of Engineering Education* 87: 343–348.

Sisti, H. M., Glass, A. L., and Shors, T. J. 2007. Neurogenesis and the spacing effect: Learning over time enhances memory and the survival of new neurons. *Learning and Memory* 14: 368–375.

Sitzmann, T., and Johnson, S. 2014. The paradox of seduction by irrelevant details: How irrelevant information helps and hinders self-regulated learning. *Learning and Individual Differences* 34: 1–11.

Sparrow, B., Liu, J., and Wegner, D. M. 2011. Google effects on memory: Cognitive consequences of having information at our fingertips. *Science* 333: 776–778.

Stickgold, R. 2005. Sleep-dependent memory consolidation. *Nature* 437: 1272–1278.

Sweller, J. 1999. *Instructional Design in Technical Areas*. Camberwell, Australia: ACER Press.

Taylor, K., and Rohrer, D. 2010. The effects of interleaved practice. *Applied Cognitive Psychology* 24: 837–848.

Tokuhama-Espinosa, T. 2014. *Making Classrooms Better: 50 Practical Applications of Mind, Brain, and Education Science*. New York: Norton.

Vago, D. R., and David, S. A. 2012. Self-awareness, self-regulation, and self-transcendence S-ART: A framework for understanding the neurobiological mechanisms of mindfulness. *Frontiers in Human Neuroscience* 6: 296.

Van Dongen, H. P. A., Maislin, G., Mullington, J. M., and Dinges, D. F. (2003). The cumulative cost of additional wakefulness: Dose–response effects on neurobehavioral functions and sleep physiology from chronic sleep restriction and total sleep deprivation. *Sleep: Journal of Sleep and Sleep Disorders Research* 26: 117–126.

Walker, M. P., Brakefield, T., Morgan, A., Hobson, J. A., and Stickgold, R. 2002. Practice with sleep makes perfect: Sleep-dependent motor skill learning. *Neuron* 35: 205–211.

Willingham, D. T. 2009. Three problems in the marriage of neuroscience and education. *Cortex* 45: 544–545.

Willingham, D. T. 2012. Neurosci and educ.–5 days, 5 ways. Day 4: Confirm a construct. December 6. http://www.danielwillingham.com/daniel-willingham-science-and-education-blog/neurosci-educ-5-days-5-ways-day-4-confirm-a-construct (accessed May 11, 2016).

Wilson, C. L., Huang, J. L., and Kraiger, K. 2013. Personality and the analysis, design, and delivery of training. In N. D. Christiansen and R. P. Tett, eds., *Handbook of Personality at Work*, 543–564. New York: Routledge.

Wulf, G., and Shea, C. H. 2002. Principles derived from the study of simple skills do not generalize to complex skill learning. *Psychonomic Bulletin and Review* 9: 185–211.

3 Facilitating the Development of Expertise

An Individual to Organizational Perspective

Alena D. Marand and Raymond A. Noe

The implication of an increased complexity in relationships among individuals, organizations, and their environment is the need for greater emphasis on multilevel theory and methods in management research (Klein & Kozlowski, 2000; Mathieu & Chen, 2010). Scholars in management and psychology recognize that we need a more thorough understanding of the emergent processes through which individual human capital translates to and affects organizational-level outcomes (e.g., Abell, Felin, & Foss, 2008; Barney & Felin, 2013; Coff & Kryscynski, 2011; Ployhart & Moliterno, 2011; Ployhart, Weekley, & Baughman, 2006). Of particular importance are the processes by and conditions under which individual expertise leads to organizational expertise.

In general, expertise at both the individual and organizational levels is associated with the accumulated knowledge and capabilities that underlie superior performance (e.g., Grant, 1996; Herling, 2000). However, no one definition of expertise has emerged; rather, expertise has been used interchangeably with a variety of constructs at various levels of analysis including competence (e.g., Herling & Provo, 2000; Jacobs, 2003), know-how (e.g., Jacobs, 2003), experience (e.g., Herling, 2000), skill (e.g., Elliot & Dweck, 2013; Grant, 1996; Herling, 2000; Herling & Provo, 2000; Parmigiani & Mitchell, 2009; Wernerfelt, 1984), and domain knowledge (e.g., Grant, 1996; Herling, 2000; Herling & Provo, 2000; Parmigiani & Mitchell, 2009; Wernerfelt, 1984). In the human resource development literature, expertise has been defined as "the optimal level at which a person is able and/or expected to perform within a specialized realm of human activity" (Swanson, 1994: 94). Two key elements persist across these definitions: (1) superior performance in a specific domain is an outcome and indicator of expertise, and (2) expertise is at one end of a developmental continuum, which requires learning or experience to achieve (e.g., Bereiter & Scardamalia, 1993; Ericsson, Krampe, & Tesch-Römer, 1993; Ericsson et al., 2006; Hoffman et al., 1995; Jacobs, 1997).

While several key elements remain the same across distinct levels of analysis some important assumptions differ. First, the nature of knowledge, skills, and capabilities are fundamentally different as we move from the individual to the organizational level. The knowledge, skills, and capabilities at the individual level reflect the individual's unique cognitive frame and behavioral characteristics. At the organizational level there is an added complexity of interpersonal interaction and a broader system of routines that only together yield outcomes of organizational level knowledge, skill, and capabilities (e.g., Nelson & Winter, 1982). At the organizational level, expertise also reflects the interdependence among its components (e.g., individual expertise, interpersonal interaction, and organizational routines), whereas individual-level expertise resides within the individual as a result of the accumulation of experiences. As a result, how such domain-specific knowledge, skills, and abilities materialize at each of these levels is inherently different. For example, although expertise may reside within key employees, if the organization is unable to leverage their expertise, say due to defunct interpersonal interactions or inoperable routines, then their expertise may go unused, or even unnoticed, thus failing to manifest into organizational-level expertise.

Key to understanding when individual-level expertise may lead to or affect organizational expertise are the underlying multilevel relationships that govern their emergence (we discuss the principles for building multilevel theory in the following text). *Emergence* refers to a bottom-up process through which individual characteristics and social interaction result in a higher-level collective, or in this case, organizational phenomenon (Klein & Kozlowski, 2000). These relationships include those among individual experts, their interpersonal interactions, and their role within or impact on broader organizational routines. Considering how emergent is conceptualized in multilevel approaches to training effectiveness may help us understand the relationship between individual, team, and organizational level of expertise (Kozlowski et al., 2000; Mathieu & Tesluk, 2010; Sitzmann & Weinhardt, 2015). These models focus on understanding how effective training at the individual level, and team level, contributes to organizational effectiveness. For example, Kozlowski et al. (2000) focus on training transfer as the primary mechanism through which training influences organizational effectiveness. Specifically, they argue that both horizontal and vertical transfer influence organizational effectiveness. *Horizontal transfer* refers to transfer of training (knowledge, skills, and expertise) across contexts at the same level. Traditionally, horizontal transfer has been the focus of training effectiveness studies that evaluate the extent to which training programs results in learning, behavior or performance change within level, that is, at the individual, team, organizational, or societal level (e.g., Aguinis & Kraiger, 2009; Arthur et al., 2003). Although horizontal transfer is important, vertical transfer is emphasized as the key linkage ("linking pin") between individual training outcomes and organizational outcomes. *Vertical transfer* refers to an "upward transfer [of learning] across different levels in the organization system," and inherently requires a multilevel perspective (Klein & Kozlowski, 2000: 159). The bottom-up emergent processes of vertical transfer are key to understanding how individual-level training outcomes contribute to team and organizational outcomes. Compilation and composition represent two different forms of emergence of vertical transfer (we discuss compilation and composition in detail in the following text). Composition emergence assumes that phenomena are the same as they emerge upward across levels. In the case of training effectiveness this means that the individuals knowledge, skills, and results gained from participating in training and applied to their jobs can be added together to understand team-level outcomes. Organizational-level expertise would be represented by the sum of outcomes across teams. Compilation emergence assumes that individual, team, and organizational outcomes represent a common domain but are different as they emerge across levels. The outcomes have the same role at the individual, team, and organizational level but they are not identical as is the case for composition. For example, training programs focusing on building employees' human capital (increasing knowledge and skills necessary for job performance) can result in increases in social capital at the team or unit level (e.g., collaboration between departments), which in turn, influences the development of organizational capital (e.g., development of better management systems, policies, and procedures). That is, training outcomes at the organizational level are based on the complex contribution of team and individual-level outcomes. We believe that to understand how individuals may exert influence on organizational expertise first requires an understanding of the nature of the higher-level phenomenon and the underlying processes that facilitate its emergence. Only then can we begin to identify the various roles that individual expertise may play in shaping the emergent organizational-level phenomena. In particular it becomes critical to identify the potential "linking pins" that bridge the gap between individual and organizational expertise. Potential "linking pins" that we discuss in this chapter are related to the organizational structures (both formal and informal) that facilitate (or constrain) individual-level experiences and behavior. These "linking pins" serve as the key mechanisms responsible for the nature of emergence, or the mode by which individual expertise is aggregated to the organizational level.

The purpose of this chapter is to provide insight into how individual expertise leads to organizational expertise. First, we review extant research on organizational-level expertise, highlighting important assumptions and trends in the literature. Second, we apply recent multilevel work that provides insight into the processes through which lower-level phenomena emerge to form higher-level organizational structures. We believe these processes are responsible for the emergence of organizational expertise. Finally, we explore the conditions under which individual-level expertise influences the emergent processes, and in turn, organizational expertise, and outline an agenda for future research.

Organizational-Level Expertise

Organizational-level expertise refers to the capacity to exploit organizational knowledge to enhance efficiency and effectiveness. Organizational knowledge has been operationalized a number of ways including knowledge held by individuals within the firm (e.g., Kogut & Zander, 1992; Simon, 1991), and individual knowledge that has been encoded into organizational routines (e.g., Levitt & March, 1988; Miner & Haunschild, 1995; Nelson & Winter, 1982; Winter, 1995), which may be reflected by norms, standard operating procedures, rules, as well as tasks or technologies that exist within the firm (e.g., Argote, 2013; Argote & Ingram, 2000; Becker, 2004). These various operationalizations imply that identifying what the organization knows is complex because it requires consideration of both individual and organization phenomena.

What the organization can "do" however, is not easily understood by simply observing its stock of knowledge, but rather, is reflected by complex organizational capabilities (e.g., Barney, 1991; 1992; Hoopes & Madsen, 2008; Kogut & Zander, 1992; Lado & Wilson, 1994; Penrose, 1959; Sears & Hoetker, 2014; Wernerfelt, 1984), or competencies (e.g., Colombo & Grilli, 2005; Foss & Knudsen, 2013). Organizational capability, or competence, has been studied from many perspectives, among which, the three most prominent are the resource-based view, the evolutionary view, and the knowledge-based view. The resource-based view takes the firm as the focal unit of analysis and assumes that it plays an active role in determining its capability position relative to close competitors. The evolutionary view assumes that firm capabilities provide an advantage to firms within an industry to the extent that they are successfully selected by the environment. Alternatively, the knowledge-based view proposes that firms differ in their performance because their capabilities differ in terms of how the underlying knowledge is managed, coordinated, and created (e.g., Grant, 1996; Kogut & Zander, 1992; 1996). Although these perspectives differ with respect to their levels of analysis and thus the core mechanisms driving performance heterogeneity, that is, differences in firm performance, we believe that they are in fact complementary because they all can help explain organizational outcomes. In the following text we briefly review each of these three perspectives in more detail.

The Resource-Based Perspective

The resource-based perspective seeks to describe when a firm may gain a competitive advantage (an outcome of expertise). Its focus is on sources of heterogeneity among organizational resources or capabilities. Specifically, the resource-based perspective argues that firms with relatively more efficient capabilities (as compared to close competitors), which cannot be easily imitated or substituted, will achieve a sustainable competitive advantage (e.g., Barney, 1991; Lippman & Rumelt, 2003; Miller & Shamsie, 1996; Peteraf, 1993; Wernerfelt, 1984). Capabilities are seen as relatively more efficient when they generate greater relative value than that generated by close competitors. Value is the gap between customer willingness to pay and supplier opportunity costs (e.g., Brandenburger & Stuart, 1996).

There are several different definitions of organizational capability within the resource-based literature. Organizational capability has been defined as the development of expertise in a given functional area (Amit and Schoemaker, 1993), as business processes strategically understood (Stalk, Evans, and Shulman, 1992), and as a standard functional classification of the firm's activities (Grant, 1991). Alternatively, Treacy and Wiersema (1993) consider capabilities as one of three possible value disciplines – operational excellence, customer intimacy, or product leadership.

Furthermore, the consideration of capabilities often includes notions of improvement and development, such that for organizational capabilities to sustain a competitive advantage in a dynamic environment they must also undergo continuous updating as a function of learning and acquiring new information from the environment (e.g., Amit & Schoemaker, 1993; Henderson & Cockburn, 1994). Amit and Schoemaker argue that for capabilities to support a sustainable competitive advantage they should sustain "repeated process or product innovations, manufacturing flexibility, responsiveness to market trends, and short development cycles" (Amit & Schoemaker, 1993: 35). Similarly, Henderson and Cockburn (1994) emphasize that organizational capabilities need not be limited to operational production and efficiency but should also include processes surrounding the allocation of the firm's resources as well as the firm's capacity to develop new capabilities, closely mirroring Lipmann and Rumelt's (1982) notion of "the production of new production functions." Similarly, Barney also makes refers to capabilities as those that "enable an organization to conceive, choose and implement strategies" (Barney, 1992: 44). Despite references to such dynamism, the resource-based view does little to explain when and which firms will gain a competitive advantage in a changing environment. What it does do well is to emphasize the nature of capabilities required for firms to gain a competitive advantage under conditions of market stability. Alternatively, the evolutionary view holds no binding assumption that firms operate within an unchanging environment, but acknowledges that the environment may swiftly change at any time, making a once expert firm obsolete if it fails to anticipate or adapt to such changes.

Evolutionary Perspective

In the evolutionary perspective, Winter (2003) defines an *organizational capability* as "a high-level routine (or collection of routines) that, together with its implementing input flows, confers upon an organization's management a set of decision options for producing significant outputs of a particular type" (Winter, 2003: 991). A *routine* is defined as a reoccurring interactive pattern of action (e.g., Cohen et al., 1996; Nelson & Winter, 1982; Pentland & Rueter, 1994). Firms' organizational capabilities are in some ways very similar to those described in the resourced-based view. However, the evolutionary view operates on distinct mechanisms including variation, selection, and retention. Organizational capabilities, consisting of socially complex bundles of "routines" that inherently vary or "mutate" (and generate further variation), are selected as a function of their "success" within a given environment. If the environment ifs generally stable, successful routines continue to persist over time (Nelson & Winter, 1982).

The central difference between the evolutionary view and the resource-based view of competitive advantage is the emphasis on the dynamism of the environment that can change the resources and capabilities necessary for competitive advantage (Nelson & Winter, 1982). The dynamic capabilities framework resulted from this emphasis on market and environmental dynamism (Teece, Pisano, & Shuen, 1997). Similar to work in both evolutionary economics and the resource-based view, the dynamics capabilities framework includes assumptions of path dependency. The dynamic capabilities framework emphasizes that the competitive advantage of firms relies on both idiosyncratic means of coordinating and combining assets, as well as their relative asset positions, and the evolution of the path(s) adopted or inherited by firms (Teece et al., 1997). The extent to which a firm's competitive advantage persists overtime, however, also depends on the stability of market demand, internal replicability of key organizational capabilities, and, similar to the resourced-based logic, imitability or replication of the firm's capabilities by competitors (Teece et al., 1997). Considering both the internal and external conditions necessary for temporary and persistent competitive advantage supports a framework that is more akin to the knowledge-based view (described in the following text) that is based not only on a combination of the firm's endowed state and exogenous changes in the environment, but also considers "internal technological, organizational, and managerial processes inside the firm" (Teece et al., 1997: 509).

The Knowledge-Based Perspective

The knowledge-based perspective considers the organization as a system that exists to coordinate the knowledge of its members. The knowledge-based perspective focuses on firms' capabilities as they relate more specifically to knowledge-related activities including knowledge management, coordination of knowledge, and knowledge creation (e.g. Grant, 1996; Kogut & Zander, 1992; 1996). According to this perspective, "the capabilities of a firm, or any organization, lie primarily in the organizing principles by which individual and functional expertise is structured, coordinated, and communicated [, where] firms are social communities which use their relational structure and shared coding schemes to enhance the transfer and communication of new skills and capabilities" (Zander & Kogut, 1995: 76). Thus, the knowledge-based perspective extends our understanding of between firm differences in capabilities and their development by unpacking the processes by which knowledge contributes to the development of firm capabilities that support a sustainable competitive advantage. Also, the knowledge-based perspective emphasizes the underlying complex social structures that facilitate such processes.

In sum, the resource-based, evolutionary, and knowledge-based perspectives propose that whether a firm will gain and sustain an advantage may be seen as a function of a firm's capability position relative to close competitors under current market conditions. Also, important are the firm's internal structures and processes supporting their capacity to alter these capabilities under changing market and environmental conditions and the extent to which competitors may imitate such expert capabilities. These perspectives have been influential in post hoc descriptions of the characteristics of firms and their capabilities that are associated with competitive advantage. However, because these perspectives consider firms' capabilities as exogenous, that is, they assume firms are endowed with certain knowledge and capabilities, they provide a limited understanding of how firm capabilities are developed and thus how and when organizational expertise emerges. We believe that multilevel theory may be the key to help us better understand the emergent processes responsible for organizational expertise. In the next section, we review extant multilevel research and apply basic principles of multilevel theory building to enhance our understanding of the emergence of organizational expertise.

Emergent Processes of Organizational Expertise

There is a considerable amount of work on multilevel phenomena that describes various processes of emergence and how to think about emergent phenomena related to organizations (e.g., Brass et al., 2004; Gittell & Weiss, 2004; Hunt & Ropo, 1995; Lepak, Smith, & Taylor, 2007; Ployhart & Moliterno, 2011; Rousseau, 1985). Klein and Kozlowski (2000) established a series of principles for building multilevel theory. First, they propose that before even addressing the multilevel relationships, the definition of the theoretical endogenous construct of interest should be clearly established. Second, the relevant lower-level units of analysis should be identified and a conceptualization provided of how they are related to higher-level outcomes. The authors describe two ways in which lower-level units "aggregate" to form the higher-level construct: (1) composition or (2) compilation. *Composition* refers to an isomorphic process of aggregation in which the phenomena are essentially equivalent as they emerge from lower to higher levels. In contrast, *compilation* forms of emergence are those that are discontinuous from lower to higher levels, that is, lower- and higher-level phenomena are conceptually distinct constructs and cannot be understood through additive processes of aggregation. Conceptualizations of the relationship between lower- and higher-level phenomena should describe the specific means through which composition or compilation ensues. Third, it is necessary to operationalization the context in which emergence occurs. Because the interaction among lower-level phenomena may be influenced by the context, it has the potential to greatly affect the nature and emergence process.

Following Klein and Kozlowski's (2000) three principles we: (1) define our construct of interest, (2) identify the lower-level units and the context within which emergence occurs, and (3) describe the relationship between lower- and higher-level units of analysis. Because our construct of interest, organizational expertise has been defined several ways, we refine its definition to develop more fine-grained theory. Specifically, the perspectives on competitive advantage discussed previously suggest two types of organizational expertise: operational expertise, that is, expertise related to efficiency in production as it relates to current markets (e.g., Lippman & Rumelt, 1982), and innovative expertise, that is, expertise related to innovation and the creation and exploitation of new markets (e.g., Teece, Pisano, & Shuen, 1997; Winter, 2003).

There are likely two distinct contexts influencing the relevance of operational and innovative expertise. Operational expertise is more likely meaningful and advantageous in a stable context where firms may develop a deep understanding of the current market environment. Innovative expertise is more valuable in dynamic environments where the demands from the market are constantly changing. Given that these two types of expertise are more likely associated with distinct contexts, we argue that the processes underlying the emergence of each of these two types of expertise are likely distinct and will for the purposes of this chapter be considered separately.

It is also possible that the market context is shaped by the behavior of firms operating within it. So while the multilevel relationship underlying expertise is likely bidirectional (i.e., firm actions affect the environmental context and vice versa), for simplicity, in this chapter we take the market environment or the context as given, focusing on the emergent processes internal to the firm. There is no doubt significant benefits can come from future research aimed at understanding processes underlying the emergence of the market environment (context) and the implications for the emergence of organizational expertise and related processes.

Next, according to Klein and Kozlowski (2000), we must next identify the relevant lower-level units of analysis and the nature of their relationship with our higher-level constructs of interest, that is, organizational expertise in operational efficiency or innovation. As highlighted earlier, the nature and relative positioning of firms' internal capabilities are critical to understanding the emergence of expertise. Furthermore, to understand whether and how a firm's capabilities evolve in such a way that leads to their expertise it is necessary to understand the social and structural elements underlying the firm's internal capabilities, which reflect the lower-level units active in the process of emergence.

While many of the same types of social and structural elements are important for the emergence of both operational and innovative expertise, the nature and configuration of such elements likely differ. For example, organizational theorists have proposed that different structures of organization are more beneficial in different environments, that is, either where innovation is required for survival in escape of obsolescence, or where firms can build on their current operational excellence. Scholars have argued that while mechanistic forms of organization are more useful in stable industries, organic structures are better for dynamic industries characterized by change and persistent volatility, that is, where innovation and adaptation is required for survival (Burns & Stalker, 1961). It is also important to note that structure may represent more than just the division and organization of roles and tasks but may reflect other formal (e.g., rules, standard operating procedures) and informal forms (e.g., experience, norms, values) both of which may have an effect on coordination (e.g., Becker, 2004).

More recently, research in the domain of social networks has found that distinct social structures lead to outcomes of greater efficiency versus greater innovation, depending on the nature of the task. Under conditions where the task depends on the cooperation among a group of individuals, cohesion is more likely to lead to higher levels of efficiency because individuals will likely share a similar understanding of the task and information flows quickly with little effort (Coleman, 1988). Alternatively, when the task requires coordinating across different groups, research suggests that sparse social structures are more effective for coordination (Burt, 1992).

These two examples show the distinct social structural requirements for different organizational tasks underlying our two higher-order constructs of interest. Efficiency is more tightly coupled with firms' capacity to integrate and coordinate knowledge in an attempt to execute their standard operating activities (also called a *first-order capability*). Innovation is more closely aligned with knowledge creation and recombination capabilities (*second-order capabilities*), which allow firms to update and develop new first-order capabilities.

Another group of lower-level units of analysis critical to understanding the emergence of organizational expertise of efficiency and innovation relates to the nature of human behavior. Research within the organization structure and design literature seeks to explain the role of organization structure in facilitating trust and control and their implications for shaping employee behavior (e.g., Creed & Miles, 1996; Ouchi, 1992). While trust and control have each been studied independently, some warn against their separation as it pertains to understanding coordination because these mechanisms offer distinct predictions for facilitating employee behavior (e.g., Burton et al., 2006). More specifically, while arguments related to trust propose returns to efficiency and performance of organizations that grant their employees greater autonomy (e.g., McEvily, Perrone, & Zaheer, 2003), logics of control suggest reduced autonomy and greater formal regulation of behavior (e.g., Eisenhardt, 1989; Jaffee, 2001). In practice, it is likely that both trust and control logics exist simultaneously within the organization and both may be required for efficient coordination (e.g., Langfred, 2004). However, it is unclear whether their relationship is synergistic (control and trust are mutually reinforcing) (e.g., Coletti, Sedatole, & Towry, 2005) or incongruous (control undermines trust) (e.g., Burton et al., 2006). Future research should study the relationship between trust and control across outcomes of innovation and efficiency. It may be that while undermining for one outcome, it may be synergistic in another.

The characteristics of knowledge also play a role in its coordination. For example, the codifiability of knowledge is an important characteristic to consider when seeking an understanding of the relationship between organizational structure, the coordinative capabilities of the firm, and the associated returns to performance (e.g., Garicano & Wu, 2012). Garicano and Wu (2012) argue that the complexity of task-oriented knowledge determines the optimal level of knowledge acquisition and whether the knowledge in the adjacent task reflects complementarities (synergies) or substitutability determines the allocation of knowledge among the members of the organization.

Finally, based on Klein and Kozlowski (2000) we must describe the relationship between the lower- and higher-level units of analysis, or rather their processes of aggregation. One means of discussing how the lower-order units translate into organizational expertise is through the process of knowledge coordination and integration. According to Grant (1996) knowledge integration is the process by which the firm coordinates and is thus able to leverage the specialized knowledge held by individuals. Examples of knowledge coordination can be seen in the treatment of a hospitalized patient whose care is contingent on the knowledge coordination among an array of specialists who have varying depths of knowledge across a diverse pool of domains.

The rather tautological definition of *knowledge integration* and the abstract example point to just how difficult it is to unpack these processes of aggregation. This is precisely where we believe future research can make critical contributions. Under what conditions do individuals successfully coordinate their knowledge? When might the system catch individual errors and when might we observe a system-level error in knowledge coordination? When is it critical for individuals to overlap in knowledge and function, and where is it most efficient for them to uniquely specialize? What are the costs and benefits associated with different means of knowledge coordination, that is, how individuals fit together in a broader system in terms of their overlap and uniqueness of knowledge and function? Are there certain means of coordination that are better for certain types of goals (e.g., quality vs. low cost)? While it is likely that many of the processes related to organizational expertise (operation and innovative) are at best partially isomorphic, and thus follow a compilation form of aggregation, there is little (if any) research to our knowledge that seeks to link the coordination of knowledge to various forms of compilation, nor a critic of whether such a depiction is nuanced enough to advance our knowledge.

Another potentially important element of aggregation is knowledge transfer. Knowledge transfer is distinct from knowledge integration because it focuses on the deliberate internal imitation of knowledge (typically at the level of a firm's subunits) by another, where there is an active role by both sender and receiver of knowledge transfer (e.g., Argote & Ingram, 2000; Szulanski, 1996). This can be considered as representing a compositional means of aggregation, or having isomorphic lower- and higher-level units. Although knowledge transfer may be necessary in the coordination and application of knowledge to carry out the firm's activities, these terms are not synonymous.

In thinking about aggregation using knowledge coordination and transfer, it can easily be seen why we might expect different key processes to play roles in either operational expertise or innovative expertise. While operational expertise is contingent on operating with a known goal within a relatively stable environment, innovative expertise often operates with a moving target in an environment that is ceaselessly changing. In each of these scenarios how knowledge is organized and coordinated should be distinctly different. Although there may be parallels in goals of achieving consensus and eliciting feedback, the variability in emergence differs significantly between to the two, that is, there less variability with a known target (operational expertise) versus a moving one (innovative expertise). Future research should seek to systematically compare the emergent processes of these two forms of organizational expertise.

Unpacking the Link between Individual and Organizational Expertise

In our preceding discussion we have described many of the components and types of potentially relevant processes, but we still do not have a clear idea of when we should expect organizational expertise to emerge. Specifically, we have yet to address how and when might individual knowledge and skill contribute to organizational expertise and ultimately a performance advantage. According to the resource- and knowledge-based views, knowledge or capabilities that are highly tacit, complex, and firm- or context-specific, because they are inimitable, may generate a sustained performance advantage (Dierickx and Cool, 1989; Lippman & Rumelt, 1982; Reed & DeFillippi, 1990; Winter, 1987). This proposition indicates that an organizational advantage may arise two ways: (1) when individuals' knowledge and skills are highly tacit, complex, or context specific, or, (2) when the organization's capability, resulting from the interaction of its expert individuals, has these characteristics.

The Human Capital Perspective

Human capital theories suggest that employees' knowledge and skills may serve as a source of sustainable competitive advantage to the extent that their valuable knowledge and skills may not be easily transferred and applied within other firms (e.g., Buchholtz, Ribbens, & Houle, 2003; Hatch & Dyer, 2004; Kor & Leblebici, 2005). In this tradition, Ployhart and Moliterno (2011) propose a multilevel model of human capital, making a distinction between knowledge, skills, and abilities as either being predominantly context specific and context generic. They argue that while ability is more likely context generic, due to its relatively stable nature over time and situations (Jensen, 1998; Kanfer, 1990), individual-level knowledge and skill vary on this dimension. That is, both knowledge and skill may be highly context specific (tightly coupled with the organizational or task environment) or context generic (applicable across several organization or task environments).

Scholars from the human capital literature also recognize that for organizations to efficiently capitalize on employee expertise, the costs of employing such individuals should be considered. For example, Campbell, Coff, and Kryscynski (2012) argue that we must consider both demand and supply side constraints on human capital mobility to understand when human capital resources might be under- or overvalued, and thus more or less likely to generate a performance advantage. Based on this logic they suggest that there might be instances when firm-specific human capital may not yield an advantage and others where general human capital may yield an advantage. In particular, low firm-specific human capital (or general human capital) is likely to yield an advantage when the workers outside options are underpriced, that is their skills are undervalued (demand-side conditions), and when workers prefer not to change firms, because of social embeddedness or geographic preference, for example (supply-side conditions). Firm-specific human capital in contrast may fail to yield an advantage when the workers outside options are overpriced, that is, their skills are overvalued (demand-side conditions), and when they prefer to change firms (supply-side conditions).

The Routine Perspective

The second path by which individuals may contribute to organizational expertise is when the product of their interactions yields a capability that is highly tacit, complex, and firm specific. Organizational-level processes related to expertise are depicted by the notion of organizational routines from the evolutionary view. Historically, the evolutionary view has not left much room for the individual, arguing that routines endure even in the face of turnover (e.g., Nelson & Winter, 1982). Persistence, despite turnover, suggests that the knowledge encoded within a routine exists beyond the scope of the individual, is held by the collective, and thus cannot be reduced to a single individual memory (Teece, 1982).

Despite the original depiction of routines as a source of functional stability and even dysfunctional rigidity (e.g., Leonard-Barton, 1992), researchers have increasingly expanded their view of routines, suggesting that they might also serve as a source of change (e.g., Feldman & Pentland, 2003). A significant portion of such research has begun to recognize the role of employees as the potential drivers of changing organizational routines (e.g. Feldman, 2000; 2003; Feldman & Pentland, 2003). Although this notion is now widely accepted, many important questions related to when and under what conditions individuals may be able to instill such change, and the nature of such change, remain to be answered.

Recent work calling for a return to "microfoundations" suggests among other things a reorientation toward understanding the role of individual-level heterogeneity in the emergence of such routines and their effects on higher-order capabilities (e.g., Abell, Felin, & Foss, 2008; Barney & Felin, 2013; Coff & Kryscynski, 2011). Felin et al. (2012) argue that the building blocks of routines, and thus organizational capabilities, consist of: (1) individuals, (2) structure, and (3) processes. More specifically the authors define *microfoundations* as "a theoretical explanation, supported by empirical examination, of a phenomenon located at analytical level N at time t (N_t). In the simplest sense, a baseline micro-foundation for level N_t lies at level $N - 1$ at time $t - 1$, where the time dimension reflects a temporal ordering of relationships with phenomena at level $N - 1$ predating phenomena at level N. Constituent actors, processes, and/or structures, at level $N - 1_{t-1}$ may interact, or operate alone, to influence phenomena at level N_t. Moreover, actors, processes, and/or structures at level $N - 1_{t-1}$ also may moderate or mediate influences of phenomena located at level N_t or at higher levels (e.g. $N + 1_{t+1}$ to $N + n_{t+n}$). In addition, while our theory focuses on the organizational routine or capability as the focal level N, the focal level N in a microfoundations inquiry may represent any collective level" (Felin et al., 2012: 1353). In their microfoundational theory of capabilities the authors posit that individuals may affect the development or evolution of routines through either individual behavior (a function of choice and rationality) or individual-level human capital (knowledge, skills, and abilities).

Felin et al. (2012) highlight that we should also consider the role of structure in the emergence of organizational routines and capabilities. In particular, they state "structures, whether at the organizational level or within an organization, specify the conditions that enable and constrain individual and collective action and establish the context for interactions within an organization. Structures may constrain behavior but they also enable efficient information processing, knowledge development and sharing, coordination and integration, and more generally, collective action" (Felin et al., 2012: 1364). Some examples of structures include rules (Davis, Eisenhardt, & Bingham, 2009), social interactions (Argote & Ingram, 2000), organizing principles (Kogut & Zander, 1992), community (Brown & Duguid, 2001), and organizational form or design (Foss, 2003; Hoopes & Postrel, 1999).

Through an examination of microfoundations, the authors posit that routines are created through interaction among individuals, structures, and processes and that in studying the emergence of organizational routines and capabilities we should focus our inquiries on seeking to understand such interactions. This suggests future research should investigate how individual choice and human capital shape organizational routines as well as the implication of certain structures for shaping the interactions of individuals with organizational routines and business processes. It is the purpose of this chapter to build on this understanding of microfoundations to further explore the emergence of organizational capabilities and the conditions under which such may lead to the emergence of organizational expertise.

The first section of this chapter focused on understanding expertise at individual and organizational levels. Next, we consider extant multilevel research, emphasizing work related to organizational expertise that complements this perspective. Finally, we discuss the linkages between individual- and organizational-level expertise and highlight directions for future research.

Developing Individual Expertise

Learning is the primary way that individuals develop expertise in organizations. Learning can occur both formally through participating in formal training and development activities as well as more naturally through social interactions and on the job. There is large and well-developed body of research focused on learning in organizations, including formal training and development and socialization (for recent reviews, see Bauer & Erdogan, 2014; Brown & Sitzmann, 2011; Noe, Clarke, & Klein, 2014). There is a less well-developed, yet important, research area that focuses on informal learning, knowledge sharing, and job crafting (e.g., Wang & Noe, 2010).

Our focus here is on those aspects of learning that are most relevant for understanding how individuals may contribute to organizational expertise. From this perspective, learning may be viewed as a system that includes formal training and development programs, socialization, informal learning, knowledge sharing, and job crafting – all of which can build expertise (e.g., Noe et al., 2014; Salas et al., 2012).

Training and Development

Formal training and development is concerned with the acquisition of expertise in organizational sponsored programs that in many cases employees are required to attend (Noe, 2013). Compared to informal learning, formal training and development programs have specific objectives or goals related to the expertise employees are expected to acquire. This expertise can include knowledge, skills, competencies, or some combination. Formal training and development includes courses and programs that employees can attend online or face to face. Also, job experiences and mentoring and coaching programs can be used for expertise development. The popularity of formal training and development is illustrated by a recent estimate that U.S. organizations spent approximately $156.2 billion on formal training and development in 2012 (Miller, 2012). The individual and organizational benefits of formal training and development programs are well established (Aguinis & Kraiger, 2009).

Socialization

Socialization is the process through which newcomers to the organization are transformed from "outsiders" to "insiders" (Feldman, 1976; 2012) or more specifically, the process by which individuals become integrated through the alignment of their values and beliefs to those of the organization (Feldman & O'Neill, 2014). Onboarding and orientation programs are formal methods organizations use to socialize employees. Socialization also occurs naturally as new employees interact with peers and managers. While such processes are unlikely directly related to the acquisition of knowledge or skill to be used as direct inputs to production or innovation, the alignment between individual and organizational values, beliefs, and norms provides individuals an understanding of the organizational climate and culture, or, alternatively, a schema for how other employees think, feel, and interpret information, as well as a guide for acceptable behaviors and social expectations, all of which are necessary for individuals to thrive within the organization (e.g., Feldman, 1981; Van Maanen & Schein, 1979).

Informal Learning

It is also important to recognize that a significant portion of expertise development occurs informally. It is estimated that informal learning accounts for almost 75% of all learning by an organization's employees (Bear et al., 2008). Informal learning includes learning that occurs outside of formal training and development is learner initiated with the intent to develop, and occurs on an as-needed basis (Bear et al., 2008; Tannenbaum et al., 2010). Informal learning includes learning from self through reflection and experimentation, learning from others, and learning through noninterpersonal sources (e.g., Internet, books, manuals)

Who learns informally and when? Individuals who are inclined to engage in proactive work behaviors, such as those who possess positive psychological resources (e.g., zest) are more likely to engage in informal learning (Noe, Tews, & Marand, 2013). Learning orientation is also a predictor of informal learning (Choi & Jacobs, 2011). In addition to individual characteristics, the organizational and task environment also serve to facilitate (or inhibit) information learning. For example, informal learning is enhanced by psychological safety (Edmonson, 1999; 2002) as well as the commitment of management to learning, an internal culture that supports learning, as well as access to social networks (Doornbos, Simons, & Denessen, 2008; Ellinger, 2005; Kyndt, Dochy, & Nijs, 2009).

Informal learning recognizes that learning and expertise development can occur socially through interactions with peers and others (Connelly et al., 2012; Hinds et al., 2001). One way to do so is through knowledge sharing, which can occur directly through face-to-face or technology-aided interactions with experts or indirectly through documenting, organizing, and capturing knowledge for others (Cummings, 2004; Pulakos, Dorsey, and Baughman, 2003). Knowledge sharing between employees and across teams allows an organization to exploit existing knowledge-based resources (Cabrera & Cabrera 2002; 2005; Damodaran & Olphert 2000). Research suggests that knowledge expertise and transfer is important for both organizational and team outcomes. For example, Maurer, Bartsch, and Ebers (2011) showed that knowledge transfer (conceptualized as the mobilization, assimilation, and use of knowledge resources) mediated the relationship between organization members' intraorganizational social capital and organizational growth and innovation. Sung and Choi (2012) found that efforts by team members to effectively utilize their knowledge base motivated proactive learning. Team knowledge utilization, but not team knowledge stock, was positively related to team creativity, which in turn predicted team financial performance. These results were stronger for teams facing high environmental uncertainty.

It is important to note that both individual differences and situational factors influence whether individuals will be motivated to seek expertise, learn, and use what they learn on the job. There are many individual differences that have been found to be important for learning and transfer of training from formal programs. These individual differences include but are not limited to general mental ability, personality (e.g., conscientiousness), self-efficacy, goal orientations, and motivation to learn (see Blume et al., 2010; Colquitt, Lepine, & Noe, 2000). These individual differences influence both the effort employees put into seeking and extracting expertise from extant learning opportunities as well as their motivation for applying the acquired knowledge on the job (Tannenbaum & Yukl, 1992).

Situational factors such as the number of explicit opportunities to use and apply acquired knowledge and skills (e.g. Quiñones et al., 1995), a continuous learning climate, support from managers and peers (Martin, 2010; Tracey, Tannenbaum, & Kavanagh, 1995), and job crafting influence learning and transfer. Research also supports the role of a learning culture in informal learning and knowledge-sharing behaviors. For example, Choi and Jacobs (2011) found that a supportive learning environment had a significant positive indirect effect on informal learning through its influence on employees' participation in formal learning courses and programs. A psychologically safe climate is important for learners' willingness to try new things, take risks, or otherwise step out of their comfort zones without fear of negative repercussions for errors. Kostopoulos and Bozionelos (2011) found psychological safety to be linearly and nonlinearly related to team exploitative and exploratory learning, respectively; exploratory and exploitative learning were additively related to team performance and mediated the relationship between psychological safety and performance.

Developing Organizational Expertise

There are several available lenses to study the development of organizational expertise including absorptive capacity from the knowledge-based view literature, exploration and exploitation from the organizational learning literature, and dynamic capabilities from insights abstracted from evolutionary economics and the resource-based view.

Absorptive Capacity

Based on the knowledge-based view, some scholars have explored organizations' capacities to develop new capabilities as a function of knowledge creation processes, which an often a necessary antecedent of innovation (e.g., Kogut & Zander, 1992; Lavie & Drori, 2012; Martin, 2010; Nahapiet & Goshal, 1998; Nonaka, 1994; Nonaka & Von Krogh, 2009; Schilling & Phelps, 2007; Smith, Collins, & Clark, 2005; Von Krogh, Ichijo, & Nonaka, 2000). One aspect of this line of research is reflected in the notion of absorptive capacity, or the ability of firms to exploit (evaluate and utilize) external knowledge with the organizational aim of innovation (Cohen & Levinthal, 1990).

The capacity of a firm to absorb external knowledge and information resides in the linkages between individuals and their interactions and is largely a function of prior related knowledge. Cohen and Levinthal's (1990) initial representation of absorptive capacity highlights the importance of boundary spanners as organizational sensors for relevant external information, which is even more crucial when operating in a turbulent environment. These boundary spanners are critical because at the organizational level, absorptive capacity reflects a trade-off between bringing in external knowledge and being able to effectively integrate such knowledge (Cohen & Levinthal, 1990). This trade-off exists because knowledge symbols and language are different across boundaries, and shared knowledge is imperative for communication and integration. More recent studies of absorptive capacity have built from a reconceptualization of the model proposed by Zahra and George (2002) that frames absorptive capacity as a process, describing how organizational knowledge is transformed from a potential to a "realized" state. This reconceptualization has been important for linking the notion of absorptive capacity to the literature on dynamic or second-order capabilities (which we will address in the following text).

Exploration and Exploitation

The literature on organizational learning is another area of research that addresses the development of organizational capabilities. Key concepts in this area are exploration and exploitation (March, 1991). Exploitation is the improvement of the firm's extant capabilities within the same domain where the firm is currently functioning and is associated with such objectives as "refinement, efficiency, selection, and implementation." Exploration is the development of capabilities in novel domains as compared to the firm's current activities, and is related to "search, variation, experimentation, and discovery" (March, 1991: 102). Teece, Pisano, and Shuen (1997) have argued that the persistence of a firm's performance advantage, and perhaps even its survival, depends on both its ability to improve its extant capabilities while simultaneously developing new capabilities. In this line of research scholars seek to understand how firms may strike a "balance" across both of these objectives, which suggests when to accept trade-offs associated with pursuing one of the other, or alternatively how firms may be able to simultaneously pursue both (e.g., Czaszar, 2013; O'Reilly & Tushman, 2008; Rivkin & Siggelkow, 2003; Siggelkow & Levinthal, 2003).

Dynamic Capabilities

Dynamic capabilities are defined as "the firm's ability to integrate, build, and reconfigure internal and external competences to address rapidly changing environments" (Teece et al., 1997: 516; also Dosi et al., 2000; Eisenhardt & Martin, 2000; Hoopes & Madsen, 2008; Winter, 2003; Zollo & Winter, 2002). According to Teece et al. (1997) dynamic capabilities consist of a system of dynamic routines that underlie its ability to learn, adapt, change, and renew over time. A dynamic capability is distinct from a first-order or operational capability, which is a discrete business-level process capable of yielding a competitive advantage in a relatively static environment (Leonard-Barton, 1992; Siggelkow, 2001; Siggelkow & Levinthal, 2005). In contrast, dynamic capabilities are those second-order capabilities that support the firm in its efforts to update its existing set of operational capabilities allowing the firm to adapt in the face of new threats or opportunities (Eisenhardt & Martin, 2000; O'Reilly & Tushman, 2008).

Many organizational-level theories of expertise assume the firm is the focal and active "learner" or developer of expertise. However, it has been well documented and generally accepted that organizations do not learn or "know," but rather, such "learning" originates in the employees of the organization, who continuously acquire, assimilate, and translate their knowledge (e.g., Simon, 1991). Conversely, Argyris and Schön articulate that "individual learning is a necessary but insufficient condition for organizational learning" (Argyris & Schön, 1978: 20). Thus, to understand the relationship between the development of individual and organizational expertise is not simply an exercise of aggregation. Rather we must understand the processes responsible for the transformation of individual expertise to organizational expertise.

Multilevel Models Related to Organizational Expertise

Scholars have proposed several different models that capture at least some of the ways that individual learning relates to organizational expertise. In these models individuals play a role in firms' so-called second-order capabilities, or the organizational capability to update its current set of productive, or first-order, capabilities. It is important to note that what scholars have referred to as first- and second-order capabilities are related to but distinct from operational and innovative expertise. Operational and innovative expertise are examples of first-order capabilities, that is, the firm's expert capability to be efficient in its current domain (operational expertise) and the firm's expert capability to create new products and services. Second-order capabilities are those that allow firms to update their first-order capabilities, or the process by which firms develop their capabilities and potentially the means through which they become expert organizations. While our focus is on expertise and the accumulation of expert knowledge and skills required to produce expert organizations, the capabilities and organizational learning perspectives do not necessitate expertise, but are concerned more broadly with organizational heterogeneity. Despite this difference in purpose, these frameworks may be informative nonetheless for furthering our understanding of the link between individual and organizational expertise. In our view, models of organizational learning, dynamic capabilities, and ambidexterity are related to but alone insufficient for explaining organizational expertise. Thus, we propose to use them as a basis and motivation for furthering research on organizational expertise.

Organizational Learning

One research area originating from organizational learning adopts an emergent perspective, illustrating how learning that occurs first at the individual level becomes shared at the group level through processes such as socialization (e.g., Huber, 1991; Kim, 1993; 1998). For example, Duncan and Weiss (1979) suggest that the processes of transferring, sharing, validating, and integrating individual knowledge are all influential in determining whether and what becomes collectively understood. Similarly, Kim (1993; 1998) proposes a model of organizational learning where not only does the organization learn through the knowledge exchange of its members but through the cocreation of shared mental models. In Kim's (1993: 10) model, organizational learning is defined as "increasing an organization's capacity to take effective action." In an alternative model Nonaka (1994) argues that organizational knowledge arises from individual knowledge that is amplified through interaction, that is through the process of knowledge conversion. In this process, knowledge is converted from one state to another across two core dimensions, tacit explicit and individual social.

Other researchers propose multilevel models of organizational learning, where organizational learning is defined as a change in the organization's knowledge as the result of experience (Argote, 2013; Fiol & Lyles, 1985). Note that organization learning is neither inherently good nor bad, and thus may or may not lead to the emergence of organizational expertise. However, both organizational learning and the emergence of organizational expertise are in parallel, contingent on experience.

Crossan, Lane, and White (1999) propose a model of organizational learning, which includes the processes of intuiting, interpreting, integrating, and institutionalizing, that suggests the link between individual and organizational levels of learning emerges from the individual level through the level of group or team. First, the processes of intuiting and interpreting occur as individuals engage in experiences and make observations, from which they draw metaphors, framing stimuli in reference to their existing cognitive framework. Next, at the group level, there is integration among individuals' interpretations of experience and observation through interaction, mutual adjustment, and the (potential) development of a shared understanding. Finally, institutionalization occurs as what is learned becomes collectively understood and is encoded into the organization's hardware, such as its routines, information systems, rules, norms, and so forth. This depiction of organizational learning recognizes the organization as an open system, links levels of analysis through social and psychological processes, assumes the bilateral impacts of cognition and action, and views organizational learning as a dynamic process. In doing so, Crossan et al.'s framework emphasizes the outcome and goal of organizational "renewal," or the concurrence of exploration and exploitation.

Argote and Miron-Spektor (2011) offer an alternative multilevel model of organizational learning. The authors suggest that organizational learning occurs through the accumulation of experience that is embedded within a context, having both active and latent components and argue that the interaction between context and experience facilitates the creation of knowledge. In this framework, experience is determined to occur at the organizational level and can happen either directly through experiential learning or indirectly through observational learning, where "a unit of task experience" is seen as a function of "its novelty, success, ambiguity, timing, and geographic location" and "the cumulative amount of experience can be characterized in terms of its heterogeneity and pace" (Argote, 2013: 35). In short, Argote and Miron-Spektor (2011) suggest that organizational learning consists of three interrelated processes: (1) knowledge creation, which stems from direct experience, (2) knowledge transfer, which is obtained observationally or vicariously, and (3) knowledge retaining, which occurs when knowledge that is created or transferred is somehow encoded and persists over time.

Dynamic Capabilities

The dynamic capabilities perspective considers the individual's role in the organization's second-order capabilities from a different perspective. Teece (2007) proposes that the microfoundations of dynamic capabilities may be captured by "the distinct skills, processes, procedures, organizational structures, decision rules, and disciplines" that underlie the three fundamental organizational-level dynamic capabilities: sensing (and shaping) opportunities and threats, seizing, and reconfiguring (Teece, 2007: 1319). Here, the role of individuals, specifically managers, are associated with "selecting and/or developing routines, making investment choices, and in orchestrating nontradable assets to achieve efficiencies and appropriate returns from innovation" (Augier & Teece, 2009: 417). The microfoundations of each dynamic capability – sensing, seizing, and reconfiguring – and the roles individuals may play within each are described in the following text.

Sensing

The capability of sensing (and shaping) opportunities and threats is associated with the organizational investment in activities related to scanning, creation, learning, and interpretation of both local and distal information (Teece, 2007). The microfoundations of such a capability consist of a combination of the cognitions and creative abilities of individuals as well as the organizational processes within which they are embedded (e.g., research and development) (Teece, 2007). Although certain individuals within the organization may have superior skills associated with sensing opportunities and threats, organizational processes are relevant in determining whether and when the appropriate information is filtered and then flows to the necessary individual(s) (Teece, 2007).

Research has also addressed other possible individual-level mechanisms beyond ability related to sensing and shaping opportunities. For example, Hodgkinson and Healey (2011) argue that affective states may have implications for how and which cognitive maps, or schema, individuals use for sensing and interpreting information. The authors also argue that there may be instances when intuition as opposed to effortful processing may yield advantages to sensing and responding to opportunities.

Seizing

Organizational seizing capabilities are required once a technological or market opportunity has been identified, and are related to the ability of the firm to exploit the focal opportunity through the development and commercialization of new products, processes, or services (Teece, 2007). Teece (2007) argues that it is often necessary for firms to invest in multiple (competing) paths, at least at early stages, as the successful exploitation of opportunities involves an organizational preparedness with respect to maintaining technological competences and complementary assets. The microfoundations of organizational seizing capabilities according to Teece (2007) are related to establishing a "good" business model, which is produced when firms are able to: "(1) analyze multiple alternatives, (2) have a deep understanding of user needs, (3) analyze the value chain thoroughly so as to understand just how to deliver what the customer wants in a cost-effective and timely fashion, and (4) adopt a neutrality or relative efficiency perspective to outsourcing decisions" (Teece, 2007: 1330). Another aspect of establishing a good business model Teece (2007) argues is determining organizational boundaries that are greatly affected by: "(1) the appropriability regime (i.e., the amount of natural and legal protection afforded the innovation by the circumstances prevailing in the market); (2) the nature of the complementary assets (cospecialized or otherwise) that an innovating enterprise possessed; (3) the relative positioning of innovator and potential imitators with respect to complementary assets; and (4) the phase of industry development (pre or post the emergence of a dominate design)" (Teece, 2007: 1331).

The role of individuals in the emergence of seizing capabilities may be related to their decision making with regard to the development and commercialization of identified opportunities (Teece, 2007). These decision-making processes Teece (2007) argues, may be susceptible to several biases, for example, there may be self-serving biases present that would favor a decision to go forward (or not) with the exploitation of an identified opportunity, which may or may not realistically lead to the optimal performance outcome at the organizational level. Teece proposes that one way to overcome such biases is for the design of "organizational structures, incentives and routines, to catalyze and reward creative action" and to develop "routines to enable the continual shedding of established assets and routines that no longer yield 'value' as this protects managers decisions from being biased by their unwarranted attachment to dead or dying assets" (Teece, 2007: 1333).

Reconfiguring

The third dynamic capability, reconfiguring, is the "ability to recombine and to reconfigure assets and organizational structures as the enterprise grows, and as markets and technologies change ... [allowing firms to] escape from unfavorable path dependencies" (Teece, 2007: 1335). The critical factors underlying such ability within a dynamic environment are related to the flexibility of the organization's structure, where business units may maintain a significant level of autonomy to be able to make and execute decisions in a timely manner, but are connected enough to other necessary business units that they may still efficiently coordinate their activities (Teece, 2007). The nature of this organizational structure should also take into account its effects on the ability of managers to manage and identify cospecialized assets (an asset whose value is determined or enhanced through its use in conjunction with other particular assets), as well as its implications for knowledge management – the ability to acquire and integrate new knowledge from the "outside" as well as preventing the "leakage" of strategic knowledge to competitors (Teece, 2007).

According to Teece (2007) these dynamic capabilities and the nature of their microfoundations allow firms to not only adapt to their evolving ecosystem – "the community of organizations, institutions, and individuals that impact the enterprise and the enterprise's customers and supplies" – but also allow them to shape such ecosystems through innovation and collaboration (Teece, 2007: 1325). Neglecting the microfoundations of organizational capabilities and such higher-level constructs are problematic because they leave an incomplete understanding of these complex.

Ambidexterity

Although Teece's (2007) microfoundational view of dynamic capabilities advocates for structural flexibility through assuming that organizations' capabilities need to be able to respond to threats and opportunities in the environment, others have suggested that our pursuit for the microfoundations of sustainable advantage more broadly should consider the pursuit of both efficiency and flexibility (e.g., Eisenhardt, Furr, & Bingham, 2010).

Organizational ambidexterity, or the capability to both explore and exploit (O'Reilly & Tushman, 2008) is one means of balancing organizational objectives of efficiency and flexibility. Like the dynamic capabilities framework, the exploration-exploitation literature suggests that excessive exploitation relative to exploration (akin to having a superior operational capability but a lack of dynamic capability) may lead to short-term performance, but is likely associated with falling into a competency trap because firms are unable to respond to environmental changes (e.g., Ahuja & Lampert, 2001; Leonard-Barton, 1992). Alternatively, firms may invest too heavily in exploration, renewing their operational capabilities, but unable to capitalize on their new capabilities relative to close competitors and thus unable to generate a relative advantage (Volberda & Lewin, 2003). Thus, balancing exploration and exploitation is key to maintaining a sustainable performance advantage (e.g., Raisch et al., 2009).

Some posit that pursuing both exploration and exploration can be done sequentially (e.g., Boumgarden, Nickerson, & Zenger, 2012; Gulati & Puranam, 2009; Nickerson & Zenger, 2002; Siggelkow & Levinthal, 2003), while others suggest that it may be managed simultaneously (e.g., O'Reilly & Tushman, 2008). However, whether done sequentially or simultaneously has distinct implications for its microfoundations and, more specifically, for the nature of the challenges facing senior management (e.g. Gupta, Smith, & Shalley, 2006). O'Reilly and Tushman (2008) suggest that to balance exploration and exploitation sequentially, managers' efforts should be focused on the shift from one strategic focus (explore or exploit) to the other; however, while managing exploration and exploitation simultaneously, managers are faced with the unique challenge of "articulat[ing] a vision and strategic intent that justifies the ambidextrous form" (O'Reilly & Tushman, 2008: 193).

To meet such unique challenges, those who are responsible for orchestrating ambidexterity likely require certain skills and abilities. Managers responsible for organizational ambidexterity must have both the ability to comprehend and the motivation to take action with respect to conflicting needs and goals (O'Reilly & Tushman, 2004). They must be able to think paradoxically (Gibson & Birkinshaw, 2004; Smith & Tushman, 2005), to multitask (Floyd & Lane, 2000; Gibson & Birkinshaw, 2004) and to search both internal and external social networks for knowledge and information (Hansen, Podolny, & Pfeffer, 2001; Subramaniam & Youndt, 2005). There are several psychological constructs that are likely relevant for understanding managers' development of ambidexterity. Good and Michel (2013) argue that there is likely a distinct cognitive ability, "individual ambidexterity," which is a combination of three critical variables: divergent thinking, focused attention, and cognitive flexibility. Learning agility, adaptability, openness to experience, and cognitive flexibility may also be important (e.g., see DeRue, Ashford, & Meyers, 2012; Gully & Chen, 2010; Pulakos et al., 2000). Future research is needed to examine whether these constructs are related to managerial ambidexterity, and to determine if managerial ambidexterity is a managerial capability that can be developed or an innate personal characteristic.

Managerial ambidexterity alone may not suffice to realize the anticipated outcome of organizational-level ambidexterity. Mom, Van den Bosch, and Volberda (2009) suggest that coordination mechanisms and the interaction of formal and informal structure (e.g., cross-function team interfaces and managerial connectedness respectively) have a significant effect on managerial ambidexterity. Others have suggested that the structure of the manager's social network is also critical for predicting ambidextrous behavior (Rogan & Mors, 2014).

Some scholars argue that ambidexterity occurs at the team level rather than individual level. These scholars propose that the top management team must be able to filter such complex information and make decisions in the face of conflicting goals (e.g., Smith & Tushman, 2005). Smith and Tushman (2005) posit that teams balance strategic contradictions through an iterative processing of information, oscillating between differentiation and integration. While differentiation clarifies distinctions between existing products and innovation, integration is the shifting from product or organizational level of analysis to identify possible synergies and to reinforce cooperation between contradicting agendas (Smith & Tushman, 2005). Top management teams that are better able to accommodate such processes reflect several characteristics. For example, top management teams that maintain a shared vision and are rewarded according to team outcomes (i.e., contingency rewards) support organizational ambidexterity (Jansen et al., 2008). Furthermore, critical to organizational ambidexterity is the acquisition by top management teams of internal and external information. Alexiev et al. (2010) found that top management teams that are heterogeneous are more likely to accommodate both internal and external advice-seeking strategies, where heterogeneity is defined as the variance in team composition along demographic, functional, and background dimensions.

The majority of individual- and team-level research on ambidexterity has focused on top management, but less is known about the human capital needs of those who are being managed, or those who are responsible for implementing strategic goals. Whether sequential or simultaneous ambidexterity, the implementation of paradoxical objectives may be just as challenging as identifying and establishing an ambidextrous strategy.

Limitations of Current Models of Organizational Expertise and Future Research Directions

Current multilevel models have several limitations that contribute to our incomplete understanding of the development of organizational expertise. One limitation is that the processes through, and conditions under which, learning at lower levels influences organizational-level constructs remain only loosely understood. For example, Argote and Miron-Spektor (2011) argue that learning that originates at the individual level affects organizational learning through the level of the group or team. Understanding how teams learn from individuals is complex because teams often have a dynamic composition, with individuals joining and departing as well as working across several teams simultaneously at different frequencies and intervals (Tannenbaum et al., 2012). Teams increasingly rely on technology and common requirements to span large geographical and cultural distances (Tannenbaum et al., 2012). Finally, there has been a trend toward giving teams greater autonomy through empowering and delayering (Tannenbaum et al., 2012).

Alternatively to representing the organization as a nested entity of groups and teams, some scholars suggest that the organization is best represented by a network of socially and dynamically embedded individuals (e.g., Murase et al., 2012). As a result, research on the emergence of organizational learning, dynamic capabilities, and ambidexterity needs to consider a more flexible and dynamic view of the organization, one that acknowledges an often multirelational and persistently changing network of individuals and their teams. For example, communities of practice have been used by organizations in an attempt to facilitate informal learning specifically relevant to a desired area of expertise (Li et al., 2009). Communities of practice facilitate knowledge acquisition, sharing, and relationship building between individuals who share a common interest (e.g., product, problem, service) but otherwise may not necessarily work on the same team or functional area. Recent work by Kirkman et al. (2011) showed how organizational communities of practice are important for development of human capital resources through knowledge sharing.

Another limitation is the lack of focused concentration on the emergent processes. While the literature points to a variety of critical units of analysis, the means by which they aggregate to impact higher-level constructs is still poorly understood. How do lower-level units aggregate to organizational expertise? Which lower-level units are more important and when? For example, while there is evidence for ambidexterity across multiple levels of analysis (O'Reilly & Tushman, 2013), we know little about the conditions under which individual, team, business unit, or organizational ambidexterity are most appropriate for developing expertise. When is individual or structural ambidexterity more important? How do different configurations of ambidexterity affect the potential emergence of organizational expertise? Given an understanding of such conditions, we could further ask, how should work be structured to support ambidexterity at each of these levels of analysis? What kinds of human capital are optimal for filling such positions? Future research should also consider the nature of internally and externally sourced information that is critical for organizational ambidexterity, as well as the characteristics of top management teams' social networks that may facilitate their access to such information. These are all important questions for furthering our understanding the process of aggregation between individual and organizational expertise.

We may ask a similar series of questions as it pertains to Teece's (2007) dynamics capabilities framework. While he points to the type of second-order capabilities firms need to be adaptable and update their first-order capabilities, we do not have a clear understanding of how the microfoundations of these capabilities aggregate to achieve firm-level outcomes, and ultimately organizational expertise. What types of knowledge and skills are associated with each of the dynamic capabilities (sensing, seizing, reconfiguring), and how much of these capabilities are driven by individual-level characteristics versus social and structural elements? Are the individuals responsible for sensing different (in cognitive characteristics or structural location) than those responsible for seizing and reconfiguring? Do these types of capabilities require individual experts or expert systems? When? Do these types of processes follow composition or compilation forms of aggregation? If evidence of both, is one more often associated with the emergence of expertise?

These examples highlight a need to better understand the process of aggregation especially as it relates to the means through which individual and structural characteristics interact. Asked broadly, whether and when do certain individual characteristics serve as complements or substitutes to the opportunities afforded to them by their structural location? For example, does an individual's

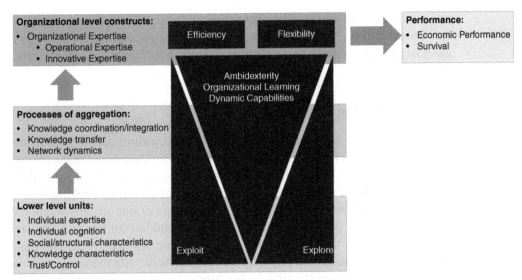

Figure 3.1. *A multilevel model of the emergence of organizational expertise.*

position within a highly connected formal role substitute or complement certain personality characteristics such as extroversion or openness? And what are the repercussions of such interactions on organizational efficiency and flexibility? These questions only scratch the surface of questions remaining to be answered about aggregation.

Lastly, it is necessary to highlight that the concept of organizational expertise has largely been ignored across these "macro"-oriented literatures. The models discussed in the chapter tend to focus on how firms may maintain an economic advantage, or how to avoid rigidities under changing environmental conditions, but do not directly address the notion of expertise. How do firms become experts in what they do? While economic performance may be a by-product of expertise, and avoiding rigidities may be necessary for long-term survival, economic performance and survival are not proof of expertise. Thus, when outcomes of performance become focal to the underlying arguments, it becomes difficult to understand the nature of its emergence and whether the organization is an expert, or if it just finds itself in a lucky position relative to competitors at a given point in time. Thus, we propose a decoupling of performance outcomes from the emergence of organizational expertise.

As a way forward, we urge scholars to develop research seeking to explain the arrows shown in Figure 3.1. The references in this chapter and factors included in this figure are not exhaustive, but identify the main sources of knowledge that we have about how individual expertise links to organizational expertise. The critical missing piece is a clear understanding of how individual- and other lower-level units of analysis are transformed to the organizational level and the conditions under which they are likely to interact in a way that produces organizational efficiency and/or flexibility. We believe that focusing on the nature and source of expertise to understand how individual and structural characteristics interact to generate organizational expertise in a given domain or in a changing environment, rather than on the potential performance outcomes, will be more likely to generate insights on which managers can act directly.

Conclusion

There has been considerable progress made with respect to our knowledge of the link between the development of individual and organizational expertise, but research has only begun to scratch the surface. This chapter highlights some of the critical assumptions that are imperative for building future multilevel research in this area, as well as some areas of opportunity where the expertise of industrial-organizational psychology and human resource scholars may be particularly useful. In addition to supporting calls for greater emphasis on multilevel organizational research, we specifically identify the need for work addressing the nature of the relationship between individuals and the organizational structures that facilitate and constrain the emergence of learning and the subsequent development of organizational expertise.

References

Abell, P., Felin, T., and Foss, N. 2008. Building micro foundations for the routines, capabilities, and performance links. *Managerial and Decision Economics* 29: 489–502.

Aguinis, H., and Kraiger, K. 2009. Benefits of training and development for individuals and teams, organizations, and society. *Annual Review of Psychology* 60: 451–474.

Ahuja, G., and Morris Lampert, C. 2001. Entrepreneurship in the large corporation: A longitudinal study of how established firms create breakthrough inventions. *Strategic Management Journal* 22: 521–543.

Alexiev, A. S., Jansen, J. J., Van den Bosch, F. A., and Volberda, H. W. 2010. Top management team advice seeking and exploratory innovation: The moderating role of TMT heterogeneity. *Journal of Management Studies* 47: 1343–1364.

Amit, R., and Schoemaker, P. J. 1993. Strategic assets and organizational rent. *Strategic Management Journal* 14: 33–46.

Argote, L., ed. 2013. *Organizational Learning: Creating, Retaining and Transferring Knowledge,* 2nd ed. New York: Springer.

Argote, L., and Ingram, P. 2000. Knowledge transfer: A basis for competitive advantage in firms. *Organizational Behavior and Human Decision Processes* 82: 150–169.

Argote, L., and Miron-Spektor, E. 2011. Organizational learning: From experience to knowledge. *Organization Science* 22: 1123–1137.

Argyris, C., and Schon, D. 1978. *Organizational Learning: A Theory of Action Approach.* Reading, MA: Addision Wesley.

Arthur, W., Jr., Bennett, W. Jr., Edens, P. S., and Bell, S. T. 2003. Effectiveness of training in organizations: A meta-analysis of design and evaluation features. *Journal of Applied Psychology* 88: 234–245.

Augier, M., and Teece, D. J. 2009. Dynamic capabilities and the role of managers in business strategy and economic performance. *Organization Science* 20: 410–421.

Barney, J. 1991. Firm resources and sustained competitive advantage. *Journal of Management* 17: 99–120.

Barney, J. B. 1992. Integrating organizational behavior and strategy formulation research: A resource based analysis. *Advances in Strategic Management* 8: 39–61.

Barney, J., and Felin, T. 2013. What are microfoundations? *Academy of Management Perspectives* 27: 138–155.

Bauer, T. N., and Erdogan, B. 2014. Delineating and reviewing the role of newcomer capital in organizational socialization. *Annual Review of Organizational Psychology and Organizational Behavior* 1: 439–457.

Bear, D. J., Tompson, H. B., Morrison, C. L., Vickers, M., Paradise, A., Czarnowsky, M., Soyars, M., and King, K. 2008. *Tapping the Potential of Informal Learning: An ASTD Research Study.* Alexandria, VA: American Society for Training and Development.

Becker, M. C. 2004. Organizational routines: A review of the literature. *Industrial and Corporate Change* 13: 643–678.

Bereiter, C., and Scardamalia, M. 1993. *Surpassing Ourselves: An Inquiry into the Nature and Implications of Expertise.* Chicago: Open Court.

Blume, B. D., Ford, J. K., Baldwin, T. T., and Huang, J. L. 2010. Transfer of training: A meta-analytic review. *Journal of Management* 36: 1065–1105.

Boumgarden, P., Nickerson, J., and Zenger, T. R. 2012. Sailing into the wind: Exploring the relationships among ambidexterity, vacillation, and organizational performance. *Strategic Management Journal* 33: 587–610.

Brandenburger, A. M., and Stuart, H. W. 1996. Value-based business strategy. *Journal of Economics and Management Strategy* 5: 5–24.

Brass, D. J., Galaskiewicz, J., Greve, H. R., and Tsai, W. 2004. Taking stock of networks and organizations: A multilevel perspective. *Academy of Management Journal* 47: 795–817.

Brown, J. S., and Duguid, P. 2001. Knowledge and organization: A social-practice perspective. *Organization Science* 12: 198–213.

Brown, K. G., and Sitzmann, T. 2011. Training and employee development for improved performance. In S. Zedeck, ed., *APA Handbook of Industrial and Organizational Psychology,* 469–503. Washington, DC: American Psychological Association.

Buchholtz, A. K., Ribbens, B. A., and Houle, I. T. 2003. The role of human capital in postacquisition CEO departure. *Academy of Management Journal* 46: 506–514.

Burns, T. E., and Stalker, G. M. 1961. *The Management of Innovation.* Champaign, IL: Academy for Entrepreneurial Leadership

Burt, R. S. 1992. *Structural Holes.* Cambridge, MA: Harvard Business School Press.

Burton, R. M., Eriksen, B., Håkonsson, D. D., and Snow, C. C. 2006. *Organization Design: The Evolving State-of-the-Art.* New York: Springer.

Cabrera, A., and Cabrera, E. F. 2002. Knowledge-sharing dilemmas. *Organization Studies* 23: 687–710.

Cabrera, E. F., and Cabrera, A. 2005. Fostering knowledge sharing through people management practices. *The International Journal of Human Resource Management* 16: 720–735.

Campbell, B. A., Coff, R., and Kryscynski, D. 2012. Rethinking sustained competitive advantage from human capital. *Academy of Management Review* 37: 376–395.

Choi, W., and Jacobs, R. L. 2011. Influences of formal learning, personal learning orientation, and supportive learning environment on informal learning. *Human Resource Development Quarterly* 22: 239–257.

Coff, R., and Kryscynski, D. 2011. Drilling for micro-foundations of human capital–based competitive advantages. *Journal of Management* 37: 1429–1443.

Cohen, M. D., Burkhart, R., Dosi, G., Egidi, M., Marengo, L., Warglien, M., and Winter, S. 1996. Routines and other recurring action patterns of organizations: Contemporary research issues. *Industrial and Corporate Change* 5: 653–698.

Cohen W. M., and Levinthal, D. A. 1990. Absorptive capacity: A new perspective on learning and innovation. *Administrative Science Quarterly* 35: 128–152.

Coleman, J. S. 1988. Social capital in the creation of human capital. *American Journal of Sociology* 94: S95–S120.

Coletti, A. L., Sedatole, K. L., and Towry, K. L. 2005. The effect of control systems on trust and cooperation in collaborative environments. *The Accounting Review* 80: 477–500.

Colombo, M. G., and Grilli, L. 2005. Founders' human capital and the growth of new technology-based firms: A competence-based view. *Research Policy* 34: 795–816.

Colquitt, J. A., LePine, J. A., and Noe, R. A. 2000. Toward an integrative theory of training motivation: A meta-analytic path analysis of 20 years of research. *Journal of Applied Psychology* 85: 678–707.

Connelly, C. E., Zweig, D., Webster, J., and Trougakos, J. P. 2012. Knowledge hiding in organizations. *Journal of Organizational Behavior* 33: 64–88.

Creed, W. D., and Miles, R. E. 1996. Trust in organizations: A conceptual framework linking organizational forms, managerial philosophies, and the opportunity cost of controls. In T. R. Tyler and R. M. Kramer, eds., *Trust in Organizations: Frontiers of Theory and Research*, 16–38. Thousand Oaks, CA: Sage.

Crossan, M. M., Lane, H. W., and White, R. E. 1999. An organizational learning framework: From intuition to institution. *Academy of Management Review* 24: 522–537.

Csaszar, F. A. 2013. An efficient frontier in organization design: Organizational structure as a determinant of exploration and exploitation. *Organization Science* 24: 1083–1101.

Cummings, J. N. 2004. Work groups, structural diversity, and knowledge sharing in a global organization. *Management Science* 50: 352–364.

Damodaran, L., and Olphert, W. 2000. Barriers and facilitators to the use of knowledge management systems. *Behaviour and Information Technology* 19: 405–413.

Davis, J. P., Eisenhardt, K. M. and Bingham, C. B. 2009. Optimal structure, market dynamism, and the strategy of simple rules. *Administrative Science Quarterly* 54: 413–52.

DeRue D. S., Ashford S. J., and Myers C. G. 2012. Learning agility: In search of conceptual clarity and theoretical grounding. *Industrial and Organizational Psychology* 5: 258–279.

Dierickx, I., and Cool, K. 1989. Asset stock accumulation and sustainability of competitive advantage. *Management Science* 35: 1504–1511.

Doornbos, A. J., Simons, R. J., and Denessen, E. 2008. Relations between characteristics of workplace practices and types of informal work-related learning: A survey study among Dutch Police. *Human Resource Development Quarterly* 19: 129–151.

Dosi, G., Nelson, R. R., and Winter, S. G. 2000. Introduction: The nature and dynamics of organizational capabilities. *The Nature and Dynamics of Organizational Capabilities* 1: 24.

Ducan, R. B., and Weiss, A. 1979. Organizational learning: Implications for organizational design. In B. Staw, ed., *Research in Organizational Behavior*, 1: 75–123. Greenwich, CT: JAI Press.

Edmondson A. 1999. Psychological safety and learning behavior in work teams. *Administrative Science Quarterly* 44: 350–383.

Edmonson, A. C. 2002. The local and variegated nature of learning in organizations: A group-level perspective. *Organization Science* 13: 128–146.

Eisenhardt, K. M. 1989. Making fast strategic decisions in high-velocity environments. *Academy of Management Journal* 32: 543–576.

Eisenhardt, K. M., and Martin, J. A. 2000. Dynamic capabilities: What are they? *Strategic Management Journal* 21: 1105–1121.

Eisenhardt, K. M., Furr, N. R., and Bingham, C. B. 2010. CROSSROADS-microfoundations of performance: Balancing efficiency and flexibility in dynamic environments. *Organization Science* 21: 1263–1273.

Ellinger, A. D. 2005. Contextual factors influencing informal learning in a workplace setting: The case of reinventing itself company. *Human Resource Development Quarterly* 16: 389–415.

Elliot, A. J., and Dweck, C. S., eds. 2013. *Handbook of Competence and Motivation.* New York: Guilford Publications.

Ericsson, K. A., Krampe, R. T., and Tesch-Römer, C. 1993. The role of deliberate practice in the acquisition of expert performance. *Psychological Review* 100: 363–406.

Ericsson, K. A., Charness, N., Feltovich, P. J., and Hoffman, R. R., eds. 2006. *Handbook of Expertise and Expert Performance.* New York: Cambridge University Press.

Feldman, D. C. 1976. A contingency theory of socialization. *Administrative Science Quarterly* 21: 433–452.

Feldman, D. C. 1981. The multiple socialization of organization members. *Academy of Management Review* 6: 309–319.

Feldman, D. C. 2012. The impact of socializing. In C. Wanberg, ed., *The Oxford Handbook of Organizational Socialization*, 215–229. New York: Oxford University Press.

Feldman, D. C., and O'Neill, O. A. 2014. The role of socialization, orientation, and training programs in transmitting culture and climate and enhancing performance. In B. Schneider and K. M. Barbera, eds., *The Oxford Handbook of Organizational Climate and Culture*, 44–64. New York: Oxford University Press.

Feldman, M. S. 2000. Organizational routines as a source of continuous change. *Organization Science* 11: 611–629.

Feldman, M. S. 2003. A performative perspective on stability and change in organizational routines. *Industrial and Corporate Change* 12: 727–752.

Feldman, M. S., and Pentland, B. T. 2003. Reconceptualizing organizational routines as a source of flexibility and change. *Administrative Science Quarterly* 48: 94–118.

Felin, T., Foss, N. J., Heimeriks, K. H., and Madsen, T. L. 2012. Microfoundations of routines and capabilities: Individuals, processes, and structure. *Journal of Management Studies* 49: 1351–1374.

Fiol, C. M., and Lyles, M. A. 1985. Organizational learning. *Academy of Management Review* 10: 803–813.

Floyd, S. W., and Lane, P. J. 2000. Strategizing throughout the organization: Managing role conflict in strategic renewal. *Academy of Management Review* 25: 154–177.

Foss, N. J. 2003. Bounded rationality and tacit knowledge in the organizational capabilities approach: An evaluation and a stocktaking. *Industrial and Corporate Change* 12: 185–201.

Foss, N. J., and Knudsen, C., eds. 2013. *Towards a Competence Theory of the Firm.* London: Routledge.

Garicano, L., and Wu, Y. 2012. Knowledge, communication, and organizational capabilities. *Organization Science* 23: 1382–1397.

Gibson, C. B., and Birkinshaw, J. 2004. The antecedents, consequences, and mediating role of organizational ambidexterity. *Academy of Management Journal* 47: 209–226.

Gittell, J. H. and Weiss, L. 2004. Coordination networks within and across organizations: A multi-level framework. *Journal of Management Studies* 41: 127–153.

Good, D., and Michel, E. J. 2013. Individual ambidexterity: Exploring and exploiting in dynamic contexts. *The Journal of Psychology* 147: 435–453.

Grant, R. M. 1991. A resource-based theory of competitive advantage: Implications for strategy formulation. *California Management Review* (Spring): 114–135.

Grant, R. M. 1996. Toward a knowledge-based theory of the firm. *Strategic Management Journal* 17: 109–122.

Gulati, R., and Puranam, P. 2009. Renewal through reorganization: The value of inconsistencies between formal and informal organization. *Organization Science* 20: 422–440.

Gully, S., and Chen, G. 2010. Individual differences, attribute-treatment interactions, and training outcome. In S. W. J. Kozlowski and E. Salas, eds., *Learning, Training, and Development in Organizations,* 3–64. New York: Routledge.

Gupta, A. K., Smith, K. G., and Shalley, C. E. 2006. The interplay between exploration and exploitation. *Academy of Management Journal* 49: 693–706.

Hansen, M. T., Podolny, J. M., and Pfeffer, J. 2001. So many ties, so little time: A task contingency perspective on corporate social capital in organizations. *Research in the Sociology of Organizations* 18: 21–57.

Hatch, N. W., and Dyer, J. H. 2004. Human capital and learning as a source of sustainable competitive advantage. *Strategic Management Journal* 25: 1155–1178.

Henderson, R., and Cockburn, I. 1994. Measuring competence? Exploring firm effects in pharmaceutical research. *Strategic Management Journal* 15: 63–84.

Herling, R. W. 2000. Operational definitions of expertise and competence. *Advances in Developing Human Resources* 2: 8–21.

Herling, R. W., and Provo, J. 2000. Knowledge, competence, and expertise in organizations. *Advances in Developing Human Resources* 2: 1–7.

Hinds, P. J., Patterson, M., and Pfeffer, J. 2001. Bothered by abstraction: The effect of expertise on knowledge transfer and subsequent novice performance. *Journal of Applied Psychology* 86: 1232–1243.

Hodgkinson, G. P., and Healey, M. P. 2011. Psychological foundations of dynamic capabilities: Reflexion and reflection in strategic management. *Strategic Management Journal* 32: 1500–1516.

Hoffman, R. R., Shadbolt, N. R., Burton, A. M., and Klein, G. 1995. Eliciting knowledge from experts: A methodological analysis. *Rational Behavior and Human Decision Processes* 62: 129–158.

Hoopes, D. G., and Madsen, T. L. 2008. A capability-based view of competitive hetero-geneity. *Industrial and Corporate Change* 17: 393–426.

Hoopes, D. G., and Postrel, S. 1999. Shared knowledge, glitches, and product development performance. *Strategic Management Journal* 29: 837–865.

Huber, G. P. 1991. Organizational learning: The contributing processes and the literatures. *Organization Science* 2: 88–115.

Hunt, J. G. J., and Ropo, A. 1995. Multi-level leadership: Grounded theory and mainstream theory applied to the case of General Motors. *The Leadership Quarterly* 6: 379–412.

Jacobs, R. 2003. *Structured On-the-job Training: Unleashing Employee Expertise in the Workplace.* Oakland, CA: Berrett-Koehler Publishers.

Jacobs, R. L. 1997. The taxonomy of employee development: Toward an organizational culture of expertise. In R. J. Torraco, ed., *AHRD Conference Proceedings*, 278–283. Baton Rouge, LA: Academy of Human Resources Development.

Jaffee, D. 2001. *Organization Theory: Tension and Change*. New York: McGraw-Hill: 1–315.

Jansen, J. J., George, G., Van den Bosch, F. A., and Volberda, H. W. 2008. Senior team attributes and organizational ambidexterity: The moderating role of transformational leadership. *Journal of Management Studies* 45: 982–1007.

Jensen, A. R. 1998. *The g Factor: The Science of Mental Ability.* Westport, CT: Praeger.

Kanfer, R. 1990. Motivation theory and industrial and organizational psychology. In M. D. Dunnette and L. Hough, eds., *Handbook of Industrial and Organizational Psychology* 1: 75–130. Palo Alto, CA: Consulting Psychologists Press.

Kim, D. H. 1993. The link between individual and organizational learning. *Sloan Management Review* 35: 35–50.

Kim, D. H. 1998. The link between individual and organizational learning. In D. A. Klein, ed., *The Strategic Management of Intellectual Capital*, 41–62. Woburn, MA: Butterworth-Heineman.

Kirkman, B. L., Mathieu, J. E., Cordery, J. L., Rosen, B., and Kukenberger, M. 2011. Managing a new collaborative entity in business organizations: Understanding organizational communities of practice effectiveness. *Journal of Applied Psychology* 96: 1234.

Kogut, B., and Zander, U. 1992. Knowledge of the firm, combinative capabilities, and the replication of technology. *Organization Science* 3: 383–397.

Kogut, B., and Zander, U. 1996. What firms do? Coordination, identity, and learning. *Organization Science* 7: 502–518.

Kor, Y. Y., and Leblebici, H. 2005. How do interdependencies among human-capital deployment, development, and diversification strategies affect firms' financial performance? *Strategic Management Journal* 26: 967–985.

Kostopoulos, K. C., and Bozionelos, N. 2011. Team exploratory and exploitative learning: psychological safety, task conflict, and team performance. *Group and Organization Management* 36: 385–415.

Kozlowski, S. W. J., Brown, K. G., Weissbein, D. A., Cannon-Bowers, J. A., and Salas, E. 2000. A multilevel approach to training effectiveness: Enhancing horizontal and vertical transfer. In K. J. Klein and S. W. J. Kozlowski, eds., *Multilevel Theory, Research, and Methods in Organizations*, 157–210. San Francisco: Jossey-Bass.

Kozlowski, S. W. J., and Klein, K. J. 2000. A multilevel approach to theory and research in organizations: Contextual, temporal, and emergent processes. In K. J. Klein and S. W. J. Kozlowski, eds., *Multilevel Theory, Research, and Methods in Organizations*, 3–90. San Francisco: Jossey-Bass.

Kyndt, E., Dochy, F., and Nijs, H. 2009. Learning conditions for non-formal and informal workplace learning. *Journal of Workplace Learning* 21: 369–383.

Lado, A. A., and Wilson, M. C. 1994. Human resource systems and sustained competitive advantage: A competency-based perspective. *Academy of Management Review* 19: 699–727.

Langfred, C. W. 2004. Too much of a good thing? Negative effects of high trust and individual autonomy in self-managing teams. *Academy of Management Journal* 47: 385–399.

Leonard-Barton, D. 1992. Core capabilities and core rigidities: A paradox in managing new product development. *Strategic Management Journal* 13: 111–125.

Lepak, D. P., Smith, K. G., and Taylor, M. S. 2007. Value creation and value capture: A multilevel perspective. *Academy of Management Review* 32: 180–194.

Levitt, B., and March, J. G. 1988. Organizational Learning. *Annual Review of Sociology* 14: 319–340.

Li, L. C., Grimshaw, J. M., Nielsen, C., Judd, M., Coyte, P. C., and Graham, I. D. 2009. Evolution of Wenger's concept of community of practice. *Implementation Science* 4: 11.

Lippman, S. S., and Rumelt, R. P. 1982. Uncertainty imitability: An analysis of interfirm differences in efficiency under competition. *The Bell Journal of Economics* 13: 418–438.

Lippman, S. A., and Rumelt, R. P. 2003. The payments perspective: Micro-foundations of resource analysis. *Strategic Management Journal* 24: 903–927.

March, J. G. 1991. Exploration and exploitation in organizational learning. *Organization Science* 2: 71–87.

Martin, H. J. 2010. Improving training impact through effective follow-up: Techniques and their application. *Journal of Management Development* 29: 520–534.

Mathieu, J. E., and Chen, G. 2010. The etiology of the multilevel paradigm in management research. *Journal of Management* 37: 610–641.

Mathieu, J. E., and Tesluk, P. E. 2010. A multilevel perspective on training and development effectiveness. In S. W. J. Kozlowski and E. Salas, eds., *Learning, Training, and Development in Organizations*, 405–442. New York: Routledge.

Maurer, I., Bartsch, V., and Ebers, M. 2011. The value of intra-organizational social capital: How it fosters knowledge transfer, innovation performance, and growth. *Organization Studies* 32: 157–185.

McEvily, B., Perrone, V., and Zaheer, A. 2003. Trust as an organizing principle. *Organization Science* 14: 91–103.

Miller, D., and Shamsie, J. 1996. The resource-based view of the firm in two environments: The Hollywood film studios from 1936 to 1965. *Academy of Management Journal* 39: 519–543.

Miller, L. 2012. *State of the Industry, 2012*. Alexandria, VA: American Society for Training and Development.

Miner, A. S., and Haunschild, P. R. 1995. Population-level learning. In L. Cummings and B. M. Staw, eds., *Research in Organizational Behavior* 17, 115–166.

Mom, T. J., Van den Bosch, F. A., and Volberda, H. W. 2009. Understanding variation in managers' ambidexterity: Investigating direct and interaction effects of formal structural and personal coordination mechanisms. *Organization Science* 20: 812–828.

Murase, T., Doty, D., Wax, A. M. Y., DeChurch, L. A., and Contractor, N. S. 2012. Teams are changing: Time to think networks. *Industrial and Organizational Psychology* 5(1): 41–44.

Nahapiet, J., and Ghoshal, S. 1998. Social capital, intellectual capital, and the organizational advantage. *Academy of Management Review* 23: 242–266.

Nelson, R. R., and Winter, S. G. 1982. *An Evolutionary Theory of Economic Change*. Cambridge: Belknap.

Nickerson, J. A., and Zenger, T. R. 2002. Being efficiently fickle: A dynamic theory of organizational choice. *Organization Science* 13: 547–566.

Noe, R. A. 2013. *Employee Training and Development*, 6th ed. Burr Ridge, IL: McGraw-Hill/Irwin.

Noe, R. A., Clarke, A. D., and Klein, H. J. 2014. Learning in the twenty-first-century workplace. *Annual Review of Organizational Psychology and Organizational Behavior* 1: 245–275.

Noe, R. A., Tews, M. J., and Marand, A. D. 2013. Individual differences and informal learning in the workplace. *Journal of Vocational Behavior* 83: 327–335.

Nonaka, I. 1994. A dynamic theory of organizational knowledge creation. *Organization Science* 5: 14–37.

Nonaka, I., and Von Krogh, G. 2009. Perspective-tacit knowledge and knowledge conversion: Controversy and advancement in organizational knowledge creation theory. *Organization Science* 20: 635–652.

O'Reilly, C. A., and Tushman, M. L. 2004. The ambidextrous organization. *Harvard Business Review* (April): 74–83.

O'Reilly, C. A., and Tushman, M. L. 2008. Ambidexterity as a dynamic capability: Resolving the innovator's dilemma. *Research in Organizational Behavior* 28: 185–206.

O'Reilly, C. A., and Tushman M. L. 2013. Organizational ambidexterity: Past, present, and future. *Academy of Management Perspectives* 27: 324–338.

Ouchi, W. G. 1992. *A Conceptual Framework for the Design of Organizational Control Mechanisms*. New York: Springer US.

Parmigiani, A., and Mitchell, W. 2009. Complementarity, capabilities, and the boundaries of the firm: The impact of within-firm and interfirm expertise on concurrent sourcing of complementary components. *Strategic Management Journal* 30: 1065–1091.

Penrose, E. T. 1959. *The Theory of the Growth of the Firm*. Oxford: Oxford University Press.

Pentland, B. T., and Rueter, H. H. 1994. Organizational routines as grammars of action. *Administrative Science Quarterly* 39: 484–510.

Peteraf, M. A. 1993. The cornerstones of competitive advantage: A resource-based view. *Strategic Management Journal* 14: 179–191.

Ployhart, R. E., and Moliterno, T. P. 2011. Emergence of the human capital resource: A multilevel model. *Academy of Management Review* 36: 127–150.

Ployhart, R. E., Weekley, J. A., and Baughman, K. 2006. The structure and function of human capital emergence: A multilevel examination of the attraction-selection-attrition model. *Academy of Management Journal* 49: 661–677.

Pulakos E. D., Dorsey D. W., and Borman W. C. 2003. Hiring for knowledge-based competition. In S. E. Jackson, A. DeNisi, and M. A. Hitt, eds., *Managing Knowledge for Sustained Competitive Advantage: Designing Strategies for Effective Human Resource Management*, 155–161. San Francisco, CA: Wiley.

Pulakos, E. D., Arad, S., Donovan, M. A., and Plamondon, K. E. 2000. Adaptability in the workplace: Development of a taxonomy of adaptive performance. *Journal of Applied Psychology* 85: 612–624.

Quiñones, M. A., Ford, J. K., Sego, D. J., and Smith, E. M. 1995. The effects of individual and transfer environment characteristics on the opportunity to perform trained tasks. *Training Research Journal* 1: 29–49.

Raisch, S., Birkinshaw, J., Probst, G., and Tushman, M. L. 2009. Organizational ambidexterity: Balancing exploitation and exploration for sustained performance. *Organization Science* 20: 685–695.

Reed, R., and DeFillippi, R. J. 1990. Causal ambiguity, barriers to imitation, and sustainable competitive advantage. *Academy of Management Review* 15: 88–102.

Rivkin, J. W., and Siggelkow, N. 2003. Balancing search and stability: Interdependencies among elements of organizational design. *Management Science* 49: 290–311.

Rogan, M., and Mors, M. L. 2014. A network perspective on individual-level ambidexterity in organizations. *Organization Science* 25: 1860–1877.

Rousseau, D. M. 1985. Issues of level in organizational research: Multi-level and cross-level perspectives. *Research in Organizational Behavior* 7: 1–37.

Salas, E., Tannenbaum, S. I., Kraiger, K., and Smith-Jentsch, K. A. 2012. The science of training and development in organizations: What matters in practice. *Psychological Science in the Public Interest* 13: 74–101.

Schilling, M. A., and Phelps, C. C. 2007. Interfirm collaboration networks: The impact of large-scale network structure on firm innovation. *Management Science* 53: 1113–1126.

Sears, J., and Hoetker, G. 2014. Technological overlap, technological capabilities, and resource recombination in technological acquisitions. *Strategic Management Journal* 35: 48–67.

Siggelkow, N. 2001. Change in the presence of fit: The rise, the fall, and the renaissance of Liz Claiborne. *Academy of Management Journal* 44: 838–857.

Siggelkow, N., and Levinthal, D. A. 2003. Temporarily divide to conquer: Centralized, decentralized, and reintegrated organizational approaches to exploration and adaptation. *Organization Science* 14: 650–669.

Siggelkow, N., and Levinthal, D. A. 2005. Escaping real (non-benign) competency traps: Linking the dynamics of organizational structure to the dynamics of search. *Strategic Organization* 3: 85–115.

Simon, H. 1991. Bounded rationality and organizational learning. *Organization Science* 2: 125–134.

Sitzmann, T., and Weinhardt, J. M. 2015. Training engagement theory: A multilevel perspective on the effectiveness of work-related training. *Journal of Management*, in press.

Smith, K. G., Collins, C. J., and Clark, K. D. 2005. Existing knowledge, knowledge creation capability, and the rate of new product introduction in high-technology firms. *Academy of Management Journal* 48: 346–357.

Smith, W. K., and Tushman, M. L. 2005. Managing strategic contradictions: A top management model for managing innovation streams. *Organization Science* 16: 522–536.

Stalk, G., Evans, P., and Shulman, L. E. 1992. Competing on capabilities: The new rules of corporate strategy. *Harvard Business Review* (March–April): 57–69.

Subramaniam, M., and Youndt, M. A. 2005. The influence of intellectual capital on the types of innovative capabilities. *Academy of Management Journal* 48: 450–463.

Sung, S. Y., and Choi, J. N. 2012. Effects of team knowledge management on the creativity and financial performance of organizational teams. *Organizational Behavior and Human Decision Processes* 118: 4–13.

Swanson, R. A. 1994. *Analysis for Improving Performance: Tools for Diagnosing Organizations and Documenting Workplace Expertise*. San Francisco: Berrett-Koehler.

Szulanski, G. 1996. Exploring internal stickiness: Impediments to the transfer of best practice within the firm. *Strategic Management Journal* 17: 27–43.

Tannenbaum, S. I., and Yukl, G. 1992. Training and development in work organizations. *Annual Review of Psychology* 43: 399–441.

Tannenbaum, S. I., Beard, R. L., McNall, L. A., and Salas, E. 2010. Informal learning and development in organizations. In S. W. J. Kozlowski and E. Salas, eds., *Learning, Training, and Development in Organizations*, 303–332. Philadelphia: Taylor and Francis.

Tannenbaum, S. I., Mathieu, J. E., Salas, E., and Cohen, D. 2012. Teams are changing: Are research and practice evolving fast enough? *Industrial and Organizational Psychology* 5: 2–24.

Teece, D. J. 1982. Towards an economic theory of the multiproduct firm. *Journal of Economic Behavior and Organization* 3: 39–63.

Teece, D. J. 2007. Explicating dynamic capabilities: The nature and microfoundations of (sustainable) enterprise performance. *Strategic Management Journal* 28: 1319–1350.

Teece, D. J., Pisano, G., and Shuen, A. 1997. Dynamic capabilities and strategic management. *Strategic Management Journal* 18 (7): 509–533.

Tracey, J. B., Tannenbaum, S. I., and Kavanagh, M. J. 1995. Applying trained skills on the job: The importance of the work environment. *Journal of Applied Psychology* 80: 239–252.

Treacy, M., and Wiersema, F. 1993. Customer intimacy and other value disciplines. *Harvard Business Review* (January–February): 84–93.

Van Maanen, J., and Schein, E. 1979. Toward a theory of organizational socialization. *Research in Organizational Behavior* 1: 209–264.

Volberda, H. W., and Lewin, A. Y. 2003. Co-evolutionary dynamics within and between firms: From evolution to co-evolution. *Journal of Management Studies* 40: 2111–2136.

Von Krogh, G., Ichijo, K., and Nonaka, I. 2000. *Enabling Knowledge Creation: How to Unlock the Mystery of Tacit Knowledge and Release the Power of Innovation*. Oxford: Oxford University Press.

Wang, S., and Noe, R. A. 2010. Knowledge sharing: A review and directions for future research. *Human Resource Management Review* 20: 115–131.

Wernerfelt, B. 1984. A resource-based view of the firm. *Strategic Management Journal* 5: 171–180.

Winter, S. 1987. Knowledge and competence as strategic assets. In D. J. Teece, ed., *The Competitive Challenge: Strategies for Industrial Innovation and Renewal*, 159–184. Cambridge, MA: Ballinger.

Winter, S. G. 1995. Four Rs of profitability: Rents, resources, routines, and replication. In C. A. Montgomery, ed., *Resource-Based and Evolutionary Theories of the Firm*, 147–178. New York: Springer.

Winter, S. G. 2003. Understanding dynamic capabilities. *Strategic Management Journal* 24: 991–995.

Zahra, S. A., and George, G. 2002. Absorptive capacity: A review, reconceptualization, and extension. *Academy of Management Review* 27: 185–203.

Zander, U., and Kogut, B. 1995. Knowledge and the speed of the transfer and imitation of organizational capabilities: An empirical test. *Organization Science* 6: 76–92.

Zollo, M., and Winter, S. G. 2002. Deliberate learning and the evolution of dynamic capabilities. *Organization Science* 13: 339–351.

4 Understanding Training Transfer from the Adaptive Performance Perspective

Jason L. Huang, Shan Ran, and Brian D. Blume

Transfer of training occurs when knowledge and skills acquired from a learning environment are generalized into different settings, people, and/or situations and maintained over time (Blume et al., 2010). Transfer of training is an important goal for organizations interested in using training to improve employee and organizational performance (Goldstein & Ford, 2002). As such, researchers often study transfer to understand whether trainees *can* and *will* utilize the newly acquired knowledge and skills on the job (Huang et al., 2012). The increase in research activities on transfer over the past 20 years or so culminated in several qualitative and quantitative reviews (e.g., Baldwin, Ford, & Blume, 2009; Blume et al., 2010; Burke & Hutchins, 2007; Cheng & Hampson, 2008; Cheng & Ho, 2001; Ford & Weissbein, 1997).

At the same time as we have seen empirical and theoretical advances in the transfer literature, the concept of adaptive performance has emerged. Adaptive performance focuses on "behaviors individuals enact in response to or anticipation of changes relevant to job-related tasks" (Jundt, Shoss, & Huang, 2015), which reflects in part individuals' ability "to transfer learning from one task to another as job demands vary" (Allworth & Hesketh, 1999: 98). Transfer research has yet to build on theories and findings from the adaptive performance literature, despite the fact that transfer performance has been subsumed as a dimension of adaptive performance (Allworth & Hesketh, 1999; Baard, Rentch, & Kozlowski, 2014; Jundt et al., 2015). By deliberately drawing from adaptive performance literature, this chapter discusses how researchers may further advance understanding of training transfer.

The chapter achieves four specific goals. First, by building a conceptual linkage between training transfer and the broader adaptive performance literature, we emphasize the difference in predictability of changes (i.e., unforeseen vs. anticipated) as a key feature that should be recognized in transfer studies. Second, using predictability as a point of departure, we conduct a qualitative review of training transfer with an explicit focus on predictors of transfer when transfer occurs in an unforeseen versus anticipated manner. Third, we discuss areas of transfer research that may benefit from explicit considerations of the nature of transfer as adaptive performance. Finally, we propose additional directions for future research.

Conceptual Linkage between Training Transfer and Adaptive Performance

Research on adaptive performance tends to incorporate training as a means to enhance individuals' capacity for adaptation. For example, Chan (2000) discussed two dominant approaches to performance adaptation: (1) the selection perspective that focuses on preexisting individual differences and (2) the training perspective that emphasizes capacity building and skill acquisition. Focusing on individuals' specific behavioral dimensions, Pulakos et al. (2000) proposed eight dimensions of adaptive performance, including: (1) handling emergencies or crisis situations; (2) handling work stress; (3) solving problems creatively; (4) dealing with uncertain and unpredictable work situations; (5) learning work tasks, technologies, and procedures; (6) demonstrating interpersonal adaptability; (7) demonstrating cultural adaptability; and (8) demonstrating physically oriented adaptability. Two examples might be someone experiencing an unanticipated delay in the delivery of materials needed to complete a project (dealing with uncertain and unpredictable work situations) or having too little time to complete work tasks (handling work stress). Clearly, learning and subsequent transfer of learning are recognized as one critical component of adaptive performance.

At the same time, training transfer entails performance adaptation. Ashford and Taylor (1990: 4) defined *individual adaptation* as "the process by which individuals learn, negotiate, enact, and maintain the behaviors appropriate to a given organizational environment." Successful adaptation occurs when individuals' behaviors meet or exceed the organization's demands. Ashford and Taylor (1990) highlighted the similarity in psychological processes underlying various types of transitions occurring at work, such as socialization, performance, adaptation, and so forth. Training transfer is one of the transitions that involve a similar process. In engaging in training activities, trainees are not only expected to demonstrate acquisition of knowledge, skills, and attitudes in the learning context, but more importantly need to show improved performance in the job context (see Goldstein & Ford, 2002). The transition from a learning context to a performance context requires trainees to maximize the fit between the newly acquired knowledge, skills, and attitudes and the demand of the transfer context. Indeed, the demand or need for individual adaptation in the transfer process is captured in Barnett and Ceci's (2002) taxonomy of transfer. That is, far transfer (i.e., transfer to a dissimilar context), as opposed to near transfer (i.e., transfer to a more similar context), involves more pronounced *changes* on various contextual dimensions. For instance, far transfer could occur in a very different physical location than the learning environment and much later in time, thus imposing a greater need for trainees to adapt to the transition from the learning context to the transfer context.

The notion that training transfer entails adaptive response on the part of the trainee makes it possible to utilize theories and findings on adaptive performance to inform transfer research. To allow for a parsimonious account of the psychological features underlying context changes in existing transfer studies, we focus on the predictability of the adaptive task context. As noted earlier, adaptive performance can occur either in response to or in anticipation of changes (Jundt et al., 2015). When changes are unforeseen, the performance context experiences sudden changes that require the individual to detect changes and respond by revising performance-related strategies. Conversely, when changes are anticipated, the performance context is characterized by new yet prescribed goals that the individual expected to pursue (Staw & Boettger, 1990; Stewart & Nandkeolyar, 2006). Analogously, the change from the learning context to the transfer context can also vary on the anticipated to unforeseen dimension. Anticipated transfer involves formal expectation to apply newly acquired knowledge and skills in a familiar task environment, whereas unforeseen transfer entails adapting newly acquired knowledge and skills to conditions marked by unfamiliarity or changes that disrupt previous familiarity.

The unforeseen versus anticipated nature of a transfer task is important because adaptive responses differ when dealing with unforeseen versus anticipated changes (LePine, Colquitt, & Erez, 2000; Stewart & Nandkeolyar, 2006). Conscientiousness, for instance, may facilitate adaptation in anticipated change contexts because of the preference that highly conscientious people have for goal achievement, and yet it can hinder adaptation in response to unforeseen changes due to the preference that they have for routine and structure (Stewart & Nandkeolyar, 2006). To appreciate the potential difference in predictor-transfer relationships occurring in unforeseen versus anticipated transfer contexts, we conduct a qualitative review of the literature, focusing on whether a predictor-transfer relationship may differ across the unforeseen versus anticipated divide. To classify existing transfer studies, we developed the following overarching decision rules. A transfer outcome falls into the anticipated category when the trainee is familiar with the transfer context and task prior to the transfer attempt. The familiarity can be due to prior work experience (e.g., transferring a customer service training back to one's job), or due to the learning experience (e.g., transferring game simulation to situations similar to those being trained under). In contrast, a transfer outcome is classified under the unforeseen category when events or conditions exist to disrupt the familiarity and requires modifications of goals, strategies, or even tasks (e.g., transferring skills to a novel situation).

It is worth noting that the classification is different from near/analogical versus far/adaptive transfer. Near versus far transfer concerns similarity between training and transfer tasks or contexts, whereas anticipated versus unforeseen transfer concerns the predictability of the change from the learning context to the transfer context. To illustrate this distinction, a far transfer situation can be anticipated if the trainees can identify how the transfer context is different from the learning context before transfer is to occur.

It should be recognized that the predictability of upcoming changes reflects a continuum, whereas unforeseen and anticipated changes represent a somewhat artificial dichotomy of the underlying continuum. Thus, it is a challenging task to identify primary transfer studies as investigations of either fully unforeseen or fully anticipated transfer. Our dichotomization of the primary transfer studies in the following text, summarized in Table 4.1, is not a definitive classification of existing studies, but rather our best collective judgment as to which category each study may fit into better, thus serving as an initial step to organize our knowledge base.

In the next section, we incorporate the primary studies included in Table 4.1 to illustrate how constructs from transfer studies might predict anticipated and unforeseen transfer. We organize predictors examined in these transfer studies into four broad categories: (1) training characteristics, (2) training interventions, (3) learning outcomes, and (4) task and work environment features. *Trainee characteristics* consist of distal individual differences particularly relevant to transfer (i.e., cognitive ability, conscientiousness, emotional stability, openness, and goal orientation) and proximal states (i.e., pretraining self-efficacy and motivation to learn). *Training interventions* include deliberate attempts to influence the trainee and the learning experience to enhance transfer. *Learning outcomes* consist of knowledge, skills, and motivational tendencies assessed at the end of training (Kraiger, Ford, & Salas, 1993). Finally, *task and work environment features* capture aspects of the transfer environment that may influence transfer.

A Qualitative Review of Predictors of Unforeseen vs. Anticipated Transfer

Based on these four categories of predictors, meta-analytic evidence suggests that the most important predictors for successful transfer across studies include cognitive ability, conscientiousness, pre- and posttraining motivation, error management instructions, and supportive work environment (Blume et al., 2010; Keith & Frese, 2008). However, we expect that foreseeability in the transfer phase moderates the strengths and/or mechanisms between some of the predictors and transfer outcomes. For each category of predictors, we will first review their expected effects and mechanisms in unforeseen versus anticipated transfer, and then summarize empirical evidence in the literature to confirm the speculated differential effects of transfer predictors.

Trainee Characteristics

Cognitive Ability
Cognitive ability enables effective and rapid process of information from the internal and external environments, and is found to be one of the most important individual determinant of job performance, training performance, and training transfer (Blume et al., 2010; Schmidt & Hunter, 1998). In predicting transfer, cognitive ability exerts direct and indirect influences. First, when trainees have no prior experiences with unexpected task or dynamic work environment, direction application of learned behaviors will be ineffective. Instead, they must

Table 4.1 *Summary and categorization of studies with anticipated and unforeseen changes*

Study	Training	Transfer	Changes
Axtell et al., 1997	interpersonal skills	current jobs	anticipated
Baldwin, 1992	interpersonal skills	unplanned encounter	unforeseen
Bell & Ford, 2007	truck driving	similar road course	anticipated
Bell & Kozlowski, 2002	radar tracking computer simulation	more difficult and complicated trial	unforeseen
Bell & Kozlowski, 2008	radar tracking computer simulation	analogical tasks similar to training tasks; adaptive tasks with more difficult and variant elements	anticipated unforeseen
Brett & VandeWalle, 1999	presentation skills	similar to training tasks	anticipated
Brown et al., 2013	interpersonal skills	current jobs	anticipated
Burke & Baldwin, 1999	supervisory skills	current jobs	anticipated
Carter & Beier, 2010	Microsoft Access	transfer tasks with new elements	unforeseen
Chen et al., 2005	flight simulation and teamwork	more dynamic and difficult mission	unforeseen
Davis & Yi, 2004	spreadsheet skills	similar to training tasks	anticipated
Day et al., 2001	aviation simulation	transfer tasks with more variant elements	unforeseen
Dierdorff & Surface, 2008	second language	language test	anticipated
Dierdorff et al., 2010	frame of reference	obtaining certification	anticipated
Ford et al., 1998	radar tracking computer simulation	more difficult and complicated tasks	unforeseen
Foster & Macan, 2002	Lego building	building more complicated model	unforeseen
Gibson, 2001	nursing	current jobs	anticipated
Gist, 1989	innovative problem solving	idea generation to different problems	unforeseen
Gist & Stevens, 1998	negotiation skills	stressful salary negotiation	unforeseen
Gist et al., 1989	use of a software	similar to training tasks	anticipated
Gist et al., 1990	negotiation skills	salary negotiation under high level of uncertainty	unforeseen
Gist et al., 1991	negotiation skills	salary negotiation with normal difficulty	anticipated
Heimbeck et al., 2003	Excel spreadsheet	tasks with more difficult elements	unforeseen
Herold et al., 2002	flight simulation	obtaining actual license	unforeseen
Holladay & Quiñones, 2003	decision-making computer simulation	tasks with more difficult and variant elements	unforeseen
Huang & Ford, 2012	driving	similar road course	anticipated
Huang et al., 2014	statistical skills	current jobs	anticipated
Johnson et al., 2012	leadership skills	current jobs	anticipated

(*cont.*)

Table 4.1 *(cont.)*

Study	Training	Transfer	Changes
Kabanoff & Bottger, 1991	creative problem solving	solving similar level problems	anticipated
Karl et al., 1993	speed reading	tasks similar to training	anticipated
Keith & Frese, 2005	PowerPoint	similar tasks	anticipated
		more difficult tasks	unforeseen
Kirkman et al., 2006	teamwork skills	current jobs	anticipated
Kozlowski et al., 2001	radar-tracking computer simulation	more complex and difficult tasks	unforeseen
Mathieu et al., 1992	proofreading	tasks similar to training	anticipated
Mathieu et al., 1993	bowling	tasks similar to training	anticipated
Morin & Latham, 2000	interpersonal skills	current jobs	anticipated
Myers, 1992	baking/motor mechanics	new jobs	unforeseen
Oakes et al., 2001	air traffic control	new jobs	unforeseen
Quiñones, 1995	decision-making computer simulation	tasks similar to training	anticipated
Ree et al., 1995	pilot simulation	more difficult and dynamic check flights	unforeseen
Richman-Hirsch, 2001	customer service	current jobs	anticipated
Rouiller & Goldstein, 1993	mandatory job skills	current jobs	anticipated
Smith-Jentsch et al., 2001	assertiveness in flight simulation	tasks similar to training	anticipated
Stanhope & Surface, 2014	second language	oral proficiency interview	anticipated
Stanhope et al., 2013	second language	test based on trained content	anticipated
Stevens & Gist, 1997	negotiation skills	salary negotiation with different elements	unforeseen
Stewart et al., 1996	self-management	current jobs	anticipated
Tews & Tracey, 2008	supervisory skills	new jobs	unforeseen
Towler & Dipboye, 2001	employment law content	solving problems	unforeseen
Tracey et al., 1995	supervisory skills	current jobs	anticipated
Tziner et al., 1991	advanced training methods	current jobs	anticipated
Warr & Bunce, 1995	supervisory skills	current jobs	anticipated
Weissbein et al., 2011	negotiation skills	salary negotiation with more difficult elements	unforeseen
Wexley & Baldwin, 1986	time management	everyday life	anticipated
Zach et al., 2007	security	more difficult and stressful simulations	unforeseen

engage in intensive information-processing activities, such as recognition and diagnosis of novel elements, flexible organization of knowledge and skills, strategies generation, and problem solving, which reveals the benefits of cognitive ability in dealing with unforeseen changes. Therefore, the direct link between cognitive ability and transfer is expected to be stronger in unforeseen, in relation to anticipated, transfer. Second, cognitive ability can also indirectly affect transfer through enhanced learning outcomes from training. Knowledge acquisition is an integral component of all training programs and a foundation of transfer performance (Kraiger et al., 1993). In particular, when transfer involves unpredictable changes, problem-solving strategies rely on the knowledge developed through training, which strengthens the indirect influence of cognitive ability on transfer outcomes. Taken together, we expect a stronger predictive validity of cognitive ability in transfer with unforeseen changes compared to anticipated changes.

Research on transferring second language skills to oral tests exemplify anticipated transfer, because speaking with an interviewer using the language is an expected task. A positive association has been found between cognitive ability and language proficiency (Stanhope & Surface, 2014; Stanhope, Pond, & Surface, 2013).

In contrast, many studies have examined unforeseen changes in transfer. For example, new hires just entered a job without prior experience (Myers, 1992; Oakes et al., 2001). Transfer tasks became unexpectedly difficult (Kozlowski et al., 2001), involved untrained components in a software (Carter and Beier, 2010), or required the use of a different tool (switching from a joystick to a keyboard; Day, Arthur, & Gettman, 2001). Aviation trainees were asked to maneuver more advanced aircrafts and complete activities more rapidly (Ree, Carretta, & Teachout, 1995). In these studies, cognitive ability was found to positively influence transfer success. Specifically, rapid knowledge acquisition and an expert-like knowledge structure receive some support as the mediating pathways (Kozlowski et al., 2001; Ree et al., 1995).

Interestingly, in the same study, Bell and Kozlowski (2008) examined both types of transfer. Zero-order correlations show that cognitive ability has a stronger association with transfer on a more complex and dynamic task ($r = .49$) than on transfer with a task similar to training ($r = .30$). This could shed a light on the further exploration of differential effects of cognitive ability in unforeseen versus anticipated transfer.

Personality

With regard to the Five-Factor Model of personality (Digman & Takemoto-Chock, 1981), conscientiousness and emotional stability are positive predictors of transfer, whereas agreeableness, extraversion, and openness tend to have smaller correlations with transfer when collapsing across studies (Blume et al., 2010). However, some stable behavioral tendencies may affect transfer differentially when transfer varies on the extent of predictability. When transfer expectations are predictable, trainees can directly apply learned behaviors without interruptions from changes in the task or context. Effort becomes the key determinant of the extent to which trainees' will exhibit the expected behaviors. Conscientious individuals tend to be organized, achievement oriented, and compliant to orders, therefore are more likely to exert effort and be self-motivated to apply learning in anticipated transfer.

When a transfer task's content or context changes dynamically beyond trainees' expectation, performance can be interrupted by fluctuation in emotions or unwillingness to explore novel elements. In these cases, emotional stability and openness to experience are desirable traits, because emotionally stable individuals tend to remain calm when dealing with unfamiliar challenges (Jundt et al., 2015), and openness to experience facilitates environmental exploration and novel solution behavior (LePine, Colquitt, & Erez, 2000; Stewart & Nandkeolyar, 2006). In contrast, conscientiousness may be a double-edged sword in unforeseen transfer because it enhances effort and self-efficacy, but it also increases self-deception of satisfactory progress, reluctance to disobey orders, and failure to alter existing behavioral patterns to solve unexpected problems (LePine et al., 2000; Martocchio & Judge, 1997; Stewart & Nandkeolyar, 2006).

A few studies have directly examined the role of personality in transfer. The expected positive effect of conscientiousness on anticipated transfer was supported in a self-leadership training program, where trainees applied training to their existing jobs (Stewart, Carson, & Cardy, 1996). Regarding unforeseen transfer, a study examined transfer of computer-simulated training to pilot certification tests, and novice pilots were to apply complex psychomotor skills to unfamiliar aircrafts. Our prediction was mostly supported, such that emotional stability and openness to experience were positively related to transfer, even after learning outcomes were accounted for in transfer performance. Interestingly, conscientiousness's influence depended on learning at the end of training: When there was a low (but not high) level of learning, trainees high on conscientiousness continued exerting effort, which promoted transfer (Herold et al., 2002).

Therefore, predictability seems to be one boundary condition that determines the relationship between personality and transfer. In particular, the mechanisms associated with conscientiousness in unforeseen transfer may be even more convoluted than our expectation, that types of training and initial learning outcomes may also interact with conscientiousness to influence transfer.

Motivational Traits
Goal orientations, a set of motivational traits, describe how individuals handle achievement situations and consist of three dimensions: (1) learning or mastery goal orientation (LGO; develop competence by learning and mastering new skills and situations); (2) performance-prove goal orientation (PPGO; seek positive evaluations); and (3) performance-avoid goal orientation (PAGO; avoid negative evaluations) (DeShon & Gillespie, 2005; VandeWalle, 1997). Among these dimensions, aggregated results converged that LGO is a moderately strong positive predictor and PAGO is a small negative predictor of transfer; whereas, divergent results exist for the effects of PPGO (Blume et al., 2010).

Specifically, LGO can be a desirable trait to facilitate transfer of training because trainees are allowed to focus on mastering newly learned knowledge and skills. However, during unforeseen transfer, trainees high on LGO can be distracted by exploring and mastering unforeseen elements, which directs attention and resources away from successful performance within a certain time limit

(DeShon & Gillespie, 2005). Therefore, the positive effect of LGO on transfer may be mitigated by unpredictability.

By contrast, high PPGO and PAGO emphasize performing over learning. The effect of PPGO remains inconsistent across studies, because trainees high on PPGO adopt both positive (i.e., continuing improvement) and negative (striving for appearance of competence) content goals in transfer (Brett & VandeWalle, 1999). Incorporating foreseeability may help untangle the complex mechanism between PPGO and transfer. When performance in value and success is relatively certain, individuals high on PPGO tend to be motivated to approach the achievement situation. However, high unpredictability can undermine trainees' opportunities to outperform others and increase the likelihood of failure. Therefore, trainees high on PPGO may be demotivated by such uncertainty for achieving better performance. In contrast, PAGO may not be as detrimental in unforeseen transfer because of the high motivation to minimize failures. In sum, we speculate that PPGO is a positive predictor of anticipated transfer, but a negative predictor of unforeseen transfer. Meanwhile, the negative influence of PAGO may be ameliorated by unpredictability of the transfer situation.

Similar to the categorization in the preceding text, changes are considered anticipated when trainees engage in transfer tasks similar to training or perform transfer in a familiar environment. For example, second languages trainees spoke to interviewers in oral tests (Dierdorff, Surface, & Brown, 2010); trainees gave presentation to audience they are familiar with (Brett & VandeWalle, 1999); professionals attended statistical training workshops and returned to their familiar daily work environment (Huang, Ford, & Ryan, 2014). Results are supportive about the positive effect of LGO and negative effect of PAGO on transfer, as well as the inconsistent effects of PPGO. When predicting anticipated transfer, PPGO can be beneficial when self-efficacy is high, but detrimental when self-efficacy is low (Dierdorff et al., 2010). Additionally, goal orientations can be conceptualized as individual characteristics with a certain level of within-person variability. Huang et al. (2014) surveyed workshop trainees weekly over six weeks and found that LGO, through its influence on motivation to transfer, had positive main effects on both initial level of transfer and transfer trajectory over time (Huang et al., 2014).

In studies categorized as unforeseen transfer, trainees performed transfer tasks that were more difficult and complex than training (Bell & Kozlowski, 2008) or involved unfamiliar software functions (Heimbeck et al., 2003). In another study, students were asked to apply learning from a lecture to solve unfamiliar practical problems (Towler & Dipboye, 2001). These studies revealed the complex interactions between goal orientations and training interventions. For instance, LGO can enhance transfer when the training encourages learning from errors or using expressive and less organized lecturing format (Bell & Kozlowski, 2008; Towler & Dipboye, 2001). The potential negative influence of PPGO and PAGO can be mitigated when the training intervention involves detailed step-by-step instructions (Heimbeck et al., 2003).

In sum, the influence of goal orientations on transfer is usually distal and may be contingent upon many moderating factors, including foreseeability of transfer, proximal states (e.g., self-efficacy), and training interventions.

Proximal States

Motivational states (i.e., motivation to learn and pretraining self-efficacy) serve as important pathways between transfer and distal predictors of ability, personality, and motivational traits (Colquitt, LePine, & Noe, 2000). Trainees' intended effort to learn and efficacy beliefs of actual outcomes from the training can be indirect determinants of transfer through their effects on learning. Thus, we do not expect pretraining motivational states to interact with predictability of transfer, which occurs posttraining.

In contrast, metacognitive activity and negative emotional states have drawn attention as meaningful additional pathways (Bell & Kozlowski, 2008; Keith & Frese, 2005). As discussed in the preceding text, unpredictable situations necessitate generation of new strategies and emotion regulation. Metacognitive activity, such as monitoring, planning, and evaluating one's cognitive functions, can facilitate trainees' engagement in "thinking about thoughts" and development of knowledge structure (Bell & Kozlowski, 2008), which can enhance trainees' new strategy generation in later transfer. Meanwhile, negative emotional states (e.g., state anxiety) require high levels of emotion regulation and drain resources from application and adaptation of important knowledge and principles. Thus, unforeseen changes during transfer could reveal the positive effect of metacognitive activities and negative effect of state anxiety on outcomes.

We speculated that motivation to learn and pretraining self-efficacy play significant roles regardless of level of predictability in transfer. Studies generally support the positive relation between pretraining self-efficacy and transfer (e.g., Gibson, 2001; Huang & Ford, 2012; Mathieu, Martineau, & Tannenbaum, 1993) and between motivation to learn and transfer (e.g., Mathieu, Tannenbaum, & Salas, 1992; Quiñones, 1995). Thus, we focus on metacognitive and emotional processes. Two studies assessed the influence of these proximal processes, and both happened to examine anticipated and unforeseen transfer within the same study. Specifically, Keith and Frese (2005) and Bell and Kozlowski (2008) separated transfer tasks into those that trainees were exposed to during training versus those with difficulty levels that trainees have not encountered. Results from these two studies suggest that metacognitive activity and emotional control (the opposite of state anxiety) had significant zero-order correlations with unforeseen transfer, and yet the corresponding correlations with anticipated transfer appeared weaker and nonsignificant.

Transfer-Related Interventions

Besides trainee characteristics, features of training design represent another set of predictors for transfer outcomes (Goldstein & Ford, 2002). Various interventions can be used before, during, or after training to facilitate learning and/or transfer. The discussion will highlight interventions aiming at promoting transfer.

In anticipated transfer, successful encoding, retention, and application of training information are the most crucial for performance by maximizing the likelihood of application of expected behaviors. Symbolic mental rehearsal (SMR), or the engagement of organizing information and mentally rehearsing behaviors by trainees, is one example of instructional technique to enable effective encoding of information (Davis & Yi, 2004). Posttraining interventions can also enhance the retention of learning, such as relapse prevention (RP). A classical RP procedure proposed by Tziner, Haccoun, and Kadish (1991) involves identifying and coping with the decay problems. Burke and Baldwin (1999) abbreviated the RP module and focused on the coping component. Additionally, posttraining goal setting, rooted from the goal-setting theory (Locke & Latham, 1990), put the emphasis on setting difficult transfer goals and promote goal commitment to motivate transfer (Morin & Latham, 2000; Wexley & Baldwin, 1986). Together, these interventions are expected to be effective when trainees can anticipate the transfer task or context.

However, unforeseen transfer is not limited to carrying out what is learned but require trainees to transform learning to meet unpredictable goals. In this case, training interventions can promote transfer using two strategies. First, interventions that enhance self-regulation at any phase of the training process can increase likelihood of trainees' tendency to monitor thought processes, adjust plans, modify behaviors, and control anxiety, which prepare trainees to handle unexpected changes. Optimistic framing is an effective technique used before and during training. For example, attributional framing instructs trainees to attribute performance to internal malleable factors such as effort and strategy, rather than stable factors such as ability and personality (Weissbein et al., 2011). Error management training frames errors positively and encourages trainees to make, explore, and learn from errors (Keith & Frese, 2005; 2008). Self-regulatory tools can also be introduced after training to help trainees monitor progress and adjust strategies (e.g., adaptive guidance; Bell & Kozlowski, 2002). Second, training that employs a variety of demonstrations and practices can develop skills corresponding to a broader array of task or contextual cues, so that trainees' exhibit a higher level of readiness and generalized self-efficacy to deal with unexpected variations between training and transfer (Holladay & Quiñones, 2003). Because trainees' active adjustment of goals and strategies are necessary for effective transfer to unforeseen changes, inflexible guidance or fixation on previous goals can hinder trainees' successful performance. Thus, goal-setting interventions may have a weak effect on outcomes in unforeseen transfer.

Most of the studied examined interventions aimed at promoting anticipated transfer occurred during employees' existing jobs with one exception that Davis and Yi (2004) conducted a lab study that asked trainees to perform a computer software task similar to training. Findings support that facilitation of encoding or retention of training information can enhance anticipated transfer (Burke & Baldwin, 1999; Davis & Yi, 2004; Tziner et al., 1991). As goal states are presumably easier to define in situations involving anticipated transfer, general posttraining goal-setting activities have been shown to be beneficial for transfer of various skills to employees' current jobs, including interpersonal (Morin & Latham, 2000), customer service (Richman-Hirsch, 2001), leadership (Johnson et al., 2012), and time management (Wexley & Baldwin, 1986). Specifically, transfer levels were similar between assigned goals and goals developed jointly by trainees and trainers (Wexley & Baldwin, 1986). Setting more than one goal can strengthen the positive effect of goal setting on transfer (Johnson et al., 2012). When contrasting different types of goals, goals targeted at performance level yielded better transfer in management development trainees than goals targeted at exhibiting specific trained behaviors at work (Brown, Warren, & Cass, 2013).

In studies of unforeseen transfer, optimistic framing of attribution or errors receives support as a positive approach to promote self-regulation (e.g., metacognitive activity, emotion control) and the subsequent performance in transfer tasks that involve new or more difficult elements (Carter & Beier, 2010; Heimbeck et al., 2003; Keith & Frese, 2005; Weissbein et al., 2011). Also, various studies suggest a number of tools to aid adaptive transfer of task or job novice performing unfamiliar tasks. For example, newly trained negotiators engaged in negotiation tasks in a different scenario, an unknown higher ceiling for salary, a different confederate, or more attacks from the confederate (Gist, Bavetta, & Stevens, 1990; Stevens & Gist, 1997). Although namely differently, these tools aimed at promoting unforeseen transfer contain similar elements, including monitoring and reflecting on progress, identifying obstacles and strategies, and seeking feedback and guidance (Bell & Kozlowski, 2002; Foster & Macan, 2002; Gist, Bavetta, & Stevens, 1990; Tews & Tracey, 2008). Moreover, Gist et al. (1990) revealed that a self-management module involving adaptive tools generated better transfer performance than goal setting. Stevens and Gist (1997) further examined framing of goals and suggested that performance-oriented goals could lead to cognitive withdrawal of trainees low on self-efficacy, which undermined transfer. By contrast, framing goals as mastery oriented led to better outcomes than performance-oriented goals, because it allowed trainees to utilize performance as feedback to reflect on progress and generate strategies.

Adaptive transfer outcomes can also be enhanced by incorporating variability in training interventions due to increased understanding of various cues for effective behaviors. Variability can be achieved by using both positive and negative behavioral models (Baldwin, 1992), instilling divergence and flexibility of thoughts (i.e., cognitive modeling; Gist, 1989), and increasing variability in practice (Holladay & Quiñones, 2003).

As expected, evidence suggests different interventions for maximizing transfer outcomes depending on the predictability of situations. For transfer with expected changes, an intervention could yield better results if it involves active maintenance of learning and motivational components (e.g., goal setting). To promote transfer with high unpredictability, improving self-regulation and gaining experience with a variety of cues can serve as the bases for generating effective interventions. Interestingly, performance-oriented posttraining goal setting is found to be most beneficial in transfer with anticipated changes, but detrimental in transfer with unforeseen changes (Brown et al., 2013; Stevens & Gist, 1997). Following Seijts and Latham (2012), it is possible that directing trainees' attention to performance goals (as opposed to learning goals) in unforeseen transfer situations hinders the formulation of new strategies.

Learning Outcomes

Learning includes cognitive (knowledge, organization, and cognitive strategies), skill (compilation and automaticity), and affective (attitudinal and motivational outcomes) categories (Goldstein and Ford, 2002; Kraiger et al., 1993). Learning outcomes are usually evaluated immediately after training. Any changes in trainee cognition, skill, and affect created by the joint effect of trainee and training characteristics serves as foundation of later transfer (Baldwin & Ford, 1988). If changes are anticipated during transfer, trainees' transfer behaviors can be a direct application of learning outcomes; whereas if changes are more unpredictable, trainees utilize learning to generate new goals and strategies.

However, a few exceptions exist. First, Kraiger et al. (1993) pointed out that how trainees organize knowledge might be as crucial as the knowledge stored. Expert-like knowledge organization can facilitate the grasp of new elements and the generation of new strategies, which will be more beneficial when predicting transfer where unforeseen changes occur. Second, skill proficiency may be more strongly associated with unforeseen rather than anticipated transfer, as more self-regulation resources are available for monitoring progress and generating new strategies. Third, generalized self-efficacy, or self-efficacy generality, resulted from training indicates trainees' confidence in dealing with a wide range of scenarios, which serves as a positive motivational force for trainees to deal with unexpected changes (Holladay and Quiñones, 2003).

Focused on the unique predictors of unforeseen transfer, we examined several studies involving more complex transfer tasks (e.g., decision making or flight simulations) compared to the training phases. These studies supported that adaptive transfer performance was better when trainee knowledge structure is similar with expert referent structure (Day et al., 2001; Kozlowski et al., 2001) or demonstrated a higher level of skills acquisition (Chen et al., 2005; Herold et al., 2002).

With regard to motivational outcomes, Holladay and Quiñones (2003) distinguished between self-efficacy generality (across situations) and intensity (level of expected performance), and discovered that self-efficacy generality, but not intensity, made a positive difference on transfer of decision-making skills. This finding underscores the importance for trainees to have confidence that they can handle variations in transfer situations.

Work and Task Environment

The transfer environment usually differs from the learning environment. Environmental factors may facilitate or hinder transfer depending on whether trainees are encouraged to and/or have opportunities and resources to apply learning. Research has focused on transfer climate, support, and level of stress as critical characteristics of the task and work environment (Blume et al., 2010; Gist & Stevens, 1998; Zach, Raviv, & Inbar, 2007). Specifically, transfer climate consists of situational cues (opportunity to apply learning) and consequences (feedback and reinforcement related to transfer), which can directly enhance transfer (Rouiller & Goldstein, 1993). Unforeseen transfers are usually accompanied by a certain level of stress, which demands trainees' personal resources. A trainee may access a greater pool of resources to react to changes and overcome unexpected obstacles when working in a supportive environment, and subsequently yield better transfer outcomes. Thus, transfer climate and support may be a more important predictor of outcomes in unforeseen transfer compared to anticipated transfer. Likewise, highly stressful transfer task can be more taxing and more negatively related to performance when unpredictability is high versus low.

Despite this expectation, there is a paucity of research examining the role of workplace support and transfer climate on unforeseen transfer. Only a few studies incorporated level of stress in unforeseen transfer. For instance, in a nine-week training of security personnel, considering the unexpected nature of terror attack simulations, introducing unanticipated weapons in combat can elevate stress experienced during transfer. A high level of stress undermines performance during a simulation when the task is complex, particularly during the early phase of transfer (Zach et al., 2007). When applying negotiation skills, beyond the changes in objectives and partners of negotiations, the level of hostility of the partner of negotiations can create variation in stress. Stress interacts with posttraining intervention to affect transfer, such that mastery-oriented supplements only foster transfer when stress level is higher (Gist & Stevens, 1998). These results demonstrate situational stress as the moderator between predictors and transfer, such that the effectiveness of intervention targeting at dealing with high demands (e.g., mastery-orientation supplements) can be revealed by stressful transfer situation.

Considering Training Transfer as Adaptive Performance

Our review in the preceding text suggests that the same predictor may have different effects on transfer depending on the anticipated/unforeseen nature of the transfer context. In particular, transfer interventions may be differentially effective for enhancing anticipated versus unforeseen changes. Beyond observed relationships, it may be of interest to note that researchers have examined different theoretically driven predictors. For instance, the finding that emotional stability predicted unforeseen transfer (Herold et al., 2002) echoed Huang et al.'s (2014) conclusion that emotional stability enables workers to react to changes.

Even when the same predictor shows similar relationships with anticipated and unforeseen transfer outcomes, we argue that the processes through which the predictor influences transfer may differ; as research suggests that adaptive responses differ between anticipated and unforeseen changes. As noted previously, cognitive ability can promote both anticipated and unforeseen transfer through the acquisition of knowledge and skills, but it may offer additional benefit when dealing with unforeseen transfer because cognitive ability will be more heavily relied upon to facilitate the revision of transfer strategies in novel situations.

It should be noted that our review focuses on predictability as one potential moderating variable in the predictor-transfer relationship. This moderating role needs to be considered in conjunction with other moderators identified in the extant literature. One of these moderators is the nature of skills being trained. Blume et al. (2010) demonstrated the need to consider the closed versus open dimension. Whereas closed skills training emphasizes identical reproduction of behaviors, open skills training emphasizes adhering to overarching principles (Yelon & Ford, 1999). Considering predictability and the nature of skills together opens the door to future research opportunities. One may examine whether open skills training is more amenable to transfer to unforeseen changes, whereas closed skills training can transfer more easily to anticipated changes. That is, perhaps open skills training's focus on principles rather than exact reproduction behaviors (i.e., characteristic of closed skills training) can result in a more flexible mind-set on the appropriate behaviors to adopt in different unexpected transfer scenarios as opposed to transferring to familiar contexts. Furthermore, researchers may begin to investigate whether predictability may interact with the closed/open nature of skills. It is likely that the need for adaptation is strongest for open skills training in unforeseen contexts, and weakest for closed skills training in anticipated contexts. Such an idea may be tested by examining the relative influence of predictors across different combinations of predictability and the nature of skills.

Building the conceptual linkage between transfer and adaptive performance also makes it important to simultaneously consider the distinction between maximum and typical measurement contexts (Klehe & Anderson, 2007; Sackett, Zedeck, & Fogli, 1988). Maximum contexts are marked by three characteristics: (1) containing explicit instruction or implicit expectation for individuals to maximize their effort; (2) provide clear cues for performance measurement; and (3) assessing individuals for a relatively short period (Sackett et al., 1988). Typical contexts, in contrast, do not include one or more of these features. As maximum performance contexts tend to result in higher motivation than typical ones, research has shown that maximum performance is better predicted by ability factors while typical performance is better predicted by motivational factors (e.g., DuBois et al., 1993; Klehe & Anderson, 2007; Witt & Spitzmuller, 2007). Parallel to the findings in the job performance literature, Huang et al.

(2012) showed that maximum transfer is more strongly predicted by cognitive ability and knowledge/skills learning outcomes, whereas typical transfer is more strongly predicted by conscientiousness and affective learning outcomes.

The joint consideration of predictability and the maximum/typical transfer context points to the need for theoretical precision in future transfer investigations. There appears to be a tendency in the transfer literature to assess unforeseen transfer in a maximum context and anticipated transfer in a typical context. Greater insight of transfer behavior will be garnered by studying unforeseen changes in a typical context and anticipated changes in a maximum context.

We highlight situations in which the need to transfer to unforeseen situations can occur dynamically in a typical context. For example, trainees transferring learning as part of a newcomer orientation program to the actual job will have to deal with a novel organizational context. Similarly, expatriates attempting to transfer learning from a cross-cultural training program to an expatriate assignment need to navigate various elements in the new culture.

Although researchers have yet to develop "a coherent framework for organizing and understanding changes" (Jundt et al., 2015: S65) in the adaptive performance literature, Pulakos et al.'s (2000) eight behavioral dimensions may be useful to dissect the behaviors instrumental for successful transfer. For example, handling work stress will facilitate transfer to the extent that the transfer context is stressful (e.g., Smith-Jentch, Salas, & Brannick, 2001), and interpersonal adaptability is important when transferring interpersonal skills training to unanticipated scenarios (Baldwin, 1992). Such a fine-grained taxonomy can be useful to index the breadth of requisite transfer behaviors.

Directions for Future Research

Having discussed ways in which transfer research may benefit from concepts and findings from the adaptive performance literature, we explore additional future research opportunities in the transfer literature. These future directions follow recent calls in the adaptive performance literature (Jundt et al., 2015; Lang & Bliese, 2009) to better understand the *process* by which individuals adapt to changes at work.

First, transfer researchers may begin to investigate the dynamic interplay between the trainee and the work environment. Training research has come a long way to recognize the dynamic nature of the trainee. That is, for relatively stable traits such as goal orientation and locus of control, researchers have designed interventions to affect their state analogs to influence learning and transfer (Bell & Kozlowski, 2008; Kozlowski et al., 2001; Weissbein et al., 2011). In contrast, most of the assessment of the work environment has followed the implicit assumption that the work environment is stable. This assumption, however, may not hold true in all transfer situations. Co-workers' support for transfer, for instance, may not be undifferentiated toward various training programs and may not remain at the same level over time. One possible contingency is the amount of effort the trainee exerts to transfer, such that co-workers offer greater support when a trainee attempts to use newly acquired skills. Another possibility is that the trainee would be proactive in reshaping his or her work environment (Berg, Wrzesniewski, & Dutton, 2010) to ensure successful transfer in the long run. Considering these possibilities leads to the potential to study the dynamic relationship (e.g., Chen et al., 2011) between the trainee and the work context.

Second, the within-person dynamics and the role of time should be integrated in the research on transfer. Huang et al. (2014) provided initial evidence that trainees indeed vary in within-person change of transfer behavior over time, and such change could be positively predicted by motivation to transfer measured at the end of the training. Given the difference across trainees on their increase (or decrease) of transfer behavior over time, it is conceivable that the same predictor may have different relationships with transfer depending on when and how transfer is assessed. We further draw from the findings by Lang and Bliese (2009) that performance adaption to changes in one's task environment can take on different shapes and share different relationships with a predictor depending on the phase of performance adaptation, thus underscoring the importance of conceptualizing and assessing within-person change over time in transfer behavior. Therefore, instead of studying transfer as an outcome at a single point in time, researchers may want to investigate transfer as a process or trajectory (Baldwin & Ford, 1988; Ford & Oswald, 2003).

Third, transfer scholars may attempt to provide ongoing interventions to facilitate transfer over time. With rare exceptions (e.g., providing self-coaching and subordinate feedback for newly hired managers; Tews & Tracey, 2008), transfer interventions tend to occur immediately after training for a short period. Consistent with the notion that transfer can manifest as a within-person process over time (Baldwin & Ford, 1988), the posttraining environment is a great prospect to influence the transfer process, particularly if interventions occur repeatedly. The need for ongoing posttraining interventions is accentuated by the constantly changing technology in today's workplace. For example, training on new technology, such as an office software program, can often cover only the basic, requisite skills, leaving out advanced skills that can potentially enhance productivity. Offering a learning-oriented goal frame as ongoing intervention, introduced and repeated as skills are acquired on the job, may not only help prevent skill decay but also lead to further learning and transfer. Indeed, such ongoing interventions can be facilitated by or delivered through technology, as trainees are likely to have easy access to content through the Internet and personal communication devices.

Finally, more transfer research is needed to understand how to enhance transfer of attitudinal training, such as diversity and ethics training. Ford, Kraiger, and Merritt (2012) noted the need to study whether changes in attitudes due to training may persist over time. We echo their assessment and further emphasize that the transfer context may present cues and dilemmas that influence such attitudes. In the case of a diversity training program, a stereotype abated due to the training may resurface after encountering a co-worker who happens to conform to the stereotype. Such a challenge of maintaining a modified attitude at work may be distinct from the process of adapting knowledge, skills, and behaviors to the work context. Drawing from research on attitude change (Wood, 2000), we propose that transfer of attitude change over a prolonged period of time may be enhanced when the following two conditions are met: (1) the trainee acquires and maintains factual information that generates attitude change; and (2) the trainee's work group comes to form a social norm that helps sustain the changed attitude. The notion that the social environment may play an exceedingly important role for the transfer of attitudes as compared to knowledge and skills may provide a fruitful area for future research.

Conclusion

In conclusion, we provide an explicit conceptual linkage between transfer and adaptive performance in this chapter. We identify predictability of transfer contexts as a key construct to consider, and further draw from the adaptive performance literature to suggest areas for future research. We hope our chapter provides actionable input for transfer research in the near future.

References

Allworth, E., and Hesketh, B. 1999. Construct-oriented biodata: Capturing change-related and contextually relevant future performance. *International Journal of Selection and Assessment* 7: 97–111.

Ashford, S. J., and Taylor, M. S. 1990. Adaptation to work transitions: An integrative approach. *Research in Personnel and Human Resources Management* 8: 1–39.

Axtell, C. M., Maitlis, S., and Yearta, S. K. 1997. Predicting immediate and longer-term transfer of training. *Personnel Review* 26: 201–213.

Baard, S. K., Rench, T. A., and Kozlowski, S. W. J. 2014. Performance adaptation: A theoretical integration and review. *Journal of Management* 40: 48–99.

Baldwin, T. T. 1992. Effects of alternative modeling strategies on outcomes of interpersonal-skills training. *Journal of Applied Psychology* 77: 147–154.

Baldwin, T. T., and Ford, J. K. 1988. Transfer of training: A review and directions for future research. *Personnel Psychology* 41: 63–105.

Baldwin, T. T., Ford, J. K., and Blume, B. D. 2009. Transfer of training 1988–2008: An updated review and agenda for future research. *International Review of Industrial and Organizational Psychology* 24: 41–70.

Barnett, S. M., and Ceci, S. J. 2002. When and where do we apply what we learn? A taxonomy for far transfer. *Psychological Bulletin* 128: 612–637.

Bell, B. S., and Ford, J. K. 2007. Reactions to skill assessment: The forgotten factor in explaining motivation to learn. *Human Resource Development Quarterly* 18: 33–62.

Bell, B. S., and Kozlowski, S. W. 2002. A typology of virtual teams implications for effective leadership. *Group and Organization Management* 27: 14–49.

Bell, B. S., and Kozlowski, S. W. 2008. Active learning: Effects of core training design elements on self-regulatory processes, learning, and adaptability. *Journal of Applied Psychology* 93: 296–316.

Berg, J. M., Wrzesniewski, A., and Dutton, J. E. 2010. Perceiving and responding to challenges in job crafting at different ranks: When proactivity requires adaptivity. *Journal of Organizational Behavior* 31: 158–186.

Blume, B. D., Ford, J. K., Baldwin, T. T., and Huang, J. L. 2010. Transfer of training: A meta-analytic review. *Journal of Management* 36: 1065–1105.

Brett, J. F., and VandeWalle, D. 1999. Goal orientation and goal content as predictors of performance in a training program. *Journal of Applied Psychology* 84: 863–873.

Brown, T. C., Warren, A., and Cass, B. 2013. The impact of behavioral goals on transfer from a management development program. In A. T. Belasen, Chair, Research on Training and Transfer of Learning. Symposium conducted at the Annual Meeting of Academy of Management, Lake Buena Vista, FL.

Burke, L. A., and Baldwin, T. T. 1999. Workforce training transfer: A study of the effect of relapse prevention training and transfer climate. *Human Resource Management* 38: 227–241.

Burke, L. A., and Hutchins, H. M. 2007. Training transfer: An integrative literature review. *Human Resource Development Review* 6: 263–296.

Carter, M., and Beier, M. E. 2010. The effectiveness of error management training with working-aged adults. *Personnel Psychology* 63: 641–675.

Chan, D. 2000. Understanding adaptation to changes in the work environment: Integrating individual difference and learning perspectives. *Research in Personnel and Human Resources Management* 18: 1–42.

Chen, G., Ployhart, R. E., Thomas, H. C., Anderson, N., and Bliese, P. D. 2011. The power of momentum: A new model of dynamic relationships between job satisfaction change and turnover intentions. *Academy of Management Journal* 54: 159–181.

Chen, G., Thomas, B., and Wallace, J. C. 2005. A multilevel examination of the relationships among training outcomes, mediating regulatory processes, and adaptive performance. *Journal of Applied Psychology* 90: 827–841.

Cheng, E. W., and Hampson, I. 2008. Transfer of training: A review and new insights. *International Journal of Management Reviews* 10: 327–341.

Cheng, E. W., and Ho, D. C. 2001. A review of transfer of training studies in the past decade. *Personnel Review* 30: 102–118.

Colquitt, J. A., LePine, J. A., and Noe, R. A. 2000. Toward an integrative theory of training motivation: A meta-analytic path analysis of 20 years of research. *Journal of Applied Psychology* 85: 678–707.

Davis, F. D., and Yi, M. Y. 2004. Improving computer skill training: Behavior modeling, symbolic mental rehearsal, and the role of knowledge structures. *Journal of Applied Psychology* 89: 509–523.

Day, E. A., Arthur Jr., W., and Gettman, D. 2001. Knowledge structures and the acquisition of a complex skill. *Journal of Applied Psychology* 86: 1022–1033.

DeShon, R. P., and Gillespie, J. Z. 2005. A motivated action theory account of goal orientation. *Journal of Applied Psychology* 90: 1096–1127.

Dierdorff, E. C., and Surface, E. A. 2008. If you pay for skills, will they learn? Skill change and maintenance under a skill-based pay system. *Journal of Management* 34: 721–743.

Dierdorff, E. C., Surface, E. A., and Brown, K. G. 2010. Frame-of-reference training effectiveness: Effects of goal orientation and self-efficacy on affective, cognitive, skill-based, and transfer outcomes. *Journal of Applied Psychology* 95: 1181–1191.

Digman, J. M., and Takemoto-Chock, N. K. 1981. Factors in the natural language of personality: Re-analysis, comparison, and interpretation of six major studies. *Multivariate Behavioral Research* 16: 149–170.

DuBois, C. L., Sackett, P. R., Zedeck, S., and Fogli, L. 1993. Further exploration of typical and maximum performance criteria: Definitional issues, prediction, and white-black differences. *Journal of Applied Psychology* 78: 205–211.

Ford, J. K., Kraiger, K., and Merritt, S. M. 2012. An updated review of the multidimensionality of training outcomes: New directions for training evaluation research. In S. W. J. Kozlowski and E. Salas, eds., *Learning, Training, and Development in Organizations*, 135–165. New York: Routlege.

Ford, J. K., and Oswald, F. L. 2003. Understanding the dynamic learner: Linking personality traits, learning situations, and individual behavior. In M. Barrick and A. M. Ryan, eds., *Personality and Work*, 229–261. San Francisco: Jossey-Bass.

Ford, J. K., Smith, E. M., Weissbein, D. A., Gully, S. M., and Salas, E. 1998. Relationships of goal orientation, metacognitive activity, and practice strategies with learning outcomes and transfer. *Journal of Applied Psychology* 83: 218–233.

Ford, J. K., and Weissbein, D. A. 1997. Transfer of training: An updated review and analysis. *Performance Improvement Quarterly* 10: 22–41.

Foster, J., and Macan, T. H. 2002. Attentional advice: Effects on immediate, delayed, and transfer task performance. *Human Performance* 15: 367–380.

Gibson, C. B. 2001. Me and us: Differential relationships among goal-setting training, efficacy and effectiveness at the individual and team level. *Journal of Organizational Behavior* 22: 789–808.

Gist, M. E. 1989. The influence of training method on self-efficacy and idea generation among managers. *Personnel Psychology* 42: 787–805.

Gist, M. E., and Stevens, C. K. 1998. Effects of practice conditions and supplemental training method on cognitive learning and interpersonal skill generalization. *Organizational Behavior and Human Decision Processes* 75: 142–169.

Gist, M. E., Bavetta, A. G., and Stevens, C. K. 1990. Transfer training method: Its influence on skill generalization, skill repetition, and performance level. *Personnel Psychology* 43: 501–523.

Gist, M. E., Schwoerer, C., and Rosen, B. 1989. Effects of alternative training methods on self-efficacy and performance in computer software training. *Journal of Applied Psychology* 74: 884–891.

Gist, M. E., Stevens, C. K., and Bavetta, A. G. 1991. Effects of self-efficacy and posttraining intervention on the acquisition and maintenance of complex interpersonal skills. *Personnel Psychology* 44: 837–861.

Goldstein, I., and Ford, J. 2002. *Training in Organizations: Needs Assessment, Development, and Evaluation,* 4th ed. Belmont, CA: Wadsworth.

Heimbeck, D., Frese, M., Sonnentag, S., and Keith, N. 2003. Integrating errors into the training process: The function of error management instructions and the role of goal orientation. *Personnel Psychology* 56: 333–361.

Herold, D. M., Davis, W., Fedor, D. B., and Parsons, C. K. 2002. Dispositional influences on transfer of learning in multistage training programs. *Personnel Psychology* 55: 851–869.

Holladay, C. L., and Quiñones, M. A. 2003. Practice variability and transfer of training: The role of self-efficacy generality. *Journal of Applied Psychology* 88: 1094–1103.

Huang, J. L., and Ford, J. K. 2012. Driving locus of control and driving behaviors: Inducing change through driver training. *Transportation Research Part F: Traffic Psychology and Behaviour* 15: 358–368.

Huang, J. L., Ford, J. K., and Ryan, A. M. 2014. Ignored no more: Within-person variability enables better understanding of training transfer. *Academy of Management Proceedings 2014*: 14097.

Huang, J. L., Blume, B. D., Ford, J. K., and Baldwin, T. T. 2012. Paths to transfer: A meta-analytic investigation of training outcomes. In M. Wang and L. Zhou, Co-chairs, *New Developments in Training Motivation and Training Transfer Research*. Symposium presented at the annual conference of Society for Industrial and Organizational Psychology, San Diego, CA, April.

Huang, J. L., Ryan, A. M., Zabel, K. L., and Palmer, A. 2014. Personality and adaptive performance at work: A meta-analytic investigation. *Journal of Applied Psychology* 99: 162–179.

Johnson, S., Garrison, L., Hernez-Broome, G., Fleenor, J., and Steed, J. 2012. Go for the goals: Relationship between goal setting and transfer of training following leadership development. *Academy of Management Learning and Education* 11: 555–569.

Jundt, D. K., Shoss, M. K., and Huang, J. L. 2015. Individual adaptive performance in organizations: A review. *Journal of Organizational Behavior* 36: S53–S71.

Kabanoff, B., and Bottger, P. 1991. Effectiveness of creativity training and its relation to selected personality factors. *Journal of Organizational Behavior* 12: 235–248.

Karl, K. A., O'Leary-Kelly, A. M., and Martocchio, J. J. 1993. The impact of feedback and self-efficacy on performance in training. *Journal of Organizational Behavior* 14: 379–394.

Keith, N., and Frese, M. 2005. Self-regulation in error management training: Emotion control and metacognition as mediators of performance effects. *Journal of Applied Psychology* 90: 677–691.

Keith, N., and Frese, M. 2008. Effectiveness of error management training: A meta-analysis. *Journal of Applied Psychology* 93: 59–69.

Kirkman, B. L., Rosen, B., Tesluk, P. E., and Gibson, C. B. 2006. Enhancing the transfer of computer-assisted training proficiency in geographically distributed teams. *Journal of Applied Psychology* 91: 706–716.

Klehe, U.-C., and Anderson, N. 2007. Working hard and working smart: Motivation and ability during typical and maximum performance. *Journal of Applied Psychology* 92: 978–992.

Kozlowski, S. W., Gully, S. M., Brown, K. G., Salas, E., Smith, E. M., and Nason, E. R. 2001. Effects of training goals and goal orientation traits on multidimensional training outcomes and performance adaptability. *Organizational Behavior and Human Decision Processes* 85: 1–31.

Kraiger, K., Ford, J. K., and Salas, E. 1993. Application of cognitive, skill-based, and affective theories of learning outcomes to new methods of training evaluation. *Journal of Applied Psychology* 78: 311–328.

Lang, J. W., and Bliese, P. D. 2009. General mental ability and two types of adaptation to unforeseen change: Applying discontinuous growth models to the task-change paradigm. *Journal of Applied Psychology* 94: 411–428.

LePine, J., Colquitt, J., and Erez, A. 2000. Adaptability to changing task contexts: Effects of general cognitive ability, conscientiousness, and openness to experience. *Personnel Psychology* 53: 563–593.

Locke, E. A., and Latham, G. P. (1990). *A Theory of Goal Setting and Task Performance.* Englewood Cliffs, NJ, US: Prentice-Hall, Inc.

Martocchio, J. J., and Judge, T. A. 1997. Relationship between conscientiousness and learning in employee training: Mediating influences of self-deception and self-efficacy. *Journal of Applied Psychology* 82: 764–773.

Mathieu, J. E., Martineau, J. W., and Tannenbaum, S. I. 1993. Individual and situational influences on the development of self-efficacy: Implications for training effectiveness. *Personnel Psychology* 46: 125–147.

Mathieu, J. E., Tannenbaum, S. I., and Salas, E. 1992. Influences of individual and situational characteristics on measures of training effectiveness. *Academy of Management Journal* 35: 828–847.

Morin, L., and Latham, G. 2000. The effect of mental practice and goal setting as a transfer of training intervention on supervisors' self-efficacy and communication skills: An exploratory study. *Applied Psychology* 49: 566–578.

Myers, C. 1992. Core skills and transfer in the youth training schemes: A field study of trainee motor mechanics. *Journal of Organizational Behavior* 13: 625–632.

Oakes, D. W., Ferris, G. R., Martocchio, J. J., Buckley, M. R., and Broach, D. 2001. Cognitive ability and personality predictors of training program skill acquisition and job performance. *Journal of Business and Psychology* 15: 523–548.

Pulakos, E., Arad, S., Donovan, M., and Plamondon, K. E. 2000. Adaptability in the workplace: Development of a taxonomy of adaptive performance. *Journal of Applied Psychology* 85: 612–624.

Quiñones, M. A. 1995. Pretraining context effects: Training assignment as feedback. *Journal of Applied Psychology* 80: 226–238.

Ree, M. J., Carretta, T. R., and Teachout, M. S. 1995. Role of ability and prior knowledge in complex training performance. *Journal of Applied Psychology* 80: 721–730.

Richman-Hirsch, W. L. 2001. Posttraining interventions to enhance transfer: The moderating effects of work environments. *Human Resource Development Quarterly* 12: 105–120.

Rouiller, J. Z., and Goldstein, I. L. 1993. The relationship between organizational transfer climate and positive transfer of training. *Human Resource Development Quarterly* 4: 377–390.

Sackett, P. R., Zedeck, S., and Fogli, L. 1988. Relations between measures of typical and maximum job performance. *Journal of Applied Psychology* 73: 482–486.

Schmidt, F. L., and Hunter, J. E. 1998. The validity and utility of selection methods in personnel psychology: Practical and theoretical implications of 85 years of research findings. *Psychological Bulletin* 124: 262–274.

Seijts, G. H., and Latham, G. P. 2012. Knowing when to set learning versus performance goals. *Organizational Dynamics* 41: 1–6.

Smith-Jentsch, K. A., Salas, E., and Brannick, M. T. 2001. To transfer or not to transfer? Investigating the combined effects of trainee characteristics, team leader support, and team climate. *Journal of Applied Psychology* 86: 279–292.

Stanhope, D. S., and Surface, E. A. 2014. Examining the incremental validity and relative importance of specific cognitive abilities in a training context. *Journal of Personnel Psychology* 13: 146–156.

Stanhope, D. S., Pond III, S. B., and Surface, E. A. 2013. Core self-evaluations and training effectiveness: Prediction through motivational intervening mechanisms. *Journal of Applied Psychology* 98: 820–831.

Staw, B. M., and Boettger, R. D. 1990. Task revision: A neglected form of work performance. *Academy of Management Journal* 33: 534–559.

Stevens, C. K., and Gist, M. E. 1997. Effects of self-efficacy and goal-orientation training on negotiation skill maintenance: What are the mechanisms? *Personnel Psychology* 50: 955–978.

Stewart, G., and Nandkeolyar, A. 2006. Adaptation and intraindividual variation in sales outcomes: Exploring the interactive effects of personality and environmental opportunity. *Personnel Psychology* 59: 307–332.

Stewart, G. L., Carson, K. P., and Cardy, R. L. 1996. The joint effects of conscientiousness and self-leadership training on employee self-directed behavior in a service setting. *Personnel Psychology* 49: 143–164.

Tews, M. J., and Tracey, J. B. 2008. An empirical examination of posttraining on-the-job supplements for enhancing the effectiveness of interpersonal skills training. *Personnel Psychology* 61: 375–401.

Towler, A. J., and Dipboye, R. L. 2001. Effects of trainer expressiveness, organization, and trainee goal orientation on training outcomes. *Journal of Applied Psychology* 86: 664–673.

Tracey, J. B., Tannenbaum, S. I., and Kavanagh, M. J. 1995. Applying trained skills on the job: The importance of the work environment. *Journal of Applied Psychology* 80: 239–252.

Tziner, A., Haccoun, R. R., and Kadish, A. 1991. Personal and situational characteristics influencing the effectiveness of transfer of training improvement strategies. *Journal of Occupational Psychology* 64: 167–177.

VandeWalle, D. 1997. Development and validation of a work domain goal orientation instrument. *Educational and Psychological Measurement* 57: 995–1015.

Warr, P., and Bunce, D. 1995. Trainee characteristics and the outcomes of open learning. *Personnel Psychology* 48: 347–375.

Weissbein, D. A., Huang, J. L., Ford, J. K., and Schmidt, A. M. 2011. Influencing learning states to enhance trainee motivation and improve training transfer. *Journal of Business and Psychology* 26: 423–435.

Wexley, K. N., and Baldwin, T. T. 1986. Posttraining strategies for facilitating positive transfer: An empirical exploration. *Academy of Management Journal* 29: 503–520.

Witt, L. A., and Spitzmüller, C. 2007. Person-situation predictors of maximum and typical performance. *Human Performance* 20: 305–315.

Wood, W. 2000. Attitude change: Persuasion and social influence. *Annual Review of Psychology* 51: 539–570.

Yelon, S. L., and Ford, J. K. 1999. Pursuing a multidimensional view of transfer. *Performance Improvement Quarterly* 12: 58–78.

Zach, S., Raviv, S., and Inbar, R. 2007. The benefits of a graduated training program for security officers on physical performance in stressful situations. *International Journal of Stress Management* 14: 350–369.

5 The Psychology of Learner Control in Training

A Multilevel, Interactionist Framework

Garett N. Howardson, Karin A. Orvis, Sandra L. Fisher, and Michael E. Wasserman

> Our culture is just a series of checks and balances. The whole idea that we're in a battle between tyranny and freedom – it's a series of pendulum swings. And the swings have become less drastic over time. (Stewart, 2010)

The opening quotation emphasizes the general societal desire to balance environmental structure with autonomous control over individual choice – to let the pendulum settle if you will. This same struggle can be found throughout the evolution of the organizational sciences (Jaffee, 2001). Early perspectives on workplace behavior emphasized standardized work processes leaving little room for individual discretion. An employee's external environment, argued such views, should regulate work behaviors more so than the individual's preferences. The principles of *scientific management* (Taylor, 1916), for example, eliminated between-worker differences in how the work was performed through standardized tools and processes. Common to this highly structured perspective is that individuals need not intuit the most effective work performance strategy, but rather that such information can be more objectively placed in employees' physical work environment through standardized tools and operating procedures. The merits of this view notwithstanding (e.g., Weber, 1922), organizational scholars also realized that, despite proving effective, not all standardization efforts worked as intended. That is, such changes to employees' environment may have simply stimulated the volitional decision-making processes that were ultimately responsible for improved productivity.

In one particularly notable example, researchers manipulated several physical features of employees' work environment (e.g., lighting). Much to the scholars' surprise, employee productivity increased regardless of the physical features manipulated, such as when productivity increased in both brighter and dimmer work environments. Eventually, scholars realized that the productivity increases stemmed not from employees' capacity to better perform the work physically, but rather from the employees' volitional increase in effort to garner favorable views from the study's researchers (Roethlisberger, 1941). Such findings implied that there was perhaps not a single, most effective work process but that several such processes might exist, any of which may improve performance.

The views, opinions, and/or findings contained in this article are solely those of the authors and should not be construed as an official position, policy, or decision of the DoD or the United States, unless so designated by other documentation.

Consequently, allowing individuals to choose among several such processes might improve worker attitudes and motivation, and through these changes, boost productivity (e.g., Maslow, 1943). The logical extreme of this perspective is that employee attitudes and motivation could be maximized with entirely autonomous and self-directed work. Perhaps unsurprisingly given the opening quotation, modern perspectives lie somewhere in between the logical extremes of absolute standardized structure and absolute worker autonomy.

Modern perspectives, known as *interactionism* (e.g., Meyer, Dalal, & Hermida, 2010; Mischel, 1968), acknowledge the role of both situational structure and individual autonomy in employee behavior. In a dangerous industrial setting, for instance, individuals might benefit greatly from standardized tools and processes to avoid injury. In such settings, all employees might have similar albeit low levels of autonomy. In a safer office environment, individuals may be given relatively high levels of autonomy with little risk. Nevertheless, not all individuals might welcome such autonomy; some may choose to leave in search of a more structured environment. In other words, one's level of autonomy is at least in part self-determined (e.g., Ryan & Deci, 2000). Consequently, interactionist views of work behavior have moved away from advocating purely structured or purely autonomous work environments' views toward understanding the specific work features that most effectively balance structure and autonomy (Meyer et al., 2010), and acknowledging that individual choices, including choices to leave the situation, must be considered.

To be sure, the interactionist ideas of balancing situational structure individual autonomy are also at the forefront of the training and adult learning literatures (e.g., Brown, Howardson, & Fisher, 2016; Gully & Chen, 2010). Instructional designers, for example, strive to balance effective pedagogical designs (i.e., situational structure) and learner motivation and attitudes given that the former by no means guarantee the latter or vice versa (e.g., Noe, Tews & Dachner, 2010; Welsh et al., 2003). For example, some of the most effective pedagogical designs purposefully impose structure to remove learner control (e.g., part task training) to prevent learners from becoming overwhelmed by the task demands (e.g., Carolan et al., 2014). A learner who has already mastered the basic task concepts, however, might find such training too highly structured and experience frustration that could lead to withdrawal. As such, the past few decades have seen a movement toward more learner-centric training delivery methods that permit greater individual control over one's training environment (Kraiger & Culbertson, 2013) with the intent that more autonomous learning will improve learner motivation and attitudes and, ultimately, learning outcomes.

This shift has been partially driven by the individualized capabilities offered in e-learning and technology-mediated training (Brown & Ford, 2002). We now have technologies that give learners more freedom over a wide variety of training-related decisions, such as where to take the training, which content to view, how quickly to progress through the training, and whether to accept advice during training. In essence, modern training and learning environments have become more autonomous and learner driven. In line with the general interactionist views in the preceding text, however, training and work learning scholars have recognized that the pendulum of one's volitional discretion to enact change on one's learning environment – termed here *learner control* – has perhaps swung too far in the purely autonomous direction (e.g., Mayer, 2004). That is, several lines of evidence demonstrate that more learner control does not necessarily result in a more effective learning experience; rather, effectively designing and delivering learner-controlled training requires balancing individual learner discretion and autonomy with the structures created by effective instructional and pedagogical designs (Brown et al., 2016). In other words, the concept of learner control is not purely an individual-level construct but is rather a constellation of interacting individual and situational constructs.

Indeed, the broader psychological literature is rich with control-related constructs addressing both situational and individual features (Skinner, 1996). To date, however, this broader literature has not been integrated into the training and work learning literatures to better understand the balance between structure and autonomy in learning environments. Thus, the purpose of this chapter is to do precisely this by advancing a comprehensive but parsimonious taxonomy and multilevel framework of learner-control constructs from an interactionist perspective. That is, our framework elucidates both the situational and individual features of learner control.

To do so, we synthesize expansive bodies of literature on the *psychology of control* and *psychology of situation strength* to argue that learner control is not a singular construct but rather a descriptive title encompassing a complex network of interacting individual and situational constructs spanning multiple levels of analyses. To make this conceptualization more parsimonious, we propose a taxonomy of learner-control constructs, accompanied by a simple multilevel framework. We argue that the learner control title encompasses *contextual control*, *actual control*, *perceived control*, *control motives*, and *control consequences*. These constructs can further be classified as individual or situational, the latter of which can be further separated into individual- and supervisor-, team-, and/ or organizational-level constructs. Figure 5.1 provides a graphical depiction of the framework.

The remaining sections of this chapter are structured as follows. We first briefly review the literature of psychological control. Next, we present a broad review of the training and adult learning literatures, the results of which we use to expound on each specific aspect of psychological control as applied to learning experiences – that is, the psychology of learner control. We conclude by suggesting several lines of future work to refine our framework and integrate diverse literatures studying the psychology of control during learning.

The General Psychology of Control

In an encyclopedic review of the psychological literature, Skinner (1996) concluded that *psychological control* is not a single construct but a broad

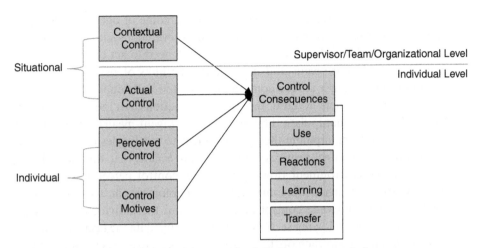

Figure 5.1. *A multilevel framework of the learner-control phenomenon.*

constellation of constructs. In her review, Skinner identified no fewer than 111 distinct operationalizations of psychological control. She synthesizes these constructs into five all-encompassing construct categories: *perceived control, contextual control,*[1] *actual control, control motives,* and *control consequences.*[2] Through this view, psychologists may better understand the diverse constructs constituting the psychological control phenomena, which are key to improving psychological and physical health (Skinner, 1996).

Here, we further refine Skinner's work and integrate psychological control with concepts from organizational research to more directly address training environments (e.g., Gully & Chen, 2010; Meyer et al., 2010). We argue that control constructs can be further classified into *individual* and *situational* constructs. *Individual control constructs* include perceived control and control motives. Perceived control refers to the individual's perception of control. Control motives refer to the amount and reasons why individuals desire control over their environment. *Situational control constructs* include actual control and contextual control. Actual control refers to the extent that the situation allows individuals to enact change and acquire desired outcomes. Contextual control is more general, occurs at higher levels of analysis, and is evaluative. Contextual control includes supervisor-, team-, and/or organizational-level qualities that communicate if and why learner control is valued. Although this refined view may inform the general study of psychological control, our focus here is on applying this view to the specific problem of learner control.

Skinner further distinguishes between the *agent-outcome, agent-means,* and *means-outcome* dimensions of psychological control. Important to this definition is the existence of an agent (i.e., the individual), a means (i.e., actions), and an outcome (i.e., desired effects). Psychological control may occur at either the agent-means or means-outcome links, but the strongest influence on behavior is when control occurs simultaneously forming a single link between the agent, means, and outcome (i.e., agent-means-outcome or agent-outcome). If either the agent-means or means-outcome link is severed, psychological control is reduced such that individuals do not perceive a need to act on their environment. Both the agent-means and means-outcome links of psychological control are formed through unique combinations of the individual and situational categories of constructs noted in the preceding sections. An individual may be able to objectively manipulate their environment (agent-means actual control) and may desire to manipulate their environment to receive desirable outcomes (means-outcome control motives), but may not *believe* that they are able to manipulate the environment (low agent-means control perceptions; Skinner, 1996). As such, the agent-outcome link of psychological control is severed by a lack of means-outcome control perceptions and the individual will refrain from acting. In the following sections, we further elucidate the agent-means and means-outcome role in each of the control construct categories identified in the preceding sections.

Perceived Control

Perceived control is an individual control construct defined as the subjective belief that an individual possesses the *ability* to produce desirable effects through actions. Perceived control being ability-based is an important distinction when placed in the context of other *desire*-based mechanisms described in later sections. Perceived control requires the existence of two distinct perceptions – perceived agent-means control and perceived means-outcome control. First, an individual must perceive the ability to actively influence the environment. This is known as perceived agent-means control (Skinner, 1996). Second, the individual must believe that influencing one's environment will produce desirable outcomes, which is known as perceived means-outcome control (Skinner, 1996). Each is discussed in more detail in the following sections.

Perceived Agent-Means Learner Control

Perceptions that an individual possesses agency and is able to manipulate the environment through action are known as perceived agent-means control. Notable examples of these control perceptions are expectancy beliefs (Vroom, 1964) and earlier conceptualizations of self-efficacy where the focus was purely on action rather than the outcomes of those actions (Bandura, 1977). These constructs focus on the subjective probability that an attempt to act on one's environment will indeed result in a change in the environment. A number of scholars have discussed agent-means control perceptions in training. For example, both Kraiger and Jerden (2007) and Karim and Behrend (2014) discuss the perception that individuals could or did enact change on their learning environment. Others (Beier & Kanfer, 2010; Colquitt & Simmering, 1998; Mathieu, Tannenbaum, & Salas, 1992) discuss learner beliefs that effort will produce a change in the environment (i.e., learner expectancy).

Perceived Means-Outcome Learner Control

Means-outcome control perceptions are beliefs that desired outcomes are contingent upon action. It is important to note that means-outcome control perceptions refer only to the probability that the desired outcome will be acquired through action, but not what specifically the desired outcome is. For example, a learner may perceive high means-outcome control for some desirable outcome that is completely irrelevant for learning (e.g., "I can skip through this training and get back to work"). Examples in the general psychology of control literature are instrumentality beliefs (Vroom, 1964), outcome expectations (Bandura, 1986, 1997), and causal attributions (Weiner, 1985). In a learning context, some learners may believe that no matter how well they perform in training, they will never master a new skill (Mathieu et al., 1992; Thomas & Mathieu, 1994). Such individuals possess low means-outcome control perceptions because skill mastery, the desirable outcome, is perceived to be entirely noncontingent upon actions taken during training. Similarly, learners who are forced to complete compliance training and pass a certification would perceive low means-outcome control because no matter how much they tried to skip through the training, they would be forced to view all of the content. Although both agent-means and means-outcome control perceptions are important, the complete link of agent-means-outcome perceptions may have the most profound impact on behavior (Skinner, 1996).

Perceived Agent-Outcome Learner Control

The hallmark of perceived control is the perception that the agent's actions will generate desired outcomes in the environment, which necessitates a complete agent-means-outcome link, or more simply an agent-outcome perception (Skinner, 1996). Vroom's expectancy theory posits that the multiplicative effect of one's expectancy and instrumentality determines an individual's will to act. This decreases if either expectancy (i.e., agent-means control perceptions) or instrumentality (i.e., means-outcome control perceptions) decreases. More recent iterations of self-efficacy theory focus on the complete agent-outcome link, defined as the "belief in one's capabilities to organize and execute the courses of action required to produce given attainments" (Bandura, 1997: 3). This definition indicates that self-efficacy may be low from either the perceived inability to act (perceived agent-means control) or from attributing attained outcomes to chance rather than to one's behavior (perceived means-outcome control; Bandura, 1997; Thomas & Mathieu, 1994). In a training context, the clear prototype for agent-outcome control perceptions is training self-efficacy, which may be conceptualized pretraining (Colquitt et al., 2000), during training (Kozlowski et al., 2001), or posttraining (Kraiger, Ford, & Salas, 1993). Drawing from the general self-efficacy definition in the preceding sections, this indicates that pretraining self-efficacy is the perception that learners can mobilize resources necessary to acquire new knowledge and skills; during training self-efficacy is the perception that individuals are successfully learning the training content; posttraining self-efficacy is the perception that the individual can mobilize resources and apply the learned knowledge and skills to their actual jobs.

Control Motives

Learner-control motives are individual-level constructs defined as the set of individual differences that determine the amount of control desired and the reasons for those desires (Skinner, 1996). In other words, control motives are individual characteristics that determine one's desire to produce a certain outcome through actions on the environment.

Agent-Outcome Learner-Control Motives

Agent-outcome motives are any characteristics that increase individuals' drive or desire to manipulate their environment in a manner that produces specific behavior-outcome contingencies. Our review identified six training-relevant constructs that fit within agent-outcome learner control motives: the Big Five personality characteristics (Costa & McCrae, 1992; Goldberg, 1999) of *conscientiousness, openness to experience, extraversion,* and *emotional stability,* and *goal orientation* (DeShon & Gillespie, 2005), as well as *training motivation* (Noe, 1986).

Conscientious individuals are task focused, organized, driven by a desire to achieve excellence, self-disciplined, and deliberate with actions. Extraverted individuals seek excitement, are assertive, and maintain high energy/activity levels. Open individuals are curious, seek intellectual opportunities, and are creative. Finally, emotionally unstable individuals frequently experience negative emotions and tend to be highly impulsive, opting for immediate rewards rather than delaying gratification (Costa & McCrae, 1992; Goldberg, 1999). Each of these Big Five traits indicates that individuals are motivated to act on their environment to produce desirable outcomes. Conscientious individuals are extremely focused (agent-means motive) because they are high achieving and prefer to be competent (means-outcome motives). Similarly, extraverted individuals prefer to interact with others in social settings (agent-means motives) because they prefer excitement and arousal (means-outcome motives). Likewise, individuals high in openness to experience seek new opportunities (agent-means motives) because they value intellectual growth (means-outcome motives). Finally, emotionally unstable individuals prefer to act immediately (agent-means motives) to secure rewards out of fear that those rewards will not be available in the future (means-outcome motives). As such, conscientiousness, extraversion, openness, and emotional stability are examples of agent-outcome learner-control motives.

Goal orientation is the general predisposition to prefer certain paths of action for accomplishing goals. Goal orientation explains both *why* individuals choose to act and precisely how they plan to act (DeShon & Gillespie, 2005). According to DeShon and Gillespie's (2005) motivated action theory account of goal orientation, individuals prefer either *mastery* or *performance* courses of action to accomplish three abstract goals: *agency, affiliation,* and *esteem.*[3]

Mastery-oriented learners pursue competence and agency goals by choosing courses of action that promote individual growth, problem exploration, and feedback seeking. Performance-oriented learners pursue affiliation and competence goals by choosing courses of action that promote social value, fairness, and impression management (DeShon & Gillespie, 2005). Training research generally finds that mastery-oriented learners do better in training than performance-oriented learners (Fisher & Ford, 1998; Schmidt & Ford, 2003). Training motivation indicates the extent to which individuals are committed to interacting with training material (agent-means motive) to acquire new knowledge and skills (means-outcome motive). Research has shown that training motivation is important in environments enabling higher learner control because motivated learners attend more to the training content when given such control (Orvis, Fisher, & Wasserman, 2009).

Agent-Means Learner-Control Motives

Agent-means control motives are individual characteristics that determine the extent to which one prefers to act on the environment. We identify two training-relevant examples of agent-means control motives. Specifically, we argue that *preferences for learner control* and *action/state orientation* are examples of agent-means control motives. Preference for learner control indicates an individual's desire to manipulate aspects of their learning environment (Kraiger & Jerden, 2007). The assumption in early learner-control research was that individuals necessarily desired more control. Research has since shown, however, that not all learners prefer control of their learning environment and that mismatches between preferred and actual control may negatively impact learning regardless of the absolute amount of control (Hannafin & Sullivan, 1996). For example, Freitag and Sullivan (1996) found that individuals given less control over the instructional material learned more than individuals given more control, as long as the low-control individuals preferred less control at the outset.

Although preferences for learner control are not well understood (Kraiger & Jerden, 2007), recent work suggests some promising possibilities. Orvis and colleagues (2009) recently found learning differences for high- and low-control learning environments, but this relationship depended on learner's personality traits. Individuals who were open to new experiences performed well when given learner control but others given less control performed worse. Conversely, individuals who prefer stable environments to variety (i.e., low openness to experience) performed best when given *less* control (Orvis et al., 2011). The authors posited that these personality characteristics manifest in specific learning situations through preferences for learner control. In other words, whereas stable-preferring individuals may desire less learner control, variety-preferring individuals may desire more control; the match between desired and actual control maximizes learning. The authors' argument suggests that preferences for control may be an agent-means manifestation of agent-outcome control motives.

Action/state orientation (Kuhl, 1985) is an individual's predisposition to either act (action) or reflect on how actions could affect one's self-concept (state). Action and state are opposite ends of a bipolar continuum so the more action oriented an individual is the more likely they are to act in a given situation and the more state-oriented they are the less likely they are to act. Research has shown that action-oriented individuals do indeed act more on their environment and perform better in both work and academic settings (Diefendorff, 2004; Diefendorff, Richard, & Gosserand, 2006; Diefendorff et al., 2000; Diefendorff et al., 1998).

Means-Outcome Learner-Control Motives

Means-outcome control motives are individual preferences that influence which behavior-outcome contingencies are formed. Stated otherwise, means-outcome learner-control motives are the reasons why learners prefer to act on an environment. For example, two learners may both wish to skip three training modules (agent-means control motives) for different reasons. One may skip the modules because she has already mastered the content of those modules. The other may skip the modules because he wants to finish the training more quickly, despite not knowing the skipped content. As such, the two learners have different motives for the same behaviors and thus different means-outcome control motives. Our review identified three means-outcome control motives relevant to training: *training valence, training relevance*, and *locus of control*.

Training valence is the inherent value that a learner ascribes to a particular learning experience (Beier & Kanfer, 2010; Colquitt et al., 2000). Training relevance is the extent to which a learner finds the content germane to realizing personal objectives or goals (Brown, 2005). Learners who perceive greater amounts of training valence and relevance are more likely to create positive behavior-outcome contingencies than learners who perceive training as less relevant or valuable. Consider the example of two learners required to attend training (i.e., have no actual agent-means control). The learner who values and finds the training relevant will be more likely to create positive behavior-outcome contingencies that attending training improves work skills. The learner who does not value the training and finds it irrelevant will create negative behavior-outcome contingencies that attending the training is wasting work time. As such, the same behavior (participating in the training) is associated with different outcomes (learning or wasted work time), creating different means-outcome contingencies as a result of training valence. Thus, training relevance and valence are examples of preferences for exactly which outcomes will be attributed to which behaviors and are means-outcome learner control motives.

Finally, locus of control (Levenson, 1973) is also an agent-outcome control motive. Locus of control refers to individuals' predisposition to believe that any outcomes produced were due to either their actions (internal) or chance environmental factors (external). Learners with an internal locus of control create different behavior-outcome contingencies than learners with an external locus of control, representing a means-outcome control motive.

Actual Control

Actual learner control is a situational construct and is the objective training design and instructional features that provide a choice over whether the learner is allowed to act in a manner consistent with personal preferences (Brown et al., 2016). Note that actual control is simply the degree to which individuals are afforded choice without reference to whether such choices are effective or ineffective for learning. That is, whereas some actual learner control may allow learners to deviate from the expert-recommended instructional designs (e.g., amount of information) other actual learner control affords choice over only superfluous design characteristics (e.g., preferred examples) that might not affect learning (Brown et al., 2016). Whether learners are allowed to alter fundamental pedagogical design features or mere convenience features can be described as deep- or surface-level actual learner control, respectively (Brown et al., 2016). In learning contexts, actual control ranges from purely learner driven (e.g., discovery learning, McDaniel & Schlager, 1990) to purely instructional driven (e.g., course lecture) with methods such as guided exploration in between (Mayer, 2004). Further, this range of actual learner control can be applied to both deep- and surface-level actual learner controls (Brown et al., 2016). Much like perceived control, actual control may refer to agent-means, means-outcome, or agent-outcome control (Skinner, 1996). For the purposes of this chapter and the framework at hand, however, we do not distinguish between deep- and surface-level actual learner controls but rather elucidate the agent-means, means-outcome, or agent-outcome components of actual learner control. Interested readers may wish to refer to Brown and colleagues (2016) for a more in-depth discussion of the surface- and deep-level actual learner control distinction.

Actual Agent-Means Learner Control

Actual agent-means control refers to any situational characteristics that facilitate or block an individual from acting. A lack of agent-means control may occur when situational constraints interrupt and prevent an individual from making a choice or acting (Heckhausen & Gollwitzer, 1987). A large portion of the training literature refers to agent-means control when discussing technological implementations of learner control. For example, Kraiger and Jerden's (2007) widely used framework notes that individuals may be allowed to influence several features of training, including *pace, content, sequence, advisory,* and *media.* Other forms of agent-means control in training may be an instructor creating a time limit for practice or testing when learners cannot act once the time limit has expired. Finally, several training designs in highly dangerous jobs purposefully remove actual agent-means control. A flight simulator removes the possibility that a trainee's actions will produce changes (e.g., crash the plane) or a military simulation may use blank rounds. Safety training often mimics job settings but does so in a manner where learner actions will not produce actual changes, such as simulating drilling procedures for an oil rig instead of drilling on an actual oilrig (e.g., Brown et al., 2016).

Actual Means-Outcome Learner Control

Actual means-outcome control is any situational factor that determines the contingency between behavior and an outcome. It is important to note that actual means-outcome control reflects objective structural characteristics of the environment and not the individual's perception of those structures. Learned helplessness studies typically use low actual means-outcome control to induce helplessness perceptions (Skinner, 1996). Individuals are given an undesirable outcome regardless of their action creating a behavioral noncontingency. Reaching the outcome is beyond the control of the individual and is low actual means-outcome control. Training contexts that provide low actual means-outcome control may be found in particularly difficult learning environments with novice learners. Regardless of effort or action, inexperienced learners will struggle to acquire new knowledge and skills (Kanfer & Ackerman, 1989). Such training environments may create a behavioral noncontingency such that even maximal amounts of effort are not likely to produce desirable outcomes. In another example, some training researchers have provided learners with a choice over material, but learners were not actually given their training choices (Baldwin, Magjuka, & Loher, 1991). Thus, although they could act on their environment, the environment created a situation in which those actions failed to produce desirable outcomes (i.e., low actual means-outcome control).

Actual Agent-Outcome Learner Control

Drawing from the preceding, actual agent-outcome control is any situational factor that increases the likelihood of action while also making desirable outcomes of those actions more probable. Recent training research has focused considerable effort on agent-outcome training interventions. *Guided exploration* creates a structure where learners interact directly with the training content and determine precisely how they progress through the training (Wood et al., 2000), which is an example of actual agent-means control. The strength of guided exploration is that the training provides suggestions for actions that will produce the most desirable outcomes (Bell & Kozlowski, 2002). The training might suggest that additional practice would benefit the learner. Exploration increases the likelihood that individuals will act, and guided exploration increases the likelihood that such actions will produce maximal benefits to learner. Thus, guided exploration is an example of actual agent-outcome control. Another strategy often combined with exploration to create positive behavior-outcome contingencies is error framing (Bell & Kozlowski, 2008; 2010) or error encouragement training (Keith & Frese, 2005; 2008). Such training designs transform a negative behavior-outcome contingency (e.g., "If I make a mistake I'm a bad learner") into a positive contingency (e.g., "If I make a mistake I'm a good learner") thereby forming another completed positive agent-means-outcome link for actual learner control.

Contextual Control

Contextual control is similar to actual control in that both are features of the situation. However, the two differ in important ways. First, contextual control occurs at higher levels of analysis, such as the team, supervisor, or organizational level. As such, contextual control interventions are necessarily more complex, difficult, and longer in scope than the shorter term and more immediate individual-level interventions on actual learner control. Because of this much broader scope, the second difference is that contextual control factors are general and do not influence specific agent-means or means-outcome aspects of control, but instead provide general guidance about which specific agent-means-outcome pathways are appropriate and desired (Skinner, 1996). That is, contextual control is evaluative and clearly indicates other control aspects that are "good" or "bad." Given its generality, contextual control does not directly influence any of the other control constructs but functions as the contextual boundary conditions that influence whether other control constructs in aggregate will have positive or negative influences on learning outcomes (e.g., Holton, 1996).

For example, an organization may be extremely safety conscious and be less likely to give individuals actual learner control for fear of an accident. The organization's safety consciousness would be openly communicated to employees making it clear that they will not have learner control, decreasing learner-control perceptions. If the company also communicates the reasons behind the lack of learner control, individuals may understand the need for less control, which would produce lower control motives. Thus, even though the organizational context places boundary constraints on the amount of actual control, such training could still be effective if appropriately attending to learners' perceived control and control motives.

Drawing from Meyer and Dalal's work (Meyer, Dalal, & Hermida, 2010; Meyer et al., 2014), we conceptualize contextual control through *situational strength*, which is defined as "implicit or explicit cues provided by external entities regarding the desirability of potential behaviors" (Meyer et al., 2010: 122). In other words, situation strength provides guidance to individuals about which behaviors are appropriate for accomplishing which desired outcomes. It is worth noting that Meyer and colleagues' (2010; 2014) conceptualization is but one of several for studying situation strength. See, for example, Brown and colleagues (2016) for an alternative conceptualization of situation strength in learner control. As with Meyer and colleagues' (2010; 2014) perspective, however, we argue that contextual learner control can therefore be classified into one of four categories: *clarity, consistency, constraints,* and *consequences.*

Clarity

Clarity is defined as "the extent to which cues regarding work training-related responsibilities or requirements are available and easy to understand" (Meyer et al., 2010: 125). In a learning context, information about work responsibilities and requirements tied to continuous learning and development would be a potential contextual control factor because such information provides clear guidance that training is valued. Consider the following scenario as an example. A particular organization clearly communicates a strong preference for self-development by allowing individuals to attend professional conferences and remain up-to-date with the major advancements in the field (e.g., Orvis & Leffler, 2011). Employees clearly understand the procedures for attending a conference, which include filling out the easily accessible and internal online forms, which will then be sent to their supervisor for approval. As such, the organization clearly communicates the presence of actual learner control (attending the conference), encourages appropriate control motives (keep knowledge up-to-date), and facilitates control perceptions (easily complete approval forms). Training-specific examples of clarity are supervisor support for training (Baldwin & Ford, 1988; Quiñones, 1995, 1997), organizational climate for training (Colquitt et al., 2000), and organizational safety culture (Hoffmann & Mark, 2006; Naveh, Katz-Navon, & Stern, 2005), to name a few.

Consistency

Consistency is defined as "the extent to which cues regarding work-related responsibilities or requirements are compatible with each other" (Meyer et al., 2010: 126). Consistency in a training context therefore refers to compatibility between cues and messages pertaining to the value of acquiring and applying new knowledge and skills. Building on the preceding example, consider that an employee attended the professional conference and mastered a new technique that will improve her work performance. Upon returning from the conference, however, the individual realizes that her supervisor's perspective has changed and employees are only allowed to use the older, more established techniques. Despite high control perceptions, motives, and actual control, the supervisor is clearly conveying that the new knowledge and skills are no longer valued, which sends inconsistent messages to the employee. As such, these inconsistent messages place a contextual boundary constraint on the learning experience's effectiveness.

Constraints

Constraints are defined as "the extent to which an individual's freedom of decision and action is limited by forces outside his or her control" (Meyer et al., 2010: 126). Ford (2008; Yelon & Ford, 1999) distinguishes between *open* and *closed* work environments (see also Brown et al., 2016). Closed environments are highly structured such that individuals' actions are to follow specific, prescribed rules. For example, air traffic controllers operate in closed environments in which actions are guided by strict standard operating procedures resulting in a prescribed course of action for each situation. Conversely, knowledge work is an example of an open environment; any given problem could have multiple, equally effective solutions. Actions are constrained more in closed than open environments (Brown et al., 2016; Brown & Klein, 2008; Ford, 2008; Yelon & Ford, 1999). No matter how much and individual desires or believes in their ability to learn a new technique, the opportunity to apply the new technique will necessarily be constrained by the nature of the work being performed, acting as another boundary situation to learner control.

Consequences

Consequences are defined as "the extent to which decisions or actions have important positive or negative implications for any relevant person or entity" (Meyer et al., 2010: 127). Industrial settings are an example where consequences are important contextual control factors. In such settings, mistakes have severe consequences in that others may be injured or even killed. Dropping a pallet of product off a forklift from 20 feet has severe consequences in that, at best, the product will be destroyed, or at worst, the pallet could strike employees in the vicinity. In such settings, individuals may understand the importance of learning to operate the forklift well and that doing so requires a low-control learning environment. Thus, individuals may still invest the effort to learn the new material even if actual control, control perceptions, and control motives are low, emphasizing the role of consequences as a learner control boundary condition.

Control Consequences

Learner-control consequences are the ultimate product of perceived learner control, learner-control motives, actual learner control, and contextual control. Put simply, consequences result from the unique profile of other learner-control constructs that influence learner behaviors and attitudes. Control consequences are classified into four categories: *use, reactions, learning,* and *transfer*.

Use

Taken together, the preceding sections suggest that learners will use actual control as they see fit for accomplishing their desired objectives or goals. Unfortunately, not all forms of learner-control use are equally as effective or productive. We conceptualize learner-control use as a bipolar construct ranging from negative control use to positive control use. The majority of training research focuses on the positive end examining learner practice and other appropriate behaviors (e.g., Bell & Kozlowski, 2008; Brown, 2001; Fisher & Ford, 1998; Ford et al., 1998; Hughes et al., 2013; Kanfer & Ackerman, 1989). Bell and Kozlowski (2008) recently found that a specific combination of training design features targeting learner-control perceptions, learner-control motives, and actual learner control encourages practice behaviors that improve both learning and attitudes. Less research, however, has focused on the negative end of this continuum by examining learner-control behaviors that actively detract from learning. For example, learners with high control perceptions who are given high actual control may act inappropriately by skipping training content.

Consider, for example, the low openness to experience, low emotional stability, and low mastery goal orientation learner who is given the option to practice new skills. In other words, the individual is given actual learner control over the training. Such individuals will likely use such control to skip the practice, in part, because practice is an opportunity to make mistakes and realize one's limited skills. Others, such as those low on training valence, might skip the training content not out of fear, but rather out of contempt that this low-value training is preventing them from performing their actual work. In both scenarios, however, the learner is acting in a way that purposefully avoids effective training features (e.g., practice). That is, the learners exercise negative learner-control use. Thus, depending on the unique profile of other learner-control constructs, learner-control use may be effective or ineffective.

Reactions

Trainee reactions are perceptions of training features that may be affectively or cognitively laden (Alliger et al., 1997). Affective reactions cover a range of affective perceptions including satisfaction, enjoyment (Brown, 2005), excitement, frustration, boredom, and calm (Howardson & Behrend, 2016). Cognitive reactions focus primarily on how relevant (Brown, 2005) or useful training content is for one's job (Alliger et al., 1997). In general, actual learner control and control perceptions that are consistent with one's control motives should improve reactions to the learning experience (Brown et al., 2016). For example, Freitag and Sullivan (1995) found that learner reactions were most positive when the level of actual control matched preferred control. Thus, learners may react best to training tailored specifically to their profile of learner control constructs.

Learning

Kraiger, Ford, and Salas (1993) denote three types of learning outcomes, *cognitive*, *skill-based*, and *affective*. Cognitive skills refer to knowledge about facts, things, and procedures and cognitive strategies that improve performance. Skill learning outcomes are psychomotor skills referring to actions that when repeatedly practiced become automatic (e.g., welding). Affective learning outcomes are motivational and attitudinal changes, such as more positive attitudes toward a training-related concept such as diversity or safety. In general, cognitive and skill-based learning should be facilitated when actual control, perceived control, and control motives align with contextual control.

Consider the scenario of an industrial manufacturing company that heavily emphasizes safety to its employees through a very strong climate for safety. In terms of the framework presented in the preceding sections, such an organization would be relatively low on contextual control. As part of its strong safety climate, the organization would create highly structured training programs relatively low in actual learner control, given the dangers of incorrectly using the industrial machinery. If, however, learners prefer a large amount of actual control, such training designs would be frustrating. Through its strong safety climate, however, the organization conveys precisely why such training designs are necessary, which likely lowers such learner-control motives prior to the training. With such low actual control designs, learners will likely also have low control perceptions. Given that learners did not expect high control training to begin with (i.e., low control motives), however, the low control perceptions align with their low control motives likely making learners more receptive to low actual control. Thus, by accepting the training, learners are more likely to acquire the necessary cognitive and skill-based information. Affective learning, however, may require a slightly different profile of learner-control constructs.

Continuing with the preceding scenario, imagine a newly hired employee proceeding through onboarding or socialization training. The company's primary focus for such training might be to make more favorable employees' attitudes toward safety. Placing individuals in a highly structured, low actual control training, however, likely will not influence learners in such ways (Brown et al., 2016). Instead, learners may require some degree of actual control to facilitate the learner-control perceptions important for improving learner attitudes. As noted previously and discussed in greater detail by Brown and colleagues (2016), however, such control should be limited to surface-level features that do not fundamentally change the training's pedagogical design. For instance, such training might be accomplished through error management training whereby learners are placed into a high-fidelity computer simulation of the industrial setting and allowed to choose their desired task strategies. Such simulation might then also demonstrate the implications of incorrect strategies, such as injuring a co-worker. Through such mistakes, learners might come to understand the importance of safety within the company, which would not occur through purely low actual control training. Thus, affective learning requires a slightly different profile of learner-control constructs than cognitive and skill-based learning (Brown et al., 2016).

Transfer

Transfer is the application of training knowledge and skills to work settings (Baldwin & Ford, 1988) and is often the focal purpose of training (Yelon & Ford, 1999). Transfer can be either near or far (Hutchins et al., 2013). Near transfer refers to situations similar to the training including transfer immediately after the training. Far transfer refers to situations different from the training including transfer after a delayed period of time. In general, transfer should be influenced by the same combination of factors that influence cognitive and skill-based learning (Brown et al., 2016).

Consider the example of communication skills transfer in an office setting. Such work settings are arguably much safer than the industrial settings mentioned previously and, as such, the organization might, for good reason, have a less strong safety climate and encourage more exploratory or trial-and-error behaviors. In other words, contextual control would be relatively high. Consequently, highly structured or low actual control training for communication skills in this office setting would be a strong departure from the actual work environment and the high contextual control. This mismatch between training and transfer environments is ineffective for encouraging actual transfer (Brown et al., 2016). Conversely, less structured or more experiential-based training (e.g., role playing) more closely matches the transfer environment and contextual control, which should improve actual transfer of training (Brown et al., 2016). Thus, like learning, transfer is maximized through an aligned profile learner-control constructs consistent with the specific work environment (i.e., contextual control).

An Agenda for Future Research

The multilevel framework in the preceding sections makes several contributions to the training and adult learning literatures. First and foremost, we clearly define and organize the nebulous construct space of learner control, arguing that learner control can be understood by classifying constructs into one of the categories depicted in Figure 5.1. Second, our framework integrates the extant training and adult learning literatures by explaining the diverse findings as to learner control's effectiveness. That is, the ultimate effectiveness of learner control rests not on one construct but on the appropriate profile of a network of interconnected constructs. Third, this framework sets the ground for subsequent work establishing a broad and general theory of psychological control in learning environments.

The framework developed in this chapter is intended to help advance research and practice. Advanced training technologies offer enormous opportunity for allowing learners to construct their own unique learning experiences, but given the range of possible learner motives and behaviors, we need to understand more about how these constructs interact to produce different outcomes. Even as research in this area works to measure actual learner-control behaviors more specifically, we need to look deeper to understand why different learners might perform the same behaviors under different patterns of agent, means, and outcome features, with varying results. Although we argue in the preceding text that learner-control effectiveness is the unique combination of learner-control constructs, we can only conjecture which specific profiles are the most effective across a wide range of settings. We see this as an active area for future research. In particular, our work could be built upon to develop a general theory of learner control that would explain each of the control consequence scenarios presented previously for use, reactions, learning, and transfer. Such a theory would prescribe the ideal balance between a learning environment's actual control and learners' perceived control and control motives for a wide range of boundary conditions created by contextual control.

The second area of future research we identified is a more nuanced view of control motives. The majority of extant training research focuses on Big Five personality traits (e.g., Colquitt et al., 2000; Wilson et al., 2013) to the exclusion of other personality facets. For example, Orvis and colleagues (2011) found that high-openness and extraverted individuals performed better in high learner-control training than low openness and less extraverted learners. The authors did not find evidence that conscientiousness was related to training performance, confirming findings that conscientiousness may only be related to training performance in certain settings (e.g., Colquitt et al., 2000; Wilson et al., 2013). One explanation for these findings is that different settings are more or less important for specific conscientiousness facets. For example, one conscientiousness facet is dutifulness, or individuals' predisposition to obey rules (Costa & McCrae, 1992; Goldberg, 1999), which could easily be a motive for less control (e.g., "I'll do what the training says"). Conversely, other conscientious facets such as orderliness could be a motive for either positive or negative control uses. As such, a facet level of personality may reveal nuances in control motives that may help explain past findings. We believe the role of personality facets in the psychology of learner control is an area ripe for future research.

Finally, another fruitful area of future research is examining changes in contextual control over time and how such changes influence lower-level learner-control constructs. For example, perhaps an organization implements new initiatives for making a more autonomous workplace or for increasing contextual control. How might employees used to less autonomy respond to new training designs with much more autonomy? That is, how might low-autonomy past experiences influence learner-control perceptions and control consequences? Perhaps, for example, only small changes would be required to greatly improve learner control given the relatively low baseline. How quickly or slowly would learners adjust to such changes? For how long would such changes be effective? What are the adverse consequences of such changes (e.g., once given autonomy, removing it might have a much greater negative effect than had they never experienced an increase in autonomy at all)? Such questions, we argue, are worthy of future research.

Conclusion

Control is not a unitary concept. Indeed the tension between individual control (e.g., choice) and situational control (e.g., constraint) is evidenced throughout psychology (Skinner, 1996). So it is with learner control. Learner control is a constellation of several constructs that, when combined, form a unique configuration of situational (i.e., contextual control, actual control) and individual (i.e., perceived control, control motives) constructs. Further, such configurations emerge from several different constructs within each of the situational and individual clusters. To date, however, learner-control research seemingly describes the overall configuration (e.g., pace, sequence) rather than understanding the processes through which the constructs interact to influence attitudes, behaviors, and learning (Brown et al., 2016).

In terms of Stewart's opening quotation, learner-control research largely conceptualizes the pendulum as fixed somewhere in between purely situational and purely individual control. Through the framework advanced in the preceding text, it is our hope that future research will more fully recognize the spectrum along which learner control constructs fall, and how different constructs along this spectrum influence learner attitudes and behaviors as well as learning outcomes. The pendulum of control will continue to swing; scholars, however, should strive to understand and influence these swings in ways that benefit *both* the learner and the organization.

Notes

1 Skinner uses the term *antecedents of control*, but here we extend her definition to be more relevant to organizational settings and renamed this category *contextual control.*

2 Skinner (1996) also identifies *control experiences*, but this construct is not well defined. As such, we chose to exclude it from our taxonomy.

3 DeShon and Gillespie's (2005) *agency, affiliation*, and *esteem* terminology corresponds to self-determination theory's (Deci & Ryan, 1985; Deci, Ryan, & Williams, 1996) *autonomy, relatedness*, and *competence.* The specific definitions of each, however, are slightly distinct. We adopted DeShon and Gillespie's (2005) terminology because their theory incorporates ideas similar to self-determination theory but also encompasses a wider range of phenomena.

References

Alliger, G. M., Tannenbaum, S. I., Bennett, W., Traver, H., and Shotland, A. 1997. A meta-analysis of the relations among training criteria. *Personnel Psychology* 50(2): 341–358.

Baldwin, T. T., and Ford, J. K. 1988. Transfer of training: A review and directions for future research. *Personnel Psychology* 41(1): 63–105.

Baldwin, T. T., Magjuka, R. J., and Loher, B. 1991. The perils of participation: Effects of choice of training on trainee motivation and learning. *Personnel Psychology* 44(1): 51–65.

Bandura, A. 1977. Self-efficacy: Toward a unified theory of behavioral change. *Psychological Review* 84: 191–215.

Bandura, A. 1986. *Social Foundations of Thought and Action.* Englewood Cliffs, NJ: Prentice-Hall.

Bandura, A. 1997. *Self-efficacy: The Exercise of Control.* New York: Freeman.

Barnett, S. M., and Ceci, S. J. 2002. When and where do we apply what we learn? A taxonomy for far transfer. *Psychological Bulletin* 128(4): 612–637.

Beier, M. E., and Kanfer, R. 2010. Motivation in training and development: A phase perspective. In S. W. J. Kozlowski and E. Salas (Eds.), *Learning Training, and Development in Organizations*, 65–97. New York: Routledge.

Bell, B. S., and Kozlowski, S. W. J. 2008. Active learning: Effects of core training design elements on self-regulatory processes, learning, and adaptability. *Journal of Applied Psychology* 93(2): 296–316.

Bell, B. S., and Kozlowski, S. W. J. 2010. Toward a theory of learner-centered training design: An integrative framework of active learning. In S. W. J. Kozlowski and E. Salas, eds., *Learning, Training, and Development in Organizations*, 263–300. New York: Routledge.

Brown, K. G. 2001. Using computers to deliver training: Which employees learn and why? *Personnel Psychology* 54: 271–296.

Brown, K. G. 2005. An Examination of the structure and nomological network of trainee reactions: A closer look at "smile sheets." *Journal of Applied Psychology* 90(5): 991–1001.

Brown, K. G., and Ford, J. K. 2002. Using computer technology in training: Building an infrastructure for learning. In K. Kraiger, ed., *Creating, Implementing, and Managing Effective Training and Development*, 192–233. San Francisco: Jossey-Bass.

Brown, K. G., Howardson, G. N., and Fisher, S. 2016. Learner control and e-learning: Taking stock and moving forward. *Annual Review of Organizational Psychology and Organizational Behavior* 3: 267–291.

Brown, K. G., and Klein, H. 2008. Third-generation instruction: "Tools in the toolbox" rather than the "latest and greatest." *Industrial and Organizational Psychology* 1(4): 472–476.

Carolan, T. F., Hutchins, S. D., Wickens, C. D., and Cumming, J. M. 2014. Costs and benefits of more learner freedom: Meta-analyses of exploratory and learner control training methods. *Human Factors* 56(5): 999–1014.

Colquitt, J. A., and Simmering, M. J. 1998. Conscientiousness, goal orientation, and motivation to learn during the learning process: A longitudinal study. *Journal of Applied Psychology* 83(4): 654–665.

Colquitt, J. A., LePine, J. A., and Noe, R. A. 2000. Toward an integrative theory of training motivation: A meta-analytic path analysis of 20 years of research. *Journal of Applied Psychology* 85(5): 678–707.

Costa, P. T., and McCrae, R. R. 1992. *Revised NEO Personality Inventory (NEO-PI-R) and NEO Five-factor Inventory (NEO-FFI) Manual*. Odessa, FL: Psychological Assessment Resources.

Deci, E. L., and Ryan, R. M. 1985. *Intrinsic Motivation and Self-determination in Human Behavior*. New York: Plenum Press

Deci, E. L., Ryan, R. M., and Williams, G. C. 1996. Need satisfaction and the self-regulation of learning. *Learning and Individual Differences* 8(3): 165–183.

DeShon, R. P., and Gillespie, J. Z. 2005. A motivated action theory account of goal orientation. *Journal of Applied Psychology* 90(6): 1096–1127.

Diefendorff, J. M. 2004. Examination of the roles of action-state orientation and goal orientation in the goal-setting and performance process. *Human Performance* 17(4): 375–395.

Diefendorff, J. M., Richard, E. M., and Gosserand, R. H. 2006. Examination of situational and attitudinal moderators of the hesitation and performance relation. *Personnel Psychology* 59(2): 365–393.

Diefendorff, J. M., Hall, R. J., Lord, R. G., and Strean, M. L. 2000. Action-state orientation: Construct validity of a revised measure and its relationship to work-related variables. *Journal of Applied Psychology* 85(2): 250–263.

Diefendorff, J. M., Lord, G. R., Hepburn, E. T., Quickle, J. S., Hall, R. J., and Sanders, R. E. 1998. Perceived self-regulation and individual differences in selective attention. *Journal of Experimental Psychology: Applied* 4(3): 228–247.

Fisher, S. L., and Ford, J. K. 1998. Differential effects of learner effort and goal orientation on two learning outcomes. *Personnel Psychology* 51:397–420.

Ford, J. K. 2008. Transforming our models of learning and development: How far do we go? *Industrial and Organizational Psychology* 1(4): 468–571.

Ford, J. K., Smith, E. M., Weissbein, D. A., Gully, S. M., and Salas, E. 1998. Relationships of goal orientation, metacognitive activity, and practice strategies with learning outcomes and transfer. *Journal of Applied Psychology* 83(2): 218–233.

Freitag, E. T., and Sullivan, H. J. 1995. Matching learner preference to amount of instruction: An alternative form of learner control. *Educational Technology Research and Development* 43(2):5–14.

Goldberg, L. R. 1999. A broad-bandwidth, public-domain, personality inventory measuring the lower-level facets of several Five-Factor models. In I. Mervielde, I. Deary, F. De Fruyt, and F. Ostendorf, eds., *Personality Psychology in Europe*, 7–28. Tilburg, The Netherlands: Tilburg University Press.

Gully, S., and Chen, G. 2010. Individual differences, attribute-treatment interactions, and training outcomes. In S. W. J. Kozlowski and E. Salas, eds., *Learning, Training, and Development in Organizations*, 3–64. New York: Routledge.

Hannafin, R. D., and Sullivan, H. J. 1996. Preferences and learner control over amount of instruction. *Journal of Educational Psychology* 88(1): 162–173.

Heckhausen, H., and Gollwitzer, P. M. 1987. Thought contents and cognitive functioning in motivational versus volitional states of mind. *Motivation and Emotion* 11: 101–120.

Hoffmann, D. A., and Mark, B. 2006. An investigation of the relationship between safety climate and medication errors as well as other nurse and patient outcomes. *Personnel Psychology* 59: 847–869.

Holton, E. F. 1996. The flawed four-level evaluation model. *Human Resource Development Quarterly* 7(1): 5–21.

Howardson, G. N., and Behrend, T. S. 2016. Coming full circle with reactions: Understanding the structure and correlates of trainee reactions through the affect circumplex. *Academy of Management Learning and Education* 15(3): 1–23.

Hughes, M. G., Day, E. A., Wang, X., Schuelke, M. J., Arsenault, M. L., Harkrider, L. N., and Cooper, O. D. 2013. Learner-controlled practice difficulty in the training of a complex task: Cognitive and motivational mechanisms. *Journal of Applied Psychology* 98(1): 80–98.

Hutchins, S. D., Wickens, C. D., Carolan, T. F., and Cumming, J. M. 2013. The influence of cognitive load on transfer with error prevention training methods: A meta-analysis. *Human Factors* 55(4): 854–874.

Jaffee, D. 2001. *Organization Theory: Tension and Change.* New York: McGraw-Hill.

Kanfer, R., and Ackerman, P. L. 1989. Motivation and cognitive abilities: An integrative/aptitude-treatment interaction approach to skill acquisition. *Journal of Applied Psychology* 74(4): 657–690.

Karim, M. N., and Behrend, T. S. 2014. Reexamining the nature of learner control: Dimensionality and effects on learning and training reactions. *Journal of Business Psychology* 29: 87–99.

Keith, N., and Frese, M. 2005. Self-regulation in error management training: Emotion control and metacognition as mediators of performance effects. *Journal of Applied Psychology* 90(4): 677–691.

Keith, N., and Frese, M. 2008. Effectiveness of error management training: A meta-analysis. *Journal of Applied Psychology* 93(1): 59–69.

Kozlowski, S. W. J., Gully, S. M., Brown., K. G., Salas, E., Smith, E. M., and Nason, E. R. 2001. Effects of training goals and goal orientation traits on multidimensional training outcomes and performance adaptability. *Organizational Behavior and Human Decision Processes* 85(1): 1–31.

Kozlowski, S. W. J., Toney, R. J., Mullins, M. E., Weissbein, D. A., Brown, K. G., and Bell, B. S. 2001. Developing adaptability: A theory for the design of integrated-embedded training systems. In E. Salas, ed., *Advances in Human Performance and Cognitive Engineering Research*, 1: 59–123. Amsterdam, The Netherlands: JAI/Elsevier Science.

Kraiger, K., and Culbertson, S. S. 2013. Understanding and facilitating learning: Advancements in training and development. In N. W. Schmitt, S. Highhouse, and I. B. Weiner, eds., *Handbook of Psychology: Volume 12 Industrial and Organizational Psychology*, 2nd ed., 244–261. Hoboken, NJ: Wiley and Sons.

Kraiger, K., and Jerden, E. 2007. A meta-analytic investigation of learner control: Old findings and new directions. In S. M. Fiore and E. Salas, eds., *Toward a Science of Distributed Learning*, 65–90. Washington, DC: American Psychological Association.

Kraiger, K., Ford, J. K., and Salas, E. 1993. Integration of cognitive, behavioral, and affective theories of learning into new methods of training evaluation. *Journal of Applied Psychology* 78(2): 311–328.

Kuhl, J. 1985. Volitional mediators cognition-behavior consistency: Self-regulatory processes and action versus state orientation. In J. Kuhl and J. Beckmann, eds., *Action Control*, 101–128. Berlin Heidelberg: Springer-Verlag.

Levenson, H. 1973. Perceived parental antecedents of internal, powerful others, and chance locus of control orientations. *Developmental Psychology* 9: 260–265.

Maslow, A. H. 1943. A theory of human motivation. *Psychological Review* 50: 370–396.

Mathieu, J. E., Tannenbaum, S. T., and Salas, E. 1992. Influences of individual and situational characteristics on measures of training effectiveness. *Academy of Management Journal* 35(4): 828–847.

Mayer, R. E. 2004. Should there be a three-strikes rule against pure discover learning? The case for guided methods of instruction. *American Psychologist* 59(1): 14–19.

McDaniel, M. A., and Schlager, M. S. 1990. Discovery learning and transfer of problem-solving skills. *Cognition and Instruction* 7(2): 129–159.

Meyer, R. D., Dalal, R. S., and Hermida, R. 2010. A review and synthesis of situational strength in organizational sciences. *Journal of Management* 36(1): 121–140.

Meyer, R. D., Dalal, R. S., Jose, I. J., Hermida, R., Chen, T. R., Vega, R. P., Brooks, C. K., and Khare, V. P. 2014. Measuring job-related situational strength and assessing its interactive effects with personality on voluntary work behavior. *Journal of Management* 40(4): 1010–1041.

Mischel, W. 1996. *Personality and assessment.* New York: John Wiley.

Naveh, E., Katz-Navon, T., and Stern, Z. 2005. Treatment errors in healthcare: A safety climate approach. *Management Science* 51(6): 948–960.

Noe, R. A. 1986. Trainees' attributes and attitudes: Neglected influences on training effectiveness. *Academy of Management Review* 11(4): 736–749.

Noe, R. A., Tews, M. J. and Dachner, A. M. 2010. Learner engagement: A new perspective for enhancing our understanding of learner motivation and workplace learning. *Academy of Management Annals* 4: 279–315.

Orvis, K. A., Fisher, S. L., and Wasserman, M. E. 2009. Power to the people: Using learner control to improve trainee reactions and learning in web-based instructional environments. *Journal of Applied Psychology* 94(4): 960–971.

Orvis, K. A., Brusso, R. C., Wasserman, M. E., and Fisher, S. L. 2011. Enabled for e-learning? The moderating role of personality in determining the optimal degree of learner control in an e-learning environment. *Human Performance* 24: 60–78.

Orvis, K. A., and Leffler, G. P. 2011. Individual and contextual factors: An interactionist approach to understanding employee self-development. *Personality and Individual Differences* 51: 172–177.

Quiñones, M. A. 1995. Pretraining context effects: Training assignments as feedback. *Journal of Applied Psychology* 80(2): 226–238.

Quiñones, M. A. 1997. Contextual influences on training effectiveness. In M. A. Quiñones and A. Ehrenstein, eds., *Training for a Rapidly Changing Workplace: Applications of Psychological Research*, 177–199. Washington, DC: American Psychological Association.

Roethlisberger, F. J. 1941. *Management and Morale*. Cambridge, MA: Harvard University Press.

Ryan, R. M. and Deci, E. L. (2000). Self-determination theory and the facilitation of intrinsic motivation, social development, and well-being. *American Psychologist* 55(1): 68–78.

Schmidt, A. M., and Ford, J. K. 2003. Learning within a learner control training environment: The interactive effects of goal orientation and metacognitive instruction on learning outcomes. *Personnel Psychology* 56: 405–429.

Skinner, E. A. 1996. A guide to constructs of control. *Journal of Personality and Social Psychology* 71(3): 549–570.

Stewart, J. 2010. Jon Stewart: The most trusted name in fake news. In T. Gross (host), *Fresh Air on National Public Radio*, October. http://www.npr.org/templates/story/story.php?storyId=130321994 (accessed November 22, 2014).

Taylor, F. W. 1916. The principles of scientific management. *Bulletin of the Taylor Society*, December. An abstract of an address given by the late Dr. Taylor before the Cleveland Advertising Club, March 3, 1915.

Thomas, K. M., and Mathieu, J. E. 1994. Role of causal attributions in dynamic self-regulation and goal processes. *Journal of Applied Psychology* 79(6): 812–818.

Vroom, V. H. 1964. *Work and Motivation*. New York: Wiley.

Weber, M. 1922. Bureaucracy. In H. Gerth and C. W. Mills, eds., *From Max Weber: Essays in Sociology*, 196–244. Oxford: Oxford University Press.

Weiner, B. 1985. An attributional theory of achievement motivation and emotion. *Psychological Review* 92: 548–573.

Welsh, E. T., Wanberg, C. R., Brown, K. G., and Simmering, M. J. 2003. E-learning: Emerging uses, empirical results and future directions. *International Journal of Training and Development* 7: 245–258

Wilson, C. L., Huang, J. L., and Kraiger, K. 2013. Personality and the analysis, design, and delivery of training. In N. D. Christiansen and R. P. Tett, eds., *Handbook of Personality at Work*, 543–564. New York: Routledge.

Wood, R. E., Kakebeeke, B. M., Debowski, S., and Frese, M. 2000. The impact of enactive exploration on intrinsic motivation, strategy, and performance in electronic search. *Applied Psychology: An International Review* 49(2): 263–283.

Yelon, S. L., and Ford, J. K. 1999. Pursuing a multidimensional view of transfer. *Performance Improvement Quarterly* 12(3): 55–78.

PART II

Understanding the Learner

6 The Role of Abilities in Learning and Training Performance

Margaret E. Beier, Anton J. Villado, and Jason G. Randall

One of the few things rarely disputed in organizational science is the importance of cognitive ability for predicting job and training performance (Schmidt & Hunter, 1998). Although research on attitudes, motivation, and other non-ability determinants of job and training performance are generally couched in qualifications about their effectiveness (e.g., "it depends"), discussions of ability-performance relations are unequivocal. And although there has been dispute about the *types* of abilities – that is, general or specific – that best predict performance, cognitive ability tends to predict job and training performance regardless of industry and job complexity. These well-established findings present an inherent challenge in writing a chapter on cognitive abilities and training performance. What can we add to the conversation? What new directions for research can we suggest?

In this chapter, we start by acknowledging that ability is a central and important determinant of training performance. The practical implication of this finding is that the use of ability measures to predict job and training performance will be effective when the outcomes are cognitive in nature (e.g., learning, skill acquisition). The scientific implications of this finding are more nuanced. In particular, the focus on a general ability predictor may overshadow other scientifically interesting relationships. In this chapter, we take a step back from the general ability-training performance relationship to examine the role of both general and specific abilities in the context of intelligence and skill acquisition theories. In particular, we discuss the usefulness of specific versus general ability predictors of training performance, and propose that the proper level of specificity for predicting skilled performance after training might lie somewhere between narrow and general abilities. Our focus is on abilities, but because abilities are related to the attentional resources available for learning in training, we include a discussion of self-regulation in the context of learning and performance in training. And because work in the 21st century is largely dependent on team performance, we consider the role of abilities in team training. Moreover, we view training outcomes as broadly encompassing cognitive, affective, and skill-based factors (Kraiger, Ford, & Salas, 1993). We conclude by presenting implications for training design, particularly as related to aptitude-by-treatment interactions and technological training. Before we describe the relationship between abilities and training, we introduce the theory underlying the currently accepted conceptualization of the construct of cognitive ability that frames our discussion.

Cognitive Ability

An exhaustive review of the evolution of modern psychometric approaches to the study of intelligence is beyond the scope of this chapter; see Ackerman (1996), Reeve, Scherbaum, and Goldstein (2015), Schneider and McGrew (2012), and Schneider and Newman (2015) for thorough and thought-provoking reviews of this literature. For our purposes, we highlight that research on human cognitive abilities is well into its second century and, since its beginning, there have been vigorous debates about both the number of cognitive abilities that exist, and their structure and organization. Notable voices in the debate include Spearman's (1904) theory of general (g) and specific ability factors, Thurstone's seven primary mental abilities (word fluency, verbal comprehension, spatial visualization, number facility, associative memory, reasoning, and perceptual speed; Thurstone, 1938), Vernon's (1971) hierarchical model of general and specific abilities, Horn and Cattell's (1966) theory of fluid and crystallized abilities, and Guilford's (1967) multiple ability model, which identified more than 120 abilities in an approach that crossed mental operation (e.g., evaluation, memory) with product (e.g., units, classes, relations) and content (e.g., figural, symbolic, semantic). In summary, at the middle of the last century, popular theories had identified anywhere from one to 120 different cognitive abilities.

The introduction of modern factor analytic techniques (and the technology that made these techniques more efficient) provided some closure to these questions. In particular, these advances made it relatively easy to identify the common variance among ability measures, and have resulted in an increased understanding of the structure and interrelatedness of human abilities. Arguably, the most significant contribution to organizing the research findings on the structure and predictive validity of cognitive abilities was conducted by Carroll (1993), who reanalyzed more than 400 datasets from the psychological literature, the military, and other sources. Emerging from Carroll's reanalysis was a hierarchical structure of cognitive abilities, called the three-stratum theory, where general mental ability (GMA – essentially Spearman's g) is comprised of common variance among lower-level abilities. GMA is at the apex or the third (highest) stratum of abilities (Carroll, 1993). Although there are alternative views on the nature of important broad abilities (Johnson & Bouchard, 2005), and although number of abilities is in flux as the theory evolves (Schneider & McGrew, 2012; Schneider & Newman, 2015), most research shows about nine relatively broad abilities on the second stratum of the ability hierarchy, which are quantitative reasoning, visual-spatial processing, auditory processing, short-term memory (memory span), long-term memory and storage, perceptual speed with elementary cognitive tasks, and decision-making speed. Broad abilities that are of particular importance to this chapter are fluid intelligence (usually defined as reasoning ability) and crystallized intelligence (broad cultural knowledge gained through education and experience). Narrower abilities exist on the first stratum of Carroll's model (more than 70 in all), and include abilities that are

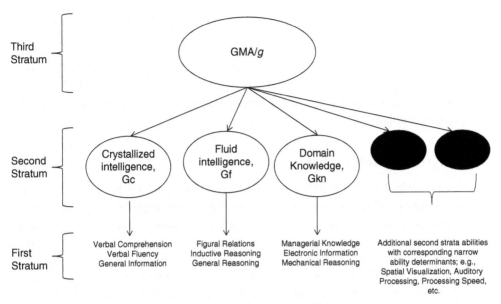

Figure 6.1. *Illustration of the CHC theory of intelligence.*

more easily operationalized into measures. For instance, verbal comprehension might be easily measured by asking for synonyms for words that differ in their frequency of use/difficulty. Performance on this type of verbal assessment would likely be correlated with measures of verbal fluency (e.g., sentence completion tests), and with tests that tap general cultural knowledge. The common variance among these vocabulary and general knowledge tests would be used to determine a crystallized intelligence factor, which is a second stratum ability.

Advances in intelligence research since the publication of Carroll's (1993) book include further integration of Carroll's three-stratum theory with Horn and Cattell's (1966) theory of fluid and crystallized intelligence into what is now known as the Cattell-Horn-Carroll (CHC) theory of ability (McGrew, 2005). Similar to Carroll's analysis, CHC is a psychometric theory that is based on examining the factor structure of abilities. Also similar to Carroll's approach, CHC recognizes a hierarchical structure of abilities through the same three strata described in the preceding text and shown in Figure 6.1.

We have included only those abilities most relevant to our discussion in the figure – fluid and crystallized intelligence and general domain knowledge – although a larger figure including a broader range of first and second strata abilities could easily be developed. Domain knowledge has been studied less frequently than other ability constructs, but we have included it here because we believe that it is an important determinant of learning in training, which we will further discuss.

Fluid Intelligence

Fluid intelligence represents a person's logical reasoning abilities and it is implicated in novel problem solving. Fluid intelligence is significantly and substantially related to working memory capacity (Ackerman, Beier, & Boyle, 2005), and is a strong predictor of learning in educational contexts for adults of all ages (Beier & Ackerman, 2005). Because it is related to memory and reasoning ability, fluid intelligence is particularly important when a person does not have prior knowledge about the content domain being taught, such as a person's first day on a new job, when people cannot rely on existing knowledge and experience.

Crystallized Intelligence

Crystallized intelligence is comprised of general cultural knowledge acquired through educational or other life experiences. Crystallized intelligence is generally measured with assessments of broadly available cultural knowledge (e.g., Who was Abraham Lincoln?), and with vocabulary tests such as one would find on standardized achievement tests used for college admissions (e.g., What is the meaning of "augur?"). Crystallized intelligence is thus an index of knowledge possessed, whereas fluid intelligence is generally considered an index of the potential to learn and acquire new knowledge (Ackerman, 1996; Salthouse, 2010).

Domain Knowledge

In contrast to crystallized intelligence, domain knowledge represents the depth and breadth of a person's experiences and as such, it is idiosyncratic in nature. That is, a person's level of domain knowledge will be a function of his or her experiences at work, at home, and in school. For example, work-related domain knowledge would include knowledge of technology, mechanical knowledge, interpersonal knowledge for effective customer service, or interpersonal knowledge for effective management (Beier & Ackerman, 2005; Motowidlo & Beier, 2010). Domain knowledge can also be considered an index of a person's level of typical intellectual engagement within their environment (Ackerman & Beier, 2004), and as such it is an index of a person's intellectual development and growth throughout the life span. This is because people who are relatively more intellectually engaged will accumulate more knowledge across the life span than those who are less engaged. For instance, people who pay attention to the news and trends in art, politics, the environment, sports, and popular culture on a day-to-day basis will accumulate more current-events domain knowledge over time compared to people who pay relatively little attention to these things either because they tend not to be engaged or because they choose not to learn about these things (Ackerman, 1996; Ackerman & Beier, 2004).

Notably, the difference between crystallized intelligence and domain knowledge may be more of depth and breadth than kind. Both domain knowledge and crystallized intelligence change over the life span, as people engage in, and learn from, different experiences. This may lead some to question whether these abilities can be considered "stable traits" versus skills that develop over time. To us, the distinction between the trait and skill is somewhat arbitrary in this context. Rather, the important distinction between these abilities is their breadth and content in terms of how well suited they are to predict a certain outcome (Wittmann & Süß, 1999). It is also notable that abilities related to knowledge are not the only cognitive abilities to change throughout the life span; memory and fluid intelligence also change throughout the life span although the trajectories are different (e.g., they are likely to decline rather than grow; Salthouse, 2010).

Domain knowledge has been identified on the second stratum of CHC theory (McGrew, 2005) and is highlighted here for three reasons. First, domain knowledge – when it is job related – is an exceedingly important determinant of job performance; for example, Hunter (1986) identified job-related domain knowledge as the main mediator of the relationship between general ability and job performance. Most importantly for this chapter, however, is the finding that domain knowledge facilitates learning in related domains (Ackerman & Beier, 2006; Beier & Ackerman, 2005).

Predicting Training Performance with General vs. Specific Abilities

General Ability

The central role of GMA in training performance cannot be disputed, and has been particularly salient since the introduction of validity generalization (meta-analytic research) on cognitive ability and job and training performance. Indeed, reviews of meta-analytic research report that the average correlation between GMA (typically operationalized in meta-analyses as a composite of various general and composite measures) and performance in job training programs is .56 (Hunter & Hunter, 1984; Schmidt & Hunter, 1998). This estimate is collapsed across occupations, but one can also expect the relationship between ability and performance to be moderated by the complexity of the occupation. For instance, the correlation between GMA and training performance is about .64 for engineering occupations and about .47 for drivers (Bertua, Anderson, & Salgado, 2005). Overall though, GMA is an important determinant of training performance regardless of occupation; it accounts for between 22 and 41% of the variance in training performance.

Hearkening back to the historical disputes about the number and structure of cognitive abilities, researchers have investigated the utility of general versus specific abilities for predicting performance in training (Brown, Le, & Schmidt, 2006; Ree & Earles, 1991). This question appeared to be largely settled two decades ago by influential papers published by Ree and colleagues (Ree, Earles, & Teachout, 1994; Ree & Earles, 1991), who demonstrated that training performance was most efficiently predicted by general ability (either composites of specific ability tests or GMA measures) because the incremental validity of specific abilities for predicting performance after general ability was accounted for was negligible (Ree & Earles, 1991). To address questions related to small samples and the rigor of the analytical methods employed by Ree and Earles (1991), Brown et al. (2006) examined the predictive validity of six specific abilities measured in the Armed Services Vocational Aptitude Battery (ASVAB) and a general ability composite of these measures. Brown and colleagues' sample comprised more than 25,000 navy trainees across 10 different schools/jobs. Like Ree and Earles, who used the ASVAB as the predictor, the outcome of interest was the trainee's final school grade in their training course. The results of Brown and colleagues' study corroborated Ree and Earles's findings; the use of specific ability predictors accounted for only negligible incremental variance over a composite ASVAB measure. Because of these influential papers, many organizational scientists and practitioners have moved away from the use and investigation of specific abilities for predicting training performance.

Researchers espousing the view that general ability is the best way to predict training performance tend to adhere to the principle of *the indifference of the indicator* (Spearman, 1904); that is, the specific content of ability items that comprise the predictor measure (i.e., ability assessment) is not important, but it is the common variance among ability items that comprises the general factor that matters (*g* in Spearman's 1904 theory; GMA in organizational science). In the context of the CHC model of intelligence described in the preceding text (McGrew, 2005), the principle of the indifference of the indicator basically ignores second-stratum abilities (fluid and crystallized abilities) and goes from stratum 1 (narrow abilities at the level of measurement) to stratum 3 (broad, GMA or *g*; Figure 6.1). As such, it is typical to see GMA measured through a single assessment that includes a range of item content (e.g., the Wonderlic; Wonderlic, 2002). These assessments are predictive of a variety of job-related behaviors, and are efficient in terms of test administration time because they tend to be short and only require one test.

Specific Abilities

Despite a lack of attention to ability theory in organizational science over the decades, researchers outside of the field (e.g., in cognitive, differential, and educational psychology) have continued to examine the structure of abilities and their validity for predicting skill acquisition, learning, and a range of behaviors relevant to training performance. Recently, researchers in organizational science interested in furthering the investigation of the role of specific abilities in performance have taken note of these advances and have called for additional research on ability theory, particularly as related to the utility of specific versus broad abilities for predicting training and job performance (Mount, Oh, & Burns, 2008; Reeve et al., 2015; Schneider & Newman, 2015). These researchers cite limitations in the research on the superiority of GMA in prediction, particularly as related to the atheoretical nature of the approach in their call to revisit abilities in organizational science (Reeve et al., 2015).

Theoretically, specific aptitudes *should* be useful predictors of training performance because of Brunswik Symmetry (Wittmann & Süß, 1999), which is the idea that the validity of a predictor will be optimized when it is matched to the criteria in terms of breadth and content. For instance, performance in training for a basic psychomotor and speeded task like typing should be best predicted by perceptual speed and psychomotor ability assessments compared to measures of GMA. In this example, GMA may also be predictive of typing performance, but more specific abilities would probably account for more variance in the outcome than GMA, because measures of psychomotor ability and perceptual speed are more closely related to the content and breadth of the outcome than GMA is (i.e., how quickly and accurately a person can type; Wittmann & Süß, 1999). Brunswik Symmetry is particularly important considering the multidimensional nature of training outcomes relevant in industrial-organizational psychology: cognitive (e.g., declarative knowledge, cognitive strategies), skill based (e.g., knowledge compilation and automaticity), and affective (attitudes and self-efficacy; Kraiger et al., 1993). Research suggests that these outcomes are independent (i.e., not highly correlated with one another and with different antecedents; Sitzmann et al., 2008), and thus, specific ability measures should optimize their prediction (Kraiger et al., 1993; Wittmann & Süß, 1999). For instance, dispositions – particularly those related to achievement motivation – would be expected to be more predictive of attitudinal training outcomes than cognitive ability predictors. Similarly, we would expect GMA predictors to be related to general cognitive outcomes (learning overall) and more specific abilities to be related to skill development in particular domains.

Revisiting the Relationship between Training Performance and Ability

As described previously, theory supports the importance of specific abilities for predicting training performance, but theoretical predictions have not been borne out in research. One reason may be related to how specific and general abilities are defined and measured. Indeed, not much attention has been given to ability measurement in organizational science over the past few decades because GMA has proven so efficient, increasing the appeal of an *indifference of the indicator* view (Spearman, 1904). But knowing what abilities are assessed when a measure is used is critically important for matching the predictor to the outcomes of interest and increasing predictive validity (Wittmann & Süß, 1999); this approach stands in stark contrast to one that ignores the items in the indicator.

Because of the breadth of the construct, ideal measures of GMA would be comprised of a range of second-strata ability measures that are linearly combined (e.g., tests of fluid, crystallized, decision-making speed). For instance, short measures of GMA tend to include a broad sampling of a small number of items reflective of verbal, knowledge, speed, and reasoning abilities (Wonderlic, 2002). It is important to consider, however, that composite ability scores can only reflect the breadth of the individual assessments that comprise them: When the individual assessments represent only a narrow range of abilities, then the composite will be similarly narrow. For example, many ability composites – for example, the ASVAB composites described in the preceding text (Brown et al., 2006; Ree & Earles, 1991) – are highly saturated with crystallized intelligence rather than being a broad representation of GMA (Roberts et al., 2000). This is because the component tests of the ASVAB are general and domain knowledge tests (e.g., mechanical comprehension, electronics information, word knowledge, paragraph comprehension), and not generally tests of memory or reasoning ability. Because the common variance related to a general factor is necessarily determined by the measures used to derive the factor, these studies are more indicative of the power of a general crystallized intelligence measure for predicting learning in training than they are indicative of the power of GMA for predicting learning in training. The finding that crystallized intelligence predicts learning in training aligns with cognitive aging research that shows the importance of prior knowledge in adult learning and development (Ackerman & Beier, 2006; Beier & Ackerman, 2005).

In summary, a better integration of ability theory into measurement in organizational science should lead to better ability prediction of training outcomes. Specifically predictors should be matched to outcomes in terms of breadth and content (Wittmann & Süß, 1999). When GMA is a relevant predictor, its measurement should be balanced in terms of the types and number of tests used to represent crystallized, fluid, domain knowledge, and other abilities on the second stratum in the CHC model (McGrew, 2005). And although many researchers rely only on matrix reasoning measures such as the Raven for assessing fluid intelligence, there is an array of available measures including problem solving, spatial, and numerical reasoning assessments (see Beier & Ackerman, 2001; 2003 for examples).

The Role of Domain Knowledge in Training Performance

The importance of crystallized intelligence and domain knowledge for learning is good news for organizational scientists because most people working in organizations are at an age where their most salient abilities are those related to domain knowledge gained through education and experience. In particular, the median age of the labor force is about 42 years, and is increasing steadily (Toossi, 2013). Most research shows that fluid intelligence starts declining in late adolescence/early adulthood and continues to descend throughout the life span (Salthouse, 2010). Although the onset of the decline differs depending on the person (e.g., some 50 year olds have the ability profile of 30 year olds, while others resemble 70 year olds), and the research design (e.g., longitudinal research tends to show the decline starting around age 30, while it starts in the early 20s in most cross-sectional studies), most research suggests that by age 30 or so, the ability to reason through novel problems and to learn completely new information is diminished for most (Hertzog et al., 2008). But people also experience stability, or even increases, in crystallized intelligence and domain knowledge as they age (Ackerman & Beier, 2003). In essence, people's ability to acquire completely novel information decreases as knowledge possessed increases through education and experience.

These changing ability trajectories make sense in the context of investment theories of intellectual development (Ackerman, 1996; Horn & Cattell, 1966). As their name implies, investment theories posit that intellectual development throughout the life span results from investment of fluid abilities (attention) toward the acquisition of general and domain knowledge (Ackerman, 1996; Cattell, 1987). Declining fluid abilities and stable/increasing crystallized abilities and domain knowledge can be considered adaptive in that as people age, they acquire a wealth of knowledge across a range of experiences at work, home, and school. New knowledge is incorporated into existing knowledge structures, minimizing the need to reason through every new situation. To be sure, as people age, the likelihood that they will encounter completely novel situations – situations in which prior experience will not be useful – shrinks. Think about, for instance, the knowledge and skills acquired through the myriad experiences of everyday life (paying taxes, handling business at the Department of Motor Vehicles, managing a budget) that are generalized to new projects and tasks. As we age, these experiences – provided people are able and willing to attend to them – lead to growth in knowledge and skills throughout the life span.

Knowledge acquired through educational and work experience is a potentially important predictor of performance in training (and on the job). The usefulness of general and domain knowledge measures has not gone unnoticed by practitioners in industrial and organizational psychology. An informal survey of industrial-organizational practitioners indicated a gap in the availability of useful measures of general work-related knowledge (Ryan & Ployhart, 2014). Measures of general knowledge could be used in training contexts to both identify training needs – as is the current practice when training needs assessment includes the examination of people who might benefit from training – but also to predict learning in training since prior knowledge is an important determinant of new learning (Beier & Ackerman, 2005). One potential measurement issue that organizational scientists will need to address is the difficulty of assessing knowledge in any normative way given the idiosyncratic nature in which knowledge develops through the life span (Lubinski, 2000).

Abilities, Learning, and Skill Acquisition in Training

According to the resource allocation model (Kanfer & Ackerman, 1989), and broader information processing theories (Kahneman, 1973; Norman & Bobrow, 1975; Wickens, 1984), people have limited attentional resources that are allocated to task learning during training. Attentional resources are generally indexed with measures of general cognitive ability (g) or working memory capacity (Kanfer & Ackerman, 1989; Randall, Oswald, & Beier, 2014). Thus, the importance of cognitive ability for training performance is manifest in its representation as the available pool of attentional resources people draw from to devote toward learning in training.

Theoretically, self-regulatory processes determine where and when to allocate attentional resources and effort during task engagement (e.g., when participating in training or on-the-job training; Kanfer & Ackerman, 1989; 1996). Self-regulation is loosely defined as any proximal motivational process that aids in the control and direction of attentional resources toward on-task efforts (Kanfer & Ackerman, 1989; Kuhl, 1984). Self-regulation is conceptualized as a skill, meaning that individuals can be taught or trained how to effectively manage their attention and effort to maximize learning and performance. Such skills include how to set effective goals, metacognitively monitor and plan, utilize different learning strategies, manage time, and structure one's environment (Sitzmann & Ely, 2011). These skills positively impact learning and performance in training precisely because they harness individuals' cognitive resources or attentional pool and manage them efficiently. Successful self-regulation helps individuals maintain successful *attention regulation*; that is, individuals who are trained in self-regulatory techniques should more frequently engage in on-task thoughts and behaviors and avoid off-task thoughts and behaviors (Randall et al., 2014).

Attention regulation is a dynamic process in part because as individuals learn or acquire skill, the frequency and impact of successes and failures in the maintenance of task focus changes. Learning any new task requires attention and focus (self-regulation) at early stages of learning (Ackerman, 1988; Anderson, 1982). As such, cognitive ability and a person's capacity for self-regulation are important determinants of learning early in training. For tasks that are relatively complex either because they require integrating large amounts of information or because they include inconsistent elements (i.e., processes that cannot be routinized) (Schneider, Dumais, & Shiffrin, 1984), cognitive ability and self-regulation will remain important predictors of performance throughout training and later on the job.

Conversely, for tasks that are relatively consistent – that include components that can be routinized – fewer attentional resources will be necessary after the skill has been practiced. For these tasks, the importance of GMA should decline over skill practice, and the importance of more narrow abilities (i.e., those at the second and first strata) should increase. However, self-regulation will remain important as the ability to monitor and maintain skilled performance over time becomes more challenging for routinized tasks (Kanfer & Ackerman, 1989; Randall et al., 2014). The type of narrower abilities (on the first or second strata) that are relevant for predicting performance and learning at later stages of practice will be predicated on the ability demands of the task being learned/practiced. For example, for tasks that tap motor skills (e.g., typing, playing a musical instrument, driving a car), psychomotor abilities (i.e., the ability to manipulate and control objects) will become increasingly important at later stages of practice (Ackerman, 1988).

Many trained tasks, however, are not psychomotor in nature, so it is useful to generalize theory about the determinants of skill acquisition beyond motor skills. Research on learning domain knowledge (declarative knowledge about an array of topics) has indicated that GMA is important for new learning, as would be predicted. Moreover, this research finds that prior levels of domain knowledge and even general cultural knowledge (crystallized intelligence) are important determinants of new learning (Beier & Ackerman, 2005). Although this research did not explicitly examine the development of knowledge structures, it is likely that knowledge possessed provides a framework in which new learning can be easily integrated, particularly if domain knowledge is in a domain related to the content being taught; for instance, general knowledge about health facilitates learning about heart disease; general knowledge about technology facilitates learning about how photocopiers work; and general financial acumen facilitates new learning about financial matters (Ackerman & Beier, 2006; Beier & Ackerman, 2005).

Admittedly, most tasks people engage in as part of their daily work life (and most tasks trained in organizations) are a complex mix of motorized skills (e.g., typing), knowledge (e.g., putting a budget together), and solving novel problems (e.g., dealing with unexpected changes in the market for one's product). These tasks also vary in terms of the extent to which they can be learned; many have components that are consistently mapped and, as such, are relatively easy to learn and automate (e.g., typing), whereas others will be a complex mixture of consistent and variably mapped tasks (e.g., completing a budget in Microsoft Excel). As such, determinants of learning and performance for most work-related tasks will be a range of narrow abilities in addition to general ability, which will be important in early phases of learning and in later phases for complex tasks. In general, however, it is important to note that a task that is attentionally demanding or difficult for one person may not be so for another. That is, a person's ability level – both general and relevant narrow abilities – will influence how easy or difficult a task is to learn (Beier & Oswald, 2012).

Regardless of the type of task trained, attentional capacity, and the ability to regulate attention are of paramount importance for learning in training. The effectiveness of diverting attentional resources away from the task being trained toward self-regulatory thoughts (e.g., self-monitoring, self-evaluation) will depend on the learners' ability level and the phase of skill acquisition (e.g., early or late in practice; Kanfer & Ackerman, 1989). If self-monitoring or self-evaluation occurs too soon or if it leads to negative, self-directed thoughts, then self-regulation may slow learning. This further reinforces the idea that cognitive ability is not a static predictor of learning and training performance because the processes of attention regulation and self-regulation are dynamic and dependent upon task demands and personal characteristics such as prior knowledge and skills, and motivation. Moreover, research on executive control theory (Kane et al., 2007; Kane & Engle, 2002) emphasizes the importance of working memory capacity (a second stratum ability) as a key regulator of such dynamic processes of attention.

Executive control (indexed using working memory capacity) represents the domain-general ability to stay focused on a goal, especially in the face of distraction or interference (Engle & Kane, 2004; Kane et al., 2007). Thus, second and third strata abilities related to executive functioning such as working memory capacity, or GMA more broadly, are key processes involved in the dynamic allocation of attention during learning and performance (Kanfer & Ackerman, 1989; Randall et al., 2014). Understanding one's limits in attentional capacity and the benefits of self-regulation in learning (Sitzmann & Ely, 2011), researchers and practitioners have demonstrated a growing interest in training strategies that might help individuals more adeptly regulate their attention in learning and skilled performance. For example, mindfulness-based interventions that help individuals stay focused on the present moment have been shown to reduce errors and stress in performance and learning environments (e.g., Jha et al., 2010; Mrazek et al., 2013; Randall, 2015; Tang et al., 2007). Thus, although evidence supports the idea that attempts to manipulate absolute levels of cognitive abilities (e.g., brain training) are unsuccessful in changing underlying abilities (e.g., Shipstead, Redick, & Engle, 2012), attempts to more successfully regulate available attentional resources through the development of self-regulatory skills that promote self-control might be more successful (Rabipour & Raz, 2012; Randall, 2015). Future research is needed to highlight the dynamic utilization of self-regulatory strategies to preserve and direct executive control throughout the learning process.

Aptitude-by-Treatment Interactions

Although we have considered how the stages of learning and practice can affect ability-performance relationships, up to now we have not considered how the design of training can interact with abilities to affect learning. The integration of experimental and differential research was emphasized more than 50 years ago in Cronbach's presidential address to the American Psychological Association. In this speech, Cronbach highlighted the power of examining individual differences in the context of experimental approaches, thus considering the variability among people as an interesting determinant of performance in a given context, rather than as a potential source of error. The ideas put forth by Cronbach have translated to the design of educational interventions – and training interventions –that acknowledge that any given training intervention will not be equally effective for all learners (Cronbach, 1957; Snow, 1989).

The most common aptitude-by-treatment interaction cited in educational research concerns cognitive ability and the structure of a training environment: Highly structured educational environments are purportedly most beneficial for relatively lower ability learners, while educational environments with less structure (e.g., discovery learning environments) are most effective with relatively higher ability learners (Snow, 1989). Ideas about the importance of the interaction between trainees' abilities and the learning environment have also been examined in organizational science, with regard to age and performance in training (Carter & Beier, 2010), and more generally as related to cognitive ability and personality traits (Campbell & Kuncel, 2001; Gully et al., 2002), and the results have generally supported the idea that individual differences can interact with training interventions to affect training outcomes.

The idea of aptitude-by-treatment interactions is particularly promising against the backdrop of technological advances in training design, which make the customization of training to individual learner needs and desires increasingly possible. One might consider, for instance, the ease with which workers older than 40 might increase the structure of an online training program to meet their needs when the training content is completely novel (i.e., increased structure when the demands on fluid ability are high) but decrease the structure when trainees have prior knowledge in a domain. But even though the aptitude-by-treatment interaction approach offers a powerful way to design maximally effective training interventions customized to the learner, there are relatively few researchers examining aptitude-by-treatment interactions in organizational science. The dearth of studies on the topic is likely a function of the difficulty of doing this work. That is, examining the interaction of individual differences and training manipulations on training performance requires random assignment of relatively large samples across training conditions. These requirements make the approach relatively restrictive, particularly for field research, although many industrial-organizational researchers have increasingly called for additional research in this area (Gully & Chen, 2010).

Abilities and Team Training

Any attempt to understand and elucidate the relationship between general and specific abilities and job or training performance must also consider the influence of context. Context is particularly important when one considers these relationships within the groups and teams. Groups are often defined as three or more individuals who perceive themselves as members of the group, recognize one another as members of the group, share a common goal, and experience collective outcomes (Arrow, McGrath, & Berdahl, 2000). Teams, by contrast, are most appropriately conceptualized a special case of a group, where members have specialized roles and a high degree of interdependency. And although the terms *group* and *team* are often used synonymously, the terms are meant to describe two different types of collective where each provides a unique context. That is, interdependency is the characteristic that differentiates groups and teams, and interdependency has implications regarding the relationship between abilities and performance. The collective nature of groups and teams, combined with the unique characteristic of interdependency inherent in teams has important implications regarding the relationship between ability and job or training performance, particularly in the operationalization of group and team ability; the unique requirement of teamwork in teams; and the importance of ability in team composition.

Team Ability

A primary consideration when discussing the relationship between abilities and performance in the team context is operationalizing ability to the level of the team. That is, ability is a psychological phenomenon that occurs at the level of the individual. As such, team ability refers to the operationalization of that individual-level ability to the team level. We use the term *team ability* to describe the distribution of ability within a group or team. The method used to operationalize individual-level ability to the team level is an important consideration, and is focused on answering the question: What is the most appropriate way to operationalize individual differences to the team level? Research investigating the relationship between abilities and performance in the team context, whether those abilities are general or specific, has focused on four primary operationalizations: mean, variance, minimum, and maximum.

Within a group context, where interdependency is not present to a great degree, it may be conceptually appealing to suggest that the appropriateness of a particular operationalization depends on the task. However, research suggests that a group's average GMA is the best predictor of group performance, regardless of the type of task being performed by the group. For example, Day et al. (2004) examined the comparative criterion-related validity of ability as a function of task type. Individuals were asked to collaborate with others to complete four different tasks that represented each of Steiner's (1966; 1972) task typology. Therefore, groups completed additive (word search and mathematical problems), compensatory (desert survival), disjunctive (Wesman PCT), and conjunctive (word jumble) tasks. The authors found that regardless of task type, the average of the individuals' GMA within the group predicted group performance better than the score of the group member with the highest or lowest GMA score. Therefore, in group contexts, regardless of whether task performance is based on the sum of individual efforts (e.g., total number of calls processed in a call center), the group's most competent member (e.g., identifying the solution to an engineering problem), the group's least competent member (e.g., total number of products produced in an assembly line shift), or whether task performance is based on various combinations of member input depending on the group's judgment (e.g., forecasting the weather), the mean GMA of a group was the best predictor of group performance. This suggests that cognitive ability is a compensatory resource within groups, such that members with differing levels of ability may compensate for one another.

Research investigating ability in *teams* has produced different results. Bell (2007) meta-analytically estimated the relationship between team performance and various compositions of team GMA and found that although the average ($\rho = .31$), minimum ($\rho = .34$), and maximum ($\rho = .27$) levels of team GMA produced similar results, the GMA of the team member with the lowest GMA score was the best predictor of overall team performance. Because teams have a high degree of interdependence, individual team members have the potential to exert a great degree of influence on team performance. Thus, in contrast to its role in groups, it appears that ability is not a compensatory resource in teams.

Teamwork Skills

Working in a team necessitates the acquisition of knowledge and skills beyond those necessary to perform an individual task. The additional knowledge and skills are brought about by the teamwork required when working on tasks with others. Teamwork refers to a team's effort to facilitate effective interaction while performing as a team, often involving processes such as communication, coordination, conflict management, and cohesion (Arthur, Villado, & Bennett, 2012; Glickman et al., 1987; Morgan et al., 1986). Teamwork is distinct from task work, such that task work consists of the behaviors required to execute team tasks. All other things being equal, learning how to perform a task as a team requires the investment of additional cognitive resources for the acquisition and execution of teamwork. That is, working in a team requires that one learn *how* to work with others, and it requires that one *does* work with others.

It may appear that the additional demands of teamwork would make working in a team that much more cognitively demanding, but teamwork knowledge and skills are relatively generic, and are therefore more generalizable than task work knowledge and skills (Stevens & Campion 1994; 1999). For example, learning how to communicate with others in one team environment may not be exactly like communicating with team members in a different environment, but it is likely to be very similar, particularly when misunderstanding the message may have critical consequences. Some teams (e.g., flight teams) may utilize readback communication protocols where the receiver of a critical message repeats the message word for word to ensure that it was received and understood. Other teams (e.g., product design teams) may utilize active listening techniques where the receiver of a critical message repeats back a paraphrased version of the original message for the same purpose. Team members who learn how to communicate critical information with team members in one environment may generalize those team communication skills to another environment. The generalizability of teamwork skills suggests that it could serve as a useful determinant of job and training performance.

Team Composition

Team composition is another important consideration when examining the relationship between abilities and team training performance. Individuals learning in a collective environment have the potential to be affected, either positively or negatively, by others who are present. For example, Day et al. (2005) examined the effect of a training partner's GMA on individual and dyadic team performance. Their results suggest that a relatively lower-ability training partner negatively affects a higher-ability trainee's task acquisition. When high-ability individuals trained with another high-ability individual, subsequent individual task performance was characteristically high. Likewise, when low-ability individuals trained with another low-ability individual, subsequent individual task performance was characteristically low. However, when high-ability individuals trained with a low-ability individual, the low-ability individual's subsequent task performance was characteristically low, but the high-ability individual's subsequent task performance was uncharacteristically low. Thus, high-ability individuals were negatively affected by a low-ability training partner. At minimum, these findings suggest that consideration of the ability composition of a team is required to optimize training outcomes for all trainees. Indeed, when the task is individual based (i.e., it will not require the trainees to perform together as a team), training focused on the individual rather than the team may be the preferred approach (Crook & Beier, 2010).

Considerations for Training Design

What are the implications of the preceding discussion for researchers and practitioners? Although the relationship between cognitive ability and learning outcomes does represent well-tread ground, our discussion has led us to the following five recommendations for research and practice; these recommendations are summarized in Table 6.1.

Expand the Consideration of Abilities

The preceding discussion argued for examining ability-learning relationships on a middle ground between narrow abilities and GMA. In particular, we argue that abilities on the second stratum of the CHC model (e.g., fluid and crystallized intelligence and general domain knowledge) are useful and theoretically interesting determinants of performance depending on the task being trained. Moreover, the assessment of second-stratum abilities should be considered when trainees are heterogeneous with respect to age. Although fluid and crystallized intelligence are correlated with each other, they are differentially correlated with age in ways that may obscure what older trainees can learn in training. When general measures are used – whether they be composites of fluid and crystallized ability measures or simply amalgams of individual items across a range of abilities – common variance among specific abilities is obscured and may disadvantage older worker selection into training programs.

In addition to the usefulness and theoretical import of crystallized intelligence for understanding what people can learn in training, we propose that domain knowledge be considered a specific ability that is relevant and interesting for predicting training performance. Indeed, researchers have acknowledged that domain-specific job knowledge is a more proximal and interesting predictor of job and training performance for years (Hunter, 1986; Schmidt & Hunter,

Table 6.1 *Recommendations for future research and training design on ability effects in training and learning*

1. Expand training research beyond GMA to include second stratum abilities, and expand the type of knowledge assessed to include domain knowledge.
2. Enhance focus on the role of domain knowledge and expertise in skill transfer after training, particularly as related to negative transfer.
3. Investigate the conditions under which the composition of various cognitive abilities within teams influences training outcomes.
4. Exploit the flexibility of technology for customizing training interventions to the unique needs of the learners, including recognition of MOOCs as a potential training method.
5. Examine how aptitude-treatment interactions might be found in the field with proper measurement and research design.

1998), but these types of measures have been discounted because their content was viewed – not as an ability – but as knowledge that could only be gained from job experience. In a training context, measures of general job knowledge could be used to meaningfully assess individual training needs, permitting customized training offerings. *Our first recommendation for future research is to expand research on second stratum abilities, and to expand the type of knowledge assessed to be domain knowledge to permit meaningful individualization of training.*

Expand Research on the Role of Abilities in Transfer

The importance of domain knowledge has been discussed mainly in terms of its positive influence on skill acquisition and learning (Ackerman & Beier, 2006; Beier & Ackerman, 2005; Motowidlo & Beier, 2010), but prior knowledge in a domain can also interfere with a person's ability to learn new skills (i.e., negative transfer). One often-cited example of negative transfer is related to Luchins's water jug problem. In this problem, participants are given three water jugs of different volumes, and are asked to find solutions for measuring specific amounts (Luchins, 1942). Luchins's water jug problems are somewhat unique in that there are shortcuts that do not require elaborate problem-solving skills to solve them. In one study, when participants were asked to solve complex arithmetic problems before the water jug problems, many of them did worse on the water jug task, particularly when the arithmetic problems were similar to the water jug problems (in terms of surface features). Similar results have been found since Luchins's influential studies, reinforcing the idea that prior examples influence the way new problems are solved, and if those examples are not relevant or applicable they will interfere with learning (Barnett & Ceci, 2002).

Although Luchins's (1942) work suggests that prior knowledge can negatively influence new learning, some researchers have found the opposite: that people become more adaptive and able to incorporate new learning into existing knowledge structures when they have extensive knowledge – or expertise – in a domain (Smith, Ford, & Kozlowski, 1997). Indeed, research in the sports domain demonstrated that the introduction of a "funny putter" (a putter with a modified handle) decremented initial performance of golf experts relative to novices in terms of the speed at which they could accurately putt. After a short amount of practice, however, golf experts could adapt to the new tool and regained their expert levels of performance in terms of both speed and accuracy (Beilock et al., 2008). In summary, the extent to which prior knowledge or expertise interferes with or facilitates new learning is not well understood. Indeed, there are likely boundary conditions related to the level of expertise, and the adaptability of the learner. *Our second recommendation for research is a call for additional focus on the role of domain knowledge and expertise in skill transfer after training, particularly as related to negative transfer.*

Expand Research on the Ability Composition of Teams

The ability composition of a team is an important determinant of team performance in training: People tend to benefit when matched with higher ability people, but not when matched with relatively lower ability people (Day et al., 2005). There are probably important qualifications to these findings that have yet to be discovered, however. For instance, as in individual training, it is likely that task complexity, team characteristics, and the interdependence of the task being trained affect the relationship between ability composition of a team and training outcomes. Moreover, it is unclear whether second-stratum abilities are important in team training; for instance, whether the existing knowledge or expertise of one member of a team would complement the lower levels of knowledge but higher fluid ability of another team member. *Our third recommendation for research is thus further investigation into the conditions under which ability composition of teams matter in training, including the team composition of different types of cognitive abilities.*

Capitalize on Technological Affordances

Our recommendations for training design echo those that have been made in the past regarding the implications of aptitude-by-treatment interactions (Campbell & Kuncel, 2001), particularly as related designing training interventions to meet the specific knowledge and ability needs of the learner. We recognize that training involves the dynamic allocation of attention to an array of activities, and that performance in training is dependent on the design of training, individual differences in attentional capacity, and self-regulatory skill. We also anticipate that technology will facilitate the design of customized training interventions. For instance, advances in training technology make it increasingly possible to use assessments of prior knowledge to identify gaps in understanding and to modify training content accordingly. Training might also be modified depending on trainee assessment of their ability levels and self-efficacy; those unsure about an area might decide to engage in fairly structured training until they feel comfortable in a domain.

Massive Open Online Courses (MOOCs) represent another technological advance that is untapped in organizational science (Cascio, 2014). There is no question, however, that people enroll in and complete MOOCs to gain workplace skills. A recent study conducted on a MOOC designed to teach computer programming in Python, for instance, found that the majority of students enrolled were industry professionals seeking training and development opportunities (35%) as opposed to university/high school students (20%) or hobbyists (14%; Beier, Rixner, Warran, & Young, 2015). Particularly relevant to this chapter is the potential for MOOCs to deliver flexible training content that can be customized to the unique ability, prior knowledge, and skill levels of trainees. *Our fourth recommendation then is for organizational scientists and practitioners to exploit the flexibility of technology for customizing training interventions to the unique needs of the learners, and to capitalize on the usefulness of MOOCs as a method to deliver organizationally relevant training.*

Further Examine Aptitude-by-Treatment Interactions

So far, our recommendations for future research and training practice assume that individual attributes of the learner can importantly interact with training environments to affect outcomes; that is, we assume aptitude treatment interactions are possible and important (Cronbach, 1957; Gully & Chen, 2010; Snow, 1989). It is notable that evidence of aptitude-by-treatment interactions is sparse, and when effects have been found, they tend to be small and – sometimes – unexpected (Carter & Beier, 2010, although see Gully & Chen, 2010 for a more optimistic assessment of the research literature). Regardless of the effect size, aptitutde-by-treatment interactions may necessitate multiple delivery methods, each tuned to a particular individual difference variable, making training costly to develop and deliver (e.g., training A for visual learners, training B for kinesthetic learners). Due to the difficulty of this work, outcomes are hard to replicate, which makes the published literature not only sparse but also confusing. One response to these disappointing results would be to abandon the pursuit of aptitude-by-treatment effects in training all together. This would assume that a uniform approach to training design works well enough given that the effects of different approaches are hard to detect. This is unfortunate because a one-size-fits-all solution for training design does not parallel what we know about different abilities and their influence on learning, and our own experiences teaching hundreds of students. Moreover, advances in technology promise to make technology-based training easier to customize for individual learner needs.

Although examining aptitude-by-treatment effects is difficult, research in this area can be strengthened when samples of learners are large and diverse, ensuring a range of individual differences, and when the training environments (i.e., treatments) are theoretically derived. In an ideal world, these studies would be experiments with random assignment and pre-post control group designs

(Shadish, Cook, & Campbell, 2001). Such designs would permit an examination of whether learning gains are a function of individual differences, training environments, or an interaction. Accumulation of evidence about how learners interact with training environments will ultimately lead to knowledge of aptitude-by-treatment interactions across studies, not just within a single study, and an understanding of how best to design training interventions for different types of learners. *Our fifth recommendation for research and practice is to further examine the illusive aptitude-by-treatment interaction; how might these effects be found in the field with proper measurement and research design?*

Conclusion

Cognitive ability is central to learning new skills and knowledge in training that ultimately leads to successful job performance. Although organizational science has known this for decades, the focus on the efficiency of a general ability predictor potentially has ignored the rich theoretical questions that are offered in the study of more specific abilities and performance (e.g., questions related to aptitude-by-treatment interactions, the structure of abilities and the composition of abilities in teams, and the measurement of general domain knowledge, to name a few). We have highlighted the importance of examining a range of abilities in organizational science and encourage scientists and practitioners alike to expand the examination and assessment of the ability-learning outcomes relationships beyond GMA.

References

Acemoglu, D., and Pischke, J. 1999. Beyond Becker: Training in imperfect labour markets. *The Economic Journal* 109(453): F112–F142.

Ackerman, P. L. 1988. Determinants of individual differences during skill acquisition: Cognitive abilities and information processing. *Journal of Experimental Psychology: General* 117: 288–318.

Ackerman, P. L. 1996. A theory of adult intellectual development: Process, personality, interests, and knowledge. *Intelligence* 22: 227–257.

Ackerman, P. L., and Beier, M. E. 2003. Trait complexes, cognitive investment, and domain knowledge. In Robert Sternberg and Elena Grigorenko, eds., *The Psychology of Abilities, Competencies, and Expertise*, 1–30. New York: Cambridge University Press.

Ackerman, P. L., and Beier, M. E. 2004. Knowledge and intelligence. In Oliver Wilhelm, ed., *Handbook of Understanding and Measuring Intelligence*, 125–139. Thousand Oaks: Sage.

Ackerman, P. L., and Beier, M. E. 2006. Determinants of domain knowledge and independent study learning in an adult sample. *Journal of Educational Psychology* 98: 366–381.

Ackerman, P. L., Beier, M. E., and Boyle, M O. 2005. Working memory and intelligence: The same or different constructs? *Psychological Bulletin* 131: 30–60.

Anderson, J. R. 1982. Acquisition of cognitive skill. *Psychological Review* 89: 369–406.

Arrow, H., McGrath, J. E. and Berdahl, J. L. 2000. *Small Groups as Complex Systems: Formation, Coordination, Development, and Adaption.* Thousand Oaks: Sage.

Arthur, W. Jr., Villado, A. J., and Bennett, W. Jr. 2012. Innovations in team task analysis: Identifying task elements, tasks, and jobs that are team-based. In G. Alliger, W. Bennett Jr., S. Gibson, and M. Wilson, eds., *The Handbook of Work Analysis in Organizations: The Methods, Systems, Applications, and Science of Work Measurement and Organizations,* 641–661. New York: Routledge/Psychology Press.

Barnett, S. M., and Ceci, S. J. 2002. When and where do we apply what we learn? A taxonomy for far transfer. *Psychological Bulletin* 128: 612–637.

Beier, M. E., and Ackerman, P. L. 2001. Current-events knowledge in adults: An investigation of age, intelligence, and nonability determinants. *Psychology and Aging* 16: 615–628.

Beier, M. E., and Ackerman, P. L. 2003. Determinants of health knowledge: An investigation of age, gender, abilities, personality, and interests. *Journal of Personality and Social Psychology* 84: 439–448.

Beier, M. E., and Ackerman, P. L. 2005. Age, ability, and the role of prior knowledge on the acquisition of new domain knowledge: Promising results in a real-world learning environment. *Psychology and Aging* 20: 341–355.

Beier, M. E., and Oswald, F. L. 2012. Is cognitive ability a liability? A critique and future research agenda on skilled performance. *Journal of Experimental Psychology: Applied* 18: 331–345.

Beier, M. E., Rixner, S., and Warren, J. 2016. Predicting performance and attrition in a Massive Open Online Course. Manuscript in preparation.

Beilock, S. L., Bertenthal, B. I., Hoerger, M. M., and Carr, T. H. 2008. When does haste make waste? Speed-accuracy tradeoff, skill level, and the tools of the trade. *Journal of Experimental Psychology: Applied* 14: 340–352.

Bell, S. T. 2007. Deep-level composition variables as predictors of team performance: A meta-analysis. *Journal of Applied Psychology* 92: 595–615.

Bertua, C., Anderson, N. and Salgado, J. F. 2005. The predictive validity of cognitive ability tests: A UK meta-analysis. *Journal of Occupational and Organizational Psychology* 78: 387–409.

Brown, K. G., Le, H., and Schmidt, F. L. 2006. Specific aptitude theory revisited: Is there incremental validity for training performance? *International Journal of Selection and Assessment* 14: 87–100.

Campbell, J. P., and Kuncel. N. R. 2001. Individual and team training. In D. H. Ones, N. Anderson, C. Viswesvaran, and H. K. Sinangil, eds., *Handbook of Industrial, Work and Organizational Psychology,* 278–312. London: Sage.

Carroll, J. B. 1993. *Human Cognitive Abilities: A Survey of Factor-Analytic Studies.* New York: Cambridge University Press.

Carter, M. and Beier, M. E. 2010. The effectiveness of error management training with working-aged adults. *Personnel Psychology* 63: 641–675.

Cascio, W. F. 2014. Leveraging employer branding, performance management and human resource development to enhance employee retention. *Human Resource Development International* 17: 121–128.

Cattell, R. B. 1987. *Intelligence: Its Structure, Growth, and Action.* New York: Elsevier.

Cronbach, L. J. 1957. The two disciplines of scientific psychology. *American Psychologist* 12: 671–684.

Crook, A. E., and Beier, M. E. 2010. When training with a partner is inferior to training alone: The importance of dyad type and interaction quality. *Journal of Experimental Psychology: Applied* 16: 335–348.

Day, E. A., Arthur, W. Jr., Miyashiro, B., Edwards, B. D., Tubré, T. C., and Tubré, A. H. 2004. Criterion-related validity of statistical operationalizations of group general cognitive ability as a function of task type: Comparing the mean, maximum, and minimum. *Journal of Applied Social Psychology* 34: 1521–1549.

Day, E. A., Arthur, W. Jr., Bell, S. T., Edwards, B. D., Bennett, W. Jr., Mendoza, J. L., and Tubré, T. C. 2005. Ability-based pairing strategies in the team-based training of a complex skill: Does the cognitive ability of your training partner matter? *Intelligence* 33: 39–65.

Engle, R. W., and Kane, M. J. 2004. Executive attention, working memory capacity, and a two-factor theory of cognitive control. In B. Ross, ed., *The Psychology of Learning and Motivation*, 145–199. New York: Academic Press.

Glickman, Albert S., Seth R. Zimmer, Craig Montero, Paula J. Guerette, Wanda J. Campbell, Ben B. Morgan Jr., and Eduardo Salas. 1987. The Evolution of Team Skills: An Empirical Assessment with Implications for Training. Tech Report Number 87-016. Arlington: Office of Naval Research.

Guilford, J. P. 1967. *The Nature of Human Intelligence*. New York: McGraw Hill.

Gully, S. M., and Gilad Chen. 2010. Individual Differences, Attribute-Treatment Interactions, and Training Outcomes. In S. W. J. Kozlowski and E. Salas, eds., *Learning, Training, and Development in Organizations*, 3–64. New York: Taylor Francis.

Gully, S. M., Stephanie C. Payne, Lee Kiechel K. Koles, and Jon-Andrew K. Whiteman. 2002. The impact of error training and individual differences on training outcomes: An attribute-treatment interaction perspective. *Journal of Applied Psychology* 87: 143–155.

Hertzog, C., Arthur F. Kramer, Robert S. Wilson, and Ulman Lindenberger. 2008. Enrichment effects on adult cognitive development: Can the functional capacity of older adults be preserved and enhanced? *Psychological Science in the Public Interest* 9: 1–65.

Horn, J. L., and Raymond B. Cattell. 1966. Refinement and test of the theory of fluid and crystallized general intelligences. *Journal of Educational Psychology* 57: 253–270.

Hunter, J. E. 1986. Cognitive ability, cognitive aptitude, job knowledge, and job performance. *Journal of Vocational Behavior* 29: 340–362.

Hunter, J. E., and Ronda F. Hunter. 1984. Validity and utility of alternative predictors of job performance. *Psychological Bulletin* 96: 72–98.

Jha, A. P., Elizabeth A. Stanley, Anastasia Kiyonaga, Ling Wong, and Lois Gelfand. 2010. Examining the protective effects of mindfulness training on working memory capacity and affective experience. *Emotion* 10: 54–64.

Johnson, W., and Thomas J. Bouchard, Jr. 2005. The structure of human intelligence: It is verbal, perceptual, and image rotation (VPR), not fluid and crystallized. *Intelligence* 33: 393–416.

Kahneman, D. 1973. *Attention and Effort*. Englewood Cliffs: Prentice-Hall.

Kane, M. J., Andrew R. A. Conway, David Z. Hambrick, and Randall W. Engle. 2007. Variation in working memory capacity as variation in executive attention and control. In A. R. A. Conway, C. Jarrold, M. J. Kane, A. Miyake, and J. N. Towse, eds., *Variation in Working Memory*, 21–48. New York: Oxford University Press.

Kane, M. J., and Randall W. Engle. 2002. The role of prefrontal cortex in working-memory capacity, executive attention, and general fluid intelligence: An individual-differences perspective. *Psychonomic Bulletin & Review* 9: 637–671.

Kanfer, R., and Ackerman, P. L. 1989. Motivation and cognitive abilities: An integrative/aptitude-treatment interaction approach to skill acquisition. *Journal of Applied Psychology* 74: 657–690.

Kanfer, R., and Ackerman, P. L. 1996. A self-regulatory skills perspective to reducing cognitive interference. In I. G. Sarason, G. R. Pierce, and B. R. Sarason, eds., *Cognitive Interference: Theories, Methods, and Findings. The LEA Series in Personality and Clinical Psychology*, 153–171. Hillsdale, NJ, England: Lawrence Erlbaum Associates Inc.

Kraiger, K., Ford, J. K., and Salas, E. 1993. Application of cognitive, skill-based, and affective theories of learning outcomes to new methods of training evaluation. *Journal of Applied Psychology* 78: 311–328.

Kuhl, J. 1984. Volitional aspects of achievement motivation and learned helplessness: Toward a comprehensive theory of action control. In B. A. Maher, ed., *Progress in Experimental Personality Research,* 13: 99–171. New York: Academic Press.

Lubinski, D. 2000. Scientific and social significance of assessing individual differences: Sinking shafts at a few critical points. *Annual Review of Psychology* 51: 405–444.

Luchins, A. S. 1942. Mechanization in problem solving: The effect of Einstellung. *Psychological Monographs* 54: i–95.

McGrew, K. S. 2005. The Cattell-Horn-Carroll theory of cognitive abilities: Past, present, and future. In Flanagan, Dawn P., and Patti L. Harrison, eds. *Contemporary Intellectual Assessment: Theories, Tests, and Issues*, 136–181. New York: Guilford Press.

Morgan, B. B. Jr., Albert S. Glickman, Elizabeth A. Woodward, Arthur S. Blaives, and Eduardo Salas. 1986. Measurement of team behaviors in a navy environment. Tech Report Number 86-014. Orlando: Naval Training Systems Center.

Motowidlo, S. J., and Margaret E. Beier. 2010. Differentiating specific job knowledge from implicit trait policies in procedural knowledge measured by a situational judgment test. *Journal of Applied Psychology* 95: 321–333.

Mount, M. K., Oh, In-Sue and Melanie Burns. 2008. Incremental validity of perceptual speed and accuracy over general mental ability. *Personnel Psychology* 61: 113–139.

Mrazek, M. D., Michael S. Franklin, Dawa T. Phillips, Benjamin Baird, and Jonathan W. Schooler. 2013. Mindfulness training improves working memory capacity and GRE performance while reducing mind wandering. *Psychological Science* 24: 776–781.

Norman, D. A., and Daniel B. Bobrow. 1975. On data-limited and resource-limited processes. *Cognitive Psychology* 7: 44–64.

Rabipour, S., and Raz, A. 2012. Training the brain: Fact and fad in cognitive and behavioral remediation. *Brain and Cognition* 79: 159–179.

Randall, J. G. 2015. Mind wandering and self-directed learning: Testing the efficacy of self-regulation interventions to reduce mind wandering and enhance online training performance. PhD diss., Rice University, Houston, TX.

Randall, J. G., Frederick L. Oswald, and Margaret E. Beier. 2014. Mind-wandering, cognition, and performance: A theory driven meta-analysis of attention regulation. *Psychological Bulletin* 140: 1411–1431.

Ree, M. J., and James A. Earles. 1991. Predicting training success: Not much more than g. *Personnel Psychology* 44: 321–332.

Ree, M. J., James A. Earles, and Mark S. Teachout. 1994. Predicting job performance: not much more than g. *Journal of Applied Psychology* 79: 518–524.

Reeve, C. L., Charles Scherbaum, and Harold W. Goldstein. 2015. Manifestations of intelligence: expanding the measurement space to reconsider specific cognitive abilities. *Human Resource Management Review* 25: 28–37.

Roberts, R. D., Ginger N. Goff, Fadi Anjoul, P.C. Kyllonen., Gerry Pallier, and Lazar Stankov. 2000. The armed services vocational aptitude battery (ASVAB): Little more than acculturated (Gc)!? *Learning and Individual Differences* 12(1): 81–103.

Ryan, A. M., and Ployhart, R. E. 2014. A century of selection. *Annual Review of Psychology* 65: 693–717.

Salthouse, T. A. 2010. *Major Issues in Cognitive Aging.* Oxford: Oxford University Press.

Schmidt, F. L., and Hunter, J. E. 1998. The validity and utility of selection methods in personnel psychology: Practical and theoretical implications of 85 years of research findings. *Psychological Bulletin* 124: 262–274.

Schneider, W. J., Dumais, and S. T., Richard M. Shiffrin. 1984. Automatic and Control Processing and Attention. In R. Parasuraman and D. R. Davies, eds., *Varieties of Attention*, 1–27. Orlando: Academic Press.

Schneider, W. J., and McGrew, K. S. 2012. The Cattell-Horn-Carroll model of intelligence. In D. P. Flanagan and P. L. Harrison, eds., *Contemporary Intellectual Assessment: Theories, Tests, and Issues*, 3rd ed., 99–144. New York: Guilford Press.

Schneider, W. J., and Newman, D. A. 2015. Intelligence is multidimensional: Theoretical review and implications of specific cognitive abilities. *Human Resource Management Review* 25: 12–27.

Shadish, W. R., Thomas D. Cook, and Donald T. Campbell. 2001. *Experimental and Quasi-Experimental Designs for Generalized Causal Inference*, 2nd ed. Boston, MA: Cengage Learning.

Shipstead, Z., Thomas S. Redick and Randall W. Engle. 2012. Is working memory training effective? *Psychological Bulletin* 138: 628–654.

Sitzmann, T., and Ely, K. 2011. A meta-analysis of self-regulated learning in work-related training and educational attainment: What we know and where we need to go. *Psychological Bulletin* 137: 441–442.

Sitzmann, T., Kenneth G. Brown, Wendy J. Casper, Katherine Ely, and Ryan D. Zimmerman. 2008. A review and meta-analysis of the nomological network of trainee reactions. *Journal of Applied Psychology* 93: 280–295.

Smith, E. M., Ford, J. K., and Kozlowski, S. W. J. 1997. Building adaptive expertise: Implications for training design strategies. In M. A. Quiñones and A. Ehrenstein, eds., *Training for a Rapidly Changing Workplace: Applications of Psychological Research*, 89–118. Washington DC: American Psychological Association.

Snow, R. E. 1989. Aptitude-treatment interaction as a framework for research on individual differences in learning. In Phillip L. Ackerman, Robert J. Sternberg, and Robert Glaser, eds., *Learning and Individual Differences: Advances in Theory and Research. A Series of Books in Psychology*, 13–59. New York: Freeman/ Times Books.

Spearman, C. 1904. General intelligence objectively determined and measured. *American Journal of Psychology* 15: 201–293.

Stevens, M. J., and Campion, M. A. 1994. The knowledge, skill and ability requirements for teamwork: Implications for human resource management. *Journal of Management* 25: 207–228.

Stevens, M. J., and Campion, M. A. 1999. Staffing work teams: Development and validation of a selection test for teamwork settings. *Journal of Management* 25: 207–228.

Thurstone, L. L. 1938. *Primary Mental Abilities.* Chicago: University of Chicago Press.

Toossi, M. 2013. Labor force projections to 2022: The labor force participation rate continues to fall. *Monthly Labor Review.* http://www.bls.gov/opub/mlr/2013/article/labor-force-projections-to-2022-the-labor-force-participation-rate-continues-to-fall.htm (accessed March 2, 2015).

Vernon, P. E. 1971. *The Structure of Human Abilities*, 2nd ed. London: Methuen.

Wickens, C. D. 1984. Processing resources in attention. In P. Raja and D.R. Davies, eds., *Varieties of Attention,* 63–102. New York: Academic Press.

Wittmann, W. W., and Süß, H. 1999. Investigating the paths between working memory, intelligence, knowledge, and complex problem-solving performances via Brunswik Symmetry. In P. L. Ackerman, P. C. Kyllonen, and R. D. Roberts, eds., *Learning and Individual Differences: Process, Trait, and Content Determinants,* 77–108. Washington DC: American Psychological Association.

Wonderlic, 2002. *Wonderlic Personnel Test & Scholastic Level Exam User's Manual.* Vernon Hills: Wonderlic, Inc.

7 Taking Charge of Your Own Learning

Self-Regulation in Training

John J. Donovan and Jessica M. Nicklin

During the past 20 years, we have witnessed a dramatic shift in the nature of work being performed in organizations, with many jobs becoming more complex and fluid in their demands on workers. As a result, today's workers are faced with the challenge of continuously updating their knowledge and skills to maximize their ability to deal with changes in their jobs (Bell & Kozlowski, 2008; Sitzmann & Ely, 2011). Taken together with the trend toward providing employees with more control over their training experiences (Kraiger & Jerden, 2007) and the increasing use of self-directed e-learning by organizations (Brown & Charlier, 2013), these changes have created significant empirical and conceptual interest in the self-regulatory processes by which employees manage their own learning through the establishment of goals, monitoring of performance relative to their goals, and adjusting their behavior or cognitions as they pursue these goals. As noted by Sitzmann and Ely (2011), self-regulation may be one of the most critical factors in determining employee effectiveness in today's organizations. The purpose of this chapter is to examine the importance of self-regulation and self-regulated learning for training in organizations, and to offer recommendations for future research and practice that can help organizations foster this type of learning among employees.

Self-Regulation and Self-Regulated Learning

Self-regulation generally refers to a collection of processes by which individuals initiate and maintain behaviors directed toward goal attainment, maximizing their well-being (Karoly, 1993). While there is general agreement upon this definition, the theoretical models forwarded to explain the processes underlying self-regulation are diverse and somewhat scattered, including goal-setting theory (Locke & Latham, 1990), social cognitive theory (Bandura, 1991), control theory (Carver & Scheier, 1998), feedback intervention theory (FIT) (Kluger & DeNisi, 1996), and resource allocation models (e.g., Kanfer & Ackerman, 1989). Further, while some models of self-regulation are rather general in nature, intended to encompass a broad array of activities and life domains (e.g., Carver & Scheier, 1998), others are more focused, limiting their propositions to self-regulation within a specific activity or domain such as student learning (e.g., Schunk & Zimmerman, 1994). However, despite these

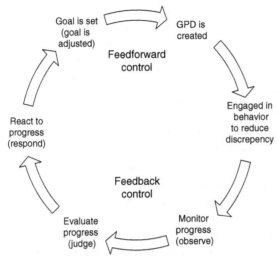

Figure 7.1. *Cycle of self-regulation.*

differences, there is some consensus about the core processes underlying self-regulation and the cyclical nature of self-regulation. Figure 7.1 presents a general model of self-regulation based upon these commonalities across the various theoretical models.

A General Model of Self-Regulation

At the most basic level, all general models of self-regulation agree that self-regulation relies on *feedforward* and *feedback* processes that revolve around the establishment (and revision) of goals or personal standards for behavior. Setting goals produces a discrepancy between current levels of performance and anticipated future outcomes (feedforward control) that is commonly referred to as a *goal-performance discrepancy* (GPD). The GPD initiates and directs behavior (effort) because of the anticipated self-satisfaction derived for achieving the goal (or the self-dissatisfaction that accompanies goal failure). Individuals are then proposed to continuously monitor and evaluate their behavior relative to their goal and adjust effort and/or strategies as needed (feedback control) to reduce the magnitude of this GPD (a process referred to as *discrepancy reduction*). Individuals may also choose to revise their goal downward (i.e., make it less challenging) as a means of reducing this discrepancy if they feel that goal attainment is unlikely or their original goal no longer holds value for them. Although there is significant disagreement among the models as to what happens upon goal attainment, models such as Bandura's social cognitive theory (1986; 1991) note that individuals who reach their goal may set more challenging goals for themselves (a process termed *discrepancy production*). In fact, Bandura (1991) suggests that in some cases people may even raise their goals to a higher standard before reaching them as a result of proximity to the goal.

To illustrate, suppose an individual wants to learn how to use a new statistical software package for data analysis at her job before the end of the year. She sets the goal of learning how to run basic analyses with the statistical software, thereby creating a discrepancy between her current performance (not knowing the software) and her anticipated outcome (having a functional knowledge of the software). This GPD (and the anticipated self-satisfaction that will result from successfully learning to use the software) encourages her to develop a plan for learning and will direct her attention toward learning the software and strategies to facilitating this learning (e.g., attending a course). While she is working on learning the software, she will actively monitor and evaluate her progress toward her goal – *Is she able to run the analyses as planned? How much time does she have left before she reaches her deadline?* Evaluating these questions and monitoring her progress will provide her with the necessary performance feedback leading her to either increase her effort or modify her goal so that her performance matches the goal (e.g., spend more time learning the software or give herself more time); thereby reducing the GPD. If she is making progress, she may even choose to raise her goal (e.g., learn more sophisticated analytic techniques) to continuously motivate herself and enhance learning outcomes.

In addition to these core processes, many self-regulation models (e.g., Bandura, 1991; Carver & Scheier, 1998) propose that individuals establish a hierarchy of goals that include both short-term, proximal goals (e.g., goals for learning a new skill in a given training session) and more distal, long-term goals (e.g., career or professional goals). Within these models, the short-term, proximal goals are viewed as comprising the lower levels of the goal hierarchy with goals becoming broader and more distal in nature as one moves up the hierarchy. These models also suggest that long-term, broad goals related to the self are facilitated by the establishment and attainment of more specific, short-term goals at lower levels of the hierarchy. Feedback intervention theory (Kluger & DeNisi, 1996) provides an excellent illustration of this notion of a goal hierarchy, suggesting that individuals establish goals at the task-detail level, the task level, and the meta-task level. Task-detail goals are the most proximal or immediate goals, focusing on the mechanics or elemental processes involved in performing or learning a task (e.g., physical action goals). Task goals focus more on the performance of a task as a whole and are where task motivation processes (e.g., progress evaluation) are generally assumed to occur. Finally, meta-task goals are higher-order, distal goals that are typically goals of the self (e.g., long-term career goals) that unfold over longer periods of time. Kluger and DeNisi (1996) suggest that meta-task goals often (but not always) control the lower-level or more proximal goals in a manner that facilitates the achievement of the meta-task or self-goals, similar to the notion of "cascading goals." Although other models of self-regulation differ in the number of levels thought to exist in these goal hierarchies (e.g., Lord et al., 2010), the goal hierarchy concept remains the same. Figure 7.2 provides an illustration of this process; the important point is that at any given time, employees are setting goals, monitoring performance, and responding to feedback at various levels of the

Figure 7.2. *Illustration of self-regulation goal hierarchy.*

goal hierarchy. Experiences in each level will thus inform and influence the goal processes at any other level.

Self-regulation is therefore a cyclical process by which individuals proactively utilize proximal and distal goal setting, performance feedback, and self-evaluation to propel themselves toward the attainment of a desired goal or end state. Within the realm of organizational training, self-regulation models are often invoked to describe how employees interested in learning new skills or competencies for their job are likely to utilize these same steps to facilitate their learning or reach a desired level of competence. As noted previously, an understanding of self-regulated learning has become increasingly important as training programs have shifted their emphasis away from tightly controlled training environments toward more learner-centered training, where trainees are viewed as active participants in their learning and are provided more control over the nature and logistics of their learning experience (Bell & Kozlowski, 2008). In self-regulated learning, individuals would follow the model in Figure 7.2 to establish goals, develop learning strategies, direct their attention toward learning, monitor their learning progress, and subsequently modify their self-regulatory processes over time (e.g., Sitzmann & Johnson, 2012).

Research on Self-Regulatory Processes

Given the diverse theoretical approaches to self-regulation that exist and the applicability of these models to many performance environments, it is not surprising that research on self-regulatory processes has come from a wide variety of sources both within and outside of the organizational training literature. From the more general domains of work motivation and individual learning, research in a variety of settings has provided strong support for the role of goals and the resulting GPDs in predicting subsequent motivational processes such as goal establishment, effort expenditure, and goal revision (Diefendorff & Chandler, 2011; Zimmerman & Schunk, 2011). With respect to performance goals, there is overwhelming evidence regarding the positive effects of challenging goals on subsequent task performance; specific, difficult performance goals produce substantially higher levels of performance than vague, easy, or do-your-best goals (Boekaerts, Pintrich, & Zeidner, 2000; Locke & Latham, 1990). In addition, research has also documented the positive effects of specific and challenging goals on effort exerted, strategy search, focused attention, and persistence (Locke & Latham, 2002), further highlighting the important of goals in predicting motivated behavior and task performance.

Research demonstrates that individuals experiencing negative GPDs (performance below their goal or standard) engage in several types of behaviors aimed at reducing the magnitude of these discrepancies, including lowering their goals (e.g., Campion & Lord, 1982; Donovan & Williams, 2003), increasing effort (e.g., Bandura & Cervone, 1983; 1986), or withdrawing from the task (e.g., Mikulincer, 1994). Similarly, this same body of research has also demonstrated the motivational impact of positive GPDs (performance above one's goal) on subsequent behaviors such as upward goal revision (e.g., Williams, Donovan, & Dodge, 2000) and changes in effort (e.g., Bandura & Cervone, 1983); individuals experiencing positive GPDs tend to raise their goals and/or increase the level of effort expended in the hopes of increasing future performance. Interestingly, there is also evidence that individuals monitor not only the magnitude of their GPD, but also the rate at which they are reducing this discrepancy, termed *velocity* (Carver & Scheier, 1998). Research suggests that individuals who sense that they are making little progress in reducing their discrepancy over successive performance episodes (i.e., low velocity) are likely to experience feelings of self-dissatisfaction and set less challenging goals for themselves as a means of addressing their GPDs (e.g., Elicker et al., 2009).

Within the organizational training domain, there has also been substantial research conducted to ascertain how performance goals and self-regulatory processes likely unfold as employees work to acquire job-relevant knowledge. In line with previous research, empirical work on the effects of performance goals in training and education programs has supported their substantial and positive impact on critical training outcomes such as learning and training performance; specific and challenging goals are associated with higher levels of learning and performance in a training context (Locke & Latham, 2002). To illustrate, recent work by Kim et al. (2012) indicated that self-set goal level was the strongest predictor of learning (as evidenced by test performance) in an educational context, while meta-analytic work by Sitzmann and Ely (2011) suggests that goal level has the largest effect on learning out of all identified self-regulatory processes. Further, goals and related processes (e.g., persistence and effort) accounted for 17% of the variance in learning over and above the effects of pretraining knowledge and cognitive ability (the strongest predictors of training performance). Taken as a whole, these findings suggest that goal setting represents one of the most critical determinants of performance in a learning or training environment. Although less voluminous, research on self-regulatory processes such as goal revision and effort expenditure in response to GPDs during training programs has also produced findings that are consistent with the general work motivation research. To illustrate, research indicates that trainees are sensitive to the presence of discrepancies between their training performance goals and their current performance, and that these discrepancies motivate individuals to engage in activities aimed at decreasing these discrepancies, such as increasing effort (e.g., Donovan, Dwight, & Schneider, 2004) or revising their goals (Donovan et al., 2008).

In sum, the research conducted to date suggests that goal setting represents a critical determinant of learning and training performance, and that these goals represent a focal point for future self-regulatory processes (e.g., effort expenditure, goal revision) that are likely to play a significant role in determining training success. Evidence of this can be seen in recent work by Sitzmann and colleagues (2009) who found that prompting during training designed to encourage effective self-regulatory processes (attention to goals, self-monitoring, and self-evaluation) had a significant, positive effect on basic and strategic learning over time. As such these processes are important factors to be considered when designing, implementing, and evaluating organizational training programs.

Individual Differences in Self-Regulation

To this point, we have discussed self-regulation and self-regulated learning as a set of generalizable processes that are assumed to operate similarly across individuals. However, we also recognize that there are significant individual differences that influence these processes and how they operate to produce learning and performance in a training context. In fact, much of the research on self-regulation conducted to date has incorporated one or more individual differences in an attempt to provide some understanding as to which factors are critical to consider when describing how learning unfolds over time. Two of the more important individual differences that are particularly relevant in training contexts are self-efficacy and goal orientation.

Self-Efficacy

Self-efficacy refers to a belief in one's capabilities to organize and execute the courses of action required to produce given attainments or behavioral outcomes (Bandura, 1997), and has long been recognized as an important factor for motivation and performance in a variety of contexts. With respect to self-regulatory processes, self-efficacy is a strong predictor of the performance goals one establishes, such that more efficacious individuals set more challenging goals for themselves (Locke & Latham, 1990; Zimmerman, 2000). Efficacious individuals also tend to exhibit higher levels of performance (Stajkovic & Luthans, 1998), although it is worth noting that there are instances in which efficacy is negatively related to performance (e.g., Vancouver & Kendall, 2006). Additionally, self-efficacy also has a significant impact on the amount of effort individuals are willing to exert in goal pursuit as well as their persistence in striving toward goal attainment; individuals high in self-efficacy exert more effort in response to a GPD and are less willing to abandon a goal in the face of a significant GPD (e.g., Bandura & Cervone, 1983).

From a training perspective, self-efficacy is essential at all stages of the training process (pretraining, during training, and posttraining). Work by Colquitt, Lepine, and Noe (2000) indicates that pretraining self-efficacy is strongly related to motivation to learn, posttraining self-efficacy, and transfer of training, and moderately related to declarative knowledge, skill acquisition, and job performance. During training, self-efficacy is important because it influences effort expenditures and perseverance. When faced with a significant GPD, those higher in self-efficacy will direct their efforts toward reducing this GPD and improving performance (Zimmerman, 2000), whereas those low in self-efficacy are more likely to direct attention toward themselves, lower their goal for their performance, or withdraw from the task all together (e.g., Donovan et al., 2008). High self-efficacy individuals are also more likely to benefit from performance feedback provided during training (e.g., Karl, O'Leary, & Martocchio, 1993) and may derive more benefit from the self-regulatory prompting mentioned previously (Sitzmann et al., 2009).

Beyond these findings demonstrating the impact of self-efficacy on performance and learning in training contexts, it is important to note that self-efficacy is also a consequence of performance and learning in training (Heggestad & Kanfer, 2000), with higher levels of performance or greater success during training leading to higher self-efficacy after the completion of training (posttraining efficacy). In other words, the development and maintenance of self-efficacy is a cyclical process whereby pretraining self-efficacy leads to positive learning outcomes, which in turn leads to higher levels of posttraining self-efficacy (Figure 7.3). This posttraining efficacy is positively related to the extent to

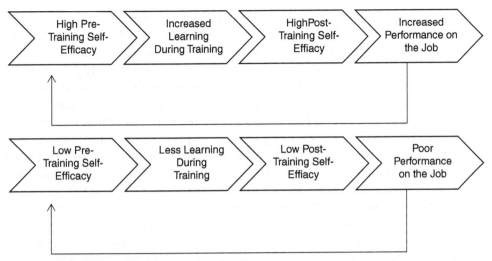

Figure 7.3. *Self-efficacy and training effects.*

which individuals transfer what they have learned during training onto their job (Colquitt et al., 2000), and may also determine the extent to which posttraining goal setting programs are effective in facilitating transfer of training (e.g., Gist, Stevens & Bavetta, 1991).

Goal Orientation

The construct of goal orientation has received quite a bit of attention in recent years in both the training and work motivation literatures (Payne, Youngcourt, & Beaubien, 2007), likely due to research demonstrating links between goal orientation and critical training variables and processes (e.g., self-efficacy, feedback seeking). *Goal orientation* refers to the goals that are implicitly pursued by individuals in achievement settings (Dweck, 1989). Current conceptualizations of goal orientation argue that there are three distinct dimensions of this construct: learning goal orientation, performance-prove goal orientation, and performance-avoid goal orientation. A strong learning orientation (alternatively referred to as a mastery orientation) is characterized by a focus on surmounting difficult challenges, gaining knowledge, and ultimately increasing task mastery. In contrast, a strong performance-avoid orientation is characterized by a focus on avoiding negative evaluations from others regarding one's competence, while performance-prove goal orientation is characterized by a focus on demonstrating one's ability by outperforming or appearing more competent than others.

At this point, it is worth noting that the significant interest in goal orientation has been accompanied by substantial disagreement and confusion as to how this variable should be conceptualized and operationalized. To illustrate, goal orientation has been variously operationalized as: (1) a dispositional trait that is assumed to be constant across situations (Phillips & Gully, 1997), (2) as a situational construct that can be manipulated through instructional design (e.g., Steele-Johnson et al., 2000), and (3) as a domain-specific individual difference that is assumed to vary across major life domains (e.g., work vs. nonwork) but stays constant within those domains (VandeWalle et al., 2001). Further, there are numerous distinct measures of goal orientation that are present in the research literature with little or no evidence demonstrating that these measures converge with one another. The result is a literature in which researchers are attempting to draw conclusions about a unified goal orientation construct, but conceptualizing and measuring goal orientations in significantly different ways. Fortunately, there appears to be some consistency in the effects of the various goal orientation dimensions across conceptualizations (trait, state, or domain-specific variable).

A large portion of the research on goal orientation has focused upon its impact on self-efficacy perceptions, which is not surprising given the importance of the self-efficacy construct in learning and self-regulatory processes. In general, these studies have shown a moderate, positive correlation between self-efficacy and learning goal orientation, while performance-avoid orientation generally exhibits a significant (albeit weak) negative relationship with self-efficacy, and performance-prove orientation does not demonstrate any consistent relationship with self-efficacy (Payne et al., 2007). Moving beyond self-efficacy, goal orientation has also been linked to a host of self-regulatory processes and outcomes that are relevant to learning and training contexts. Several studies suggest that goal orientation is linked to feedback-seeking behaviors, a critical component of the self-monitoring function in self-regulatory models. Research has generally shown that the degree to which individuals seek out feedback is positively correlated with the strength of one's learning goal orientation and negatively correlated with their level of performance-avoid goal orientation, while the effects of a strong performance-prove orientation are inconsistent (Payne et al., 2007). Goal orientation has also been examined as it relates to responses to GPDs, with research suggesting that a learning goal orientation may be associated with a greater willingness to raise one's goals after performance and a general tendency to increase effort when faced with a negative GPD, while a strong performance avoid-orientation may be linked to a tendency to abandon goals after goal failure (e.g., Donovan & Hafsteinsson, 2006; Donovan et al., 2008). Although fewer in number, a handful of studies have also demonstrated that goal orientation may be linked to the learning strategies and metacognitive processes exhibited by individuals acquiring new skills (e.g., Schmidt & Ford, 2003). Interestingly, a handful of studies have also found that the effects of goal orientation on self-regulatory and motivational processes may depend on task characteristics. For example, research by Steele-Johnson and colleagues (e.g., Steele-Johnson et al., 2000) suggests that the beneficial effects of a strong learning goal orientation may be lessened when individuals are asked to perform routine, simple, or nonchallenging tasks.

From a training and self-regulated learning perspective, the general consensus is that a learning goal orientation enhances self-regulatory effectiveness in a learning environment, and that self-regulated learning is optimized when trainees have a strong learning goal orientation and this is matched with learning goals outlined in the training (e.g., Kozlowski et al., 2001). To illustrate, Bell and Kozlowski (2008) found that trainees that received a learning intervention designed to prime a learning goal orientation subsequently were more likely to adopt a learning goal orientation for the task at hand. This situation-specific learning orientation was associated with increased levels of self-efficacy and intrinsic motivation, which in turn facilitated both learning and transfer performance. In contrast, trainees in this study with a strong performance-avoid goal orientation demonstrated lower levels of self-efficacy, which resulted in lower levels of transfer performance. These results and other similar findings clearly demonstrate the beneficial effects of a strong learning orientation and associated learning-based goals (Pintrich, 2000) and hint at the potentially deleterious effects of a strong performance-avoid orientation. Taken together with the research discussed in the preceding text, these findings indicate that goal orientation represents a critical influence on the effectiveness of self-regulatory processes and self-regulated learning.

Contextual Influences on Self-Regulation

While there is no doubt that characteristics of the learner such as self-efficacy and goal orientation play a substantial role in determining self-regulatory processes and associated learning outcomes, there are also several factors outside of the learner (i.e., factors in the training context) that can impact self-regulated learning. Although an exhaustive review of these factors is beyond the scope of this chapter, we will highlight three factors that we believe to be particularly important: the nature of feedback provided during training, the nature of the task being performed, and the presence of multiple performance goals.

Feedback

Research on the effects of feedback on self-regulatory process and learning performance has existed for well more than a century (Kluger & DeNisi, 1996), yet there are several significant questions about the effects of feedback that remain unanswered. For example, while we have generally accepted and supported the basic proposition that feedback regarding one's performance is a critical element of self-regulated learning and that goal setting without feedback has limited effects (e.g., Erez, 1977), we know much less about the effects of different types of feedback (e.g., normative vs. absolute feedback). To illustrate, virtually all the empirical work on self-regulatory processes to date has focused exclusively on the effects of feedback sign (i.e., a negative or positive GPD), with little attention given to other feedback characteristics. Given the many different forms that feedback can take during learning and evidence that some forms of feedback may actively undermine learning and subsequent performance, it is important for us to identify critical characteristics of feedback that can enhance (or undermine) effective self-regulation in learning environments. To this end, Kluger and DeNisi (1996) developed FIT in an attempt to both document the variable effects that feedback can have on performance and provide some initial identification of factors that may be responsible for these variable effects (see also Butler & Winne, 1995).

At its core, FIT is similar to the models of self-regulation discussed previously in that it argues that a comparison of performance relative to one's goal drives self-regulatory behavior and that individuals are motivated to reduce any discrepancies that exist (i.e., GPDs). Further, FIT proposes that individuals have multiple levels of goals or standards for behavior that include goals at the self, task, and task detail level, and that feedback that directs attention to or away from these levels will have variable effects on performance. Initial meta-analytic results presented by Kluger and DeNisi (1996) suggest a host of factors that may determine whether feedback has positive or negative effects on subsequent performance. For example, feedback that directs attention to the self-level through normative comparisons or threats to self-esteem tended to reduce the effectiveness of performance feedback, while feedback that provided individuals with velocity information or provided cues that support learning enhanced the effectiveness of feedback on subsequent performance. Despite the promise of this model and the initial meta-analytic results, there have been very few studies conducted to date to provide additional tests of the FIT model or elaborate upon its initial hypotheses. Of these studies, none have originated in the organizational training or learning literatures, which is quite surprising given the potential importance of these findings for informing the design and implementation of organizational training programs. While this lack of research is disappointing, the model warrants consideration when providing feedback during training, as it not only highlight feedback characteristics that may enhance or harm self-regulatory processes, but also provides evidence that the effects of feedback are much more nuanced than previously thought.

Nature of the Task

Beyond any feedback given during task learning, the nature of the task may also impact self-regulatory processes and learning outcomes. To illustrate, training individuals for complex skills or behaviors is likely to require a significant amount of effort as learners encounter challenges and deal with many more opportunities for failure, as compared to learning relatively simple skills or behaviors. These challenges are likely to create a learning environment where the effects of a strong learning goal orientation are particularly positive and pronounced, while the harmful outcomes associated with a strong performance-avoid orientation are likely to be magnified (e.g., Steele-Johnson et al., 2000). Training for complex or challenging behaviors and skills also places even more emphasis on the role of learner self-efficacy, as learners high in self-efficacy have been shown to be able to address the challenges that accompany such learning and persist in the face of hurdles or actual failure (Zimmerman, 2000). In contrast, learners low in self-efficacy are unlikely to be able to effectively handle the demands of learning these complex tasks and are more likely to disengage from the task or abandon their performance goals in the face of adversity (Zimmerman, 2000), both of which are undesirable outcomes from an organizational perspective. These and other findings indicating that key elements of the self-regulation process (e.g., goal setting; Locke & Latham, 2002; Schunk, 1990) are likely to be impacted by the task being performed, clearly suggest that organizations should be attentive to the nature of the task they are training to either guard against nonoptimal learning outcomes (e.g., disengagement or learned helplessness) or modify the training environment so as to reduce the complexity of the task being presented to learners (e.g., through spacing of materials).

Multiple Goals

As noted in our introduction, the very nature of the work that employees are being asked to perform has changed substantially in recent years, with jobs becoming more fluid and multidimensional. As a result, employees are now being asked to allocate their attention and effort across multiple tasks at any given point in time, both on the job and during organizational training efforts (Lord et al., 2010). In line with this trend, recent research has begun to explore how the presence of multiple (and perhaps conflicting) task goals may impact self-regulatory processes and learning.

Although still in its infancy, this research indicates that GPDs continue to play a critical role in guiding self-regulatory efforts, both in terms of effort exerted and time spent attending to a given goal (at the expense of other goals). In general, individuals direct their time and attentional resources toward goals with the largest, negative GPDs or the goals they are perceived to be most difficult (e.g., Erez, Gopher, & Arzi, 1990; Schmidt & DeShon, 2007) when they believe that attainment of all goals is possible. However, when they perceive that the attainment of all goals is unlikely, they focus their resources on the goal with the smallest discrepancy (i.e., the goal they are closest to attaining). From a training perspective, this suggests that individuals may be ignoring their strongest developmental needs (i.e., tasks with the largest GPD) when they believe that attainment of all training goals is unlikely due to time constraints or other limiting factors (e.g., low perceived ability).

Perhaps more importantly, the research allocation perspective suggests that self-monitoring and self-evaluation activities associated with goal setting may divert attentional resources away from the task learning processes that are essential during training programs (e.g., Kanfer & Ackerman, 1989), thus inhibiting task performance and learning. When coupled with the presence of more than one goal (and multiple instances of self-monitoring and self-evaluation), this diversion of resources away from task learning is likely to substantially undermine training efforts (learning and transfer) for novel tasks where trainee expertise and resources are limited.

Considered as a whole, these findings suggest that organizations may want to limit the number of goals trainees are exposed to during training, particularly when the trainees are novices or are faced with challenging time constraints. This also suggests that organizations conducting training should seek to minimize distractions associated with work demands outside of the training program so that trainees can direct their full resources toward learning and mastering the task at hand.

Organizational Training: Practice vs. Science

Up to this point, we have focused our attention on summarizing conceptual and empirical work on models of self-regulation and self-regulated learning and have identified key themes and findings that hold implications for how we run our organizational training programs. However, as evidenced in many areas of human resource management, it is often the case that the practices used in organizations do not incorporate or consider significant findings in the relevant research literatures (i.e., a science-practice gap exists; Rynes, 2012). Therefore, we sought to assess the extent to which core findings from the self-regulation research literature were being incorporated into training practices in organizational settings. To this end, we conducted a survey of training professionals to obtain their perspectives on several topics, including how key self-regulatory constructs (goal setting, feedback) were being used in their own training programs and their perceptions of the training research literature.

A convenience sample of 15 training professionals with an average of 18.2 years of work experience across a range of industries (e.g., accounting, pharmaceutical, manufacturing) in the northeastern United States responded to a brief online survey assessing these key issues. The responses provided to these survey questions (summarized in Table 7.1) revealed several interesting findings regarding the extent to which well-established research findings on training and self-regulated learning were being applied in organizational training programs.

One of the core findings noted in our review of the self-regulation literature was that goals for training performance generally had strong, beneficial effects on learning and performance (Sitzmann & Ely, 2011). When asked about the extent to which their training programs utilized goal-setting programs, only 27% of respondents indicated that their organization utilized a formal goal-setting program for their trainees. Thirty-three percent noted that goals were used informally or sporadically in their training efforts, while 40% indicated that goal setting was not utilized in any format in their organizational training. This finding is somewhat surprising and troubling, given both the training literature demonstrating the effects of performance goals on important outcomes and the broader recognition of the power of goal setting (Locke & Latham, 2002). Of those who indicated that they used goals in some form during their training programs, only 50% responded that their organization provided some training for

Table 7.1 *Survey of training professionals (n = 15)*

Goal Setting

Q: To what extent do your training programs utilize goal setting for trainees?

27%   Formal goal setting us used in all training programs
33%   Goal setting used informally or sporadically
40%   No goal setting occurs in our training programs

Q: If you utilize goal setting, do you instruct trainees on how to set effective goals or provide them with strategies to facilitate goal attainment?

50%   Provide training on how to set goals
38%   Provide trainees with strategies to facilitate goal attainment
25%   Do not provide training in goal setting or strategies for goal attainment

Feedback

Q: Do your training programs provide trainees with performance feedback?

40%   Provide formal performance feedback
27%   Provide feedback informally or sporadically
33%   Provide no performance feedback to trainees

individuals as to how to set effect goals (e.g., SMART goals), while 38% noted that their organization provided trainees with strategies they could employ to facilitate goal attainment. In addition, for those organizations that utilized goal setting, the content of these goals ranged from team performance goals to goals that were derived from higher level strategic objectives to goals that represented vague organizational outcomes (e.g., "address identified training needs"). Interestingly, only one individual noted that her organization allowed trainees to set and revise their own goals for training performance. Taken as a whole, these responses suggest that organizational training programs are not fully leveraging our understanding of the benefits of establishing challenging and specific goals for training performance or, in some cases, are establishing goals that are likely to hinder learning and training performance.

A second core self-regulatory construct discussed in our earlier review of the research was performance feedback. A key takeaway message from this research was that goal setting without feedback is unlikely to be effective and the wrong types of feedback can be detrimental to learning and performance (Kluger & DeNisi, 1996). Forty percent of our survey respondents indicated that their organization provided formal and consistent performance feedback for trainees, while the remaining individuals noted that their organization either provided informal feedback (27%) or no feedback at all (33%) to trainees regarding their performance. Of those that provided feedback in some form, most provided feedback through open discussion (either with a team or a peer) or through the trainer, while some provided feedback using self-assessment quizzes. As with the responses to our goal-setting questions, these results suggest that training programs are either not fully aware of the importance of providing trainees with the right types of performance feedback, or choose not to provide feedback for some practical or philosophical reason.

Although the responses to our survey questions were completed by only a small sample of training professions, the results nonetheless suggest that there may be significant science-practice gaps that exist in today's organizational training programs. More specifically, despite our extensive findings documenting the beneficial effects of specific, difficult goals on learning and performance and our research documenting the important of feedback, neither of these principles seems to be applied in a consistent manner in organizational training. While some would suggest that it is normal for there to be a "lag" in seeing research findings used in applied settings, it is important to realize that the literature supporting both goal setting and feedback has been around for decades. For example, the implications of the findings from goal-setting research for organizational training programs were noted in the third edition of Goldstein's seminal book on training in organizations, which was published in 1993. Clearly there is some work that needs to be done in integrating these and other self-regulatory research findings into the design and implementation of our organizational training programs.

Future Research Directions

The literature on self-regulation has provided the field with a significant body of evidence regarding how self-regulatory processes may unfold during training and learning. To facilitate additional progress and the generation of practical knowledge, we have three recommendations for future research.

Clarification of the Goal Orientation Construct

Given substantial interest in the goal orientation construct in the training field, yet significant confusion as to how this variable should be conceptualized, we would like to see research move toward a unified perspective on goal orientation. As noted, the diverse operationalizations of goal orientation that have been used to date create an unwieldy situation in which researcher are attempting to make generalized conclusions about a single goal orientation construct using measures and definitions that may be incompatible. In the hopes of generating a more cohesive body of knowledge regarding this construct, research would benefit from adopting a multifaceted model of goal orientation, which recognizes that goal orientation exists at multiple levels (dispositional, domain-specific, situational). That is, rather than trying to decide which conceptualization of goal orientation is "best" (e.g., disposition vs. state), researchers should explicitly recognize that goal orientation can be amenable to situational influence (e.g., priming instructions) *and* stable over time (dispositional), and that individuals may adopt different goal orientations in various life domains (e.g., work vs. nonwork environments).

A framework recently proposed by Donovan et al. (2013; Figure 7.4) provides an example of the type of model that could be utilized to guide research

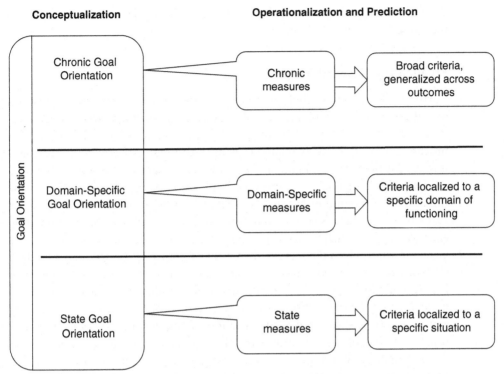

Figure 7.4. *Multilevel conceptualization and operationalization of the goal orientation construct (adapted from Donovan et al., 2013).*

on goal orientation's effects on self-regulated learning. Key elements of this model include: (1) adoption of a common terminology to differentiate between different conceptualizations of goal orientation (chronic, domain-specific, and state goal orientation); (2) researchers precisely specifying which operationalization they are employing in their research and limiting their conclusions to that specific form of goal orientation; (3) recognition that while there is likely some overlap among these orientations, individuals may display different orientations at different levels (e.g., one's goal orientation in a given learning context may be distinct from their chronic or dispositional goal orientation tendencies); and, (4) a concerted effort on the part of researchers to "match" their operationalization of goal orientation to the outcomes they are interested in predicting, such that the level of specificity in their outcomes is matched by the level of specificity at which they measure the goal orientation construct (cf., Azjen, 1991; Fishbein & Azjen, 1975). Although following these suggestions would require time and effort on the part of researchers and necessitate reclassifying previous research based upon the conceptualization used, these changes would be accompanied by the emergence of clearer and more consistent relationships between goal orientation and motivational constructs and a reduction in the conceptual confusion that currently exists (Payne et al., 2007). This will create a more precise and focused research literature that facilitates drawing conclusions about the role of goal orientation in self-regulated learning.

Broaden Our Research Focus

Furthermore, research should move beyond an examination of the main effects of self-regulatory variables (i.e., goals, self-efficacy, feedback) to consider additional research questions that enhance our understanding of key motivational processes impacting self-regulated learning. Although a thorough discussion is not feasible here, we highlight a few key questions that warrant future attention.

First, although there is a growing body of research focused on assessing the impact of computer-assisted or virtual training (e.g., Brown, Charlier, & Pierotti, 2012), there is surprisingly little work to determine what factors influence use of and attrition from these programs. This area of inquiry is particularly important given the increased amount of control given to today's learners (Bell & Kozlowski, 2002) and the significant interest in virtual or online training. To illustrate, respondents to our survey of training professionals (Table 7.1) indicated that the vast majority (64%) believe their organization will be making a move toward self-directed, virtual training. Thus, the question of what factors lead to the use of and attrition from these programs seems particularly critical. Fortunately, we are starting to see research emerging in this area, primarily from Sitzmann and colleagues (e.g., Sitzmann, 2012), suggesting that trainee characteristics such as self-efficacy and conscientiousness may represent important determinants of attrition from training programs. Recent work by Brown and Charlier (2013) also propose several factors that likely influence use of e-learning, such as individual workload, perceived ease of use, and the climate for desired change. In line with these recent studies, we recommend that future research devote more attention to examining the impact of individual differences and contextual factors on both the use of and attrition from virtual or self-directed learning programs in organizations. A clearer understanding of how self-regulatory processes unfold during these learning programs, as well as a foundational knowledge of the individual, organizational, and contextual factors that can enhance the use of these programs or reduce attrition would benefit the field of training tremendously. For example, we would argue that research in this area needs to more explicitly examine how individuals embed this type of training within their work day to identify individual (e.g., polychronicity), job-related (e.g., workload), and contextual (e.g., managerial support for training) factors that are associated with effective learning versus those that derail these learning efforts and lead individuals to abandon these programs.

Second, we believe the field would benefit from conceptualizing performance as a trajectory of learning, rather than simply as an outcome of training examined at a single point in time. This suggestion is not new, having been espoused for years by both researchers and practitioners (e.g., Thoresen et al., 2004), yet our research continues to focus on performance measured at a single point in time. As noted by Chen and Mathieu (2008), the conceptualization of performance as a trajectory holds significant potential to both advance our understanding of behavior and performance in a training context and increase the efficiency of our training programs. Although research in the more general training and employee performance literatures has acknowledged the concept of performance trajectories (e.g., Hofmann et al., 1992), the self-regulation literature has largely overlooked this perspective. We recommend that researchers follow the lead of recent work (e.g., Chen & Mathieu, 2008; Yeo et al., 2009) examining performance from a more dynamic perspective and attempt to model self-regulatory processes as they relate to these performance trajectories. To illustrate, we believe research in this area would benefit from repeated-measures research designs in which multiple measurements of learning and performance are collected before, during, and after training to model growth, development, and maintenance of learning, rather than focusing exclusively on performance at a single point in time. While this type of research is clearly more difficult and time consuming, we believe that this type of research provides us with significantly more valuable information that is directly applicable to today's organizational training programs.

Finally, given the work by Kluger and DeNisi (1996) highlighting the many characteristics of feedback, we urge researchers to treat feedback in a more nuanced manner that carefully considers the many characteristics (e.g., normative vs. nonnormative feedback) when investigating the effects of feedback on learning and self-regulation. Far too many studies treat feedback as an all or nothing phenomenon or simply examine feedback sign as a predictor of self-regulatory processes. This approach to studying feedback limits our knowledge of the types of feedback that may maximize learning and training performance, ultimately hindering our ability to properly design training programs that facilitate effective self-regulation. As a starting point, we would suggest that researchers consider conducting foundational studies that utilize analytical approaches such as policy capturing to isolate the features/types of feedback that are most salient to learners and have the largest impact on subsequent learning and/or self-regulatory behavior. This would serve as the groundwork for future research examining how the manipulation of these identified factors could be used in organizational settings to enhance learning or effective self-regulation.

Increase the Accessibility of Research Findings

One key takeaway message from our survey of training professionals was that the field of training and development could benefit from a more concerted effort on the part of researchers to present their findings in both accessible outlets (e.g., trade publications) and use terminology that facilitates the use of research findings in organizational settings, while also utilizing research settings that are viewed as being generalizable to organizational training environments. To illustrate, virtually all the literature examining goal revision in response to performance feedback has been conducted utilizing college student participants in artificial environments with little consequences for high or low levels of learning or task performance. One can see how training professionals may view this research setting as being ill suited to inform their organization as to how actual employees will act when participating in organizational training programs with significant implications for their success as employees. In line with this, our survey of training professionals indicated that only 27% of these individuals felt that the training research literature was very helpful in informing them about how to design or implement training programs within their organization. We believe that efforts to increase the accessibility of our research findings to training and development professionals could have a significant impact on the state of training in organizations and substantially reduce the "science-practice gap" that currently exists.

Recommendations for Organizational Training Programs

Organizational training programs have undergone a significant shift in recent years toward the increased use of virtual training tools (e.g., self-authored videos, virtual communication channels, self-guided online coursework), as technological advances have made these virtual learning solutions more accessible to the typical organization. To this point, 63% of the respondents from our survey of training professionals expect their own organizations to increase their use of virtual, asynchronous learning programs in the future. One outcome of this shift toward asynchronous/virtual learning is that today's organizational training programs are providing trainees with increasing control over their training experiences (training content, timing, etc.). This emphasis on self-directed learning clearly underscores the importance of effective self-regulation in training contexts, as trainees will be largely responsible for their own learning and skill acquisition. However, regardless of whether training occurs face to face or in the virtual space, it is evident from the literature reviewed that there are several important considerations for motivating employees in training contexts. Table 7.2 summarizes our key recommendations for practitioners to ensure that they adequately facilitate the self-regulation of trainees to optimize training programs.

Goal Setting and Self-Regulation

First and foremost, it is evident from our survey of training professionals that most companies are not using any formal goal setting in their training programs. This is curious given that there is a plethora of empirical support for the effectiveness of goal setting, both in and outside of training contexts (e.g., Locke & Latham, 2002; Sitzmann & Ely, 2011). Therefore, we recommend that *prior to beginning a training program, trainers and managers assign or encourage individuals to establish difficult and specific learning goals (Recommendation #1)*. For instance, an employee entering a training course for clerical skill development would benefit from setting specific and difficult learning goals, such as typing 45

Table 7.2 *Recommendations for encouraging self-regulated learning in training contexts*

1. Prior to training, managers should encourage or assign trainees difficult and specific training goals.
2. Trainers and supervisors should participate in self-regulation training prior to developing training programs to adequately assist trainees in their self-regulatory processes during training.
3. Trainers should (a) limit the number of goals trainees are exposed to during training, (b) avoid placing too much emphasis on self-monitoring and self-evaluation, and (c) minimize distractions during training. This will help trainees direct attention toward goal relevant training tasks.
4. Feedback during training should focus on learning, velocity, and goal setting. This will enhance self-efficacy, self-regulation, and performance.
5. Trainers should prime a learning orientation in training environments by instructing trainees to make and learn from errors during training, so long as the training tasks are novel, complex, or challenging.

words per minute by the end of the course. The goals should focus on understanding new concepts, mastering new tasks, and learning new skills; not on displaying performance relative to others (Winters & Latham, 1996). Further, these goals should be developed with the organization's strategic goals and the goals of the employee (and their team, if applicable) in mind to minimize conflict or competing demands during these programs. This information should be collected as a part of the organizations' normal training needs assessment and would ensure that the organization is accounting for the organizational environment trainees are working in. These appropriately designed goals will serve to direct attention toward goal-relevant activities that are consistent with their context and away from distractions, while also increasing effort, strategy search, and persistence, ultimately leading to higher performance levels (e.g., Locke & Latham, 1990; 2002).

Recall that goal-setting produces a negative GPD between one's current and anticipated level of performance. The GPD not only provokes action (because negative GPDs are dissatisfying), but it also provides important feedback information as individuals continuously monitor their progress relative to goals set. Thus, in the case of the clerical employee, we expect that the GPDs will motivate her to engage in behaviors aimed at reducing the discrepancy (e.g., Donovan et al., 2004) and she will continuously receive performance feedback by monitoring her own performance.

An important caveat is that if employees are encouraged to set difficult and specific learning goals, managers, supervisors, and trainers *must* be comfortable with supporting goal setting and self-regulation processes. To illustrate, consider the trainee that set a training goal of reaching 45 words per minute by the end of the seven-day class, but at day four, she is only at 38 words. What is she to do? If trainees become discouraged during training and do not persist toward accomplishing their goals, this is harmful for both the organization and the individuals – time and money are wasted. Thus, a trainer or supervisor can help trainees navigate these perceived difficulties, lending to more adaptive self-regulatory strategies and supporting goal striving. However, this is only true if the trainers themselves have the requisite knowledge of effective goal setting and self-regulation, and unfortunately, our survey results suggest that most trainers likely do not. Therefore, we recommend that *trainers and supervisors participate in self-regulation training prior to developing training programs* (*Recommendation #2*). If trainers are not prepared, then we can't reasonably expect trainees to effectively self-regulate and make progress toward attaining their learning goals.

This draws attention to another important point; *it is critical that trainers: (a) limit the number of goals trainees are exposed to during training, (b) avoid placing too much emphasis on self-monitoring and self-evaluation, and (c) minimize distractions during training* (*Recommendation #3*). Trainees may become overwhelmed when faced with too many demands on their attentional resources, particularly when they are novices with regard to the content of a training program (see Kanfer & Ackerman, 1989). Therefore, trainers should encourage trainees to identify a select few specific and challenging learning goals for training. Although we recommend that organizations encourage trainees to engage in goal setting and self-regulation, we caution that self-monitoring and self-evaluation should be kept to a minimum at first, to not distract trainees from learning the intended knowledge and skills. Furthermore, when identifying goals and strategies, it is likely that trainees will avoid working toward the goals that are perceived as the most challenging, and focus attention on the tasks with the smallest GPD (e.g., Erez et al., 1990). Thus, trainers should also educate trainees on how to select and prioritize the most important tasks, and help direct their attention to the tasks with the biggest GPDs (most need) for the most learning and development to occur.

Interestingly, this recommendation dovetails nicely with recent interest in the gamification of training programs that has emerged in the nonacademic training literature (e.g., McGonigal, 2011). Gamification generally emphasizes placing trainees in a simplified learning task environment that both restricts their focus to relevant activities and provides clear and unambiguous rules, goals, and feedback, while also directing individuals to attend to areas where they are most in need of development. Although the research literature on gamification is rather sparse, these efforts may nonetheless represent a viable means of helping learners effectively self-regulate when learning new or novel tasks, while also maintaining or increasing learner engagement (particularly in self-directed, virtual learning environments).

Individual and Organizational Considerations

Trainers should also focus on providing feedback that enhances (rather than undermines) self-efficacy, self-regulation, learning, and performance. As noted by Kluger and DeNisi (1996), the nature of feedback provided to learners is often overlooked or given little thought. This is problematic because not all feedback is beneficial for learning and performance, and some forms of feedback that would appear to be positive on the surface (e.g., overly positive feedback or "cheerleading") may be detrimental to performance. Kluger and DeNisi suggested that feedback that emphasizes learning; focuses on velocity (defined as the rate of progress one is making toward their goal) and effective goal setting and self-monitoring; and minimizes attention to the self is likely to yield impressive gains in performance. If we return to our previous example, the clerical trainee should feel most efficacious and motivated during training when feedback focuses on learning the task (e.g., here is another technique to improve key strokes) and on goal setting (e.g., look at your progress so far this week). Although additional research is needed to fully understand how different types of feedback influence training outcomes, we recommend that *trainers provide feedback to trainees in a manner that enhances self-efficacy, self-regulation, and performance by focusing on learning, velocity, and goal setting (Recommendation #4)*.

Consistent with a focus on *learning*, we recommend that training programs be created in such a way that primes a learning goal orientation (taking on difficult challenges, gaining knowledge, and increasing task mastery). As discussed previously, a learning goal orientation is associated with higher levels of self-efficacy, feedback seeking behaviors, and effort when faced with negative GPDs (Donovan et al., 2008; Payne et al., 2007). While goal orientation is considered by some to be a dispositional trait, it is possible to foster a learning goal orientation through instructions and interventions in the training environment (e.g., Kozlowski et al., 2001). In line with our first recommendation (setting learning goals), one strategy to prime a learning orientation during training to instruct and encourage trainees to make and learn from errors during training (Frese et al., 1991). These instructions frame errors as a natural part of the learning process and deemphasize performance evaluation. Returning to our previous example, if the clerical trainee is told that "errors are a natural part of the training process; you can learn from your typing mistakes and develop a better understanding of typing strategy," she will be more likely to develop a learning orientation, leading to enhanced self-efficacy, effort expenditure, and performance. This priming of a learning orientation may also be facilitated by framing the training as sequence of learning objectives and discussing the use of performance scores as useful diagnostic feedback, rather than as an evaluation on the part of the trainer or organization (e.g., Kozlowski et al., 2001).

It is important to note however, that priming a learning goal orientation is expected to be most effective when matched with corresponding learning goals and learning-focused feedback. To illustrate, in a typical organizational training environment focused on increasing job-related competencies (rather than those being used for selection or to ensure that errors do not occur), it would not be useful to prime a learning goal orientation if the goal of training is framed in a comparative (e.g., to be the "fastest typer in the room") or performance-focused manner (e.g., to "make the fewest number of errors"), as these directly contradict the notion of learning goals and likely create goal conflict and confusion among trainees.

Similarly, priming a learning goal orientation is likely to be most beneficial when tasks are novel, difficult, or complex. This orientation would be less beneficial in situations in which the tasks are routine or easy, as these tasks do not require complex problem solving, strategy, or mastery. For example, it would not be advantageous to instruct someone to make errors on a task with which she is already intimately familiar or is particularly easy. Thus, taken together, our last recommendation is that: *In novel, complex, and challenging programs, trainers should prime a learning orientation by instructing trainees to make and learn from errors during training (Recommendation #5).* In these environments, we expect organizations to get the most out of their training efforts when trainees adopt a strong learning orientation and subsequently establish learning goals to match this orientation.

Conclusions

Today's employees exist in a complex and dynamic world, where workplaces are diverse and dispersed, technology is advancing at a rapid pace, the Baby Boomers are retiring, and there is a great demand for highly skilled technical workers. Simply put, there is a high demand for training and development. This, coupled with the fact that training professionals are expecting to see a rise in the use of virtual training and asynchronous learning in the near future, highlights the relevance and importance of self-regulatory processes in training contexts. While a gap seems to exist between researchers and practitioners with regard to the use of goal setting in training programs; the data doesn't lie – goal setting is an effective means of improving learning from training programs because it engages self-regulatory processes that are essential to learning. Goal setting can be augmented by setting difficult and specific long- and short-term goals, directing attention toward goal-relevant tasks (and away from irrelevant tasks), providing appropriate feedback, enhancing self-efficacy, and priming a learning orientation. Moving forward, researchers should make a concerted effort to disseminate training motivation research to practitioners, and practitioners should familiarize themselves with the training motivation literature. This exchange will result in extraordinary benefits for individuals and organizations involved in employee training and development.

References

Ajzen, I. 1991. The theory of planned behavior. *Organizational Behavior and Human Decision Processes* 50: 179–211.

Bandura, A. 1986. *Social Foundations of Thought and Action: A Social Cognitive Theory.* Englewood Cliffs, NJ: Prentice Hall.

Bandura, A. 1991. Social cognitive theory of self-regulation." *Organizational Behavior and Human Decision Processes* 50: 248–287.

Bandura, A. 1997. *Self-efficacy: The Exercise of Control.* New York: Freeman.

Bandura, A., and Cervone, D. 1983. Self-evaluative and self-efficacy mechanisms governing the motivational effects of goal systems. *Journal of Personality and Social Psychology* 45: 1017–1028.

Bandura, A., and Cervone, D. 1986. Differential engagement of self-reactive influences in cognitive motivation. *Organizational Behavior and Human Decision Processes* 38: 92–113.

Bell, B. S., and Kozlowski, S. W. J. 2002. Goal orientation and ability: Interactive effects on self-efficacy, performance, and knowledge. *Journal of Applied Psychology* 87: 497–505.

Bell, B. S., and Kozlowski, S. W. J. 2008. Active learning: Effects of core training design elements on self-regulatory processes, learning, and adaptability. *Journal of Applied Psychology* 93: 296–316.

Boekaerts, M., Pintrich, P. R., and Zeidner, M., eds., 2000. *Handbook of Self-Regulation.* San Diego, CA: Academic Press.

Brown, K. G. 2001. Using computers to deliver training: Which employees learn and why? *Personnel Psychology* 54: 271–296.

Brown, K. G., and Charlier, S. D. 2013. An integrative model of e-learning use: Leveraging theory to understand and increase usage. *Human Resource Management Review* 23: 37–49.

Brown, K. G., Charlier, S. D., and Pierotti, A. 2012. E-learning in work organizations: Contributions of past research and suggestions for the future. In G. P. Hodgkinson and J. K. Ford, eds. *International Review of Industrial and Organizational Psychology*, 27, 89–114. Chichester, UK: John Wiley and Sons.

Butler, D. L., and Winne, P. H. 1995. Feedback and self-regulated learning: A theoretical synthesis. *Review of Educational Research* 65: 245–281.

Campion, M. A., and Lord, R. G. 1982. A control systems conceptualization of the goal setting and changing process. *Organizational Behavior and Human Performance* 30: 265–287.

Carver, C. S., and Scheier, M. F. 1998. *On the Self-Regulation of Behavior.* New York: Cambridge University Press.

Chen, G., and Mathieu, J. E. 2008. Goal orientation dispositions and performance trajectories: The roles of supplementary and complementary situational inducements. *Organizational Behavior and Human Decision Processes* 106: 21–38.

Colquitt, J. A., Lepine, J. A., and Noe, R. A. 2000. Toward an integrative theory of training motivation: A meta-analytic path analysis of 20 years of research. *Journal of Applied Psychology* 85: 676–707.

Diefendorff, J. M., and Chandler, M. M. 2011. Motivating employees. In S. Zedeck, ed., *Handbook of Industrial and Organizational Psychology*, 65–135. Washington, DC: American Psychological Association.

Donovan, J. J., and Hafsteinsson, L. G. 2006. The impact of goal-performance discrepancies, self-efficacy and goal orientation on upward goal revision. *Journal of Applied Social Psychology* 36: 1046–1099.

Donovan, J. J., and Williams, K. J. 2003. Missing the mark: Effects of time and causal attributions on goal revision in response to goal-performance discrepancies. *Journal of Applied Psychology* 88: 379–390.

Donovan, J. J., Bateman, T., and Heggestad, E. D. 2013. Individual differences in work motivation: Current directions and future needs. In N. Christiansen and R. P. Tett, eds., *Handbook of Personality at Work*, 101–128. New York: Psychology Press/Routledge.

Donovan, J. J., Dwight, S. A., and Schneider, D. 2004. Goal revision processes in an organizational context. Manuscript presented at the 19th *Annual Conference of the Society for Industrial and Organizational Psychology*. Chicago, April.

Donovan, J. J., Lorenzet, S. J., Dwight, S. A., and Schneider, D. 2008. Self-regulation in training: The effects of goal-performance discrepancies on subsequent goals and effort. Paper presented at the 23rd *Annual Conference of the Society for Industrial and Organizational Psychology*. San Francisco.

Dweck, C. S. 1989. Motivation. In A. Lesgold and R. Glaser, eds., *Foundations for a Psychology of Education*, 87–136. Hillsdale, NJ: Erlbaum.

Elicker, J. D., Lord, R. G., Ash, S. R., Kohari, N. E., Hruska, B. J., McConnell, N. L., and Medvedeff, M. E. 2009. Velocity as a predictor of performance satisfaction, mental focus, and goal revision. *Applied Psychology: An International Review* 59: 495–514.

Erez, M. 1977. Feedback: A necessary condition for goal setting/performance relationship. *Journal of Applied Psychology* 62: 624–627.

Erez, M., Gopher, D., and Arzi, N. 1990. Effects of goal difficulty, self-set goals, and monetary rewards on dual task performance. *Organizational Behavior and Human Decision Processes* 47: 247–269.

Fishbein, M., and Azjen, I. 1975. *Belief, Attitude, Intention, and Behavior: An Introduction to Theory and Research*. Reading, MA: Addison-Wesley.

Frese, M., Brodbeck, F., Heinbokel, T., Mooser, C., Schleiffenbaum, E., and Thiemann, P. 1991. Errors in training computer skills: On the positive function of errors. *Human–Computer Interaction* 6: 77–93.

Gist, M. E., Stevens, C. K., and Bavetta, A. G. 1991. Effects of self-efficacy and post-training intervention on the acquisition and maintenance of complex interpersonal skills. *Personnel Psychology* 44: 837–861.

Heggestad, E. D., and Kanfer, R. 2000. Individual differences in trait motivation: Development of the motivational trait questionnaire. *International Journal of Educational Research* 33: 751–777.

Hofmann, D. H., Jacobs, R., and Gerras, S. J. 1992. Mapping individual performance over time. *Journal of Applied Psychology* 77: 185–195.

Kanfer, R., and Ackerman, P. L. 1989. Motivation and cognitive abilities: An integrative aptitude/treatment interaction approach to skill acquisition. *Journal of Applied Psychology* 74: 657–690.

Karl, K. A., O'Leary-Kelly, A. M., and Martocchio, J. J. 1993. The impact of feedback and self-efficacy on performance in training. *Journal of Organizational Behavior* 14: 379–394.

Karoly, P. 1993. Mechanisms of self-regulation: A systems view. *Annual Review of Psychology* 44: 23–52.

Kim, K., Oh, I., Chiaburu, D. S., and Brown, K. G. 2012. Does positive perception of oneself boost learning motivation and performance? *International Journal of Selection and Assessment* 20: 257–271.

Kluger, A. N., and DeNisi, A. 1996. The effects of feedback interventions on performance: A historical review, a meta-analysis, and a preliminary feedback intervention theory. *Psychological Bulletin* 119: 254–284.

Kozlowski, S. W., Gully, S. M., Brown, K. G., Salas, E., Smith, E. M., and Nason, E. R. 2001. Effects of training goals and goal orientation traits on multidimensional training outcomes and performance adaptability. *Organizational Behavior and Human Decision Processes* 85: 1–31.

Kraiger, K., and Jerden, E. 2007. A meta-analytic investigation of learner control: Old findings and new directions. In S. M. Fiore, and E. Salas, eds., *Toward a Science of Distributed Learning*, 65–90. Washington, DC: American Psychological Association.

Locke, E. A., and Latham, G. P. 1990. *A Theory of Goal Setting and Task Performance.* Englewood Cliffs, NJ: Prentice-Hall.

Locke, E. A., and Latham, G. P. 2002. Building a practically useful theory of goal setting and task motivation: A 35-year odyssey. *American Psychologist* 57: 705–717.

Lord, R. G., Diefendorff, J. M., Schmidt, A. M., and Hall, R. J. 2010. Self-regulation at work. *Annual Review of Psychology* 61: 543–568.

McGonigal, J. 2011. *Reality Is Broken: Why Games Make Us Better and How They Can Change the World.* New York: Penguin Press.

Mikulincer, M. 1994. *Human Learned Helplessness: A Coping Perspective.* New York: Plenum Press.

Payne, S. C., Youngcourt, S. S., and Beaubien, J. M. 2007. A meta-analytic examination of the goal orientation nomological net. *Journal of Applied Psychology* 92: 128–150.

Phillips, J. M., and Gully, S. M. 1997. Role of goal orientation, ability, need for achievement, and locus of control in the self-efficacy and goal setting process. *Journal of Applied Psychology* 82: 792–802.

Pintrich, P. R. 2000. The role of goal orientation in self-regulated learning. In M. Boekaerts, P. R. Pintrich, and M. Zeidner, eds., *Handbook of Self-Regulation*, 451–502. San Diego, CA: Academic.

Rynes, S. L. 2012. The research-practice gap in I/O Psychology and related fields: Challenges and potential solutions. In S. W. J. Kozlowski, ed., *The Oxford Handbook of Organizational Psychology*, 409–452. New York: Oxford University Press.

Schmidt, A. M., and DeShon, R. P. 2007. What to do? The effects of discrepancies, incentives, and time on dynamic goal prioritization. *Journal of Applied Psychology* 92: 928–941.

Schmidt, A. M., and Ford, J. K. 2003. Learning within a learner control training environment: The interactive effects of goal orientation and metacognitive instruction on learning outcomes. *Personnel Psychology* 56: 405–429.

Schunk, D. H. 1990. Goal setting and self-efficacy during self-regulated learning. *Educational Psychologist* 25: 71–86.

Schunk, D. H, and Zimmerman, B. J., eds., 1994. *Self-Regulation of Learning and Performance: Issues and Educational Applications.* Hillsdale, NJ: Lawrence Erlbaum Associates.

Sitzmann, T. 2012. A theoretical model and analysis of the role of self-regulation in the attrition process. *Learning and Individual Differences* 22: 46–54.

Sitzmann, T., and Ely, K. 2011. A meta-analysis of self-regulated learning in work-related training and educational attainment: What we know and where we need to go. *Psychological Bulletin* 137: 421–442.

Sitzmann, T., and Johnson, S. K. 2012. When is ignorance bliss? The effects of inaccurate self-assessments of knowledge on learning and attrition. *Organizational Behavior and Human Decision Processes* 117: 192–207.

Sitzmann, T., Bell, B. S., Kraiger, K., and Kanar, A. M. 2009. A multilevel analysis of the effect of prompting self-regulation in technology-delivered instruction. *Personnel Psychology* 62: 697–734.

Stajkovic, A. D., and Luthans, F. 1998. Self-efficacy and work related performance: A meta-analysis. *Psychological Bulletin* 124: 240–261.

Steele-Johnson, D., Beauregard, R. S., Hoover, P. B., and Schmidt, A. M. 2000. Goal orientation and task demand effects on motivation, affect, and performance. *Journal of Applied Psychology* 85: 724–738.

Thoresen, C. J., Bradley, J. C., Bliese, P. D., and Thoresen, J. D. 2004. The big five personality traits and individual job performance growth trajectories in maintenance and transitional job stages. *Journal of Applied Psychology* 89: 835–853.

Vancouver, J. B., and Kendall, L. N. 2006. When self-efficacy negatively relates to motivation and performance in a learning context. *Journal of Applied Psychology* 91: 1146–1153.

VandeWalle, D., Cron, W. L., and Slocum, J. W. 2001. The role of goal orientation following performance feedback. *Journal of Applied Psychology* 86: 629–640.

Williams, K. J., Donovan, J. J., and Dodge, T. L. 2000. Self-regulation of performance: Goal establishment and goal revision process in athletes. *Human Performance* 13: 159–180.

Winters, D., and Latham, G. 1996. The effect of learning versus outcome goals on a simple versus a complex task. *Group and Organization Management* 21: 236–250.

Yeo, G., Loft, S., Xiao, T., and Kiewitz, C. 2009. Goal orientations and performance: Differential relationships across levels of analysis and as a function of task demands. *Journal of Applied Psychology* 94: 710–726.

Zimmerman, B. J. 2000. Self-efficacy: An essential motive to learn. *Contemporary Educational Psychology* 25: 82–91.

Zimmerman, B. J., and Schunk, D. H., eds., 2011. *Handbook of Self-Regulation of Learning and Performance*. New York: Routledge.

8 Genuine and Perceived Demographic Differences in Training and Development

Tracy C. McCausland and Eden B. King

Social, political, and technological changes have given rise to a workforce comprised of people from a wide range of gender, ethnic, religious, age, and cultural groups. Indeed, the U.S. Census (2013) projects that the proportion of ethnic minorities will exceed the white majority of the U.S. working adult population by the year 2039. Already a number states (California, Texas, New Mexico, and Hawaii) and cities (Baltimore, Dallas, Detroit, Los Angeles, Philadelphia, Phoenix, St. Louis, and San Jose) have majority minority populations (Wazwaz, 2015). The U.S. Census also reveals a population that includes 38 million people born in other countries, more than 40 different religious identity groups, and an aging workforce. Diversity is clearly a reality in contemporary organizations. Unfortunately, evidence on the outcomes of organizational diversity is inconclusive.

On the one hand, evidence suggests that diversity of opinion, expertise, and experience can facilitate decision making and idea generation (Milliken & Martins, 1996). On the other hand, diversity can give rise to problems such as incivility, reduced cohesion, stifled communication, and, sometimes, poorer unit performance (see Joshi & Roh, 2009; van Knippenberg & Schippers, 2007). Thus, the important question is not whether diversity is associated with positive outcomes, but how to ensure that such outcomes are encouraged through effective diversity management practices (see Guilluame et al., 2013; Shore et al., 2009).

An important piece of this diversity management puzzle is equality in developmental experiences; to maximize the benefits of a diverse workforce, all employees need access to high-quality training opportunities. Indeed, the substantial gap between the skills that are required in contemporary organizations and those that are available in the global labor market (Udland, 2016) underscores the need to ensure that *all* workers are engaged in effective training programs. Unfortunately, evidence suggests that all people do not have the same access to development opportunities such as higher education (e.g., Meyer et al., 2013), Moreover, of focus in this chapter, employees do not benefit equally from training programs (e.g., Gully & Chen, 2010; King et al., 2012; McCausland et al., 2015; Shapiro, King, & Quiñones, 2007).

In this chapter, we discuss two dominant scholarly explanations for demographic group differences in training outcomes. The first reason is that there may be genuine, average differences in the individual differences that contribute to training outcomes such as self-efficacy, goal orientation, and motivation to learn (Salas et al., 2012). The second reason for demographic group differences in training is that trainer and trainee expectations – stereotypes – about group members create different training experiences. To describe these perspectives and relevant evidence, we synthesize and examine extant literature on genuine and perceived demographic differences in the training domain. In addition, we introduce possible remedies with hope of kindling efforts to ensure that all workers have equal opportunities to gain job knowledge and skills.

Genuine Demographic Group Differences Relevant to Training

The specific objectives of training programs vary substantially with tasks, learner experience, and organizational contexts, but the overarching premise of training and development activities is that trainees will gain positive learning outcomes in cognitive, affective, and/or skill-based domains (Kraiger, Ford, & Salas, 1993). That is, "learning may be evident from changes in cognitive, affective, or skill capacities" (Kraiger et al., 1993: 311). Here we consider major demographic categories that have salience in the working world – gender, race, age, disability, religion, pregnancy or maternal status, and obesity – that may impact the acquisition of these learning outcomes.

Existing meta-analyses on training have not reported gender or ethnic differences in outcomes, but Colquitt et al. (2000) concluded that the limited evidence of gender differences in training contexts was inconsistent and atheoretical. In the case of ethnicity, Gully and Chen (2010: 18) stated that, "research on the effects of race, nationality, and ethnicity on training outcomes appears relatively scarce." The three meta-analyses that include age differences in training outcomes (Colquitt, LePine, and Noe, 2000; Kubeck et al., 1996; Ng & Feldman, 2008) suggest that age is negatively related to training outcomes in terms of task mastery, declarative knowledge, posttraining self-efficacy, and completion times. Scant research has directly considered training outcomes for the other demographic groups – disability, religion, pregnancy or maternal status, and obesity. Taken together, this pattern of findings suggests that: (1) few overall gender differences likely exist in training outcomes, (2) younger workers may, on average, benefit more from training than older workers, and (3) we do not know whether differences exist among people from different ethnic, ability, religious, family status, and body size groups. The preliminary and limited nature of these conclusions points to the need to explore when and why demographic group memberships might matter.

According to Gully and Chen (2010), the extent to which affective, cognitive, and skill-based learning objectives are achieved in any developmental experience can be explained through intervening mechanisms of information processing capacity, attentional focus and metacognitive processing, motivation and effort allocation, and emotional regulation and control. Though once understudied (Noe, 1986), several individual difference variables have been identified as compelling, proximal pretraining factors that influence these processes, including cognitive ability, self-efficacy, and goal orientation (for a summary, see Salas & Cannon-Bowers, 2001). To the extent that there are robust group differences in these variables, we should anticipate differences in training outcomes.

We next discuss the extent to which empirical evidence suggests that each of these interindividual differences variables reliably relate to key demographic characteristics before turning to some of the contextual features that likely create or exacerbate these differences. It is important to recognize at the onset that these arguments are inextricably intertwined; genuine, average-level differences in variables that influence training effectiveness likely derive from some of the same stereotypic expectations that influence training effectiveness. This self-reinforcing cycle likely exacerbates the challenge of ensuring universal opportunity for benefiting from training programs. Although we discuss the evidence of genuine and perceived differences in benefits from training separately, we nonetheless view these as inherently linked phenomena.

Demographic Group Differences in Cognitive Ability Test Scores

Gully and Chen (2010) argued convincingly, based on multiple meta-analytic estimates (e.g., Colquitt et al., 2000; Hunter & Hunter, 1984), that cognitive ability is a strong predictor of training outcomes. Indeed, an indicator of the ability to learn, general cognitive ability, is "associated with the increased ability to acquire, process, and synthesize information, allowing for more rapid acquisition, application, and generalization of knowledge to new domains" (Gully & Chen, 2010: 9). It is therefore important to consider whether evidence suggests that there are consistent subgroup differences in cognitive ability that could ultimately influence training outcomes.

Evidence assessing demographic differences in general cognitive ability is voluminous, multidisciplinary, and hotly debated. For some groups, there do seem to be small but consistent differences in performance on tests of general cognitive ability (Sackett et al., 2001; see Chapter 6 for more detailed description of specific mental abilities). We focus here on these differences in *test performance* – rather than cognitive ability– to recognize that there are numerous explanations for these differences (e.g., item biases, testing contexts, educational resources) that are not indicative of differences in general cognitive ability.

Gender, Race, and Age
In their review of adverse impact in personnel selection procedures, Hough, Oswald, and Ployhart (2001) summarized existing findings pertaining to gender, race, and age differences in cognitive ability test scores. Focusing on general mental ability (rather than its facets), the authors reported approximate mean level differences of -1.0 for black/white, -.5 for Hispanic/white, .2 for East Asian/white, .0 for women/men, and -.4 for older/younger adults. This can be interpreted to suggest that scores on cognitive ability tests favor white, Asian, and younger adults, particularly compared to black and Hispanic adults, and that there are no overall differences in the general mental ability test scores of men and women.

Disability

For the even less-studied subgroups of people from different ability, religious, parental status, and body size groups, there is preliminary evidence to suggest that there may be some overall, omnibus differences in cognitive ability test scores. Certainly, some types of disability would influence scores on cognitive ability tests (e.g., dyslexia), but physical disabilities are unlikely to have any influence on such performance, provided that any necessary accommodations are made to allow for a fair testing environment.

Religion

In the case of religion, a meta-analysis of 63 studies yielded a small to moderate negative correlation between scores on intelligence measures and religiosity (mean r = -.23 among adults; Zuckerman, Silberman, & Hall, 2013). These findings were explained by potential differences in conformity, analytic versus intuitive styles of thinking, and sources of coping, and point to an interesting direction for future scholarship on the intersection between religion and work.

Parental Status

Focusing next on parents and pregnant women, there is no theoretical reason to anticipate that becoming a parent (or carrying a fetus) would impact cognitive ability test scores beyond the impact of sleep deprivation (Lim & Dinges, 2010). Literature on pregnancy and parenting instead focuses more appropriately on *children's* intelligence test scores in relation to their parents' experiences and backgrounds.

Obesity

A recent systematic review and meta-analysis on the relationship between obesity and intelligence (Yu et al., 2010) included 26 studies across the developmental life span. The results suggest that in children (weighted mean difference of obese vs. nonobese preschoolers = -15.1), obesity was negatively correlated with performance on tests of general intelligence. However, the overall relationship between intelligence test scores and obesity was eliminated when participants' education was considered, suggesting that obesity may be more directly related to education than intelligence.

Taking these findings together, there is reason to anticipate that there may be overarching subgroup differences in training outcomes. To the extent that cognitive ability test scores relate to training outcomes, we would expect that white and Asian, younger, less religious, and thinner trainees would gain more knowledge and skill on average from training than black, Hispanic, older, more religious, and obese trainees. Importantly, the extent to which people from each of these groups are likely to gain confidence or attitude change is an open question.

Demographic Group Differences in Self-Efficacy

If cognitive ability represents the "can do" capability for training, self-efficacy represents the "belief that one can do." The belief in one's ability to achieve the outcomes of interest, whether affective, cognitive, or skill based, has an important impact on trainee motivation and performance. Colquitt et al. (2000) reported strong meta-analytic relationships between self-efficacy and motivation to learn ($r = .42$) and transfer of training ($r = .47$) as well as job performance ($r = .22$). Whether gender, race, age, religion, parental status, and body size differences exist in self-efficacy is therefore an important question in the interest of maximizing training outcomes. Substantial research on subgroup differences in self-efficacy (and the closely related constructs of self-esteem and core self-evaluations, which represent more general views of one's value and worth) has been conducted over the past 50 years.

Gender

Indeed, meta-analytic studies of gender differences in self-esteem that include nationally representative samples show small, yet consistent differences favoring men and boys across the life span (e.g., Kling et al., 1999). That is, on average, men tend to view themselves as having more worth and value than do women. Similarly, an international examination focusing on gender differences in science, technology, engineering, and math performance and attitudes found that men tend to have greater self-confidence in mathematics and greater overall self-efficacy (Else-Quest, Hyde, & Linn, 2010). These differences were strongest in countries wherein there were gender discrepancies in school enrollment, proportional share of research jobs, and representation in parliamentary or government roles, pointing to cultural determinants of men and women's self-concept.

Race

A counterintuitive finding regarding the self-esteem of ethnic minorities has emerged in multiple meta-analyses: People from some ethnic minority backgrounds tend to report higher levels of self-esteem than do people from the majority (white) group. The general results of Gray-Little and Hafdahl's meta-analysis (2000) comparing the academic self-esteem of black and white youth are generally consistent with the broader study of Twenge and Crocker (2002), which showed that black people on average have somewhat higher self-esteem than white people (ds $= .15 - .20$). Importantly, the self-esteem of white people tended to be higher than that of Hispanic, American Indian, and especially Asian people. Thus, ethnic group differences in self-esteem emerge in distinct patterns depending on the specific cultural heritage, suggesting that there are unique dynamics and relationships that foster self-esteem between and within some ethnic groups. Interestingly, these meta-analytic effects varied with age such that the patterns reversed among older black and white people (Twenge & Crocker, 2002).

Age

In a separate study of self-esteem contrasting chronological age and birth cohort relations, Twenge and Campbell (2001) found that scores on the Rosenberg self-esteem scale increase with age. Though there was also evidence in nonmonotonic change during adolescence, as well as some evidence of birth cohort effects, self-esteem seems to have a weak positive association with age. Additional evidence suggests that increases in self-esteem may stall after young adulthood (Huang, 2010), when the self-concept may stabilize.

Disability

The label or classification of disability may influence the degree to which people see themselves as capable and worthy. Evidence suggests that the degree to which disability status reduces self-esteem seems to be dependent upon the nature of the disability (e.g., minor vs. major), age, and adjustment. For example, a meta-analysis of people with mental illness showed a strong relationship between internalized stigma of mental illness and self-esteem (random effect size = -.55; Livingston & Boyd, 2010). In a study of women with physical disabilities, the severity of disability was negatively related with self-esteem ($r = -.17$; Nosek et al., 2003). In general, having a disability may cause people to question their self-esteem and, possibly, self-efficacy.

Religion

Religiosity, to the contrary, seems to bolster views of the self as competent. Religiosity may provide meaning and purpose as well as strong social support systems that enhance views of the self. Indeed, the degree to which people practice organized religion and believe in a higher power seems to be positively correlated with their self-concept (Ellison, 1991; Krause, 1995; Schieman, Pudrovska, & Milkie, 2005; Wilson & Musick, 1996).

Parental Status

Strong theoretical rationale suggests that being or becoming a parent may confer similar psychological benefits. According to an expansionist perspective of work and family (Barnett & Hyde, 2001), and in line with role enrichment theories (e.g., Greenhaus & Powell, 2006), involvement in multiple roles in different contexts can yield enhancements in each domain. This boost may include self-efficacy; a person's success in one role may help them feel more competent in another role. Qualitative data suggest that the ways women see their abilities in work and pregnancy roles are indeed interrelated (Ladge, Clair, & Greenberg, 2012), and data from a Norwegian survey suggest that mothers reported higher self-esteem than women without children (Hansen, Slagsvold, & Moum, 2009). This rationale and limited evidence suggests that there may be some benefits of parenthood to self-efficacy.

Obesity

Conversely, people who are obese may be particularly likely to report low self-efficacy. Obese individuals often see themselves as culpable for their condition and hold negative beliefs and attitudes about being heavy. This translates into low levels of self-esteem (Crandall & Biernat, 1990; Crocker, Cornwell, & Major, 1993), and likely low self-efficacy.

In sum, evidence suggests that men and people who are black, older, religious, and thinner may have more positive views of their own abilities than women and people who are from other ethnic groups, younger, less religious, and heavier. To the extent that self-efficacy (and self-esteem) gives rise to training outcomes, these differences may yield demographic group disparities in training effectiveness.

Demographic Group Differences in Goal Orientation

Goal orientation, whether conceptualized as trait or state variability in orientation toward achievement, represents the extent to which individuals desire to demonstrate their ability (performance goal orientation) as compared to their desire to demonstrate their ability or competence in the task (learning goal orientation; Dweck, 1986). A slightly newer variable of scholarly attention than cognitive ability and self-efficacy, goal orientation has nonetheless been linked consistently with training outcomes. Overall, higher levels of learning goal orientation promote more positive training outcomes, whereas higher levels of performance goal orientation seem to have a negative impact on training effectiveness (e.g., Brett & VandeWalle, 1999; Heimbeck et al., 2003; Kozlowski et al., 2001). This may be due to the distinct motivational profiles of these orientations – individuals who are motivated to engage and understand versus individuals who are motivated to be successful and avoid failure – that create different approach and avoidance patterns in response to training tasks.

The growing body of evidence on goal orientation has paid little attention to potential demographic differences. A meta-analysis of correlates of goal orientation (Payne, Youngcourt, & Beaubien, 2007) indicated that, "we found no substantial bivariate relationships between trait goal orientation (GO) and sex and age. That said, it might be fruitful to examine interactions between GO dimensions and these demographic characteristics . . . [and] the relationship between GO and ethnicity might also be explored as more cross-cultural GO research is conducted" (143). A striking lack of evidence of demographic differences in goal orientation makes it impossible to derive reliable predictions.

Summary

The preceding review of empirical evidence on interindividual differences for learning outcomes and intervening mechanisms suggests that there are genuine demographic differences on key variables related to training and development. Certainly, this conclusion is concerning; yet these interpretations should be considered with caution given: (1) the lack of evidence to directly tie many demographic groups with cognitive and skill-based learning outcomes, (2) the complex relationship between perceived and genuine differences described in the preceding text, and (3) the limited evidence in many areas. Next, we review an alternative, although inextricably linked, approach to explaining demographic differences in training, which draws from the fundamental principles of social perception and cognition.

Perceived Demographic Group Differences Relevant to Training

According to social categorization perspectives (e.g., Tajfel, 1981), people automatically perceive and categorize other people based on their membership to known and socially meaningful groups. Different groups of people are often associated with characteristics *typical* of that group, which are guided by mental structures learned through socialization and personal experiences. In turn, these mental structures (i.e., schemas) influence how people select, interpret, and remember information. Ultimately, these characterizations translate into oversimplified labels. A stereotype is just an exaggerated belief about a category of people (Allport, 1979) and stereotyping occurs when identical characteristics are assigned to all persons in a particular group, regardless of actual variation between group members (Aronson, Wilson, & Akert, 2010).

To the extent that stereotypes are based on accurate experiences, they may be an efficient and useful manner to organize knowledge about the social world. They impose structure and meaning on complex perceptual processes. However, to the extent that stereotypes are used to justify behavior toward a whole group of people, blind to individuating information, they are harmful (Allport, 1979). Adaptive or maladaptive, favorable or unfavorable, the role of stereotypes in training merit further discussion because regardless of whether an individual endorses them, stereotypes are widely shared and known to most (Johns, Schmader, & Martens, 2005). This underscores the possible – albeit likely unintended – consequences of stereotypes. Specifically, stereotypes may affect interpersonal judgments (i.e., evaluations of others) as well as intrapersonal judgments (i.e., evaluations about the self). As such, we will organize our discussion of how stereotypes may alter the training experience from these two vantage points. Indeed, our emphasis on a dual perspective (evaluations of others and the self) as well as supporting rationale aligns with a comprehensive stereotype-based theory supported by meta-analytic evidence (Leslie, Mayer, & Kravitz, 2014).

Stereotypes Influence Trainers' Evaluations

The stereotype content model (Cuddy, Fiske, & Glick, 2007; Fiske et al., 2002) offers a theoretical explanation, supported by empirical results, of why we should be mindful of others' stereotypes. The theory posits that the content of stereotypes varies along the dimensions of warmth (e.g., warm, tolerant, sincere) and competence (e.g., competent, capable, confident) and the appraisal of a group's standing on warmth and competence stems from the assessment of a group's standing on status and competition. Fiske and colleagues argue that these fundamental perceptions of warmth and competence may be derived from survival (i.e., evolutionary) motives; it is important from an evolutionary perspective to know whether others are likely to harm you and whether they have the necessary abilities to do so. Across diverse samples of participants, groups perceived as high status are viewed as possessing competence and groups perceived as competitors are viewed as lacking warmth (Cuddy et al., 2007; Eckes, 2002; Fiske et al., 2002). These dimensions form a 2 (warmth: high, low) by 2 (competence: high, low) matrix facilitating four warmth-competence combinations (warm-incompetent, warm-competent, cold-incompetent, cold-competent).

Each combination is associated with a distinct affective reaction (pity, admiration, contempt, and envy, respectively). These affective reactions may in turn predispose individuals to exhibit behaviors corresponding to a particular emotion (Caprariello, Cuddy, & Fiske, 2009; Talaska, Fiske, & Chaiken, 2008). For example, an individual experiencing contempt (an affective reaction) toward a target may result in that individual showing less interest, terminating the interaction sooner, and/or displaying less positivity (e.g., Hebl et al., 2002) as compared to if that individual was experiencing admiration for the target. Whether these behaviors are positive (e.g., encouragement) or negative (e.g., harassment), the basis for this behavior is the target's group membership, which is discrimination. Of course, discrimination is most commonly associated with unfair treatment and thus negative behaviors are of primary concern.

Stereotypes provide perceivers with initial expectations about the attributes and behaviors that members of a particular group are likely to display, which can influence judgments in two predictable ways (Biernat & Vescio, 2002). First, stereotype-based expectations can serve as interpretive frames that guide the encoding and processing of information (e.g., older trainees have a lower ability to learn; Heilman, 1984). Second, stereotype-based expectations can serve as benchmarks for which a particular group is compared (e.g., this trainee learns quickly. . . *for an older employee*; Hilton & von Hippel, 1996). Reliance on stereotypes for initial assessments may be more likely when available information is limited or ambiguous (Fiske & Neuberg, 1990; Heilman, Martell, & Simon, 1988). Moreover, in line with the prototype matching process (Heilman, 1983; Perry, 1994), the salience of a stereotype may be highlighted (or not) in certain contexts (e.g., industries, companies, jobs). Specifically, an individual is compared to what is prototypical under the circumstances (e.g., a prototypical trainee) and the greater the discrepancy between the individual and the prototype, the more an individual's group membership will be emphasized.

In the current context, there is reason to anticipate subgroup differences in training and developmental outcomes stemming from trainers' stereotypic expectations. To be clear, we do not argue that stereotypes will *always* result in discriminatory behavior; however, under certain circumstances, research suggests that the likelihood of stereotype-based expectations influencing behaviors may be increased. For instance, when a perceiver is not motivated or able to devote sufficient resources to observe, assess, and incorporate individuating information then the perceiver will be unable to thoughtfully consider and potentially revise his/her initial evaluation. One condition under which this assessment process may be bypassed is when the immediate environment is demanding (e.g., time pressures, juggling multiple requirements) causing cognitive resources to be limited (i.e., "cognitive busyness"). Consequently, individuals rely more heavily on automatic processing (i.e., using stereotypes) as opposed to controlled processing (i.e., pursing accurate information). In addition to limited resources, the maintenance or revisal of these initial stereotype-based expectations also depends on other condition such as confirmation biases (i.e., the tendency to search for, interpret, or recall information in a way that confirms one's beliefs), flexibility of expectations, and the strength of disconfirming evidence (Jussim, 1986). For example, a white trainer who has little exposure to Hispanic people and has insufficient time to get to know a particular Hispanic trainee may make stereotypic assumptions about their ability and motivation.

In the remainder of this section, anchored in the principles of the stereotype content model, we discuss the limited body of work investigating the extent to which stereotypes of social groups may guide trainers' expectations and ultimately affect training and development outcomes.

Gender

As evident by the ambivalent sexism framework (Glick & Fiske, 1996), sex-related stereotypes have received an abundance of theoretical and empirical attention. Research suggests that the perceptions of women are contingent on context, such that women who work outside the home (i.e., occupy non-traditional roles) are viewed as being low on warmth and high on competence (Cuddy, Fiske, & Glick, 2004; Eckes, 2002). Given this warmth-competence combination, they are viewed as worthy of respect, but elicit jealousy and/or animosity (see Cuddy et al., 2007). In turn, we would not expect business women to be disadvantaged in training. Indeed, in a formal training setting, there is little to no evidence suggesting a systematic bias against women in the form of lower trainer evaluations.

Race

Similar to sex, racially based stereotypes are dependent upon context. Accordingly, black professionals – like business women – are perceived as competent, but lacking warmth (Fiske et al., 2002). Given the higher standing on competence, one would not expect black professionals to be disadvantaged. However, poor blacks (that may nonetheless be working) are viewed as low on warmth and competence, suggesting this assessment will elicit contempt, which could translate into poorer training outcomes. We do note that in other contexts (e.g., education) research has provided evidence of lowered expectations and differential treatment because of perceived intellectual inferiority (e.g., Rubovits & Maehr, 1973).

Age

Based on extensive research investigating the content of age stereotypes in the workplace (e.g., Finkelstein, Ryan, & King, 2013; Posthuma & Campion, 2009), older workers are perceived to be high on warmth (more stable, dependable, and trustworthy), but also low on competence (resistant to change, lower ability to learn, and technophobic). This mixed stereotype of high warmth and low competence has shown to elicit emotions such as pity and sympathy (Fiske et al., 2002), which – in a training environment – is likely to create lower access and expectations for success (e.g., mastery of the material, time to complete), as compared to their younger counterparts. Scholars have speculated that stereotype-based expectations are contributing to older trainees' poorer performance (see Landy, Shankster-Cawley, & Moran, 1995; Shore & Goldberg, 2004) and only recently has this hypothesis received empirical attention. In an experimental study, researchers experimentally manipulated the perceived age in trainer-trainee dyads (all participants age 30 or below) through false photos and voice distortion software (McCausland et al., 2015). Findings support, as compared to younger trainees, ostensibly older trainees evoked negative expectancies when training for a new, technological task, which ultimately manifested in poorer training interactions and trainer evaluations of trainee performance. However, trainee performance was not ultimately affected. However, it should be noted that if these results held in programs where the only measure of trainee success was trainer evaluation, then older trainees would have been judged to be less successful than younger trainees.

An interesting boundary condition to this finding may depend on the familiarity of the skill or knowledge to be acquired. For instance, if the task is completely novel, as in the previously discussed study (McCausland et al., 2015), then a negative relationship between age and expectations may emerge. However, if the task can take advantage of and build upon an existing knowledge and skill base, stereotypic expectations could convey a complicated story. In fact, older workers may be advantaged in such situations because older trainees are believed to be experienced, knowledgeable, and hardworking (Finkelstein et al., 2013). In contrast, younger workers are perceived to be inexperienced, and – according to middle-aged workers – lazy and unmotivated (Finkelstein et al., 2013). When and how learning related, age stereotypes are relevant and may affect others' behavior merits future attention.

Disability

Similar to older employees, disabled persons are also often viewed as having high warmth and low competence (Cuddy, Norton, & Fiske, 2005; Fiske et al, 2002), thus tending to elicit pity and/or a paternalistic response (Cuddy et al., 2007). Extending findings from older trainees, one could reasonably assume that disabled individuals may provoke similar expectations (i.e., a lower expectation for success than a nondisabled person) and therefore receive differential treatment from a trainer leading to poorer training outcomes. Although – to our knowledge – this social group has not been examined empirically in a training context.

Parental Status

There is no evidence – that we are aware of – directly investigating the influence of parental status on trainer expectations. Indeed, most trainers would likely be unaware of this information because parenthood is not an observable characteristic. Nonetheless, there is extant research to suggest that parental status, if known, may impact others' judgments of competence (Cuddy, Fiske, & Glick, 2004; Ridgeway & Correll, 2004) and commitment (Correll, Benard, & Paik, 2007; King, 2008). Interesting, working fathers do not appear affected by parenthood, if anything they benefit from this status in terms of perceived warmth as compared to working men with no children. However, motherhood negatively affects working mothers, such that perceived competence and commitment decreases, as compared to women with no children. By extension, these decrements in perceived competence and commitment would likely be accompanied with lower trainer expectations for success. Following this logic, we expect pregnant women to be subject to the same expectations of working mothers, and, visible pregnancy may exacerbate these already negative judgments.

Religion

Perhaps the most studied religious groups are Jews, Christians, and Muslims (Fiske et al., 2002). Indeed, Jews are frequently used as the exemplar for the mixed stereotype of high on competence and low on warmth. By contrast, Christians are assumed to be the cultural default group (i.e., in-group) and perceived as high on both competence and warmth. Finally, Muslims are evaluated to be nondescript, or rather middle of both the competence and warmth dimensions. Taken together, it appears that Christians would be most benefited from their religious affiliation in terms of trainers' evaluations, followed by Jews, and then Muslims. Again, we are not aware of empirical research on this topic.

Obesity

Stereotypes held about obese individuals, as compared to average-weight individuals, appear to be uniformly negative (less active, self-disciplined, intelligent, and successful; Hebl, 1997; Pingitore et al., 1994; Ryckman et al., 1989) such that obese individuals are rated low on warmth and competence (Hebl et al., 2012). Experimentally manipulating weight (by depicting a false photograph of a trainee as either obese or average), influenced trainer expectations and evaluations of the training and trainee (Shapiro, King, & Quiñones, 2007). Specifically, relative to trainers of the average weight trainees, trainers of obese trainees expected less success and less work ethic from their obese trainees as well as evaluated the overall training experience more negatively. In addition, individuals portrayed as obese trainees (note that individuals were unaware of the picture manipulation) evaluated their trainer and training more negatively, as compared to individuals portrayed as average weight trainees. Although trainees in the obese condition did not perform more poorly on the task, exploratory analyses suggest that trainees portrayed as obese with *inflexible trainers* (i.e., individuals unwilling to revise initial expectations) performed worse on the task.

Stereotypes Influence Trainees' Self-Evaluations

As previously reviewed, the content of stereotypes is widely known (Johns et al., 2005) such that the characteristics deemed typical to a social group are known to individuals outside of that social group, as well as to those within that social group. Therefore, assuming the far-reaching effects of stereotypes are limited to perceivers (i.e., out-group members) is unrealistic. On the contrary, there is evidence to suggest that stigmatized groups internalize and come to endorse societal expectations associated with stereotypes. To the extent that people are situationally or chronically preoccupied with negative stereotypes about their group, they may possess fewer of the cognitive and emotional resources that are required to learn new information and skills (Gully & Chen, 2010). In addition, Roberson and Kulik (2007) argue that initial poor performance on such tasks can be negatively reinforcing as frustrations rise and motivations decline. In the following we discuss research surrounding stereotype threat – broadly defined as the concern about the risk of confirming a negative, group-relevant stereotype (e.g., Steel, 1997; Steele & Aronson, 1995; Steele, Spencer, & Aronson, 2002); that is, stereotype threat is "the apprehension people feel when performing in a domain in which their group is stereotyped to lack ability" (Aronson & Inzlicht, 2004: 830).

Stereotype threat is precipitated by the priming of relevant stereotypes due to certain situational cues; therefore, stereotype threat is a context-dependent phenomenon (e.g., women have low abilities *in math*). Stereotype threat differs from stereotype priming in that the target internalizes this fear, which – in turn – places additional burdens on the target to disprove the stereotype, ultimately interfering with the learning process (Marx, 2012). Moreover, the internalization of this fear may be initiated from the targets' personal evaluations (self-as-source) or the targets' fear of other's evaluations (other-as-source; Shapiro & Neuberg, 2007).

Self-as-source threat stems from one's recognition of belonging to a negatively stereotyped group, which can occur even when one knows that others are unaware of this group membership (e.g., only Jackson knows his diagnosis of clinical depression). Other-as-source stereotype threat occurs when an individual believes that his/her stereotype-relevant is available to others, at the time of one's performance. Key to other-as-source categorization is the *believed* public visibility of one's stereotype-relevant performance; even though, the stereotype-relevant behavior can occur privately (e.g., only Jackson knows his performance on a stereotype-relevant exam). Much of the stereotype threat research examines threats encountered by ethnic minorities and women (e.g., Nguyen & Ryan, 2008), but emerging research confirms that other groups may experience similar challenges (see Roberson & Kulik, 2007). We argue that both self- and other-sources of threat can impact the way that people from diverse backgrounds experience and perform in training contexts.

Gender

The overwhelming majority of stereotype threat research as it pertains to gender has focused on the ways that stereotypes of women's math and leadership abilities can lead to their underperformance in these domains (see Nguyen & Ryan, 2008). And, indeed, it is possible that women who are involved in training programs that focus on these masculine-stereotyped domains are susceptible to stereotype threat effects. Importantly, however, stereotype threat can impact any domain in which a stereotype exists and is accessible. In the case of gender and training, this means that both men and women can also experience apprehension and reduced-performance stereotyped domains. For example, women may underperform in difficult physical training contexts and men may underperform in challenging interpersonal training programs. Indeed, men made more errors on an emotion identification task when they were reminded that, "men are not as apt as women to deal with affect" (Koenig & Eagly, 2005). It follows that the nature of the training task and its framing can determine how it is interpreted – and how it impacts the involvement, experience, and performance of both men and women – through the lens of gender stereotypes. Indeed, employees might even be less likely to attend training that raises stereotype confirmation concerns.

Race

Stereotype threat research has demonstrated that black and Latino people are aware of stereotypes that they lack intellectual ability, and that activating these stereotypes can give rise to underperformance through stereotype threat (Steele & Aronson, 1995). This powerful stereotype about the greater cognitive abilities of majority racial group members (i.e., white people) compared to minority racial group members is persistent and pervasive (Fiske et al., 2002; Katz & Braly, 1933). Given this, it would be surprising if stereotype threat did *not* emerge for racial minorities in any training task that is cognitively oriented. Like gender, however, there are domains in which some racial minority groups are positively stereotyped. For example, in tests of "natural athletic ability," white – and other not black – men were susceptible to stereotype threat effects on their performance (Stone et al., 1999). In contrast to cognitively loaded domains, training that emphasizes athletic or other physical abilities may therefore make white men vulnerable to stereotype threat.

Age

A growing body of evidence has directly assessed the ways in which age stereotypes create stereotype threat. Lamont, Swift, and Abrams (2015) summarized this research in a meta-analysis of 22 published and 10 unpublished papers. The results confirmed that age stereotypes do give rise to a small to medium stereotype threat effect overall (d = .28), and that this effect is largest in tests of cognitive performance. Only two studies were identified that considered skill acquisition specifically, so the effect of threat in training cannot be isolated using meta-analysis. Yet, findings that memory and cognitive performance of older people were impacted by stereotype threat suggests that training performance would be similarly influenced. It is possible, though untested, that stereotypes about younger workers could influence their performance in stereotyped domains, such as those requiring "wisdom," "patience," or "technological savvy" (see Finkelstein et al., 2013).

Disability

People with disabilities are also aware of and concerned about stereotypes regarding their abilities (Shapiro, 2011). People with a head injury, for example, performed worse on cognitive tests after stereotypes about their abilities were made salient (Suhr & Gunstad, 2002). Interestingly, Silverman and Cohen (2014) found that affirming the value of blind participants broke down chronic stereotype threat effects and bolstered their self-confidence, ultimately improving their performance in a skill-training program. These findings not only confirm the influence of stereotype threat on training performance for people with disabilities, but also suggest a strategy for overcoming these effects.

Religion

People who are religious tend to identify strongly with that part of their identity and eschew negative stereotypes of their group (Shapiro, 2011). Yet nonetheless, when considering their religion, people report substantial other-as-source stereotype threats; that is, they are concerned about how other people perceive their group and how their performance may reflect on their group. We would not anticipate that religion would be highly salient in most training contexts, but in cases where it is (e.g., for people who are visibly identified as members of a minority religion), religious minorities may be apprehensive about how they appear to others.

Parental Status

We could not identify any research that has directly assessed the role of stereotype threat on parents' beliefs, emotions, or behaviors. Yet, there is compelling reason to anticipate that – like other targets of negative stereotypes – parents can also be impacted by the detrimental effects of stereotype threat.

Obesity

Stereotypes of obese people as lazy, unreliable, and low-skilled may permeate obese employee's self-views. Indeed, as Carlson and Seacat (2014) summarize, evidence suggest that obese people often experience reduced self-esteem, depression, and anxiety as a result of a negative self-concept. Research has also shown that stereotype threat can negatively influence health-related behaviors of obese people (Major et al., 2014; Seacat & Mickelson, 2009). To the extent that obese trainees are reminded of negative stereotypes that are relevant to the training task, they may similarly experience negative cognitive, emotional, and performance implications while engaged in training.

Taken together, this rationale and evidence suggests that some genuine group differences might impact training effectiveness, but that the role of stereotypes in shaping both trainers' and trainees' expectations and behaviors cannot be overlooked. We next describe future research opportunities to explore and address each of these potential sources of inequality.

Future Research Directions

Given the evidence for demographic-based differences in training, one particular concern is the how to adapt training to meet the needs of certain demographic groups. In the following section, we explore three distinct approaches in making efforts toward eliminating these subgroup discrepancies: culturally competent trainers, individually tailored training programs, and group-specific training programs.

Culturally Competent Trainers

This avenue for reducing subgroup discrepancies focuses on modifying the expectations and behaviors of trainers. The basic idea is to increase the cultural competence of trainers, thereby reducing the stereotypes that influence training outcomes. It is noteworthy that this approach follows an identity-conscious, rather than identity-blind, perspective (Konrad & Linnehan, 1995), requiring that trainers explicitly acknowledge potential subgroup stereotypes and differences that are relevant to training. As an example, culturally competent trainers might be aware of stereotypes about the development of older workers, and so could actively compensate for both their own stereotypes and the stereotype threat potentially experienced by older trainees.

The question of how to increase trainers' cultural competence is, of course, complex. Evidence about reducing and avoiding discrimination is limited both in frequency and scope (Paluck & Green, 2009). Recent meta-analyses (Bezrukova et al., 2014; Kalinoski et al., 2013) suggest that the best practices in diversity training programs – the goals of which typically focus on enhancing cultural competence– include several elements. First, diversity training programs are most effective when they are paired with more comprehensive or systematic efforts to increase diversity and inclusion. Second, diversity programs that target not only awareness of diversity issues but also specific skills relevant to diversity are the most effective. Third, diversity programs that occur over a period promote more positive outcomes than single, short programs. To increase the cultural competence of trainers, then, the trainers must engage in targeted and systematic experiences that bolster their awareness and skills.

Individually Tailored Training Programs

Following the aptitude–treatment interaction approach (Snow, 1989), this avenue involves modifying the content and/or delivery of training to meet the unique needs of individual trainees. To overcome the potentially destructive effects of stereotypes and stereotype threat, it might be helpful to directly address and reduce the specific stereotypes that are relevant for trainees considering the training task. For example, to avoid the effects of stereotypes and stereotype threat for older workers being trained on a cognitively demanding and technologically rich task, both trainers and trainees should be reminded of the learning potential of potentially targeted trainees through techniques such as automatic matching of pictured images in training materials with the demographic characteristics of individual trainees. Building efficacy among trainees may reduce stereotype threat apprehension and directly contradicting trainers' stereotypes might improve their instruction (see McCausland, 2014). Implementing such tailored approaches requires careful analysis of the trainees' demographics relative to dominant stereotypes and in relation to the nature of the task being trained. Matching the approach with the specific threat experienced by the particular set of trainees is likely to yield the most productive outcomes (Shapiro, Williams, & Hambarchyan, 2013).

Group-Specific Training Programs

Group-specific training programs refer to learning opportunities that are designed for and available to specific groups of workers. Of course, how groups are determined is critically important. When group membership is based on a psychological construct (e.g., expertise) or a job-relevant specialization, then this recommendation is unlikely to be problematic because, indeed, this practice is quite common. For example, an organization offers continuous training on a particular software program; however, courses are made available only to software engineers and broken into three versions, depending on expertise: Level I, II, and III. In contrast, when group membership is based on a demographic characteristic then this recommendation immediately becomes contentious, with good reason. Legal realities (such as the Age Discrimination in Employment Act of 1967) that prohibit differential access to opportunities as a function of age are likely to make widespread implementation unrealistic and ill-advised; however, there is some evidence to suggest this approach may be beneficial for certain demographic groups.

Preliminary research for chronological age – from domains outside of the training literature – warrant discussion. Avery, McKay, and Wilson (2007) found that when older workers were satisfied with their co-workers, perceived age similarity among co-workers was associated with higher levels of engagement for older workers, as compared to younger workers. Libermann et al. (2013) examined the influence of age similarity for teams on individual team members' health and found, the health of older and younger team members (as compared to middle-age team members) was negatively affected in age diverse teams. Interestingly, it was not age diversity per se, but the stereotypes that older and younger team members held, that exacerbated the negative impact. This suggests that by creating homogenous training groups, it is possible that stereotypes and stereotype threats are reduced, or that they are simply less salient. This, of course, allows for students' cognitive resources to be devoted to learning as opposed to worrying about disproving well-known stereotypes.

Conclusion

In this chapter, we examined literature on demographic group differences in training outcomes through two primary perspectives: (1) genuine, average differences in the individual differences and (2) perceived differences stemming from stereotype-based expectations. Additionally, we introduced possible remedies to reduce such demographic-group differences. In the training domain, demographic groups continue to be an understudied topic and it is our hope that this review will spark future investigation to better understand and eliminate such learning-related discrepancies so that all workers have equal opportunities to gain the requisite knowledge and skills.

References

Allport, G. W. 1979. *The Nature of Prejudice.* Cambridge, MA: Perseus Books.

Aronson, E., Wilson, T. D., and Akert, R. M. 2010. Interpersonal attraction: From first impressions to close relationships. *Social Psychology* 286–321.

Aronson, J., and Inzlicht, M. 2004. The ups and downs of attributional ambiguity: Stereotype vulnerability and the academic self-knowledge of African American college students. *Psychological Science* 15: 829–836.

Avery, D. R., McKay, P. F., and Wilson, D. C. 2007. Engaging the aging workforce: The relationship between perceived age similarity, satisfaction with coworkers, and employee engagement. *Journal of Applied Psychology* 92: 1542–1556.

Barnett, R. C., and Hyde, J. S. 2001. Women, men, work, and family: An expansionist Theory. *American Psychologist* 56: 781–796.

Bezrukova, Y., Spell, C. S., Perry, J. L., and Jehn, K. A. 2014. A meta-analytical integration of over 40 years of research on diversity training evaluation. In *Academy of Management Proceedings* 14813. Briarcliff, NY: Academy of Management.

Biernat, M., and Vescio, T. K. 2002. She swings, she hits, she's great, she's benched: Shifting judgment standards and behavior. *Personality and Social Psychology Bulletin* 28: 66–76.

Brett, J. F., and VandeWalle, D. 1999. Goal orientation and goal content as predictors of performance in a training program. *Journal of Applied Psychology* 84(6): 863–873.

Caprariello, P. A., Cuddy, A. J. C., and Fiske, S.T. 2009. Social structure shapes cultural stereotypes and emotions: A causal test of the stereotype content model. *Group Processes and Intergroup Relations* 12: 147–155.

Carlson, J. H. and Seacat, J. D. 2014. Multiple threat: Overweight/obese women in the workplace. *Industrial and Organizational Psychology* 7: 482–487.

Colquitt, J. A., LePine, J. A., and Noe, R. N. 2000. Toward an integrative theory of training motivation: A meta-analytic path analysis of 20 years of research. *Journal of Applied Psychology* 85: 678–707.

Correll, S. J., Benard, S., and Paik, I. 2007. Getting a job: Is there a motherhood penalty? *American Journal of Sociology* 112: 1297–1339.

Crandall, C., and Biernat, M. 1990. The ideology of anti-fat attitudes. *Journal of Applied Social Psychology* 20: 227–243.

Crocker, J., Cornwell, B., and Major, B. 1993. The stigma of overweight: Affective consequences of attributional ambiguity. *Journal of Personality and Social Psychology* 64: 60–70.

Cuddy, A. J. C., Fiske, S. T., and Glick, P. 2004. When professionals become mothers, warmth doesn't cut the ice. *Journal of Social Issues* 60: 701–718.

Cuddy, A. J. C., Fiske, S. T., and Glick, P. 2007. The BIAS Map: Behaviors from intergroup affect and stereotypes. *Journal of Personality and Social Psychology* 92: 631–648.

Cuddy, A. J. C., Norton, M. I., and Fiske, S. T. 2005. This old stereotype: The stubbornness and pervasiveness of the elderly stereotype. *Journal of Social Issues* 61: 265–283.

Dweck, C. S. 1986. Motivational processes affecting learning. *American Psychologist* 41: 1040–1048.

Eckes, T. 2002. Paternalistic and envious gender stereotypes: Testing predictions from the stereotype content model. *Sex Roles* 47: 99–114.

Ellison, C. G. 1991. Religious involvement and subjective well-being. *Journal of Health and Social Behavior* 32: 80–99.

Else-Quest, N. M., Hyde J. S., and Linn, M. C. 2010. Cross-national patterns of gender differences in mathematics: A meta-analysis. *Psychological Bulletin* 136: 103–127.

Finkelstein, L., Ryan, K., and King, E. B. 2013. What do the young (old people think of me? Content and accuracy of age-based metastereotypes. *European Journal of Work and Organizational Psychology* 22: 633–657.

Fiske, S. T., and Neuberg, S. L. 1990. A continuum model of impression formation, from category-based to individuating processes: Influence of information and motivation on attention and interpretation. In M. P. Zanna, ed., *Advances in Experimental Social Psychology* 23: 1–74. New York: Academic Press.

Fiske, S. T., Cuddy, A. J. C., Glick, P., and Xu, J. 2002. A model of (often mixed) stereotype content: Competence and warmth respectively follow from perceived status and competition. *Journal of Applied Psychology* 82: 878–902.

Glick, P., and Fiske, S. T. 1996. The ambivalent sexism inventory: Differentiating hostile and benevolent sexism. *Journal of Personality and Social Psychology* 70: 491–512.

Gray-Little, B., and Hafdahl, A. R., 2000. Factors influencing racial comparisons of self-esteem: A quantitative synthesis. *Psychological Bulletin* 126: 26–54.

Greenhaus, J. H., and Powell, G. N. 2006. When work and family are allies: A theory of work-family enrichment. *Academy of Management Review* 31: 72–92.

Guillaume, Y. R. F., Dawson, J. F., Woods, S. A., Sacramento, C. A., and West, M. A. 2013. Getting diversity at work to work: What we know and what we still don't know. *Journal of Occupational and Organizational Psychology* 86: 123–141.

Gully, S. M., and Chen, G. 2010. Individual differences, aptitude-treatment interactions, and learning. In S. W. J. Kozlowski and E. Salas, eds., *Learning, Training, and Development in Organizations*, 3–64. New York: Routledge Academic.

Hansen, T., Slagsvold, B., and Moum, T. 2009. Childlessness and psychological well-being in midlife and old age: An examination of parental status effects across a range of outcomes. *Social Indicators Research* 94(2): 343–362.

Hebl, M. 1997. *Nonstigmatized individuals' reactions to the acknowledgment and valuation of a stigma by physically disabled and overweight individuals.* PhD Diss. Baker Library, Dartmouth College.

Hebl, M., Ruggs, E., Singletary, S., and Beal, D. L. 2012. Perceptions of obesity across the lifespan. *Obesity* [Special Issue] 16: S46–S52.

Hebl, M. R., Foster, J., Mannix, L. M, and Dovido, J. F. 2002. Formal and interpersonal discrimination: A field study of bias toward homosexual applicants. *Personality and Social Psychology Bulletin* 28: 815–825.

Heilman, M. 1983. Sex bias in work settings: The lack of fit model. *Research in Organizational Behavior* 5: 269–298.

Heilman, M., Martell, R., and Simon, M. 1988. The vagaries of sex bias: Conditions regulating the underevaluation, equivaluation, and overevaluation of female job applicants. *Organizational Behavioral and Human Decision Processes* 41: 98–110.

Heilman, M. E. 1984. Information as a deterrent against sex discrimination: The effects of applicant sex and information type on preliminary employment decisions. *Organizational Behavior and Human Performance* 33(2): 174–186.

Heimbeck, D., Frese, M., Sonnentag, S., and Keith, N. 2003. Integrating errors into the training process: The function of error management instructions and the role of goal orientation. *Personnel Psychology* 56: 333–361.

Hilton, J. L., and von Hippel, W. 1996. Stereotypes. *Annual Review of Psychology* 47: 237–271.

Hough, L. M., Oswald, F. L., and Ployhart, R. E. 2001. Determinants, detection and amelioration of adverse impact in personnel selection procedures: Issues, evidence and lessons learned. *International Journal of Selection and Assessment* 9: 152–194.

Huang, C. 2010. Mean-level change in self-esteem from childhood through adulthood: Meta-analysis of longitudinal studies. *Review of General Psychology* 14: 251–260.

Hunter, J. E., and Hunter, R. F. 1984. Validity and utility of alternative predictors of job performance. *Psychological Bulletin* 96: 72–98.

Johns, M., Schmader, T., and Martens, A. 2005. Knowing is half the battle: Teaching stereotype threat as a means of improving women's math performance. *Psychological Science* 16: 175–179.

Joshi, A., and Roh, H. 2009. The role of context in work team diversity research: A meta-analytic review. *Academy of Management Journal* 52: 599–627.

Jussim, L. 1986. Self-fulfilling prophecies: A theoretical and integrative review. *Psychology Review* 93: 429–445.

Kalinoski, Z. T., Steele-Johnson, D., Peyton, E. J., Leas, K. A., Steinke, J., and Bowling, N. A. 2013. A meta-analytic evaluation of diversity training outcomes. *Journal of Organizational Behavior* 34: 1076–1104.

Katz, D., and Braly, K. 1933. Racial stereotypes of one hundred college students. *Journal of Abnormal and Social Psychology* 28: 280–290.

King, E. B. 2008. The effect of bias on career advancement of working mothers: Disentangling legitimate concerns from inaccurate stereotypes as predictors of career success. *Human Relations* 61: 1677–1711.

King, E. B., Botsford, W., Hebl, M. R., Kazama, S., Dawson, J. F., and Perkins, A. 2012. Benevolent sexism at work: Gender differences in the distribution of challenging developmental experiences. *Journal of Management* 38(6): 1835–1866.

King, E. B., Hebl, M. R., Botsford Morgan, W., and Ahmad, A. 2013. Experimental field research on sensitive organizational topics. *Organizational Research Methods* 16: 501–521.

Kling, K. C., Hyde, J. S., Showers, C. J., and Buswell, B. N. 1999. Gender differences in self-esteem: A meta-analysis. *Psychological Bulletin* 125: 470–500.

Koenig, A. M., and Eagly, A. H. 2005. Stereotype threat in men on a test of social sensitivity. *Sex Roles* 52(7–8): 489–496.

Konrad, A. M., and Linnehan, F. 1995. Formalized HRM structures: Coordinating equal employment opportunity or concealing organizational practices? *Academy of Management Journal* 38(3): 787–820.

Kozlowski, S. W. J., Gully, S. M., Brown, K. G., Salas, E., Smith, E. M., and Nason, E. R. 2001. Effects of training goals and goal orientation traits on multidimensional training outcomes and performance adaptability. *Organizational Behavior and Human Decision Processes* 85: 1–31.

Kraiger, K., Ford, J. K., and Salas, E. 1993. Application of cognitive, skill-based, and affective theories of learning outcomes to new methods of training evaluation. *Journal of Applied Psychology* 78: 311–328.

Krause, N. 1995. Religiosity and self-esteem among older adults. *Journal of Gerontology: Social Sciences* 50: 236–246.

Kubeck, J. E., Delp, N. D., Haslett, T. K., and McDaniel, M. A. 1996. Does job-related training performance decline with age? *Psychology and Aging* 11: 92–107.

Ladge, J., Clair, J. A., and Greenberg, D. 2012. Cross-domain identity transition during liminal periods: Constructing multiple selves as "Professional and Mother" during pregnancy. *Academy of Management Journal* 55: 1264–1294.

Lamont, R. A., Swift, H. J., and Abrams, D. 2015. A review and meta-analysis of age-based stereotype threat: Negative stereotypes, not facts, do the damage. *Psychology of Aging* 30: 180–193.

Landy, F. J., Shankster-Cawley, L., and Moran, S. K. 1995. Advancing personnel selection and placement methods. In A. Howard, ed., *The Changing Nature of Work*, 252–289. San Francisco: Jossey-Bass.

Leslie, L. M., Mayer, D. M., and Kravitz, D. A. 2014. The stigma of affirmative action: A stereotyping-based theory and meta-analytic test. *Academy of Management Journal* 57: 964–989.

Libermann, S. C., Wegge, J., Jungmann, F., and Schmidt, K. H. 2013. Age diversity and individual team member health: The moderating role of age and age stereotypes. *Journal of Occupational and Organizational Psychology* 86: 184–202.

Lim, J., and Dinges, D. F. 2010 A quantitative analysis of the impact of short-term sleep deprivation on cognitive variables. *Psychological Bulletin* 136(3): 375–389.

Livingston, J. D., and Boyd, J. E. 2010. Correlates and consequences of internalized stigma for people living with mental illness: A systematic review and meta-analysis. *Social Science and Medicine* 71: 2150–2161.

Major, B., Hunger, J. M., Bunyan, D., and Miller, C. T. 2014. The ironic effects of weight stigma. *Journal of Experimental Social Psychology* 51: 74–80.

Marx, D. M. 2012. Differentiating theories: A comparison of stereotype threat and stereotype priming effects. *Stereotype Threat: Theory, Process, and Application* 124–140.

McCausland, T. C., King, E. B., Bartholomew, L., Feyre, R., Ahmad, A., and Finkelstein, L. M. 2015. The technological age: The effects of perceived age in technology training. *Journal of Business Psychology* 1–16.

Meyer, H. D., John, E. P. S., Chankseliani, M., and Uribe, L., eds. 2013. *Fairness in Access to Higher Education in a Global Perspective Reconciling Excellence, Efficiency, and Justice.* Rotterdam, The Netherlands: Springer Science and Business Media.

Milliken, F. J., and Martins, L. L. 1996. Searching for common threads: Understanding the multiple effects of diversity in organizational groups. *Academy of Management Review* 21: 402–433.

Ng, T. W. H., and Feldman, D. C. 2008. The relationship of age to ten dimensions of job performance. *Journal of Applied Psychology* 93: 392–423.

Nguyen, H.-H. D., and Ryan, A. M. 2008. Does stereotype threat affect test performance of minorities and women? A meta-analysis of experimental evidence. *Journal of Applied Psychology* 93: 1314–1334.

Noe, R. A. 1986. Trainees' attributes and attitudes: Neglected influences on training effectiveness. *Academy of Management Review* 11(4): 736–749.

Nosek, M. A., Hughes, R. B., Swedlund, N., Taylor, H. B., and Swank, P. 2003. Self-esteem and women with disabilities. *Social Science Medicine* 56(8): 1737–1747.

Paluck, E. L., and Green, D. P. 2009. Prejudice reduction: What works? A review and assessment of research and practice. *Annual Review of Psychology* 60: 339–367.

Payne, S. C., Youngcourt, S. S., and Beaubien, J. M. 2007. A meta-analytic examination of the goal orientation nomological net. *Journal of Applied Psychology* 92: 128–150.

Perry, E. L. 1994. A prototype matching approach to understanding the role of applicant gender and age in the evaluation of job applicants. *Journal of Applied Social Psychology* 24: 1433–1473.

Pingitore, R., Dugoni, B. L., Tindale, R. S., and Spring, B. 1994. Bias against overweight job applicants in a simulated employment interview. *Journal of Applied Psychology* 79: 909–917.

Posthuma, R. A., and Campion, M. A. 2009. Age stereotypes: Common stereotypes, moderators, and future research directions. *Journal of Management* 35: 158–188.

Ridgeway, C. L., and Correll, S. J. 2004. Motherhood as a status characteristic. *Journal of Social Issues* 60: 683–700.

Roberson, L., and Kulik, C. T. 2007. Stereotype threat at work. *Academy of Management Perspectives* 21: 24–40.

Rubovits, P., and Maehr, M. 1973. Pygmalion black and white. *Journal of Personality and Social Psychology* 25: 210–218.

Ryckman, R. M., Robbins, M. A., Kaczor, L. M., and Gold, J. A. 1989. Male and female raters' stereotyping of male and female physiques. *Personality and Social Psychology Bulletin* 15(2): 244–251.

Sackett, P. R., Schmitt, N., Ellingson, J. E., and Kabin, M. B. 2001. High-stakes testing in employment, credentialing, and higher education: Prospects in a post-affirmative-action world. *American Psychologist* 56: 302–318.

Salas, E., and Cannon-Bowers, J. A. 2001. The science of training: A decade of progress. *Annual Review of Psychology* 52: 471–499.

Salas, E., Tannenbaum, S. I., Kraiger, K., and Smith-Jentsch, K. A. 2012. The science of training and development in organizations: What matters in practice. *Psychological Science* 13: 74–101.

Schieman, S., Pudrovska, T. and Milkie, M. A. 2005. The sense of divine control and the self-concept: A study of race differences in late life. *Research on Aging* 27: 165–196.

Seacat, J. D., and Mickelson, K. D. 2009. Stereotype threat and the exercise/dietary health intentions of overweight women. *Journal of Health Psychology* 14: 556–567.

Shapiro, J., and Neuberg, S. L. 2007. From stereotype threat to stereotypes threats: Implications of multi-threat framework for causes, moderators, mediators, consequences, and interventions. *Personality Social Psychology Review* 11: 107–130.

Shapiro, J. R., King, E. B., and Quiñones, M. A. 2007. Expectation of obese trainees: How stigmatized trainee characteristics influence training effectiveness. *Journal of Applied Psychology* 92: 239–249.

Shapiro, J. R., Williams, A. M., and Hambarchyan, M. 2013. Are all interventions created equal? A multi-threat approach to tailoring stereotype threat interventions. *Journal of Personality and Social Psychology* 104: 277–288.

Shore, L. M., and Goldberg, C. B. 2004. Age discrimination in organizations. In R. L. Dipboye and A. Colella, eds., *Psychological and Organizational Bases of Discrimination at Work*. Mahwah, NJ: Lawrence Erlbaum.

Shore, L. M., Chung-Herrera, B. G., Dean, M. A., Ehrhart, K. H., Jung, D. I., Randel, A. E., and Singh, G. 2009. Diversity in organizations: Where are we now and where are we going? *Human Resource Management Review* 19(2): 117–133.

Silverman, A. M., and Cohen, G. L. 2014. Stereotypes as stumbling-blocks how coping with stereotype threat affects life outcomes for people with physical disabilities. *Journal of Personality and Social Psychology* 40: 1330–1340.

Snow, R. E. 1989. Aptitude-treatment interaction as a framework for research on individual differences in learning. In P. L. Ackerman, R. J. Sternberg, and R. Glaser, eds., *Learning and Individual Differences: Advances in Theory and Research*, 13–59. New York: Freeman.

Steele, C. M. 1997. A threat in the air: How stereotypes shape intellectual identity and performance. *American Psychologist* 52: 613–629.

Steele, C.M., and Aronson, J. 1995. Stereotype threat and the intellectual test performance of African Americans. *Journal of Personality and Social Psychology* 69: 797–811.

Steele, C. M., Spencer, S. J., and Aronson, J. 2002. Contending with group image: The psychology of stereotype and social identity threat. In M. Zanna, ed., *Advances in Experimental Social Psychology*, 34: 379–440. New York: Academic Press.

Suhr, J. A., and Gunstad, J. 2002. "Diagnosis threat": The effect of negative expectations on cognitive performance in head injury. *Journal of Clinical and Experimental Neuropsychology* 24: 448–457.

Tajfel, H. 1981. *Human Groups and Social Categories: Studies in Social Psychology*. Bath, England: Cambridge University Press.

Talaska, C. A., Fiske, S. T., and Chaiken, S. 2008. Legitimating racial discrimination: A meta-analysis of the racial attitude-behavior literature shows that emotions, not beliefs, best predict discrimination. *Social Justice Research: Social Power in Action* 21: 263–296.

Twenge, J. M., and Campbell, W. K. 2001. Age and birth cohort differences in self-esteem: A cross-temporal meta-analysis. *Personality and Social Psychology Review* 5: 321–344.

Twenge, J. M., and Crocker, J. 2002. Race and self-esteem: Meta-analyses comparing Whites, blacks, Hispanics, Asians, and American Indians and comment on Gray-Little and Hafdahl (2000). *Psychological Bulletin* 128: 371–408.

Udland, M. 2016. There's something wrong with the U.S. labor market. *Business Insider.* http://www.businessinsider.com/labor-market-skills-gap-widening-2016-5 (accessed May 22, 2017).

van Knippenberg, D., and Schippers, M. C. 2007. Work Group Diversity. *Annual Review of Psychology* 58(1): 515–541.

Wazwaz, N. 2015. It's official: The US is becoming a minority-majority nation. *U.S. News & World Report*, July 6.

Wilson, J., and Musick, M. 1996. Religion and marital dependency. *Journal for the Scientific Study of Religion* 35: 30–40.

Yu, Z. B., Han, S. P., Cao, X. G., and Guo, X. R. 2010. Intelligence in relation to obesity: A systematic review and meta-analysis. *Obesity Reviews* 11: 656–670.

Zuckerman, M., Silberman, J., and Hall, J. A. 2013. The relation between intelligence and religiosity a meta-analysis and some proposed explanations. *Personality and Social Psychology Review* 17(4): 325–354.

PART III

Designing the Intervention

9 Enhancing Training Transfer by Promoting Accountability in Different Work Contexts

An Integrative Framework

Michael J. Tews and Lisa A. Burke-Smalley

With knowledge workers abounding in today's service-based economy, organizations continue to invest in training and learning opportunities to enhance human capital. According to the Association for Talent Development's *2014 State of the Industry Report*, U.S. organizations spend $1,208 per employee/per year on training. Clearly, one of the primary goals of such training investments is to enhance positive transfer, or the degree to which learning from training is applied to the job, and to produce relevant changes in employee and job performance (Burke, Hutchins, & Saks, 2013; Grossman & Salas, 2011). Unfortunately, there is empirical evidence that little of what has been acquired during training is transferred to the workplace (Saks, 2002). Given less than ideal transfer rates, means to promote transfer represent a key challenge for training scholars and practitioners alike (Burke, 2001). If trainees fail to successfully transfer new knowledge and skills, training expenditures are ultimately poor investments.

Many studies over the last few decades have examined methods for promoting transfer. For example, research has focused on enhancing transfer through posttraining interventions such as goal-setting and self-management training (e.g., Brown, 2005; Burke & Baldwin, 1999; Richman-Hirsch, 2001; Taylor, Russ-Eft, & Chan, 2005; Tews & Tracey, 2008), transfer climate (e.g., Holton, Bates, & Ruona, 2000; Rouiller & Goldstein, 1993; Tracey & Tews, 2005), and supervisory and peer support (e.g., Cromwell & Kolb, 2004; Hutchins, Burke, & Berthelsen, 2010; Lim & Johnson, 2002). Furthermore, various exhaustive reviews have summarized the existing body of research on transfer of training (Blume et al., 2010; Burke & Hutchins, 2007; Grossman & Salas, 2011). While there is evidence that transfer is influenced by various individual trainee characteristics, training design, and different aspects of organizational support, there is less clarity on which antecedents matter most (Hilbert, Preskill, & Russ-Eft, 1997), though some have offered their insights (Grossman & Salas, 2011).

Despite advances in transfer research, we contend that overall the body of research lacks synthesis (Blume et al., 2010) and remains principally atheoretical. The training and development field has organizing frameworks to help classify transfer elements (such as before, during, and after training; Broad, 2005), yet further theoretically grounded guidance would help design specific transfer strategies to use in different workplace contexts. Toward this end, the goal of the present chapter is to create an integrative conceptual framework that is theory driven and provides context-relevant implications for stakeholders of training transfer design.

The fundamental premise of this chapter is that accountability may be lacking in organizations for trainees to apply what they have learned in training on the job. As Kopp (2006) claims, transfer seems to be viewed as "nice-to-have," and often stakeholders are not held accountable for transfer success in a meaningful way. Drawing on Schlenker and colleagues' (1994; 1997) model of accountability and Yelon and Ford's (1999) multidimensional model of transfer, the present chapter delineates means to enhance accountability for training transfer in different work contexts. Burke and Saks (2009) recently applied Schlenker's framework to transfer in general, and in this chapter we go further by considering work context. Specifically, this chapter focuses on the means to promote accountability for transfer of open and closed skills performed under either supervised or autonomous working conditions. It is important to consider the nature of the skill and degree of supervision because these dimensions affect ease of proficiency acquisition, latitude in adapting skills, responsibility for monitoring posttraining behavior, and the level of posttraining support required.

The structure of the chapter is as follows. First, we will review previous research related to accountability and transfer of training. Then, we will provide an overview of Schlenker and colleagues' (1994; 1997) model of accountability and Yelon and Ford's (1999) multidimensional model of transfer. We then synthesize these theoretical perspectives and articulate strategies to promote accountability for transfer in various work contexts.

The Importance of Accountability in Training Transfer

Frink and Klimoski (1998) defined *accountability* as a perceived need to justify an action to some audience that has reward or sanction power. From a management perspective, when individuals know they will be held accountable for their behaviors and decisions, they are more motivated to focus on achieving specific outcomes, use self-regulatory strategies, and exert greater effort and persist in overcoming obstacles. Organizations have a range of formal mechanisms and informal mechanisms to influence perceived accountability (Frink & Klimoski, 1998). Formal accountability mechanisms may include performance reviews, promotions or demotions, disciplinary action, and incentives like merit or bonus pay. Informal mechanisms may include cultural norms, peer influence, and coaching from supervisors. While accountability has been studied in decision making, selection, and performance appraisal contexts, it has been examined to a lesser extent in the training context (i.e., DeMatteo, Lundby, & Dobbins, 1997). In the training transfer domain, accountability addresses the extent to which transfer is expected from trainees (Brinkerhoff & Montesino, 1995; Burke & Saks, 2009).

We contend that accountability can be deficient with respect to transfer on several fronts. At a general level, training may be perceived as an isolated event, divorced from the natural work environment. In this respect, trainers may be held accountable only for designing and delivering an effective training session, without an eye toward transfer. Furthermore, training practitioners and managers may not be fully aware of the typically limited rates of transfer and merely assume that transfer spontaneously occurs. Extending these arguments, supervisors may not be cognizant of the transfer problem, or they might also view promoting transfer as someone else's responsibility. Following that trainers and supervisors may not focus on transfer, trainees may not place a priority on transfer and instead direct their efforts toward what they perceive to be more pressing demands or more likely rewarded. Given these challenges, it is important to strengthen responsibility mechanisms to help ensure that transfer is maximized (Broad & Newstrom, 1992).

The inclusion of accountability in transfer models and measures is surprisingly lacking despite various studies presenting direct or indirect implications for integrating accountability in transfer interventions (Burke & Saks, 2009). In another study by Baldwin and Magjuka (1991), it was demonstrated that trainees expecting some form of follow-up assessment after training reported stronger intentions to transfer. In commenting on this finding, Tannenbaum and Yukl (1992) stated: "The fact that their supervisor would require them to prepare a post-training report or undergo an assessment meant that they were being held accountable for their own learning and apparently conveyed the message that the training was important" (418). In addition, DeMatteo and colleagues (1997) conducted a systematic manipulation of training accountability in a lab setting and found that accountability interventions (either a postdiscussion with the trainer or a video critique) produced more note taking, learning, and trainee satisfaction if the trainees were notified *prior* to the training of such assessments. Longenecker (2004) also identified enhancing accountability for application, such as requiring posttraining reports from trainees, as a key learning imperative articulated by managers. Saks and Belcourt (2006) subsequently found such accountability mechanisms to be significantly related to transfer. Further support for the role of accountability in transfer can be found in Taylor, et al.'s (2005) meta-analysis of 117 behavioral modeling studies that demonstrated a larger effect for transfer when sanctions and rewards were instituted in trainees' work environments, such as the incorporation of newly learned skills into performance reviews.

Transfer climate constructs, which encompass a variety of support mechanisms to facilitate transfer, also highlight the need for accountability in directing transfer. Rouiller and Goldstein (1993) conceptualized transfer climate as encompassing two dimensions – situational cues and consequences. Situational cues included goal cues, social cues, and task and structural cues. Consequences included feedback and rewards. Tracey, Tannenbaum, and Kavanagh (1995) found support for the relationship between transfer climate and transfer, with Tracey and Tews's (2005) conceptualization of transfer climate encompassing organizational support, managerial support, and job support. Organizational support refers to policies, and reward systems to support training. Managerial support refers to managers encouraging learning and supporting transfer. Finally, job support refers to whether jobs are designed to promote continuous learning. While such transfer climate constructs may not have explicitly identified accountability as a specific factor, they point to the importance of responsibility and consequences associated with transfer.

More recent research further signals the importance of accountability in the context of transfer. In an empirical study, Cheramie and Simmering (2010) found that learners low in conscientiousness exhibited higher levels of learning when they perceived accountability for training outcomes as high, and concluded that "organizations should implement formal controls to increase perceived accountability and improve learning" (44). Lastly, Saks and Burke (2012), in another empirical investigation, provided evidence that training evaluation frequency was related to higher rates of transfer in organizations when organizations measured behavioral change and results-oriented criteria after training (as compared to trainee satisfaction or learning).

Schlenker's Accountability Theory and Training Transfer

Schlenker and colleagues' (1994; 1997) theory of accountability (i.e., responsibility) provides an overarching theoretical framework that we contend can usefully guide transfer research (Burke & Saks, 2009). Schlenker et al. (1994) argue that accountability is a key mechanism through which social entities control the behavior of members. In particular, accountability reflects "being answerable to audiences for performing up to prescribed standards that are relevant to fulfilling obligations, duties, expectations, and other charges" (Schenkler, 1997: 249). When individuals are held responsible by others for adhering to a course of action, they can be evaluated with respect to a relevant event. Moreover, when individuals perceive themselves as accountable for executing a course of action, individuals become more motivated to follow prescribed behaviors and achieve goals and objectives. Thus, enhancing responsibility helps guarantee that organizational members adhere to performance expectations.

Fundamentally, designing accountability into the transfer process enhances stakeholders' sense of ownership and responsibility for skill enhancement such that trainers, trainees, and managers face a source of discomfort from the organization if they do not follow through on their obligation to transfer learning to their job. As Schlenker (1997) claims, gaps between an employee's behavior and "oughts," such as "I ought to transfer skills I learn"; "I ought to hold my employees responsible for transfer"; or "I ought to share evidence of my training program's influence on behavioral change with top managers," produce a state of incompleteness. To embed accountability in transfer of training, individuals must understand what transfer behaviors are expected of them, how their actions will be measured, and what rewards or sanctions will be imposed for transfer or lack thereof (Santos & Stuart, 2003).

Schlenker et al. (1994) argue that accountability "involves an evaluative reckoning in which individuals are judged" (634). The essential facets of accountability include inquiry, accounting, and verdict. That is, questions are raised about how well a person performs (inquiry), evidence is presented and evaluated (accounting), and the person is rewarded or punished (verdict). All such evaluations, whether by others or by the actor him- or herself, involve information about three key variables: prescriptions, identity, and event. *Prescriptions* refer to expectations, rules, and standards of conduct to guide an individual's behavior, which may be formal or informal, explicit or tacit. *Identity* refers to attributes of the actor, such as his or her roles, values, commitments, and aspirations. The *event* refers to a focal course of action that is anticipated or has transpired. Promoting accountability to engage in future desired behaviors, such as training transfer, should focus on these variables and the links between them.

Schlenker et al. (1994) connect these three variables to form three links that contain the adhesive glue to bind individuals to situations and courses of action. Strengthening these links increases responsibility and, thereby, accountability. The *prescription-event* link relates to whether a clear set of expectations applies to a given event, resulting in goal and process clarity. In the context of transfer, the prescription-event link reflects expectations for the use and application of trained skills. When the link is strong, individuals have clear goals for transfer and know how to proceed to meet them. The *prescription-identity* link relates to whether prescriptions are applicable to individuals by virtue of their roles and other personal characteristics, serving to enhance a sense of ownership of a course of action. This link captures the extent to which individuals believe transfer is important because of their role in an organization or their personal sense of obligation. Finally, the *identity-event link* relates to whether individuals are connected to the event and have control and freedom over their actions. In the context of transfer, this link reflects the extent to which individuals have personal control over their transfer behavior.

The three variables and their links are presented graphically in Figure 9.1, known collectively as "the responsibility triangle" (Schlenker et al., 1994: 635). To summarize, a strong prescription-event link requires goal and process clarity; the prescription-identity link necessitates a sense of ownership of the goal and process by individuals; and the identity-event link requires individuals' perceived control over the event. When these links are strong, individuals' self-regulatory systems engage, and they become more determined, committed to goals, and "unwavering in pursuing them despite obstacles, distractions, and temptations" (Schlenker, 1997: 268). Moreover, when people feel more personally responsible, they are less apt to make excuses and engage in avoidance strategies (Schlenker, 1997). By overlaying accountability mechanisms across stakeholders involved

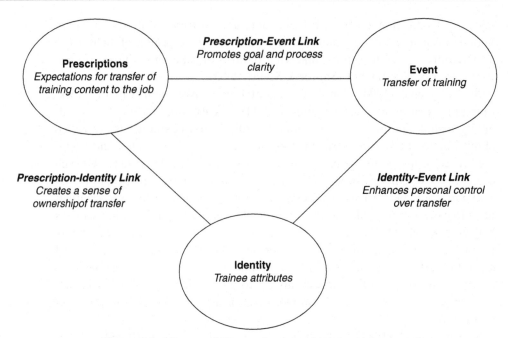

Figure 9.1. *Accountability mechanisms driving training transfer.*

in training transfer, a "psychological adhesive" connects these critical parties to common expectations for and commitment to transfer outcomes.

Burke and Saks (2009) recently applied Schlenker's (1994; 1997) model specifically to transfer of training. In particular, they articulated the accountability linkages for trainers, trainees, and supervisors to ensure these stakeholders focus on transfer enhancement. According to Burke and Saks (2009), trainers should have clear expectations for incorporating transfer enhancement in training programs (prescription-event link), a clear sense of duty to include transfer in training content (prescription-identity link), and control over developing training that focuses on focal skills as well as transfer (identity-event link). Trainees should have clear goals for transfer (prescription-event link), a clear sense of obligation to apply what they have learned (prescription-identity link), and personal control over opportunities to transfer (identity-event link). Finally, supervisors should have clear performance expectations to aid their employees in transfer (prescription-event link), an obligation to focus on trainee transfer (prescription-identity link), and personal control to help facilitate trainee transfer (identity-event link) (Burke & Saks, 2009).

Burke and Saks further propose practical strategies to enhance accountability among these different stakeholders. Trainers, for example, can clearly establish transfer expectations prior to training, devote time specifically to transfer enhancement during training sessions, and systematically evaluate the extent to which trainees use new knowledge and skills on the job. In turn, trainees can set specific goals with supervisors for transfer before training, commit to transfer during training, and document as well as share their learning posttraining.

Table 9.1 *Stakeholder accountability mechanisms for transfer*

Stakeholder	Prescription-Event Link	Prescription-Identity Link	Identity-Event Link
Trainer	Should have clear expectations for incorporating transfer enhancement in training programs	Should have a clear sense of duty to include transfer strategies in training	Should have control over developing training that targets focal skills and transfer
Trainee	Should have clear goals for transfer	Should have a clear sense of obligation to apply what has been learned	Should have personal control over opportunities to transfer
Supervisor	Should have clear performance expectations to aid their employees in transfer	Should have a personal obligation to focus on trainee transfer to the job	Should have personal control to help facilitate trainee transfer

With respect to supervisors, they can discuss transfer objectives with trainees prior to their training, prepare a list of activities to commit to after training to promote transfer among their employees, provide rewards and incentives for transfer, and include transfer in employee performance appraisals. As such, Burke and Saks's application of Schlenker's (1994; 1997) model provides theoretically derived strategies to enhance the transfer of training, as summarized in Table 9.1.

Notwithstanding the value of their contribution, we contend that accountability strategies should vary based on the work context. Toward this end, we extend Burke and Saks's (2009) work to promote trainee accountability in various work *contexts*, specifically in terms of the nature of the trained skill set and the degree of supervision the trainee is subject to, as originally crafted by Yelon and Ford (1999) and described next.

Yelon and Ford's Multidimensional Framework of Transfer

Most models of training transfer present prescriptions and theoretical relationships presumably applicable to all trained tasks. However, such universalistic models may not be appropriate in all contexts. To better delineate the conditions for successful transfer, Yelon and Ford (1999) developed a multidimensional transfer of training model. By multidimensional, Yelon and Ford are referring to two dimensions of the skill set to be performed that should be considered when selecting among transfer strategies. The first dimension of the Yelon and Ford model is *task adaptability*, and the second dimension is the *degree of employee supervision*.

The first dimension of the framework, task adaptability, refers to the extent to which the task to be performed ranges from closed to open. Performing a closed task involves responding to predictable situations with standardized responses. In contrast, performing an open task involves responding to variable situations with adaptive, tailored responses. There is one best way to perform closed tasks; whereas there are multiple ways to perform open tasks that are contingent upon the situation at hand. Examples of closed tasks include preparing food in a fast food restaurant, cleaning a hotel room, filling out a report, and checking in an airline passenger. Examples of open tasks include facilitating discussions in a training session, performing a role in a stage play, motivating employees, and responding to difficult customers.

Yelon and Ford's (1999) second dimension is the degree of supervision under which trained skills are performed on the job. This dimension ranges from heavy supervision to autonomous working conditions. Under heavily supervised conditions, supervisors can closely monitor employee performance on trained skills, provide positive and constructive feedback, and administer appropriate rewards. Further, under such conditions, employees may be more apt to engage in appropriate behaviors with the knowledge of close observation. Under autonomous working conditions, however, employees have more discretion whether to engage in trained behaviors and must be more responsible for ensuring that behaviors are appropriately executed.

Based on these two dimensions – task adaptability and degree of job supervision – Yelon and Ford (1999) developed a corresponding 2 × 2 matrix. The resulting four cells in the Yelon and Ford model include: (1) supervised trainees and closed skills; (2) autonomous trainees and closed skills; (3) autonomous trainees and open skills; and (4) supervised trainees and open skills. For each cell, Yelon and Ford then provide differentiated strategies to enhance transfer, as summarized in Table 9.2.

Supervised Trainees and Closed Skills

For supervised trainees performing closed skills, trainees are required to execute specific standards under the guidance of their supervisors. With respect to employee selection, organizations should choose candidates with a detail orientation and willingness to follow direction. Training content should focus on declarative knowledge, procedural knowledge, shaping favorable attitudes toward adhering to standards, and cooperating with supervisors. Yelon and Ford (1999) also recommend high-fidelity training, training in specific and detailed procedures, providing practice opportunities to facilitate automaticity, and providing trainees with detailed procedural checklists. Once on the job, supervisors should manage adherence to standards and provide appropriate incentives and rewards.

Autonomous Trainees and Closed Skills

Yelon and Ford's (1999) prescriptions for autonomous trainees and closed skills diverge from supervised trainees with closed skills on several fronts. On

Table 9.2 *Exemplar transfer enhancement strategies from* Yelon and Ford's (1999) *multidimensional framework*

	Supervised Trainees	Autonomous Trainees
Closed Skill	• Select trainees with a detail orientation and willingness to follow direction • Train detailed procedures and provide detailed procedural checklists • Shape/reward favorable attitudes toward adhering to standards and cooperating with supervisors • Supervisors should manage adherence to standards	• Select trainees with a detail orientation and the ability work independently • Train detailed procedures and provide detailed procedural checklists • Shape/reward favorable attitudes toward seeking support and train meta-cognitive competence to help trainees monitor their behavior • Provide avenues for trainees to obtain needed on-the-job support
Open Skill	• Select trainees with a learning orientation and willingness to follow direction • Train strategic knowledge, meta-cognitive competence, and favorable attitudes toward experimentation • Train favorable attitudes toward cooperation with supervisors • Train supervisors in the target skills to best manage trainees on the job	• Select trainees with a learning orientation and ability to work independently • Train strategic knowledge, meta-cognitive competence, and favorable attitudes toward experimentation • Train how to overcome on-the-job obstacles • Provide avenues for trainees to obtain needed on-the-job support

a selection front, hiring those with a learning orientation is advised as such individuals persist in challenging situations that might more often occur when working independently. To help ensure trainees are motivated to perform the closed skill, trainers should relate the skill to trainees' personal and job goals. Trainers should also engender favorable attitudes toward seeking support to help ensure that trainees perform skills effectively posttraining. Regarding specific instructional strategies, trainees should discuss their intentions to use the closed skill, perform an obstacle assessment and create a response plan, and practice meta-cognitive skills to reflect on their behavior. Once on the job, there should be avenues for trainees to obtain any needed guidance.

Autonomous Trainees and Open Skills

Again, the difference between an open skill and closed skill is that there is not necessarily one best way to perform an open skill. Performing an open skill requires attention to contingency variables to determine a course of action. That is, successful performance requires strategic knowledge – information about when and why to use a particular knowledge or skill on the job (Kraiger,

Ford, & Salas, 1993). Accordingly, training for an open skill requires attention to strategic knowledge to determine when and how trainees should perform trained skills. To enhance the flexibility required for performing open skills, trainers could develop meta-cognitive competence and favorable attitudes toward experimentation. Regarding individual differences on which to select employees, those with a learning orientation may also be better able to learn and transfer open skills. Such individuals focus on developing new skills, attempt to understand their tasks, and successfully achieve self-referenced standards for success (Button, Mathieu, & Zajac, 1996). Related to the autonomous nature of the skill being performed, the prescriptions for transfer are similar to those discussed in the preceding text for autonomous trainees performing closed skills.

Supervised Trainees and Open Skills

For supervised trainees with open skills, training should include many of the strategies advised for such skills performed autonomously. To successfully transfer open skills in a heavily supervised work setting, the following three strategies may be appropriate. First, training employees with favorable attitudes toward cooperation with supervisors may facilitate productive supervisor-subordinate relationships. Second, training supervisors in the target skills may lead to better management of trainees on the job. Third, the trainee and supervisor should jointly perform an obstacle assessment to determine potential barriers to transfer and means to overcome them.

Context-Dependent Transfer Accountability Strategies

Yelon and Ford's (1999) multidimensional framework and Burke and Saks's (2009) application of Schlenker's accountability model (1994, 1997) have each independently advanced research on transfer of training. Burke and Saks have highlighted the importance of the prescription-event, prescription-identity, and identity-event links to increase accountability and articulated transfer strategies to strengthening these links. That said, Burke and Saks did not address means to strengthen these links in different work contexts. Yelon and Ford's work is valuable as they emphasized the importance of context for transfer and delineated strategies appropriate for different skills and degrees of supervision, but they did not position their model and corresponding transfer strategies in the context of accountability. Yelon and Ford's framework thus represents a useful means to extend Burke and Saks's accountability work. It should be noted that not all the original transfer strategies proposed by Yelon and Ford are necessarily applicable to the three accountability links, nor are all their transfer strategies exhaustive. However, they serve as a valuable guide and foundation. Rather than treat these two theoretical perspectives as independent, we suggest that value is to be gained by integrating them to provide greater theoretical precision on how best to foster accountability for training transfer.

Toward this end, we articulate context-dependent transfer accountability strategies. For each of Schlenker's (1994; 1997) three links, several strategies are discussed for specific contexts. Namely, to strengthen each of the prescription-event, prescription-identity, and identity-event links, we propose how to modify transfer enhancement strategies for closed and open skills and, within each skill set, for supervised and autonomous working conditions. When doing so, we also discuss strategies to overcome challenges that might weaken these links. In practice, human resource practitioners combine strategies to bolster the prescription-event, prescription-identity, and identity-event linkages for their specific context.

Bolstering the Prescription-Event Link

In this section, we discuss means to strengthen the prescription-event link for transfer. Fundamentally, the foundation for bolstering this link, and thereby enhancing goal and process clarity, is trainees knowing *what* and *how* to transfer. The strategies in this section address how to articulate to individuals that they should focus on the transfer of newly acquired skills and the standards to which they should adhere. Using diverse and complementary strategies helps ensure that trainees do not revert to old patterns of behavior, divergent personal preferences, or superordinate prescriptions advocated by irrelevant others (Dose & Klimoski, 1995). In order, we discuss strategies to explicitly communicate expectations for transfer and the use of reward systems to indirectly communicate expectations for transfer, while including strategies to overcome challenges of competing job responsibilities.

Communicating Transfer Expectations

The communication of transfer expectations is relatively straightforward for closed skills, given that the successful execution of closed skills requires following standard procedures. Yelon and Ford (1999) advocate high-fidelity training, training in specific and detailed procedures, and providing trainees with detailed procedural checklists, and these strategies will likely serve to enhance the prescription-event link. Because there is one best way to execute a closed skill, there must be a high degree of fidelity between training content and job requirements, which may be obtained through careful needs assessment (Broad, 2005). When closed skills are supervised, supervisors may also require training in the standards so they can manage behavior consistently. When supervisors' standards differ from training standards, trainees will more likely follow the supervisors' standards, given the inherent power supervisors possess. The reinforcement of closed skills is arguably more challenging with autonomous employees, as supervisors cannot readily reinforce the closed skill. Thus, a greater responsibility is placed on organizations to appropriately select conscientious workers and on trainers to ensure that skills are fully learned during training. In these situations, accessible on-the-job reference information and trainer follow-ups may also be needed to cement standards.

Communication of expectations for transfer is less straightforward for open skills. A strong prescription-event link requires clear expectations, yet open skills need to be adapted to a variety of situations. This requirement for adaptation could be translated as ambiguity. It may not always be clear how to execute open skills, nor is it feasible to delineate all possible variations of open skill adaptation. In this respect, trainees should be taught general principles that can be applied to different situations (Yelon & Ford, 1999). Trainers should identify a manageable, yet diverse, set of response-by-situation models to help trainees develop skill adaptability. Moreover, we contend that boundaries should be established to ensure individuals execute adaptation within limits and possess an apt sensitivity to what degree of variability is acceptable. Given that all possible variations cannot be prescribed, trainees may also need to be encouraged to seek guidance and support and socialized to comply with general principles and company values.

When employees are supervised transferring an open skill, supervisors can help them refine their skill in adapting to different situations by incorporating feedback from customers, co-workers, and other key constituents where appropriate. In doing so, supervisors are further reinforcing performance expectations and strengthening the prescription-event link. A challenge is that some supervisors could be tempted to micromanage the open skill. Supervisors likely have expertise and could possess particular ideas for how open skills should be transferred. That said, appropriately selected and trained supervisors in these situations should allow employees to adapt the skill within the general principles and parameters taught in training. Along the same lines, supervisors need to communicate through informal coaching or more formal performance appraisal that exercising discretion and making sound decisions are inherent components of open skills. If supervisors micromanage or if employees do not make their own decisions, an open skill may ultimately devolve into a closed skill, which could render employees inflexible and at times ineffective.

When employees are working autonomously to transfer an open skill, posttraining interventions could strengthen the prescription-event link. For example, requiring employees to complete action plans and follow-up reports detailing how they intend to use or have used trained skills could be valuable (Tews & Tracey, 2008). Interventions such as these could signal to trainees that transfer is important and motivate individual effort toward applying new knowledge and skills. In this respect, they direct individuals toward transfer and further skill development, rather than other demands. Further, such interventions represent a vehicle to reinforce training content and expectations that may not have been fully cemented during training. Following that open skills are often more complex than closed skills, open skills are less apt to have been fully learned during training. Accordingly, training content and performance expectations may need to be further learned on the job. One caveat is that these posttraining interventions reflect additional work for individuals. To ensure use of these interventions, they should be simple and easy to use, and there can be accountability mechanisms built into systems such as performance reviews to help guarantee they become a part of trainees' work routines.

Rewarding Transfer

Reward systems could strengthen the prescription-event link by signaling that transfer is important in organizations (Dose & Klimoski, 1995). One challenge of rewarding the transfer of any particular skill is that the skill may only represent one aspect of an employee's job performance. It is often the case that an employee's *total* job performance is rewarded, not just a specific behavior, such as transferring one skill. Consequently, trainees may perceive little connection between transfer and rewards obtained. Another issue is that the rewards for transfer may not have enough value to motivate employee effort. That said, if transfer is not rewarded meaningfully, employees may not transfer and may instead focus on tasks where such recognition is present.

Yelon and Ford (1999) suggest rewarding adherence to standards for closed skills. When such skills are supervised, it may be relatively easy to reward both behavior and results. In the context of a receptionist following a script, a supervisor could reward adherence to the script and ratings of customer satisfaction. However, when such skills are performed autonomously, rewards may need to only focus on results because results are the only source of easily accessible information (e.g., ratings of customer satisfaction). When a closed skill is relatively simple, which is sometimes the case, informal recognition may be more appropriate and feasible than formal rewards. To the extent that a closed skill has less economic value than other skills, managers may need to reward a closed skill primarily with informal recognition, feedback, and praise. Of course, this strategy depends on the closed skill in question.

With respect to open skills, Yelon and Ford (1999) suggest rewards for experimentation. Rewards should focus on experimentation as opposed to performance because open skills may not be fully learned in training due to their inherent complexity and the need for adaptation on the job. When open skills are supervised, supervisors could certainly reward trainee experimentation. However, supervisors typically reward maximum performance, which is reduced by experimentation. Accordingly, it may be unclear what to reward when transfer does not meet expectations, and rewarding effort such as experimentation is fraught with ambiguity. Therefore, supervisors may need to allow for a "penalty free" period of experimentation after training that does not affect the reward system.

When autonomous employees perform open skills, rewarding experimentation is more difficult. Managers may need to base rewards on objective measures of experimentation. If none exist, managers and trainees may have no choice but to use measures of outcomes, such as focusing on patient recovery rates or student evaluations of instruction. In such cases, however, employees do not have full control over such measures, and metrics may decline posttraining if individuals are experimenting. These arguments are certainly not meant to undermine the potential value of rewards in promoting transfer, but rather highlight that if not properly designed, reward systems could send mixed messages and weaken the prescription-event link.

Managing Other Job Responsibilities

Finally, careful attention needs to be paid to managing the trainee's total set of job responsibilities to free attention and time to practice the trained skill. When work demands are high, individuals will focus on core job responsibilities and immediate job performance in lieu of focusing on transfer (Marx, 1982). Temporarily curtailing job responsibilities is perhaps most relevant for open skills when further skill learning is required on the job, as compared to closed skills that are relatively straightforward. That said, not all closed skills are simple skills, and even simple skills may require further learning on the job. Managing job responsibilities to accommodate transfer is relatively straightforward when trained skills are closely supervised as supervisors directly manage employee workloads. When the trained skill is autonomously performed, trainers bear a stronger responsibility for helping trainees best manage their job responsibilities to accommodate transfer.

Bolstering the Prescription-Identity Link

The prescription-identity link in Schlenker's (1994; 1997) framework is the extent to which prescriptions apply to individuals by virtue of who they are. In the transfer context, the extent to which the trained skill is required and perceived as appropriate by a trainee is a function of both his or her formal role and personal attributes. When individuals view prescriptions as consistent with their identities, they are more apt to transfer the trained skill (Burke & Saks, 2009). Strengthening this link requires an alignment between the transfer expectations and the trainee's perceptions of their appropriateness. As Schlenker (1997) argues, when goals are not ennobling and the prescription is perceived to have little value, individuals will avoid them. If trainees' identities are threatened, individuals are more likely to engage in avoidance strategies, such as delaying or concealing attempts to follow prescriptions for transfer, distracting others so as not to notice their transfer efforts or lack thereof, or perhaps discrediting those who seek to hold them accountable for transfer. As means to bolster this link, we discuss selecting employees whose individual differences match the skill set and the degree of supervision and inculcating favorable attitudes toward the skill and supervision context. In addition, we discuss strategies for managing the challenge of mismatches between prescriptions and trainees' overall job.

Selecting Employees

A long-run strategy for maximizing fit between transfer prescriptions and trainees' identities is selecting employees with individual differences congruent with a skill set and degree of supervision. While many individual differences could be positioned in the context of Yelon and Ford's (1999) framework, here we will highlight a few exemplars. Although conscientiousness is important irrespective of context (Colquitt, LePine, & Noe, 2000), the orderliness and dutifulness facets of conscientiousness are likely particularly important for executing closed skills that require adherence to strict standards (Costa, McCrae, & Dye, 1991). General mental ability is also one of the most dominant predictors of training success (Colquitt et al., 2000), but is certainly more important for open skills high in complexity. As discussed by Yelon and Ford, a learning orientation is also key for open skills as they require adaptation, reflection, and problem solving. Noe, Tews, and Marand (2013) recently demonstrated that zest, where individuals approach life with eagerness, energy, and anticipation (Peterson & Seligman, 2004), was a significant predictor of informal learning. Following that open skills require informal learning on the job, zest should be relevant to this skill set. Regarding degree of supervision, the compliance facet of agreeableness is especially relevant for supervised trainees (Costa et al., 1991), whereas a proactive personality is especially germane for autonomous trainees because such individuals are unconstrained by situational forces and persevere until they achieve desired results (Parker & Sprigg, 1999).

Promoting Favorable Attitudes

Another strategy is for trainers and supervisors, where appropriate, to inculcate favorable attitudes toward the specific skill and supervision context (Tracey et al., 1995). Links are weaker when a prescription appears arbitrarily imposed or to only benefit the person imposing it (DeHart-Davis, 2009). For closed skills, trainers could focus on strengthening attitudes toward the standards and the process of executing them, noting adverse consequences of deviations. Imposing nonvalued standards is likely less of an issue for closed skills performed under supervision due to the nature of a close employee-supervisor working relationship. With respect to open skills, trainers could attempt to enhance trainees' appreciation for creativity, risk taking, problem solving, and the ability to adapt principles in different contexts. When skills will be transferred under close supervision, trainers could develop in trainees positive attitudes toward supervision, accepting feedback from others, and the benefits of teamwork. Supervisors should accept some adaptation and variation and confer with trainees to gain their acceptance of prescriptions. In turn, for autonomously performed open skills, trainers could target the benefits of working independently, freedom, and self-determination. Extending the aforementioned arguments, a potentially fruitful strategy is to leverage trainees' individual differences by linking them to the specific characteristics of the skill to be transferred. For example, for closed skills, trainers could appeal to trainees' orderliness and dutifulness, and for autonomously performed skills, trainers would appeal to trainees' proactive personality.

Limiting Mismatches

One challenge that may weaken the prescription-identity link is a mismatch between prescriptions for a specific skill set and the overall nature of an individual's job. That is, the link could be compromised when trained skills are inconsistent with the overall set of responsibilities for a given job and the degree of supervision an individual typically receives at work (Mathieu & Martineau, 1997). There appears to be an implicit assumption in the transfer literature that there is congruence on this front, which may not always be the case. For example, an administrative assistant who normally performs closed tasks may be trained in more complex project management skills. As another example, a college professor who normally performs autonomously may be evaluated three times a semester in his or her use of a new classroom management technology, a potential affront to autonomy. In such instances, trainees may resist transfer if they are given prescriptions inconsistent with their identity and job.

To overcome this challenge and strengthen the prescription-identity link, practitioners can either limit mismatches or acknowledge them when they are necessary. Furthermore, alternative strategies should be employed to minimize identity threats depending on whether trainees will be expanding or narrowing the scope of their work. When moving from closed to open skills or supervised to autonomous working conditions, trainers should seek to explicitly expand the trainee's identity to encompass the new task. For example, trainers and supervisors could appeal to an individual's need for growth, development, and autonomy. However, when moving from open to closed skills or from autonomous to supervised working conditions, people may experience threats to their perceived competence because they are being constrained. To limit identity threats in these instances, trainers should seek to appeal to trainees' willingness and ability to do the task well for the benefit of the organization and recognize and reward their sacrifice.

Bolstering the Identity-Event Link

The identity-event link reflects the extent to which the actor has personal control over the event; higher perceived control enhances felt responsibility (Dose & Klimoski, 1995). In the context of transfer, this link is stronger when individuals have confidence in their ability to successfully use new knowledge and skills and favorably influence the desired outcome of transfer, namely improved job performance. Self-efficacy beliefs, which have been demonstrated to have a positive impact on behavior across a wide set of domains (Bandura, 1986; Judge & Bono, 2001; Stajkovic & Luthans, 1998), are central to strengthening the identity-event link (Schlenker, 1997).

Bandura (1986) defined self-efficacy as individuals' "judgments of their capabilities to organize and execute courses of action required to attain designated types of performances" (391). Wood and Bandura (1989) contend that self-efficacy beliefs relate to individuals' perceived capabilities "to mobilize the motivation, cognitive resources, and courses of action to meet given situational demands" (408). Self-efficacy beliefs may include both traitlike individual differences (Chen, Gully, & Eden, 2001; Judge, Erez, & Bono, 1998; Judge, Locke, & Durham, 1997) and task-specific states that can be enhanced through mastery experiences (Bandura, 1986; Stajkovic & Luthans, 1998). As such, strengthening self-efficacy to strengthen the identity-event link could be achieved by careful employee selection and providing posttraining support (Gist & Mitchell, 1992) including goal-setting and self-management training, to which we now turn. A major challenge to strengthening this link is unrealistic expectations.

Selecting Employees

Two traits could be used in the selection process to facilitate trainees' perceived personal control. The first is generalized self-efficacy (GSE), which refers to the extent to which an individual has an enduring belief that he or she is capable of accomplishment irrespective of the situation or task demands (Chen et al., 2001; Judge et al., 1998; Judge et al., 1997). Given that those higher in GSE believe they can succeed in any achievement situation, they likely will have confidence in their ability to transfer. In addition, the perceived ability to learn and solve problems (PALS), which relates to self-efficacy in acquiring new knowledge and skills and effective problem solving, may have particular relevance for transfer of training (Tews, Michel, & Noe, 2011). Although PALS has not been examined in the context of learning explicitly, Tews and colleagues demonstrated that PALS was significantly related to job performance for managers and entry-level employees. Moreover, PALS was found to explain additional variance in performance beyond general mental ability, personality, and similar constructs related to learning and problem and solving. In the context of Yelon and Ford's (1999) model, GSE and PALS are more relevant for open skills and for those autonomously performed as they place greater demands on individuals. GSE and PALS are likely less relevant for closed, supervised work because its standardized nature reduces the importance of human judgment and creativity.

Providing Posttraining Support

A variety of goal-setting interventions may bolster accountability for autonomous employees, particularly those performing open skills. In an early study in this area, Wexley and Nemeroff (1975) demonstrated in the development of managerial and negotiation skills that trainees who received assigned goals, coupled with on-the-job coaching sessions with trainers, exhibited superior on-the-job performance compared to trainees who attended classroom training only. Richman-Hirsch (2001) illustrated that goal-setting training focused on action planning within the formal classroom resulted in better customer service performance for trainees who participated in this supplement compared to those who received classroom training only. Furthermore, Tews and Tracey (2008) demonstrated that a self-coaching program designed to improve the transfer of interpersonal skills for managers resulted in higher posttraining performance and self-efficacy beliefs for trainees compared to those who received classroom training only. This intervention involved trainees completing written self-assessments in which they reflected on their performance and established learning and performance goals for several weeks after completing the formal training.

Self-management training, which is similar to goal-setting interventions, could also have relevance for transferring autonomously performed skills. Self-management training is training in the formal classroom environment designed to equip individuals with skills necessary to support successful transfer (Marx, 1982; Richman-Hirsch, 2001). This training typically involves lectures and discussions on these self-management strategies, as well as opportunities for trainees to establish goals for themselves, identify potential challenges to successful performance, and develop specific strategies to facilitate transfer (Richman-Hirsch, 2001). It should be noted that while accountability mechanisms typically involve an external audience to evaluate an individual's performance (Frink & Klimoski, 1998), by definition, autonomous trainees lack such an audience much of the time. Consequently, autonomous trainees must serve as the first line of accountability, making self-management training and related techniques necessary vehicles. Some research has demonstrated a positive impact for self-management training on posttraining performance (Noe, Sears, & Fullenkamp, 1990; Tziner, Haccoun, & Kadish, 1991), but other studies have not (Burke, 1997; Gaudine & Saks, 2004; Richman-Hirsch, 2001; Wexley & Baldwin, 1986). Self-management training may rely too heavily on individuals to manage their performance on the job. One potential means to improve its effectiveness is to have trainees formally meet with supervisors or trainers, which would increase the degree of accountability and allow for follow-up coaching and advice.

Minimizing Unrealistic Expectations

Unrealistic expectations for a successful event diminish the strength of the identity-event link (Schlenker, 1997), representing a key challenge. Accordingly, successful attempts at transfer should not be perceived as too difficult. Given that closed skills are relatively easier to acquire than open skills, initial proficiency may be expected sooner posttraining for closed skills; however, not all closed tasks are simple, so proficiency is not always quickly attained. Supervisors should be sure there is enough time and excess trainee capacity to facilitate transfer. Because open skills are more complex, supervisors need to pull back in initial proficiency expectations even more than for closed skills and reward (formally and informally) progression. Supervisors should place a greater emphasis for open skills on learning goals, where individuals are allowed to focus on further skill acquisition, effort, challenge, and errors (Kozlowski et al., 2001). When skills are autonomously performed, trainees bear a greater responsibility for setting realistic transfer goals to enhance their personal control. Moreover, for autonomously performed skills, there is a greater need for goal-setting and self-management training to help trainees traverse the transfer process.

Guidelines for Practice

We have identified several useful strategies in the preceding sections to strengthen the prescription-event, prescription-identity, and identity-event links

Table 9.3 *Transfer conditions for supervised closed skills*

Example Job: Fast Food Restaurant Cook Focal Skill to Transfer: Making Food to Standards		
Transfer Requirement	*Accountability Link*	*Trainee Conditions Necessary for Transfer*
Trainees must follow precise standards under closely supervised conditions	Prescription-Event: The extent to which clear and unambiguous expectations exist for transfer	Trainees require precise standards for skill application and following direction from supervisors
	Prescription-Identity: The extent to which prescriptions are relevant to trainees by virtue of their role, values, or other personal attributes	Trainees value adhering to precise standards and willingly accept direction
	Identity-Event: The extent to which trainees have personal control over their ability to transfer	Trainees have the capacity to adhere to standards and follow direction

to enhance accountability and transfer in different contexts. The framework encourages careful consideration of what happens during training and in the broader organization to increase trainees' role clarity, sense of ownership, and perceived control over transfer. A common theme throughout this chapter has been that one size does not fit all and that careful consideration must be paid to the nature of the skill and the conditions under which the skill will be performed. It is important that practitioners not necessarily assume that a transfer strategy that worked well in one context will work well in another. Practitioners should be well versed in a broad set of transfer accountability strategies, as there is no quick fix.

The complexity and challenges of transfer highlight the importance of conducting a careful needs assessment to determine the specific context for transfer and the availability of support and accountability mechanisms to facilitate the application of new knowledge and skills. Along the same lines, multiple stakeholders should be involved in the needs assessment process and the implementation of accountability strategies. Transfer is not the responsibility of one, but of many stakeholders – trainers, supervisors, and trainees.

We summarize the conditions that must be satisfied to bolster Schlenker's (1994; 1997) three accountability links in Yelon and Ford's (1999) four contexts in Tables 9.3–9.6. These tables provide a useful reference for practitioners to design strategies for transfer; a sample job and task is provided for each context to help the reader. In designing transfer strategies, practitioners should strive to bolster all three links. Consider the context of actors developing a character role, a supervised open skill. To address the prescription-event link, the actors would require clear outcome goals for putting on a good performance, clear expectations for skill

Table 9.4 *Transfer conditions for autonomous closed skills*

Example Job: Hotel Guest Room Attendant Focal Skill to Transfer: Cleaning a Guest Room to Standards		
Transfer Requirements	*Accountability Link*	*Trainee Conditions Necessary for Transfer*
Trainees must follow precise standards under autonomous working conditions	Prescription-Event: The extent to which clear and unambiguous expectations exist for transfer	Trainees require precise standards for skill application and clear expectations for taking responsibility for monitoring standards themselves
	Prescription-Identity: The extent to which prescriptions are relevant to trainees by virtue of their role, values, or other personal attributes	Trainees value adhering to precise standards and working independently
	Identity-Event: The extent to which trainees have personal control over their ability to transfer	Trainees have the capacity to adhere to standards and work independently

Table 9.5 *Transfer conditions for autonomous open skills*

Example Job: Supervisor Focal Skill to Transfer: Motivating Employees		
Transfer Requirements	*Accountability Link*	*Necessary Trainee Conditions for Transfer*
Trainees must adapt skill autonomously	Prescription-Event: The extent to which clear and unambiguous expectations exist for transfer	Trainees require clear outcome goals and clear expectations for skill adaptation and taking responsibility for monitoring their performance
	Prescription-Identity: The extent to which prescriptions are relevant to trainees by virtue of their role, values, or other personal attributes	Trainees value skill experimentation and working independently
	Identity-Event: The extent to which trainees have personal control over their ability to transfer	Trainees have the capacity to adapt skills and work independently

Table 9.6 *Transfer conditions for supervised open skills*

Example Job: Actor Focal Skill to Transfer: Character Development		
Transfer Requirements	*Accountability Link*	*Trainee Conditions Necessary for Transfer*
Trainees must adapt skill under supervised conditions; must have receptivity to take direction	Prescription-Event: The extent to which clear and unambiguous expectations exist for transfer	Trainees require clear outcome goals and clear expectations for skill adaptation and taking direction from supervisors
	Prescription-Identity: The extent to which prescriptions are relevant to trainees by virtue of their role, values, or other personal attributes	Trainees value skill experimentation and are open to taking direction from others
	Identity-Event: The extent to which trainees have personal control over their ability to transfer	Trainees have the capacity to engage in skill experimentation and take direction from others

adaptation in developing their characters, and clear expectations that they will be directed and not be wholly autonomous. To address the prescription-identity link, the actors must value skill adaption, as well as value and be receptive to taking direction. Finally, to address the identity-event link, the actors must perceive that they have the ability to create a well-developed character. We acknowledge that designing accountability strategies may not always be easy, and they may not be necessary at all times. However, we encourage practitioners to make the attempt for knowledge and skill sets of particular strategic importance.

Future Research

By integrating Schlenker's (1994; 1997) and Yelon and Ford's (1999) frameworks, we have offered a number of strategies to enhance transfer. Some of these propositions were empirically referenced, but others remain theoretical. While we have identified several potentially viable transfer enhancement strategies, organizations may be using a host of additional strategies. Descriptive research would therefore be valuable to generate data on accountability strategies already being employed in workplaces. To extend the contribution of this chapter, research is needed to test the extent to which the strategies offered herein are effective. A fundamental tenet of this chapter is that situational specificity matters. As such, when validating these strategies, context must either be experimentally manipulated or measured and modeled in survey research. In addition to assessing the direct influence of the strategies on transfer, research could examine trainees' perceptions of goal/process clarity, ownership of transfer, and personal control as mediators in strategy-transfer relationships. Such work would validate the hypothesized central role of accountability for transfer.

An area in need of research is how best to promote favorable trainee attitudes toward performing open and closed skills under varying degrees of supervision. One challenge to development of favorable attitudes may be threats to an individual's identity. For example, performing a closed skill under supervised working conditions may likely be resisted by those who prefer to perform open skills autonomously. Research would be worthwhile that compares whether a discussion-based training format where trainees generate the benefits and importance of executing a specific skill yields more favorable attitudes than an approach where trainers communicate the benefits. Following Deci and Ryan's self-determination theory (2002), which posits that individuals seek to be self-directed agents, such an approach might yield potentially high returns.

We suggest several specific comparisons to validate our proposed integrated model. One potentially useful comparison is to examine the value of a single strategy across different contexts. For example, research could examine the different effects of self-management training for open versus closed skills. Given the complexity inherent in open skills, we would hypothesize that self-management training would be more effective in facilitating transfer in this context. Another useful comparison is to assess the effectiveness of different strategies that address a specific link. Both personality characteristics and perceived role breadth were argued to influence the prescription-identity link, and research would be worthwhile that examines which matters more.

Further, research would be valuable that examines the relative importance of the different links in a particular context. While the combination of all links forms the social adhesive to promote accountability, the links may not always be of equal importance in specific situations. We believe that the prescription-event link may be more important than the prescription-identity link for supervised closed skills and that the prescription-identity link is more important than the prescription event-link for autonomous open skills. Testing such relationships is warranted to ascertain whether greater precision is in fact necessary or whether a more a parsimonious set of strategies suffice.

These avenues for research could be addressed either through survey research or through experimental manipulations. A survey of employees could assess training context, training design and delivery, work environment support, individual differences, and transfer, preferably with data collected at multiple points in time. In an ideal design, employees from a large organization or across multiple organizations would be sampled to provide the necessary variability for comparative studies. Although it is difficult to secure such samples for training research, the increased availability of online panels through *Qualtrics*, for example, makes such research more feasible. When conducting transfer studies across contexts, the nature of the job, performance, and focal training content are likely different. Thus, researchers must pay careful attention to the selection of dependent variables that are applicable across contexts and lend themselves to meaningful comparisons. In this regard, measures of transfer should be general (e.g., "I successfully apply material from training on the job") as opposed to content specific (e.g., "I successfully apply customer skills from training on the job").

Experimental studies could also be conducted in the field to further substantiate cause-and-effect relationships. Given the challenge of access to organizations, experimental research with samples of working students may also be valuable. The aforementioned DeMatteo et al. (1997) lab study is a useful exemplar. In their 2 × 2 design, they studied two accountability interventions and their temporal position (before vs. after training) using a student sample and measured students' satisfaction and learning. Although DeMatteo and colleagues did not measure transfer, it is feasible to do so with the advent of mobile technologies such as *Socrative®* that enable researchers to survey individuals with simple questions by phones, tablets, and laptops about their transfer of class learning to the workplace.

Conclusion

In this chapter, we provided a synthesized framework for transfer of training that is theory driven, integrative, and context sensitive. By integrating the work of Schlenker and colleagues (1994; 1997) and Yelon and Ford (1999), this chapter has discussed how to enhance trainees' role clarity, sense of ownership, and perceived control over transfer for open and closed skills performed either under supervised or autonomous working conditions. Promoting transfer of training represents a perennial challenge for scholars and practitioners. Yet, promoting transfer is critical to ensure that employees possess the knowledge and skills to succeed in today's competitive and dynamic business environments. It is our hope that this chapter has provided a useful framework for understanding accountability issues associated with transfer, guiding future research efforts, and facilitating transfer design in practice.

References

Association for Talent Development. 2014 state of the industry report. https://www .td.org/Professional-Resources/State-Of-The-Industry-Report (accessed March 1, 2015).

Baldwin, T. T., and Magjuka, R. J. 1991. Organizational training and signals of importance: Linking pretraining perceptions to intentions to transfer. *Human Resource Development Quarterly* 2: 25–36.

Bandura, A. 1986. *Social Foundations of Thought and Action*. Englewood Cliffs, NJ: Prentice Hall.

Bates, R. A. 2003. *Managers as Transfer Agents: Improving Learning Transfer in Organizations*. San Francisco: Jossey Bass.

Blume, B. D., Ford, J. K., Baldwin, T. T., and Huang, J. L. 2010. Transfer of training: A meta-analytic review. *Journal of Management* 39: 1065–1105.

Brinkerhoff, R. O., and Montesino, M. U. 1995. Partnerships for training transfer: Lessons from a corporate study. *Human Resource Development Quarterly* 6: 263–274.

Broad, M. L. 2005. *Beyond Transfer of Training: Engaging Systems to Improve Performance*. San Francisco: John Wiley and Sons.

Broad, M. L., and Newstrom, J. W. 1992. *Transfer of Training: Action-Packed Strategies to Ensure High Payoff from Training Investments*. Reading, MA: Addison-Wesley.

Brown, T. C. 2005. Effectiveness of distal and proximal goals as a transfer-of-training intervention: A field experiment. *Human Resource Development* 16: 369–387.

Burke, L. A. 1997. Improving positive transfer: A test of relapse prevention training on transfer outcomes. *Human Resource Development Quarterly* 8: 115–128.

Burke, L. A. 2001. *High-Impact Training Solutions: Top Issues Troubling Trainers*. Westport, CT: Quorum Books.

Burke, L. A., and Baldwin, T. 1999. Workforce training transfer: A study of the effect of relapse prevention training and transfer climate. *Human Resource Management* 38: 227–242.

Burke, L. A., and Hutchins, H. 2007. Training transfer: An integrative literature review. *Human Resource Development Review* 6: 263–296.

Burke, L. A., and Saks, A. M. 2009. Accountability in training transfer: Adapting Schlenker's model of responsibility to a persistent but solvable problem. *Human Resource Development Review* 8: 382–402.

Burke, L. A., Hutchins, H., and Saks, A. 2013. Best practices in training transfer. In M. Paludi, ed., *The Psychology for Business Success*, 3, 115–132. Westport, CT: Praeger Publishing.

Button, S. B., Mathieu, J. E., and Zajac, D. M. 1996. Goal orientation in organizational research: A conceptual and empirical foundation. *Organizational Behavior and Human Decision Processes* 67: 26–48.

Chen, G., Gully, S.M., and Eden, D. 2001. Validation of a new general self-efficacy scale. *Organizational Research Methods* 4: 62–83.

Cheramie, R., and Simmering, M. 2010. Improving individual learning for trainees with low conscientiousness. *Journal of Managerial Psychology* 25: 44–57.

Colquitt, J., LePine, J. A., and Noe, R. 2000. Toward an integrative theory of training motivation: A meta-analytic path analysis of twenty years of research. *Journal of Applied Psychology* 85: 678–707.

Costa Jr., P. T., McCrae, R. R., and Dye, D. A. 1991. Facet scales for agreeableness and conscientiousness: a revision of the NEO personality inventory. *Personality and Individual Differences* 12: 887–898.

Cromwell, S. E., and Kolb, J. A. 2004. An examination of work-environment support factors affecting transfer of supervisory skills training to the workplace. *Human Resource Development Quarterly* 15: 449–471.

Deci, E., and Ryan, R. 2002. *Handbook of Self-determination Research*. Rochester, NY: University of Rochester Press.

DeHart-Davis, L. 2009. Green tape: A theory of effective organizational rules. *Journal of Public Administration Research and Theory* 19: 361–384.

DeMatteo, J., Lundby, K., and Dobbins, G. 1997. The effects of accountability on performance in training. *Training Research Journal* 3: 39–57.

Dose, J., and Klimoski, R. 1995. Doing the right thing in the workplace: Responsibility in the face of accountability. *Employee Responsibilities and Rights Journal* 8: 35–56.

Frink, D., and Klimoski, R. 1998. Toward a theory of accountability in organizations and human resources management. *Research in Personnel and Human Resources Management* 16: 1–51.

Gaudine, A. P., and Saks, A. M. 2004. A longitudinal quasi-experiment on the effects of posttraining transfer interventions. *Human Resource Development Quarterly* 15: 57–76.

Gist, M. E., and Mitchell, T. R. 1992. Self-efficacy: A theoretical analysis of its determinants and malleability. *Academy of Management Review* 17: 183–211.

Grossman, R., and Salas, E., 2011. The transfer of training: What really matters. *International Journal of Training and Development* 15: 103–120.

Hilbert, J., Preskill, H., and Russ-Eft, D., eds., 1997. *Evaluating Training*. Alexandria, VA: ASTD.

Holton, E. F., Bates, R., and Ruona, W. E. A. 2000. Development of a generalized learning transfer system inventory. *Human Resource Development Quarterly* 11: 333–360.

Hutchins, H., Burke, L. A., and Berthelsen, A. M. 2010. A missing link in the transfer problem? Understanding how trainers learn about training transfer. *Human Resource Management* 49: 599–618.

Judge, T. A., and Bono, J. E. 2001. Relationship of core self-evaluations traits–self-esteem, generalized self-efficacy, locus of control, and emotional stability – with job satisfaction and job performance: A meta-analysis. *Journal of Applied Psychology* 86: 80–92.

Judge, T. A., Erez, A., and Bono, J. E. 1998. The power of being positive: The relation between positive self-concept and job performance. *Human Performance* 11: 167–187.

Judge, T. A., Locke, E. A., and Durham, C. C 1997. The dispositional causes of job satisfaction: A core evaluations approach. *Research in Organizational Behavior* 19: 151–188.

Kopp, D. M. 2006. Trainer self-loathing. *Human Resource Development Quarterly* 17: 351–357.

Kozlowski, S. W., Gully, S. M., Brown, K. G., Salas, E., Smith, E. M., and Nason, E. R. 2001. Effects of training goals and goal orientation traits on multidimensional training outcomes and performance adaptability. *Organizational Behavior and Human Decision Processes* 85: 1–31.

Kraiger, K., Ford, J. K., and Salas, E. 1993. Application of cognitive, skill-based, and affective theories of learning outcomes to new methods of training evaluation. *Journal of Applied Psychology* 78: 311–328.

Lim, D. H., and Johnson, S. D. 2002. Trainee perceptions of factors that influence learning transfer. *International Journal of Training and Development* 6: 36–48.

Longenecker, C. O. 2004. Maximizing transfer of learning from management education programs: Best practices for retention and application. *Development and Learning in Organizations* 18: 4–6.

Marx, R. D. 1982. Relapse prevention for managerial training: A model for maintenance of behavioral change. *Academy of Management Review* 7: 433–441.

Mathieu, J., and Martineau, J. 1997. Individual and situational influence on training motivation. In J. K. Ford, ed., *Improving Training Effectiveness in Work Organizations*, 193–222. Mahwah, NJ: Lawrence Erlbaum.

Noe, R. A., Sears, J. A., and Fullenkamp, A. M. 1990. Relapse training: Does it influence trainees' post-training behavior and cognitive strategies? *Journal of Business and Psychology* 4: 317–328.

Noe, R. A., Tews, M. J., and Marand, A. D. 2013. Individual differences and informal learning in the workplace. *Journal of Vocational Behavior* 83: 327–335.

Parker, S. K., and Sprigg, C. A. 1999. Minimizing strain and maximizing learning: The role of job demands, job control, and proactive personality. *Journal of Applied Psychology* 84: 925–939.

Peterson, C., and Seligman, M. E. 2004. *Character Strengths and Virtues: A Handbook and Classification*. New York: Oxford University Press.

Richman-Hirsch, W. L. 2001. Post-training interventions to enhance transfer: The moderating effects of work environments. *Human Resource Development Quarterly* 12: 105–120.

Rouiller, J. Z., and Goldstein, I. L. 1993. The relationship between organizational transfer climate and positive transfer of training. *Human Resource Development Quarterly* 4: 377–390.

Saks, A. M. 2002. So what is a good transfer of training estimate? A reply to Fitzpatrick. *The Industrial-Organizational Psychologist* 39: 29–30.

Saks, A. M. and Belcourt, M. 2006. An investigation of training activities and transfer of training in organizations. *Human Resource Management* 45: 629–648.

Saks, A. M., and Burke, L. A. 2012. An investigation into the relationship between training evaluation and the transfer of training. *International Journal of Training and Development* 16: 118–127.

Santos, A., and Stuart, M. 2003. Employee perceptions and their influence on training effectiveness. *Human Resource Management Journal* 13: 27–45.

Schlenker, B. R. 1997. Personal responsibility: Applications of the triangle model. *Research in Organizational Behavior* 19: 241–301.

Schlenker, B. R., Britt, T. W., Pennington, J. W., Murphy, R., and Doherty, K. J. 1994. The triangle model of responsibility. *Psychological Review* 101: 632–652.

Stajkovic, A. D., and Luthans, F. 1998. Self-efficacy and work-related performance: A meta-analysis. *Psychological Bulletin* 124: 240–261.

Tannenbaum, S. I., and Yukl, G. 1992. Training and development in work organizations. *Annual Review of Psychology* 43: 399–441.

Taylor, P. J., Russ-Eft, D. F., and Chan, D. W. L. 2005. A meta-analytic review of behavior modeling training. *Journal of Applied Psychology* 90: 692–709.

Tews, M. J., and Tracey, J. B. 2008. An empirical examination of posttraining on-the-job supplements for enhancing the effectiveness of interpersonal skills training. *Personnel Psychology* 61: 375–401.

Tews, M. J., Michel, J. W., and Noe, R. A. 2011. Beyond objectivity: The performance impact of the perceived ability to learn and solve problems. *Journal of Vocational Behavior* 79: 484–495.

Tracey, J. B., and Tews, M. J. 2005. Construct validity of a general training climate scale. *Organizational Research Methods* 8: 353–374.

Tracey, J. B, Tannenbaum, S., and Kavanagh, M. 1995. Applying trained skills on the job: The importance of the work environment. *Journal of Applied Psychology* 80: 239–252.

Tziner, A., Haccoun, R., and Kadish, A. 1991. Personal and situational characteristics influencing the effectiveness of transfer of training improvement strategies. *Journal of Occupational Psychology* 64: 167–177.

van Wijk, R., Jansen, J. J. P., and Lyles, M. A. 2008. Inter- and intra-organizational knowledge transfer: A meta-analytic review and assessment of its antecedents and consequences. *Journal of Management Studies* 45: 830–853.

Wexley, K. N., and Baldwin, T. T. 1986. Post-training strategies for facilitating positive transfer: An empirical exploration. *Academy of Management Journal* 29: 508–520.

Wexley, K. N., and Nemeroff, W. 1975. Effectiveness of positive reinforcement and goal-setting as methods of management development. *Journal of Applied Psychology* 60: 446–450.

Wood, R., and Bandura, A. 1989. Social cognitive theory of organizational management. *Academy of Management Review* 14: 361–384.

Yelon, S., and Ford, K. 1999. Pursuing a multi-dimensional view of transfer. *Performance Improvement Quarterly* 12: 58–77.

10 Building Deep Specialization through Intentional Learning Activities

J. Kevin Ford, Jessica M. Webb, and Morgan Showler

> Any company has the potential to build deep specialization. Think about those job roles that define your company's competitive advantage. In most, these roles are in research, engineering, or manufacturing. Start here – and ask your business leaders to define what an expert really is. Study these people and use them as models to build deep specialization programs for others. (Bersin, 2009)

Work is becoming more knowledge driven and global in scope requiring a deeper combination of information, experience, understanding, and problem-solving skills that can be applied to decisions and actions around strategically critical situations (Kraiger & Ford, 2007). This reality highlights the need for enhancing the development of deep specialization for functional experts in key or "mission critical" jobs that are important for future growth (Ziebell, 2008). For example, at Intel, 80% of their worldwide staff works in technical positions (Bersin, 2009). This company and others like it are dependent on the level of knowledge and expertise in specialized areas. For example, the nuclear industry sets criteria for job position risk assessment with the highest level being jobs where: (1) individuals have critical and unique knowledge or skills that can have the potential for significant reliability and safety impacts, (2) years of training and experience are required, and (3) there are no ready replacements available (International Atomic Energy Agency, 2006).

The importance of understanding and enhancing deep specialization is particularly relevant today in response to the imminent retirement of such experts (i.e., the "grey tsunami") in many strategic business areas, especially in the United States (Moon, Hoffman, & Ziebell, 2009). It is important to not only understand in broad terms the distribution of expertise by job category, but also to identify what type of expertise (what tasks, skills, knowledge) is likely to be lost (risk assessment) through expected promotions, turnover, and retirements and to create processes to address expertise loss and strategically develop talent where there will be critical shortages before they occur (Ziebell, 2008).

As noted by Schein (1993), an individual's career can be studied as a series of movements along three different dimensions: (1) moving up in the hierarchy; (2) moving laterally across various subfields; and (3) moving toward the centers of influence in an organization. The concept of deep specialization in core areas that are critical to organizational success is targeted toward this third, and less researched, career movement. As noted by Bersin (2009), it is time to rethink the traditional career pyramid by increasing efforts to develop and enhance deep levels of skills and knowledge and hence accelerate the time it takes to become an expert in a career field. While organizations rely on experts in critical jobs to achieve strategic goals, they often do not fully appreciate or understand the impact of expertise on day to day operations (Borton, 2007; Prietula & Simon, 1989).

Organizations often focus on bringing newcomers up to speed on a job to get immediate value out of the investment of recruitment, selection, and initial training costs (Byham, 2008). Less attention is paid to longer-term developmental strategies to facilitate the move to deep specialization (Lord & Hall, 2005; Ziebell, 2008). Identifying effective strategies for long-term development is a critical step in considering how to speed up the development cycle. Given that it can take years of training, learning activities, and work experiences to develop deep specialization in a technical career field, it is important to identify key levers to accelerate individual development (Hoffman et al., 2014).

The purpose of this chapter is to examine intentional learning strategies that can be enacted to develop individuals in highly specialized jobs throughout the course of their career. There have been some attempts to focus not just on training in isolation but on continued development throughout a career (e.g., Caligiuri & Tarique, 2014; Cerasoli et al., 2014). Salas and Rosen (2009) reviewed the literature on the development process as individuals move from novice to expert and provided a framework for understanding the characteristics of expertise, as well as discussed how expertise can be developed and maintained. Based on this framework, they developed 17 principles for developing expertise at work (e.g., provide variability in learning activities). While the framework and principles have value, only one of the 17 principles dealt explicitly with differences in learning strategies to support learning needs through transitions from beginner to intermediate and to advanced learners.

The present chapter explores changing developmental needs and effective learning strategies as an individual moves from a relative newcomer to becoming a valued employee with deep specialization. We first identify three key characteristics that evolve as individuals develop expertise in their job and performance indicators that are associated with this evolution. The chapter then provides a framework for the goals of development over time. The final section provides insights into strategies for building knowledge and skills as a person progresses toward expertise.

The Road to Expertise

The goal of development is the achievement of consistent, superior performance through enhanced mental and physical processes. This goal is pursued by providing employees experience, training, and on-the-job learning activities that have a "developmental punch" (Ford & Kraiger, 1995; Kraiger & Ford, 2007; Quiñones, Ford, & Teachout, 1995). Researchers have begun to identify the depth of knowledge and skill building that characterize deep specialization in a career field (Ericsson, Nandagopal, & Roring, 2009; McCall, 2004). This section discusses the shifts that occur to change a person's status from a relative novice to expert, as well as indicators of expert performance.

Qualitative Shifts That Define Expertise

Dreyfus and Dreyfus's (1986) identify five developmental stages: novice, advanced beginner, competent, proficient, and expert. Variants of this stage model exist, adding terms such as *naivete, initiate, apprentice,* and *journeyman* (Alexander, 2003; Hoffman, 1996; Hoffman et al., 1995; Kinchin & Cabot, 2010). Research generally supports that there is a stepwise (but not necessarily linear) progression of skill and practice in developing expertise (Dall'Alba & Sandberg, 2006; Kinchin & Cabot, 2010). During the beginning phase, novices are focused on learning facts and using deliberate reasoning, and they rely on general strategies across situations. By the competent stage, learners have begun to organize related pieces of information into mental models and have routinized many (but not all) types of processes. By the time learners have reached the expert stage, they can deliberately reason about their own intuitions regarding a situation or problem and generate new rules or strategies to use (see Dreyfus & Dreyfus, 1986).

The stage models highlight that the knowledge of an apprentice is thus not just an incomplete version of the knowledge of an expert (Lajoie, 2003). Rather, there are three key qualitative shifts that occur over time. One shift concerns depth of knowledge. With deep specialization, the knowledge of the learner has become proceduralized and principled so that individuals can not only recall facts and figures as an advanced beginner can, but the person can distinguish between situations when that knowledge (or skill) is applicable and when it is not (Ericsson & Charness, 1994). The ability to apply this type of knowledge leads individuals to use their depth of knowledge in the appropriate context and at the appropriate time to achieve superior performance. Over the course of various job experiences, individuals learn rules and heuristics and can test the boundaries of those heuristics to recognize constraints of the problem space (Ericsson & Charness, 1994). As learners encounter a greater number of situations, pattern recognition increases. Consequently, an individual with deeper knowledge can do a better job of relating information to changing demands and predicting what might happen next given the current situation. For instance, Dreyfus and Dreyfus (1986) posit that a difference between competent and proficient performers is that competent individuals lack the "know-how" of understanding how to approach a problem, while proficient individuals have many more experiences that allow them to think and act more automatically.

A second qualitative shift concerns the complexity of a learner's mental models or ways of organizing knowledge. As individuals gain experience with a task or job, they begin to form relational knowledge that defines how various pieces of information fit together (Klein & Hoffman, 1993). Learners who have achieved deep specialization have well-defined mental models that help them recognize connections between seemingly disparate pieces of information that then lead to problem solutions. In particular, they possess knowledge structures that contain both problem definitions and specific solutions while learners who are at the earlier stages tend to possess separate knowledge structures for problem definitions and solutions (Ericsson & Charness, 1994). Thus, when exposed to a domain early in a career, individuals focus on the fundamental elements of the problem and seek out evidence to confirm or disconfirm their hypotheses. Over time, they look at the features of the problem and the overall situational patterns, and reflect on job experiences that may have been similar. In this way, individuals progressively focus more on the entire situation holistically to see the interconnectedness of features within the problem space to move forward to a solution (Salas & Rosen, 2009). This understanding of interconnectedness leads to well-organized schemas such that when individuals are confronted with a problem that requires the knowledge stored in long-term memory, the brain recalls the schema and it is place in working memory (Prietula & Simon, 1989; Salas & Rosen, 2009). As a result, this knowledge no longer places as large of a burden on an individual's working memory. Experts rely less on context-free information, instead focusing on the context of the situation and their past personal experience in related contexts and settings (Farrington-Darby & Wilson, 2006). For example, high-level programmers can mentally group steps within a task so that when they see a particular symptom or problem, they can identify several alternative strategies to take and can rank order these strategies in terms of their likelihood of success (Ford & Schmidt, 2000).

A third qualitative shift involves the development of effective self-regulatory skills that include the ability to know what the appropriate strategies are for facilitating further knowledge and skill acquisition (Lord & Hall, 2005). Individuals who have achieved deep specialization are able to more accurately monitor or assess their own mental states, more likely to know when they have understood task-relevant information, and more likely to discontinue a problem-solving strategy that would ultimately prove to be unsuccessful (Salas & Rosen, 2009). They are also better able to estimate the number of trials they will need to accomplish a task. For example, highly valued information technologists have superior understanding of programming tasks and of ideal working strategies, and have a better awareness of their own performance strategy options (Sonnentag, 1998).

Performance Indicators of Expertise

As individuals increase in knowledge and skill level, they become increasingly reliant on the situation to inform them of the problem, take a more holistic approach to recognizing patterns in the problem, base decision making on intuition, and become absorbed in their performance. As noted by Dreyfus (2006), those who reach high levels of expertise "do not solve problems, and do not make decisions; they do what normally works" (24). Individuals who have reached this high level can also begin to contribute to their domain by generating new knowledge creatively (Ericsson & Charness, 1994).

Researchers have begun to explore performance characteristics that can be used to determine if a person has obtained expert status (Germain & Tejeda, 2012; Van der Heijden & Verhelst, 2002; Weiss & Shanteau, 2003). As noted by the Electric Power Research Institute, although it may take up to 25 years to become an expert in mission-critical activities, a proportion of utility personnel with that level of tenure are not recognized as having expertise; they have simply become very good (i.e., proficient) at what they do (see Ziebell, 2008). Hoffman et al. (2014) provided behaviorally based indicators to distinguish between those who are proficient and those considered to be expert in a specialized area. Some of the indicators of experts include: (1) is highly regarded by peers because of their highly organized body of knowledge; (2) shows consummate skill (i.e., has qualitatively different strategies and has economy of effort); (3) deals effectively with rare cases; (4) recognizes aspects of a problem that make it novel and brings strategies to solve tough cases; and (5) contributes new knowledge and procedures. Hoffman and Hanes (2003) provide evidence that experts at particular highly skilled jobs (e.g., repairing large turbines) can be identified by plant managers and fellow engineers based on these characteristics.

Framework for Understanding the Development of Deep Specialization

While research on expertise has expanded our understanding of underlying characteristics and expected changes in performance from novice to expert, the majority of expertise studies have focused on tasks in well-defined domains such as chess masters, hockey players, and pianists (e.g., Ericsson, 2006). In addition, the emphasis in these studies has been on differences between experts and novices with less focus on the developmental challenges of moving an individual from a novice to a competent level and from a competent level to deep specialization.

In well-defined, highly focused tasks the strategy of deliberate practice has been highlighted as a key impetus for development (Ericsson, Krampe, & Tesch-Romer, 1993). In comparison, problems in highly technical jobs, such as product development engineers for the auto industry or power plant operators, are much more ill-defined and varied, thus posing several challenges for developing deep specialization. These types of jobs require complex learning within dynamic situations so that individuals can learn how to generalize information and strategies from one type of problem situation to new, unpredictable problems. For example, when dealing with a traffic accident, police officers must learn how to attend to various pieces of information they obtain about the actions of the drivers involved both directly from witnesses and indirectly from the accident scene. They must develop general strategies for how to obtain this information and how to make judgments as to the accuracy of the information, which they

Table 10.1 *Heuristic model of development toward deep specialization*

	Routine Expertise	Adaptive Expertise
Training	Design for Complex Skills: • Contextual interference • Augmented feedback • Scaffolding Targeted practice	Guided discovery Frame changing Adaptive thinking
Work Experience	Deliberate performance: • Estimation • Experimentation • Extrapolation • Explanation Cognitive apprenticeship	On-the-job learning Developmental job assignments

then employ dynamically across accident situations altering those strategies as needed based on the specific context (such as when, e.g., there are no witnesses and information provided by the involved drivers' conflicts). While moving through the stages of expertise, there is also an interplay between immediate demands for performance and longer-term expertise development, as individuals are required to perform at high levels each day while learning to perform tasks that they have not yet faced.

Table 10.1 presents a framework for thinking about the development of deep specialization for highly complex skills within specialized jobs. The model consists of two dimensions; the first dimension targets the expected outcomes of developmental activities. The conceptual approach or framework that has utility when examining development over time involves thinking in terms of the need for building routine or for building adaptive expertise (Hatano & Inagaki, 1986; Holyoak, 1991). The second dimension of the framework focuses on the two major types of learning activities for developing skills – through formal training or through work experience (Ford & Kraiger, 1995). Research consistently shows that organizations that invest more in training have higher levels of productivity (Kim & Ployhart, 2014; Sung & Choi, 2014; Zwick, 2006). Learning activities can also be incorporated into the work experience of the learner to facilitate building the depth of knowledge, organized mental models, and strong self-regulatory processes required as individuals move toward deep specialization (Sonnentag, 2000).

Routine and Adaptive Expertise

Hatano and Inagaki (1986) and Holyoak (1991) have distinguished between developing routine and adaptive expertise. Routine expertise focuses on knowledge and skills that individuals apply to well-learned and familiar contexts and situations. Through learning activities, individuals compile declarative knowledge into procedural, condition-action knowledge and continued practice leads to automatic and efficient performance. Adaptive expertise involves the capability to integrate simultaneously multiple sources of knowledge for use in addressing changing conditions and unfamiliar situations.

Hoffman et al. (2014) have noted characteristics of tasks that impact the need for routine or adaptive expertise, such as whether situations are relatively static or dynamic. In dynamic conditions (relevant for many work tasks), goals are often shifting and may even be competing with other goals and problems are often ill-structured and information is incomplete and ambiguous (Oransanu & Connoly, 1993). Action feedback loops are often lengthy in dynamic situations, making the connection between behavioral cause and effect more difficult to establish. Dynamic conditions also require an individual to be able to recall multiple perspectives and schemas to determine the meaning of the situation or problem before moving to solutions.

Although routine experts can solve familiar problems quickly and accurately, they have difficulty with novel problems or situations. In contrast, adaptive experts are said to be able to invent new procedures based on their knowledge and make predictions regarding possible outcomes that may occur depending on the strategy taken. Adapting requires an understanding of deeper principles underlying the task, executive-level capabilities to recognize and identify changed situations and knowledge of whether the existing repertoire of strategies can be applied (Smith, Ford, & Kozlowski, 1997). If the situation requires individuals to reconfigure procedures, extensive knowledge about a variety of procedures as well as how to select and combine them is necessary. The progression from competent to adaptive expert requires that decision making and indeed an understanding of the particular situation is intuitive such that it may "take longer to reach than any of the intermediate stages, if it's ever reached at all" (Kinchin & Cabot, 2010: 155).

The concepts of routine and adaptive expertise are consistent with calls from instructional design researchers to distinguish between training for recurrent and nonrecurrent skills. As noted by Young et al. (2014), for more novice or advance beginner learners, the aspects that need to be developed are recurrent skills (i.e., practicing tasks that are consistent from problem situation to problem situation). This development of recurrent skills continues throughout a career as an individual comes to automatize certain tasks and develops more efficient and effective strategies relevant to these recurrent skills. When moving beyond basic competency, there is a need to also develop nonrecurrent skills in which the effectiveness of behaviors differs across problem situations. Thus, the development of nonrecurrent skills builds upon the foundations laid by developing competencies in the recurrent skills.

Learning Activities

Much of the empirical work on understanding learning and transfer of learning has focused on relatively simple tasks (Wulf & Shea, 2002). Recent work has emphasized that learning complex skills is different than learning simple skills during training and work experience, and that principles of learning must reflect that reality (Wulf & Shea, 2002). In addition, while there has been much research on work experience as helping build complex leadership skills, less attention has been paid to the role of experience in building complex skills in highly technical and specialized jobs. The following sections will provide strategies for developing complex skills in such specialized jobs through both more formal training design and on-the-job learning principles within an organizational setting.

Training for Complex Skills

Complex learning must target the integration of knowledge, skills, and attitudes and the transfer of what is learned to work (van Merriënboer, Kirschner, & Kester, 2003). Cognitive load theory provides a foundation for discussing the instructional design principles that facilitate learning while not overwhelming the learner with the complexity of the tasks to be learned.

Cognitive load theory focuses on how cognitive resources are distributed in a learning situation and how the amount of resources is negatively related to the processing of working memory (Chandler & Sweller, 1991). It has been used as a guiding framework to describe an expertise reversal effect, or the change in the effectiveness of particular learning techniques as an individual progresses through stages of expertise (Kalyuga et al., 2003). When teaching complex skills, novices and advance beginners need much more structured information (e.g., low intrinsic cognitive load) than competent performers to understand the basics and learn productively. As skill level increases, this same amount of structure is no longer productive to learning. The intrinsic cognitive load (associated with performing the essential aspects of the task) then becomes extraneous load (associated with the nonessential aspects of the task) such that the information provided is redundant to the individual and prevents them from learning new information (Kalyuga, 2007). For example, with newer employees, working memory can only process a limited number of elements at any given time, which can create a bottleneck for learning (Young et al., 2014). To facilitate learning, extraneous load must be decreased.

Learning from Work Experience

Developing routine or adaptive expertise requires not only formal training but also systematic and intentional work experiences that build upon trained skills. Ford et al. (1992) identified three ways of operationalizing work experience, including the breadth or number of different trained tasks performed on the job, the activity level or the number of times each of these tasks is performed, and the task type or the difficulty of the tasks performed on the job. In a meta-analytic review by Quiñones et al. (1995), they found that the different measures of work experience were differentially related to performance outcomes. Tesluk and Jacobs (1998) built on the work of Quiñones and colleagues and described work experience as having quantitative (amount, time) and qualitative (variety, challenge, complexity) components. In addition, they identified density and timing as interactional components (different combinations of quantitative and qualitative aspects of experience). Density focuses on the intensity of work experiences. For example, if a person obtains experience in a variety of challenging situations, that person will have more density of experience than someone with the same tenure level who is given relatively fewer challenging assignments. The timing dimension refers to "when a work experience occurs relative to a longer sequence of successive experiences such as those that characterize a career" (329). For example, having a mentor who observes and immediately provides detailed feedback on how to improve following a challenging assignment facilitates learning. This dimension captures the notion that specific work experiences can be ordered or sequenced in ways that maximize motivational, learning, and performance outcomes depending on the developmental need of the learner.

Strategies for Developing Deep Specialization

In this section, we examine intentional strategies that can facilitate the development of expertise. We emphasize the different approaches for each of the four cells in Table 10.1.

Building Routine Expertise through Training

The literature on the training of complex tasks highlights three principles that fit with building routine expertise. In addition, there is an emerging literature on building skills to achieve routine expertise through targeted and intensive practice of key skills – especially given advances in training technologies such as virtual reality and serious gaming.

Incorporate Appropriate Instructional Design Principles
According to Koedinger and colleagues (2008), learning principles consist of multiple instructional techniques that, when combined, create multiple possible instructional and learning paths. Of these, the most researched instructional design principles for facilitating learning of complex tasks are contextual interference, augmented feedback, and scaffolding.

Contextual interference is defined as the factors within the training environment that can enhance or inhibit learning. When learning a skill, contextual interference is specified through a practice schedule. Usually, contextual interference manifests as blocked practice (i.e., practicing all trials on a task before transitioning to another task) or random practice (i.e., transitioning between trials on different tasks). The contextual interference effect provides evidence that high contextual interference (random practice) results in better learning and transfer of simple skills (Shea & Morgan, 1979). However, the opposite appears to be true for learning complex skills – especially for novice learners attempting to learn a complex motor skill. According to Wulf and Shea (2002), low contextual interference (blocked practice) is better for learning complex skills. The cognitive load when learning a complex skill is considerably higher than when learning simple skills due to the need for more memory and attentional resources. When individuals are starting to learn a complex task and have had little practice, low contextual interference will have a more positive impact on learning. As Wulf and Shea conclude, "the results seem to indicate that when the tasks are more difficult because of high attention, memory, and or motor demands (or when learners are relatively inexperienced), random practice may overload the system and thus disrupt the potential benefits of random practice" (188). The implication is that as the individual practices the complex skill more often and becomes more efficacious, introducing high contextual interference may benefit performance by allowing for better learning transfer to varied contexts and settings.

Another principle for facilitating complex skill learning is augmented feedback. Feedback consists of providing knowledge of results or knowledge of performance to individuals. Wulf and Shea (2002) argue that augmented feedback should be delivered frequently during complex skill practice trials to effectively transfer learning at the onset of practicing a new complex skill. By delivering frequent feedback for a task that could possibly overload individuals' cognitive resources, learners obtain critical and specific performance information that helps them to understand their current learning progress and adapt their strategies and behaviors to improve. This helps learners to develop a working understanding of generally successful and unsuccessful principles and strategies and to learn to self-reflect on their performance, increasing the likelihood that complex skills will transfer to real-world contexts. In this way, individuals are able to develop their own checks and balances to their learning system.

The third principle of scaffolding includes strategies that support learning over time as a learner develops (van Merriënboer, Kirschner, & Kester, 2003). Van Merriënboer et al. (2003) argue that instructors should structure learning tasks from easy to difficult over time and to vary the context in which these tasks occur to encourage generalization. From this perspective, as individuals progress, the amount of instructor support received should be reduced (e.g., fading). They encourage instructors to use supportive information (e.g., information that supports learning and performance; the productive intrinsic load) up front before starting any instruction on a set of tasks. As individuals progress through the tasks, instructors should provide procedural information (e.g., how to perform the task) just in time to not overload working memory. Scaffolding reflects a strategy that facilitates enhancing awareness and self-regulation as well as building knowledge and skills (Azevedo, Cromley & Seibert, 2004; Najjar, 2008). For instance, for relatively new learners, it is important to provide more structured opportunities for learning. At earlier stages of development, trainees need guidance as to what to practice and how to practice it so that they can develop enduring, successful practice habits and experience (Barzilai & Blau, 2014). However, for intermediate learners (those building routine expertise), an emphasis on developing independent learning and self-monitoring is most likely beneficial, as employees at this stage are more prepared to take charge of their own learning. Advanced learners benefit most from access to mentor guidance, as they are able to engage effectively in self-regulated learning, but may not yet have the experience that more senior employees can draw from when making decisions. Thus, instructional design principles suggest that moving from novice to expert involves adapting learning strategies from instructor-guided, structured, and focused on more simple tasks in early stages of learning toward more independently directed, variable, and focused on more complex tasks across situations in advanced stages of learning.

Targeted Practice

A critical component in starting and sustaining the process of building toward routine expertise is through deliberate practice (Ericsson et al., 1993). As noted by Ericsson (2006), executing proficiently during routine work may not lead to further improvement. Instead, improvements depend on deliberate efforts to continually refine and enhance one's skills.

Advances in new training technologies allow for much more targeted and intensive practice than through traditional training programs. Technologies such as virtual reality (VR) and simulation training provide a safe environment in which to make mistakes and observe the consequences of actions. Scenarios can stimulate the senses, incorporate interactivity and cause and effect linkages, as well as include a cycle of judgments, behaviors, and feedback that allow for high physical and psychological fidelity (Ford & Meyer, 2014).

With simulation and VR training, learning occurs by immersing the trainee in media rich contexts that are similar to those encountered in real life (Brooks, 1999). A VR training system can simulate many different types of situations and learning events within a short time frame (Gupta, Anand, Brough, Schwartz, & Kavetsky, 2008). VR training applications are now more numerous, more powerfully realistic, and more innovative. VR technology has been applied to areas such as driving simulators (Cockayne & Darken, 2004), medical situations such as surgical procedures (Hague & Srinivasan, 2006), military tactics (Knerr, 2007), and aircraft maintenance tasks (Bowling, Khasawneh, Kaewkuekool, Jiang, & Gramopadhye, 2008).

The evidence for the effectiveness of VR is striking for training very specific skills within discrete tasks such as medical procedures. Hague and Srinivasan (2006) found that simulators lessened the time taken to complete a given surgical task in the operating room and lead to no differences in error rates in comparison with traditional clinical training. Larsen and colleagues (2009) examined studies on training for laparoscopic surgery through randomized controlled trials and found that VR training led to the equivalence of the experienced gained from 25 surgeries and reduced the time to complete operations. McGaghie, Issenberg, Cohen, Barsuk and Wayne (2012) showed that simulation with embedded deliberate practice enhanced specific clinical skill acquisition goals over traditional clinical medical training efforts. Larsen et al. (2012) found that operating time was reduced by 17% to 50% through VR training depending on the simulator type and training principles incorporated. They also found that deliberate practice was a superior approach than training based on a fixed time or fixed numbers of repetitions. Interestingly, Bongers, and colleagues (2015) incorporated problems into the laparoscopic skills simulator that a trainee was forced to address while continuing with the simulated operation. Results indicated that while the interruptions impacted all trainees' performance the intervention group (that received problems) was significantly faster in solving problems on the posttest evaluation.

Building Routine Expertise through Work Experience

Glaser and Chi (1988) noted the need to know how expertise is acquired and how beginning learners can be presented with the appropriate experiences to build competency. Strategies for incorporating intentional developmental job experiences into work to build functional depth are just becoming more a focus of research efforts. Two intentional development strategies that are most promising for developing routine expertise through work experiences include deliberate performance and intentional efforts to enhance self-regulatory skills via cognitive apprenticeship.

Deliberate Performance

Deliberate performance is defined as "effort to increase domain expertise while engaged in routine work activity" (Fadde & Klein, 2010: 5). Similar to just-in-time training, deliberate performance involves leveraging everyday job situations as learning opportunities, but with a focus on building expert-like mental frameworks and situational awareness that allow an individual to approach decision making and problem solving more efficiently (Fadde & Klein, 2010). Fadde and Klein (2010) suggest four deliberate performance strategies that can be used to build routine expertise while performing day-to-day work activities: estimation, experimentation, extrapolation, and explanation.

Estimation involves weighing what is known about a task or project and how it might be related to other tasks or projects, as well as how it could be affected by the environment. The individual can then be asked to approximate the amount of time and resources needed to complete it prior to working on the task. For example, an engineer could be prompted to estimate the amount of time and effort that would be needed to troubleshoot an electrical problem and then be asked to reflect after completing the task on why or why not the prediction was accurate.

Experimentation allows an individual to try out different strategies for accomplishing a task or goal and then to make adjustments based on whether the strategy was successful or not. The individual is pushed to consider alternative strategies and to try them out and reflect, often with a mentor, on what strategies worked best and why.

Extrapolation is using some prior situation that was completed successfully or unsuccessfully (whether through direct experience or the experience of others) as a reference point for thinking about why success was achieved or how things might have been done differently to prevent a negative outcome.

Explanation involves having the individual discuss the steps taken on a project, explain why things were done the way they were, justify the order of the steps taken, and explain what cues prompted different responses and why. Explaining actions can help the learner make better sense of those actions, the situation, and the feedback loop to identify more effective strategies, understand the bottlenecks in the system, and make improvements.

Though few have examined deliberate performance in the workplace, researchers have investigated deliberate practice on the job. One successful instance of incorporating deliberate practice into the workplace was described by Sonnentag and Kleine (2000). They measured systematic attempts at deliberate practice by insurance agents during work through regularly performing key tasks with the aim of developing their competence. They found that the more time agents spent on deliberate practice above the number of cases handled and the amount of time on the job, the higher their rated performance was. Overall, mental stimulation (e.g., imagining difficult situations with a client and mentally exploring what to do) and asking for feedback were determined to be the main aspects that were practiced in a deliberate way while working on the job. As Fadde and Klein (2010) note, the most difficult part of deliberate performance is to make sense of the feedback received in the workplace environment. By estimating and experimenting (similar to the notion of mental stimulation), on-the-job learners are able to make inferences about their environment, consider strategies to test those inferences on their own or with colleagues, and receive feedback from their environment on the success of those strategies.

Cognitive Apprenticeship

Another strategy for building expertise through work experience is through the promotion of self-regulation during task performance (Salas & Rosen, 2009). Research has shown that self-monitoring and metacognition are useful in improving performance by fostering awareness of progress toward a task or goal (Fiorella, Vogel-Walcutt, & Fiore, 2012; Pintrich, Wolters, & Baxter, 2000).

Lajoie (2003) describes a "cognitive apprenticeship model" that can be used to enhance cognitive and metacognitive processes in technical troubleshooting tasks while on the job. The model was developed to help facilitate the transfer and enhancement of skills from the initial extensive training program to help learners continue to learn on the job and accelerate the development of proficiency. The approach focuses on identifying how experts go about troubleshooting problems, and then using that type of information to develop realistic job situations and problems and to help build an intelligent tutoring system to use as a performance aid. The learners can then obtain extensive practice and build skills relevant to how experts approach and solve the troubleshooting tasks while at work. The apprenticeship includes the use of realistic problems through computer simulation of the job environment and the intelligent tutoring system to provide a safe environment for coaching support. Lajoie (2003) noted that after 24 hours of practice on this system, airmen who had been on the job for six months were able to troubleshoot test station failures at a level similar to others who had been on the job for four years. In addition, the more time learners spent in the tutoring environment, the fewer steps taken to solve the problem and the closer trainees' troubleshooting processes were to expert processes and solutions.

Research on the cognitive apprenticeship strategy demonstrates that making learners aware of the strategies in identifying and solving problems that experts use can help guide practice and learning processes by building stronger self-regulatory skills. During the workday, an individual can be prompted to recognize patterns (identification of successful vs. unsuccessful strategies), feedback seeking (looking for additional information regarding performance progress), and the development of long-term goals. Thus, self-regulation can be a vehicle for engaging in a form of deliberate practice while performing job-relevant work. Such systems also allow individuals to learn from mistakes through work in simulated environments; the intelligent tutoring system can then help pinpoint areas in need of more development. These opportunities are important not only because they provide learners with the ability to experiment and make mistakes outside the context of their job performance, but also because they push learners to move beyond their current achievement and competency levels. Providing immediate, constructive, and high-quality feedback to learners as they navigate these learning tasks allows them to make adjustments and strategize with an emphasis on development rather than on performance, as is typically the case for formal job tasks. By providing employees with opportunities to more quickly tackle advanced skill development, the timeline that might be expected for developing expertise is shortened as they develop critical skills and cognitions earlier and independent of job title or formal job tasks.

Building Adaptive Expertise through Training

Adaptability has been conceptualized as the capacity to alter one's performance in response to shifting challenges and the ability to anticipate changes and to modify strategies (Ely, Zaccaro, & Conjar, 2009). Three processes that help to build adaptability are guided discovery learning, cognitive frame changing, and adaptive thinking training.

Guided Discovery Learning

The traditional learning approach (especially for building routine expertise) uses a deductive approach in which trainees are explicitly instructed on the complete task and its concepts, rules, and strategies. In contrast, research indicates the importance of taking an inductive approach to build more learning depth, as well as to promote adaptive expertise (Smith et al., 1997). In this discovery learning process, individuals must explore a task or situation to infer and learn the underlying rules, principles, and strategies for effective performance. As noted by Mayer (2004) and Kirschner, Sweller, and Clark (2006), it is also clear that guided discovery learning is more effective than pure discovery. Research also indicates that guided discovery learning is more effective for individuals with experience and some level of competency on the task (Taylor, Russ-Eft, & Chan, 2005). A recent meta-analysis by Hutchins et al. (2013) found that exploratory learning provided more benefits as guidance increased and for far transfer more than near transfer.

There are several reasons why guided rather than pure discovery learning is beneficial (Ford & Schmitt, 2000). First, in the discovery learning approach, individuals are typically more motivated to learn because they are responsible for generating correct task strategies and are thus more actively engaged in learning. Second, discovery learning allows learners to use hypothesis testing and problem-solving learning strategies. In contrast to the traditional deductive learning approach, this active process requires more conscious attention for its application and adds depth to the learning process. Third, individuals engaged in exploratory learning are also likely to experiment with a greater range of strategies. The development of these strategies for discovering information helps individuals to identify novel or unpredictable job situations and, thus, promote a search for new ways to approach the situation. The new knowledge that is acquired by trying out alternative strategies can then become better integrated with the learner's existing knowledge.

There are several ways to implement a guided discovery approach to learning for perceptual-motor and problem-solving tasks. Guidance can include the following types: giving partial answers to problems, providing leading questions or hints to the learner, varying the size of steps in instruction (part vs. whole learning), and providing prompts without giving solutions. In addition, guidance can be given to learners on how to form hypotheses and test out those ideas in an effective way. For example, trainees can be presented with case studies of previous situations and asked to draw inferences about effective and ineffective responses to these situations. From these specific incidents, general principles of effective response can be generated and discussed.

Cognitive Frame Changing

Cognitive frame changing (DeYoung, Flanders, & Peterson, 2008; Ohlsson, 1992) is the process of breaking free of inappropriate assumptions, increasing insight problem solving, and creating or adopting new task-relevant strategies. To the extent that individuals can switch cognitive frames, they will be better able to find solutions to complex, novel problems and adapt their skills to meet unanticipated environmental demands (Ely et al., 2009). McKenzie and colleagues (2009) found that successful performers must also possess the ability to manage opposing demands. As noted by Quinn and Cameron (1988), individuals must "have the capacity to see problems from contradictory frames, to entertain and pursue alternative perspectives" (45) so as to learn strategies for fulfilling competing expectations.

Learning strategies that can enhance an individual's ability to react to and anticipate job challenges are emerging and being incorporated into training scenarios (Zaccaro et al., 2009). In terms of fostering cognitive frame-changing skills, Ely et al. (2009) propose that experiential variety. Similarly, Nelson,

Zaccaro, and Herman (2010) expanded on the frame-changing nature of these training approaches and noted that training that varies surface characteristics is appropriate for building routine expertise, but that adaptive expertise requires structural variation that includes varying the problem domain so that trainees must change their preferred strategy or approach.

In a series of studies, Ansburg and Dominowski (2000) examined the effects of different learning strategies on improving verbal insight problem solving. They found that strategic information provision before and during training to help guide trainees, in combination with practice involving surface variation, led to an increase in insight problem solving (i.e., cognitive frame-changing skills). In addition, designating time during training for elaborating on problems and facilitating the search for finding structural similarities between problems was found to increase insight problem solving. This approach is clearly different from the emphasis on developing routine expertise through repetitive practice to reach a certain standard or criterion of success.

Cognitive frame changing requires accurate situational assessments and critical thinking. As noted by van den Bosch and de Beer (2007), traditional training programs often provide insufficient opportunities for learning the situational nuances that make application of an already learned procedure either appropriate or inappropriate. Developing the ability to assess situations requires practicing cases from different perspectives so that learners have more opportunities to recognize various situational factors that can impact the effectiveness of different strategies and to recognize appropriate cues and their interdependencies. This experience-based interactive problem-solving approach is based on realistic and challenging work issues that require skills beyond foundational competency in a job domain. By engaging in practice experiences under controlled and safe conditions, the learner can gain a better understanding of situation-response relationships.

Klein (2004) describes two studies that compared critical thinking training design with a traditionally designed training program. The critical thinking program allowed learners to produce different explanations for events, question assumptions of situational assessments, and critique and revise strategies. Trainers provided support and feedback on the critical thinking process by asking key questions and challenging assumptions. They also would use the "devil's advocate" procedure to push for deeper thinking about an issue. Results indicated that the critical thinking training led to higher levels of augmentation (e.g., explaining conflicting evidence, criticizing assumptions) and stronger contingency planning (e.g., anticipating alternative courses of events in the plan and the quality of precautionary steps to be taken).

Adaptive Thinking Training
Adaptive thinking training was developed for the military to help teach soldiers how to think as well as how to fight. Adaptive thinking is one component of the adaptability model developed by Pulakos et al. (2000). The training focuses on the deliberate practice of thinking skills to enhance problem identification,

analysis, and problem solving so that the learner comes closer to the mental models of (and the methods employed by) experts. In this way, trainees can respond effectively to complex tasks under changing conditions and with ambiguous or missing information. The approach relies on developing (through discussions with experts in a domain) a set of themes or elements that should be considered when thinking through an ambiguous and changeable situation. For example, in the military, important elements of thinking might be seeing the big picture, using all assets available, visualizing the battlefield, and considering timing (Shadrick & Lussier, 2004; Shadrick & Lussier, 2009). Trainees are presented with a variety of scenarios and are encouraged to incorporate thinking elements into their understanding of the issues and developing possible solutions. Then, they discuss and defend what considerations they had relevant to the scenario, are presented with the expert model, and are given individualized feedback including a discussion about why certain elements were considered and incorporated into the expert model.

Evaluation of the adaptive thinking training has shown increases in the percent of critical information identified by learners as relevant to the scenario, as well as performance gains (Shadrick et al., 2007). Adaptive thinking training has also been expanded to include training teams (e.g., Zimmerman et al., 2012). For example, Schaefer et al. (2009) report on the training of planning teams that must respond to crises such as power grid shutdowns and industrial plant explosions using adaptive thinking training methods; they found improved cognitive task performance as a result of the team training. While these training approaches have been incubated in military settings, the notion of enhancing skills is quite relevant for building deep specialization in other industries as well.

Building Adaptive Expertise through Work Experience

Barneff and Koslowski (2002) note that performance is affected by longer-term, more extensive life experiences than those developed from short-term training and development programs. Thus, there is a need to understand and study more directly the effect of more extensive and long-term experience. Nelson, Zaccaro, and Herman (2010) stress that factors such as experiential variety need to be incorporated into work experience, as well as formal training activities. Similarly, Tannenbaum et al. (2010) discuss the importance of studying informal learning that occurs on the job. They note that four key informal learning components are the intent to learn and develop, experience and action, feedback, and reflection. This process of informal learning becomes even more important after an individual gains competency in the job, as they now have the foundational knowledge, mental models, and self-regulatory skills to grow and develop toward deep specialization.

Two major strategies for building expertise through work experience are creating learning opportunities within the current job and assigning challenging job assignments to broaden one's skill base beyond the immediate job, thus enhancing understanding of how systems work in the organization.

On-the-Job Learning

A critical component of employees being able to learn while performing on the job is to tackle challenges above their current skill level. Tannenbaum et al. (2010) contend that meaningful learning from these types of opportunities requires intentional steps ensure tolerance for deviation (learning from mistakes), tolerance of inefficiency, and feedback from mentors to drive reflection. Strategies for enhancing learning during these challenging job experiences can be taken prior to task performance, during task performance, and after task performance (Ford & Schmidt, 2000; Ford et al., 1992).

Nelson et al. (2010) describe the importance of preperformance instruction to facilitating the development of adaptive expertise. While based on training research, the findings have direct implications for improving performance in the job domain. Preperformance briefings by supervisors or mentors might review what types of situations are likely to occur while performing a task and how to respond to them. The briefs can also highlight different ways of thinking about the upcoming task and the problems embedded in that task so as to prompt more critical thinking.

During task performance, mentors can be available to provide adaptive guidance (Bell & Kozlowski, 2002). Adaptive guidance refers to support given to the person performing a task by providing diagnostic task-related information, timely suggestions on how to improve performance, and encouragement to seek alternative strategies when appropriate. This support is particularly important for developing strategic task skills that include an understanding of how to integrate various pieces of information related to a task and gaining a broader contextual understanding of when to use specific strategic skills. Strategic skills are needed in complex work domains that are malleable and require learners to shift their behavior and cognitions in response to changing situations. Adaptive guidance can help learners to move beyond the acquisition of basic task skills involving declarative and procedural knowledge and an emphasis on simple, routinized operations (Kanar & Bell, 2013)

Once the task has been completed, mentors can aid in the learning experience by conducting after-action reviews. Chatham (2009) discusses the development of the Top Gun approach that incorporated a strong emphasis on after-action reviews to force individuals to confront what happened and why and how different strategies might have been appropriate. Ellis and Davidi (2005) showed that performance of soldiers on a navigation exercise improved when debriefed on failures and successes compared to those who were debriefed only about failures. These findings suggest that focusing on reasons for success and reasons for failures enhanced the development of useful mental models. Tannenbaum and Cerasoli (2013) note that the essential elements of after-action reviews include active self-learning in which participants engage in discovery with a clear intent for learning in a nonjudgmental way, and a focus on specific events and performance episodes rather than general performance, and receive input from outside observers. They conducted a meta-analysis of after-action reviews and found that such reviews improve effectiveness by about 25%, with the average effect size similar for simulated training environments and real work settings.

Developmental Job Assignments

McCall (2004) notes that experience in the form of job assignments should form the core of development. This focus on job assignments requires understanding what experiences are developmental and what people can learn from those experiences. Some types of jobs and tasks are likely to be more developmental than others (McCauley & Brutus, 1998). In addition, different kinds of developmental assignments are most likely associated with different kinds of learning. A strong research base has identified key developmental assignments of leaders, such as handling unfamiliar responsibilities, creating change, dealing with job overload, handling external pressure, and influencing others without formal authority (McCauley, Ruderman, Ohlott, & Morrow, 1994).

Variety in assignments throughout one's career is clearly as important for highly technical and specialized jobs as it is for developing leaders. Developmental assignments are needed for facilitating the creation of a broad and holistic perspective, enhancing skills, and building adaptive expertise. Not surprisingly, engineers at Intel are encouraged to move into developmental assignments associated with new projects so as to work on a range of projects that build overall experience and judgment (Bersin, 2009). Similarly, Sonnentag (1995) found that highly proficient (adaptive) software professionals had worked in a variety of projects with more difficult programming languages as compared to those with routine expertise.

Hoffman et al. (2014) highlight the importance of developing high levels of proficiency in employees in organizationally critical job and skill areas as quickly as possible. While researchers acknowledge the need for continuous learning to build functional depth and develop high levels of proficiency (Salas & Rosen, 2009), what intentional developmental job experiences should be incorporated into work has not been identified. Thus, it is an open question as to how generalizable the results from managerial development studies on learning from job experiences by McCauley et al. (1994) are to highly technical, mission-critical job domains. For example, job transitions, while an important component of management development, may not be as critical for individuals who are likely to stay (and are needed to stay) in core technical jobs. Thus, future research is needed to identify these developmental experiences. Individual and/or focus group interviews with employees at different stages on the road to expertise in highly specialized fields could be useful next steps. The focus of these interviews would be to uncover work experiences and learning opportunities that have helped move them from relative newcomers to routine and then adaptive experts. The data from the interviews could be used to categorize the key learning opportunities, and based on those categories, survey items can be written by category on the learning opportunities similar to the approach taken by McCauley et al. (1994). The developed survey of learning experiences that facilitate the move to routine and/or adaptive expertise cam be used to predict the level of expertise achieved over time

In addition, as noted by McCall (2004): "People do not automatically learn from experience. They can come away with nothing, the wrong lessons, or only some of what they might have learned" (128). Thus, using targeted assignments as part of a development system for building deep specialization in highly technical skills must also be linked other development strategies like coaching, providing role models, and intentional training experiences.

Discussion

A recent popular press book, called *Outliers*, made claims based on this type of research (Gladwell, 2008) by touting the conclusion that it takes 10,000 hours of practice to become an expert in a domain. It is also estimated that to obtain expertise, the amount of "deliberate practice" (intensive, continual repetition) of a skill requires 10 years or 10,000 hours of practice (e.g., Charness et al., 2005; Ericsson, 2006; Ericsson et al., 1993). These claims have become a catchall conclusion that as can be seen by the discussion in this chapter is not likely to generalize to core, highly technical jobs at work. Such estimates do not provide insight into the variety of learning strategies through training and work experience that can be incorporated into the workplace to accelerate the development of expertise. Our chapter has attempted to provide some insight into the variety of learning strategies that have been found relevant in the development of expertise.

Thus, in this chapter, we have stressed the importance of considering both training and systematic job experience factors that can help build routine and adaptive expertise over time in highly technical and critical jobs. For example, it is clear that expertise is more than a function of job tenure and number of hours worked. As noted by the Electric Power Research Institute, while it may take up to 25 years to become an expert in mission-critical activities, a proportion of utility personnel with that level of tenure are not recognized as having expertise, as they have simply become very good (proficient) at what they do (see Ziebell, 2008). Our frameworks points to the need for intentional strategies to develop adaptive expertise as well as routine expertise to build deep specialization.

Another takeaway from the research is that the time to move from newcomer to competent is likely to be shorter than the time required to move from competent to expert. The progression from competent to expert requires that "decision making and indeed an understanding of the particular situation is intuitive such that it may take longer to reach than any of the intermediate stages, if it's ever reached at all" (Kinchin & Cabot, 2010: 155). Much effort is often focused on bringing newcomers up to speed and developing them into competent performers. While this makes sense, as organizations want to get value out of the investment of recruitment, selection, and initial training costs (Byham, 2008), less attention is often paid to the intentional strategies needed to move an individual from competent to expert (Ziebell, 2008). A corollary to this idea is that the time to move from newcomer to competent and from competent to proficient is most likely longer for the more nonroutine and difficult tasks within a job compared to the simpler and more routine tasks in a job. While this may seem obvious, thinking in this way questions the conclusions often drawn regarding estimates of 10,000 hours of practice needed to become expert in a domain. Our chapter has highlighted the challenges in building expertise as well as identifying that the strategies for building routine expertise are different from strategies to enhance adaptive expertise. Finally, it is also likely that individuals identified as having expertise within a job domain will differ in terms of which tasks that they are considered as an expert and/or in what situations they are considered to be the "go to person." It is likely that a person will have some tasks within the job where he/she has a particularly valuable skill and thus possesses critical knowledge that would be difficult to quickly replace. It is important to understand what training and job experiences have led to expertise in particular tasks but not others within a job domain. Such research will help identify the more effective learning strategies. In addition from a practical perspective, identifying what areas a person is expert in and in what situations they are the "go to" person provides a critical baseline for understanding the impact of impending retirements on loss of organizational expertise.

References

Alexander, P. A. 2003. Development of expertise: The journey from acclimation to proficiency. *Educational Researcher* 32: 10–14.

Ansburg, P. I., and Dominowski, R. L. 2000. Promoting insightful problem solving. The Journal of Creative Behavior 34: 30–60.

Azevedo, R., Cromley, J. G., and Seibert, D. 2004. Does adaptive scaffolding facilitate students' ability to regulate their learning with hypermedia? *Contemporary Educational Psychology* 29: 344–370.

Barneff, S., and Koslowski, B. 2002. Adaptive expertise: Effects of type of experience and the level of theoretical understanding it generates. *Thinking and Reasoning* 8: 237–267.

Barzilai, S., and Blau, I. 2014. Scaffolding game-based learning: Impact on learning achievements, perceived learning, and game experiences. *Computers and Education* 70: 65–79.

Bell, B. S., and Kozlowski, S. W. J. 2002. A typology of virtual teams: Implications for effective leadership. *Group and Organization Management* 27(1): 14–49.

Bersin, J. 2009. Deep specialization for competitive advantage. http://www.astd .org/Publications/Newsletters/LX-Briefing/LXB-Archives/2009/11/Deep-Specialization-for-Competetive-Advantage (accessed November 27, 2009).

Bongers, P. J., Diederick van Hove, P., Stasssen, P. S., Dankelman, J., and Schreuder, H. 2015. A new virtual-reality training module for laparoscopic surgical skills and equipment handling: Can multitasking be trained? A randomized controlled trial. *Journal of Surgical Education 72*: 184–191.

Borton, G. 2007. Measuring the business impact of employee proficiency and employee job life cycle. *Management Services* (Autumn): 28–33.

Bowling, S. R., Khasawneh, M. T., Kaewkuekool, S., Jiang, X. C., and Gramopadhye, A. K. 2008. Evaluating the effects of virtual training in an aircraft maintenance task. *International Journal of Aviation Psychology* 18: 104–116.

Brooks, F. P. 1999. What's real about virtual reality? *IEEE Computer Graphics and Applications* 19(6): 16–27.

Burton, A. M., Shadbolt, N. R., Rugg, G., and Hedgecock, A. P. 1990. The efficacy of knowledge elicitation techniques: A comparison across domains and levels of expertise. *Knowledge Acquisition* 22: 167–178.

Byham, W. C. 2008. *Strong Start to Job Success*. White paper. Development Dimensions International, Pittsburgh, PA.

Caligiuri, P., and Tarique, I. 2014. Individual-level accelerators of global leadership development. In J. S. Osland, M. Li, and Y. Wang, eds., *Advances in Global Leadership*, 8: 251–267.

Carbonell, K. B., Stalmeijer, R. E., Könings, K. D., Segers, M., and van Merriënboer, J. J. 2014. How experts deal with novel situations: A review of adaptive expertise. *Educational Research Review* 12: 14–29.

Cerasoli, C. P., Alliger, G. M., Donsbach, J. S., Mathieu, J. E., Tannenbaum, S., and Orvis, K. A. 2014. *What is informal learning and what are its antecedents? An integrative and meta-analytic review*. Research Note 2014-03. U.S. Army Research Institute for the Behavioral and Social Sciences, Fort Belvoir, VA.

Chandler, P., and Sweller, J. 1991. Cognitive load theory and the format of instruction. *Cognition and instruction* 8: 293–332.

Charness, N., Tuffiash, M., Krampe, R., Reingold, E., and Vasyukova, E. 2005. The role of deliberate practice in chess expertise. *Applied Cognitive Psychology* 19: 151–165.

Chatham, R. E. (2009). The 20th century revolution in military training. Development of Professional Expertise: Toward Measurement of Expert Performance and Design of Optimal Learning Environments. In K. A. Ericsson, ed., *Development of Professional Expertise: Toward Measurement of Expert Performance and Design of Optimal Learning Environments*, 27–60. Cambridge, UK: Cambridge University Press.

Cockayne, W., and Darken, R. 2004. The application of human ability requirements to virtual environment interface design and evaluation. In D. Diaper and N. Stanton, eds., *The Handbook of Task Analysis of Human Computer Interaction*, 401–421. Mahwah, NJ: LEA.

Dall'Alba, G., and Sandberg, J. 2006. Unveiling professional development: A critical view of stage models. *Review of Educational Research* 76: 383–412.

DeYoung, C. G., Flanders, J. L., and Peterson, J. B. 2008. Cognitive abilities involved in insight problem solving: An individual differences model. *Creativity Research Journal,* 20: 278–290.

Dreyfus, H. L. 2006. Intuitive, deliberative, and calculative models of expert performance. In K. A. Ericsson, N. Charness, P. Feltovich, and R. R. Hoffman, eds., *Handbook of Expertise and Expert Performance*, 17–28. Cambridge: Cambridge University Press.

Dreyfus, H. L., and Dreyfus, S. E. 1986. *Mind over Machine*. New York: Simon and Schuster.

Dreyfus, H. L., and Dreyfus, S. E. 2005. Peripheral vision expertise in real world contexts. *Organization Studies* 26: 779–792.

Ellis, S., and Davidi, I. 2005. After-event reviews: Drawing lessons from successful and failed experience. *Journal of Applied Psychology* 90(5): 857–871.

Ely, K., Zaccaro, S. J., and Conjar, E. A. 2009. Leadership development: Training design strategies for growing adaptability in leaders. In C. Cooper and R. Burke, eds., *The Peak Performing Organization*. London: Routledge.

Ericsson, E. 1996. *The Road to Excellence: The Acquisition of Expert Performance in the Arts and Sciences, Sports, and Games*. Mahwah, NJ: LEA.

Ericsson, K. A. 2004. Deliberate practice and the acquisition and maintenance of expert performance in medicine and related domains. *Academic Medicine* 79: S70–S81.

Ericsson, K. A. 2006. The influence of experience and deliberate practice on the development of superior expert performance. In K. A. Ericsson, N. Charness, P. Feltovich, and R. R. Hoffman, eds., *Handbook of Expertise and Expert Performance*, 683–706. Cambridge: Cambridge University Press.

Ericsson, K. A., and Charness, N. 1994. Expert performance: Its structure and acquisition. *American Psychologist* 49: 725.

Ericsson, K. A., Krampe, R. T., and Tesch-Römer, C. 1993. The role of deliberate practice in the acquisition of expert performance. *Psychological Review* 100: 363–406.

Ericsson, K. A., Nandagopal, K., and Roring, R. W. 2009. Toward a science of exceptional achievement. *Annals of the New York Academy of Sciences* 1172: 199–217.

Fadde, P. J., and Klein, G. A. 2010. Deliberate performance: Accelerating expertise in natural settings. *Performance Improvement* 49: 5–14.

Farrington-Darby, T., and Wilson, J. R. 2006. The nature of expertise: A review. *Applied Ergonomics* 37: 17–32.

Fiorella, L., Vogel-Walcutt, J. J., and Fiore, S. 2012. Differential impact of two types of metacognitive prompting provided during simulation-based training. *Computers in Human Behavior* 28: 696–702.

Ford, J. K., and Kraiger, K. 1995. The application of cognitive constructs to the instructional systems model of training: Implications for needs assessment, design, and transfer. In C. L. Cooper and I. T. Robertson, eds., *International Review of Industrial and Organizational Psychology*, 1–48. Chichester, UK: Wiley.

Ford, J. K., and Meyer, T. 2014. Advances in training technology: Meeting the workplace challenges of talent development, deep specialization and collaborative learning. In M. D. Coovert and L. F. Thompson, eds., *The Psychology of Workplace Technology*, 43–76. New York, NY: Routledge.

Ford, J. K., and Schmidt, A. M. 2000. Emergency response training: Strategies for enhancing real-world performance. *Journal of Hazardous Materials* 75: 195–215.

Ford, J. K., Quiñones, M. A., Sego, D. J. and Sorra, J. S. 1992. Factors affecting the opportunity to perform trained tasks on the job. *Personnel Psychology* 45: 511–527.

Germain, M. L., and Tejeda, M. J. 2012. A preliminary exploration on the measurement of expertise: An initial development of a psychometric scale. *Human Resource Development Quarterly* 23: 203–232.

Gladwell, M. 2008. *Outliers: The Story of Success*. New York: Little, Brown and Company.

Glaser, R., and Chi, M. T. H. 1988. Overview. In M. T. H. Chi, R., Glaser, and M. J. Farr, eds., *The Nature of Expertise*, XV–XXVIII. Hillsdale, NJ: Lawrence Erlbaum Associates.

Gupta, S. K., Anand, D. K., Brough, J. E., Schwartz, M., and Kavetsky, R. A. 2008. *Training in Virtual Environments*. College Park, MD: Calce Press.

Hague, S., and Srinivasan, S. 2006. A meta-analysis of the training effectiveness of virtual reality surgical simulators. *Transactions on Information Technology in Biomedicine* 10: 51–58.

Hatano, G., and Inagaki, K. 1986. Two courses of expertise. In H. Stevenson, J. Azuma, and K. Hakuta, eds., *Child Development and Education in Japan*, 262–272. New York: W. H. Freeman.

Hoffman, R. R. 1996. How can expertise be defined? Implications of research from cognitive psychology. In R. Williams, W. Faulkner, and J. Fleck, eds., *Exploring Expertise*, 81–100. Edinburgh: University of Edinburgh Press.

Hoffman, R. R., ed., 2007. *Expertise Out of Context: Proceedings of the Sixth International Conference on Naturalistic Decision Making*. Mahwah, NJ: LEA.

Hoffman, R. R., and Hanes, L. F. 2003. The boiled frog problem. *IEEE: Intelligent Systems* (July–August): 68–71.

Hoffman, R. R., Coffey, J. W., Ford, K. M., and Novak, J. D. 2006. A method for eliciting, preserving, and sharing the knowledge of forecasters. *Weather and Forecasting* 21: 416–428.

Hoffman, R. R., Shadbolt, N. R., Burton, A. M., and Klein, G. 1995. Eliciting knowledge from experts: A methodological analysis. *Organizational Behavior and Human Decision Processes* 62: 129–158.

Hoffman, R. R., Ward, P., Feltovich, P. J., DiBello, L., Fiore, S. M., and Andrews, D. H. 2014. *Accelerated Expertise*. New York: Psychology Press.

Holyoak, K. J. 1991. Symbolic connectionism: Toward third generation theories of expertise. In K. A. Ericsson and J. Smith, eds., *Towards a General Theory of Expertise*, 301–335. Cambridge: Cambridge University Press.

Hutchins, S. D., Wickens, C. D., Carolan, T. F., and Cumming, J. M. 2013. The influence of cognitive load on transfer with error prevention training methods: A meta-analysis. *Human Factors* 55: 864–874.

International Atomic Energy Agency. 2006. *Risk Management of Knowledge Loss in Nuclear Industry Organizations*. Vienna, Austria: International Atomic Energy Agency.

Jacobs, R., Kafry, D., and Zedeck, S. 1980. Expectations of behaviorally anchored rating scales. *Personnel Psychology* 33: 595–640.

Kalyuga, S. 2007. Expertise reversal effect and its implications for learner-tailored instruction. *Educational Psychology Review* 19: 509–539.

Kalyuga, S., Ayres, P., Chandler, P., and Sweller, J. 2003. The expertise reversal effect. *Educational Psychologist* 38: 23–31.

Kanar, A. M., and Bell, B. S. 2013. Guiding learners through technology-based instruction: The effects of adaptive guidance design and individual differences on learning over time. *Journal of Educational Psychology* 105(4): 1067–1081.

Kim, Y., and Ployhart, R. E. 2014. The effects of staffing and training on firm productivity and profit growth before, during, and after the Great Recession. *Journal of Applied Psychology* 99: 361–389.

Kinchin, I. M., and Cabot, L. B. 2010. Reconsidering the dimensions of expertise: From linear stages towards dual processing. *London Review of Education* 8: 153–166.

Kinicki, A. J., Bannister, B. D., Hom, P. W., and DeNisi, A. S. 1985. Behaviorally anchored rating scales vs. summated rating scales: Psychometric properties and susceptibility to rating bias. *Educational and Psychological Measurement* 45: 535–549.

Kirschner, P. A., and van Merriënboer, J. J. G. 2008. Ten steps to complex learning: A new approach to instruction and instructional design. In T. L. Good, ed., *21st Century Education: A Reference Handbook*, 244–253. Thousand Oaks, CA: Sage.

Kirschner, P. A., Sweller, J., and Clark, R. E. 2006. Why minimal guidance during instruction does not work: An analysis of the failure of constructivist, discovery, problem-based, experiential, and inquiry-based teaching. *Educational Psychologist* 41: 75–86.

Klein, G. 1997. Developing expertise in decision making. *Thinking and Reasoning* 3: 337–352.

Klein, G. 2004. *The Power of Intuition*. New York: Doubleday.

Klein, G. A., and Hoffman, R. R. 1993. Seeing the invisible: The perceptual cognitive aspect of expertise. In M. Rabinowitz, ed., *Cognitive Science Foundations of Instruction*, 203–226. Mahwah, NJ: Lawrence Erlbaum Associates.

Koedinger, K. R., Booth, J. L., and Klahr, D. 2008. Instructional complexity and the science to constrain it. *Science* 342: 935–937.

Kraiger, K., and Ford, J. K. 2007. The expanding role of workplace training: Themes and trends influencing training research and practice. In L. L. Koppes, ed., *Historical Perspectives in Industrial and Organizational Psychology*, 281–309. Mahwah, NJ: Lawrence Erlbaum Associates.

Lajoie, S. P. 2003. Transitions and trajectories for studies of expertise. *Educational Researcher* 32: 21–25.

Larsen, C. R., Oestergaard, J., Ottesen, B. S., and Soerensen, J. L. 2012. The efficacy of virtual reality simulation training in laparoscopy: A systematic review of randomized trials. *Acta Obstetricia et Gynecologica Scandinavica* 91: 1015–1028.

Larsen, C. R., Soerensen, J. L., Grantcharov, T. P., Dalsgaard, T., Schouenborg, L., Ottosen, C., Schroeder, T. V., and Ottesen, B. S. 2009. Effect of virtual reality training on laparoscopic surgery: Randomized controlled trial. *BMJ* 338: b1802.

Lord, R.G. and Hall, R.J. 2005. Identity, deep structure and the development of leadership skills. *The Leadership Quarterly* 16: 591–615.

Mayer, R. E. 2004. Should there be a three-strikes rule against pure discovery learning? *American Psychologist* 59(1): 14–19.

McCall, M. W. 2004. Leadership development through experience. *The Academy of Management Executive* 18: 127–130.

McCauley, C. D., and Brutus, S. 1998. *Management Development Through Job Experiences*. Greensboro, NC: Center for Creative Leadership.

McCauley, C. D., Ruderman, M. N., Ohlott, P. J., and Morrow, J. E. 1994. Assessing the developmental components of managerial jobs. *Journal of Applied Psychology* 79: 544–560.

McGaghie, W. D., Issenberg, S. B., Cohen, E., Barsuk, J. H., and Wayne, D. B. 2012. Does simulation based medical education with deliberate practice yield better results than traditional clinical education? A meta-analytic comparative review of the evidence. *Academy Medical* 86: 706–711.

McKenzie, J., Woolf, N., van Winkelen, C., and Morgan, C. 2009. Cognition in strategic decision making. A model of non-conventional thinking capacities for complex situations. *Cognition in Strategic Decision Making* 27: 209–232.

Moon, B., Hoffman, R., and Ziebell, D. 2009. How did you do that? Utilities develop strategies for preserving and sharing expertise. *Electric Perspectives* 34 (January–February): 20–29.

Najjar, M. 2008. On scaffolding adaptive teaching prompts within virtual labs. *International Journals of Distance Education Technologies* 6(2): 35–54.

Nelson, J. K., Zaccaro, S. J., and Herman, J. L. 2010. Strategic information provision and experiential variety as tools for developing adaptive leadership skills. *Consulting Psychology Journal: Practice and Research* 62: 131–142.

Ohlsson, S. 1992. Information-processing explanations of insight and related phenomena. In M. T. Keane and K. J. Gilhooly, eds., *Advances in the Psychology of Thinking*, 1–44. New York, NY: Harvester Wheatsheaf.

Oransanu, J., and Connolly, T. 1993. The reinvention of decision making. In G. A. Klein, J. Oransanu, R. Calderwood, and C. E. Zsambok, eds., *Decision Making in Action: Models and Methods*, 3–20. Norwood, CT: Ablex.

Prietula, M. J., and Simon, H. A. 1989. The experts in your midst. *Harvard Business Review* 67: 120–124.

Pintrich, P. R., Wolters, C. A., and Baxter, G. P. 2000. Assessing metacognition and self-regulated learning. In G. Schraw and J. C. Impara, eds., *Issues in the Measurement of Metacognition*, 43–97. Lincoln, NE: Buros Institute of Mental Measurements.

Pulakos, E. D., Arad, S., Donovan, M. A., and Plamondon, K. E. 2000. Adaptability in the workplace: Development of a taxonomy of adaptive performance. *Journal of Applied Psychology* 85: 612–624.

Quinn, R. E., and Cameron, K. S. 1988. Paradox and transformation: A framework for viewing organization and management. In R. E. Quinn and K. S. Cameron, eds., *Paradox and Transformation: Toward a Theory of Change in Organization and Management*. Cambridge, MA: Ballinger.

Quiñones, M. A., Ford, J. K., and Teachout, M. S. 1995. The relationship between work experience and job performance: A conceptual and meta-analytic review. *Personnel Psychology* 48: 887–910.

Salas, E., and Rosen, M. A. 2009. Experts at work: Principles for developing expertise in organizations. In S. W. J. Kozlowski and E. Salas, eds., *Learning, Training, and Development in Organizations*, 99–134. New York: Taylor and Francis.

Schaefer, P. S., Shadrick, S. B., Beaubien, J., and Crabb, B. T. 2008. *Training effectiveness assessment of Red Cape: Crisis action planning of execution* (Research Report 1885). Arlington, VA: U. S. Army Research Institute for the Behavioral and Social Sciences.

Schein, E. H. 1993. *Career Anchors*, 2nd ed. San Francisco: Jossey-Bass.

Shadrick, S. B., and Lussier, J. W. 2004. Assessment of the "think like a commander" training program. Research Report 1824. U.S. Army Research Institute for the Behavioral and Social Sciences, Arlington, VA.

Shadrick, S. B., and Lussier, J. W. 2009. Training complex cognitive skills: A theme-based approach to the development of battlefield skills. In K. A. Ericson, ed., *Development of Professional Expertise*, 286–311. Cambridge: Cambridge University Press.

Shadrick, S. B., Lussier, J. W., and Fultz, C. 2007. *Accelerating the development of adaptive performance: Validating the Think Like a Commander training* (ARI Research Report 1868). Arlington, VA: U. S. Army Research Institute for the Behavioral and Social Sciences.

Shea, J. B., and Morgan, R. L. 1979. Contextual interference effects on the acquisition, retention, and transfer of a motor skill. *Journal of Experimental Psychology: Human Learning and Memory* 5: 179–187.

Smith, E., Ford, J. K., and Kozlowski, S. W. J. 1997. Building adaptive expertise: Implications for training design strategies. In M. Quiñones and A. Ehrenstein, eds., *Training for the 21st Century: Applications of Psychological Research*, 89–118. Washington, DC: American Psychological Association.

Sonnentag, S. 1995. Excellent software professionals: Experience, work activities, and perceptions by peers. *Behaviour and Information Technology* 14: 289–299.

Sonnentag, S. 1998. Expertise in professional software design: A process study. *Journal of Applied Psychology* 83: 703–715.

Sonnentag, S. 2000. Expertise at work: Experience and excellent performance. In C. Cooper and I. Robertson, eds., *International Review of Industrial and Organizational Psychology* 15: 223–264. Chichester, UK: John Wiley.

Sonnentag, S., and Kleine, B. 2000. Deliberate performance at work: A study with insurance agents. *Journal of Occupational and Organizational Psychology* 73: 87–102.

Sung, S. Y., and Choi, J. N. 2014. Do organizations spend wisely on employees? Effects of training and development investments on learning and innovation in organizations. *Journal of Organizational Behavior* 35: 393–412.

Tannenbaum, S. I., and Cerasoli, C. P. 2013. Do team and individual debriefs enhance performance? A meta-analysis. *Human Factors* 55: 231–245.

Tannenbaum, S. I., Beard, M., and Salas 2010. Informal learning and development in organizations. In S. W. J., Kozlowski and E. Salas, eds., *Learning, Training, and Development in Organizations*, 303–332. New York: Taylor and Francis

Taylor, P. J., Russ-Eft, D. F., and Chan, D. W. 2005. A meta-analytic review of behavior modeling training. *Journal of Applied Psychology*, 90: 692–709.

Tesluk, P. E., and Jacobs, R. R. 1998. Toward an integrated model of work experience. *Personnel Psychology* 51: 321–355.

Van den Bosch, K., and de Beer, M. M. 2007. Playing a winning game: An implementation of critical thinking training. In R. R. Hoffman, ed., *Proceedings of the Sixth International Conference on Naturalist Decision Making*, 177–198. Mahwah, NJ: Lawrence Erlbaum Associates.

Van der Heijden, B. I. J. M. 2000. The development and psychometric evaluation of a multidimensional measurement instrument of professional expertise. *High Ability Studies* 11: 9–39.

Van der Heijden, B. I. J. M. and Verhelst, N. D. 2002. The psychometric evaluation of a multidimensional measurement instrument of professional expertise. *European Journal of Psychological Assessment* 18: 165–178.

Van der Maas, H. L. J., and Wagenmakers, E. 2005. A psychometric analysis of chess expertise. *American Journal of Psychology* 118: 29–60.

van Merriënboer, J. J., and Kirshchner, P. A. 2007. *Ten Steps to Complex Learning*. Mahwah, NJ: LEA.

van Merriënboer, J. J., Kirschner, P. A., and Kester, L. 2003. Taking the load off a learner's mind: Instructional design for complex learning. *Educational Psychologist* 38: 5–13.

Weiss, D. J., and Shanteau, J. 2003. Empirical assessment of expertise. *Human Factors* 45: 104–116.

Wulf, G., and Shea, C. H. 2002. Principles derived from the study of simple skills do not generalize to complex skill learning. *Psychonomic Bulletin and Review* 9: 185–211.

Young, J. Q., van Merriënboer, J., Durning, S., and Cate, O. T. 2014. Cognitive load theory: Implications for medical education: AMEE guide no. 86. *Medical Teacher* 36: 371–384.

Zaccaro, S. J., Banks, D., Kiechel-Koles, L., Kemp, C., and Bader, P. 2009. *Leader and team adaptation: The influences and development of key attributes and processes.* Tech. Rep. No. #1256. U.S. Army Research Institute for Behavioral and Social Sciences.

Ziebell, D. 2008. *Program on Technology Innovation: Accelerating the Achievement of Mission-Critical Expertise: A Research Roadmap.* Report 1016710. Palo Alto, CA: Electric Power Research Institute.

Zimmerman, B. J., Sestokas J. M., Burns, C. A., Bell, J., and Manning, D. 2012. *Methods and tools for training crisis response.* Research Note 2012-07. U.S. Army Research Institute for the Behavioral and Social Sciences.

Zwick, T. 2006. The impact of training intensity on establishment productivity. *Industrial Relations* 45: 26–46.

11 The Science and Practice of Simulation-Based Training in Organizations

Shannon L. Marlow, Christina N. Lacerenza, Denise Reyes, and Eduardo Salas

A report completed by the Association for Talent Development (2014) illustrates that organizations are increasingly shifting from relying on conventional training techniques to implementing technology-based forms of training. One such training strategy that arose as a function of technological advances is simulation-based training (SBT). This approach is becoming increasingly prevalent within organizations (Summers, 2004) because of its capacity to meet a multitude of training needs. It offers advantages beyond traditional training techniques, such as lectures, by delivering salient information but coupling that delivery with the opportunity to practice (Bell, Kanar, and Kozlowski, 2008). Specifically, simulations are ideal for delivering instruction pertaining to new technology and furthering the ability of employees to work within the complex, dynamic conditions that characterize the modern workplace (Day, 2014). For example, simulations can recreate an environment that would otherwise be too difficult, costly, or dangerous to provide training within, such as a mass causality scenario for health care workers (Heinrichs et al., 2008). Simulations are also ideal for targeting technical skills or furthering understanding of new technology being implemented within an organization (e.g., Aggarwal et al., 2007). Given the ability of SBT to address the growing needs of organizations, it is unsurprising that this training medium is becoming more commonly implemented.

As the use of SBT increases, there is a corresponding need to review the evidence for its use. Our purpose in this chapter is to provide both researchers and practitioners a comprehensive understanding of the state of SBT in science and practice. First, we begin by defining SBT and discussing some of the advantages and disadvantages associated with using this technique. Second, we review the science that informs this training technique. Next, we outline the multitude of ways in which SBT is currently being utilized in practice and briefly discuss how organizations can most effectively design SBT by outlining best practices gleaned from the literature. Finally, we close by suggesting future directions for research initiatives that will benefit both scientific understanding and practical applications of SBT.

Defining Simulation-Based Training

SBT is an amalgamation of simulation (i.e., an artificial environment designed to mirror reality; Bell et al., 2008) and training (i.e., the acquisition of attitudes, cognitions, knowledge, and skills through a systematic program; Goldstein, 1991). Moreover, SBT can be defined as "any synthetic practice environment that is created in order to impart these competencies (i.e., attitudes, concepts, knowledge, rules, or skills) that will improve a trainee's performance" (Salas, Wildman, and Piccolo, 2009: 2008). SBT is proven to be effective (e.g., Aggarwal et al., 2007; Gaba et al., 2001; McGaghie et al., 2006; Steadman et al., 2006) and offers several advantages to organizations.

The U.S. workforce has shifted to being more knowledge based, among other changes (e.g., increased diversity) and, correspondingly, employees are required to be increasingly skilled in more complex areas (Bogdanowicz and Bailey, 2002; Burke and Ng, 2006). For example, organizations have become more reliant upon employees who are successfully able to adapt to perpetually changing circumstances (Huang et al., 2014) and researchers suggest that this skill, referred to as *adaptivity*, should be trained using active learning strategies; active learning methods can be encompassed within SBT (Bell and Kozlowski, 2007). In addition, global virtual teams and telecommuting are becoming more common (e.g., Reichard, Serrano, and Wefald, 2013), increasing the need for training methods that can be delivered to those who are not physically present. SBT offers the elasticity to be implemented from almost anywhere at any time, thereby reducing the need for inconveniences associated with traditional, classroom-based training (Summers, 2004).

A recent trend within the selection industry is providing applicants and new job incumbents a realistic job preview (RJP) during the hiring and training processes. RJPs can be defined as materials and/or representations that provide candidates with realistic information, which can be positive and/or negative in nature, about a job (Breaugh and Starke, 2000). RJPs are associated with decreased turnover (Phillips, 1998; Premack and Wanous, 1985). SBT provides organizations the ability to train employees while delivering a RJP to them by immersing them in a realistic practice environment (Cannon-Bowers and Bowers, 2009) that may reduce turnover (Phillips, 1998).

Another primary advantage of SBT is that it provides learners an opportunity for monitored practice without endangering others (Deering et al., 2007) and affords trainees the ability to practice with reduced risks to life and capital (Gordon et al., 2001); this is especially beneficial for training teams or individuals that need to acquire skills necessary for dealing with high-stress, dynamic, and/or complex situations (e.g., military soldiers, emergency medicine technicians, pilots). In regard to the educational domain, traditional teaching mechanisms within the management education domain have been criticized for placing an emphasis on teaching theory without providing opportunities to practice (Lane, 1995), and SBT may provide an answer to this critique (Salas et al., 2009). SBT also allows for reduced training time, but similar developmental capabilities in comparison to traditional training methods (Lane, 1995). In addition, SBT can be affordable as some of the most simplistic and free forms of SBT (e.g., Tinsel Town; Devine et al., 2004) are effective for certain goals. Other advantages to SBT include increased engagement (Keys and Wolfe, 1990) and more enhanced outcomes than traditional education and training programs (e.g., McGaghie et al., 2011).

Evidence indicates that it is possible to cultivate training outcomes at the individual, group, and organizational level with SBT (McGaghie et al., 2011). At the individual level, research suggests that SBT improves knowledge, skill, and ability levels of trainees (e.g., Sweeney et al., 2014). For instance, McKinney and colleagues (2013) meta-analytically demonstrated that SBT produced positive changes in cardiac auscultation skills. These researchers also found that hands-on practice with a simulator appeared to be important for effectiveness. In addition, Singer and colleagues (2013) found that first-year medical residents who were trained with a SBT program outperformed traditionally trained third-year residents on a clinical skills assessment.

At the team level, research has shown SBT to improve team performance and processes (e.g., Kaplan, Lombardo, and Mazique, 1985; Shapiro et al., 2004). Specifically, Sweeney and colleagues (2014) tested the effectiveness of a SBT program within emergency department teams and found a significant increase in communication efficiency. Shapiro and colleagues (2004) further found that simulation-based teamwork training also contributed to a greater improvement of clinical team performance in comparison to didactic training.

However, despite these many benefits, it is important to note that there are certain disadvantages associated with these programs. According to Funke (1998), one drawback is that it is hard to compare across individual trainee outcomes because most SBT environments are dynamic. Relatedly, a plethora of behavioral data is typically produced following SBT, making it difficult for researchers and practitioners to analyze the data (Funke, 1998). Moreover, complex SBT programs can be very costly and may require additional supervision to implement (e.g., Preisler et al., 2015; Shetty et al., 2014). Jacobs and Baum (1987) noted that adopting a SBT program might not be the most cost-effective strategy, which suggests that smaller companies may want to implement more traditional training methods. Thus, practitioners must consider if SBT is ideal for meeting their training needs before choosing to implement this technique. Reviewing the science underlying the effectiveness of SBT can help in determining when to implement this strategy.

The Science of Simulation-Based Training

Although there is not an integrated theory in which SBT is grounded, broad theoretical advancements in the science of training have shaped training practices like SBT. The science of training has expanded at a rapid rate over the past few decades, contributing new theoretical frameworks and constructs that illuminate the conditions under which training is most effective (Salas and Cannon-Bowers, 2001). One common thread across these models is the necessity of taking a systematic approach to the design, delivery, and assessment of training. This point is consistent with empirical evidence, which consistently indicates that when training is systematic, it is effective across multiple levels of analysis (Aguinis and Kraiger, 2009; Arthur et al., 2003; Keith and Frese, 2008).

The systems approach, which advocates viewing "training as a system embedded in an organizational context" (Salas and Cannon-Bowers, 2001: 491), has informed the development of a conceptual model detailing the specific stages that should be taken when implementing SBT (Salas et al., 2005). Specifically, Salas et al. (2005) delineated the following training principles as necessary to the success of SBT interventions: (1) completion of a training needs analysis, (2) development of task competencies, (3) specification of training objectives, (4) design of training events, (5) development of performance measures, (6) diagnosis of performance, and (7) delivery of feedback and debriefing. We propose an augmented framework. Specifically, we suggest that performance measures should be developed *before* training events are designed, which we discuss in the following text. We also note that if observers are rating the performance of the trainees, they should receive the appropriate training to increase rater accuracy (Lievens, 2001; Woehr and Huffcut, 1994). The adapted framework is presented in Figure 11.1.

First, conducting a needs analysis results in information regarding where training needs are most pronounced and where specific deficiencies lie (Moore and Dutton, 1978). This information can be leveraged to determine what competencies should be targeted with the training program and, relatedly, learning objectives. Once the objectives have been clearly delineated, ideal and minimum levels of performance can be defined to correspond to the learning objectives. Performance measures can then be created based upon the previously defined levels of performance. Next, simulation scenarios or specific events can be developed that require the use of the chosen competencies. This evokes scenario-based training, which advocates embedding events within training that require the use of the targeted competencies as well as the opportunity for the trainee to recognize when they should apply the skills (Fowlkes et al., 1998). Embedding events in such a manner also provides observers the opportunity to anticipate and measure the desired skills at predefined intervals throughout the SBT, reducing confusion in measurement and ultimately standardizing evaluation, feedback, and debriefing processes. At this phase, measures should be modified to ensure that they are appropriately paired with these events. For example, an observer measure should be created to follow the order in which competencies are triggered within the SBT. Observers should also receive the appropriate training before providing ratings. Finally, the performance data should be utilized to inform feedback and debriefing such that prescriptive information is provided regarding the targeted competencies. Feedback can be delivered in a

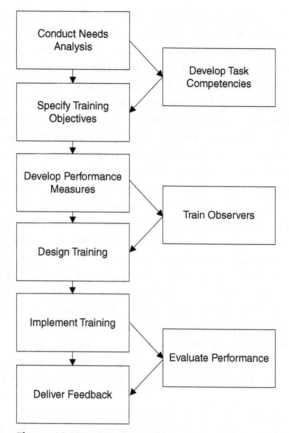

Figure 11.1. *Adapted system-based approach to developing simulation-based training.*

traditional manner (e.g., a trainer delivers feedback) but it can also be embedded within the training scenario such that trainees discover it through debriefing and dialogue within the events.

Following these steps ensures that a systematic approach grounded in empirical evidence is taken. However, it is unknown which features specific to simulations lead to effective training outcomes. In other words, it is not precisely known how or why SBT is effective in facilitating targeted results or why some studies have indicated that it is more effective than other training techniques (e.g., Keys and Wolfe, 1990). Compounding this problem, Cannon-Bowers and Bowers (2009) noted that although training research has begun to consistently take a systematic approach, research examining the effectiveness of simulations has yet to fully parallel this trend.

As there are a plethora of underlying features in any one training intervention, it is difficult to precisely determine how such interventions lead to targeted outcomes. This ambiguity is especially salient to the study of SBT, as most SBT interventions are implemented in practice (Summers, 2004), where a myriad of factors are prone to vary, such the setting of the training, the sample,

Table 11.1 *Simulation-based training features integral to success*

Training Feature	Definition	Source
Interactivity	Degree to which trainees interact with trainers, the system, and/or other trainees	Kozlowski and Bell, 2007
Fidelity	Degree to which the simulation depicts reality or recreates a real-world system	Alessi, 2000; Meyer et al., 2012
Feedback	Information received regarding different aspects of performance	Komaki et al., 1980
Debriefing	The process through which trainees are guided through making sense of what they have learned and how to generalize it to real-world situations	Fanning and Gaba, 2007; Lederman, 1983

and scenarios used. However, although research conducted on SBT is largely nascent, the literature has begun to examine several components of training and how they can be used within the specific context of SBT to further training effectiveness. Specifically, interactivity, fidelity, and feedback and debriefing are components that research has begun to assess. These features are summarized in Table 11.1.

Interactivity

Kozlowski and Bell (2007) identified interactivity as an integral component of SBT. This refers to the "characteristics that can influence the potential degree and type of interaction between users of the system, between trainers and trainees, and potentially, between teams or collaborative learning groups" (Bell et al., 2008: 1421). *Interactivity* refers to the interaction between the system and the trainee and is related to learner control (Lepper and Malone, 1987). Kraiger and Jerden (2007) found that, in the case of computer-based training, trainees with a higher degree of learner control exhibited increased declarative and procedural knowledge as compared to trainees without this feature. However, the effect was small.

A recent meta-analysis completed by Karim and Behrend (2014) further explored two dimensions of learner control, perceived learner control (i.e., individuals self-report perceiving control over the learning experience), and objective learner control (i.e., different features of the training are manipulated such that trainees actually have some degree of control over the learning experience, such as choosing the training modules to complete), and found that each dimension demonstrated a different relationship with learning. Perceived learner control had stronger relationships with learning outcomes than more objective measures of learner control, suggesting that other aspects (e.g., motivation) may play a large role in these relationships. Other work suggests that trainees may not make sufficient use of control over training materials and may even make poor decisions that negatively influence learning or performance outcomes (e.g., Brown, 2001). However, taken as a whole, the findings of research conducted on learner control suggest that this feature can marginally increase learning outcomes but the nature and level of interactivity within SBT should be chosen carefully, informed by the desired training competencies and outcomes.

Fidelity

Fidelity is the degree to which the simulation accurately portrays reality (Alessi, 2000) by representing a real-world system (Meyer et al., 2012). Fidelity was originally conceptualized as being either high or low, but researchers have begun to denounce this distinction as too simplistic (Beaubien and Baker, 2004; Bowers and Jentsch, 2001) and have instead begun more frequently conceptualizing fidelity as multidimensional. One particularly influential typology of fidelity was described by Rehmann, Mitman, and Reynolds (1995); this typology includes equipment, environment, and psychological fidelity. Equipment fidelity is the degree to which the simulation recreates the actual system (e.g., the tools and technology) trainees will later be required to interact with while performing. In other words, this aspect of fidelity can be defined as how accurately the simulation portrays the displays, controls, and other features of any equipment trainees will use on the job. For example, if a simulation for a surgical team was designed such that all equipment (e.g., surgical tools) provided mirrored that found in the real operating room, the simulation would be rated as high in equipment fidelity.

The second aspect of fidelity, environment fidelity, can be defined as the degree to which the simulation replicates the task environment. The task environment includes features such as sensory information and motion cues. For example, if an aircraft simulation did not include environmental elements that would be experienced in flight, such as motion, it would not be labeled high on this dimension. Rehmann et al. (1995) noted the importance of this dimension in ensuring learning, as it enhances realism experienced by the trainees and can more closely evoke the actual environment trainees will later be required to apply newly learned skills within.

Finally, the third dimension described within the taxonomy delineated by Rehmann et al. (1995), psychological fidelity, refers to the extent to which the cues and consequences of the task are realistically portrayed within the simulation. For example, if a simulation created for surgical teams lacked the appropriate consequences of surgical error (e.g., indicating patient harm in some manner), it would be considered low in psychological fidelity. Bowers and Jentsch (2001) noted that often simulations were built to have high environment and equipment fidelity, at a high cost, but psychological fidelity was not always emphasized. It has been argued that psychological fidelity can "minimize the transfer problem by closing the gap between training and the real-world task" (Kozlowski and Deshon, 2004: 27). Kozlowski and Deshon (2004) posited that enhancing psychological fidelity, rather than primarily focusing on other aspects of fidelity, may enable cost-effective simulations that maximize transfer.

Feedback and Debriefing

Research has consistently indicated that feedback, or information received from an outside source regarding performance, is critical in ensuring transfer in all training contexts (e.g., Kluger and DeNisi, 1996; Komaki, Heinzmann, and Lawson, 1980). It serves several critical functions, such as highlighting discrepancies between ideal and current levels of performance, which can motivate trainees to attain higher levels of performance (Locke and Latham, 1990). It can also provide information to trainees regarding how to rectify prior errors they have committed (Ilgen, Fisher, and Taylor, 1979).

Specificity and immediacy of feedback are components of feedback posited to affect the degree to which feedback positively affects training outcomes (Annett, 1969; Bernardin and Beatty, 1984; Kluger and DeNisi, 1996; Kopelman, 1986). Specificity refers to the degree of detail provided within the feedback as well as the extent to which the feedback refers to actual instances of performance (Annett, 1969). Immediacy can be defined as the timeliness with which feedback is delivered after performance has occurred (Daft and Lengel, 1986). The traditional view of feedback held that feedback was most effective for furthering training outcomes when it was delivered frequently and immediately. However, Schmidt and Bjork (1992) suggested that consistent feedback is not always beneficial for transfer; specifically, they posited that withholding feedback provides trainees with needed time to think critically about their errors and make predictions about the type of behavior needed to facilitate higher levels of performance. Although this will lead to more mistakes during training, this is argued to ultimately enhance training transfer.

In line with the idea that feedback is not indefinitely effective in facilitating learning, more recent studies have begun to suggest it is only successful when designed in accordance with the training context (Watling et al., 2012). A recent meta-analysis indicated that feedback delivery may be effective in SBT, but the effectiveness of the feedback is contingent on the level of experience of the trainees and when it is delivered (Hatala et al., 2014). Specifically, feedback was more effective when delivered at the end of a practice attempt, also referred to as terminal feedback, for more experienced trainees; it was more effective when delivered during each practice attempt, referred to as concurrent feedback, for less experienced trainees. Similarly, other findings suggest that terminal feedback leads to better outcomes for simple tasks and concurrent feedback is more effective for facilitating training outcomes in complex tasks (Wulf and Shea, 2004). This is in accordance with the suggestions of Schmidt and Bjork (1992) described in the preceding text. Multiple sources of feedback were also found to lead to enhanced training effectiveness, as compared to one source (Hatala et al., 2014). Thus, depending on the sample and the nature of the task being trained, feedback should be structured accordingly for SBT interventions.

Similar to feedback, debriefing has also been identified as an integral component of training and, like feedback, can be embedded within the simulation. Debriefing is the process through which trainees are guided through analyzing, making sense of, and learning how to generalize what they have learned to other situations (Fanning and Gaba, 2007; Lederman, 1983). Arafeh and colleagues (2010) emphasized that debriefs should be structured around learning objectives and targeted at facilitating transfer, focusing on the internal mental framework of the learners. Internal mental frameworks refer to trainees' knowledge structures built around previous knowledge and experience. These frameworks guide trainees' behavior (Rudolph et al., 2007) and the goal of a debrief should be to change those frameworks such that new knowledge gleaned from the training scenario is integrated for future reference.

The Practice of Simulation-Based Training

SBT has been utilized in the aviation and military industry for decades (Moorthy, Vincent, and Darzi, 2005). However, although SBT may have initially burgeoned within the military and aviation industry, the application of this delivery method now crosses industries. For example, SBT has been incorporated into domains such as education and management (Salas et al., 2009). Particularly within the past few decades, SBT has been widely implemented within the medical industry (e.g., Andreatta et al., 2011; McKinney et al., 2013; Zendejas et al., 2013; Zevin, Aggarwal, and Grantcharov, 2012). Based on annual revenues of the largest simulation companies, Summers (2004) estimated that there is a worldwide market between $623 and $712 million. The increased popularity of SBT may be due to the match between this training mechanism's strengths and current market needs, such as the capacity of SBT to train both technical and nontechnical skills across a multitude of domains.

Simulation-Based Training in Practice across Industries

The military has historically utilized SBT in a variety of ways, providing soldiers with a scenario that cannot otherwise be replicated, delivering custom training for the learner, and offering multiple practice sessions for skill retention (TRADOC, 2011). SBT has also been frequently used in aviation (Moorthy et al., 2005). Reducing human error is often a primary goal of the use of this intervention in the aviation context. Closely aligned with SBT is crew resource management (CRM), a training program developed in the 1980s to target specific teamwork skills (Helmreich, 1997). Several studies also indicate that low-fidelity simulations are an effective means of fostering skills through CRM (Baker et al., 1993; Bowers et al., 1992).

Yet another area where SBT is commonly utilized is the health care domain (e.g., Gaba et al., 2001). The health care sector is always working to improve patient safety; however, as they are limited by the amount of patient interactions, SBT allows practitioners to develop cognitive and psychomotor skills in the absence of actual patient interaction (Motola et al., 2013). Research indicates that SBT is also an effective approach to training technical skills in the medical industry, with scenarios ranging from cardiopulmonary bypass emergencies, coronary artery bypass graft operations, and anesthesia crisis resource management capable of fostering the necessary associated skills (Gaba et al., 2001; Tokaji et al., 2012; Wahr et al., 2013).

Management education is another area where simulations are beginning to be used more frequently for training purposes. There has been an increased demand for this training technique in educational settings because training has been shown to be a critical factor in improving performance and maintenance of skills (Salas and Bowers, 2001). SBT can provide students with an opportunity to actively engage in applying learned concepts rather than just learning theory (Lane, 1995). More corporations are beginning to follow this trend after observing the widespread use of SBT in the military and aviation industries.

Businesses are constantly changing so simulations must evolve to accommodate any associated training needs (Fripp, 1997). For example, production is exponentially growing, markets are globalizing, there is an increasing number of stakeholders from diverse areas, and social and environmental issues are also influencing the work environment (Fripp, 1997). As simulations can be designed to emulate virtually any scenario, organizations are increasingly opting to implement them. For example, a computerized simulation called MyMuse was used for a management accounting course to illustrate the complexities that occur in a business setting (Wynder, 2004); the simulation provided students with an opportunity to instantly test ideas that would otherwise require a long time to implement. Students had the freedom to exercise their creative problem-solving skills by dealing with customer satisfaction, demand, and short-term profitability. Such simulations can help trainees learn how to deal with unstructured tasks and acquire higher-level skills.

In a business setting, managerial training is particularly important for project management. Project management typically involves delivering a specific output under a limited budget and time frame (Zwikael and Sadeh, 2007). Numerous studies support the usage of SBT for management education so that project managers can gain the necessary experience and expertise for accomplishing their assigned tasks (Keys and Wolfe, 1990; Washbush and Gosen, 2001; Zantow, Knowlton, and Sharp, 2005). For example, Cohen and colleagues (2014) recently utilized SBT as an approach to project management training for systems engineers. Project Team Builder was used to integrate both the technical and managerial concerns that are unique to the demands of a systems engineer. In this simulation, trainees are guided through every phase of a project (i.e., initiation, conceptual design, planning, and implementation). Project Team Builder was evaluated positively by users ranging from beginning systems engineering students to systems engineers at various experience levels.

The banking industry has also recognized SBT for management operations such as BankSim, and simulation games such as BankExec, the Stanford Bank Game, and Bank President (Koppenhaver, 1993). These computer simulations incorporate bank functions while addressing management issues that are necessary for bankers to successfully operate a bank. BankSim, for example, requires trainees to work in teams. Each team must analyze their financial statements, create goals, and develop strategies to further the accomplishment of previously identified goals. The two-week simulation emulates a two-year management experience equipped with a computer printout of the team's financial standing, call reports, and regulatory agency examination of books and records (Koppenhaver, 1993). Moreover, Faria and Dickinson (1994) analyzed both academic and management training simulations for sales management, and noted that Sales Management Simulation deals with all aspects of a sales manager's job. Given the realistic setting, it has been suggested that this simulation can serve to train new employees, screen current or prospective managers, and serve as ongoing management training (Faria and Dickinson, 1994). This conclusion heightens the importance of investing time and resources into ensuring the simulation accurately portrays the targeted tasks.

This section has elaborated on the use of SBT across industries. However, it should be noted that conventional forms of training may be equally as effective in some cases. Therefore, organizations must evaluate whether the use of SBT is the best choice to meet their training needs. Ultimately, SBT has the potential to be effective in creating changes in knowledge, skill, and ability level; however, it must be implemented in the right way to engender such outcomes. As such, we now discuss how practitioners should design their SBT programs to ensure effectiveness.

Developing Simulation-Based Training

Following suit with the push for improving SBT development skills within industry, researchers argue that extensive preparation is required for SBT programs to reach their full training potential (Keys and Wolfe, 1990; Tannenbauem and Yukl, 1992; Thornton and Cleveland, 1990). The extensive research on SBT has shed some light on what preparatory steps and design techniques need to be utilized by practitioners to ensure training effectiveness. For example, Thornton and Cleveland (1990) recommend that management training simulations include examples of effective management behaviors coupled with descriptions of managerial competencies. In addition, several researchers have noted the importance of implementing a structured debrief after the simulation (Keys and Wolfe, 1990; Thornton and Cleveland, 1990), as discussed previously.

In an attempt to encourage scientists and practitioners to design SBT programs aligned with this science, we have identified best practices (see Table 11.2) informed by salient theory and evidence as well as a synthesis of previously suggested best practices (e.g., Rosen et al., 2008). Following these best practices can enhance the effectiveness of SBT. Although much has been learned about how to design and implement SBT, which has led to the delineation of best practices such as the ones provided here, there are many areas where additional research is required to further understand how and when SBT is effective.

Table 11.2 *Best practices for designing systematic SBT programs*

1. **Maximize Psychological Fidelity**
   (Bowers and Jentsch, 2001; Salas, Bowers, and Rhodenizer, 1998)
   - Develop scenarios that successfully emulate the task characteristics and demands that trainees will later be expected to contend with on the job.
   - Guide the process of synthetic task design with the behavioral and cognitive requirements of the actual task.
   - Utilize a solid theoretical framework to increase psychological fidelity.
   - Ensure that the training evokes components of self-regulation, including cognitive, motivational, and behavioral mechanisms.

2. **Align Level of Training with Level of Practice**
   (Klein and Kozlowski, 2000; Salas and Cannon-Bowers, 2001)
   - Evoke teamwork competencies with training delivered at the team level.
   - Incorporate theoretically and empirically based training competencies.
   - Design the training program so that it evokes the use of the trained competency.
   - Account for the level of interdependence of the task.
   - Deliver team level training for tasks that are high in interdependence (i.e., require cooperation among team members).

3. **Implement Feedback and Debriefing Sessions**
   (Fanning and Gaba, 2007; Kluger and DeNisi, 1996)
   - Predicate the timing and implementation of feedback in SBT on observed performance levels, learning objectives, and relevant theory.
   - Craft feedback such that it makes salient the goals of the training intervention.
   - Structure feedback to address strengths and weaknesses in the competencies being trained and make references to specific, observable instances of behavior.
   - Incorporate the following features when constructing a debrief: (1) identify the impact of the experience, (2) identify and consider the processes that developed, (3) clarify the facts, concepts, and principles, (4) identify the ways in which emotion was involved, and (5) identify the different views that each of the participants formed.

4. **Use an automated performance measurement system**
   (Salas et al., 2009; Schreiber, Watz, and Winston, 2003)
   - Use the automated process during both the execution phase and the postexecution phase to provide performance diagnosis to inform performance evaluations.
   - Adapt or use predeveloped systems such as: Performance Effectiveness Tracking System (Schreiber et al., 2003) and Distributed Interactive Simulation.
   - Utilize push-to-talk buttons to allow for the collection of data pertaining to communication patterns.

5. **Train and guide observers using protocols**
   (Cook et al., 2009; Hasenbosch and Ross, 2013; Holt, Hansberger, and Boehm-Davis, 2002).
   - Provide observers with prescriptive information about how to measure trainees.
   - Include an elaborate description of all the dimensions that are being rated and provide practice scenarios (e.g., pilot sessions, previous sessions, or sample sessions).
   - Use a script that identifies typical events based on theory.
   - Schedule meetings between the observers to discuss any discrepancies after observer training.
   - Provide feedback to observers who are not aligned with the standard rating.
   - Require observers to rate sessions after the reliability is established.
   - Monitor and regularly deliver feedback throughout the rating process to ensure proper protocol is being followed.

(cont.)

Table 11.2 (*cont.*)

---

6. **Utilize measures that are specific to learning outcomes and focus on observable behaviors**
(Rosen et al., 2010; Weaver et al., 2010)
   - Ensure that the foundation of a training evaluation is in accordance with the learning objectives.
   - Prepare training evaluations such that they represent the assessment of trainee's performance within the training environment.
   - Implement measures of observable behaviors.
7. **Incorporate deliberate and repetitive practice**
(McGaghie et al., 2011)
   - Provide trainees with the opportunities to exercise targeted competencies.
   - Ensure that the trainer guides practice such that the competencies are properly interpreted and practiced.
   - Utilize role-play or scenario-based practice sessions.
   - Assign trainees specific roles via the instructor or script within role-play activities and isntruct them to utilize the trained concepts to successfully complete their role.
   - Design scenario-based training programs to mirror a real-world environment and provide trainees the opportunity to execute tasks similar to what they would experience on the job.
   - Incorporate repetitive practice sessions.

Suggestions for Future Research

Although SBT has been extensively studied over the past decade, several questions have yet to be addressed. Therefore, in the following section we discuss several future directions for research examining SBT. We suggest the following areas for future study in SBT: using additional measures, exploring mechanisms of SBT effectiveness, examining how the effectiveness of SBT may differ under varying conditions, determining minimally necessary fidelity levels, and examining the influence of technological advances on the use and effectiveness of SBT.

Use Additional Measures

One primary limitation of the SBT literature concerns the type of outcomes generally examined. Several researchers have noted that SBT studies generally collect self-report data encompassing affective reactions rather than more systematic, objective indicators of performance and transfer (Salas and Cannon-Bowers, 2001; Wideman et al., 2007). Future empirical studies examining the effectiveness of SBT should include more objective, systematic learning and performance metrics. This aligns with the call of researchers to incorporate observable measures of behaviors within training endeavors that map onto actual behaviors required on the job (Weaver et al., 2010). Bell and colleagues (2008) suggested that, in addition to using more objective and robust measures, future research should also examine a broader range of outcomes. For example, rather than primarily focusing on assessing performance, measures such as adaptability, transfer, and other more implicit measures of knowledge should also be evaluated.

Explore Mechanisms

Bell and colleagues (2008) further suggested that future research should address the mechanisms through which instructional features of simulations facilitate targeted outcomes. Specifically, they posited that the areas of content, immersion, interactivity, and communication can all be utilized to achieve training objectives. However, they noted that prior work addressing the utility of different training features remains limited. More work is needed in this area to garner a better understanding of how different training features can be implemented to achieve optimal levels of training outcomes. Although work has been completed addressing which features can improve training (e.g., McGaghie et al., 2010), it is not precisely known through which learning mechanisms or cognitive processes and at what time these features are able to contribute to enhanced learning. Although initial work assessing how several features utilized in SBT interventions contribute to overall training effectiveness has been completed, further work investigating additional features and under what conditions they are necessary should be conducted.

Examine Relative Effectiveness

As an extension of the research agenda outlined in the preceding text, another direction for future work includes determining when SBT is most effective. As SBT scenarios can require extensive time and money to develop and implement, depending upon the scenarios constructed (Summers, 2004), it is critical that organizations prioritize when to use SBT. Salas and colleagues (2009) noted that, in the context of management education, it is largely unknown when SBT is more effective than other training techniques. However, this is a common thread across a majority of contexts where SBT is implemented and understanding remains limited regarding when SBT is most beneficial. Thus, future research should examine when to implement SBT and under which circumstances it is more effective than more conventional training approaches. For example, as previously discussed, personnel that must work in dynamic conditions characterized by high complexity may especially benefit from SBT (Salas et al., 2009) whereas employees who work in relatively stable conditions may benefit equally from primarily information and demonstration-based methods.

Determine Minimally Necessary Fidelity Levels

Another question that has remained largely unanswered is the degree to which fidelity is necessary for facilitating targeted training outcomes. This is especially important given the degree to which fidelity can drive the price of developing the SBT intervention (Summers, 2004). Although there is evidence that a low-fidelity simulator can be as effective as a high-fidelity simulator in facilitating targeted results (e.g., Norman, Dore, and Grierson, 2012), additional work exploring potential moderators could further illuminate the relationship between fidelity and learning outcomes. For example, all aspects of fidelity, as detailed in the taxonomy described by Rehmann and colleagues (1995), may be integral to facilitating learning in employees working in fields where a high degree of precision is required (e.g., surgeons) but may be less necessary for producing effective training outcomes in employees working in other fields.

Examine the Effect of Technological Advances

Future work should also examine the impact of advances in computer technology, such as virtual reality, that will allow training to be delivered in a routine and ongoing fashion. As the price of technology continues to lower, organizations can more frequently incorporate more technologically advanced forms of training (e.g., Blackmur et al., 2013). This will enable trainees to receive high-fidelity forms of training on a more frequent basis than was previously possible. This raises the question of whether the line between simulations and real work environments will grow increasingly blurred. As trainees are eventually able to move seamlessly between simulations and the actual environment experienced on the job, it is important to examine the impact this will have on training effectiveness.

In sum, future research should seek to primarily address under which conditions SBT is most effective and whether the necessity of certain features of SBT is contingent upon different factors and processes. This includes examining a variety of potential moderators, including elements such as individual differences and organizational features. Additional measures of effectiveness (e.g., objective measures of employee performance) should also be incorporated into studies of SBT. Future work should also examine the impact of more advanced forms of technology being increasingly available to supplement training practices. In answering these questions, a more nuanced understanding of SBT will be attained and subsequently allow for its more successful implementation; this will enable organizations to prioritize when to utilize SBT and ultimately promote enhanced performance within employees.

Conclusion

The purpose of this chapter was to provide a comprehensive understanding of the science of SBT by reviewing theory that should guide it use. We also sought to provide an explanation of the current state of SBT in practice, by discussing the domains where this training technique is most commonly implemented as well as providing several examples of simulations that have been successfully utilized. We also offered suggestions regarding how to best design and implement SBT, informed by relevant literature, for practitioners. Finally, we concluded by discussing several areas where more research is needed in this area. By gaining familiarity with the theory underlying SBT, understanding how it is currently implemented in practice, and following the best practices outlined within this chapter, training developers can create an appropriate and effective strategy for training that efficiently and effectively improves employee knowledge, skill, and performance.

Acknowledgements

This work was supported in part by contract NNX16AB08G with the National Aeronautics and Space Administration (NASA) and contract NBPF03402 with the National Space Biomedical Research Institute (NSBRI) to Rice University. The views expressed in this work are those of the authors and do not necessarily reflect the organizations with which they are affiliated or their sponsoring institutions or agencies.

References

Aggarwal, R., Ward, J., Balasundaram, I., Sains, P., Athanasiou, T., and Darzi, A. 2007. Proving the effectiveness of virtual reality simulation for training in laparoscopic surgery. *Annals of Surgery* 246(5): 771–779.

Aguinis, H., and Kraiger, K. 2009. Benefits of training and development for individuals and teams, organizations, and society. *Annual Review of Psychology* 60: 451–474.

Alessi, S. 2000. Designing educational support in system-dynamics-based interactive learning environments. *Simulation and Gaming* 31(2): 178–196.

Andreatta, P., Chen, Y., Marsh, M., and Cho, K. 2011. Simulation-based training improves applied clinical placement of ultrasound-guided PICCs. *Supportive Care in Cancer* 19(4): 539–543.

Annett, J. 1969. *Feedback and Human Behaviour: The Effect of Knowledge of Results, Incentives and Reinforcement on Learning and Performance.* Oxford: Penguin Books.

Arafeh, J. M. R., Hansen, S. S., and Nichols, A. 2010. Debriefing in simulated-based learning: Facilitating a reflective discussion. *Journal of Perinatal and Neonatal Nursing* 24(4): 302–311.

Arthur Jr., W., Bennett Jr., W., Edens, P. S., and Bell, S. T. 2003. Effectiveness of training in organizations: A meta-analysis of design and evaluation features. *Journal of Applied Psychology* 88: 234–245.

Association for Talent Development. 2014. *2014 State of the Industry Report.* Alexandria, VA: American Society for Training and Development.

Baker, D., Prince, C., Shrestha, L., Oser, R., and Salas, E. 1993. Aviation computer games for crew resource management training. *The International Journal of Aviation Psychology* 3(2): 143–156.

Beaubien, J. M., and Baker, D. 2004. The use of simulation for training skills in health care: How low can they go? *Quality and Safety in Health Care* 13: 151–156.

Bell, B. S., and Kozlowski, S. W. J. 2007. Advances in technology-based training. In S. Werner, ed., *Managing Human Resources in North America*, 27–42. New York: Routledge.

Bell, B. S., Kanar, A. M., and Kozlowski, S. W. J. 2008. Current issues and future directions in simulation-based training in North America. *International Journal of Human Resource Management* 19(8): 1416–1436.

Bernardin, H. J., and Beatty, R. W. 1984. *Performance Appraisal: Assessing Human Behavior at Work*. Boston: Kent Pub Co.

Blackmur, J. P., Clement, R. G. E., Brady, R. R. W., and Oliver, C. W. 2013. Surgical training 2.0: How contemporary developments in information technology can augment surgical training. *The Surgeon, Journal of the Royal Colleges of Surgeons of Edinburge and Ireland* 11(2): 105–112.

Bogdanowicz, M. S., and Bailey, E. K. 2002. The value of knowledge and the values of the new knowledge worker: Generation X in the new economy. *Journal of European Industrial Training* 26(2/3/4): 125–129.

Bowers, C. A., and Jentsch, F. 2001. Use of commercial, off-the-shelf, simulations for team research. In E. Salas, ed., *Advances in Human Performance and Cognitive Engineering Research*, 1, 293–317. Amsterdam: Elsevier Science/JAI Press.

Bowers, C. A., Salas, E., Prince, C., and Brannick, M. 1992. Games teams play: A method for investigating team coordination and performance. *Behavior Research Methods, Instruments, and Computers* 24: 503–506.

Breaugh, J. A., and Starke, M. 2005. Research on employee recruitment: So many studies, so many remaining questions. *Journal of Management* 26(3): 405–434.

Brown, K. G. 2001. Using computers to deliver training: Which employees learn and why? *Personnel Psychology* 54: 271–296.

Burke, R. J., and Ng, E. 2006. The changing nature of work and organizations: Implications for human resource management. *Human Resource Management Review* 16(2): 86–94.

Cannon-Bowers, J. A., and Bowers, C. 2009. Synthetic learning environments: On developing a science of simulation, games, and virtual worlds for training. In S. W. J. Kozlowski and E. Salas, eds., *Learning, Training, and Development in Organizations*, 229–261. New York: Routledge/Taylor and Francis Group.

Cohen, I., Iluz, M., and Shtub, A. 2014. A simulation-based approach in support of project management training for systems engineers. *Systems Engineering* 17(1): 26–36.

Cook, D. A., Dupras, D. M., Beckman, T. J., Thomas, K. G., and Pankratz, V. P. 2009. Effect of rater training on reliability and accuracy of mini-CEX scores: A randomized, controlled trial. *Journal of General Internal Medicine* 24(1): 74–79.

Daft, R. L., and Lengel, R. H. 1986. Organizational information requirements, media richness and structural design. *Management Science* 32(5): 554–571.

Day, R. D. 2014. *Leading and Managing People in the Dynamic Organization*. New York: Psychology Press.

Deering, S., Brown, J., Hodor, J., and Satin, A. J. 2007. Simulation training and resident performance of singleton vaginal breech delivery. *Obstet Gynecol* 107(1): 86–89.

Devine, D. J., Habig, J. K., Martin, K. E., Bott, J. P., and Grayson, A. L. 2004. Tinsel town: A top management simulation involving distributed expertise. *Simulation and Gaming* 35(1): 94–134.

Fanning, R. M., and Gaba, D. M. 2007. The role of debriefing in simulation-based learning. *Simulation in Healthcare* 2(2): 115–125.

Faria, A. J., and Dickinson, J. R. 1994. Simulation gaming for sales management training. *Journal of Management Development* 13(1): 47–59.

Fowlkes, J., Dwyer, D. J., Oser, R. L., and Salas, E. 1998. Event-based approach to training (EBAT). *The International Journal of Aviation Psychology* 8(3): 209–221.

Fripp, J. 1997. A future for business simulations? *Journal of European Industrial Training* 21(4): 138–142.

Funke, J. 1998. Computer-based testing and training with scenarios from complex problem-solving research: Advantages and disadvantages. *International Journal of Selection and Assessment* 6(2): 90–96.

Gaba, D. M., Howard, S. K., Fish, K. J., Smith, B. E., and Sowb, Y. A. 2001. Simulation-based training in anesthesia crisis resource management (ACRM): A decade of experience. *Simulation and Gaming* 32(2): 175–193.

Goldstein, I. L. 1991. Training in work organizations. In M. D. Dunnette and L. M. Hough, eds., *Handbook of Industrial Organizational Psychology*, 2nd ed., 2: 507–620. Palo Alto, CA: Consulting Psychologists Press.

Gordon, J. A., Wilkerson, W. M., Shaffer, D. W., and Armstrong, E. G. 2001. "Practicing" medicine without risk: Students' and educators' responses to high-fidelity patient simulation. *Academic Medicine* 76(5): 469–472.

Hasenbosch, S., and Ross, P. 2013. Communication analysis for virtual mission preparation: Moving beyond simple replay. *Proceeding of SimTecT*, 62–68. Adelaide: Simulation Australia.

Hatala, R., Cook, D. A., Zandejas, B., Hamstra, S. J., and Rydges, R. 2014. Feedback for simulation-based procedural skills training: A meta-analysis and critical narrative synthesis. *Advances in Health Sciences Education* 19(2): 251–272.

Heinrichs, W. L., Youngblood, P., Harter, P. M., and Dev, P. 2008. Simulation for team training and assessment: Case studies of online training with virtual worlds. *World Journal of Surgery* 32: 161–170.

Helmreich, R. L. 1997. Managing human error in aviation. *Scientific American* 276(5): 62–67.

Holt, R. W., Hansberger, J. T., and Boehm-Davis, D. A. 2002. Improving rater calibration in aviation: A case study. *International Journal of Aviation Psychology* 12(3): 305–330.

Huang, J. L., Ryan, A. M., Zabel, K. L., and Palmer, A. 2014. Personality and adaptive performance at work: A meta-analytic investigation. *Journal of Applied Psychology* 99(1): 162–179.

Ilgen, D. R., Fisher, C. D., and Taylor, M. S. 1979. Consequences of individual feedback on behavior in organizations. *Journal of Applied Psychology* 64: 349–371.

Jacobs, R. L., and Baum, M. 1987. Simulation and games in training and development: Status and concerns about their use. *Simulation and Games* 18(3): 385–94.

Kaplan, R. E., Lombardo, M. M., and Mazique, M. S. 1985. A mirror for managers: Using simulation to develop management teams. *The Journal of Applied Behavioral Science* 21(3): 241–253.

Karim, M. N., and Behrend, T S. 2014. Reexamining the nature of learner control: Dimensionality and effects on learning and training reactions. *Journal of Business and Psychology* 29: 87–99.

Keith, N., and Frese, M. 2008. Effectiveness of error management training: A meta-analysis. *Journal of Applied Psychology* 93: 59–69.

Keys, B., and Wolfe, J. 1990. The role of management games and simulations in education and research. *Journal of Management* 16: 307–336.

Klein, K. J., and Kozlowski, S. W. J., eds., 2000. *Multilevel Theory, Research, and Methods in Organizations: Foundations, Extensions, and New Directions.* San Francisco: Jossey-Bass.

Kluger, A. N., and DeNisi, A. 1996. The effects of feedback interventions on performance: A historical review, a meta-analysis and a preliminary feedback intervention theory. *Psychological Bulletin* 119(2): 254–284.

Komaki, J., Heinzmann, A. T., and Lawson, L. 1980. Effect of training and feedback: Component analysis of a behavioral safety program. *Journal of Applied Psychology* 65(3): 261–270.

Kopelman, R. E. 1986. *Managing Productivity in Organizations: A Practical, People-Oriented Perspective.* New York: McGraw-Hill.

Koppenhaver, G. D. 1993. An evaluation of three bank management simulations: Preliminary results. *Financial Practice and Education* 3(2): 89–96.

Kozlowski, S. W. J., and Bell, B. S. 2007. A theory-based approach for designing distributed learning systems. In S. M. Fiore and E. Salas, eds., *Toward a Science of Distributed Learning*, 15–39. Washington, DC: American Psychological Association.

Kozlowski, S. W. J., and DeShon, R. P. 2004. a psychological fidelity approach to simulation-based training: Theory, research and principles. In S. G. Schiflett, L. R. Elliott, E. Salas, and M. D. Coovert, eds., *Scaled Worlds: Development, Validation, and Applications*, 75–99. Burlington, VT: Ashgate.

Kraiger, K., and Jerden, E. 2007. A meta-analytic investigation of learner control: Old findings and new directions. In S. M. Fiore and E. Salas, eds., *Toward a Science of Distributed Learning*, 65–90. Washington, DC: American Psychological Association.

Lane, D. C. 1995. On a resurgence of management simulations and games. *The Journal of Operational Research Society* 46(5): 604–625.

Lederman, L. C. 1983. Differential learning outcomes in an instructional simulation: Exploring the relationship between designated role and perceived learning outcome. *Communications Quarterly* 32: 198–204.

Lepper, M. R., and Malone, T. W. 1987. Intrinsic motivation and instructional effectiveness in computer-based education. In R. E. Snow and M. J. Farr, eds., *Aptitude, Learning, and Instructions: Cognitive and Affective Process Analysis*, 255–286. Hillsdale, NJ: Erlbaum.

Lievens, F. 2001. Assessor training strategies and their effects on accuracy, interrater reliability, and discriminant validity. *Journal of Applied Psychology* 86(2): 255–264.

Locke, E. A., and Latham, G. P. 1990. Work motivation and satisfaction: The light at the end of the tunnel. *Psychological Science* 1(4): 240–246.

McGaghie, W. C., Issenberg, S. B., Petrusa, E. R., and Scalese, R. J. 2006. Effect of practice on standardized learning outcomes in simulation-based medical education. *Medical Education* 40(8): 792–797.

McGaghie, W. C., Issenberg, S. B., Petrusa, E. R., and Scalese, R. J. 2010. A critical review of simulation-based medical education research: 2003–2009. *Medical Education* 44(1): 50–63.

McGaghie, W. C., Issenberg, S. B., Cohen, E. R., Barsuk, J. H., and Wayne, D. B. 2011. Does simulation-based medical education with deliberate practice yield better results than traditional clinical education? A meta-analytic comparative review of the evidence. *Academic Medicine* 86(6): 706–711.

McKinney, J., Cook, D. A., Wood, D., and Hatala, R. 2013. Simulation-based training for cardiac auscultation skills: Systematic review and meta-analysis. *Journal of General Internal Medicine* 28(2): 283–291.

Meyer, G. F., Wong, L. T., Timson, E., Perfect, P., and White, M. D. 2012. Objective fidelity evaluation in multisensory environments: Auditory cue fidelity in flight simulation. *PloS ONE* 7(9): 1–14.

Moore, M. L., and Dutton, P. 1978. Training needs analysis: Review and critique. *Academy of Management Review* 3(3): 532–545.

Moorthy, K., Vincent, C., and Darzi, A. 2005. Simulation-based training is being extended from training individuals to teams. *BMJ: British Medical Journal* 330(7490): 493–494.

Motola, I., Devine, L. A., Chung, H. S., Sullivan, J. E., and Issenberg, S. B. 2013. Simulation in healthcare education: A best evidence practical guide. AMEE Guide No. 82. *Medical Teacher* 35(10): e1511–e1530.

Norman, G., Dore, K., and Grierson, L. 2012. The minimal relationship between simulation fidelity and transfer of learning. *Medical Education* 46(7): 636–647.

Phillips, J. M. 1998. Effects of realistic job previews on multiple organizational outcomes: A meta-analysis. *The Academy of Management Journal* 41(6): 673–690.

Preisler, L., Svendsen, M. B. S., Nerup, N., Svendsen, L. B., and Konge, L. 2015. Simulation-based training for colonoscopy: Establishing criteria for competency. *Medicine* 94(4): e440.

Premack, S. L., and Wanous, J. P. 1985. A meta-analysis of realistic job preview experiments. *Journal of Applied Psychology* 70(4): 706–719.

Rehmann, A. J., Mitman, R. D., and Reynolds, M. C. 1995. *A Handbook of Flight Simulation Fidelity Requirements for Human Factors Research*. Technical Report No. DOT/FAA/CT-TN95/46. Wright-Patterson, AFB, OH: Crew Systems Ergonomics Information Analysis Center.

Reichard, R. J., Serrano, S. A., and Wefald, A. J. 2013. Engaging followers at a distance: Leadership approaches that work. In M. C. Bligh and R. E. Riggio, eds., *Exploring Distance in Leader-Follow Relationships: When Near Is Far and Far Is Near*, 107–135. New York: Routledge.

Rosen, M. A., Salas, E., Wilson, K. A., King, H. B., Salisbury, M., Augenstein, J., Robinson, D. W., and Birnbach, D. J. 2008. Measuring team performance in simulation-based training: Adopting best practices for healthcare. *Simulation in Healthcare* 3(1): 33–41.

Rosen, M. A., Weaver, S. J., Lazzara, E. H., Salas, E., Wu, T., Silvestri, S., Schiebel, N., Almedia, S., and King, H. B. 2010. Tools for evaluating team performance in simulation-based performance. *Journal of Emergencies, Trauma, and Shock* 3(4): 353–359.

Rudolph, J. W., Simon, R., Rivard, P., Dufresne, R. L., and Raemer, D. B. 2007. Debriefing with good judgment: Combining rigorous feedback with genuine inquiry. *Anesthesiology Clinics* 25(2): 361–376.

Salas, E., and Cannon-Bowers, J. A. 2001. The science of training: A decade of progress. *Annual Review of Psychology* 54: 471–499.

Salas, E., Bowers, C. A., and Rhodenizer, L. 1998. It is not how much you have but how you use it: Toward a rational use of simulation to support aviation training. *The International Journal of Aviation Psychology* 8(3): 197–208.

Salas, E., Wildman, J. L., and Piccolo, R. F. 2009. Using simulation-based training to enhance management education. *Academy of Management Learning and Education* 8(4): 559–573.

Salas, E., Rosen, M. A., Held, J. D., and Weissmuller, J. J. 2009. Performance measurement in simulation-based training: A review and best practices. *Simulation and Gaming* 40(3): 328–376.

Salas, E., Wilson, K. A., Burke, C. S., and Priest, H. A. 2005. Using simulation-based training to improve patient safety: What does it take? *Joint Commission Journal on Quality and Patient Safety* 31(7): 363–371.

Schmidt, R. A., and Bjork, R. A. 1992. New conceptualizations of practice: Common principles in three paradigms suggest new concepts for training. *Psychological Science* 3(4): 207–217.

Schreiber, B. T., Watz, B. A., and Winston, B. 2003. Objective human performance measurement in distributed environment: Tomorrow's needs. *Proceedings of Interservice/Industry Training, Simulation and Education Conference*. Orlando, FL: National Security Industrial Association. http://www.iitsecdocs.com/volumes/2003 (accessed April 18, 2017).

Shapiro, M. J., Morey, J. C., Small, S. D., Langford, V., Kaylor, C. J., Suner, S., Salisbury, M. L., Simon, R., and Jay, G. D. 2004. Simulation-based teamwork training for emergency department staff: Does it improve clinical team performance when added to an existing didactic teamwork curriculum? *Quality and Safety in Health Care* 13(6): 417–421.

Shetty, S., Zevin, B., Grantcharov, T. P., Roberts, K. E., and Duffy, A. J. 2014. Perceptions, training experiences, and preferences of surgical residents toward laparoscopic simulation training: A resident survey. *Journal of Surgical Education* 71(5): 727–733.

Singer, B. D., Corbridge, T. C., Schroedl, C. J., Wilcox, J. E., Cohen, E. R., McGaghie, W. C., and Wayne, D. B. 2013. First-year residents outperform third-year residents after simulation-based education in critical care medicine. *Simulation in Healthcare: Journal of the Society for Simulation in Healthcare* 8(2): 67.

Steadman, R. H., Coates, W. C., Huang, Y. M., Matevosian, R., Larmon, B. R., McCullough, L., and Ariel, D. 2006. Simulation-based training is superior to problem-based learning for the acquisition of critical assessment and management skills. *Critical Care Medicine* 34(1): 151–157.

Summers, G. J. 2004. Today's business simulation industry. *Simulation and Gaming* 35(2): 208–241.

Sweeney, L. A., Warren, O., Gardner, L., Rojek, A., and Lindquist, D G. 2014. A simulation-based training program improves emergency department staff communication. *American Journal of Medical Quality* 29(2): 115–123.

Tannenbaum, S. I., and Yukl, G. 1992. Training and development in work organizations. *Annual Review of Psychology* 43(1): 399–441.

Thornton, G. C., and Cleveland, J N. 1990. Developing managerial talent through simulation. *American Psychologist* 45(2): 190–199.

Tokaji, M., Ninomiya, S., Kurosaki, T., Orihasi, K., and Sueda, T. 2012. An educational training simulator for advanced perfusion techniques using a high-fidelity virtual patient model. *Artificial Organs* 36(12): 1026–1035.

TRADOC. 2011. The U.S. Army learning concept for 2015. TRADOC PAM 525-8-2. http://www.tradoc.army.mil/tpubs/pams/tp525-8-2_CH1.pdf (accessed April 18, 2017).

Wahr, J. E., Prager, R. L., Abernathy III, J. H., Martinez, E. A., Salas, E., Seifert, P. C., Groom, R. C., Spiess, B. D., Searles, B. E., Sundt III, T. M., Sanchez, J. A., Shappell, S. A., Culig, M. H., Lazzara, E. H., Fitzgerald, D. C., Thourani, B. H., Eghtesady, P., Ikonomidis, J. S., England, M. R., Sellke, F. W., and Nussmeier, N. A. 2013. Patient safety in the cardiac operating room: Human factors and teamwork a scientific statement from the American Heart Association. *Circulation* 128(10): 1139–1169.

Washbush, J., and Gosen, J. 2001. An exploration of game-derived learning in total enterprise simulations. *Simulation and Gaming* 32(3): 281–296.

Watling, C., Driessen, E., Van Der Vleuten, C. P. M., and Lingard, L. 2012. Learning from clinical work: The roles of learning cues and credibility judgments. *Medical Education* 46(2): 192–200.

Weaver, S. J., Salas, E., Lyons, R., Lazzara, E. H., Rosen, M. A., DiazGranados, D., Grim, J. G., Augenstein, J. S., Birnbach, D. J., and King, H. 2010. Simulation-based team training at the sharp end: A qualitative study of simulation-based team training design, implementation, and evaluation in healthcare. *Journal of Emergencies, Trauma, and Shock* 3(4): 369–377.

Wideman, H. H., Owston, R. D., Brown, C., Kushniruk, A., Ho, F., and Pitts, K. C. 2007. Unpacking the potential of educational gaming: A new tool for gaming research. *Simulation and Gaming* 38(1): 10–30.

Woehr, D. J., and Huffcutt, A. I. 1994. Rater training for performance appraisal: A quantitative review. *Journal of Occupational and Organizational Psychology* 67(3): 189–205.

Wulf, G., and Shea, C. H. 2004. Understanding the role of augmented feedback: The good, the bad, and the ugly. In A. M. Williams and N. J. Hodges, eds., *Skill Acquisition in Sport: Research, Feedback, and Practice*, 121–144. London: Routledge.

Wynder, M. 2004. Facilitating creativity in management accounting: A computerized business simulation. *Accounting Education* 13(2): 231–250.

Zantow, K., Knowlton, D. S., and Sharp, D. C. 2005. More than fun and games: Reconsidering the virtues of strategic management simulations. *Academy of Management Learning & Education* 4(4): 451–458.

Zendejas, B., Brydges, R., Hamstra, S., and Cook, D. A. 2013. State of the evidence on simulation-based training for laparoscopic surgery: A systematic review. *Annals of Surgery* 257(4): 586–593.

Zevin, B., Aggarwal, R., and Grantcharov, T. P. 2012. Simulation-based training and learning curves in laparoscopic roux-en-y gastric bypass. *British Journal of Surgery* 99(7): 887–895.

Zwikael, O., and Sadeh, A. 2007. Planning effort as an effective risk management tool. *Journal of Operations Management* 25(4): 755–767.

12 Augmented Reality Systems in Training

Joseph R. Keebler, Brady S. Patzer, Travis J. Wiltshire, and Stephen M. Fiore

With the advent of low-cost wearable computing devices, smartphones, and heads up displays, we are approaching an era of human-technology integration that is unparalleled in the past. Augmented reality (AR) represents a useful tool for human-technology integration. AR, defined in the broadest sense, is the integration of physical reality with digital information overlays, such as visual or auditory information. The major difference between AR and virtual reality is that with AR there is always a component of the physical reality present (Stevens, 1995). More specifically, AR often enhances reality through the display of information that is not normally accessible directly through the users' senses.

AR systems have existed in some form or another for more than five decades, but only recently have become affordable for a consumer market. The first AR systems were developed at Harvard in the 1960s, and were further refined at NASA, the U.S. Air Force, MIT, and UNC over the next two decades (Krevelen & Poleman, 2010). The term *augmented reality* wasn't used to refer to these types of systems until the 1990s (Caudell & Mizell, 1992)

AR has evolved over the past two decades since the term was originally coined. Historically, many have argued that an AR system must use a head mounted display (HMD). However, many modern systems have shown that AR can exist outside of HMDs. In fact, AR technologies have moved away from such displays (Azuma, 1993). A modern definition entails that 3D objects be integrated into real environments for a system to be considered "augmented reality." Nevertheless, this definition has not always held true as AR systems developed. For instance, systems have augmented the auditory or tactile information provided to the AR user (Azuma, 1993; Krevelen & Poleman, 2010). This change in the definition of the term has been accompanied by the development of devices and software that streamline the creation of AR and its availability at a consumer level – such as with smart mobile devices – allowing for the rapid advancement of AR applications. In summary, we believe that one of the best definitions of AR systems was devised in Krevelen and Poleman's review of the technology (Krevelen & Poleman, 2010). The authors discuss three key aspects that identify a system as being "AR." For the remainder of this chapter, AR is defined as a system that: (1) combines real and virtual objects in a real environment, (2) registers real and virtual objects with each other, and (3) runs dynamically in three dimensions in real time.

AR systems have been implemented in a wide range of contexts, from training environments in health care and industry settings, to high-risk professions including the cockpits of fighter jets and police force facial recognition software for identifying criminals (Newman, 2014). Further, AR has implications for aiding those with cognitive deficits (Chang, Kang, & Huang, 2013), educating children (Dieterle, 2009), and creating museum displays (Lydens, Saito, & Inoue, 2007).

To narrow the focus for this chapter, we will focus on the potential learning and training outcomes of these systems, as well as performance enhancement capabilities within operational environments. In addition, we will discuss potential next steps and future directions for AR technology, research, and application in training systems.

Taxonomies of Augmented Reality Systems

Although AR and virtual reality are highly similar, there are a few key differences that make the two types of technology quite unique from one another. The role that physical reality plays is one of the major differentiating factors between the two types of systems. By definition, AR requires that some aspect of physical reality is used in the augmented system. Thus, the distinguishing factor is that AR supplements the real world, whereas virtual reality creates an entirely artificial environment that replaces the real world (Azuma, 1993). Some have mapped this on a continuum spanning from real environments on one end to entirely virtual environments on the other, with AR falling in between the two (see Figure 12.1; Milgram et al., 1994; Mistry, Maes, & Chang, 2009).

Another useful taxonomy considers a set of factors concerned with how one's body relates to the system, coupled to the amount of artificiality the system creates. These dimensions have been used to classify AR systems. Figure 12.2 summarizes this idea – the x-axis equals the dimension of immersion of the physical body (i.e., low immersion remains in reality vs. high immersion is entirely in a virtual environment) while the y-axis equals the dimension of artificiality of environment (level of actual physical/reality presented vs. level of synthetic reality presented) (Benford et al., 1998).

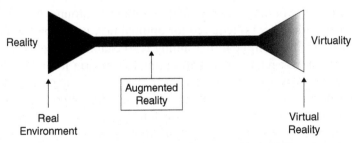

Figure 12.1. *Adapted version of Milgram et al.'s (1994) reality-virtuality continuum.*

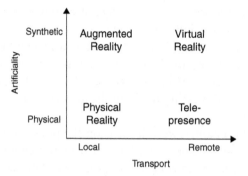

Figure 12.2. *Adapted version of Benford et al.'s (1998) classes of shared space in mixed reality.*

If we examine the requirements for AR versus virtual reality, we find that they differentiate across three subsystems (Azuma, 1997): scene generation, display device, and tracking/sensing. Specifically, AR does not need to create scenery – instead it overlays virtual information on a real-world environment so it can use much simpler displays then virtual reality. The major difference, and the aspect of AR that usually needs to be more advanced compared to virtual reality, is the tracking and sensing of the virtual objects in relation to the real world. In other words, the coupling of the virtual image to its location is a key component of the efficacy of a given AR system. This leaves the challenge for AR systems to match expectations due to their existence in an ever-changing dynamic environment, whereas virtual reality does not face the same issue because it entirely fabricates the environment, leaving no room for error in regard to the computer's ability to respond to outside environmental cues.

In summary, AR and virtual reality appear to be different species of virtual environments, differentiated by the ratio of virtual to physical reality, with AR being associated with a high level of physical reality embedded with virtual information, and virtual reality being a virtual environment that may or may not have some aspects of physical reality apparent to the user.

Integrating Augmented Reality into Training Environments

An ideal training environment is designed around the knowledge, skills, and attitudes (KSAs) required for optimal task performance (Goldstein & Ford, 2002). The main goal of training is to enable trainees to familiarize with and adopt task-related KSAs to optimally perform job-related tasks. In the past, technology has been used as a tool to teach knowledge, skills, and abilities within training environments. Moreover, AR offers the opportunity to improve on-the-job training by providing learning opportunities while a trainee is in the work environment. Currently, there are several components of a training environment in which AR can be integrated to afford for KSA acquisition in trainees.

Augmented Reality as a Learning Tool for Embedded Training

Studies performed on learning tasks have used AR as a supplementary tool because the premise of AR is that it augments some aspect of the real environment. Several studies have documented the benefit that AR has on improving learning outcomes during a task. First, it seems that AR may help motivate individuals to learn (Chang, Morreale, & Medicherla, 2010), although further work is needed to understand why this occurs. Additionally, AR can be used as a tool to demonstrate complex systems. For example, Liarokapis and colleagues (2004) used AR to demonstrate systems in a mechanical engineering course (Liarokapis et al., 2004). The AR was implemented onto a tabletop environment, allowing the trainee to interact with multimedia while learning. Students interacted with 3D models of real objects being discussed in class to understand the mechanism of a camshaft in relation to other engine components (Liarokapis et al., 2004).

To determine whether an AR system is useful in education, Radu (2014) conducted a systematic review that identified several themes in successful AR learning system. Evidence from literature on successful AR learning system suggests that systems should meet all the following statements:

1. The application transforms the problem representations such that difficult concepts are easier to understand.
2. The application presents relevant educational information at the appropriate time and place, providing easy access to information and/or reducing extraneous learner tasks.
3. The application directs learner attention to important aspects of the educational experience.
4. The application enables learners to physically enact, or to feel physically immersed in, the educational concepts.
5. The application permits students to interact with spatially challenging phenomena. (9)

Augmented Reality as Feedback during On-the-Job Training

AR can provide feedback in real time. For instance, the display could reveal whether the trainee conducted a task correctly. For example, assembly tasks require the user to identify different components and bring them together in a systematic order to assemble the final product. Typically, these tasks are guided by a drawing of the components in a paper-based format (Hou & Wang, 2010). On-the-job training can instead use AR as a cognitive aid during the assembly decision process, allowing the user to manipulate components and receive guidance in the form of vocal instructions, animations, video, or visual cues (e.g., arrows highlighting important components) that are directly related to the steps required to perform each task (Hou & Wang, 2010). This form of guidance while performing tasks or learning new skills may decrease the cognitive load required to interpret instructional information, such as an assembly manual, and enable the user to divert more of their working memory capacity to learning and performing a task. In fact, evidence of improved skill transfer of training to an actual task was reported for an assembly task using AR over conventional two-dimensional engineering drawings (Boud et al., 1999). Results of the experiment suggested that training to perform the assembly task using AR led to shorter task performance time because the AR system allowed the trainees to reference the virtual information for guidance and begin to develop their motor skills while learning the task (Boud et al., 1999). Given this apparent effect, future research will need to disentangle whether learning was hindered in the face of better performance. In other words, participants are performing the tasks better due to the AR, but they aren't learning as well as more traditional methods due to overreliance on the AR system.

Integrating Augmented Reality into Medical Environments

Recently, AR has been increasingly used in medical settings. AR systems are being designed to afford practice prior to patient contact, and in some cases during procedures with patients. In the following text, we review the evidence AR implementation in medical education and medical procedures within the past five years.

Augmented Reality in Medical Education

AR as an education tool has many of the potential benefits of simulation-based training, such as allowing health care providers to maintain or master skills outside of actual patient scenarios, without the repercussions associated with errors (Alaraj et al., 2013; Ungi et al., 2011).

Multimodal (e.g., haptic and visual information) AR training systems have been proposed as a platform for medical residents learning neurosurgical procedures (Alaraj et al., 2013). For example, a ventriculostomy is a procedure that attempts to provide relief to those who have brain injury, hydrocephalus, or brain tumors by draining some of their cerebrospinal fluid (Yudkowsky et al., 2013). Residents who were trained to perform the ventriculostomy using an AR system showed increased performance in both the simulated practice sessions and subsequent surgical procedures on real patients (Yudkowsky et al., 2013).

Bruellmann and colleagues (2013) developed a reliable method for assisting endodontic studies by creating a system that identifies root canal orifices and tooth types. They posit that AR imaging can be overlaid onto the site to aid an endodontic surgeon in detecting where root canals were after they have been filled (Bruellmann et al., 2013).

Ungi et al. (2011) examined medical student accuracy of needle placement for percutaneous facet joint injection. Results showed improvement in successful needle placement for those trained using AR guided placement tools versus students who were trained without the assistance of AR. The authors suggest that the time required to learn the skill proficiently may be less when students are trained using the AR guided training method.

AR has also been investigated in laparoscopic skills training. Vera et al. (2014) conducted a study that investigated the efficacy of a laparoscopic skills training that overlays guidance from a mentor onto the trainees laparoscopic monitor while they are performing a surgical task. Using the augmented reality telementoring (ART) tool, the mentor can essentially show the trainee how to perform complex sutures (Vera et al., 2014).

Results indicate that the trainees who received the AR telementoring developed adequate skills faster, performed the suturing tasks faster, and made fewer errors than the students that did not receive the AR telementoring (Vera et al., 2014). Volonte et al. (2011) suggests that AR visualization techniques can have an impact on laparoscopic surgery by making surgeries easier, faster, and safer (Volonte et al., 2011).

AR applications have been implemented and tested from mobile technologies, such as phones and tablets. One example is the mobile augmented reality blended learning environment (mARble; von Jan et al., 2012; Albrecht et al., 2013). This system allows medical students to become immersed in the topic that they are studying and enable simulation of events that rarely occur. See Figure 12.3 for an example of the mARble system visualization.

Albrecht and colleagues (2013) conducted a study examining the implementation of the mARble system in a third-year medical student cohort who was learning to treat gunshot wounds. They examined knowledge and attitudinal outcomes between students who used the mobile AR system and those that used traditional textbook material. Results indicated that AR led to increased knowledge integration and decreased feelings of numbness and fatigue, which may suggest that AR motivates trainees to learn (Albrecht et al., 2013). However, the authors note that it is difficult to determine whether the results were due to the mode of learning (i.e., AR or textbook) or if a confounding factor impacted learning, such as the approach to training. Specifically, textbooks required individuals to learn on their own, while the AR system encouraged social interaction while learning and it may be this difference in the learning experience that accounts for the observed results.

AR has been studied within the anatomy education realm as well. Anatomy knowledge is foundational for medical education (Chien, Chen, & Jeng, 2010). Because it is difficult to get a sense for the 3D structures of anatomy using textbook images, AR has been used as a substitute (Chien, Chen, & Jeng, 2010). One example is the miracle system, which is an AR training tool designed to teach bone structure and abdomen anatomy (Figure 12.4; Blum et al., 2012).

The miracle system provides the trainee with a reflection of the world, much like a mirror, and augments the visual scene so that the anatomy of their abdomen is displayed on the trainee's body. This visualization allows users to see the layout of the bone or organ anatomy within the abdomen. Additionally, the authors suggest that this system could be beneficial in demonstrating the crucial steps that will be performed during a surgery to patients (Blum et al., 2012).

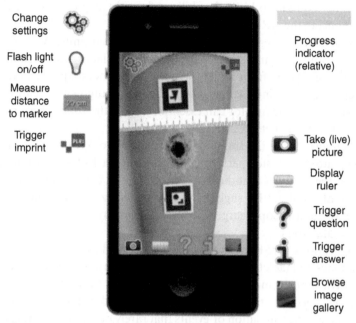

Change settings

Flash light on/off

Measure distance to marker

Trigger imprint

Progress indicator (relative)

Take (live) picture

Display ruler

Trigger question

Trigger answer

Browse image gallery

Figure 12.3. *Example of the mARble system visualization from von Jan et al. (2012).*

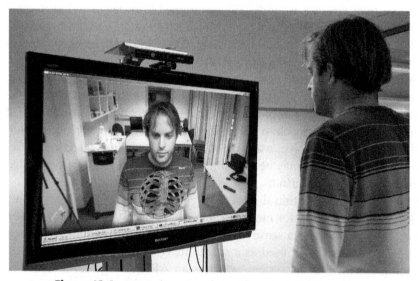

Figure 12.4. *Mirracle system from Blum et al. (2012).*

Other anatomy training systems take into consideration multiple modes of information presented to the trainee in an effort to maximize learning. For instance, the BodyExplorerAR allows a trainee to interact with anatomy using the tactile, auditory, and visual senses (Samosky et al., 2012). The BodyExplorerAR system uses a projector to overlay anatomy onto a physical mannequin. The visualization allows the trainee to interact with the AR by requesting additional information about an organ, viewing physiological information, listening to simulated heart sounds, or interacting with the mannequin in ways akin to interactions with real patients. For example, the trainee can listen to the heart beat of the simulated patient, examine the electrocardiogram, simulate the injection of a drug, and observe the change in a patient's heart rate and sounds (Samosky et al., 2012). Thomas, John, and Delieu (2010) describe the Bangor Augmented Reality Education Tool for Anatomy (BARETA), which is a system that allows trainees to touch and see AR content (Thomas, John, & Delieu, 2010). The aforementioned AR tools are a promising avenue for anatomy training. However, additional investigation is required to validate training systems and examine the role of multimodal learning in aiding training outcomes.

Augmented Reality as an Aid during Procedures

Marzano and colleagues (2013) present a successful AR guided surgery that performed an artery-first pancreatico-duodenectomy in a 77-year-old patient. The surgery required real-time interaction between the surgeon and a computer scientist controlling the AR system to ensure that the AR was accurately overlaid onto the patient. The authors state that utilizing the AR system afforded the surgeon the ability to understand the appropriate dissection planes and margins during the surgery to reduce the chance of unintentionally damaging surrounding areas (Marzano et al., 2013).

Research conducted on the integration of AR in laparoscopic surgery suggests that AR can be a useful tool to add depth cues to an otherwise 2D visualization and afford surgeons with a more comprehensive view of the operating field by digitally integrating images into the workflow (Kang et al., 2014). AR systems are helpful for 3D visualizations as surgeons were able to easily identify the major organs during AR visualization and were more accurate with their procedures (Kang et al., 2014; Lopez-Mir et al., 2013).

However, there is evidence that suggests that using AR during surgical procedures can hinder health care provider's ability to detect relatively obvious stimuli. Dixon and colleagues (2013) performed a study that found that surgeons who performed an endoscopic navigation task using AR provided anatomical contours were more accurate in navigating the endoscope, but were less likely to identify critical complications and foreign bodies when compared to surgeons who did not use AR (Dixon et al., 2013). This suggests that the use of AR led to an attentional tunneling effect, essentially distracting the surgeon from relatively obvious (and important) stimuli. Errors such as this could be potentially dangerous in an applied setting, where patient well-being is at risk.

Limitations of Augmented Reality in the Medical Setting

Overall, it seems that AR may be a useful tool for affording skill acquisition and improving performance in medical settings. However, there are some limitations to the implementation of AR in these environments. First, training systems need to be developed with a target audience in mind and tested with specific trainees (e.g., surgical residents) before being implemented fully into curricula. Second, trainees' experience levels should be accounted for so that the training system is designed around a specified level of experience. Third, the innate learning requirements of an AR-based environment need to be considered (Alaraj et al., 2013); proficiency with the system is particularly critical when that system is being used with real patients.

Although there has been evidence supporting the effectiveness of AR-based training in medicine as outlined within this section, more research is needed to determine whether skills learned during training will transfer to an actual work task, and how potential deleterious effects on performance, like the tunneling effect, can be averted. We discuss future research in the next section.

Future Directions for Research and Practice in Augmented Reality

As we have demonstrated in the preceding text, AR has become increasingly pervasive and beneficial in the medical domain for purposes of training and improving workplace performance. Of course, the potential for such technologies is profound and research has only begun to scratch the surface regarding the many possibilities. More, the increasing adoption of technology in the workplace is rapidly changing the way work is done. It seems as if the limits of what is possible with this technology seem to only be constrained by what humanity can imagine. Highly sophisticated AR systems have been conceived of and visualized in popular science fiction films, such as *Minority Report* and *Iron Man*, and such examples only serve to highlight what is on the not too distant horizon. With the increasing adoption of not only mobile phones with AR capabilities, but also wearable technologies such as Google Glass, future research is needed to investigate the implications of AR for improving training and workplace performance. We cannot claim to comprehensively cover all the possibilities here, but we hope to outline several proximal areas of research worth pursuing. In particular, we discuss how AR could be used to augment learning and accelerate training, improve human-machine system interactions, and improve social and team interaction in the workplace.

Augmenting Learning and Accelerating Training

Prior work has shown that AR systems can be used to augment learning (e.g., Keebler et al., 2014) and, perhaps, accelerate the training process. Recent technological advances have been applied to the learning sciences with the aim of developing intelligent systems that can adapt to a learner to accelerate the learning process. Generally a subfield of the learning and cognitive sciences called *accelerated learning* has focused specifically on how to reduce the amount of training required for a given domain, improve retention of knowledge, and put individuals on a path to developing adaptive expertise (Hoffman et al., 2009;

Hoffman et al., 2013). The learning and training environment, particularly in the workplace, is increasingly becoming a multimodal engagement in which learning materials are distributed across technological systems (i.e., computers), artifacts (i.e., books), and people (i.e., a mentor). Further, many modern training tasks are performance based in which it is often not feasible to refer to training materials. Regardless of the type of training, what is important for accelerating the learning process is an emphasis on the integration of knowledge directly into the environment, as well as the development of the metacognitive capacities involved in learning. This is another area where AR could be applied in future research to augment learning and accelerate training. Specifically, the following question should be addressed by future work: How can AR be used to accelerate the learning process by facilitating the integration of knowledge and developing metacognitive capacities?

In general, AR applied to learning has focused on presenting information in novel ways such as providing three-dimensional representations of anatomical structures, which are commonly taught with two-dimensional representations. Future research applying AR to learning should move beyond just developing new ways to represent information to focusing on ways to integrate knowledge. For example, when a learner is reading information in a text, AR displays could provide prompts that indicate how that information is related to prior knowledge. Further, the gap between learning from instructional materials and their application in real-world contexts, as well as transfer from one learning context to the next, is potentially abridged. AR could provide the mechanism to remind learners or trainees of relevant information they acquired during training as it is relevant to the present workplace task.

Another application of AR is that it could be used to deliver prompts during the training process that induce metacognitive capacities (e.g., Fiore & Vogel-Walcutt, 2010; Wiltshire et al., 2014). For example, an AR display could show text-based prompts to a trainee while they are preparing for a performance session that activates prior knowledge related to the task, prompts during the task that elicit monitoring of performance, and prompts after the task that elicit reflection on performance during the task. Such strategies have been argued to be essential for accelerating learning and developing expertise and have not yet been administered through an AR system.

In sum, research on AR applied to learning should investigate: (1) how AR can facilitate the integration of knowledge with preexisting knowledge during learning and performance, (2) how AR can facilitate the connection of learned content with the actual environment and novel situations, and (3) how AR can provide prompts that engage a learning in metacognition before, during, and after training.

Augmenting Human-Machine System Interaction

All too often the modern-day work environment is characterized by increasingly complex technological systems for which effective performance is often predicated by in-depth knowledge of the system and continually updated information regarding how that system is performing. As system complexity has increased, so too have the interfaces designed to convey information regarding system statuses and performance. Evidence for this claim can be seen by examining, for example, images of nuclear power plant control rooms, the cockpits of modern aircraft, or the International Space Station Mission Control room. Indeed, many of these domains have been subject to study by the field of cognitive engineering: an interdisciplinary approach that applies knowledge and techniques from cognitive science to study and design better human-machine systems (see Wilson, Helton, & Wiggins, 2013 for review). Common across complex domains characterized as human-machine systems is the need for technology to convey information regarding the system such that the human understands the system and what actions they can perform. This is another area future research and advances in AR should pursue. In particular, the following question should be addressed – in what ways can AR be used to help system users cope with information complexity of the technology?

The answer to this question is likely domain specific. For example, in domains such as nuclear power or space flight, the work environment is information dense with many displays. AR could provide a simple and unobtrusive technological capacity for cueing the operator to the appropriate display at a given time. Additionally, it could be used as a visual-spatial storage space to offload cognitive demands for memory-intensive tasks. For example, if there are several pieces of information from one display that need to be compared with information on another display, then an AR system could allow for storage of this information in a mobile display. Alternatively, in domains in requiring human operation of autonomous systems (e.g., human-robot interaction), AR displays could be used to provide information about how those systems are performing as well as their location. Ultimately, the application of AR to improving work in human-machine systems will be contingent on the domain, but could likely be determined by focusing on: (1) identifying the most salient and task-critical pieces of information, and (2) determining how the information could be conveyed with AR to reduce the complexity commonly associated with the domain to lead to better workplace performance.

Augmenting Social and Team Interaction at Work

The modern workplace is fundamentally a social environment in which effective performance requires coordination that spans the boundaries of biological and technological systems (i.e., across humans, resources, and technology; Hutchins, 1995; Malone & Crowston, 1994). In the workplace, joint activities between humans are commonplace and are typically geared toward aligning actions, knowledge, and objectives of team members who have different, albeit interdependent, roles (e.g., Rico et al., 2008). Essential to these joint actions is that the individuals involved can understand each other's intentions and other mental states to bring about the desired changes in the environment (e.g., accomplishing a task; Knoblich, Butterfill, & Sebanz, 2011). This is one area we suggest that future AR research and development could be applied. The general question here is: How can AR be used to enrich an individual's understanding of the social environment such that it helps them interact with team members and others to better accomplish their work?

One of the most robust areas of computer vision research in this regard is the detection of basic emotions from human facial expressions (e.g., Janssen et al., 2013). Indeed, recent applications, particularly for Google Glass have focused on leveraging this capability to enrich the user's information regarding the social environment. Specifically, applications have already been developed that augment a user's view of the environment by layering it with social information such as the displayed emotion of an individual being observed.

While these technological capabilities are just recently being developed for the purposes of AR, the implications for the workplace, we can speculate, are far reaching. For example, how often is it that we misinterpret the mood or intention of one of our colleagues or co-workers? Or misremember the last time we spoke with someone? Or in a large company, forget an employee's name? Augmentations could alleviate these problems. AR in combination with computer vision techniques can provided an augmented and enriched view of the social environment. Future research should identify: (1) the many possible types of social information that could be displayed with AR systems (e.g., intentions, emotions, actions, beliefs, personal history) and (2) examine the effects that displaying such information has on the interactions, relationship development, and, ultimately, effective task completion.

Conclusion

AR is an emerging technology that has several implications in training systems. With enhancements in technology used to create AR (e.g., cameras) the application of the technology will continue to increase. Corporations such as Microsoft have invested heavily in devices like the Hololens – an advanced wearable AR system that will enable individuals to interact in a virtual space overlaid on reality without having to rely on a complex computing system to accompany the augmentation. The potential for AR, especially as simulation-based training systems, is quite high – with appropriate implementation, refinement, and evaluation, AR systems could forever change the way we train. But the potential for AR extends much further, as integration of these systems into daily work could alter the information that is available in real time. Overlaying needed information in real time potentially removes the need to ever cross-reference information from other sources, enhancing human performance in the workplace beyond current capabilities.

References

Alaraj, A., Charbel, F. T., Birk, D., Tobin, M., Luciano, C., Banerjee, P. P., …, Roitberg, B. 2013. Role of cranial and spinal virtual and augmented reality simulation using immersive touch modules in neurosurgical training. *Neurosurgery* 72(1): 115–123.

Albrecht, U.-V., Folta-Schoofs, K., Behrends, M., and von Jan, U. 2013. Effect of mobile augmented reality learning compared to textbook learning on medical students: Randomized controlled pilot study. *Journal of Medical Internet Research* 15(8): e182.

Azuma, R. 1993. Tracking requirements for augmented reality. *Real World: Communications of the ACM* 36(7): 50–51.

Azuma, R. T. 1997. A survey of augmented reality. *Presence: Teleoperators and Virtual Environments* 6(4): 355–385.

Benford, S., Greenhalgh, C., Reynard, G., Brown, C., and Koleva, B. 1998. Understanding and constructing shared spaces with mixed-reality boundaries. *ACM Trans. Computer-Human Interaction* 5(3):185–223.

Blum, T., Kleeberger, V., Bichlmeier, C., and Navab, N. 2012. Miracle: An augmented reality magic mirror system for anatomy education. *IEEE Virtual Reality*: 115–116.

Boud, A. C., Haniff, D. J, Baber, C. and Steiner, S. J. 1999. Virtual reality and augmented reality as a training tool for assembly tasks. *IEEE International Conference on Information Visualization*: 32–36.

Bruellmann, D. D., Tjaden, H., Schwanecke, U., and Barth, P. 2013. An optimized video system for augmented reality in endodontics: A feasibility study. *Clinical Oral Investigations* 17: 441–448.

Caudell, T. P. and Mizell, D. W. 1992. Augmented reality: An application of heads-up display technology to manual manufacturing processes. In *Proc. Hawaii Int'l Conf. on Systems Sciences*: 659–669. Kauai, Hawaii: IEEE CS Press.

Chang, Y. J., Kang, Y. S., and Huang, P. C. 2013. An augmented reality (AR)-based vocational task prompting system for people with cognitive impairments. *Research in Developmental Disabilities* 34(10): 3049–3056.

Chang, G., Morreale, P., and Medicherla, P. 2010. Applications of augmented reality systems in education. In D. Gibson and B. Dodge, eds., *Proceedings of Society for Information Technology and Teacher Education International Conference 2010*, 1380–1385. Chesapeake, VA: AACE.

Chien, C.-H., Chen, C.-H., and Jeng, T.-S. 2010. An interactive augmented reality system for learning anatomy structure. *Proceedings of the International MultiConference of Engineers and Computer Scientists* 1: 1–6.

Dieterle, E. 2009. Neomillennial learning styles and River City. *Children Youth and Environments* 19(1): 245–278.

Dixon, B. J., Daly, M. J., Chan, H., Vescan, A. D., Witterick, I. J., and Irish, J. C. 2013. Surgeons blinded by enhanced navigation: The effect of augmented reality on attention. *Surgical Endoscopy* 27: 454–461.

Fiore, S., and Vogel-Walcutt, J. J. 2010. Making metacognition explicit: Developing a theoretical foundation for metacognitive prompting during scenario-based training. *Proceedings of the Human Factors and Ergonomics Society Annual Meeting* 54(27): 2233–2237.

Goldstein, I. L., and Ford, J. K. 2002. The needs assessment phase. *Training in Organizations*, 34–84. Belmont, CA: Wadsworth Cengage Learning.

Hoffman, R. R., Feltovich, P. J., Fiore, S. M., Klein, G., and Ziebell, D. 2009. Accelerated learning. *Intelligent Systems, IEEE* 24(2): 18–22.

Hoffman, R. R., Ward, P., Feltovich, P. J., DiBello, L., Fiore, S. M., and Andrews, D. H. 2013. *Accelerated Learning: Training for High Proficiency in a Complex World.* New York: Psychology Press.

Hou, L., and Wang, X. 2010. Using augmented reality to cognitively facilitate product assembly process. In S. Maad, ed., *Augmented Reality*, 99–112. http://cdn .intechopen.com/pdfs/6761/InTech-Using_augmented_reality_to_cognitively_ facilitate_product_assembly_process.pdf.

Hutchins, E. 1995. How a cockpit remembers its speeds. *Cognitive Science* 19(3): 265–288.

Janssen, J. H., Tacken, P., de Vries, J. J. G., van den Broek, E. L., Westerink, J. H., Haselager, P., and Ijsselsteijn, W. A. 2013. Machines outperform laypersons in recognizing emotions elicited by autobiographical recollection. *Human–Computer Interaction* 28(6): 479–517.

Kang, X., Azizian, M., Wilson, E., Wu, K., Martin, A. D., Kane, T. D., …, Shekhar, R. 2014. Stereoscopic augmented reality for laparoscopic surgery. *Surgical Endoscopy* 28: 2227–2235.

Keebler, J. R., Wiltshire, T. J., Smith, D., Fiore, S. M., and Bedwell, J. S. 2014. Shifting the paradigm of music instruction: Implications of embodiment stemming from an augmented reality guitar learning system. Frontiers in Psychology. *Theoretical and Philosophical Psychology* 5: 471.

Knoblich, G., Butterfill, S., and Sebanz, N. 2011. Psychological research on joint action: Theory and data. In Brian H. Ross, ed., *Advances in Research and Theory*, 59–101. London: Academic Press.

Van Krevelen, D. W. F., and Poleman, R. 2010. A Survey of Augmented Reality Technologies, Applications, and Limitations. *The International Journal of Virtual Reality* 9(2): 1–20.

Liarokapis, F., Mourkoussis, N., White, M., Darcy, J., Sifniotis, M., Petridis, P., … Lister, P. 2004. Web3D and augmented reality to support engineering education. *World Transactions on Engineering and Technology Education* 3(1). Melbourne, Australia: UICEE.

Lopez-Mir, F., Naranko, V., Fuertes, J. J., Alcaniz, M., Bueno, J., and Pareja, E. 2013. Design and validation of an augmented reality system for laparoscopic surgery in a real environment. *BioMed Research International* 2013: 1–12.

Lydens, L., Saito, Y., and Inoue, T. 2007. Digital technology at the National Science Museum of Japan. *Journal of Museum Education* 32(1): 7–16.

Malone, T. W., and Crowston, K. 1994. The interdisciplinary study of coordination. *ACM Computing Surveys (CSUR)* 26(1): 87–119.

Marzano, E., Piardi, T., Soler, L., Diana, M., Mutter, D., Marescaux, J., and Pessaux, P. 2013. Augmented reality-guided artery-first pancreatico-duodenectomy. *Journal of Gastrointestinal Surgery* 17: 1980–1983.

Milgram, P., Takemura, H., Utsumi, A., and Kishino, F. 1994. Augmented reality: A class of displays on the reality-virtuality continuum. *Proceedings of Telemanipulator and Telepresence Technologies* 2351: 282–292.

Mistry, P., Maes, P, and Chang, L. 2009. WUW – wear Ur World: A wearable gestural interface. *Proceedings CHI EA*: 4111–4116.

Newman, L. H. 2014. Dubai police will wear Google Glass with facial recognition software to ID crooks. *Slate*. http://www.slate.com/blogs/future_tense/2014/10/ 03/dubai_police_will_use_facial_recognition_and_google_glass_to_look_for_ wanted.html (accessed September 17, 2016).

Radu, I. 2014. Augmented reality in education: A meta-review and cross-media analysis. *Personal Ubiquitous Computing*: 1–11.

Rico, R., Sánchez-Manzanares, M., Gil, F., and Gibson, C. 2008. Team implicit coordination processes: A team knowledge–based approach. *Academy of Management Review* 33(1): 163–184.

Samosky, J. T., Nelson, D. A., Wang, B., Bregman, R., Hosmer, A., Mikulis, B., and Weaver, R. 2012. BodyExplorerAR: Enhancing a mannequin medical simulator with sensing and projective augmented reality for exploring dynamic anatomy and physiology. *Proceedings of the 6th International Conference on Tangible and Embedded Interaction*: 263–270.

Stevens, J. E. 1995. The growing reality of virtual reality. *BioScience*, 45(7): 435–439.

Thomas, R. G., John, N. W., and Delieu, J. M. 2010. Augmented reality for anatomical education. *Journal of Visual Communication in Medicine* 33(1): 6–15.

Ungi, T., Yeo, C. T., U-Thainual, P., McGraw, R. C., and Fichtinger, G. 2011. Augmented reality needle guidance improves facet joint injection training. *Proceedings of SPIE 7964, Medical Imaging 2011: Visualization, Image-Guided Procedures, and Modeling*: 79642E.

Vera, A. M., Russo, M., Mohsin, A., and Tsuda, S. 2014. Augmented reality telementoring (ART) platform: A randomized controlled trial to assess the efficacy of a new surgical education technology. *Surgical Endoscopy* 28: 3467–3472.

Volonte, F., Pugin, F., Bucher, P., Sugimoto, M., Ratib, O., and Morel, P. 2011. Augmented reality and image overlay navigation with OsiriX in laparoscopic and robotic surgery: Not only a matter of fashion. *Journal of Hepatobiliary Pancreatic Science* 18: 506–509.

von Jan, U., Noll, C., Behrends, M., and Albrecht, U.-V. 2012. mARble: Augmented reality in medical education. *Biomedical Technology* 57: 67–70.

Wilson, K. M., Helton, W. S., and Wiggins, M. W. 2013. Cognitive engineering. Wiley Interdisciplinary Reviews: *Cognitive Science* 4(1): 17–31.

Wiltshire, T. J., Rosch, K., Fiorella, L., and Fiore, S. M. (2014). Training for collaborative problem solving improving team process and performance through metacognitive prompting. *Proceedings of the Human Factors and Ergonomics Society Annual Meeting* 58(1): 1154–1158.

Yudkowsky, R., Luciano, C., Banerjee, P., Schwartz, A., Alaraj, A., Lemole, G. M., … Frim, D. 2013. Practice on an augmented reality/haptic simulator and library of virtual brains improved residents' ability to perform a ventriculostomy. Simulation in healthcare: *The Journal of the Society for Simulation in Healthcare* 8(1): 25–31.

13 One (Lesson) for the Road? What We Know (and Don't Know) about Mobile Learning

Michael E. Wasserman and Sandra L. Fisher

Nearly everyone has a mobile phone with web capabilities. Recent data suggests that even in emerging economies, large numbers of citizens have access to web-enabled phones and use them voraciously. *The Economist*, not known for hyperbole, noted that more than half of the adult population, worldwide, has a web-enabled smartphone and estimates that 80% will have one by 2020 (The Economist, 2015). This is great news for consumers – it is inexpensive and easy to keep in touch with one's elderly Aunt Betty and Uncle Dale or post photos of breakfast pastries at the cool new bakery on Stonegate Drive, and makes it easy to settle random trivia bets about questions such as, "Does Mr. T's real last name begin with the letter 'T'?" Tighter integration with the lives of friends and family, immediate weather data, directions, and winning said trivia bets (Mr. T was indeed born Lawrence Tureaud) are generally viewed as advancing quality of life. This advance is especially notable in emerging economies, where access to crop information (McCole et al., 2014), health advice (Chang et al., 2013), and basic services such as banking (Shaikh & Karjaluoto, 2015) has greatly improved the quality of life for millions.

The ubiquity of web-enabled mobile devices should also be great news for educators and training professionals. And seventh-grade teachers, college professors, piano instructors, and corporate trainers across the globe should be thrilled that mobile technology has made possible the ultimate goal of effective training: anywhere, anytime! Indeed we have anecdotal evidence of successful implementation of mobile learning solutions across a variety of educational, governmental, and industrial settings (Deriquito & Domingo, 2012; Mercado & Murphy, 2012; Messier & Schroeder, 2014; Sharples, Corlett, & Westmancott, 2002). However, a careful review of the relevant research from the education, psychology, and information technology literatures suggests that we know little about mobile learning and that the mobile learning ecosystem is shifting rapidly.

Similar to the early days of web-based training (e.g., Hall, 1997), use of mobile learning in organizations has outpaced rigorous research on the topic. Thus, in this chapter, we will identify what we do and do not know and improve our understanding of the trajectories that technology platforms, learning content, and learner attitudes are traveling along. We will explore both foundational and emerging research and identify a few areas of focus that will help practitioners and researchers better leverage mobile learning to move us closer to the goal of effective training anywhere, anytime.

What Is Mobile Learning?

Mobile learning is defined in many ways across the different literatures. Practitioners and researchers each take different approaches to defining mobile learning to suit their needs in different disciplines, including education, training, psychology, and information technology. The variety of definitions makes it difficult to identify and understand key terminology, theory, and developing best practices. For example, one definition provided by an educational technology organization is "the ability to obtain or provide educational content on personal pocket devices" (mobl21, 2015: par. 1). Similarly, the Association for Talent Development defined *mobile learning* in 2010 as deploying learning content on a mobile device in a way that allows organizations to provide new learning possibilities for workers who are not tied to a specific location (Woodill, 2010). These definitions are grounded in the use of a specific class of devices, which makes it difficult to use from a research perspective. A construct that is solely reliant on ever-changing technology will be short lived, and will make it challenging for the field to accumulate a body of knowledge over time.

In the academic literature, definitions also tend to focus on specific attributes of mobile learning such as connectivity, accessibility, immediacy, portability, and customizability as key elements (Korucu & Alkan, 2011; Laouris & Eteokleous, 2005; Traxler, 2009). The general approach is that mobile learning means learning anywhere, anytime. However, we see a wide range of learning activities within this approach, ranging from asynchronous access to written materials to sets of short, video-enhanced, interactive modules, or even synchronous video-based instruction (Laouris & Eteokleous, 2005; Paul, 2014).

These important variations in the definition and use of mobile learning across the literature lead to some interesting questions. To what extent is mobile learning "device driven"? Does it matter if a learner is using a laptop, a mobile phone, or just a book for learning? Perhaps the key is location. Does it matter if the learner is in the office, on the subway, or on an airplane? Alternatively, it may be the interaction between device and location. If a learner completes training on a mobile phone while sitting at a desk in the office, is that mobile learning? What about reading a book while on an airplane? Clearly, the existing definitions in the literature do not fully circumscribe the mobile learning context.

The range of critical aspects of the various definitions of mobile learning can be distilled into four broad themes based around devices, time and place, social interaction, and context. We discuss each of these themes, and then explore two important dynamics of mobile learning – accessibility and distractibility – as opposing forces in the future development of mobile learning. We then examine mobile learning in the traditional training cycle to more clearly identify opportunities and challenges moving forward. Finally, we discuss some research opportunities for mobile learning that may help mobile learning stakeholders (both individuals and organizations) better understand the mechanisms that can yield the best return on both time and financial investments.

Themes in Defining Mobile Learning

We reviewed literature on mobile learning from more than 20 years of research in the education, psychology, and information technology literatures. This review suggests that there are four broad themes embedded in the various definitions of mobile learning. The first theme is device based (e.g., mobl21, 2015; Motiwalla, 2007; Saccol et al., 2010; Wang, Wu, & Wang, 2009). These definitions distinguish mobile learning from other types of learning in that the learner uses a portable, Internet-enabled device. The implication is that if the learner is using a mobile technology device, the learner is engaging in mobile learning. Completing training on a PC that is physically connected to the wall is clearly not mobile learning. The construct of mobile learning is clearly derived from a technological perspective, and is not meant to cover reading a book on the airplane. But then, if a manager uses her smartphone to complete training in her office, is that mobile learning?

This leads to the second theme within mobile learning definitions: time and place (e.g., Denk, Weber, & Belkfin, 2007; Korucu & Alkan, 2011). This theme focuses on when and where the learner is engaging in the training or learning. Many authors set the defining feature of mobile learning as taking place, literally "anytime, anywhere" (Korucu & Alkan, 2011) and includes any learning that happens when the learner is not at a fixed, predetermined location (Crompton, 2014). In this class of definitions, mobile learning would mean that the learner is engaging in a learning activity:

(1) in a place other than in her/his traditional learning location (classroom, office, job site, training site, etc.), and/or
(2) at a time other than when the learner would traditionally engage in learning activities (outside of normal work shifts or typical school hours, etc.).

While the type of device *permits* mobility, it is the time and place dimension that determines more directly if the learning is actually mobile. This is similar to the distinction within the learner control literature of learner control tools being offered versus learners using them or not (Brown, Howardson & Fisher, 2016; Howardson et al., Chapter 5 this volume). It matters little if learner control (or mobility) is possible if no learner uses it.

The third theme is the social aspect of mobile learning. Many authors include a social dimension in their definitions of mobile learning, arguing that mobile learning inherently involves social interaction and collaboration (e.g., Crompton, 2014; Koole, 2009; Sharples, 2005). For example, mobile learning can be shared with relevant individuals (colleagues, suppliers, customers, etc.) or shared with loosely or completely unrelated individuals (nonwork friends, family). The social context is created using either social communication tools built directly into the mobile learning platform or learners' own communication tools/apps such as Facebook and Twitter. Learners may communicate with specified co-workers or trainees or with members of their own professional and personal networks. The social aspect of mobile learning may also occur in person, as learners may share content on a mobile device in a social manner, such watching videos together or receiving help on a knowledge assessment. This social functionality of mobile learning is similar to Kraiger's (2008) discussion of third-generation learning as the role of learner-to-learner interaction becomes an important function of training in general. However, despite the centrality of social interaction in many mobile learning definitions, we argue that the social aspect is one *possible* feature of mobile learning, but it is not a necessary condition. A learner could be using a smartphone or tablet to learn something away from his or her traditional location, outside of the traditional time, but be doing it without direct interaction with other learners.

The fourth aspect of mobile learning we derived from our review is the intended usage context in which the learning event takes place (Traxler, 2009). By this we mean how learners are expected to use, apply, and retain the knowledge and skills addressed in the training. A mobile learning program can be designed to help users learn new content that they would use in the near future, to review or refresh knowledge and skills learned earlier, or to provide immediate performance support. One unique characteristic of many mobile learning tools is that they can be easily used as performance support tools on the job. Training designers report that users are demanding extremely short training modules, less than five minutes at a time (Roberts, 2012). It seems likely that in this length of time, learning objectives may include some explicit knowledge that needs to be memorized but less tacit knowledge that requires deep and complex understanding. Learning modules may build together to help learners develop a new skill or decision-making expertise, but these would need to be carefully crafted to bring together the elements of knowledge, provide opportunities for practice, and give feedback.

Brown, Charlier, and Pierotti (2012) made a clear distinction between information and instructional learning resources. In their typology, an information learning resource is one that provides easy access and retrieval of information that can be used to help develop job-related knowledge or for learning something as needed. Sometimes information needs to be retrieved to complete a task and the user has no intent of learning it. In this case, the retrieval process does not qualify as a learning event. Similarly, Pimmer and Gröhbiel (2008) argue that retrieval of information is not learning. Thus, even informational learning resources delivered through mobile technology should have the goal of helping employees learn something rather than relying on that external source each time they need the information. Mobile learning platforms may serve a dual role as both learning stimulus and easily accessed performance support, a role of which those dusty training binders on everyone's cubicle bookshelves would be envious.

Now we return to the questions posed at the beginning of this section about what is mobile learning and what is not. The inherent technological nature of the construct eliminates reading a book on a plane as mobile learning. We are unwilling to tie the construct specifically to a particular technology, but it clearly is meant to be technology enabled. What if that traveler is reading a book on an e-reader? He or she is using appropriate technology, is out of the office, and perhaps on nonwork time. The e-reader has a social component where it can mark the most commonly highlighted passages by all readers on that platform. Thus, it would seem to meet the social criterion. The usage context of this experience is less well defined. The reader is probably not using it as an immediate performance support tool, but may be trying to identify one or two leadership principles that could be applied at work. Imagine another passenger on the airplane who is using the seat-back entertainment system to learn some Japanese while flying to Tokyo. This passenger seems like he or she is using a type of mobile training. It involves technology and is conducted out of the office and away from work time. It may lack the social component, unless the passenger is trying out some new words and phrases on the person in the next seat. He or she may have specific goals for applying the new language skill upon arrival in Tokyo. We could go on, but at this point in the evolution of mobile learning, we advocate defining it broadly, including knowledge development in both training for immediate knowledge and skills for longer-term development.

It will be important for researchers to clearly operationalize the instances of mobile learning that they are studying and developing to help build a common understanding of the related phenomena. We build off of Kukulska-Hulme (2010), Sharples, Taylor, and Vavoula (2007), and Traxler (2009) and offer a definition of mobile learning as *knowledge and skill building using technological tools that allow learners on-demand access to instructional resources untethered to or enhanced by geographic location.*

Thus, the core of mobile learning is knowledge and skill development with tools that are connected and portable. Beyond connected and portable, mobile learning can be: (1) customized to learner needs in terms of time and location and (2) social in that information can be easily shared with peers and instructors both formally and informally. Most interestingly, the combination of customization and socially connected can result in the ability to tailor a learning program to the capabilities of specific devices, and be *situationally connected* – that is offering learning experiences that are relevant to the learner's location in time and space at the exact moment the learning occurs. For example, the training module can change based on the device's GPS and sensors and on the location and conditions in which the learner finds him/herself (plant location, weather conditions, type of equipment, etc.). This can be a mild intervention, such as showing videos on equipment once you near that equipment (situated learning), or extensive intervention, such as using augmented reality (AR) where the camera view from the phone will include layers of data that will help a learner see things that she or he could not see otherwise, embedded within the actual physical scene that she or he views through his or her device (Wojciechowski & Cellary, 2013). In the most extreme sense of situational connectedness, the learner can be taught or shown material based on exactly what she or he is seeing at that very moment and be connected with peers who can offer expertise at the moment that expertise is needed to enhance learning.

One important question is how our definition of mobile learning differs from e-learning. To sharpen the focus on understanding mobile learning, the next section addresses similarities and differences between e-learning and mobile learning.

E-learning vs. Mobile Learning

> Proponents of mobile learning are still struggling to find a literature and rhetoric distinct from conventional tethered e-learning. (Traxler, 2007: 16)

A major definitional problem is disentangling e-learning and mobile learning. This problem arises because computing power has become smaller and increasingly portable. The ability to retrieve documents, watch video, take assessments, and communicate with video and audio in real time has moved from desktop and laptop technology that people use in an indoors, officelike, or classroom setting to something pocketable and useable anytime, anywhere with a smartphone, tablet, or watch. Technology has freed learners from being tethered to a classroom or their desk.

Technology advances have created a lag in addressing the e-learning/mobile learning boundary. Mobile learning has been viewed as either an evolutionary step in the e-learning continuum (e.g., Mostakhdemin-Hosseini and Tuimala, 2005) or as a separate subset of e-learning (e.g., Georgiev, Georgieva, & Smrikarov, 2004). Others argue that there is a more important, nuanced distinction. For example, Sharples (2009) suggests that "mobile learning creates new contexts for learning through interactions between people, technologies, and settings" (18).

For the purposes of this chapter, we consider mobile learning to be an evolutionary step beyond e-learning but also with the potential to be fundamentally separate from e-learning. We believe it to be a step along the path of e-learning that creates opportunities and challenges that were unthinkable in the 1990s. It is evolutionary because it shares many of the same learning and learner requirements as more traditional e-learning. There are significant concerns about learner motivation, learner control over various activities, and persistence and drop-out rates. This may be because e-learning typically offers greater control to learners, and increases the psychological distance between the learner and instructor and other learners. With less direct accountability, the relationships between instructor and learner and among learners change, and this holds in both e-learning and mobile learning.

Mobile learning offers similar opportunities for learning "anytime, anywhere" as we saw in early descriptions of e-learning (DeRouin, Fritzsche, & Salas, 2004), although now the "anywhere" element is taken to a greater extreme. Finally, both e-learning and mobile learning offer customizability. As Traxler (2007) pointed out, "Learning that used to be delivered 'just in case' can now be delivered 'just in time, just enough, just for me'" (14). Traxler was describing mobile learning, but that description could just as easily be applied to many instances of e-learning.

We also think mobile learning has the potential to exist as a separate category from e-learning, both as a different type of educational/training intervention and as a technology to create different types of learning processes. One mobile learning practitioner suggested that "[m]obile learning is a bigger deal than most organizations realize. . . . It represents an amazing disruption and opportunity in how we educate" (Daniel Burrus, quoted in Roberts, 2012: para. 4). Mobile learning, as an intervention, can allow interaction with content in more flexible and location-aware ways. It can also better integrate learning with social technologies that can enhance the richness and applicability of knowledge development (Roberts, 2012). Mobile learning offers location-aware abilities to customize the learning content to the exact location of the learner. An example of this is AR applications, where learners use display technology (e.g., phones, headsets, glasses) to overlay digital content onto their visible surroundings. The result is that components or hazards can be identified or instructions can be visually displayed within the user's line of sight (Westerfield, Mitrovic, & Billinghurst, 2015). These are related to the intentionality of the training designer to leverage the valuable aspects of mobile technology in terms of the length of learning modules, the use of video, the use of camera and other sensing technologies on the mobile device, and the ability to conduct real-time assessment. All of these support the possibility of thinking about mobile learning as a distinct process from e-learning.

The current state of mobile learning, however, is largely analogous to the early days of e-learning when training developers simply recorded lectures or put Microsoft PowerPoint slides online and called it e-learning. We now see sophisticated e-learning programs that offer guidance, adapt to learners, and integrate complex gaming techniques. We expect that mobile learning will follow a similar trajectory. Mobile learning practice is currently in its infancy, with many mobile learning programs consisting of little more than delivery of Microsoft Word or PDF documents to a mobile platform (Roberts, 2012). Creating learning modules that leverage mobile technology in terms of social sharing, instant feedback, location-specific customization and tools for real-time performance support, and longer-term transfer of training may lead to a unique class of training material distinct from traditional e-learning. We believe it makes sense to deal with mobile learning and e-learning as related categories along the evolutionary path, but with mobile learning having unique characteristics and capabilities that can and should be leveraged in unique ways.

In summary, mobile learning consists of education and training that use easily transportable and web-enabled technologies to allow significant flexibility in the learning environment. Mobile learning can be different from both traditional classroom learning and e-learning because of how the learning process is both affected by and affects location and time. Mobile learning offers the advantage of making learning material accessible across time, location, and device beyond what e-learning can offer and the idea of *situational connectedness* separates mobile learning from e-learning.

But, should we rush headlong into AR and situational connectedness? There is a potential dark side to mobile learning that must be addressed. By the very nature of attempting to learn on a mobile device that wants to let you know every time an e-mail or tweet arrives, learners will be exposed to distractions. Further, being out in the world rather than in a relatively controlled environment of the office or classroom invites more distraction.

Two Key Forces That Drive Effective Mobile Learning

Two potentially opposing forces are relevant in the design and deployment of mobile learning: accessibility and distractibility.

Accessibility

Accessibility is one key attribute of mobile learning. As described in the preceding text, learning on a mobile device is intended to be convenient. Most mobile learning uses a multipurpose device that in many cases a user already owns and uses, and this device can be used almost anytime, anywhere, in any conditions. The notion of *accessibility*, or closely related terms such as *access* or *convenience*, is a consistent component of almost every definition currently in use in the research and practitioner literatures.

Accessibility impacts both the training designer and the training consumer. From the training design perspective, where and when the trainee uses the training materials should be of concern. The duration of learning events, the type of methods used (simple vs. complex) and the type of media used (video vs. text) may all need to change depending on how mobile the trainees will be. On the other side, the device and operating system become relevant to designers in determining how to best reach the intended learners. For example, should the tool be browser based or app based? Is the training program designed to take advantage of existing social networks or operate in isolation? These platform decisions are important components of accessibility.

Distractibility

The second key attribute of mobile learning as it is designed and practiced today is *distractibility*. Distractibility is something that is not generally at the surface of most mobile learning definitions, but it underlies much discussion in many of the existing published papers in this domain. Distraction is a cognitive state whereby individuals shift attention away from a primary task and toward a secondary, noncritical task, and this shift is not typically intentional (Lleras, Buetti, & Mordkoff, 2013). This construct has been well studied in the psychology literature, in the workplace related to task attention, and in the educational research in terms of learning effort and retention (e.g., Appelbaum, Marchionni, & Fernandez, 2008; Fang, 2009; Lavoie & Pychyl, 2001).

The distractibility of the user and the situation are likely key factors in the user's ability to attend to, process, store, and even apply information provided in mobile learning. Mobile devices are designed for constant notifications and multitasking. While multitasking is recognized as a common requirement of many job environments, and skill in multitasking is listed as a required or desired ability in many job postings, much research has found negative effects of multitasking on performance (Appelbaum et al., 2008). The social aspect of mobile learning is often viewed as a benefit. Users can share perspectives or opinions, offer additional information, provide critical feedback, or ask questions of peers or instructors in real time. This same benefit, however, can also be a negative impact if peers are distracting each other with off-task information, providing irrelevant information or asking unrelated questions. The availability of social media on the core learning device offers additional opportunities for distraction, as demonstrated in studies examining student use of laptops in college classrooms (e.g., Fang, 2009; Lavoie & Pychyl, 2001). Learners may also confuse surface-level social media interaction with learning. Someone could find an idea in the training interesting and use a social media channel to "share" the information. This learner may feel that he or she has done something to participate in the training, but the simple act of sharing does not mean that the information was processed in a way that leads to real learning.

Even though these aspects of mobile learning that interject real-time information and allow social interaction are intended to benefit the learner, they may ultimately serve to distract the learner and decrease the effectiveness of the learning event. One mechanism for examining distractibility is through interruptions. At this point, there has been little research on the impact of interruptions on training effectiveness and we do not know what the ultimate impact will be (Noe, Clark, & Klein, 2014). However, Sitzmann et al. (2010) demonstrated that even very brief interruptions from simulation technical difficulties inserted into an online training program led to decreases in short-term learning and increases in attrition, although high training motivation insulated learners from these negative effects. Further, offering learners too many choices can be distracting, especially in an e-learning environment, and can disrupt focus on the learning task at hand (Scheiter & Gerjets, 2007).

Mobile learning also has potential to distract learners from other important activities, either in their work or home lives, such as a meeting or a family dinner. At the extreme, learners could be participating in mobile learning to such an extent that it reduces job performance. Stanko and Beckman (2015) examined the need for organizations to exhibit boundary control over the interplay between personal and work-related activities that are facilitated by personal technologies, such as cell phones. They defined individual use of informational and communication technologies as an event that would shift employees' attention away from work. With mobile learning, however, we see potential role conflict within the workspace as employees must decide how to handle incoming messages and prompts about mobile learning events that may conflict with other job requirements. Mobile learning could also serve to increase work-life conflict if the implication of the "anytime, anywhere" learning environment is that learning is done at home outside of work time. In the next section, we examine the implications of mobile learning, focusing on these two characteristics of accessibility and distractibility, in the context of the traditional instructional design process.

Mobile Learning in the Traditional Training Cycle

In this section we examine the impact of mobile learning on three key phases of the instructional design process (Goldstein & Ford, 2002): needs assessment, design/development, and evaluation (see Table 13.1). To provide context for this review, we use a variety of mobile learning scenarios from the workplace setting (Pimmer & Gröhbiel, 2008), looking at sales representatives, engineers, nurses, and apprentices. We examine issues related to accessibility and distractibility in each of the three phases.

Needs Assessment

Needs assessment is often divided into three components: organizational assessment, task assessment, and individual assessment.

Organizational Analysis

The organizational analysis broadly addresses factors that may affect the success of the training such as goals, resources, and climate (Goldstein & Ford, 2002). At the organizational level, there are several factors that should be examined when planning a mobile learning program, including the mix of employees, features of the job, devices in use at the organization, and features of the organizational climate for training.

Employee mix. There is a general assumption in much of the practitioner literature that because members of the millennial generation have grown up with ubiquitous mobile devices, these users will prefer or even demand training on this platform. Companies that follow fads to recruit and retain talent might cater to this demographic and offer mobile learning on platforms that millennials use. Even if younger employees do prefer mobile learning, there is little evidence that matching learner preferences to the training results in better learning (Pashler et al., 2008).

Job flexibility. Given the anytime, anywhere nature of mobile learning, one important part of organizational analysis is determining if jobs offer sufficient flexibility to gain value from the accessibility characteristic of mobile learning. Eaton (2003) defines *flexibility* as "the ability to change the temporal and spatial boundaries of one's job" (148). Following this definition, jobs can be flexible in many ways, including location of the work, timing of task performance, and choosing when to take breaks. Consider a mobile learning application in which nursing staff were asked to record and post videos demonstrating how to operate infrequently used hospital equipment (Pimmer & Gröhbiel, 2008). In the nursing environment, choices around work location and timing of task

Table 13.1 *Mobile learning in the instructional design cycle*

Phase	Key Concerns
Needs Assessment	
Organizational Analysis	Employee mix
	Flexible nature of jobs
	Policy on devices (provided by organization or BYOD)
	Climate/culture
Task Analysis	Learning vs. performance support
	Collecting task data
Person Analysis	Skill in using mobile devices
	Individual differences (motivation, self-control)
Design and Development	Modularized content
	Learner control
	Situationally connected instruction
	Design for small screens
	Coproduction of content
	Refresher modules
Evaluation	Using mobile devices to collect evaluation data

performance can be limited. Shifts are scheduled, the location is set, and emergencies can happen at any time. It could be quite difficult for a nurse to take the time to record or view mobile learning material in the face of competing demands for continual patient care. The mobile technology may fit well with the distributed location of nurses all across a hospital or doctor's office, but they may need more structured time to dedicate to learning. Limited job flexibility may actually reduce the overall accessibility of mobile learning resources.

Organizations with a distributed workplace in which employees are often out of the office may have not only the opportunity to use mobile learning, but also a greater need for flexible mobile learning solutions that match the flexibility of the job. For example, salespeople who travel frequently would benefit from the enhanced accessibility of mobile learning, using it between appointments or during travel to brush up on new product features, pricing schedules, or organizational compliance requirements (Pimmer & Gröhbiel, 2008). Thus, from an organizational needs assessment perspective, it is important to note the extent to which it is possible for learners to engage in mobile learning as well as the extent to which the environment creates a demand for mobile learning.

Device selection. As part of the organizational level assessment for mobile learning, it will be important for designers to know if the organization provides common mobile devices such as smartphones and tablets to employees or if it uses a "bring your own device" (BYOD) policy. If the organization provides the same devices to all employees, it will be easier to develop mobile learning programs within a single hardware and software environment. Attributes such as screen size, processor speed, battery life, and software compatibility vary across devices (Liu, Han & Li, 2010). Organizations with a BYOD policy may have challenges implementing certain types of training strictly on a mobile platform if they cannot be certain that everyone has access to an appropriate device. A 2016 industry survey suggests that over half (59%) of organizations have a BYOD policy (Maddox, 2016). Training designers will need to know what kind of devices are in use and how many employees have access to these devices, and provide alternative access to training materials if some employees do not have appropriate devices. With the BYOD policy, accessibility of mobile learning is not evenly assured.

Climate/Culture. Organizational climate is another characteristic that may impact the success of mobile learning and should be investigated during the training needs analysis. Climate for training includes aspects of an organization's environment such as supervisory and support for training, and policies and procedures that emphasize the importance of training (Tracey & Tews, 2005) and is associated with more positive training results. Organizational climate is generally a more effective predictor when it describes a specific aspect of employee perceptions. For example, in addition to climate for training, climate for training transfer has been examined as an important predictor of transfer (Goldstein & Ford, 2002). Thus, we may find a more specific climate for mobile learning that examines the extent to which managers, peers, and organizational policies are supportive of the flexibility needed for effective mobile learning. In the case of mobile learning, other aspects of organizational climate or culture may also affect the success of such initiatives. For example, if we expect that mobile learning should be completed outside of typical work hours, an organization with a strong cultural value for work-life balance may experience more resistance from employees and consequently less success with mobile learning. Even if the mobile learning is technologically accessible, culture or climate will likely affect employees' willingness to access it.

Task Analysis

The task level analysis details what trainees should learn and the conditions under which the tasks should be performed (Goldstein & Ford, 2002). As discussed previously, mobile learning can and has been used for a variety of training topics, and the basic process for describing desired tasks and conditions should not change. Two areas that may change are determining what should be learned versus merely accessible, and opportunities for more effective data collection.

Learning vs. performance support. Mobile learning may affect task analysis in a fundamental way, as the easy accessibility of information through mobile technology may change the types of learning outcomes required. As noted by Traxler (2009), "Finding information rather than possessing it or knowing it becomes the defining characteristic of learning generally and of mobile learning especially" (14). As discussed earlier, Brown et al. (2012) distinguish between informational and instructional learning resources, and the purpose of the mobile learning activity must be clearly stated during the task analysis phase. The learning goal may be related to how to use the platform to find needed information rather than learning the information.

There are several examples of this shift in task analysis. In example with nurses recording and viewing video, instead of learning how to use the medical equipment, the nurses would need to learn how to access and use the database to call up the needed video when preparing to use the equipment. Similarly, Pimmer and Pachler (2014) report that IBM switched from a strategy of providing mini-courses that could be accessed anytime, anywhere to a system of "in-field performance support" (196). This support was available not just anytime, but at the right time. For example, before attending an important meeting with clients, the performance support system would allow IBM employees to download a checklist with critical information to cover during the meeting. The learning outcome is then not what needs to be covered during the meeting, but what resources are available and how to access them.

In the mobile learning context, task analysis may become more about defining the task performance conditions that require "just in case" learning in advance. Goldstein and Ford (2002) describe a "level of recall" scale used in task analysis that allows incumbents to specify if they only need general familiarity with a task and can look up the details, or if they need full recall of the task to perform it "without referring to source documents" (69). Task analysis for mobile learning applications should address how quickly and how often performance is required. For infrequent tasks, performance support tools may be the better option. For frequent tasks, or tasks that require immediate performance, advance learning may still be required. In the nursing example, we certainly hope that in a medical emergency the nurses do not need to pause and view a three-minute video on how to operate the necessary life-saving equipment. However, the on-demand approach may be very effective for physical therapy equipment or adjusting the hospital bed for patient comfort.

Collecting task data. Technologies associated with mobile learning may offer opportunities for improving the process of task analysis through more effective data collection. Rather than relying on retroactive reports of the most important tasks on a job, for example, employees could use their mobile phone to create diary entries about the tasks they are performing at a specified time or when prompted through a text message. Employees could easily take photos or record video of important tasks or situational features. However, scheduling of such data collection should be done carefully to limit the distractions introduced into the work environment.

Person Analysis

The phase of person analysis addresses which employees need the training and if they are prepared to participate in the training (Goldstein & Ford, 2002). This section focuses on individual skill levels and characteristics related to training preparedness in the mobile learning context.

Skill using devices. In the mobile learning environment, one important prerequisite is skill using the device(s) on which the training will be delivered. Even if the company has a BYOD policy and employees are using their own devices, they may not know how to use the specific features required in the mobile learning environment and some guidance on this might be required. In the nursing example, they may use their own smartphones to record videos demonstrating use of equipment. Most people probably have sufficient smartphone skills to complete the recording. However, they may be less familiar with the necessary steps to edit the videos and upload them to a central repository. Accessibility of mobile learning could be reduced if the intended users do not have sufficient skill with the devices to fully engage with the content.

Individual differences. A broader view of person analysis, and an often-studied topic in the training literature, examines other individual difference characteristics that are associated with successful training performance. We would expect the traditional factors of trainee motivation, self-efficacy, and locus of control (Sitzmann & Ely, 2011) to be relevant predictors of success with mobile learning. Further, given the distractibility inherent in mobile learning, we would expect learners with better capacity to deal with multitasking to be more suited to the mobile learning environment. Grawitch and Barber (2013) found that individuals who are low in self-control perform better in multitasking situations when they express a preference for polychronicity, or engaging in multiple tasks at once. Polychronicity was unrelated to performance when participants had high self-control. Other individual differences potentially associated with success in mobile learning include readiness for mobile learning (Liu et al., 2010), the ability to self-manage learning, and comfort with mobile learning technologies.

Results of the person analysis could impact mobile learning initiatives in several ways. If employees are not skilled in using relevant features of the mobile devices, or if motivation is very low, the organization may decide against using mobile learning at that point in time. Another option is to address some of these characteristics as part of pretraining preparation, such as taking time during staff meetings to discuss the approach and boost employee self-efficacy for participating in mobile learning. A third approach is to address the individual readiness or skill concerns as part of the mobile learning. This is discussed more in the section on design and development in the following text.

Design and Development

Modularized Content

One design strategy used for mobile learning is to create shorter modules of content to minimize interference from distractions. *Bite sized* is a phrase often used to describe the amount of information to be delivered in mobile learning resources (Traxler, 2009). If the learner is distracted, concentrating for a short period to comprehend the small piece of information may be more effective. Another term for this is *microlearning*, defined as "a short, focused learning nugget (often 3–5 mins long or shorter) that is designed to meet a specific learning outcome" (Pandey, 2016: para. 3). With sales representatives, microlearning modules could be developed to address features of individual products, changes to the sales process, or refreshers on individual organizational policies regarding returns, repeat orders, or sales bonuses.

Modularizing content also would help address variation in learner skills or readiness. Some of the intended learners may have expert-level video editing and processing skills while others are limited to taking short videos of family events that they never watch again. Offering a series of short modules at the beginning of the learning program would allow learners to enhance their skills as needed to fully benefit from the mobile learning. Other modules could help learners plan an appropriate series of learning events, or make suggestions on how to anticipate and address potential learning distractions.

Learner Control

It is not clear to what extent mobile learning should be instructor guided or user guided. Some authors seem to assume that mobile learning will provide substantial or complete learner control (Cook, Pachler, & Bachmair, 2011; Liu et al., 2010), controlling at least the time and place of learning. Mobile learning may facilitate socially constructed learning with learner-to-learner interaction (Kraiger, 2008), but given the inconsistent research findings about the effectiveness of learner control (Brown et al., 2016; Kraiger & Jerden, 2007) it would seem wise to consider how to include appropriate guidance from the program or instructor. Consider a situation in which apprentices use their mobile phones to create an electronic learning diary (Pimmer & Gröhbiel, 2008). Each day, learners prepare diary entries describing what they have learned and how they can use these skills in the future. The learners were allowed to choose how to enrich their diaries with media (i.e., photos, videos), but the diary entries were guided by daily questions from the program instructors rather than allowing learners to completely choose their own topics. As in regular e-learning, the objectives of training and the resulting design may dictate different levels or amounts of control. Novice learners may require more guidance from the training program on fundamental learning activities, but be given surface-level control to enhance motivation and engagement (Brown et al., 2016).

Situationally Connected Instruction

As mentioned earlier, mobile technologies offer the possibility of delivering relevant training material when the learner is in a designated location. With the salesperson training, for example, critical information about customer accounts could be delivered to the employee's mobile phone as he or she approaches the customer site. Location-aware instruction has been used to provide information about sites in a city that learners pass by while on a walking tour (Cook et al., 2011), or as users approach a painting or other display at a museum (Specht, 2014). This type of location-aware instruction provides greater context to the learners, maximizing the relevance of the information. Conducting learning outside of a designated classroom space also increases potential for distractions, of course, but initial evidence presented by Cook and colleagues suggested that learners found the location-aware experience to be highly engaging and interesting. The AR applications discussed earlier are interesting examples of how situationally connected learning can be a defining characteristic of mobile learning.

Situationally connected learning could also relate to the social configuration of the learning community. Sometimes learning requires a focused relationship between the teacher/trainer and the learner, especially when the teacher/trainer has specialized, expert knowledge that she or he can impart to the learner. This can happen on an ad hoc basis when both parties are online and willing to interact. Other times, peer-based, learner-to-learner interaction is best for real-time feedback – at times where the teacher/trainer is not available, or at times when peers are located nearby for real-time interaction. Other times, a training platform can offer suggested interactions (teacher/trainer or peer) based on the specific type of learning situation and the location or availability of others in the learning community. As location-aware devices and artificial intelligence become more advanced, the design of these types of training scenarios can become more mainstream.

Design for Small Screens

Many mobile learning programs are intended to be used on a range of devices that typically include mobile phones. While screen size has been steadily increasing, there is still typically much less space available on a mobile phone screen than a laptop screen. Designers need to adjust the amount of text presented, level of detail that can be shown in videos, and associated learning activities. Further, as mentioned earlier, AR creates new design opportunities and challenges. Finally, virtual reality (VR) headsets become a more complex design context.

The web design and app design communities offer tools and techniques for accommodating a variety of screen sizes, enhancing usability, and even designing for "fat fingers" as an input device instead of a desktop mouse (e.g., StartApp, 2014). Of greater concern to the training designer is what types of interactive exercises may successfully be used on small screens. These might include hand-held language translation using a smartphone camera or identification of parts with a device that only needs one hand to operate, such as in tight spaces. Small screens present design limitations, such as restricting the number of choices that can be presented on screen or in a drop-down box. However, smartphones also offer opportunities in use of the tilt sensors as an input device for exercises where location or motion is important (e.g., driving simulations) or on-screen tools such as easy-to-manipulate sliders or video control bars within the user interface.

Pimmer and Gröhbiel (2008) described a mobile learning example in which engineers view training content on VR display headsets while they are repairing machines. VR headsets can display a significant amount of detail, including text, images, and embedded video. They also restrict the learner's visibility to the physical world around them. This has the often significant advantage of reducing distractions, but could also be a disadvantage, or even a risk, for a learner who needs better situational awareness because of physical danger or a need for vigilance in a training environment (e.g., in a factory or in a retail outlet). But for dedicated, protected training events, headset goggles seem to have significant potential to add content to an immersive and situationally sensitive learning environment.

Coproduction of Learning Content

Many mobile learning platforms offer the potential for coproduction of learning content, but it is not clear to what extent this is a useful feature of mobile learning. Cook et al. (2011) suggested that coproduction may be important for engaging students, although their evidence on this point is from primary and secondary education. Pimmer and colleagues (Pimmer & Gröhbiel, 2008; Pimmer & Pachler, 2014) have found that in peer-to-peer training, such as with the videos produced by nurses, the employees did not always have the necessary technical or training design skills to produce their own content. A training program that allowed or required coproduction may need to include a module specifically on how to achieve that. In contrast, if learners are more engaged in the learning activity because they are producing some of their own content, then distraction is less likely to be a concern (Fang, 2009).

Refresher or Relapse Prevention

One opportunity for training design in the mobile environment is to use the mobile technology to build in refresher or relapse prevention modules that can be pushed out to learners after they have completed training. In their meta-analysis of training transfer, Blume et al. (2010) found very small and inconsistent effect sizes for the use of posttraining relapse prevention interventions on transfer performance (ρ = -.06, 95% CI = -.19 – .08). They noted there were few studies that examined relapse prevention techniques (n = 6) and including them at the end of a training session tends not to be effective because the trainees are tired. Mobile learning may provide an alternative route for communicating key learning points to trainees in the weeks and months following the learning event. The social aspect of mobile learning could enhance social support, further promoting transfer of knowledge and skills. Alternatively, the use of mobile devices to provide electronic performance support may minimize concerns about transfer in many contexts. Again, this depends on the nature of the task as discussed in the preceding text.

Evaluation

Mobile learning may help overcome some of the barriers to posttraining evaluation, such as lack of access to trainees after they complete the training, lack of staff to conduct the evaluation, performance apprehension for testing conducted in the work environment, and extended time lags (Ghodsian, Bjork, & Benjamin, 1997). It is easier for evaluation surveys to reach trainees through mobile devices. Testing within the work environment may be as simple as responding to a series of questions delivered on a mobile phone to determine if the trainee has retained knowledge three and six months after the training program. However, organizations should consider further risk of interrupting and distracting employees through requests for evaluation data.

Mobile technologies may not be appropriate for carrying out evaluations of all learning outcomes, but certainly could be used for reactions and knowledge outcomes through surveys delivered through e-mail, web services such as Survey Monkey, or apps. Testing a former trainee's knowledge without the use of support materials could be problematic, as it would be difficult to ensure that the trainee is only using his or her memory (and not the available training or performance support material) to answer test questions. This may redefine the training outcome measured, changing it from "demonstrates six-month recall of procedures for using physical rehabilitation equipment" to the broader "describes correct procedure for using physical rehabilitation equipment in ten minutes or less." The outcome of interest may shift to having the ability to locate and use the information in a short period. Further, use of mobile devices to collect data on important transfer outcomes could also make it easier to collect data at multiple points in time and from multiple sources (e.g., from trainees and their supervisors), addressing one of the concerns Blume et al. (2010) raised about the quality of the training transfer literature.

As introduced in the preceding text, one innovative approach to collecting evaluation data in mobile learning is requiring apprentices to use mobile phones to create an electronic learning diary, reflecting and even documenting through pictures what they have learned each day (Pimmer & Gröhbiel, 2008; Pimmer & Pachler, 2014). This type of data collection could allow researchers and training managers to assess learning trajectories over time. Requiring apprentices to provide input at a particular time each day, or whenever they had free time, could minimize the risks of distraction. Extending this idea one step further, trainees could record video of themselves performing a particular skill such as repairing a machine or using new foreign-language vocabulary. These visual artifacts could be sent to and scored by experts, who could provide feedback to learners and to program designers.

Conclusions and Future Research Directions

Mobile learning clearly offers opportunities for making training more accessible and engaging to learners. These opportunities need to be considered in the context of managing the simultaneous potential for distractions that could limit the effectiveness of the learning and detract from other aspects of work performance or home life. Unfortunately, the existing body of research on mobile learning to help training designers navigate these opposing forces is still quite limited. Further, the research base in mobile learning at the present time is largely anchored in educational settings examining how students learn rather than in work organizations looking at how employees learn. The few studies looking at mobile learning in corporate settings report on some interesting implementations, but tend to have small samples and offer largely descriptive reviews of the training rather than rigorous evaluation. Thus, we see many possible directions for future research to expand on the ideas described in the preceding text and test the application of existing theories and models in this new context to leverage the accessibility while managing distractions. In the following text, we review potential research directions for the topic of mobile learning.

First, regarding strategic choices, research is needed on the extent to which mobile learning should be considered a formal training activity that is developed and implemented by the organization versus an informal way of sharing information and learning through social media. Noe et al. (2014) noted both the importance of informal learning and the rise of social media as a training method. Both trends are related to Kraiger's (2008) discussion of third-generation learning, where learning becomes much more focused on interactions between the learners. Research is needed that investigates the effectiveness of mobile learning techniques for informal, social types of learning compared to more formal, instructor-led training. Informal training may be more suitable for the frequent interruptions likely to occur in mobile learning environments, while more formal training may require face-to-face or computer-based distance learning methodologies.

Second, mobile learning offers the opportunity to reach learners where they are located, expand learner-to-learner interaction, and add location-based features to training. These factors are important in understanding the accessibility and distractibility aspects of mobile learning. This offers potential for increased convenience and effectiveness of organizational training (accessibility), but also carries risks of decreased learning effectiveness and job performance as a result of off-task interruptions during the training process (distractibility). It would also be interesting to research potential positive effects of distraction and interruption in the mobile learning environment, such as learner exploration of additional learning resources introduced through a social exchange. Future research in mobile learning should continue to examine how to leverage the convenience and accessibility while creating designs that help control or minimize problems due to distractions.

A third design topic that needs more research is coproduction of learning content. The process of coproduction is not new (e.g., Kotze & Du Plessis, 2003). Consider how many university professors require students to deliver presentations in front of the class, presumably both to test the student's knowledge and to share knowledge with other students. Mobile learning offers more opportunities for sophisticated coproduction, and coproduction using mobile learning tools may help further enhance trainee engagement (Cook et al., 2011). However, there are many questions about the feasibility and effectiveness of coproduction. First, what are the attentional processes involved in the coproduction of learning content? To what extent do learners focus on the material to be learned, or are they distracted by the content production process? Second, what is the impact of using content produced by other learners rather than by a training designer or other expert? It would be interesting to test different types of peer contributions and how they influence learning behaviors and outcomes. Viewing peer-submitted materials may encourage continued use and deeper processing if learners perceive an emotional or social connection with the other learners. These peer-produced materials may be perceived as more relevant to the learners' own situation, perhaps leading to better retention and transfer of training (Blume et al., 2010). Alternatively, peer-produced materials that are unprofessional or simply incorrect may overload or distract learners from key learning points. Some kind of "scoring" or "ratings" of peer content so that expert judged material was shown first may be useful in minimizing negative outcomes.

More research is also needed on the interaction between different features of training environments to determine how, where, and when learners can best leverage mobile learning. For example, are certain types of training best completed in a low-distraction environment, or directly in the workplace setting, as opposed to during a commute or while multitasking on a conference call? Complexity of learning objectives might also come into play in such research. For example, a study that compares learning effectiveness in high- and low-distraction environments for declarative and procedural knowledge training outcomes could help provide guidance in training design choices. Here we caution researchers to avoid testing whether particular mobile learning interventions work, but to focus on generalizable aspects of the training intervention. Development of measures to specifically describe and compare levels of accessibility and distractibility would assist in this direction. Ultimately, from the practitioner perspective, instruction and assistance for learners on how best to use mobile learning, similar to what DeRouin et al. (2004) offered in their guidelines for effective e-learning, may be warranted.

Even though there is some evidence to suggest that younger employees (i.e., millennials or digital natives) prefer mobile learning over face-to-face learning or even "old fashioned" e-learning, there is little concrete evidence that it is more effective. Research in learner control has examined the extent to which preferences for different aspects of learner control are related to training outcomes, finding some support that trainees with certain personality characteristics are better suited for learner control environments (see Howardson et al., Chapter 5 this volume; Orvis et al., 2011). Further investigation of this matching hypothesis in mobile learning is warranted. For example, we might expect that extraverted learners are better suited for mobile learning environments that include a substantial social component. This would be an interesting context in which to explore the individual difference aspect of distractibility as well. Are there consistent differences between learners in their ability to manage distractions inherent in the mobile learning environment? Conscientiousness might be an important predictor of the ability to manage distractions in the learning environment.

The more traditional approach of training students and employees "just in case" the knowledge or skill is needed in the future is very different from what mobile learning advocates argue is the "just in time" nature of mobile learning

(Pimmer & Pachler, 2014). This shift should enhance transfer of training, as the newly learned knowledge or skill can be put to use immediately. However, if trainees know they can always access the information again, will that negatively affect motivation to transfer? In contrast, it is possible that mobile learning could enhance transfer of training through a social effect. We know that peer and supervisor support is a consistent, positive predictor of transfer (Blume et al., 2010). In a mobile learning environment, trainees may use the technology to share information with peers and supervisors, or others in their network, about training they have experienced and intentions to use this material. It would be interesting to examine if stated social intentions to use knowledge or skills acquired through mobile learning would affect transfer. Imagine a learner posting something to social media describing a training program, or texting a co-worker about it. This may create social expectations that facilitate transfer (Blume et al., 2010), enhancing motivation to transfer through social support.

Researchers should investigate trajectories of motivation throughout the mobile learning experience, examining pretraining motivation, shifts in motivation during the training experience, and how learners are motivated to retain knowledge and skills for the future. Research in an online learning environment has shown that motivation to learn can change over time in a multipart training program (Sitzmann et al., 2009). If a mobile learning program relies on microlearning to enhance engagement and minimize problems with distractibility, similar decreases in motivation to learn would be problematic. Future research should examine differences in training motivation at multiple points within a mobile learning program, comparing effects for microlearning with longer learning programs.

Conclusion

The shift to methods and models of mobile learning will have a significant effect on both training designers and the consumers of training. Mobile learning offers the opportunity for situational connectedness and greater accessibility for many. Mobile learning also may suffer from the distractibility of learners that ultimately reduces learning effectiveness. In this chapter, we have outlined several ways to examine and analyze the design and delivery of training in a mobile context. However, there is almost no rigorous research on the consumption of training in a mobile context. That is ground fertile for further research. In answering these types of questions empirically in the future, we can improve the accessibility and the effectiveness of employee training.

References

Appelbaum, S. H., Marchionni, A., and Fernandez, A. 2008. The multi-tasking paradox: Perceptions, problems, and strategies. *Management Decision* 46(9):1313–1325.

Blume, B. D., Ford, J. K., Baldwin, T. T., and Huang, J. L. 2010. Transfer of training: A meta-analytic review. *Journal of Management* 36(4): 1065–1105.

Brown, K. G., Charlier, S., and Pierotti, A. 2012. E-Learning at work: Contributions of past research and suggestions for the future. In G. P. Hodgkinson and J. K. Ford, eds., *International Review of Industrial and Organizational Psychology*, 27: 89–114.

Brown, K. G., Howardson, G., and Fisher, S. L. 2016. learner control and e-learning: Taking stock and moving forward. *Annual Review of Organizational Psychology and Organizational Behavior* 3: 267–291.

Chang, L. W., Njie-Carr, V., Kalenge, S., Kelly, J. F., Bollinger, R. C., and Alamo-Talisuna, S. 2013. Perceptions and acceptability of mHealth interventions for improving patient care at a community-based HIV/AIDS clinic in Uganda: A mixed methods study. *AIDS Care* 25(7): 874–880.

Cook, J., Pachler, N., and Bachmair, B. 2011. Ubiquitous mobility with mobile phones: A cultural ecology for mobile learning. *E-Learning and Digital Media* 8(3): 181–195.

Crompton, H. 2014. A diachronic overview of technology contributing to mobile learning: A shift towards student-centred pedagogies. In M. Ally and A. Tsinakos, eds. *Increasing Access through Mobile Learning*: 7–15. Vancouver, BC: Commonwealth of Learning.

Denk, M., Weber, M., and Belfin, R. 2007. Mobile learning – challenges and potentials. *International Journal of Mobile Learning and Organisation* 1(2): 122–139.

Deriquito, M., and Domingo, Z. 2012. Mobile learning for teachers in Asia. UNESCO Working Paper Series on Mobile Learning. http://unesdoc.unesco.org (accessed August 28, 2016).

DeRouin, R. E., Fritzsche, B. A., and Salas, E. 2004. Optimizing e-learning: Research-based guidelines for learner controlled training. *Human Resource Management* 43(2/3): 147–162.

Eaton, S. C. 2003. If you can use them: Flexibility policies, organizational commitment, and perceived performance. Industrial Relations. *A Journal of Economy and Society* 42(2): 145–167.

The Economist. 2015. Planet of the phones. February 28. http://www.economist.com/news/leaders/21645180-smartphone-ubiquitous-addictive-and-transformative-planet-phones (accessed August 29, 2016).

Fang, B. 2009. From distraction to engagement: Wireless devices in the classroom. *Educause Quarterly* 32(4): 4–9.

Georgiev, T., Georgieva, E., and Smrikarov, A. 2004. *M-Learning – a new stage of e-learning*. Proceedings of the International Conference on Computer Systems and Technologies-CompSysTech, 1–5.

Ghodsian, D., Bjork, R. A., and Benjamin, A. S. 1997. Evaluating training during training: Obstacles and opportunities. In M. A. Quiñones and A. Ehrenstein, eds. *Training for a Rapidly Changing Workplace*, 63–88. Washington, DC: American Psychological Association.

Goldstein, I. L., and Ford, J. K. 2002. *Training in Organizations*, 4th ed. Belmont, CA: Wadsworth Publishing.

Grawitch, M. J., and Barber, L. K. 2013. In search of the relationship between polychronicity and multitasking performance: The importance of trait self-control. *Journal of Individual Differences* 34(4): 222–229.

Hall, B. 1997. *Web-based Training*. New York: Wiley and Sons.

Koole, M. L. 2009. A model for framing mobile learning. In M. Ally, ed., *Mobile Learning: Transforming the Delivery of Education and Training*, 25–47. Athabasca, AB: Athabasca University Press.

Korucu, T., and Alkan, A. 2011. Differences between m-learning (mobile learning) and e-learning, basic terminology and usage of m-learning in education. *Social and Behavioral Science* 15: 1925–1930.

Kotze, T. G., and Du Plessis, P. J. 2003. Students as "co-producers" of education: A proposed model of student socialisation and participation at tertiary institutions. *Quality Assurance in Education* 11(4): 186–201.

Kraiger, K. 2008. Transforming our models of learning and development: Web-based instruction as enabler of third generation instruction. *Industrial and Organizational Psychology: Perspectives on Science and Practice* 1: 454–467.

Kraiger, K., and Jerden, E. 2007. A meta-analytic investigation of learner control: Old findings and new directions. In S. M. Fiore and E. Salas, eds., *Toward a Science of Distributed Learning*, 65–90. Washington, DC: American Psychological Association.

Kukulska-Hulme, A. 2010. Learning cultures on the move: Where are we heading? *Educational Technology and Society* 13(4): 4–14.

Laouris, Y., and Eteokleous, N., 2005. We need an educationally relevant definition of mobile learning. www.mlearn.org.za/CD/papers/Laouris%20&%20Eteokleous .pdf (accessed April 24, 2017).

Lavoie, J. A. A., and Pychyl, T. A. 2001. Cyberslacking and the procrastination superhighway: A web-based survey of online procrastination, attitudes, and emotion. *Social Science Computer Review* 19(4): 431–444.

Liu, Y., Han, S., and Li, H. 2010. Understanding the factors driving m-learning adoption: A literature review. *Campus-Wide Information Systems* 27(4): 210–226.

Lleras, A., Buetti, S., and Mordkoff, J. T. 2013. When do the effects of distractors provide a measure of distractibility? In B. H. Ross, ed., *Psychology of Learning and Motivation*, 261–315. San Diego, CA: Academic Press.

Maddox, T. 2016. BYOD, IoT and wearables thriving in the enterprise. *TechProResearch*. http://www.techproresearch.com/article/byod-iot-and-wearables-thriving-in-the-enterprise (accessed April 17, 2017).

McCole, D., Culbertson, M. J., Suvedi, M., and McNamara, P. 2014. Addressing the challenges of extension and advisory services in Uganda: The Grameen Foundation's Community Knowledge Worker Program. *Journal of International Agricultural and Extension Education* 21(1): 6–18.

Mercado, J. E., and Murphy, J. 2012. *Evaluating Mobile Device Usage in the Army. Proceedings of the 2012 Conference on Education and Training Modeling and Simulation (ETMS'12)*. San Diego, CA: The Society for Modeling and Simulation International.

Messier, S., and Schroeder, S. 2014. 6 elements of a successful iPad implementation. https://www.iste.org/explore/articledetail?articleid=219 (accessed August 15, 2016).

mobl21. 2015. Mobile learning basics. http://www.mobl21.com/Basics_Of_Mobile_ Learning.pdf (accessed August 20, 2016).

Mostakhdemin-Hosseini, A., and Tuimala, J. 2005. Mobile learning framework. IADIS International Conference Mobile Learning 2005. Qawra, Malta.

Motiwalla, L. F. 2007. Mobile learning: A framework and evaluation. *Computers and Education* 49: 581–596.

Noe, R. A., Clarke, A. D. M., and Klein, H. J. 2014. Learning in the twenty-first century workplace. *Annual Review of Organizational Psychology and Organizational Behavior* 1: 245–275.

Orvis, K. A., Brusso, R. C., Wasserman, M. E., and Fisher, S. L. 2011. E-nabled for e-learning? The moderating role of personality in determining the optimal degree of learner control in an e-learning environment. *Human Performance* 24: 60–78.

Pandey, A. 2016. 5 killer examples: How to use microlearning-based training effectively. *eLearning Industry*. April 11. https://elearningindustry.com/5-killer-examples-use-microlearning-based-training-effectively (accessed August 25, 2016).

Pashler, H., McDaniel, M., Rohrer, D., and Bjork, R. 2008. Learning styles concepts and evidence. *Psychological Science in the Public Interest* 9(3): 105–119.

Paul, T. V. 2014. An evaluation of the effectiveness of e-learning, mobile learning, and instructor-led training in organizational training and development. *Journal of Human Resource and Adult Learning* 10(2): 1–13.

Pimmer, C., and Gröhbiel, U. 2008. Mobile learning in corporate settings: Results from an expert survey. Paper presented at the MLearn08 conference.

Pimmer, C., and Pachler, N. 2014. Mobile learning in the workplace: Unlocking the value of mobile technology for work-based education. In M. Ally and A. Tsinakos, eds. *Increasing Access through Mobile Learning*, 193–204. Vancouver, BC: Commonwealth of Learning.

Roberts, B. 2012. From e-learning to mobile learning. *HRMagazine* 57(8): 61–65.

Saccol, A. Z., Reinhard, N., Schlemmer, E., and Barbosa, J. L. V. 2010. M-learning (mobile learning) in practice: A training experience with IT professionals. *Journal of Information Systems and Technology Management* 7(2): 261–280.

Scheiter, K., and Gerjets, P. 2007. Learner control in hypermedia environments. *Educational Psychology Review* 19(3): 285–307.

Shaikh, A. A., and Karjaluoto, H. 2015. Mobile banking adoption: A literature review. *Telematics and Informatics* 32(1): 129–142.

Sharples, M. 2005. Learning as conversation: Transforming education in the mobile age. *Proceedings of Seeing, Understanding, Learning in the Mobile Age*: 147–152.

Sharples, M. 2009. Methods for evaluating mobile learning. In G. N. Vavoula, N. Pachler, and A. Kukulska-Hulme, eds., *Researching Mobile Learning: Frameworks, Tools and Research Designs*, 17–39 Oxford: Peter Lang Publishing Group.

Sharples, M., Corlett, D. and Westmancott, O. 2002. The design and implementation of a mobile learning resource. *Personal and Ubiquitous Computing* 6: 220–234.

Sharples, M., Taylor, J., and Vavoula, G. N. 2007. A theory of learning for the mobile age. In R. Andrews and C. Haythornthwaite, eds. *The SAGE Handbook of E-learning Research*, 221–247. London: Sage.

Sitzmann, T., and Ely, K. 2011. A meta-analysis of self-regulated learning in work-related training and educational attainment: What we know and where we need to go. *Psychological Bulletin* 137(3): 421–442.

Sitzmann, T., Ely, K., Bell, B. S., and Bauer, K. N. 2010. The effects of technical difficulties on learning and attrition during online training. *Journal of Experimental Psychology: Applied* 16(3): 281–292.

Sitzmann, T., Brown, K. G., Ely, K., Kraiger, K., and Wisher, R. A. 2009. A cyclical model of motivational constructs in web-based courses. *Military Psychology* 21(4): 534–551.

Specht, M. 2014. Design of contextualized mobile learning applications. In M. Ally and A. Tsinakos, eds., *Increasing Access through Mobile Learning*, 61–73. Vancouver, BC: Commonwealth of Learning.

Stanko, T. L., and Beckman, C. M. 2015. Watching you watching me: Boundary control and capturing attention in the context of ubiquitous technology use. *Academy of Management Journal* 58(3): 712–738.

StartApp. 2014. Top tips for building exceptional mobile apps – and what not to do! http://www.startapp.com/blog/top-tips-building-exceptional-mobile-apps (accessed August 12, 2016).

Tracey, J. B., and Tews, M. J. 2005. Construct validity of a general training climate scale. *Organizational Research Methods* 8(4): 353–374.

Traxler, J. 2007. Defining, discussing and evaluating mobile learning: The moving finger writes and having writ. . . . *The International Review in Open and Distance Learning* 8: 1–13.

Traxler, J. 2009. Current state of mobile learning. In M. Ally, ed., *Mobile Learning: Transforming the Delivery of Education and Training*, 9–24. Edmonton, AB: AU Press.

Wang, Y-S., Ming-Cheng Wu, M-C, and Wang, H-Y. 2009. Investigating the determinants and age and gender differences in the acceptance of mobile learning. *British Journal of Educational Technology* 40(1): 92–118.

Westerfield, G., Mitrovic, A., and Billinghurst, M. 2015. Intelligent augmented reality training for motherboard assembly. *International Journal of Artificial Intelligence in Education* 25(1): 157–172.

Wojciechowski, R., and Cellary, W. 2013. Evaluation of learners' attitude toward learning in ARIES augmented reality environments. *Computers and Education* 68: 570–585.

Woodill, G. 2010. Getting started with mobile learning. https://www.td.org/Publications/Magazines/TD/TD-Archive/2010/12/Getting-Started-with-Mobile-Learning (accessed August 22, 2016).

14 Time and Thinking

An Alternative to Traditional Learning and Development Activities

Gillian B. Yeo and Sharon K. Parker

Learning and development are important for employees and organizations (e.g., Birdi, Allan, & Warr, 1997; Maurer, Weiss, & Barbeite, 2003). Learning refers to changes in knowledge, skills, attitudes, or behaviour (e.g., Noe et al., 1997). Development refers to a form of growth, characterized by successive changes that move the individual towards a qualitatively distinct state (Moshman, 1998; Parker, 2014). Learning and development are presumed to lead to positive outcomes in both professional (e.g., job performance, promotability, leadership potential) and personal (e.g., well-being, identity formation, nonwork competencies (Birdi et al., 1997; Maurer et al., 2003; Zoogah, 2010) domains.

In this chapter, we propose that time and the associated thinking offer a unique pathway to learning and development, in comparison with traditional learning and development activities. Traditional activities have been categorized into employee assessment (e.g., 360-degree feedback), job experiences (e.g., temporary work assignments), relationships (e.g., mentoring programs) and formal courses/programs (e.g., professional development courses; Noe et al., 1997). Because time in these activities promotes greater learning and development, most work in this area has searched for levers that can be used to increase participation in such activities (e.g., Birdi et al., 1997; Hurtz & Williams, 2009; Major, Turner, & Fletcher, 2006; Maurer et al., 2003). However, these activities typically require scheduling time for the individual to engage in learning and development experiences. We argue that an emphasis on "action" might hold individuals back from maximizing their long-term potential. We call for more attention to "slack time" (similar to layperson conceptualizations of "free time" or "quiet time") as a crucial enabler of learning and development in the workplace.

Individuals, organizations, and society at large have tended to place little value on slack time. To the extent that periods of nonactivity are built into a work day, they are often the first thing to go when things get busy or the pressure to produce intensifies (Daudelin, 1996; Elsbach & Hargadon, 2006). For example, Google's "20% time," which reflects the portion of time that is set aside to work on individuals' own projects, is now referred to as "120% time" to indicate that staff tend to work on personal projects outside of work hours because of increased pressure for production (Mims, 2013). Similarly, the popular press describes an epidemic of people believing they are "too busy" to leave portions of work time free of activity (Kreider, 2012; Seiter, 2014).

There are exceptions to this rule, often motivated by the desire for greater innovation. In 1948, 3M introduced an "Innovation Time Off (ITO)" initiative of "10% downtime" per week. More recently, an Australian IT company, Atlassian, has "ShipIt" days – there are four per year that last 24 hours for employees to focus on a non-work-related project (Atlassian, 2016). Some companies offer sabbaticals (paid time off work) to foster recuperation and self-improvement (Kane, 2015). These sabbaticals range from one week to one year and employees have used the nonwork time for travel, volunteering, education, and connecting with family. These initiatives have not been informed by data, but indicate that some practitioners believe time that is not filled with specific allocated work activities is important both professionally and personally. These practices are consistent with our contention that time, in and of itself, is important for fostering learning and development.

More specifically, we consider the role of slack time in triggering various forms of thinking. We focus on thinking because our investigation indicates that slack time is critical for thinking and that, in turn, thinking offers an alternative pathway to learning and development relative to traditional development activities. Moreover, the benefits of traditional activities notwithstanding, we suggest thinking, and ultimately learning and development, will not be maximized if individuals' work time is filled with activities. By devaluing slack time, we are missing a unique pathway to employee growth.

The heuristic model guiding our work is shown in Figure 14.1. We begin by discussing concepts related to time, including slack time. Next, we review the literature on five forms of thinking for which slack time appears to be an important factor, and that likely influence professional and personal outcomes. Delving into the dynamic learning and development process that is likely triggered by slack time and thinking is beyond the scope of this chapter, as is a detailed treatment of potential antecedents or moderators. However, we depict these links in Figure 14.1 as a platform for further research. We also touch on these ideas in our discussion of implications for future research and practice.

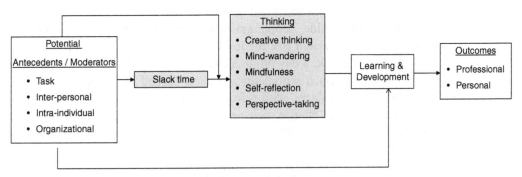

Figure 14.1. *Heuristic model of time and thinking.*
Note. The constructs in the shaded boxes are the core focus on this chapter.

Time as a Key Construct

In this section, we discuss general ideas about time within contemporary society. We then discuss the more specific concept of slack time.

Notions of Time in Contemporary Society

Time, at least in Western cultures, is viewed as a limited, scarce resource – we only have 24 hours per day, and as time passes, or is "used up," we cannot get it back (Kasser & Sheldon, 2009). Consequently, time is viewed as a resource that needs to be controlled to enhance productivity (Fried & Slowik, 2004). A control strategy that many have adopted is to "do" as much as possible with one's time (Rosa, 2003). This strategy is evident from time-use studies that show that we are maximizing work time by eating faster, sleeping less, reducing pauses and intervals between tasks, and engaging in more multitasking than previously – basically, we pack every moment of our day with activity (Kahneman et al., 2004; Turnbull, 2004). This phenomenon is referred to as the "busy trap," wherein responses such as "I'm so busy" to the question "How are you?" can represent boasts disguised as a complaint (Kreider, 2012). It is not surprising, then, that the modern workplace is described as experiencing a "time famine" – there is a perception of too much to do and not enough time to do it in (Mogilner, Chance, & Norton, 2012; Szollos, 2009). More broadly, society at large is experiencing an accelerated pace of life, which refers to increased speed and compression of activities in everyday life (Rosa, 2003; Szollos, 2009).

Views regarding a meaningful life might explain the tendency – at least in some countries or cultures – to pack every moment with activity. To understand this phenomenon, Rosa (2003) draws on Ancillon's observations from the 19th century – that people's notion of "the good life" is a life rich in experiences and capacities. Rosa notes that one way to achieve a fulfilled life is to realize as many opportunities as possible from what the world has to offer. This is a tall feat given that the world has more to offer than can be experienced in a single lifetime. However, accelerating our pace of life – such as by taking half the time to realize a goal – can double what we can do within our lifetime. We further argue that on the flipside, people are hesitant to let a moment pass without activity because that would risk the loss of potentially valuable opportunities. As such, taking a break, a day off, or slowing down can be viewed as "wasting time" or "laziness." Such sentiments are likely fuelled by the increasing time pressure within workplaces arising from global markets and enhanced competition, technological change, new employment arrangements, and more. In the learning and development space, we see evidence of this activity-time compression. Both our work and nonwork time is filled with structured activities designed to foster learning, achieve more and fulfil our potential. For example, it is common for development programs to boast providing staff access to online learning resources "24/7" (e.g., Allianz Insurance, 2016).

There are exceptions to this accelerated pace of life. Many of these are described under the banner of the "slow movement" (Honoré, 2004; Szollos, 2009) that reflects a deceleration of life, such as by taking time out in monasteries or in yoga courses for the purpose of improving well-being and/or facilitating more successful coping with and achievements within the fast pace of life (Rosa, 2003). A related movement is "take back your time," which advocates for increased value of leisure time and associated paid time off work in an effort to challenge the epidemic of overscheduling and time famine. Consistent with these ideologies, in this chapter we propose an alternative, some might argue riskier, strategy to attain professional and personal benefits, namely to leave some portions of time open without demanding activities (i.e., to actively create slack time) to facilitate various forms of thinking presumed to facilitate learning and development.

Slack Time and Related Concepts

Slack time refers to the perceived or actual availability of time that requires little or no cognitive demands. We see slack time as a form of a "slack resource" because it is a portion of time characterized by a stock of excess cognitive capacity relative to the situational demands (Voss, Sirdeshmukh, and Voss, 2008), even if the "time" has been deliberately crafted out of a demanding day. Voss et al. (2008) proposed that slack resources are characterized according to the rarity and absorption of the resource. In terms of resource rarity, a slack resource can range from being rare (scarce and unique) to generic (commonly available); and in terms of resource absorption a continuum is proposed from absorbed (currently committed but could be redeployed if necessary) to unabsorbed (currently uncommitted and could be deployed). We conceptualize slack time as a rare resource because of its scarce nature, that is, unabsorbed. Our conceptualization of slack time as a rare resource means that we see slack time as being meaningful only in situations in which slack time is atypical, or not the norm, as opposed to situations in which slack time is very common (e.g., when being unemployed).

Going beyond Voss et al.'s (2008) framework, we propose that slack time can be concentrated, such as when you block out a two-hour period in your diary or dispersed, such as when you use the full duration of a scheduled two-hour period for a primary task, but the task does not require full resource capacity. Slack time is a malleable construct as it can change over time (e.g., a meeting cancellation can increase both actual and perceived slack time; whereas illness could reduce it) and it can be conceptualized over varying time scales (e.g., hours, days, months). Slack time can also vary across domains (e.g., across tasks or the work/home boundary) and individuals – both perceived (e.g., individuals high on time urgency may perceive less slack time than their counterparts) and actual (e.g., full-time workers may have less slack time than part-time workers). Finally, slack time is not a predetermined consequence of one's workload (although, of course, slack time is likely to be affected by one's demands). For example, slack time can reflect conscious efforts in which an individual creates portions of time that place little or no demand on his or her cognitive resources, even in the context of high workload.

We now highlight overlaps and distinctions between slack time and similar constructs in the literature. First, we discuss three constructs that use the term *slack*. The engineering literature defines *slack time* as the amount of time a task can be delayed without causing another task to be delayed or impacting the completion date of a given project (BusinessDictionary.com, 2016). This meaning is similar to our concept in that it refers to a period that is unabsorbed; however, the engineering term is more restrictive because the purpose of that unabsorbed time is to be on standby in case unexpected delays occur. The engineering conceptualization is also objective, whereas ours encompasses both objective and subjective components.

The human resources and macro-organizational behaviour literatures define *slack resources* as a stock of excess resources available to an organization (Voss et al., 2008). The underlying concept is similar, however, slack resources are conceptualized at the organizational level – usually using objective indicators such as numerical ratios – and as such tend to focus on higher level resources such as human resource, financial, and operational slack (Dolmans et al., 2014).

Finally, the cognitive psychology literature uses the term *resource slack* – with particular focus on the resources of time and money – to refer to the perceived surplus of a given resource available to complete a focal task (Zauberman & Lynch, 2005). This definition is a narrower, more task-specific conceptualization that relates to our notion of perceived, dispersed slack time at the task level.

Next, we discuss two constructs from the organizational psychology and social anthropology literatures that do not refer to the term *slack*: time affluence and time pressure.

Time affluence is not explicitly defined in the literature, however, its measures imply that it refers to an individual's perception of how much available spare time he or she has (Kasser & Sheldon, 2009; Mogilner et al., 2012). This concept has some overlap with our notion of slack time – indeed, one of the items used by Zauberman and Lynch (2005) to measure resource (time) slack was used by Mogilner et al. (2012) to measure time affluence – "On the following scale, please circle a number that reflects how much available spare time you have (-5 very little available time to 5 lots of available time)." However, although time affluence might result in slack time (because time affluence implies that one has a set of task requirements with a generous time allocation) slack time does not imply time affluence. For example, busy and overloaded individuals (low in time affluence) can consciously create some slack time in their workday.

Time pressure has been described as a subjective experience felt when the amount of work exceeds the time available (Sonnentag & Fritz, 2014). As such, time pressure relates to the rate at which resources need to be expended whereas slack time refers to the amount of time that places little or no demands on cognitive resources. There could be a negative association between slack time and time pressure, such that the more slack time, the less time pressure experienced;

however, this correlation is unlikely to be perfect. There may be little or no slack time, but the resource requirements are such that the task can be completed without experiencing time pressure. Likewise, an individual might create slack time at work, even though a large part of his or her working hours are characterized by high time pressure.

Slack Time, Thinking, and Professional/Personal Outcomes

We propose that slack time promotes various forms of thinking that have implications for learning and development, and ultimately lead to professional and personal outcomes. We review the literature on five forms of thinking that have potential links with slack time and likely foster learning and development. We review each thinking concept, the theory and empirical evidence relating to professional and personal outcomes, and then the antecedents of the thinking concept with a particular focus on those antecedents related to time.

Creative Thinking

Creative thinking refers to generating novel and useful ideas (Amabile et al., 1996). Theory and research in this literature support the view that creative thought and output facilitate professional (e.g., performance) and personal (e.g., well-being) outcomes (for reviews see Anderson, Potocnik, & Zhou, 2014; Zhou & Hoever, 2014).

This literature has examined time-related antecedents of creativity. We review this work in relation to time in general, resource slack, and time pressure. Mednick (1962) proposed that time is important for creativity because novel ideas are far removed from initial problems. Amabile (1983) highlighted time as an environmental factor in her componential theory of organization creativity and innovation, arguing that time is required to think creatively about a problem so that different perspectives can be explored. Similarly, it is argued that creative insights are not quick "aha!" moments but rather result from protracted periods of sustained effort (Gruber, 1981). Gilson, Litchfield, and Gilson (2014) argued that time is important for creativity because it is required for gathering information, generating ideas, integrating perspectives and developing something novel. These authors highlighted a cognitive pathway, in which time should allow exploration of knowledge such that divergent associations are developed as more obvious ideas are used up, and a motivational pathway, in which time allows movement from less novel, safer ideas to more nonroutine ideas. Many authors have concluded that individuals should "take their time" if they want a creative solution and that organizations should give employees time for creative work (Runco, 2004; Shalley & Gilson, 2004). Empirical evidence for the ideas about time in general is limited (Anderson et al., 2014). Relevant research is primarily qualitative, showing that employees frequently mention time as critical for creativity (for a review see Amabile et al., 1996).

The literature on resource slack generally operationalizes the construct as financial slack (Greve, 2003). Resource slack is thought to enable individuals to explore and develop creative ideas (Bledow et al., 2009; Voss et al., 2008). Empirical results have been mixed, showing positive effects of financial slack on investment in research and development (Greve, 2003), negative effects on research and development investment in declining organizations (Latham & Braun, 2009), and no effect of resource availability on innovation implementation (Choi & Chang, 2009). These inconsistent findings may reflect that, although surplus time and other resources allow exploration, tangible results are not guaranteed (Bledow et al., 2009). Similarly, Shalley and Gilson (2004) advised a balance between allocating enough time to be creative but not too much time, as extreme levels may trigger boredom and reduce motivation.

The bulk of time-related work in the creativity literature relates to time pressure. Researchers acknowledge conflicting arguments (Gilson et al., 2014; Ohly & Fritz, 2010; Zhou & Hoever, 2014). The arguments for a negative impact align with those for time per se, that is, time pressure may be detrimental for creativity because the fast pace is not conducive to delving deeply into problems or fully exploring solutions. By contrast, time pressure may focus attention through necessity. Researchers have attempted to reconcile these views using a curvilinear hypothesis (Baer & Oldham, 2006; Ohly & Fritz, 2010) derived from activation theory (Gardner, 1986; Scott, 1966). This theory assumes that activation increases with increased time pressure, and that intermediate levels of activation are associated with optimal engagement because it matches the individual's characteristic levels of activation. Low or high levels of time pressure are assumed to correspond with deviations from employees' characteristic levels of activation, resulting in lower engagement. Meta-analytic work indicates wide variability in the relationship between time pressure and creativity (Harrison et al., 2006). Time pressure has been negatively (Amabile et al., 2003), positively (Ohly & Fritz, 2010), and nonsignificantly (Amabile & Gryskiewicz, 1989) related to creativity. There is some evidence for a curvilinear effect (Ohly, Sonnentag, & Pluntke, 2006), though further boundary conditions appear to be important such as openness to experience and organizational support for creativity (Baer & Oldham, 2006).

Mind Wandering

Mind wandering is defined as "a situation in which executive control shifts away from a primary task to the processing of personal goals" (Smallwood & Schooler, 2006: 946). It has been examined predominantly within performance contexts, with meta-analytic evidence indicating a detrimental link between mind wandering and performance (Randall, Oswald, & Beier, 2014). Tasks from primary studies include reading comprehension (Smallwood, McSpadden, & Schooler, 2008), listening to lectures (Risko et al., 2012), and list learning (Smallwood et al., 2003).

Researchers also believe that mind wandering is beneficial for some outcomes, through servicing personal goals that extend beyond current task-related issues

(Baird, Smallwood, & Schooler, 2011; Smallwood, Ruby, and Singer, 2013). There is a growing body of empirical work supporting these ideas, by demonstrating beneficial links between mind wandering and a range of non-task-related phenomena including creativity (Baird et al., 2012), autobiographical planning (Baird et al., 2011), and consolidation of self-memories (Smallwood et al., 2011).

There is relatively little work on the antecedents of mind wandering (Christoff, 2012; Smallwood, 2013). However, there is consensus that the initiation of mind wandering is a goal-driven process. The "current concerns hypothesis" was proposed by Klinger, Gregoire, and Barta (1973) and adopted by others in the field (e.g., McVay & Kane, 2010; Smallwood & Schooler, 2006). This hypothesis states that when mind wandering occurs, it is because the individual's most salient experiences or concerns are external to the primary task being performed (Randall et al., 2014). Studies have examined indicators of current concerns – such as thoughts regarding personal and primed goals (Stawarczyk et al., 2011), self-reflection, and primed self-memories (Smallwood et al., 2011) – and shown that they do relate to mind wandering.

Studies have also examined the impact of concepts related to cognitive resources. Regarding situational effects, research suggests that mind wandering is triggered in contexts that have low cognitive resource demands. Mind wandering has been shown to be associated with reduced attentional demands (Smallwood et al., 2009) and task practice (e.g., Smallwood et al., 2003). Regarding individual differences in cognitive resource availability, meta-analytic evidence shows that mind wandering is more prevalent in individuals with low working memory or ability (Randall et al., 2014). Within-person research may reconcile these seemingly inconsistent results by showing that individuals with high cognitive capacity engage in more mind wandering when they experience low task demands compared to when they experience high task demands.

Related research derives from that on brain structures. The "default network," which is a large-scale brain system involving a set of medial and lateral brain regions (Andrews-Hanna, 2012) is associated with passive "resting" states or "task-induced deactivation" (Mazoyer et al., 2001), and has been shown to be active when participants report mind wandering (e.g., Mason et al., 2007). This research suggests that portions of time characterized by rest or deactivation are likely to promote mind wandering. To the extent that high slack time is characterized by lower demands on cognitive resources, these studies suggest that our notion of dispersed slack time (i.e., slack time experienced while engaged in a primary task) may be positively associated with mind wandering.

Arguments diverge regarding the mechanisms underlying the maintenance of mind wandering. The control x concerns hypothesis (Smallwood et al., 2013) assumes that the maintenance of mind wandering is a controlled, resource-demanding process. Mind wandering is assumed to rely on the same limited capacity of cognitive resources as on-task thoughts. Thus, current concerns provide the impetus to engage in mind wandering, and then these experiences are supported by controlled processing that redirects resources away from the external task towards internal thought. The control failure x concerns hypothesis (McVay & Kane, 2010) assumes that the maintenance of mind wandering does not require cognitive resources, but rather reflects a disruption of executive control. These authors suggest that mind wandering reflects a default mode of processing whereby thoughts about higher order goals flow in an uncontrolled, resource-free manner.

Mindfulness

Despite varied definitions (Brown, Ryan, & Creswell, 2007), researchers converge on the notion that mindfulness is a form of cognition that involves bringing attention to experiences (both internal and external) occurring in the present moment, and being aware of them in a nonjudgemental or accepting way (e.g., Baer & Oldham, 2006; Brown & Ryan, 2003; Hulsheger et al., 2013). Attention is defined as a process of focusing conscious awareness, providing heightened sensitivity to a limited range of experience (Brown & Ryan, 2003). Awareness is the "background radar" of consciousness, registering internal and external stimuli – thus one may be aware of stimuli without them being at the centre of attention (Brown & Ryan, 2003; Brown et al., 2007). Mindfulness is considered a psychological state that varies within individuals; however, it is also conceptualized as a more stable trait (Dane, 2011). Empirically, most research on naturally occurring (as opposed to induced) mindfulness has assessed it as a trait (for a review see Glomb et al., 2011).

Mindfulness research originated in clinical disciplines, so most work has focussed on personal outcomes. Most of this research has examined the impact of intervention programs that have a mindfulness training component (Brown et al., 2007; Brown & Ryan, 2003). This literature has demonstrated beneficial effects of mindfulness on a range of health and well-being indicators (for meta-analyses and reviews see Brown et al., 2007; Chiesa & Serretti, 2009; Dane, 2011). More recently, researchers have demonstrated beneficial effects of mindfulness on professional outcomes, including job satisfaction (Hulsheger et al., 2013), work engagement (Leroy et al., 2013), and cognitive functioning (Mrazek et al., 2013).

Theoretical explanations for effects of mindfulness centre on the benefits of present moment attention/awareness and nonjudgemental acceptance. The arguments underlying these benefits relate to self-control in the regulation of cognitive resources. Researchers argue that focussing attention and awareness on the present moment disengages, or disrupts, automatic thoughts and behaviour patterns that are triggered by a broader lens of consciousness (Brown & Ryan, 2003; Brown et al., 2007). These automatic reactions (e.g., preoccupation with other concerns, rumination, habitual processing) are thought to be detrimental in and of themselves and also through the self-control requirements that draw on limited regulatory resources (e.g., Baumeister et al., 1998). Thus, the disruption of these automatic reactions is thought to remove the need for self-control and conserve resources (Brown & Ryan, 2003; Brown et al., 2007;

Hulsheger et al., 2013). Similarly, nonjudgemental acceptance is characterized by the absence of self-control of cognitive resources (Holzel et al., 2011) – indeed, by definition, it means doing so without controlling or avoiding experiences (Alberts, Schneider, & Martijn, 2012; Wolever et al., 2012).

There is little work on the antecedents of mindfulness (Brown & Ryan, 2003; Brown et al., 2007). However, most of these ideas centre on the notion that mindfulness is a human capacity that differs across individuals (Brown & Ryan, 2003; Brown et al., 2007; Dane, 2011). Developmental and social factors have been highlighted as potential barriers to mindfulness – such as chronic experiences of control or feelings of threat, and conditions that foster high ego involvement or contingent self-worth (Brown et al., 2007). More directly related to our focus on time, a traditional focus in this literature has been to cultivate mindfulness through meditation practices (Kabat-Zinn, 1990). Meta-analytic evidence supports the notion that meditation practice enhances mindfulness (Chiesa & Serretti, 2009; Glomb et al., 2011). However, the multicomponent nature of mindfulness programs, in conjunction with a generally low level of research design rigor, makes it difficult to isolate specific antecedents (Brown et al., 2007; Chiesa & Serretti, 2009).

The notion of time as a potential antecedent of mindfulness has not been explicit in this literature; however, its role is inherent in the design of programs aimed at cultivating mindfulness using intervention programs. The Mindfulness Based Stress Reduction program (Chiesa & Serretti, 2009) is a standardized meditation program created in 1979 that integrates Buddhist mindfulness meditation with contemporary psychological clinical practice. The program covers: (1) body scan (which is a gradual sweeping of attention through the body, focusing noncritically on sensations/feelings that incorporates breath awareness and relaxation); (2) sitting meditation (which involves mindful attention on the breath and a state of nonjudgemental awareness of streams of thoughts; and (3) Hatha yoga (gentle, basic yoga classes that include postural and breathing exercises). This program and its variants tend to run for eight weeks, with homework exercises set each day (roughly 30 minutes per day in total; Williams & Penman, 2011). Therefore, it appears that time is needed to practice these techniques, as well as to engage in mindful thought once the capacity for mindful thought has been developed. However, the potential separation of time as an antecedent and mindfulness as a state fostered by time has not been discussed theoretically or disentangled empirically.

There are also hints at the role of time in discussions of the conceptualization of mindfulness. This work uses phrases such as "mental gap" (or the decoupling of consciousness from mental content; Brown et al., 2007) and "fertile void" (from gestalt approaches to therapy, e.g., Perls, Hefferline, and Goodman, 1951) to describe the mechanisms associated with letting go of self-control, disrupting automatic reactions, and fostering present moment attention and nonjudgemental acceptance. The literature is not clear regarding the causal ordering among these concepts, but there is suggestion that concepts such as "relaxation experiences" (Marzuq & Drach-Zahavy, 2012) and "relaxed attention" (Brown et al.,

2007; Perls et al., 1951) can deactivate self-control and promote the "mental gap" implicated in mindful thought. It seems plausible that slack time would be a necessary condition for fostering these types of relaxation concepts and, more broadly, the chain of cognitive processes implicated in mindfulness.

Self-Reflection

Self-reflection and self-awareness (and less often, self-focus) are used interchangeably to represent a cognitive activity wherein attention is directed inward towards the self and involves inspection of one's thoughts, feelings, and behaviors (e.g., Daudelin, 1996; Duval & Wicklund, 1972). The social psychology literature distinguishes between trait and state self-focus. Trait self-focus is usually measured with the Self-Consciousness Scale (Fenigstein et al., 1975), whereas the corresponding state is often measured by the Situational Self-Awareness Scale (Govern & Marsch, 2001). A distinction is made between public and private forms of trait self-consciousness and state self-awareness. The public form is characterized by attentiveness to features of one's self that are presented to others (e.g., physical features) whereas the private form involves attentiveness to the internal aspects of one's self (e.g., memories, feelings; Fenigstein et al., 1975; Govern & Marsch, 2001). A final distinction is Trapnell and Campbell's (1999) separation of private self-consciousness into rumination and reflection sub-components. *Rumination* is a neurotic form of self-attentiveness characterized by dwelling on negative aspects of oneself, motivated by perceived threats, losses, or injustices to the self and purportedly associated with distress and dysfunctional thinking styles. *Reflection* is an intellectual form of self-attentiveness characterized by a more open and accepting approach to introspection, motivated by philosophical curiosity and purportedly associated with more adaptive outcomes.

The dominant theory concerning the outcomes of self-reflection/self-awareness is Objective Self Awareness Theory (Duval & Wicklund, 1972; see also Carver and Scheier, 1981). This theory concerns the consequences of focusing attention on the self (Silvia & Phillips, 2013) and draws on the concepts of the self, standards, and attentional focus (Silvia & Duval, 2001). The theory proposes that when attention is directed inward towards the self, this focus automatically triggers an evaluation process by which the individual compares the self to relevant standards. If a discrepancy is detected, negative affect arises, which prompts the individual to change the self to reduce that discrepancy or avoid awareness of that discrepancy. Carver and Scheier (1981) argued that Objective Self Awareness Theory (Duval & Wicklund, 1972) describes a self-regulatory negative feedback loop proposed within control theory. However, these feedback loops are construed differently in each theory (Pyszczynski & Greenberg, 1987). Duval and Wicklund (1972) argued that self-awareness is aversive whenever a negative discrepancy arises, whereas Carver and Scheier (1981) argued that it is only when the individual perceives a low probability of reducing a negative discrepancy that self-awareness is aversive.

Early work in this literature aligned with Duval and Wicklund's (1972) view that self-awareness is an aversive state – based on the assumption that discrepancies and negative affect were inevitable (Duval & Wicklund, 1972; Silvia & Duval, 2001). Therefore, this theory prompted work on the detrimental effects of self-awareness on personal outcomes, as evident in self-awareness theories of depression (Pyszczynski & Greenberg, 1987), alcoholism, and suicide (Baumeister, 1991) and supporting empirical evidence (for a review see Ingram, 1990).

More recent work has been influenced by Carver and Scheier's (1981) control theory and proposes beneficial outcomes. Regarding personal outcomes, Silvia and O'Brien (2004) proposed that self-awareness has positive outcomes if the person has realistic standards and is optimistic about his or her ability to meet the standards. These authors found beneficial effects in the literature for outcomes including perspective taking, self-control, and self-esteem. With regard to professional outcomes, the leadership literature shows that leader self-awareness can be beneficial for outcomes such as leader effectiveness (Atwater & Yammarino, 1992; Fleenor et al., 2010). This work proposes that if a leader perceives a discrepancy between how they see themselves and how they believe others to perceive them, this mismatch will prompt action to reduce the discrepancy. Accurate assessments are thus expected to lead to positive outcomes because they help employees correct mistakes and tailor their behaviour to meet organizational demands.

Thus, the positive and negative outcomes demonstrated for self-reflection and self-awareness have been reconciled by some researchers by identifying boundary conditions (Carver & Scheier, 1981; Silvia & O'Brien, 2004). As noted earlier, another angle for reconciling this work has been to distinguish between adaptive and maladaptive forms of self-focussed attention such as reflection and rumination (Trapnell & Campbell, 1999).

There is little work on antecedents of self-reflection/self-awareness. When antecedents are mentioned, the common theme is that the trigger for self-directed attention is an external event or experience (Daudelin, 1996; Gray, 2007) – in particular, one that creates a state of tension or uncertainty. For example, Feedback Intervention Theory (Kluger & DeNisi, 1996), which is based on a control theory framework, proposes that feedback, particularly that which is normative, can trigger attention to the self. The antecedent states are generally thought to trigger self-directed attention and the ensuing process of reflection automatically (Ellis, Mendel, & Nir, 2006; Nesbit, 2012). We are not aware of research that has directly tested the link between experience and self-reflection/self-awareness; however, this link is implied in research that uses techniques such as guided memory recall to manipulate self-awareness (e.g., Govern & Marsch, 2001).

The potential role of time in triggering self-reflection/self-awareness is not raised often. However, researchers converge on the notions that: (1) self-reflection cannot occur without time to think, and (2) modern work places more value on action than reflection and allows little time for reflection (Daudelin, 1996; Gray, 2007; Raelin, 2002). Daudelin (1996) hints at potential mechanisms underlying the link between time and reflection that relate to resource capacity. She suggests that activities that do not require the brain's full attention trigger a spontaneous process of reflection by momentarily suspending the flow of unrelated information into the brain. She suggests that such activities include mindless, physical activities such as jogging or mowing the lawn, as well as habitual routines such as showering or driving a familiar route (for related ideas, see Elsbach & Hargadon, 2006).

Perspective Taking

Definitions of perspective taking converge on it being an effortful cognitive process that entails trying to understand or consider another's viewpoint (Hoever et al., 2012). A more precise definition is that "perspective taking occurs when an observer tries to understand in a nonjudgmental way the thoughts, motives and/or feelings of a target as well as why they think and/or feel the way they do" (Parker, Atkins, & Axtell, 2008: 151). This definition refers to perspective taking as a malleable state, however it is also conceptualized as a stable trait (e.g., Davis, 1980).

Parker et al. (2008) integrated the literature to examine the link between perspective taking and outcomes. Parker et al. noted that the literature lacked an overarching theoretical framework but there was some commonality underlying the arguments. Being aware of and understanding a broad spectrum of factors (e.g., perceptions, cognitions, motivations, affect) associated with a broad range of targets (e.g., colleagues, organizations) or events (e.g., task-related, environmental) from multiple perspectives is assumed to represent a form of advanced cognition that is advantageous for decision making and goal accomplishment (Parker & Axtell, 2001).

Empirical research has demonstrated beneficial links between perspective taking and a range of outcomes. Examples of professional outcomes include contextual performance (Parker & Axtell, 2001), empathy for customers (Axtell et al., 2007), and creativity (Grant & Berry, 2011; Hoever et al., 2012). Examples of personal outcomes include relationship satisfaction (Franzoi, Davis, & Young, 1985), communication satisfaction (Park & Raile, 2010) and stereotyping (Galinsky & Moskowitz, 2000). Parker et al. (2008) also argued that perspective taking has potential negative outcomes (e.g., exploitation, preferential treatment). However, they noted that little work has explored such possibilities.

Discussions regarding the antecedents of perspective taking are limited but converge around two themes – one that is developmental and one that relates to cognitive resources. In terms of developmental trajectories, Piaget's work (1932) demonstrates that young children learn to attend to the viewpoints of others through a natural process of developing cognitive maturity. Kohlberg's (1976) stages of moral reasoning situates perspective taking at the highest stage – individuals are proposed to progress through the six stages at a slow pace, and it is thought that many adults are unlikely to reach the highest level (see also Bartunek, Gordon, & Weathersby, 1983).

With regard to cognitive resources, there is agreement that perspective taking is an intentional, goal-driven process governed by controlled processing and requires resources for execution (Horton & Keysar, 1996; Parker et al., 2008; Rosnagel, 2000). The antecedents identified for perspective taking are forms of cognitive resource capacity or allocation. It is thought that the greater ability that some individuals have to take the perspective of others is indicative of higher levels of cognitive complexity (the capacity to identify complex connections amongst differentiated aspects of a stimulus; Parker & Axtell, 2001). Intraindividual changes in perspective taking are assumed to be explained by malleable factors that represent different effort requirements or resource demands (Parker et al., 2008; Rosnagel, 2000). Indeed, Parker et al.'s (2008) review resulted in an integrative framework that included the predictors of the perspective taker's capacity for perspective taking (e.g., abilities and knowledge), demands of the perspective-taking situation (e.g., task complexity, work demands), and the effort expended to engage in perspective taking.

Time-related constructs have not received much treatment, but are flagged as potential factors under the banner of resource demands. Parker et al. (2008) speculated that work demands such as time pressure may interfere with management effectiveness, for example, by reducing motivation to attend to the perspective of a subordinate. In terms of empirical evidence, Horton and Keysar (1996) showed that time pressure reduced perspective taking in a communication task. Rosnagel (2000) proposed cognitive load may explain this finding – in support, they showed that verbal instructions were adapted in line with the target's perspective under low cognitive load but not under high cognitive load.

Summary

In summary, all five forms of thinking reviewed have demonstrated important implications for professional and/or personal outcomes. Of primary interest here, these literatures also discuss potential links between slack time and thinking, and to a lesser extent, underlying mechanisms regarding the initiation and maintenance of thought.

The creativity literature houses the most concentrated body of work that directly examines the link between time and thinking. Many scholars have theorized that having sufficient time is important for creative thinking, and although there is some evidence that this is true, there is also contrary and null evidence. The bulk of work has focused on time pressure but as we note in the preceding text, that is conceptually different to our proposed concept of slack time.

The mind-wandering literature does not refer to time per se. However, the arguments regarding the mechanisms that underlie the initiation and maintenance of mind wandering have implications for slack time. There is consensus in this literature that the initiation of mind wandering is automatic and goal driven, but arguments diverge regarding its maintenance. The current concerns hypothesis (Smallwood et al., 2013) assumes that the maintenance of mind wandering is resource demanding, whereas the control failure X concerns hypothesis

(McVay & Kane, 2010) assumes that it is a default mode of thought that flows spontaneously in a resource-free manner unless disrupted by task-directed attention. The arguments within this latter hypothesis relating to deactivated task and/or brain states particularly resonate with our notion of slack time.

In the mindfulness literature, there is little mention of time, but arguments suggest that time is needed for the practice of, and engagement in, mindful thought. Arguments regarding the benefits of mindfulness suggest that its initiation disrupts negative automatic thought processes, which removes the need for self-control and thus is maintained in a resource-free manner. A distinct contribution from this literature is the notion that present focused thoughts need to be nonjudgemental and accepting in nature (also see mention of this by Parker et al., 2008, in relation to perspective taking). Similarly, the self-reflection literature contrasts an open, accepting form of reflection from negatively focussed rumination. Thus, the nonjudgemental and accepting features may be critical for understanding when various forms of thinking are likely to be adaptive or maladaptive for development outcomes. There is little mention of time in the self-reflection literature, except to mention that time is needed for thinking. Regarding the mechanisms involved in reflection, it is proposed that activities that do not require full attention trigger a spontaneous flow of thought (Daudelin, 1996). In the perspective-taking literature, some work touches on the potential link between time pressure and perspective taking, with evidence consistent with the notion that, as a resource-demanding form of thought, perspective taking requires time to devote the necessary resources to its engagement and maintenance. Consensus in this literature appears to be that the initiation of perspective taking is goal driven and effortful (e.g., Parker et al., 2008).

Implications for Research and Practice

Theoretical Integration

We have proposed that slack time potentially fosters important forms of thinking, which in turn can lead to professional and personal outcomes through learning and development. Given the constraints of space, our focus has been on the link between slack time and thinking, and empirical evidence linking thinking to professional/personal outcomes. We recognise that further theorizing is needed to specify how slack time influences thinking, and how thinking in turn relates to the dynamic process of learning and development. We suggest that a self-regulatory framework (Lord et al., 2010) will be a useful platform to work with. Despite being isolated from each other, most of the "thinking" literatures reviewed in the preceding text draw on the notion of self-regulation. The way in which self-regulation theories are drawn on varies, yet the aspects of differentiation may point to mechanisms that will be critical for understanding the links of interest here. For example, the propositions differ in terms of whether the form of thinking is resource demanding, whether it is a goal-driven process, and whether its initiation and/or maintenance is governed by controlled or automatic processes; and the resulting arguments for the direction or nature of effects also differ.

The evidence is far from definitive, but we speculate that slack time triggers various forms of thinking in a resource-free manner, which has long-term benefits for learning and development. Slack time refers to a portion of time characterized by little or no cognitive resource demands. During slack time, therefore, there should be less chance for task-oriented thoughts and associated controlled processing to dominate. Said another way, slack time may be associated with the absence of control, or an experience of "letting go of control." Without controlled processing, thinking may be more likely to flow in a resource-free manner (e.g., see McVay & Kane, 2010). A key implication of this idea is that thinking triggered by slack time may not deplete limited resources, providing a win-win situation in which one may reap the benefits of that thinking without the cost of depletion. These ideas may seem at odds with popular wisdom. The layperson may assume that "doing nothing" is "wasteful/lazy" and that one is more likely to "get ahead" by filling his or her time with activity. However, activity-time compression is likely to come at a cost of resource depletion (and thus may outweigh the potential benefits of those activities). Experiencing or intentionally scheduling time with little or no demands on cognitive resources may be a more assured pathway to success, especially over the longer term, because it has the potential to trigger thinking that has beneficial outcomes without the cost of resource depletion. Research drawing on ego-depletion theory to investigate the resource-depleting nature of self-control may be useful for testing the notion that higher levels of slack time are associated with less resource depletion and greater well-being and performance benefits than lower levels of slack time. Further, these experimental studies could be combined with neuroscientific research to examine whether periods of time thought to represent higher slack time and lower resource depletion are associated with activation of the default brain network that is thought to represent states of rest or task-induced deactivation (e.g., Andrews-Hanna, 2012).

Our ideas regarding slack time and letting go of control contrast with the view within self-regulation theories that emphasizes the benefits of self-control (Baumeister et al., 1998). The notions of exploration versus exploitation discussed in the creativity literature are useful for reconciling these opposing views. Our speculations suggest that the traditional strategy of activity-time compression for "getting ahead" relies on self-control to allocate our limited availability of resources judiciously and efficiently. We allocate our limited time to planned activities, and use self-control to stay focussed on the task, resist distractions or temptations, and push through fatigue. The focus of such self-controlled efforts, even implicitly, appears to be targeted towards exploitation, which refers to the creation of value through existing or minimally modified competencies that sustain long-term viability (March, 1991; Voss et al., 2008). In contrast, slack time may encourage individuals to "let go of control" and to foster exploration, which, although viewed as riskier because it has uncertain payoffs, is thought to have potential for creating novel competencies with long-term benefits (March, 1991; Voss et al., 2008). Thus, we suspect that slack time and the associated experience of letting go of control are required to experience spontaneous, non-judgemental thinking that has the potential to promote the types of exploratory thinking that lead to long-term personal and professional benefits.

Consequences of Slack Time

More work is needed on identifying and conceptualizing the types of thinking that are important when considering the consequences of slack time, as well as consideration of other potential outcomes.

First, it is important to acknowledge that although this chapter has focussed on the potential benefits of slack time; it may not be desirable for some people or in some situations. For example, slack time might prompt rumination for some individuals, which is generally believed to have detrimental outcomes (Trapnell & Campbell, 1999). Smillie et al. (2006) showed that individuals with high neuroticism showed greater performance improvement compared to their counterparts on busier work days or when expending more effort than usual, and argued that this is because the higher need to direct their cognitive resources to on-task activities meant there were fewer resources available for their usual negative thoughts. On the flipside, then, it is possible that increased slack time is detrimental for such individuals through increased rumination. More broadly, it is possible that slack time has a curvilinear effect such that a moderate amount is beneficial for triggering positive thinking patterns but too much could trigger negative patterns. For example, long-term unemployed people may experience uncharacteristically high levels of slack time, which may feed into negative thought spirals.

We speculate that slack time is important for triggering thinking with certain characteristics – for example thinking that is solitary, spontaneous, and nonjudgemental – and that this type of thinking is important for generating thoughts that are novel, exploratory, and future focussed. As a first step, however, we need to develop a taxonomy of thinking that is relevant to this topic. At a minimum, one could consider where various forms of thinking fall on various continuums. Example continuums include temporal focus (i.e., past, present, or future), person focus (intrapersonal or interpersonal), and task focus (on-task or off-task). These continuums describe salient features; however, they are not mutually exclusive and thus not easily portrayed in a two-dimensional matrix. For example, self-reflection is unequivocally characterized as a self-focused cognition (under the person focus category), however, it could vary in terms of temporal focus (e.g., reflecting on the self's past and/or future) and task focus (e.g., reflecting on events that are task and/or off-task related). Other considerations for a taxonomy include how the thinking was initiated (spontaneously or deliberately) and the function that it serves (e.g., proactive or adaptive). Future work could draw from and extend our review to propose a taxonomic framework with associated measures that differentiate thinking along various continuums, and empirically test proposed links among slack time, thinking, and outcomes that fall out of that framework.

Regarding learning and development, we suspect that the forms of thinking we have considered here are especially important for promoting holistic and long-term oriented development. Although we have not delved deeply into notions of adult development, having instead adopted a generic definition, we suggest the particular relevance of concepts like psychological growth. Staudinger and Kunzmann (2005) identified psychological growth as a kind of positive personality development characterized "by increases in certain virtues such as insight, integrity, self-transcendence, and the striving toward wisdom" (321). They argued that psychological growth requires that we be continuously "challenged by new experiences and we need to emancipate ourselves in thinking and feeling, and transcend the structures within which we have been socialized" (321). Ultimately, such forms of growth, we assert, will be enabled by slack time and the resulting opportunities for thinking.

In this chapter, we have focussed on the potential cognitive states (i.e., thinking) that are triggered by slack time. However, there are likely to be motivational and emotional consequences as well. For example, if slack time triggers a self-reflective process regarding one's standing on various goals, it may indirectly prompt associated emotions such as dissatisfaction and motivational states such as implementation intentions aimed at reducing those discrepancies.

Triggers and Boundary Conditions

The potential links among slack time, thinking, and outcomes raise questions regarding what factors may trigger these pathways and what factors may influence the direction or strength of the relationships.

There is a growing literature on the importance of breaks for the recovery process (e.g., Fritz et al., 2013). The notion of breaks implies time away from work, however, such breaks may or may not be filled with activity (e.g., attending a training seminar could be considered a break from work; a vacation break can be filled with non-work-related activity). Our arguments suggest that breaks characterized by little or no demand on cognitive resources (i.e., slack time) will be more likely to trigger thinking and associated benefits. Emerging evidence indirectly supports our arguments – a social networking company called Draugiem used a time-tracking productivity app (DeskTime) to show that the 10% of employees with the highest productivity took on average, a break of 17 minutes every 52 minutes. Moreover, one of the most common ways in which these most productive workers spent this time was to take a walk – which presumably could have been a solitary act that promoted slack time and thinking (Evans, 2014). Future research could examine the organizational features likely to promote taking breaks (e.g., autonomy, modularized work), and whether various features of the breaks (e.g., length, activity-time compression) influence slack time, thinking, and associated outcomes.

We discussed earlier the fact that workload is increasing in the modern workplace and that it works against the desire to schedule activity-free time. This suggests that one method for promoting slack time may be to reduce the amount of work that is required. Alternatively, it may be fruitful to relax deadlines so that the same amount of work can be completed at a slower pace. The "slow movement" is gaining momentum and shows promise for promoting slack time and associated forms of thinking (Honoré, 2004). Research could investigate these ideas by conceptualizing the concept of "slow work" (e.g., taking longer than usual to do a task) and investigating whether it enhances thinking through slack time more so than reducing workload per se.

Another avenue for promoting slack time is to consider work strategies. Employees are increasingly experiencing the need to juggle multiple goals (Unsworth, Yeo, & Beck, 2014), and the usual strategy for dealing with this situation is to multitask (Levitin, 2015). However, Levitin (2015) reviews neuroscientific research highlighting the costs of multitasking for well-being and performance. There may be potential for the alternative strategy of single tasking to lead to equal or even more productivity than multitasking by fostering periods of slack time.

Another strategy for dealing with high workload and multiple goals is to approach work in a structured, task-oriented manner which is presumably associated with controlled processing (McVay & Kane, 2010; Smallwood, 2013). A contrasting approach to work is "play," which is a behavioural orientation to performing activities, characterized by elements such as a flexible association between means and ends, being free from external constraints, and perceiving time during play as an internal experience rather than as clock time (Mainemelis & Ronson, 2006). There is a long history of research on how children can learn through play (Lieberman, 1977), and growing recognition of how those principles can also apply to adults (Brown, 2009). For example, there is evidence that a relatively unstructured approach to work, characteristic of play, can facilitate cognitive processes such as divergent thinking and mental transformations (Mainemelis & Ronson, 2006) as well as having broader benefits for performance and well-being (Brown, 2009). It is possible that play is a vehicle for promoting the experience and/or creation of slack time and associated benefits for learning and development.

Conclusion

In conclusion, although it is early days in regards to this topic, it is likely that important implications for both individuals and organizations will flow as these ideas for slack time are developed and tested. To fully maximize individuals' thinking, and hence their learning and development, we suggest that they need to be proactive in creating and/or preserving periods of slack time. At the same time, organizations will benefit from putting in place practices and work designs that support and enable periods of slack time for employees. We hope that the ideas put forward in this chapter help stimulate research to guide such practical application.

References

Alberts, H. M., Schneider, F., and Martijn, C. 2012. Dealing efficiently with emotions: Acceptance-based coping with negative emotions requires fewer resources than suppression. *Cognition and Emotion* 26: 863–870.

Allianz Insurance. 2016. Employee benefits. https://www.allianzlife.com/about/careers/benefits (accessed August 28, 2016).

Amabile, T. 1983. *The Social Psychology of Creativity*. New York: Springer-Verlag.

Amabile, T., and Gryskiewicz, S. 1989. The creative environment scales: Work environment inventory. *Creativity Research Journal* 2: 231–253.

Amabile, T., Conti, R., Coon, H., Lazenby, J., and Herron, M. 1996. Assessing the work environment for creativity. *The Academy of Management Journal* 39: 1154–1184.

Amabile, T., Mueller, J., Simpson, W., Hadley, C., Kramer, S., and Fleming, L. 2003. Time pressures and creativity in organisations: A longitudinal field study. *HBS Working Paper*: 2–73.

Anderson, N., Potocnik, K., and Zhou, J. 2014. Innovation and creativity in organizations: A state-of-the-science review, prospective commentary, and guiding framework. *Journal of Management* 40: 1297–1333.

Andrews-Hanna, J. R. 2012. The brain's default network and its adaptive role in internal mentation. *Neuroscientist 18*: 251–270.

Atlassian. 2016. ShipIt. https://www.atlassian.com/company/shipit (accessed August 28, 2016).

Atwater, L. E., and Yammarino, F. J. 1992. Does self-other agreement on leadership perceptions moderate the validity of leadership and performance predictions? *Personnel Psychology* 45(1): 141–164.

Axtell, C. M., Parker, S. K., Holman, D., and Totterdell, P. 2007. Enhancing customer service: Perspective taking in a call centre. *Journal of Work and Organizational Psychology* 16: 141–168.

Baer, M., and Oldham, G. R. 2006. The curvilinear relationship between experienced creative time pressure and creativity: Moderating effects of openness to experience and support for creativity. *Journal of Applied Psychology* 91: 963–970.

Baird, B., Smallwood, J., and Schooler, J. W. 2011. Back to the future: Autobiographical planning and the functionality of mind-wandering. *Consciousness and Cognition* 20: 1604–1611.

Baird, B., Smallwood, J., Mrazek, M. D., Kam, J. W. Y., Franklin, M. S., and Schooler, J. W. 2012. Inspired by distraction: Mind wandering facilitates creative incubation. *Psychological Science* 23:1117–1122.

Bartunek, J. M., Gordon, J. R., and Weathersby, R. P. 1983. Developing "complicated" understanding in administrators. *The Academy of Management Review* 8: 273–284.

Baumeister, R. F. 1991. *Escaping the Self*. New York: Basic Books.

Baumeister, R. F., Bratslavsky, E., Muraven, M., and Tice, D. M. 1998. Ego depletion: Is the active self a limited resource? *Journal of Personality and Social Psychology* 74: 1252–1265.

Birdi, K., Allan, C., and Warr, P. 1997. Correlates and perceived outcomes of four types of employee development activity. *Journal of Applied Psychology* 82(6): 845–857.

Bledow, R., Frese, M., Anderson, N., Erez, M., and Farr, J. 2009. A dialectic perspective on innovation: Conflicting demands, multiple pathways, and ambidexterity. *Industrial and Organizational Psychology* 2: 305–337.

Brown, K. W., and Ryan, R. M. 2003. The benefits of being present: Mindfulness and its role in psychological well-being. *Journal of Personality and Social Psychology* 84: 822–848.

Brown, K. W., Ryan, R. M., and Creswell, D. 2007. Mindfulness: Theoretical foundations and evidence for its salutary effects. *Psychological Inquiry: An International Journal for the Advancement of Psychological Theory* 18: 211–237.

Brown, S. L. 2009. *Play: How it Shapes the Brain, Opens the Imagination, and Invigorates the Soul*. New York: Penguin Group.

BusinessDictionary.com. 2016. Slack. http://www.businessdictionary.com/definition/slack.html (accessed August 28, 2016).

Carver, C., and Scheier, M. F. 1981. *Attention and Self-Regulation: A Control Theory Approach to Human Behavior*. New York: Springer-Verlag.

Chiesa, A., and Serretti, A. 2009. Mindfulness-based stress reduction for stress management in healthy people: A review and meta-analysis. *Journal of Alternative and Complementary Medicine* 15: 593–600.

Choi, J. N., and Chang, J. Y. 2009. Innovation implementation in the public sector: An integration of institutional and collective dynamics. *Journal of Applied Psychology* 94: 245–253.

Christoff, K. 2012. Undirected thought: Neural determinants and correlates. *Brain Research* 1428: 51–59.

Dane, E. 2011. Paying attention to mindfulness and its effects on task performance in the workplace. *Journal of Management* 37: 997–1018.

Daudelin, M. W. 1996. Learning from experience through reflection. *Organizational Dynamics* 26: 36–48.

Davis, M. H. 1980. A multidimensional approach to individual differences in empathy. *JSAS Catalog of Selected Documents in Psychology* 10: 85.

Dolmans, S. A. M., van Burg, E., Reymen, I. M. M. J., and Romme, A. G. L. 2014. Dynamics of resource slack and constraints: Resource positions in action. *Organization Studies* 35(4): 511–549.

Duval, T. S., and Wicklund, R. A. 1972. *A Theory of Objective Self Awareness*. New York: Academic.

Ellis, S., Mendel, R., and Nir, M. 2006. Learning from successful and failed experience: The moderating role of kind of after-event review. *Journal of Applied Psychology* 91: 669–680.

Elsbach, K. A., and Hargadon, A. B. 2006. Enhancing creativity through "mindless" work: A framework of workday design. *Organization Science* 17: 470–483.

Evans, L. 2014. The exact amount of time you should work every day. http://www.fastcompany.com/3035605/how-to-be-a-success-at-everything/the-exact-amount-of-time-you-should-work-every-day (accessed August 28, 2016).

Fenigstein, A., Scheier, M. F., and Buss, A. H. 1975. Public and private self-consciousness: Assessment and theory. *Journal of Consulting and Clinical Psychology* 43: 522–527.

Fleenor, J. W., Smither, J. W., Atwater, L. E., Braddy, P. W., and Sturm, R. E. 2010. Self–other rating agreement in leadership: A review. *The Leadership Quarterly* 21: 1005–1034.

Franzoi, S. L., Davis, M. H., and Young, R. D. 1985. The effects of private self-consciousness and perspective taking on satisfaction in close relationships. *Journal of Personality and Social Psychology* 48: 1584–1594.

Fried, Y., and Slowik, L. H. 2004. Enriching goal-setting theory with time: An integrated approach. *Academy of Management Review* 29(3): 404–422.

Fritz, C., Ellis, A. M., Demsky, C. A., Lin, B. C., and Guros, F. 2013. Embracing work breaks: Recovering from work stress. *Organizational Dynamics* 42: 274–280.

Galinsky, A. D., and Moskowitz, G. B. 2000. Perspective-taking: Decreasing stereotype expression, stereotype accessibility, and in-group favouritisim. *Journal of Personality and Social Psychology* 78: 708–724.

Gardner, D. G. 1986. Activation theory and task design: An empirical test of several new predictions. *Journal of Applied Psychology* 71: 411–418.

Gilson, L. L., Litchfield, R. C., and Gilson, P. W. 2014. An examination of the relationship between time and creativity. In A. Shipp and Y. Fried, eds., *Time and Work: How Time Impacts Individuals*, 141–162. East Sussex, UK: Psychology Press.

Glomb, T. M., Duffy, M. K., Bono, J. E., and Yang, T. 2011. Mindfulness at Work. In J. Martocchio, H. Liao, and A. Joshi, eds., *Research in Personnel and Human Resource Management*, 30: 115–157.

Govern, J. M., and Marsch, L. A. 2001. Development and validation of the Situational Self-Awareness Scale. *Consciousness and Cognition* 10: 366–378.

Grant, A. M., and Berry, J. W. 2011. The necessity of others is the mother of invention: Intrinsic and prosocial motivations, perspective taking, and creativity. *Academy of Management Journal* 54(1): 73–96.

Gray, D. E. 2007. Facilitating management learning: Developing critical reflection through reflective tools. *Management Learning* 38: 495–517.

Greve, H. R. 2003. A behavioural theory of RandD expenditures and innovations: Evidence from shipbuilding. *Academy of Management Journal* 46: 685–702.

Gruber, H. E. 1981. On the relation between "a ha" experiences and the construction of ideas. *History of Science* 19: 41–59.

Harrison, M. M., Neff, N. L., Schwall, A. R., and Zhao, X. 2006. A meta-analytic investigation of individual creativity and innovation. Paper presented at the *Annual conference of the Society for Industrial and Organisational Psychology*, Dallas, TX.

Hoever, I. J., van Knippenberg, D., van Ginkel, W. P., and Barkema, H. G. 2012. Fostering team creativity: Perspective taking as key to unlocking diversity's potential. *Journal of Applied Psychology* 97: 982–996.

Holzel, B. K., Lazar, S. W., Gard, T., Schuman-Olivier, Z., Vago, D. R., and Ott, U. 2011. How does mindfulness meditation work? Proposing mechanisms of action from a conceptual and neural perspective. *Perspectives on Psychological Science* 6: 537–559.

Honoré, C. 2004. *In Praise of Slowness: How a Worldwide Movement is Challenging the Cult of Speed*. San Francisco, CA: Harper Collins.

Horton, W. S., and Keysar, B. 1996. When do speakers take into account common ground? *Cognition* 59: 91–117.

Hulsheger, U. R., Alberts, H. J. E. M., Feinholdt, A., and Lang, J. W. B. 2013. Benefits of mindfulness at work: The role of mindfulness in emotion regulation, emotional exhaustion, and job satisfaction. *Journal of Applied Psychology* 98: 310–325.

Hurtz, G. M., and Williams, K. J. 2009. Attitudinal and motivational antecedents of participation in voluntary employee development activities. *Journal of Applied Psychology* 94: 635–653.

Ingram, R. E. 1990. Self-focused attention in clinical disorders: Review and a conceptual model. *Psychological Bulletin* 107: 156–176.

Kabat-Zinn, J. 1990. *Full Catastrophe Living: Using the Wisdom of Your Body and Mind to Face Stress, Pain and Illness.* New York: Delacorte.

Kahneman, D., Krueger, A. B., Schkade, D. A., Schwarz, N., and Stone, A. A. 2004. A survey method for characterizing daily life experience: The day reconstruction method. *Science* 306(5702): 1776–1780.

Kane, C. 2015. These 21 companies will pay you to take time off. *Fortune*, March 16. http://fortune.com/2015/03/16/paid-sabbaticals (accessed August 28, 2016).

Kasser, T., and Sheldon, K. M. 2009. Time affluence as a path toward personal happiness and ethical business practice: Empirical evidence from four studies. *Journal of Business Ethics* 84: 243–255.

Klinger, E., Gregoire, K. C., and Barta, S. G. 1973. Physiological correlates of mental activity: Eye movements, alpha, and heart rate during imagining, suppression, concentration, search, and choice. *Psychophysiology* 10: 471–477.

Kluger, A., and DeNisi, A. 1996. The effects of feedback interventions on performance: A historical review, a meta-analysis, and a preliminary feedback intervention theory. *Psychological Bulletin* 119(2): 254–284.

Kohlberg, L. 1976. *Collected Papers on Moral Development and Moral Education.* Cambridge, MA: Center for Moral Education.

Kreider, T. 2012. The "busy" trap. *The New York Times*, June 30. http://opinionator.blogs.nytimes.com/2012/06/30/the-busy-trap/?_r=1 (accessed August 28, 2016).

Latham, S. F., and Braun, M. 2009. Managerial risk, innovation, and organizational decline. *Journal of Management* 35: 258–281.

Leroy, H., Anseel, F., Dimitrova, N. G., and Sels, L. 2013. Mindfulness, authentic functioning, and work engagement: A growth modeling approach. *Journal of Vocational Behaviour* 82: 238–247.

Levitin, D. 2015. *The Organized Mind: Thinking Straight in the Age of Information Overload.* New York: Penguin.

Lieberman, J. N. 1977. *Playfulness: Its Relationship to Imagination and Creativity.* New York: Academic Press.

Lord, R., Diefendorff, J., Schmidt, A., and Hall, R. 2010. Self-regulation at work. *Annual Review of Psychology* 61: 543–568.

Mainemelis, C., and Ronson, S. 2006. Ideas are born in fields of play: Towards a theory of play and creativity in organisational settings. *Research in Organizational Behavior* 27: 81–131.

Major, D. A., Turner, J. E., and Fletcher, T. D. 2006. Linking proactive personality and the Big Five to motivation to learn and development activity. *Journal of Applied Psychology* 91: 927–935.

March, J. G. 1991. Exploration and exploitation in organisational learning. *Organization Science* 2: 71–87.

Marzuq, N., and Drach-Zahavy, A. 2012. Recovery during a short period of respite: The interactive roles of mindfulness and respite experiences. *Work and Stress: An International Journal of Work, Health and Organisations* 26: 175–194.

Mason, M. F., Norton, M. I., Van Horn, J. D., Wegner, D. M., Grafton, S. T., and Macrae, C. N. 2007. Wandering minds: The default network and stimulus-independent thought. *Science* 315(5810): 393–395.

Maurer, T. J., Weiss, E. M., and Barbeite, F. G. 2003. A model of involvement in work-related learning and development activity: The effects of individual, situational, motivational, and age variables. *Journal of Applied Psychology* 88: 707–724.

Mazoyer, P., Zago, L., Mellet, E., Bricogne, S., Etard, O., Houde, F., Crivello, F., Joliot, M., Petit, L., and Tzourio-Mazoyer, N. 2001. Cortical networks for working memory and executive functions sustain the conscious resting state in man. *Brain Research Bulletin* 54: 287–298.

McVay, J. C., and Kane, M. J. 2010. Does mind wandering reflect executive function or executive failure? Comment on Smallwood and Schooler (2006) and Watkins (2008). *Psychological Bulletin* 136: 188–197.

Mednick, S. A. 1962. The associative basis of the creative process. *Psychological Review* 69: 220–232.

Mims, C. 2013. Google engineers insist 20% time is not dead – it's just turned into 120% time. *Quartz*, August 16. http://qz.com/116196/google-engineers-insist-20-time-is-not-dead-its-just-turned-into-120-time (accessed August 28 2016).

Mogilner, C., Chance, Z., and Norton, M. I. 2012. Giving time gives you time. *Psychological Science* 23: 1233–1235.

Moshman, D. 1998. Cognitive development beyond childhood. In D. Kuhn, R. Siegler, and W. Damon, eds., *Handbook of Child Psychology*, 5th ed., 2: 947–978. New York: Wiley.

Mrazek, M. D., Franklin, M. S., Phillips, D. T., Baird, B., and Schooler, J. W. 2013. Mindfulness training improves Working Memory Capacity and GRE performance while reducing mind wandering. *Psychological Science* 24: 776–781.

Nesbit, P. L. 2012. The role of self-reflection, emotional management of feedback, and self-regulation processes in self-directed leadership development. *Human Resource Development Review* 11: 203–226.

Noe, R. A., Wilk, S. L., Mullen, E., and Wanek, J. 1997. Employee development: Issues in construct definition and investigation of antecedents. In J. Ford and Associates, eds., *Improving Training Effectiveness in Work Organizations*, 153–189. Mahwah, NJ: Lawrence Erlbaum Associates.

Ohly, S., and Fritz, C. 2010. Work characteristics, challenge appraisal, creativity, and proactive behaviour: A multilevel study. *Journal of Organizational Behaviour* 31: 543–565.

Ohly, S., Sonnentag, S., and Pluntke, F. 2006. Routinisation, work characteristics and their relationships with creative and proactive behaviours. *Journal of Organizational Behaviour* 27: 257–279.

Park, H. S., and Raile, A. N. W. 2010. Perspective taking and communication satisfaction in coworker dyads. *Journal of Business and Psychology* 25: 569–581.

Parker, S. K. 2014. Beyond motivation: Job and work design for development, health, ambidexterity, and more. *Annual Review of Psychology* 65: 661–691.

Parker, S. K., and Axtell, C. M. 2001. Seeing another viewpoint: Antecedents and outcomes of employee perspective taking. *Academy of Management Journal* 44: 1085–1100.

Parker, S. K., Atkins, P. W. B., and Axtell, C. M. 2008. Building better workplaces through individual perspective taking: A fresh look at a fundamental human process. *International Review of Industrial and Organizational Psychology* 23: 149.

Perls, F., Hefferline, R. F., and Goodman, P. 1951. *Gestalt Therapy: Excitement and Growth in the Human Personality*. London: Souvenir Press.

Piaget, J. 1932. *The Moral Judgement of the Child*. London: Paul Keegan.

Pyszczynski, T., and Greenberg, J. 1987. Self-regulatory perseveration and the depressive self-focusing style: A self-awareness theory of reactive depression. *Psychological Bulletin* 102: 122–138.

Raelin, J. A. 2002. "I don't have time to think!" versus the art of reflective practice. *Reflections* 4: 66–75.

Randall, J., Oswald, F., and Beier, M. 2014. Mind-wandering, cognition and performance: A theory-driven meta-analysis of attention regulation. *Psychological Bulletin* 140(6): 1411–1431.

Risko, E. F., Anderson, N., Sarwal, A., Engelhardt, M., and Kingstone, A. 2012. Everyday attention: Variation in mind wandering and memory in a lecture. *Applied Cognitive Psychology* 16: 234–242.

Rosa, H. 2003. Social acceleration: Ethical and political consequences of a desynchronised high-speed society. *Constellations* 10: 4–33.

Rosnagel, C. 2000. Cognitive load and perspective-taking: Applying the automatic-controlled distinction to verbal communication. *European Journal of Social Psychology* 30: 429–445.

Runco, M. A. 2004. Creativity. *Annual Review of Psychology* 55: 657–687.

Scott, W. E. 1966. Activation theory and task design. *Organizational Behaviour and Human Performance* 1: 3–30.

Seiter, C. 2014. Why you need to stop thinking you are too busy to take breaks. *Fast Company*, October 2. http://www.fastcompany.com/3034928/the-future-of-work/why-you-need-to-stop-thinking-you-are-too-busy-to-take-breaks (accessed August 28 2016).

Shalley, C. E., and Gilson, L. L. 2004. What leaders need to know: A review of social and contextual factors that can foster or hinder creativity. *The Leadership Quarterly* 15: 33–53.

Silvia, P. J., and Duval, T. S. 2001. Objective self-awareness theory: Recent progress and enduring problems. *Personality and Social Psychology Review* 5: 230–241.

Silvia, P. J., and O'Brien, M. E. 2004. Self-awareness and constructive functioning: Revisiting "The Human Dilemma." *Journal of Social and Clinical Psychology* 23: 475–489.

Silvia, P. J., and Phillips, A. G. 2013. Self-awareness without awareness? Implicit self-focused attention and behavioral self-regulation. *Self and Identity* 12: 114–127.

Smallwood, J. 2013. Distinguishing how from why the mind wanders: A process-occurrence framework for self-generated mental activity. *Psychological Bulletin* 139: 519–535.

Smallwood, J., and Schooler, J. W. 2006. The restless mind. *Psychological Bulletin* 132: 946–958.

Smallwood, J., McSpadden, M., and Schooler, J. W. 2008. When attention matters: The curious incident of the wandering mind. *Memory and Cognition* 36(6): 1144–1150.

Smallwood, J., Ruby, F. J. M., and Singer, T. 2013. Letting go of the present: Mind-wandering is associated with reduced delay discounting. *Consciousness and Cognition* 22: 1–7.

Smallwood, J., Baracaia, S. F., Lowe, M., and Obonsawin, M. 2003. Task unrelated thought whilst encoding information. *Consciousness and Cognition* 12(3): 452–484.

Smallwood, J., Fitzgerald, A., Miles, L. K., and Phillips, L. H. 2009. Shifting moods, wandering minds: Negative moods lead the mind to wander. *Emotion* 9(2): 271.

Smallwood, J., Schooler, J. W., Turk, D. J., Cunningham, S. J., Burns, P., and Macrae, C. N. 2011. Self-reflection and the temporal focus of the wandering mind. *Consciousness and Cognition* 20: 1120–1126.

Smillie, L. D., Yeo, G., Furnham, A., and Jackson, C. J. 2006. Benefits of all work and no play: The relationship between neuroticism and performance as a function of resource allocation. *Journal of Applied Psychology* 91: 131–155.

Sonnentag, S., and Fritz, C. 2014. Recovery from job stress: The stressor-detachment model as an integrative framework. *Journal of Organizational Behaviour* 36(S1): S72-S103.

Staudinger, U. M., and Kunzmann, U. 2005. Positive adult personality development: Adjustment and/or growth? *European Psychologist* 10: 320–329.

Stawarczyk, D., Majerus, S., Maj, M., Van der Linden, M., and D'Argembeau, A. 2011. Mind-wandering: Phenomenology and function as assessed with a novel experience sampling method. *Acta Psychologica* 136: 370–381.

Szollos, A. 2009. Toward a psychology of chronic time pressure: Conceptual and methodological review. *Time and Society* 18: 332–350.

Take back your time. 2016. https://www.takebackyourtime.org (accessed August 28 2016).

Trapnell, P. D., and Campbell, J. D. 1999. Private self-consciousness and the Five-Factor Model of Personality: Distinguishing rumination from reflection. *Journal of Personality and Social Psychology* 76: 284–304.

Turnbull, S. 2004. Perceptions and experience of time-space compression and acceleration: The shaping of leaders' identities. *Journal of Managerial Psychology* 19: 809–824.

Unsworth, K. L., Yeo, G. B., and Beck, J. 2014. Multiple goals: A review and derivation of general principles. *Journal of Organizational Behaviour* 35(8): 1064–1078.

Voss, G. B., Sirdeshmukh, D., and Voss, Z. G. 2008. The effects of slack resources and environmental threat on product exploration and exploitation. *Academy of Management Journal* 51: 147–164.

Williams, M., and Penman, D. 2011. *Mindfulness: A Practical Guide to Finding Peace in a Frantic World*. London: Piatkus.

Wolever, R. Q., Bobinet, K. J., McCabe, K., Mackenzie, E. R., Fekete, E., Kusnick, C. A., and Baime, M. 2012. Effective and viable mind-body stress reduction in the workplace: A randomized controlled trial. *Journal of Occupational Health Psychology* 17(2): 246.

Zauberman, G., and Lynch, J. G. 2005. Resource slack and propensity to discount delayed investments of time versus money. *Journal of Experimental Psychology: General* 134: 23–37.

Zhou, J., and Hoever, I. J. 2014. Research on workplace creativity: A review and redirection. *Annual Review of Organizational Psychology and Organizational Behavior* 1: 333–359.

Zoogah, D. B. 2010. Why should I be left behind? Employees' perceived relative deprivation and participation in development activities. *Journal of Applied Psychology* 95: 159–173.

15 Developing Latino Talent

Miguel A. Quiñones

In our rapidly evolving business landscape, organizations must adapt and remain relevant by tapping into an increasingly diverse employee talent pool. This chapter explores the challenges and opportunities for organizations presented by the fast-growing Hispanic or Latino population in the United States.[1] Specifically, the gap between the size of the Latino population relative to their representation among the upper levels of corporations is explored. A solution to this apparent bottleneck in moving Latino up the corporate hierarchy is presented and an illustrative example of a successful approach to address this challenge is discussed. The bottom line is that organizations must take a proactive and systematic approach to identifying and developing Latino talent within their ranks to remain competitive and advance their business objectives.

A Changing Landscape

Organizations are confronting what has been referred to as a VUCA world characterized by volatility, uncertainty, complexity, and ambiguity (Bennett & Lemoine, 2014). For example, in the city of Dallas, which in 2015 was the ninth largest city in the United States, the economy has been very healthy and continues to pick up steam. However, the arrival of an Ebola patient to a local hospital on September 20, 2014 threw the city into chaos and the real possibility of economic impact due to fear of travel into the city was something that business leaders had to consider. Luckily, everyone's worst fears were not realized. Nevertheless, this type of environment, where events seem to come out of nowhere, demands adaptability, nimbleness, and the ability to develop innovative solutions to problems.

Another aspect of this VUCA world is the changing nature of the marketplace in which businesses operate. Witness, for example, the dramatic change in attitudes toward same-sex marriage over the past 10 years (Pew Research Center, 2015a) or the declining car ownership rates of young millennials (Badger, 2014). Even how customers access information and products continues to evolve at a time when the purchasing power of the middle class is stagnant or decreasing (Pew Research Center, 2014). In fact, the most recent *Southern Methodist*

---

[1] Although the terms Hispanic, Latino, and Latina have distinct meanings, they will be used interchangeably in this chapter.

University (SMU) Cox CEO Sentiment Survey found that business leaders today put the changing customer needs and expectations as their top concern going forward (Quiñones & Rasberry, 2015). Clearly, organizations need to connect with their customers more closely than ever before.

The ability to adapt to a volatile world and connect with a changing customer base is increasingly dependent on the quality of the people working in and running an organization. However, just as the customer base is changing, the labor force from which organizations draw their talent is also undergoing a dramatic shift. Numerous surveys find that companies are having a difficult time filling key positions (PwC 18th Annual Global CEO Survey, 2015). The talent pool from which they are drawing is also much more diverse than ever. The millennial generation (individuals born between 1982 and 2004), is the most diverse generation ever with 43% being nonwhite compared with 28% of boomers (Pew Research Center, 2014). Thus, organizations have to compete much more fiercely for talent from a pool that is very different then what they are used to.

The single-largest demographic trend influencing both the consumer as well as the labor markets in the United States is the dramatic growth of the Hispanic population. According to census data, the U.S. Hispanic population grew by 48% from 2000 to 2011 and is now estimated to be more than 52 million, or 17% of the total U.S. population (Brown and Patten, 2014). In fact, Latinos accounted for 54% of the overall population growth in the United States from 2000 to 2014 (Stepler & Lopez, 2016). Among 18 to 24 year olds, Hispanics now make up more than 20% of the population. Even more astonishing, Hispanics will account for more than 75% of the labor force growth from now until 2020 (Rochhar, 2012). These findings make it clear that to meet the challenges and opportunities presented by the current and future economic, social, and demographic landscape, organizations are going to have to find ways to connect to and tap the talents of the fast-growth Hispanic population.

Hispanic Talent Is Not Reaching the Top

Despite the growing importance of Hispanics for organizations' success, the record concerning their advancement in Corporate America is not encouraging. Senator Robert Menendez's (D-NJ) *2014 Corporate Diversity Report* that surveyed 69 Fortune 100 companies found that Hispanics occupied only around 4.9% of board and 2.9% of executive positions (Menendez, 2015). Similarly, the Hispanic Association on Corporate Responsibility (HACR), in their annual Corporate Inclusion Index, finds significant Hispanic underrepresentation in board and executive positions among Fortune 100 companies (Hispanic Association for Corporate Responsibility, 2013). The same report found that responding companies had an average hiring rate for Hispanics of 12% but a 17% attrition rate for the same demographic. Also, an analysis of Equal Employment Opportunity (EEO) data by the *Latino Leadership Initiative* at SMU found that Hispanics have a much lower conversion rate from middle management to executive positions than whites (Quiñones, 2010).

This evidence suggests that organizations have a two-pronged challenge related to Hispanic talent. First, they must be able to attract and retain this increasingly mission-critical source of talent. Second, they need to find ways to move this talent up the corporate hierarchy. If they can't solve these two challenges, organizations risk not being able to advance their corporate objectives and fail to innovate new products and services in an ever-changing competitive marketplace. In fact, a recent survey of global CEOs found that talent availability is the biggest barrier to achieving growth for their organizations (PwC 18th Annual Global CEO Survey, 2015). Increasingly, this talent shortage will be caused by the inability to tap into the growing Hispanic population.

Potential Reasons for the Hispanic Talent Gap

There are many possible explanations for the gap in hiring, retention, and advancement among Hispanics. Factors such as biases in the selection process, differential development, and advancement opportunities, and unique Hispanic traits and cultural scripts can account for this gap. Each will be discussed in the following text.

Bias

First, there is a large body of work demonstrating bias against nonwhites in the hiring process (Ruggs et al., 2013). For example, Hosoda, Nguyen, and Stone-Romero (2012) found that applicants with a Hispanic accent were rated as less suitable for an open position and less likely to be promoted to management than applicants without an accent (see also Gluszek and Dovidio, 2010). In general, racial minorities are sometimes viewed as not possessing qualities required for the position (e.g., leadership capacity) as well as possessing traits that translate into lower work performance (e.g., less educated, lazy). Not only does this bias translate into fewer opportunities to enter and move up the organizational ladder, but also overt and subtle discrimination has been shown to have negative physical and psychological health outcomes (Jones et al., 2016).

Prior Experience and Exposure

The Hispanic talent gap can also be partially explained by real differences in experiences, exposure, and preparation for higher-level roles. For example, studies have long demonstrated the importance of mentoring relationships for career progression and success (Eby et al., 2008). Mentors can help their protégés navigate organizational politics, provide valuable feedback, as well as impart knowledge and wisdom regarding job-specific issues (Tonidandel, Avery, & Phillips, 2007). However, there is evidence to suggest that Hispanics may not have as many mentoring opportunities as other groups (Blancero & DelCampo, 2005).

Also, Hispanics are disproportionately more likely to be mentored by other Hispanics, who tend to lack influence within the organization (Ragins, 1997).

Cultural Scripts

Finally, cultural scripts common among Hispanics can impact behavior and perceptions that impede progress and advancement in organizations (cf., Dabbah & Poiré, 2006). For example, a general cultural characteristic among Spanish-speaking countries is power distance, or the acceptance of hierarchical power structures (cf., Hofstede, 2001). This cultural trait means that, in general, Hispanics are taught to be respectful of authority. This can lead others to wrongfully conclude that Hispanics are lacking ambition or do not have "executive presence." Thus, when the time comes to select high-potential individuals to receive specialized leadership training or high-visibility assignments, Hispanics may be overlooked.

It is likely that the Hispanic talent gap in organizations is due to a combination of these and other factors. However, it is important to note that these subtle biases in identifying potential and doling out developmental opportunities can remain hidden from view. This leads organizational leaders to express frustration with the talent gap and throw their hands up in resignation. However, what organizations need to do is commit to a proactive, thoughtful, and systematic approach to talent development that focuses on all segments of their talent pool, especially traditionally overlooked groups such as Hispanics.

Creating a Development Pipeline

Recent changes in the supply and demand for talent have increased the need for organizations to develop a robust internal pipeline of top leadership talent (Cappelli, 2008). This pipeline begins when new talent is selected into an organization, continues when they are subsequently identified as having potential for higher levels of responsibility, and individuals are then given experiences and exposure to round out their skill set to be promoted (Charan, Drotter, & Noel, 2011). Therefore, concerted efforts need to be made at these stages in the pipeline.

Recruitment

The challenge of developing a strong pipeline of Hispanic talent begins at the recruitment stage. Reaching a culturally and ethnically diverse workforce requires different approaches than organizations traditionally use (Rodriguez, 2007). For example, Hispanics overindex (use at a higher rate that their numbers would predict) on their use social media with Facebook and Instagram serving as favorite platforms (Pew Research Center, 2015b). Additionally, Hispanics tend to score higher on measures of collectivism and power distance suggesting that they may be differentially attracted to organizations with a structure and culture that matches those tendencies (Guerrero & Posthuma, 2014; Stone & Deadrick, 2015). Finally, Hispanics are younger than other demographic groups, a fact that is likely to impact their job search strategies and preferences. The implications of these differences can be profound for generating a strong and diverse pool of job applicants.

Given these factors, organizations must examine and alter their recruitment practices to successfully tap into this talent pool. Rodriguez (2007) recommends that organizations take a long-term view and focus on creating an employment brand that is welcoming to Latinos. This requires a knowledge of the Latino culture, demonstrable career opportunities for advancement for Latinos, and an active involvement in the Latino community. Expanding channels used to communicate career opportunities that take advantage of the above-average use of social media is also critical. Finally, involving current Latino employees, executives, and employee resource or affinity groups in the recruitment process will go a long way toward communicating that Latinos are not only welcome but also can thrive in this organization.

Selection

Even with a diverse applicant pool, biases in the selection process can result in fairly homogeneous hires. In fact, there is ample evidence that applicants from traditionally underrepresented groups can be disproportionately excluded during an organization's typical selection process (Barron, Hebl, & King, 2011; Ruggs et al., 2013). Dipboye and Halverson (2004) identify several factors that can contribute to discrimination in the workplace such as individually held stereotypes and biases, flawed policies and practices that favor specific groups, and organizational pressures for conformity and "fit" within the prevailing organizational culture. Thus, for organizations to tap into all sources of talent within the labor market, they need to make some changes to their hiring practices.

The most important change that an organization can make to their employee selection process is to understand the nature of the job they are hiring for and identify objective and job-relevant attributes that drive performance for that job (Schmitt, 2014). It is in situations in which selection criteria are vague and subjective that stereotypes and biases tend to creep in (Huffcutt, 2011). This problem is especially true within the context of the most commonly used selective process, the employment interview, where there is room for interviewers to focus on job-irrelevant factors and ask questions that tend to confirm preexisting biases (Rivera, 2012). One of the most effective ways to combat bias in interviews is to employ standardized and structured questions that evaluate all applicants on the same job-relevant factors (McCarthy, Van Iddekinge, and Campion, 2010). Other recommendations include increasing the diversity of interviewers, ensuring that any other selection tools such as preemployment tests are not biased, and validating the selection process against job performance.

Development

The final component of the talent pipeline involves identifying high-potential individuals to receive targeted developmental experiences and subsequent promotions to higher levels of responsibility (Ready, Conger, and Hill, 2010). Unfortunately, it has long been known that employees from underrepresented groups tend to be rated lower in potential for promotion, even after controlling for several relevant factors such as experience and education (e.g., Landau, 1995). Unfortunately, commonly used tools such as the nine-blocker, which rates employees on the dimensions of current performance and future potential, leave room for subjective bias (Brook, 2014). Furthermore, talent review meetings where decisions regarding who has potential for future promotions can favor individuals who have strong advocates or "sponsors" that can speak on the candidate's behalf. Unfortunately, underrepresented groups are less likely to have such advocates (Thomas and Gabarro, 1999). There is also anecdotal evidence suggesting that minorities are more likely to be rated as "ready later" or "ready in three years" when managers are asked to indicate the promotion potential of their people (SMU Latino Leadership Initiative, 2015).

This reality points to the need for a reevaluation of the processes by which companies identify high-potential employees. A good starting point would be clear and objective methods to identify criteria for judging potential (see McCall, 1998). Utilizing tools such as standardized assessments, or performance in special assignments where clear performance measures are established, would help put all candidates for promotion on equal footing. It is also clear that the role and availability of sponsors in the talent review process needs to be revisited. At one extreme, one could require that everyone being discussed should be represented by someone who knows his or her performance and skill set. At the other extreme, decisions about who should be considered a high potential could be based completely on "objective" criteria such as job performance ratings and assessment scores. Beyond these mechanical changes, it is imperative that Hispanics, like other employees, need to have sponsors who know them well and are credible enough in the organization to open doors to developmental opportunities.

Once high-potential employees are identified, they should be assigned to developmental experiences that prepare them for the next promotion and beyond. Unfortunately, organizations seldom have a clear understanding of the developmental value of different assignments and experiences as well as the prerequisites for success in a given position (McCauley et al., 1994). Fortunately, research has identified the following experiences as particularly developmental for managerial and executive roles (McCall, 2010; McCall, Lombardo, & Morrison, 1988):

- Initial supervisory assignment – Understand the difference between doing and leading
- Task force assignments – Learn to influence without formal authority and understand different points of view

- Line to staff switches – How to create value in a completely different area while gaining exposure to corporate strategy and culture
- Leading a turnaround – Being decisive and courageous while making difficult choices
- Starting something new – Being innovative and resourceful while pulling together a new team
- Certain bosses – Working under good and bad bosses gives exposure to what works and what doesn't
- Overcoming hardships – Teaches resilience, resourcefulness, and courage

There is ample evidence linking these developmental experiences with promotion rates and leadership performance (McCall et al., 1988). Therefore, fair processes should be established to determine which employees are exposed to them.

Evaluation

To ensure that they are tapping into this fast-growing talent pool, it is imperative that organizations develop metrics to evaluate the effectiveness of their efforts. Without deliberate attention to evaluation, good intentions will fail to result in meaningful outcomes as managers and leaders are not held to account for making significant progress. Unfortunately, the ultimate evaluation will come when organizations who don't track their progress wake up one day and realize that they don't have the talent they need to execute their plans.

When devising an evaluation regime, the metrics chosen should focus on the entire employment life cycle from recruitment to separation (see Edwards, Scott, & Raju, 2003). In terms of recruitment, evaluation should first focus on how the organization is perceived as a place of employment by potential employees, or what is commonly referred to as their employment brand (Sartain & Schumann, 2006). Whether collected through focus groups, formal surveys, or reading comments on social media sites, this data can serve as an early warning system to subsequent difficulties in recruiting from diverse talent pools. Other recruitment metrics include tracking the numbers, quality, and composition of applicants identified from different sources (word of mouth, referrals, social media, job boards, etc.).

Selection metrics should focus on the performance of different applicant groups on interviews, tests, and other valid processes used to make hiring decisions. Any differences between groups can signal potential biases and should be investigated. It is important that all selection tools be validated against unbiased criteria based on an analysis of the drivers of job performance. The composition of resulting hires should also be compared to that of the general population as well as the applicant pool to check for adverse impact (i.e., differential selection rates by demographic subgroup).

Development efforts can be evaluated in several ways. First, lists such as those of "high potentials" and succession plans should be examined to see if they systematically exclude particular groups. If so, then the process and criteria used to place employees on those lists should be scrutinized. Second, organizations should document access to developmental experiences such as leadership programs, high-profile assignments, and mentorship opportunities. Finally, the progress of employees throughout the organization should be tracked using metrics such as time in position, last promotion, and the composition of the leadership pipeline at all levels including the C-suite.

To detect leaks in the leadership pipeline, organizations should also collect and evaluate their turnover rates. This date should be analyzed not only by demographic group but also by dimensions such as voluntary/involuntary, avoidable/unavoidable, and functional/dysfunctional turnover. This last dimension refers to the ease of replacing these employees (e.g., skills that are in high demand) and how strategically relevant they are to the future of the organization (e.g., fast-growing divisions). By using the various metrics described in the preceding text, a groups companies recognized the need to develop a comprehensive program to accelerate the development of their Latino talent. This program is described in the following text.

An Illustrative Case: The Corporate Executive Development Program

A group of Fortune 1000 companies examined the career paths of various demographic groups and found that Latinos were reaching middle management quicker than other groups but tended to stall there. Recognizing the untenable nature of this dynamic, these corporations, through their affiliation with the National Hispanic Corporate Council (NHCC), developed a blueprint for a program that could accelerate the careers of these Latino leaders and propel them into the ranks of vice president and beyond. This blueprint identified a core set of competencies that these organizations felt were critical for success at the executive level. The competencies included in the CEDP are described in Table 15.1.

After an exhaustive nationwide search, the NHCC chose the SMU Cox School of Business as a partner to help bring their blueprint to life. Several factors led to this selection including a history and reputation for successfully partnering with corporations to develop executive education programs, a commitment to Latino leadership development, our Dallas location at the forefront of the demographic changes taking place across the country, and the increasing prominence of the Dallas-Fort Worth area as the central business district of the United States. With the blueprint as a guide, SMU Cox was tasked with designing and executing a transformative experience that could have a measurable impact on the careers of participants within their organizations. The result was the Corporate Executive Development Program (CEDP).

Participants

The target audience for the CEDP are mid-level functional or general Latino managers from Fortune 1000 companies with potential for advancement into

Table 15.1 *Competencies targeted by CEDP*

Competency	Description
Self-Awareness	Understanding one's behavioral tendencies, responses, strengths, and weaknesses.
Understanding Hispanic Cultural Scripts	Knowledge of cultural elements of Latino culture that impact behavior and perceptions of that behavior.
Developing and Deploying Social Capital	Building mutually beneficial relationships that advance personal, professional, and organizational goals.
Adaptability	Ability to assess situational demands along with the flexibility to adapt behavior to match those demands.
Developing and Leading Teams	Understanding the characteristics of successful teams, managing the stages of team development, and avoiding common team dysfunctions.
Building Trust and Influence	Understanding the impact of trust on speed and cost of execution, applying critical behaviors that establish and build trust, and repairing trust when broken.
Understanding and Leveraging Differences	Sensitivity and appreciation for different perspectives and approaches.
Holding Oneself and Others Accountable	Skills in holding courageous conversations with anyone in the organization regardless of positional authority.
Developing Others through Coaching and Mentoring	Understanding the role of coaching and mentoring on organizational performance and the ability to establish strategic mentoring relationships.
Thinking Globally and Strategically	Understanding the drivers of global economic activity and the implications for organizational performance.
Leading Change and Innovation	Knowledge of the phases of organizational and individual change and ability to lead others through change.
Navigating Corporate Culture	Having political skills and the ability to read the "unspoken rules" of an organization.

executive positions. Participants to the program are nominated by their supervisor as well as talent managers from their human resources department. They have different levels of acculturation and come from (or are descendent from) a wide range of Latin American countries, including Brazil. The sponsoring organization pays the full cost of the program and associated travel expenses. The program is organized into consecutive cohorts, with the first one selected in 2011. Since then, approximately 168 Latino professionals have completed the CEDP over six cohorts. These participants represent all functional areas including marketing, finance, operations, and human resources and come from throughout the United States and beyond.

Program Design

The CEDP is composed of four broad elements that work in concert to increase its relevance and impact. These include: (1) formal classroom instruction, (2) assessment and feedback, (3) exposure to highly seasoned Hispanic executives, and (4) an action learning team project. The program is divided into three phases that take place over a nine-month period.

The formal instruction component of the program employs an inside-out structure that starts with individual-level concepts and culminates with an organizational-level perspective. Each of the three phases consists of four days of instruction on the SMU campus. The three instructional phases of the program are: (1) Leading with Authenticity, (2) Leading High Performance Teams, and (3) Becoming a Corporate Leader.

Each phase contains specific sessions led by highly experienced instructors utilizing several proven pedagogical methods such as cases, role plays, group activities, hands-on exercises, and simulations. The goal of Phase 1 is to increase the participants' level of self-awareness, adaptability, intercultural competence, and emotional intelligence. Phase 2 focuses on group and interpersonal skills such as developing trust, building teams, holding others accountable, driving innovation, and coaching others. Finally, Phase 3 is aimed at corporate-wide competencies such as developing social capital, navigating corporate culture, leading change, and understanding the global economic landscape. Table 15.2 summarizes the topics covered in each of the CEDP phases.

A unique aspect of the CEDP is the presence of three executive advisors who are current or recently retired Hispanic corporate executives. These advisors perform several roles throughout the program. First, they are present during all instructional sessions to provide a linkage between the content presented and application to a corporate environment, as well as to inject a Hispanic cultural lens to the discussion. For example, during a discussion on accountability, the advisors could observe that, in their experience, Hispanics tend to have difficulty saying no to requests and may become overcommitted and let some obligations slip through the cracks. That observation would spur a further conversation around cultural scripts and how they can impact one's behavior and others' perceptions.

In addition to having access to executive advisors, CEDP participants also have the opportunity to receive and act upon feedback throughout the program. During Phase 1, participants are given the results of a 360-degree assessment instrument tapping into the program competencies described in the preceding text. This assessment is completed by supervisor(s), peers, and direct reports from their organization. Program participants work with their assigned executive advisors to make sense of the results and develop an action plan for closing any critical gaps and identifying key strengths. Throughout the program, executive advisors are also in a position to give participants direct feedback regarding their behavior and performance in class sessions and the team project. The use of multiple feedback methods and opportunities enriches the experience, builds self-awareness, and sets participants up for meaningful development.

Another element of the CEDP that helps drive individual development and skill application is the capstone team project. The purpose of the project is to give participants the opportunity to apply the program content within a team context while developing an enterprise-wide perspective. The project leverages

Table 15.2 *CEDP instructional phases and modules*

Instructional Phase	Modules
Phase 1: Leading with Authenticity	• Understanding and leveraging the power of culture • Behavior change for successful people (360-degree feedback) • Increasing adaptability through situational awareness • Developing emotional and social intelligence • Reaching high performance across cultures: multicultural dexterity • Establishing your leadership brand for maximum impact and visibility
Phase 2: Leading High Performance Teams	• Developing trust, influence, and accountability • Leading high-performance teams • Coaching and mentoring • Executive panel on global leadership • Innovation and human-centered design
Phase 3: Becoming a Corporate Leader	• Developing an executive presence mind-set • Strategically building social capital • Understanding the global economy • Leading and sustaining change (a simulation) • Collaboration across boundaries • Understanding and navigating corporate culture

the perspectives and knowledge of the participants, who come from a variety of industry and functional backgrounds. The project teams (ranging in size from five to seven depending on the size of the overall cohort) are given the challenge to develop a venture that is financially viable but also addresses a social need. To date, team projects have tackled issues such as childhood obesity, education, texting and driving, fair trade, and environmental sustainability, to name a few.

Program participants work on their team projects while on the SMU campus and remotely when they are between program phases. During Phase 1 of the program, teams complete a team charter outlining expectations of each other as well as their team values. An executive advisor is assigned to each team to monitor team progress and provide candid feedback. This feedback can range from encouraging specific team members to apply program concepts during team meetings to pointing out behaviors they observe that can impact the participant's effectiveness and career progression. In our experience, teams take the project very seriously and devote a large amount of time to creating a quality deliverable. Before they leave campus at the conclusion of Phase 1, project teams agree on their communication method and frequency and set a schedule for working on their project. Each of the teams' executive advisor participates in these virtual meetings to provide feedback and general guidance. Upon returning to campus for Phase 2, the teams give a brief update on their progress that includes the general topic or issue they chose to tackle as well as the approach taken. During Phase 3, teams present their final projects to their classmates, company sponsors, and other program guests. These presentations are followed by a graduation ceremony culminating their nine-month journey.

Program Impact

By all measures, the CEDP has been a huge success. First, and perhaps most importantly, approximately 70% of CEDP participants have received opportunities to move into positions with significant increases in scope and responsibility (including promotions to vice president and beyond). Feedback from corporate sponsors also has been positive indicating that the program provides them another tool for developing their high-potential Latino professionals as well as for attracting and retaining top talent. Participants give the program consistently high marks in ratings of program sessions as well as the overall experience. Preliminary research conducted with CEDP participants also shows that the program has helped them improve in the competencies identified by the original blueprint. For example, participants have reported greater awareness of the role that culture plays in their behavior, higher levels of self-awareness, more intentional development of their social capital, and more confidence in leading their teams.

Future Research

Although we know a great deal regarding the importance of leadership development for moving individuals into higher levels of responsibility and scope in organizations, there are still areas that require further study (see DeRue & Myers, 2014 for a comprehensive review). We know, for example, that experience is one of the primary sources of learning for leaders, that some situations are more developmental than others, and that certain personal characteristics are associated with higher degrees of learning (McCall, 2010). However, DeRue and Myers (2014) argue that future research must broaden its focus from an individualistic (leader) perspective to include followers and the organization.

What this means for Latino leadership development is that, in addition to ensuring that high-potential Latinos are afforded development opportunities, non-Latinos in the organization may need development that challenges their potentially narrowly held views of what a leader looks and sounds like. Thus, it is not just Latinos that need to raise their awareness of traditional Latino cultural scripts but also their supervisors and potential followers. This will ensure that the proper attributions are made for specific behaviors and untested assumptions about leadership potential or performance do not go unchallenged.

A second area of future research concerns the balance between developing leaders that align an organization's current goals with the need for leaders that provide a unique perspective that can lead to innovations in new products and services. Changing expectations from customers as well as demographic and technological changes call for different ways of doing things. This suggests that organizations need to be more open to different leadership styles as well as individuals with different backgrounds. How an organization successfully manages this transition as well as the culture, policies, and practices that reinforce this shift need to be identified.

Research is also needed to explore the impact of culturally relevant leadership development. As described, the CEDP relies heavily on contextualizing leadership behaviors within Latino culture. Participants report that this aspect of the program helps them build self-awareness and become more intentional about how they behave and how they are perceived. Future studies should examine this process and the factors that affect who is impacted most. In addition, it is also important to identify the most important and relevant cultural factors that should be incorporated into development experiences. Finally, it would be interesting to determine if contextualizing leadership development within a participant's culture helps them internalize a leader identity (DeRue, Ashford, & Cotton, 2009).

Day and Sin (2011) documented the existence of different leadership development trajectories across individuals. This line of research should be pursued further as it is consistent with the finding by some SMU Latino Leadership Initiative partner companies where Latinos tended to reach middle management at significantly higher rates but tended to stall there. It is possible that the factors that help propel an individual through different stages vary. Identifying these factors will go a long way to ensuring that all sources of leadership talent within organizations are developed.

Conclusion

Organizations are only as effective as the quality of the human capital they possess. Thus, it is critical that no source of talent goes untapped, especially in our rapidly changing business environment. With the increase in the number of Latinos in the labor force, organizations need to ensure that they are attracting, selecting, and developing this mission-critical talent if they are to remain competitive. The techniques outlined in this chapter as well as the specific approach developed in the CEDP can help organizations do just that.

References

Badger, E. 2014. The many reasons millennials are shunning cars. *Washington Post*, October 15. https://www.washingtonpost.com/news/wonk/wp/2014/10/14/the-many-reasons-millennials-are-shunning-cars (accessed August 10, 2016).

Barron, L.G., Hebl, M., and King, E.B. 2011. Effects of manifest ethnic identification on employment discrimination. *Cultural Diversity and Ethnic Minority Psychology* 17(1): 23–30.

Bennett, N., and Lemoine, G. J. 2014. What a difference a word makes: Understanding threats to performance in a VUCA world. *Business Horizons* 57: 311–317.

Blancero, D.M. and DelCampo, R.G. 2005. Hispanics in the workplace: Experiences with mentoring and networking. *Employment Relations Today* 32(2): 31–38.

Brook, J. 2014. Boost the nine-box talent grid. *Training Journal* September: 5–8.

Brown, A. and Patten, E. 2014. Statistical portrait of Hispanics in the United States, 2012. *Pew Research Center.* http://www.pewhispanic.org/2014/04/29/statistical-portrait-of-hispanics-in-the-united-states-2012 (accessed May 15, 2016).

Cappelli, P. 2008. *Talent on Demand: Managing Talent in an Age of Uncertainty.* Boston, MA: Harvard Business Press.

Charan, R., Drotter, S., and Noel, J. 2011. *The Leadership Pipeline.* San Francisco: Jossey Bass.

Dabbah, M., and Poiré, A. 2006. *The Latino Advantage in the Workplace: Use Who You Are to Get Where You Want to Be.* Clearwater, FL: Sphinx Publishing.

Day, D. V., and Sin, H. P. 2011. Longitudinal tests of an integrative model of leader development: Charting and understanding developmental trajectories. *Leadership Quarterly* 22: 545–560.

DeRue, D. S., and Myers, C. G. 2014. Leadership development: A review and agenda for future research. In D. Day, ed., *Oxford Handbook of Leadership and Organizations,* 829–852. New York: Oxford University Press.

DeRue, D. S., Ashford, S. J., and Cotton, N. C. 2009. Assuming the mantle: Unpacking the process by which individuals internalize a leader identity. In L. M. Roberts, and J. E. Dutton, eds., *Exploring Positive Identities and Organizations: Building a Theoretical and Research Foundation,* 217–236. New York: Routledge

Dipboye, R. L., and Halverson, S. K. 2004. Subtle (and not so subtle) discrimination in organizations. In R. W. Griffin and A. M. O'Leary-Kelly, eds., *The Dark Side of Organizational Behavior,* 131–158. San Francisco: Jossey-Bass.

Eby, L. T., Allen, T. D., Evans, S. C., Ng, T. W. H., and DuBois, D. L. 2008. Does mentoring matter? A multidisciplinary meta-analysis comparing mentored and non-mentored individuals. *Journal of Vocational Behavior* 72: 254–267.

Edwards, J. E., Scott, J. C., and Raju, N. S. 2003. *The Human-Resources Program-Evaluation Handbook.* Thousand Oaks, CA: Sage.

Gallegos, P. V., and Ferdman, B. M. 2007. Identity orientations of Latinos in the United States: Implications for leaders and organizations. *The Business Journal of Hispanic Research* 1: 26–41.

Gluszek, A., and Dovidio, J. F. 2010. The way they speak: A social psychological perspective on the stigma of nonnative accents in communication. *Personality and Social Psychology Review* 14: 214–237.

Guerrero, L., and Posthuma, R. A. 2014. Perceptions and behaviors of Hispanic workers: A review. *Journal of Managerial Psychology* 29: 616–643.

Hispanic Association for Corporate Responsibility. 2013. Corporate Inclusion Index. Washington, DC: HACR.

Hofstede, G. 2001. *Culture's Consequences.* Thousand Oaks, CA: Sage.

Hosoda, M., Nguyen, L. T., Stone-Romero, E. F. 2012. The effect of Hispanic accents on employment decisions. *Journal of Managerial Psychology* 27(4): 347–364.

Huffcutt, A.I. 2011. An empirical review of the employment interview construct literature. *International Journal of Selection and Assessment* 19(1): 62–81.

Jones, K. P., Peddie, C. I., Gilrane, V. L., King, E. B., and Gray, A. L. 2016. Not so subtle: A meta-analytic investigation of the correlates of subtle and overt discrimination. *Journal of Management* 42(6): 1588–1613.

Kennedy, G. M., and Wissoker, D. A. 1994. An analysis of the correlates of discrimination facing young Hispanic job-seekers. *American Economic Review* 84: 674–83.

Landau, J. 1995. The relationship of race and gender to managers' ratings of promotion potential. *Journal of Organizational Behavior* 16(4): 391–400.

Lee, D. L., and Ahn, S. 2012. Discrimination against Latina/os: A meta-analysis of individual-level resources and outcomes. *The Counseling Psychologist* 40: 28–65.

McCall, M. Lombardo, and Morrison, A. M. 1988. *The Lessons of Experience*. New York: Free Press.

McCall, M. W. 1998. *High Flyers: Developing the Next Generation of Leaders*. Boston, MA: Harvard Business Press.

McCall, M. W. 2010. Recasting leadership development. *Industrial and Organizational Psychology* 3: 3–19.

McCarthy, J. M., Van Iddekinge, C. H., and Campion, M. A. 2010. Are highly structured interviews resistant to demographic similarity effects? *Personnel Psychology* 63: 325–359.

McCauley, C. D., Ruderman, M. N., Ohlott, P. J., and Morrow, J. E. 1994. Assessing the developmental potential of jobs. *Journal of Applied Psychology* 79(4): 544–560.

McCauley, C. D., and McCall, M. W. 2014. *Using Experience to Develop Leadership Talent*. San Francisco: Jossey-Bass.

Menendez, Senator Robert. 2015. 2014 Corporate Diversity Survey. June.

Pew Research Center. 2014. For most workers, real wages have barely budged. https://www.washingtonpost.com/news/wonk/wp/2014/10/14/the-many-reasons-millennials-are-shunning-cars (accessed August 10, 2016).

Pew Research Center. 2014. *Hispanic Nativity Shift*. http://www.pewhispanic.org/2014/04/29/hispanic-nativity-shift (accessed August 10, 2016).

Pew Research Center. 2015a. Changing attitudes on gay marriage. http://www.pewforum.org/2015/07/29/graphics-slideshow-changing-attitudes-on-gay-marriage (accessed August 10, 2016).

Pew Research Center. 2015b. Social media update 2014. http://www.pewinternet.org/files/2015/01/PI_SocialMediaUpdate20144.pdf (accessed August 10, 2016).

PwC 18th Annual Global CEO Survey. 2015. http://www.pwc.com/gx/en/ceo-survey/2015/assets/pwc-18th-annual-global-ceo-survey-jan-2015.pdf (accessed August 10, 2016).

Quiñones, M. A. 2010. Getting more Hispanics to the top. *Forbes*. August 23.

Quiñones, M. A., and Rasberry, R. 2015. Dark clouds gathering? Results of the 2015 SMU Cox CEO Sentiment Survey. *DCEO Magazine*. November/December.

Ragins, B. R. (1997). Diversified mentoring relationships in organizations: A power perspective. *Academy of Management Review* 22(2): 482–521.

Ready, D. A., Conger, J. A., and Hill, L. A. 2010. Are you a high potential? *Harvard Business Review*. June.

Rivera, L. A. 2012. Hiring as cultural matching: The case of elite professional service firms. *American Sociological Review* 77(6): 999–1022.

Rochhar, R. 2012. Labor force slows, Hispanic share grows. Pew Research Center. http://www.pewhispanic.org/2012/02/13/labor-force-growth-slows-hispanic-share-grows (accessed September 1, 2016).

Rodriguez, R. 2007. *Latino Talent: Effective Strategies to Recruit, Retain, and Develop Hispanic Professionals*. Hoboken, NJ: Wiley and Sons.

Romero, E. J. 2004. Hispanic identity and acculturation: Implications for management. *Cross Cultural Management* 11: 62–71.

Ruggs, E. N., Law, C., Cox, C. B., Roehling, M. V., Werner, R. L., Hebl, M. R., and Barron, L. 2013. Gone fishing: I-O psychologists' missed opportunities to understand marginalized employees' experiences with discrimination. *Industrial and Organizational Psychology* 6(1): 39–60.

Sanchez, J. I., and Brock, P. 1996. Outcomes of perceived discrimination among Hispanic employees: is diversity management a luxury or a necessity? *Academy of Management Journal* 39: 704–19.

Sartain, L., and Schumann, M. 2006. *Brand from the Inside*. San Francisco: Jossey-Bass.

Schmitt, N., ed. 2014. *The Oxford Handbook of Personnel Assessment and Selection*. Oxford University Press.

Shorey, H. S., Cowan, G., and Sullivan, M. P. 2002. Predicting perceptions of discrimination among Hispanics and Anglos. *Hispanic Journal of Behavioral Sciences* 24: 3–22.

SMU Latino Leadership Initiative. 2015. Attracting, retaining and developing Latino talent. Symposium presented on the SMU Campus. Dallas, Texas.

Stepler, R., and Lopez, M. H. 2016. U.S. Latino population growth and dispersion has slowed since onset of the Great Recession. http://www.pewhispanic.org/2016/09/08/latino-population-growth-and-dispersion-has-slowed-since-the-onset-of-the-great-recession (accessed August 10, 2016).

Stone, D. L. and Deadrick, D.L. 2015. Challenges and opportunities affecting the future of human resource management. *Human Resource Management Review* 25: 139–145.

Thomas, D. A., and Gabarro, J. J. 1999. *Breaking Through: The Making of Minority Executives in Corporate America*. Boston: Harvard Business School Press.

Tonidandel, S., Avery, D., and Phillips, M. 2007. Maximizing returns on mentoring: Factors affecting subsequent protégé performance. *Journal of Organizational Behavior* 28(1): 89–110.

PART IV

Special Topics

16 Training and Development in Small and Medium Enterprises

Melissa S. Cardon and Stephen D. Valentin

The vast majority of businesses around the world are small and medium enterprises (SMEs) and they are central to job growth in established and emerging economies (Loan-Clarke, Boocock, Smith, & Whittaker, 1999). While definitions vary by geography, SMEs typically employ between 0 and 200 (European classification) or 0 and 500 employees (U.S. Small Business Association classification). Regardless of the upper bound concerning the exact size of such firms (which will be addressed in more detail in the following text), SMEs play a pivotal role in sustaining employment and creating income and prosperity of an economy (Lange, Ottens, & Taylor, 2000). For example, the total population of European Union firms with 20 or more employees is 1.5 million, of which 80% have 20–100 employees (European Commission, 2000). One study of the U.K. economy reports that of the 1.2 million firms with employees, only 32,000 had more than 50 employees, and only 7,000 had more than 250, indicating that SMEs comprised more than 99% of the total population of firms at that time (Smith & Whittaker, 1998). In Scotland, 99% of all businesses employ fewer than 50 people (Lange et al., 2000), and in Japan, 70% of all employees are working in SMEs (Gamage & Sadoi, 2008). These numbers are similar in the United States, where small firms represent 99.7% of all employer firms, and since 1995 have generated 64% of new jobs and paid 44% of the total U.S. private payroll (Brown, 2014). Having a vibrant SME population can be a means of reducing unemployment, promoting flexibility and innovation, and improving the health of an economy (Loan-Clarke et al., 1999; Storey, 1994).

Despite the importance and prevalence of small and medium-size firms in economies around the world, there is very little research on how such firms train and develop their employees, despite repeated calls over many years (Cardon & Stevens, 2004; Cassell, Nadin, Gray, & Clegg, 2002). There is an assumption that training is a good thing for firms and will enhance individual and organizational performance, as is discussed in the rest of this book. Yet a very small percent of small firms make any investment in training for any employee category (Barclays Bank, 1994; Loan-Clarke et al., 1999; Storey & Westhead, 1997; Westhead & Storey, 1996), and the training they do engage in is likely to be very different from that provided in larger organizations. Hence there is an important need to better understand training and development in SMEs, because small firms are not simply "scaled down" versions of larger organizations (Storey, 1994), and they face very real distinctions in how human resource decisions are made (Heneman, Tansky, & Camp, 2000).

Interestingly, the majority of research related to training and development in entrepreneurship or small business management is focused on training the entrepreneur rather than on training employees of SMEs. We focus instead on research concerning training and development of employees of SMEs, leaving discussion of entrepreneurship education (how to train people to be entrepreneurs or small business owners) out of our review and discussion. However, those interested in learning more about entrepreneurship education are encouraged to read further on competencies entrepreneurs need (Solomon, Duffy, & Tarabishy, 2002), suggestions for ways to train entrepreneurs (Ulrich & Cole, 1987), the importance of entrepreneurial training (Lans et al., 2004), and the impact of entrepreneurship education programs (Fayolle, Gailly, & Lassas-Clerc, 2006). There is also considerable work on the different training needs of male and female entrepreneurs around the world (Birley, Moss, & Saunders, 1987; Ekpe, Razak, & Mat, 2013; Kao & Chiang, 2000; Nagesh & Murthy, 2008; Premalatha, 2010).

Training employees within small and medium firms is crucial because once an entrepreneur grows the firm enough to hire the first employee, human resource decisions concerning that employee will impact the potential for individual and organizational performance (Leung, Foo, & Chaturvedi, 2013). We also focus on SMEs, regardless of their age, not just nascent, new, or emerging firms (Cardon & Stevens, 2004). This is an important distinction because while all new firms start small, not all SMEs are new. There is a vast population of small and medium firms that are mature, and may not be trying to grow, but instead seeking to maintain their current size. This population of SMEs may face different training and development needs than entrepreneurs who are starting new firms with a clear goal of growth.

We define SMEs as firms that have between 0 and 250 employees, based on prior work. Although there is some variation in the upper bound of what scholars and practitioners consider a medium firm (Loan-Clarke et al., 1999), there is consistency across studies on human resource practices in SMEs over the past 40 years that firms with fewer than approximately 200–250 employees face very different human resource management (HRM) challenges than large organizations (more on this in the following text). We also note that some scholars have found key differences within the category of SMEs and break these firms into smaller groups based on organizational size, such as 10–19, 20–49, 50–99, and 100–199 employees (de Kok, Uhlaner, & Thurik, 2006; Loan-Clarke et al., 1999) with some studies even providing specific labels of microfirms (0–4 employees), small firms (5–19 employees), and medium firms (20–100 employees) (Kotey & Folker, 2007; Kotey & Sheridan, 2004; Kotey & Slade, 2005) based on the Australian Bureau of Statistics' definitions. In the following text, we discuss specific findings concerning how size of organization within the overall category of SMEs influences the extent of training provided, type and content of such training, and perceptions of effectiveness or impact of training.

The purpose of this chapter is to review research on training and development in SMEs, updating reviews done previously of HRM practices in SMEs including that of Cassell and colleagues (Cassell et al., 2002), Heneman, Tansky, and Camp (2000), and Cardon and Stevens (2004), and digging deeper into studies specifically focused on training and development. We first discuss why and how training and development is different in SMEs versus large firms, then examine the current state of knowledge concerning methods and content of training and development of employees of SMEs. We examine research findings concerning the impact of training and development on organizational outcomes such as growth and performance, both in terms of the perceptions small business owners have of the relationship between training and firm performance, and in terms of empirical evidence concerning this relationship. Interestingly, there is a fair amount of work on how small and medium firms train their employees in specific countries such as Britain, China, Japan, Sweden, and Spain, among others, which we review, before discussing our overall thoughts on the current state of knowledge about SME training and development and identifying opportunities for future research.

Training and Development Differences by Organization Size

Key distinctions between SMEs and large firms include who makes training decisions, resource constraints, control vulnerability, and concerns over employee turnover. First, in SMEs it is the business owner who is most likely to make training decisions, unlike in large firms where there is typically a dedicated human resource person responsible for such decisions (Banks, Bures, & Champion, 1987). This is an important distinction because research has shown that a single manager is typically the most important influence on providing development for employees, where having one person take on that responsibility leads to much greater likelihood of employees receiving development opportunities (Kock, Gill, & Ellström, 2008). Small firms are less likely to have a human resources professional or in-house training advocate, and as a result, training needs may not be a priority in the firm (de Kok et al., 2006). In addition, SME owners may or may not find value in training of employees based on their personal and professional backgrounds. For example, there is a large population of SME owners who started their firms because they did not find formal large organizations or educational institutions particularly valuable or helpful, so they may not want to send their employees to such programs (Lange et al., 2000). SME owners may also not want to invest in training because they do not believe there is a link between training and profits (Keep & Mayhew, 1996; Lange et al., 2000; Storey & Westhead, 1997; Westhead & Storey, 1996), and instead view it as an expense with little upside potential. In addition to the possibility that training is avoided and specifically decided against (Cannon, 1997), it also could be that SME owners are not aware of external training opportunities (Westhead & Storey, 1996) or are simply too busy managing operational issues to think strategically about employee development (Smith et al., 2002; Watkins, 1982). Whatever the specific motivation, the first key difference in training in SMEs and large firms is simply who makes decisions about training, because these decisions are much more likely to be in the hands of the overall business owner and operator, rather than a dedicated human resources professional, and therefore training will receive less intentional focus and planning in SMEs than in large firms.

A second key difference between SMEs and large firms is the severe resource constraints of smaller firms, including both money and time. Cost of training has been identified as one of the most important reasons for why SMEs do not invest in formal training, in particular (Curran et al., 1997; de Kok & Uhlaner, 2001; Hill & Stewart, 2000; Kirby, 1990; Kotey & Folker, 2007; Lange et al., 2000; Loan-Clarke et al., 1999; Reid, 1987). Because of financial constraints, small firms are less likely to invest in things that are not essentially to current business operations (Loan-Clarke et al., 1999; Storey & Westhead, 1997), including general training programs, and also cannot devote resources to specialized programs that would meet the specific needs of the small firm because of even higher costs associated with custom programs (de Kok & Uhlaner, 2001; Notebloom, 1993). In addition to the financial cost, SME managers are often concerned about lost productivity that results from employees engaging in formal training (Curran et al., 1997; Hill & Stewart, 2000), leaving fewer managers left to handle the work load (Loan-Clarke et al., 1999; Storey & Westhead, 1997; Westhead & Storey, 1996). For example, in one study of Scottish SMEs, 30% indicated financial constraints and 15% lost production time as reasons for not investing in formal training programs, such as lifelong learning activities offered by the government (Lange et al., 2000). That same study indicated that while 40% of small companies engaged in formal training, on average, they trained only 50% of their employees. Clearly, concerns over resource constraints of time and money experienced by SMEs significantly reduce the training opportunities they provide to employees.

A third key difference is that SMEs are much more sensitive to control issues than are larger firms. At a very basic level, formal training may be avoided by SME owners because they prefer autonomy and independence over accepting external input (Curran et al., 1997; Smith et al., 2002). In addition, some SME owners may feel threatened by employees who have greater skill sets than they do, especially in family-owned firms (Loan-Clarke et al., 1999), because of a perceived threat to control of their firm (Harris, Reid, & McAdam, 2004; Kotey & Folker, 2007). Anecdotally, some SME owners want to appear to be in control of their firms, and to believe they are in control of their firms, and therefore worry that training their employees might diminish either their ability or perception of being in control.

Fourth, in both family and nonfamily firms, SME owners also appear to be highly concerned that investing in skill development of their employees will only lead to these employees being poached by other organizations (Cassell et al.,

2002; Curran et al., 1997; Loan-Clarke et al., 1999). This may lead to SMEs investing more in hiring employees with necessary skills (perhaps by poaching them from other firms) rather than in developing current employees (Cassell et al., 2002; Lange et al., 2000). This approach to employee development is especially problematic in small and medium firms because there is not much room for advancement within these firms, especially the smallest among them, which leads to more labor movement across firms than within them (Curran et al., 1997). In very small firms, loss of even one skilled employee can have a significant impact on productivity and ability to meet sales goals, and even in medium firms where there is still often a family and friendship-based culture, loss of a skilled employee can substantially change not only productivity of the firm, but also the culture and ability to recruit new talent.

Because of the key differences between SMEs and larger firms of who makes training decisions, substantial resource constraints, perceived vulnerability to loss of control, and concerns about losing trained employees, the type and content of training in SMEs is very different than that of larger firms. We discuss this point next.

Training Methods in Small and Medium Enterprises

Perhaps the clearest finding concerning training in small and medium firms is that it is primarily informal rather than formal. Small firms often report that they do no training of employees because they often do not consider informal training as "real" training (Ross, 1993; Smith et al., 2002), and they rarely carry out formal training needs analysis or use a systematic approach (Kotey & Folker, 2007). One study suggested that SMEs have 24% of employees untrained compared to 4% in large enterprises (Storey & Westhead, 1997). Indeed, because the literature on training typically takes a large firm view, which tends to focus more on formal training, there is very little research or knowledge focused on informal training in SMEs (Kotey & Folker, 2007). Yet, "the importance of informal training is difficult to over-state. Not only is informal in-house training important, but for many small firms it is their only form of training. For others, it is their preferred mode of training; external training is often regarded as second best in terms of their ability to meet their needs" (Curran et al., 1997: 97)

Informal training is important to small firms as a method of skill and knowledge acquisition (Hill & Stewart, 2000; Jones, Morris, & Rockmore, 1995; Kotey & Folker, 2007; Sirmon & Hitt, 1992), and may include socialization (which can include formal and informal elements), on-the-job training, and knowledge sharing (see Chapter 3 by Marand and Noe in this volume). SMEs are more willing to engage in informal training when there is a direct link between costs and benefits (Lange et al., 2000). Small firms often train new employees by watching them work and correcting their performance as they go (Kotey & Slade, 2005), especially in micro-sized firms. As such, training in smaller firms tends to be ad hoc (Cassell et al., 2002; Marlow &

Patton, 1993). In small firms, owners/managers typically take direct responsibility for employee training, and teach them the owners' preferred method of doing things (Kotey & Slade, 2005; Timmons, 1999). Such informal training is not only less expensive, but can also be infused into daily operations of the firm, and is focused on not only employee-specific needs (Curran et al., 1997; Hill & Stewart, 2000), but also firm-specific needs, which addresses the concerns with losses in productivity and control discussed in the preceding text. Informal training is also effective in small firms because employees learn on-site while their skills are being used and where their skills will need to be maintained (Lange et al., 2000). This allows employees to learn how to solve problems as they arise, which creates a more multitalented labor force, which is highly suited to the SME environment (Kotey & Folker, 2007; Smith et al., 2002). Informal human resources practices, including training, allow smaller firms to be more flexible in coping with environmental uncertainty, too (de Kok & Uhlaner, 2001; Hill & Stewart, 2000). Because informal practices are not codified in formal, written policies, they can be more easily changed by owners with less resistance and complaint than if they had been written down, codified, and perceived by employees as a contract.

SMEs do conduct some formal training, such as orientation for new employees (Kotey & Slade, 2005). Yet the formal training that is provided to employees in these firms is likely to be reactive, occurring based on poor performance on the part of an employee (Banks et al., 1987; Lange et al., 2000) or if an external need is identified for it (Smith & Whittaker, 1998). The focus of such training is typically on individual employee skill development for their current job, rather than more comprehensive or general training for future skills the employee might need (Lange et al., 2000).

Some SMEs also provide "bite-size training" where employees get small focused lessons from specific formal courses tailored to the needs of a particular organization or job, rather than broader or more generalized training (Lange et al., 2000), which may take more time. Some evidence also suggests that small firms tend to use trade associations, short college seminars (less than five days), and in-house personnel as the most common sources of training and development (Banks et al., 1987) although training delivery methods have changed substantially since the time of that study and therefore such preferences may have also changed.

There is also heterogeneity within SMEs concerning the type and content of training they engage in, based on individual and organizational factors, such as company size, strategy, technology, culture, and environment (de Kok & Uhlaner, 2001). Smith et al. (2002) developed a comprehensive model of individual and organizational factors, as well as aspects of formal training, that triggers SME adoption of a specific formal training program, and Kotey and Folker (2007) examine the effect of size and whether the firm is family owned on adoption of informal and formal training programs in SMEs. We focus on differences in SME training based on the size of the firm, as well as based on whether it is a family firm, which appear to be two critical factors impacting SME training.

Size of Firm

Even within the category of SMEs, some have more sophisticated HRM practices than others (Hill & Stewart, 2000), including the formalization of their training program (de Kok & Uhlaner, 2001). Some of this sophistication may be due to growth strategies. The majority of small firms are concerned with survival rather than growth and innovation (Curran et al., 1997) and many small firms choose to remain small or medium in size, rather than the small size being simply a matter of a large firm that has not yet bloomed (Cardon & Stevens, 2004). However, some small firms do aspire to grow at least to become a medium firm, and those with growth orientations are more likely to find value of more formalized HRM practices and therefore to invest in training (Loan-Clark et al., 1999), especially formal training.

Many studies of training in SMEs do not explicitly consider whether the firm seeks growth or not, but instead examine how training varies based on the size of the firm. In general, greater company size is associated with more formalized training practices (de Kok & Uhlaner, 2001; Koch & McGrath, 1996). This may be because informal styles of management communication are stretched when firms have 20 or more employees (Roberts, Sawbridge, & Bamber, 1992). The strain on management time and energy limits the ability of owner-managers to conduct training, and they may therefore turn their attention from training employees to training managers. Then, owners expect managers to train entry-level employees (Kotey & Slade, 2005).

Some have also argued that firms above a certain size or with more opportunities for internal promotion need to provide more formal training and development opportunities to retain their employees (Loan-Clarke et al., 1999; Smith et al., 2002) and to demonstrate legitimacy as an organization (Kock et al., 2008). This focus on training may be less about skill development and more about having signs recognized in the marketplace of being a legitimate organization, which may be important to their ability to both recruit new employees and gain customers (Kock et al., 2008). That said, at least one study found that resource availability, rather than external stakeholder expectations, was more important to the adoption of formal training and development by SMEs (de Kok & Uhlaner, 2001). Regardless of the motivation for such investments, Loan-Clark et al. (1999) found that investments in training were significantly higher in firms that have 20–49 employees than those that have 10–19 employees, and significantly higher in firms with 50–99 employees than those with 20–49 employees, but there were no significant differences between firms that have 50–99 and 100–199 employees.

Family Firms

Interestingly, a fair amount of research has been done differentiating training and development in SMEs based on whether they are family owned (de Kok et al., 2006). The general agreement appears to be that there is far less formal management training done in family than in nonfamily firms (Cromie, Stephenson, & Montieth, 1995; Loan-Clarke et al., 1999). One of the most comprehensive and detailed studies of training examined the type of training provided and the provider of that training based on firm size and whether it was family owned. The sample included 448 family and 470 nonfamily SMEs in the United Kingdom (Kotey & Folker, 2007). They found that for nonfamily firms, informal training is dominant but that training becomes more formal, structured, and development oriented for firms with 20–49 employees. In contrast, for family firms, formal training programs increased for firms with 20–49 employees, but not those with 50–99 employees. For firms that have 100–199 employees, there are very few differences between family- and nonfamily-owned firms (Kotey & Folker, 2007). We encourage readers to see Table 8 (229) of Kotey and Folker (2007) for detailed information on these differences in family versus nonfamily firms of differing sizes. In a separate study of 551 SMEs in the United Kingdom, nonfamily organizations were found to invest significantly more time and money in managerial training and development than firms where the founding family was still represented (Loan-Clarke et al., 1999). Thus it appears that family ownership of an SME may influence the formalization of training, especially at smaller organizational sizes.

Training Content in Small and Medium Enterprises

The benefit of training to organizations is not just the person acquiring the skill and therefore being able to produce more output, but also the increase in the company's ability to flexibly shift its focus between sectors and branches and to innovate in the marketplace, which is essential for both keeping labor and capital employed and for maintaining competitiveness of the business (Booth & Snower, 1990; Lange et al., 2000). Very small firms need flexibility and speedy response times to changing strategic priorities and environmental variables (Kotey & Slade, 2005). Therefore their training is often focused on generalized skill sets and jobs rather than more specialized ones (Bacon et al., 1996; de Kok & Uhlaner, 2001; Wagner, 1997).

For very small microfirms, training is typically only that which is required by law, such as health and safety legislation compliance (Smith & Whittaker, 1998). In very small firms (10–50 employees), training might only occur in the form of annual team outings with employees (de Kok & Uhlaner, 2001). Service-sector SMEs may also provide training emphasizing building and maintaining customer relationships (Loan-Clarke et al., 1999; Wong et al., 1997). Other training topics most needed include management skills, communication skills, leadership, problem solving, motivation, and decision making (Banks et al., 1987) – soft skills that can be utilized regardless of how the firm strategy or size adapts. Skill development in SMEs has also been focused on problem solving and multitasking (Chittenden & Robertson, 1994; Smith et al., 2002), both essential aspects of small firm operations. For somewhat larger SMEs, competitive pressures may lead to customer wanting higher quality or customized products or services, and quicker delivery times, which has led to a demand for improved individual competence with technical knowledge, flexibility, responsibility, and ability to cooperate with others and work in teams (Kock et al., 2008). Training on such areas related to work process and daily routines appears to be the dominant focus of SME training (Kock et al., 2008), whether informal or formal in nature.

Training Effectiveness for Small and Medium Enterprises

A key question is whether training is worth the investment for SME firms. While empirical data on training and development practices in SMEs, especially specific methods or content, and the outcomes associated with such practices, is quite minimal, the research that does exist seems to suggest that training is important and effective for SMEs. Some scholars have even suggested that small business failure almost invariably stems from poor managerial competence (Jennings & Beaver, 1995), and a major factor determining such competence is the education, training, and experience of senior managers in these firms (Loan-Clarke et al., 1999). Prior research has found relationships between training in SMEs and outcomes of survival, success in ability to achieve organizational objectives, and firm performance, including growth. We discuss each of these outcomes further in the following text.

First, scholars have argued that training can enhance the survival rate of small firms, as well as firm performance (English, 2001; Kotey & Folker, 2007). Survival is a very real concern among SMEs, not just due to liabilities of newness found in emerging firms (Hannan & Freeman, 1984; Stinchcombe, 1965), but also because of liabilities of smallness (Bruderl & Schussler, 1990; Ranger-Moore, 1997), which every small firm faces. Beyond mere survival, firms clearly also aspire to succeed. Despite the fact that many SME owners do not feel providing formal training will help the competitiveness of their business (Smith et al., 2002), one study found that 43% of companies who use such practices say they do help them attain business objectives (Cassell et al., 2002). Reid and Harris (2002) found that the most successful SMEs provide more employee training than average (Kotey & Folker, 2007).

Better organizational performance is also a key intended outcome of training efforts. This relationship may be even more apparent in small firms simply because there are fewer degrees of separation between the lowest level employee and the owner/manager of the firm (Lange et al., 2000). Prior research has found clear relationships between training and performance in SMEs (Carlson, Upton, & Seaman, 2006; Chandler & McEvoy, 2000; de Kok & Uhlaner, 2001; Kotey & Folker, 2007; Litz & Stewart, 2000; Sels et al., 2006; Singh, Garg, & Deshmukh, 2009), including profitability (Cosh, Duncan, & Hughes, 1998; Gamage & Sadoi, 2008) and firm growth (Carlson et al., 2006; Mabey, 2008). That said, these relationships are not always present. For example, Sels et al. (2006) found that training only has an effect on productivity if it is rooted in strategic planning and careful attention to employee needs analysis. Family firms also experience a much weaker relationship between investment in training and organizational performance, perhaps because firms with a family member still involved invest much less heavily in training of employees (Loan-Clarke et al., 1999). Further, research in large firms (Wright et al., 2005) indicates that the relationship between human resources practices and firm performance goes to zero when you control for past performance. This suggests that good performance may drive good human resources as much as the reverse effect. We know of no studies examining the causality among firm performance and investments in different forms of training in SMEs.

Very few studies have tried to further understand the mechanism through which training impacts organizational performance in SMEs. Pajo and colleagues (Pajo, Coetzer, & Guenole, 2010) found evidence that one reason formal training of employees leads to better firm performance is because providing such training increases feelings of perceived organizational support among employees. Such feelings lead to higher job satisfaction and affective commitment, which reduce exit intentions and turnover, both of which influence organizational performance. The positive and strong relationships between organizational commitment to employees and company performance may be even stronger in small businesses than in others (Muse et al., 2005). Sels et al. (2006) also found a causal set of relationships among training and development, employee knowledge and skills, motivation, productivity, and organizational performance. These results confirm prior findings that firms that invest in employee training are likely to have lower turnover, higher productivity, and enhanced financial performance (Chandler & McEvoy, 2000). Another study showed that after receiving training, 70% of employees were more confident and willing to take on more responsibilities within the company, as well as additional training (Devins & Johnson, 2003). Finally, a study of Swedish SMEs found that using a combination of formal and informal training in the organization was the most successful combination for developing greater competence among employees (Kock & Ellström, 2011), which is an important driver of firm performance. Taken together these results suggest that training in SMEs can have substantial positive effects on employees and SME firms.

International Research on Training in Small and Medium Enterprises

The majority of research on training in SMEs done in the last decade has been done in countries outside of the United States. In several countries there seems to be a concerted effort on the part of the government to ensure skill development and lifelong learning among the working population, and they are encouraging firms to invest in such learning for their employees (Kock et al., 2008; Lange et al., 2000; Smith & Whittaker, 1998). Research focused on training and development of employees in SMEs has been conducted in Sweden (Kock et al., 2008), India, China (Singh et al., 2009; Zheng, O'Neill, & Morrison, 2009), the Netherlands (de Kok & Uhlaner, 2001), Spain (Arocena,

Núñez, & Villanueva, 2007), Scotland (Lange et al., 2000), England (Smith & Whittaker, 1998), Australia (Kotey & Slade, 2005), Germany, Norway, and the United Kingdom (Mabey, 2008). Government programs to support and promote competence development in SMEs exist in the European Union (Devins & Johnson, 2003; Kock et al., 2008), China (Singh et al., 2009; Zheng et al., 2009), and India (Singh et al., 2009), among other places. Findings are consistent and strong that employees of SMEs (here in Britain) are part of a "disadvantaged group" that receives less training than they should (Devins & Johnson, 2003; Devins, Johnson, & Sutherland, 2004). The speculation is that small firms find government programs are not tailored to their specific needs and are instead created initially for larger companies and adapted (but not necessarily well) for small firm adoption (Smith & Whittaker, 1998).

Many of the studies done around the world have similar findings that are reported in the earlier sections of this chapter – that size of the firm and whether it is a family business or not are two of the largest influences on the investment of training and development (de Kok & Uhlaner, 2001; Loan-Clarke et al., 1999). Others suggest country-specific differences, such as Singh and colleagues (Singh et al., 2009), who argue that Chinese SMEs give more focus to cost reduction and relationship management than SMEs in other countries do, and in particular, that Chinese adoption of training and development may not mirror a Western strategy due to cultural emphasis on hierarchy, collectivism, and respect for seniority (Cunningham & Rowley, 2007).

Discussion

The key conclusion we can draw from prior research is that SME firms are not homogenous (Kotey & Slade, 2005); they are not all informally organized with correspondingly informal HRM practices (de Kok & Uhlaner, 2001). Instead, specific characteristics of the organization including size and ownership structure (family owned or not) make a difference to the type, content, and extent of training they provide, as do specific characteristics of the owners. The SME population is continuously shifting, with frequent firm entries and exits (Cassell et al., 2002), making future long-term training needs difficult to plan (Smith et al., 2002; Storey, 1994). Because of this uncertainty, employees in small firms have to be multiskilled and able to adapt to changing market and organizational conditions (Lange et al., 2000). Due to the combination of limited resources and particularly limited slack resources in terms of funds to afford training, facilities in which to provide it, or time for employees to disengage from their primary job duties long enough to focus on skill development, training tends to be informal and ad hoc in SMEs.

The barriers for SMEs in formal management development are outlined quite well by Smith and Whittaker (1998), who note these barriers include the lack of qualified senior management, operational and often crisis-led approaches to managing (Watkins, 1982), firms focused on lifestyle rather than growth (Banfield, Jennings, & Beaver, 1996), preference for informal development (Murphy & Young, 1995), and learning by doing (Johnson & Gubbins, 1992; Margerison, 1991). Small firms may also struggle with recognizing the need for training, or may not believe there is any value in training (Banfield et al., 1996; Smith & Whittaker, 1998). We note, however, that these factors depend in large part on firm size and age, as the category of SME includes firms from 0 to 250 employees (and in some studies up to 500 employees), regardless of growth intentions, and there are clear differences in resource slack based on where a firm falls within this size spectrum and based on whether the firm is trying to expand. The smallest organizations are less likely to invest in formal training and when they do they will invest fewer dollars than medium or large firms (Loan-Clarke et al., 1999). However, when firms reach a certain size, which appears to be somewhere between 20 and 50 employees, employee specialization of skills increases (Kotey & Slade, 2005), and the owner has to start delegating more tasks to others (Jennings & Beaver, 1995), including training.

Opportunities for Future Research on Training and Development in Small and Medium Enterprises

Based on our review of the literature discussed in the preceding text, we find several areas ripe for future research, including a strong need for more empirical research, greater emphasis in heterogeneity of human resources practices in SMEs, more comprehensive studies with multiple training and firm variables incorporated, better reflection of labor market conditions surrounding the SMEs, and stronger emphasis on SME owners as decision makers concerning training of employees in their firms. We expand on each in the following text.

First, we simply need more data on training in SMEs. There is a clear mismatch between, on the one hand, the prevalence of small firms in worldwide economies and the reality that effective management of human resources is one of the most important problems faced by SMEs, and, on the other hand, the acute shortage of research on practices used by such firms or their impact on the organization or its employees (Cassell et al., 2002; Chandler & McEvoy, 2000; Williamson, 2001). Despite this gap having been noted repeatedly and for many years, the review done in this chapter, more than 10 years after the calls for more research in this area began, found significantly more studies based outside of the United States rather than within it, and with primarily incremental insights offered into the specific training and development practices, motivations, or outcomes for firms that fall into the SME category. Many (but not all) of the conclusions drawn are based on small samples (12 or 16 firms, e.g.), and we simply need more data on what firms are really doing focused specifically on training of employees. Possibilities for pursuing such research include partnering with the Society for Human Resource Management to utilize their database of firms (including SMEs) and human resources practices, or creating a new large-scale database by partnering with entrepreneurship-focused organizations, such as the Small Business Administration, the Kauffman Foundation, or some other entrepreneurial institute or center.

Second, we note that in addition to heterogeneity of small firms, there is heterogeneity of HRM adoption in small firms (de Kok & Uhlaner, 2001). We need to dig further into heterogeneity of SMEs, not just based on size or overall formalization of HRM, but also based on specific and nuanced practices and organizational leaders' motivations for pursing them, and employee motivations for engaging in them, as well as the outcomes that result, both good and bad, for both the organization and the individual employee. For example, many existing studies of HRM in SMEs measure different aspects of HRM such as training investment, formalized incentive programs, and having written job descriptions, but they then merge these together into one overall measure of HRM formalization. We need a better understanding of why firms invest in some HRM initiatives and not others, and with what effect on employees and the organization. Interestingly, related work has been done in a sample of organizations of all sizes (5 to 6,000 employees) by Toh and colleagues (2008). They found five different bundles of human resources practices that typically go together, where two bundles do not include providing a variety of training methods or evaluating training effectiveness, and three bundles do. Not surprisingly, they found that the cost minimizer and contingent motivator human resources bundles are significantly negatively related to organizational size (meaning smaller organizations are more likely to fall into these categories), and these are the two categories that use human resources bundles that do not include using a variety of training methods/techniques or doing systematic training evaluations.

Third, within the area of training and development we need a deeper understanding of the choices SMEs are making. Just as we know that training outcomes can vary from understanding of material, enjoyment of the training, and ability to apply the material learned on the job, for example, we need to understand why firms choose informal versus formal training for different types of employees, what specific content they are providing in such training, and how employees are utilizing that training within the organization. While one study cannot cover all bases, we need more comprehensive studies that include training methods, content, provider, and impact, along with data on owner characteristics, firm characteristics, and employee characteristics so that rather than drawing conclusions for SMEs as a homogenous body, we can start to better understand the intricacies of the different approaches to training they have, much as the Cunningham and Rowley (2007) study did for HRM in China. In addition to owner demographic characteristics, more sophisticated studies that examine owner goals, mind-set, beliefs, values, and emotions felt for the firm and/or employees, and how these guide choices concerning firm strategy and human resources practices would be novel.

Fourth, there may also be important distinctions in training investment based on the labor markets in which the SME operates. For example, if needed skill sets are readily available in the local market and affordable, then small firms may do better to hire the skills they need, rather than train employees they already have. In contrast, if those skills are either scarce or unaffordable, then training is more important. Lepak and Snell (1999) suggested that where required firm skills are valuable and unique (specialized in the firm), the firm should engage in internal development, including training and career development. Where skills are valuable but not unique, firm should pursue strategy of acquisition (hire the skills you need). Finally, where human resources are low in value, outsourcing the needs or allying with a partner may be the best approach (de Kok & Uhlaner, 2001; Lepak & Snell, 1999). Despite these suggestions from prior research, further empirical examination of such relationships is clearly needed.

Fifth, we noted earlier in the chapter that one distinction between SMEs and larger firms when it comes to training is that in an SME the owner is the key decision maker concerning training, and is also often the provider of informal training. Because it is often the owner of the firm that makes training decisions in SMEs, and because they often do not want employees who know more about technologies and systems than they do, businesses that are owned by highly trained and educated people are much more likely to have employees with greater skill levels (Lange, Ottens, & Taylor, 2000), either because they provide the training and role modeling of those skills themselves, or because they understanding the value of such training and offer employees more opportunities to receive formalized training external to the firm. Research is needed that examines characteristics of the owners of these firms and how these may impact training decisions.

Cautions for Future Research

We want to note three cautions concerning how research on training and development of employees in SMEs should be conducted. First, we need to be cognizant that not all small firms are simply new firms that are destined to grow, and because of this, we should maintain clear definitions of what we mean by small firms and what we mean by new firms. Scholars should be specific as to whether they are studying small firms that are small because they are in the process of becoming larger, and small firms that intend to and likely will remain small.

Second, our review of the literature points out the lack of clear agreement on what we mean by SMEs, which limits our ability to compare and generalize across studies. Not only do scholars not share the same definition of SME based on firms of 200, 250, or even 500 employees as the upper limit, our measurement of number of employees may also not be consistent, as some include full-time employees, and some include all employees regardless of full- or part-time status and temporary contract or permanent employees. We advocate for a greater focus on how many of which specific types of employees SMEs invest in for what types and content of training.

Third, we encourage research that expands the definition of *training* to include different types of informal training, such as socialization, informal learning, mentoring, coaching, and other forms of knowledge sharing, as discussed by Marand and Noe in Chapter 3 in this volume. Although the conclusion often drawn is that SMEs do not engage in training, because some business owners and scholars may not include informal training in their definitions, our conclusion is instead that SMEs are engaging in training but that it is primarily informal in nature. Small firms can support learning of employees in cost-effective ways through greater utilization of different forms of informal training, and more empirical work is needed to examine and evaluate such possibilities.

Conclusion

The need to study the interaction of firm size and HRM practices has long been recognized (Cardon & Stevens, 2004; Heneman et al., 2000; Kotey & Slade, 2005), but the state of the literature has not caught up to this recognized need (Coetzer, 2006; Hill & Stewart, 2000). The research that has been done on training and competence development shows that competence development occurs in a variety of forms and under diverse conditions (Kitching & Blackburn, 2002; Matlay, 1998; Saru, 2007). SMEs clearly differ from large firms in how important they think training is (Kitching, 2008; Kock & Ellström, 2011; Ram, 2000), and in the ways they think about and implement training and development of their employees. Just as there is a need for effective HRM practices in the small firm (Audretsch & Thurik, 2000; 2001), there is also a clear need for further study of such practices as well (de Kok & Uhlaner, 2001). We strongly encourage more in-depth and nuanced examinations of: (1) what SMEs are doing in terms of training their employees; (2) organizational, environmental, and individual characteristics that impact these decisions; and (3) the implications of these T&D choices for their employees and their organizations, both in the short and long term.

References

Arocena, P., Núñez, I., and Villanueva, M. 2007. The effect of enhancing workers' employability on small and medium enterprises: Evidence from Spain. *Small Business Economics* 29: 191–201.

Audretsch, D. B., and Thurik, A. R. 2000. Capitalism and democracy in the 21st century: From the managed to the entrepreneurial economy. *Journal of Evolutionary Economics* 101: 17–34.

Audretsch, D. B., and Thurik, A. R. 2001. What is new about the economy: Sources of growth in the managed and entrepreneurial economies. *Industrial and Corporate Change* 10: 267–315.

Bacon, N., Ackers, P., Storey, J., and Coates, D. 1996. It's a small world: Managing human resources in small businesses. *International Journal of Human Resource Management* 71: 82–100.

Banfield, P., Jennings, P. L., and Beaver, G. 1996. Competence-based training for small firms – An expensive failure? *Long Range Planning* 291: 94–102.

Banks, M. C., Bures, A. L., and Champion, D. L. 1987. Decision making factors in small business: Training and development. *Journal of Small Business Management* 25(1): 19–25.

Barclays Bank. 1994. *Bridging the Skills Gap*. London: Barclays.

Birley, S., Moss, C., and Saunders, P. 1987. Do women entrepreneurs require different training? *American Journal of Small Business* 12(Summer): 27–35.

Booth, A. L., and Snower, D. J., eds., 1990. *Acquiring Skills: Market Failures, Their Symptoms and Policy Responses*. Cambridge: Cambridge University Press.

Brown, J. M. 2014. How important are small businesses to local economies? *Houston Chronicle*. http://smallbusiness.chron.com/important-small-businesses-local-economies-5251.html (accessed May 18, 2017).

Bruderl, J., and Schussler, R. 1990. Organizational mortality: The liabilities of newness and adolescence. *Administrative Science Quarterly* 35: 530–547.

Cannon, T. 1997. Management development and business performance: What do we know and what do we need to know? *Managing the Solution*. London: Management Charter Initiative.

Cardon, M. S., and Stevens, C. E. 2004. Managing human resources in small organizations: What do we know? *Human Resource Management Review* 14(3): 295–323.

Carlson, D. S., Upton, N., and Seaman, S. 2006. The impact of human resource practices and compensation design on performance: An analysis of family-owned SMEs. *Journal of Small Business Management* 44(4): 531–543.

Cassell, C., Nadin, S., Gray, M., and Clegg, C. 2002. Exploring human resource management practices in small and medium sized enterprises. *Personnel Review* 31(5/6): 671–692.

Chandler, G. N., and McEvoy, G. M. 2000. Human resource management, TQM, and firm performance in small and medium-size enterprises. *Entrepreneurship: Theory and Practice* (Fall): 43–57.

Chittenden, F., and Robertson, M. 1994. Small firms and the prospect of recovery: A note on policy. *Small Business and Enterprise Development* 1: 54–60.

Coetzer, A. 2006. Managers as learning facilitators in small manufacturing firms. *Journal of Small Business and Enterprise Development* 133: 351–362.

Cosh, A., Duncan, J., and Hughes, A. 1998. *Investment in Training and Small Firm Growth and Survival: An Empirical Analysis for the UK 1987–95*. London: Department of Education and Employment.

Cromie, S., Stephenson, B., and Montieth, D. 1995. The management of family firms: An empirical investigation. *International Small Business Journal* 13: 11–34.

Cunningham, L. X., and Rowley, C. 2007. Human resource management in Chinese small and medium enterprises. *Personnel Review* 36(3): 415–439.

Curran, J., Blackburn, R., Kitching, J., and North, J. 1997. Small firms and workforce training: Some results, analysis and policy implications from a national survey. In M. Ram, D. Deakins, and D. Smallbone, eds., *Small Firms: Enterprising Futures*, 90–101. London: Paul Chapman Press.

De Kok, J. M. P., and Uhlaner, L. M. 2001. Organization context and human resource management in the small firm. *Small Business Economics* 174: 273–291.

De Kok, J. M. P., Uhlaner, L. M., and Thurik, A. R. 2006. Professional HRM practices in family owned-managed enterprises. *Journal of Small Business Management* 44(3): 441–460.

Devins, D., and Johnson, S. 2003. Training and development activities in SMEs: Some findings from an evaluation of the ESF Objective 4 Programme in Britain. *International Small Business Journal* 21(2): 205–218.

Devins, D., Johnson, S., and Sutherland, J. 2004. Employer characteristics and employee training outcomes in UK SMEs: A multivariate analysis. *Journal of Small Business and Enterprise Development* 11(4): 449–457.

Ekpe, I., Razak, R. C., and Mat, N. B. 2013. The performance of female entrepreneurs: Credit, training and moderating effect of attitude towards risk taking. *International Journal of Management* 303: 10–13.

English, J. 2001. *How to Organize and Operate a Small Business.* Sydney, Australia: Allen and Unwin.

European Commission, 2000. *The quality of vocational training: Proposal for Action.* Brussels: Directorate General for Training and Education.

Fayolle, A., Gailly, B., and Lassas-Clerc, N. 2006. Assessing the impact of entrepreneurship education programmes: A new methodology. *Journal of European Industrial Training* 30(9): 701–720.

Gamage, A., and Sadoi, Y. 2008. Determinants of training and development practices in SMEs: A case of Japanese manufacturing firms. *Sri Lankan Journal of Human Resource Management* 21: 46–61.

Hannan, M. T., and Freeman, J. 1984. The population ecology of organizations. *American Sociological Review* 49: 149–164.

Harris, R. I. D., Reid, R. S., and McAdam, R. 2004. Employee involvement in family and non-family owned businesses in Great Britain. *International Journal of Entrepreneurial Behavior and Research* 10(1/2): 49–58.

Heneman, R. L., Tansky, J. W., and Camp, S. M. 2000. Human resource management practices in small and medium-sized enterprises: Unanswered questions and future research perspectives. *Entrepreneurship: Theory and Practice* 25: 11–27.

Hill, R., and Stewart, J. 2000. Human resource development in small organizations. *Journal of European Industrial Training* 24(2/4): 105–117.

Jennings, P. L., and Beaver, G. 1995. The managerial dimension of small business failure. *Briefings in Entrepreneurial Finance* 44: 185–200.

Johnson, S., and Gubbins, A. 1992. Training in small and medium enterprises: Lessons from North Yorkshire. In K. Caley, E. Chell, F. Chittenden, and C. Mason, eds., *Small Enterprise Development: Policy and Practice in Action*, 28–42. London: Paul Chapman Publishing.

Jones, F. F., Morris, M. H., and Rockmore, W. 1995. HR practices that promote entrepreneurship. *HR Magazine* 40(5): 86–88.

Kao, R. W. Y., and Chiang, L. C. 2000. Training and development of women entrepreneurs in China: A conceptual model. *Journal of Enterprising Culture* 81: 85–102.

Keep, E., and Mayhew, K. 1996. Evaluating assumptions that underline training policy. In A. L. Booth and D. J. Snower, eds., *Acquiring Skills: Market Failures, Their Symptoms and Policy Responses*, 303–334. London: Centre for Economic Policy Research.

Kirby, D. 1990. Management education and small business development: An exploratory study of small firms in the UK. *Journal of Small Business Management* 28: 78–87.

Kitching, J. 2008. Rethinking UK small employers' skill policies and the role of workplace learning. *International Journal of Training and Development* 12(2): 100–120.

Kitching, J., and Blackburn, R. 2002. *The Nature of Training and Motivation to Train in Small Firms*. London: Kingston University Small Business Research Centre.

Koch, M. J., and McGrath, R. G. 1996. Improving labor productivity: Human resource management policies do matter. *Strategic Management Journal* 17: 335–354.

Kock, H., and Ellström, P. E. 2011. Formal and integrated strategies for competence development in SMEs. *Journal of European Industrial Training* 35(1): 71–88.

Kock, H., Gill, A., and Ellström, P. E. 2008. Why do small enterprises participate in a programme for competence development? *Journal of Workplace Learning* 20(3): 181–194.

Kotey, B., and Folker, C. 2007. Employee training in SMEs: Effect of size and firm type–family and nonfamily. *Journal of Small Business Management* 45(2): 214–238.

Kotey, B., and Sheridan, A. 2004. Changing HRM practices with firm size. *International Journal of Small Business and Enterprise Development* 11(4): 474–485.

Kotey, B., and Slade, P. 2005. Formal human resource management practices in small growing firms. *Journal of Small Business Management* 43(1): 16–40.

Lange, T., Ottens, M., and Taylor, A. 2000. SMEs and barriers to skills development: A Scottish perspective. *Journal of European Industrial Training* 24(1): 5–11.

Lans, T., Wesselink, R., Biemans, H. J. A., and Mulder, M. 2004. Work-related lifelong learning for entrepreneurs in the agri-food section. *International Journal of Training and Development* 8: 73–89.

Lepak, D. P., and Snell, S. A. 1999. The human resource architecture: Toward a theory of human capital allocation and development. *Academy of Management Review* 24(1): 31–48.

Leung, A., Foo, M. Der, and Chaturvedi, S. 2013. Imprinting effects of founding core teams on HR values in new ventures. *Entrepreneurship Theory and Practice* 37(1): 87–106.

Litz, R. A., and Stewart, A. C. 2000. Trade-name franchise membership as a human resource management strategy: Does buying group training deliver "true value" for small retailers? *Entrepreneurship: Theory and Practice* 25(1): 125–135.

Loan-Clarke, J., Boocock, G., Smith, A. J., and Whittaker, J. 1999. Investment in management training and development by small businesses. *Employee Relations* 21(3): 296–310.

Mabey, C. 2008. Management development and firm performance in Germany, Norway, Spain and the UK. *Journal of International Business Studies* 39(8): 1327–1342.

Margerison, C. 1991. Adding value through management. *Target Management Development Review* 8(3): 13–19.

Marlow, S., and Patton, D. 1993. Managing the employment relationship in the small firm: Possibilities for human resource management. *International Small Business Journal* 11(4): 57–64.

Matlay, H. 1998. The paradox of training in the small business sector of the British economy. *Journal of Vocational Education and Training* 49(4): 573–589.

Murphy, J., and Young, J. 1995. Marketing development and small business: Exploring emergent issues. *Management Learning* 26(3): 319–330.

Muse, L. a., Rutherford, M. W., Oswald, S. L., and Raymond, J. E. 2005. Commitment to employees: Does it help or hinder small business performance? *Small Business Economics* 24(2): 97–111.

Nagesh, P., and Murthy, M. 2008. The effectiveness of women entrepreneurship training program: a case study. *The Icfai University Journal of Entrepreneurship Development* 3: 24–40.

Notebloom, B. 1993. Firm size effects on transaction costs. *Small Business Economics* 5: 283–295.

Pajo, K., Coetzer, A., and Guenole, N. 2010. Formal development opportunities and withdrawal behaviors by employees in small and medium-sized enterprises. *Journal of Small Business Management* 48(3): 281–301.

Premalatha, U. M. 2010. An empirical study on the impact of training and development on women entrepreneurs in Karnataka. *The IUP Journal of Soft Skills* 4(3): 49–64.

Ram, M. 2000. Investors in people in small firms: Case study evidence from the business services sector. *Personnel Review* 29(1): 69–91.

Ranger-Moore, J. 1997. Bigger may be better, but is older wiser? Organizational age and size in the New York life insurance industry. *American Sociological Review* 62: 903–920.

Reid, R. S., and Harris, R. I. D. 2002. The determinants of training in SMEs in Northern Ireland. *Education and Training* 44(8): 443–450.

Reid, S. 1987. Designing management education and training programs for service firm entrepreneurs. *Journal of Small Business Management* 25(1): 51–60.

Roberts, I., Sawbridge, D., and Bamber, G. 1992. Employee relations in small firms. In B. A. Towers, ed., *Handbook of Industrial Relations Practice*, 240–257. London: Kogan.

Ross, K. 1993. Training and evaluation in SMEs: Manufacturing enterprises in the West Midlands. *Local Economy* 8(2): 143–154.

Saru, E. 2007. Organisational learning and HRD: How appropriate are they for small firms? *Journal of European Industrial Training* 31(1): 36–51.

Sels, L., De Winne, S., Delmotte, J., Maes, J., Faems, D., and Forrier, A. 2006. Linking HRM and small business performance: An examination of the impact of HRM intensity on the productivity and financial performance of small businesses. *Small Business Economics* 26(1): 83–101.

Singh, R. K., Garg, S. K., and Deshmukh, S. G. 2009. The competitiveness of SMEs in a globalized economy. *Management Research Review* 33(1): 54–65.

Sirmon, D. G., and Hitt, M. A. 1992. Managing resources: Linking unique resources, management, and wealth creation in family firms. *Entrepreneurship: Theory and Practice* 27(4): 339–358.

Smith, A. J., and Whittaker, J. 1998. Management development in SMEs: What needs to be done? *Small Business and Enterprise Development* 5(2): 176–185.

Smith, A. J., Boocock, G., Loan-Clarke, J., and Whittaker, J. 2002. IIP and SMEs: Awareness, benefits and barriers. *Personnel Review* 31(1): 62–85.

Solomon, G. T., Duffy, S., and Tarabishy, A. 2002. The state of entrepreneurship education in the United States: A nationwide survey and analysis. *International Journal of Entrepreneurship Education* 11: 1–21.

Stinchcombe, A. L. 1965. Social structure and organizations. In J. G. March, ed., *Handbook of Organizations*, 142–193. Chicago: Rand McNally.

Storey, D. J. 1994. Understanding the small business sector. CENGAGE Learning EMEA. http://sro.sussex.ac.uk/18241 (accessed May 18, 2017).

Storey, D. J., and Westhead, P. 1997. Management training in small firms: A case of market failure? *Human Resource Management Journal* 7(2): 61–71.

Timmons, J. A. 1999. *New Venture Creation: Entrepreneurship for the 21st Century*. New York: Irwin McGraw-Hill.

Toh, S., Morgeson, F. P., and Campion, M. A. 2008. Human resource configurations: Investigating fit with the organizational context. *Journal of Applied Psychology* 93(4): 864–882.

Ulrich, T. A., and Cole, G. S. 1987. Toward more effective training of future entrepreneurs. *Journal of Small Business Management*, 25(4): 32–39.

Wagner, J. 1997. Firm size and job quality: A survey of the evidence from Germany. *Small Business Economics* 9: 411–425.

Watkins, D. 1982. Management development and the owner/manager. *Small Business Research*, 193–215.

Westhead, P., and Storey, D. J. 1996. Management training and small firm performance: Why is the link so weak? *International Small Business Journal* 14: 13–24.

Williamson, I. O. 2001. Employer legitimacy and recruitment success in small business. *Entrepreneurship: Theory and Practice* 26(Fall): 27–42.

Wong, C., Marshall, J. N., Alderman, N., and Thwaites, A. 1997. Management training in small and medium-sized enterprises: Methodological and conceptual issues. *The International Journal of Human Resource Management* 8(1): 44–65.

Wright, P. M., Gardner, T. M., Moynihan, L. M, and Allen, M. R. 2005. The relationship between HR practices and firm performance: Examining causal order. *Personnel Psychology* 58: 409–446.

Zheng, C., O'Neill, G., and Morrison, M. 2009. Enhancing Chinese SME performance through innovative HR practices. *Personnel Review* 38(2): 175–194.

17 Team Training

Knowing Much, but Needing to Know Much More

Erich C. Dierdorff and J. Kemp Ellington

Teams have become an increasingly preferred work arrangement across a wide variety of industries (Bell, 2007; Devine et al., 1999; Salas, Stagl, & Burke, 2004). The effective deployment of work teams is also recognized as a high-performance work practice, with meta-analytic evidence demonstrating positive but modest relationships with multiple organizational outcomes, including financial success, productivity, and growth (Combs et al., 2006). Of course, the effective deployment of teams requires that those teams are indeed well constructed and highly functioning. That is, the use of teams alone does not make a high-performance work practice per se, but rather the positive effect occurs when the proper systems supporting the formation and management of teams are in place. Toward this end, an enormous body of literature has accrued on how to develop successful teams (Aguinis & Kraiger, 2009; Ilgen et al., 2005; Mathieu et al., 2008; Salas, et al., 2008).

Team training is one of the critical elements promoting team effectiveness. In general, team training refers to a systematic "set of tools and methods that, in combination with required competencies and training objectives, form an instructional strategy" (Salas & Cannon-Bowers, 1997: 254). Although a wide variety of tools and methods are often brought to bear in team training (Salas & Cannon-Bowers, 1997), the ultimate instructional goal of any team training effort is to inculcate a set of learning outcomes that underlie team functioning. Scholars typically separate team training from team building (Tannenbaum, Beard, & Salas, 1992), where team training consists of systematic and formal instruction aimed at improving specific competencies relevant to the team's tasks while team building involves less systematic interventions focused on much broader issues (e.g., trust building) that are not directly linked to the team's immediate tasks (Klein et al., 2009; Salas et al., 1999). The learning outcomes of team training more specifically span cognitive, behavioral, and affective outcomes that support effective team processes and performance (Ellis et al., 2005; Rapp & Mathieu, 2007). As examples, team training often seeks to increase situational awareness and shared mental models (cognitive outcomes), promote cooperation and coordination (behavioral outcomes), and foster team cohesion and efficacy (affective outcomes).

Team training has been the focus of substantial empirical research, especially over the past two decades. Results from this body of work have been generally favorable, with the evidence collectively indicating that team training indeed promotes effective team functioning. For instance, meta-analysis results have suggested that approximately one-fifth of the variance in team performance can be accounted for by team training interventions (Salas et al., 2008). Such supportive findings may make one wonder whether the field of team training needs additional scholarship. That is, with such convincing evidence that team training "works," what else remains to be investigated?

We believe, as do others (e.g., Salas & Gorman, 2010), that there are several critical needs remaining to be addressed by team training scholarship, and that it would be regrettable to be complacent. With this in mind, the primary goal of this chapter is to shift the conversation from "does team training work?," to questions of "why and when does team training work?" This shift entails moving scholarship from a training evaluation mind-set – one that emphasizes measuring the attainment or change in knowledge, skill, or attitudes as a function of a training intervention – to a training effectiveness perspective, where emphasis is on ascertaining the various factors that influence learning during training and the transfer of trained competencies to other settings (Aguinis & Kraiger, 2009).

To accomplish this goal, we organize the chapter in three broad sections. First, we review empirical literature to provide a foundation from which to discuss what is reasonably known and what remains to be understood regarding team training. Because there have been several previous qualitative and quantitative reviews of team training (Denson, 1981; Dyer, 1984; Salas, Nichols, & Driskell, 2007; Salas et al., 2004), our review begins with a recent meta-analysis by Salas et al. (2008). We also restrict our review to research that directly examines team training, excluding studies that more generally examine team performance or team learning but do not directly test an instructional strategy. Next, we discuss several broader workplace trends and forces that amplify the need to expand team training scholarship. Finally, we present three areas that we feel are particularly beneficial for future research to address in terms of both the practice and science of team training.

What We Know About Team Training

The existing knowledge base on team training is substantial, providing guidance as to the effectiveness of team training interventions for diverse team-level outcomes. Salas et al. (2008) conducted a comprehensive quantitative integration of this literature, incorporating empirical studies from university, military, business, aviation, and medical domains. Their study confirms that, overall, team training "works" – with a moderate, positive effect across all outcomes (estimated true correlation of $\rho = .34$, $k = 52$). Regarding specific types of team-level criteria, previous research has examined outcomes that are consistent with taxonomies of learning outcomes (Kraiger, Ford, & Salas, 1993). Table 17.1 lists the types of outcomes common to team training, and includes illustrative examples of each type. Examining these specific criteria separately suggests that team training has a moderate, positive effect on cognitive ($\rho = .42$,

Table 17.1 *Examples of team training outcomes*

Outcome Type	Illustrative Examples	k	ρ
Cognitive	Collective knowledge, decision-making strategies, situational awareness, shared mental models, transactive memory, role clarity	12	.42
Affective	Interpersonal trust, team efficacy, group cohesion, commitment to team, perceived effectiveness of team processes	16	.35
Behavioral	Communication, collaborative problem solving, coordination, cooperation, assertiveness	25	.44
Performance	Quantity, quality, accuracy, efficiency, effectiveness	40	.39

Note. Number of effect sizes (k) and population estimates (ρ) from Salas et al. (2008).

$k = 12$), affective ($\rho = .35$, $k = 16$), behavioral or process ($\rho = .44$, $k = 25$), and performance outcomes ($\rho = .39$, $k = 40$; Salas et al., 2008). Again, these findings indicate that team training is an effective intervention for improving a variety of outcomes important for team functioning.

In practice, team training can also include a range of content, strategies, and team characteristics. Fortunately, the existing literature is also informative about which factors influence the consequences of team training. First of all, broadly speaking, team training typically focuses on improving the knowledge and skill necessary to perform the tasks required of the team (i.e., task work), the knowledge and skill required to work together as a team (i.e., teamwork), or some combination of both (Salas et al., 1992). Salas et al. (2008) examined the extent to which this training content moderates the effectiveness of team training, and found that task work and teamwork training (as well as a combination of the two) were positively associated with cognitive (task work, $\rho = .30$, $k = 4$; teamwork, $\rho = .52$, $k = 2$; mixed, $\rho = .51$, $k = 6$), affective (task work, $\rho = .11$, $k = 1$; teamwork, $\rho = .41$, $k = 11$; mixed, $\rho = .36$, $k = 4$), behavior/process (task work, $\rho = .28$, $k = 3$; teamwork, $\rho = .44$, $k = 13$; mixed, $\rho = .56$, $k = 9$), and performance outcomes (task work, $\rho = .35$, $k = 6$; teamwork, $\rho = .38$, $k = 17$; mixed, $\rho = .40$, $k = 17$). Though the authors suggest caution in interpreting the results due to a low number of effect sizes, teamwork and mixed content team training were associated with more favorable affective and behavioral/process outcomes than task work training.

Beyond this broad distinction of focusing on task work versus teamwork, there are also numerous specific strategies that have been developed to train teams to function and perform more effectively (see Table 17.2 for illustrative examples of team training strategies). Although Salas et al. (2008) were able to examine 10 different team training strategies, their study indicated that the majority of these approaches have not been sufficiently investigated. The two strategies that have been examined more extensively include coordination training/crew resource management (CRM; $\rho = .47$, $k = 33$) and cross-training ($\rho = .44$, $k = 14$), both of which had moderate, positive effects on outcomes.

Table 17.2 *Examples of team training tactics*

Tactic	Common Goals or Elements
Assertiveness Training	Developing strategies that support initiating communication and proactive problem-solving relevant to the team goals and tasks
Communication Training	Fostering awareness of different communication forms, improving communication efficiency, increasing communication quality and effectiveness in the team
Crew Resource Management	Enhancing situational awareness and group-based decision making, developing capacities to conduct action briefings, applying conflict-resolution procedures, avoiding of cognitive errors, and so forth
Cross-training	Developing within-team capacities to understand and perform the tasks and responsibilities of other team members in the team
Task Delegation Training	Developing knowledge about the functions, roles, responsibilities, and expectations of all team members
Self-correction (team dimension) Training	Developing team debriefing strategies that involve effectively diagnosing performance problems and generating effective solutions
Team Adaptation and Coordination Training	Recognizing and utilizing available resources, such as people, information, and technology; enhancing communication, coordination and cooperation among team members
Simulation-Based Team Training	Developing teamwork competencies (e.g., cooperation, coordination mental models) while learning or demonstrating technical skills in settings that mimic real-world demands and tasks

However, it is worth noting that a previous meta-analysis focusing exclusively on intact teams by Salas, Nichols, and Driskell (2007) found that the extent to which cross-training was employed was not predictive of team training effectiveness, therefore research is needed to better understand the conditions under which this approach is effective.

Finally, the Salas et al. (2008) meta-analysis also examined the moderating effect of two different characteristics of teams. First, intact teams with a shared history whose membership was more stable fared more favorably on certain outcomes than ad hoc teams whose members were typically strangers brought together for a short term. This result was particularly true for performance outcomes (intact, $\rho = .54$, $k = 8$; ad hoc, $\rho = .38$, $k = 32$), but less so for others such as behavior/process outcomes (intact, $\rho = .48$, $k = 8$; ad hoc, $\rho = .44$, $k = 17$). And second, there was also some evidence that team size may moderate the outcomes of team training. The authors categorized teams as small (2 members), medium (3–4 members), and large (5+ members), and found that team performance improved most in large teams (small, $\rho = .39$, $k = 12$; medium, $\rho = .34$, $k = 15$; large, $\rho = .50$, $k = 13$), whereas behavioral processes improved most for small teams (small, $\rho = .59$, $k = 10$; medium, $\rho = .33$, $k = 7$; large, $\rho = .49$, $k = 8$).

Researchers have made further contributions to the team training literature since the quantitative integration by Salas et al. (2008), which includes two review articles. The first review was a quantitative synthesis by Delise et al. (2011). These authors conducted a meta-analysis of team training, which included between subjects, within subjects, and crossed designs. Their findings largely replicated those of Salas et al. (2008), however, Delise et al. extended the previous meta-analysis by further dividing performance outcomes into subjective (e.g., team member or expert perception of performance) and objective task-based skill (e.g., points earned in a simulation, accuracy). Like the Salas et al. meta-analysis, team training was again positively related with cognitive ($d = 1.37$, $k = 6$), affective ($d = .80$, $k = 7$), and behavior/process ($d = .64$, $k = 9$) outcomes. In addition, Delise et al. found that team training was also positively related to both subjective ($d = .88$, $k = 6$) and objective ($d = .76$, $k = 13$) task-based skill outcomes. Although the effect sizes varied to a degree across outcomes, team training did not have a significantly stronger association with any of the specific team effectiveness criteria.

The second review article by Weaver, Dy, and Rosen (2013) was a qualitative synthesis of the team training literature, focusing specifically on research in the medical and health care domain. This review indicates that many team-training strategies are being implemented in health care settings, including coordination training and cross-training, but other approaches are also being employed such as assertiveness training, error management training, and guided team self-correction. Notably, many of the studies in the medical and health care domain reviewed by Weaver et al. not only replicate the previous findings regarding outcomes such as teamwork processes, but also show team training to have positive effects on more specific criteria such as clinical care processes and patient outcomes.

Regarding recent primary studies in team training, scholars have continued to examine different team training strategies. For example, CRM training, which was originally developed and largely applied in the aviation industry, has seen continued application in the health care domain (e.g., Clay-Williams et al., 2013) and has also been recently applied in the automotive industry (Marquardt, Robelski, & Hoeger, 2010). Results from these studies support the generalizability of CRM training, showing positive effects on teamwork knowledge, behavior, and attitudes. Cross-training tactics have also seen continued investigation (e.g., Ellis & Pearsall, 2011; Espevik, Johnsen, & Eid, 2011; Gorman, Cooke, & Amazeen, 2010). For instance, Ellis and Pearsall (2011) found that the impact of cross-training was moderated by job demands, such that cross-training was less influential when demands were low, but resulted in higher mental model accuracy, greater information allocation, and less tension when job demands were high. These authors suggest that such results indicate that cross-training may act as a buffer to the negative effects of job demands in teams. Finally, although few, some studies have examined newer team training tactics. For example, a study by Rentsch et al. (2010) experimentally tested and found support for the effects of using an information board to facilitate team knowledge building in problem-solving teams.

Recent research in team training has continued to expand to include teams that collaborate virtually. In both national and multinational organizations employees are often geographically dispersed; however, various communication and collaboration technologies (e.g., e-mail, teleconferencing, videoconferencing, discussion boards, shared online work spaces) allow employees to work interdependently as a team to accomplish common goals. Although earlier work (e.g., Kirkman et al., 2006; Rosen, Furst, & Blackburn, 2006) began to build the foundation for research on training distributed teams, since 2008 the research in the domain is sparse. Two notable exceptions are studies from Martinez-Moreno et al. (2014) and Rentsch et al. (2014). Martinez-Moreno et al. examined the conflict-management strategies of trained versus untrained synchronous computer-mediated communication teams. These authors specifically analyzed the content of the teams' chat communications and found results suggesting that virtual teams that received self-guided training to improve team functioning used more functional and less dysfunctional conflict-management strategies than teams that did not receive training. Noting the difficulties distributed teams often face in building team knowledge, Rentsch et al. examined the impact of a team training strategy targeting information sharing (previously developed with face-to-face teams by Rentsch et al., 2010). Teams communicated using chat and an information board in the training group in completing a problem-solving task. Results showed that, compared to untrained teams, those receiving training shared more unique information, showed greater knowledge transfer among team members, developed more congruent task schemas, and generated higher quality problem solutions.

Though much of the research on team training to date has focused primarily on the previously mentioned team-level outcomes, recent research has begun to examine factors that shape individual learning and acquisition of team training content. For example, we examined relationships between individual goal orientations and self-regulated learning (self-efficacy and metacognition) in a simulation-based team training context (Dierdorff & Ellington, 2012). We found that these preferences for different types of goals were predictive of the growth and posttraining level of individual self-regulation. Furthermore, individual goal orientations interacted with the average goal preferences of the team, suggesting that team composition shapes the extent to which members actively monitor and manage their own learning during team training. For instance, when individuals high in learning goal orientation were in teams of high average learning goal orientation across members, these individuals engaged in greater rates of metacognition, whereas when individuals high in avoid-performance goal orientation were within teams of high average avoid-performance goal orientation they engaged in lower rates of metacognition. Moreover, average levels of metacognition among a team's members positively predicted team-level cooperation and decision-making quality. In another study, we also focused on individual learning in team training, and found that trainees who more actively self-regulated their learning during team training were subsequently better able to individually demonstrate their declarative and procedural knowledge after the team training event (Ellington & Dierdorff, 2014). Interestingly, this relationship was amplified for those who were trained in teams that performed well in team training (both declarative and procedural knowledge), and for those in teams with high cooperation quality during the team training (procedural knowledge). From a practical standpoint, this suggests that trainers may need to provide additional instruction to trainees in poorer performing, less cooperative teams, or take steps to ensure trainees have an opportunity to learn in a highly cooperative context. Importantly, these two studies highlight the interplay between individuals and the team context in shaping learning during team training.

Trends Amplifying the Need for Team Training Research

As mentioned at the beginning of this chapter, teams continue to be a pervasive approach to structuring work in today's organizations and team training has been a key way organizations facilitate the performance of their teams. Yet, the nature of team-based work has evolved in several substantive ways since the dawn of this millennium, and we posit that team training research has not necessarily kept pace with this evolution. Tannenbaum et al. (2012) recently summarized the evolving nature of teams by noting: "Today, most teams operate in a more fluid, dynamic, and complex environment than in the past. They change and adapt more frequently, operate with looser boundaries, and are more likely to be geographically dispersed. They experience more competing demands, are likely to be more heterogeneous in composition, and rely more on technology than did teams in prior generations" (3).

Trends such as these hold multiple implications for expanding research on team training. For example, the increased prevalence of virtual and distributed teams necessitates different forms of teamwork behavior than traditional teams, and presents more pronounced challenges that are due to team members being temporally and geographically separated from one another (Salas & Gorman, 2010; Stagl et al., 2007). One obvious difference for these kinds of teams is the increased reliance on technology-mediated communication to accomplish team tasks. Another difference is the extent to which teams are culturally diverse, especially with respect to globally distributed teams. Moreover, as Gibson et al. (2014) recently pointed out, both geographic dispersion and technology-mediated communication frequently intersect when we consider the rising use of global virtual teams in today's world of work.

With respect to virtual teams, scholars have argued that it is important to recognize that such teams vary in their level of virtuality, where virtuality is defined as the extent to which team members use technology to execute team processes and coordinate and synchronize team member interactions, as well as the overall amount of informational value provided by the technology (Kirkman & Mathieu, 2005). Meta-analytic research by Mesmer-Magnus and colleagues (2011) supports the idea of varying levels of virtuality and further reveals that team virtuality reduces the overall openness of information sharing, which is even more important for virtual teams compared to face-to-face teams. These authors also found that particularly high levels of virtuality can hinder information sharing in general among team members. Regarding compositional heterogeneity in teams, research that examines diversity along a host of dimensions (e.g., functional, demographic, cultural) has generally shown that, at least in earlier stages of a team's life cycle, more diverse teams have more process difficulties and lower team performance (Gibson et al., 2014). Results from meta-analysis further show that the negative effects of cultural diversity are amplified in larger teams with higher tenure and more task complexity (Stahl et al., 2010).

Still other research finds that when virtuality and cultural diversity intersect in teams, unique challenges to effective team processes and performance are created (Gibson et al., 2014). For example, Glickson and Erez (2013) found that in virtual teams using computer-mediated communication, cultural diversity shaped how emotion displays were interpreted, with members in more culturally diverse teams viewing positive emotions as more appropriate and negative emotions as more inappropriate than members in more homogenous virtual teams. Other evidence indicates that levels of technical experience using electronic collaboration tools among team members affect relationships between diversity and creativity, with larger differences in technical experience exacerbating the negative effects of within-team nationality differences on levels of creativity (Martins & Shalley, 2011).

Team tenure is now often short-lived, which results in much more fluidity of team membership (Tannenbaum et al., 2012). Some estimates suggest that 78% of individuals spend two years or less with a single work team (Thompson, 2008). Still further, team-related knowledge and skills are not always trained in intact teams, but rather delivered to individuals directly or in temporary teams as part of more general leadership development programs (Salas et al., 2012). As an example, one of the central executive development programs at General Electric's corporate university instructs team-related competencies while individuals are in temporary teams completing various exercises and simulations over the course of two weeks. Participants then rejoin their existing teams at work and must not only generalize what they have learned to the new setting, but also coach others on their teams to use the trained behaviors.

All of these trends exemplify shifts in the nature of team functioning as well as the context in which teams function. Thus, these trends have implications for team training research and practice because when we train teams, we do so to facilitate a collective capacity for effective performance. The future of team training research therefore requires that we confront the challenges of distance, diversity, and dynamic membership. This also emphasizes the importance and value of a training effectiveness approach that again extends team training research beyond "it works" to a deeper understanding of when and why it works, as well as how these trends are shaping team training outcomes.

Looking to the Future of Team Training Research

As our review of the recent literature revealed, empirical work since the Salas et al. (2008) meta-analysis has continued to find supportive evaluation results for team training. In addition, this research has begun to explore factors that amplify or attenuate the effectiveness of team training on both team-level and individual-level outcomes. Although one conclusion from the substantial body of empirical support might be that the scholarship on team training is rather mature and thus few important questions remain to be studied, we believe that this is not the case considering the trends discussed in the preceding text. Toward this end, we see at least three key areas for future research to address to move forward the current body of literature on team training, both in terms of scholarship and practice.

Linking Different Tactics to Different Outcomes

Regarding instructional interventions, more research is needed to gain a deeper understanding of how different team training techniques ultimately come to influence different kinds of team outcomes. Although the importance of such research has been recognized for some time (see Salas et al., 2007, e.g.), the body of work in this area remains small. There are several intriguing and practical questions that can be examined. For instance, while we know that a variety of team training tactics are employed and are generally effective (Salas et al., 2008), there is insufficient research to reveal which tactics or instructional components are *most or least* effective across the different learning outcomes of team training (i.e., cognitive, behavioral, and affective outcomes). Some common team training components would appear to have obvious relevance for inculcating certain outcomes, such as critical thinking and team knowledge components facilitating cognitive outcomes like decision-making strategies and team cognition; however, other components or tactics do not seem to hold obvious connections, such as self-guided training, stress training, and communication training, which could impact multiple types of outcomes. Moreover, several other tactics and components have been suggested as potentially valuable for team learning, but have yet to be empirically examined. For example, process mapping has been proposed as a technique to foster shared mental models for problem-solving teams (see Fiore & Schooler, 2004). This material is summarized in Table 17.3. Research that investigates the effectiveness of different components of team training, both in isolation and in combination, across different types of team training outcomes would be a welcome addition to the literature.

Uncovering the linkages between tactics and outcomes is paramount to team training effectiveness. It is axiomatic to state that theories from the team learning literature *should* directly inform team training. This literature has in fact provided many pertinent factors for understanding how teams function, such as team efficacy, shared mental models, and psychological safety, but at the same time empirical examinations of how to best *train* these key factors

Table 17.3 *Summary of areas for future team training research*

Linking Different Tactics to Different Outcomes	
Aligning instructional components with outcomes	• Which instructional components are most/least effective for the variety of learning outcomes used in team training?
Closing the theoretical-empirical gap in team learning	• What are the most effective techniques to train the factors identified in team learning theory (e.g., team efficacy, shared mental models, and psychological safety, collective knowledge)?
Applying established individual-level training techniques	• Are individual-level training techniques supported by research also effective for team training (e.g., behavioral modeling, error management)? • What is the best approach for integrating these individual-level methods into team training design? • How can self-regulation tactics be best integrated into team training to facilitate both individual-level and team-level outcomes?
Examining newer individual-level training techniques	• Do mindfulness interventions in team training promote more effective team outcomes? How does mindfulness shape the relational and social processes required for team functioning? Can mindfulness facilitate other team-level outcomes (e.g., situational awareness, team cognition, coordination)? • Do process-mapping techniques facilitate team-level outcomes such as collective knowledge, error detection, team mental models, and so forth? What are the most effective approaches to design process-mapping techniques into team training?
Designing team training from a process perspective	• When should specific interventions be introduced into team training to maximize effectiveness (e.g., early or late in training, posttraining)? • How should particular team training components be sequenced to maximize individual-level and team-level learning? • Which instructional approaches are most effective for team processes such as transition, action, and interpersonal processes?
Moving Beyond the Intervention Environment	
Building evidence for team training transfer	• To what extent does team training transfer to the work environment (i.e., near, far, novel transfer)? Does transfer vary across different team training techniques? • What are the best methods to promote the maintenance and generalization of team learning in the work environment? • Are the same factors that predict transfer in general training research also important for team training transfer? • Are team-level analogs such as team efficacy and/or team compositional variables such as motivation or social support important for team training transfer?
Extending measurements of team training transfer	• How do different measures depict and assess team training transfer (e.g., cycle times, time-to-proficiency)? • What factors shape team performance trajectories over time ("transfer curves") after team training events?

Placing team training in context	• How does team training fit within the broader multiteam systems that characterize many organizations?
	• Are factors such as superordinate goals, between-team interdependence, shared expertise, and task redundancy relevant for team training transfer?
	• Do social network ties between teams promote vertical transfer of team training across an organization?
	• How well does team training generalize when some members move to other teams that have not received formal training?
	• When must we train the entire intact team?
	• How can we best train multiple teams during team training and how does this learning impact the broader multiteam system?

Meeting the New Reality of Teams

Addressing the fluidity of team membership	• To what extent is team training transportable from team to team?
	• Under what circumstances is it beneficial to train only central members of a team or those with certain strategic roles? What team-level factors influence the individual-level acquisition and transfer of team training content?
	• What dynamic team composition characteristics are influential?
Investigating informal learning in teams	• What factors are associated with informal learning in teams?
	• How does team regulation shape the emergence of informal team learning?
	• How can individual-level informal learning be transported to other teams?
Using technology to facilitate team training	• What aspects can collaborative technology effectively replace when compared to face-to-face and interpersonally oriented team training?
	• How can organizations train the use of technology in teams and the factors that facilitate the benefits of this technology?
	• How can simulation-based team training be used to facilitate both task work and teamwork?
Expanding research to geographically dispersed and virtual teams	• How effective are conventional team training techniques when used in virtual environments? What factors shape this effectiveness?
	• Are the knowledge and skills that reflect cooperation and coordination different in face-to-face versus virtual team training?
	• To what extent does the virtuality of teams impact the effectiveness of specific team training techniques?
	• How can the factors that promote distributed/virtual team performance (e.g., transactive memory systems) be best included in team training?
	• How do aspects of diversity found in team research (e.g., cultural, functional, demographic) affect learning processes during team training?
	• How can team training best address the short-term difficulties (e.g., increased conflict, lower performance, etc.) that often face heterogeneous teams?

remains largely unspecified. Empirical evidence that points to the relative effectiveness of specific tactics across different learning outcomes would hold substantial utility for team training practitioners too, as such data could directly inform instructional designs to allow for efficient design and delivery as well as increased instructional precision directed toward desired learning outcomes. Along these lines, future research must first seek to close the gap between theoretical and empirical scholarship in the broader team performance literature. Literally dozens of theoretical models of team functioning exist, yet few have been empirically tested (see Salas & Gorman, 2010). However well developed, these theoretical models often stop short of prescribing the kinds of methods one could use to actually influence the essential variables that are identified as key mechanisms in the proposed models. Not only does this create quite a quandary for those who wish to use such theories to inform team training research, it also substantially inhibits application to instructional designs in team training practice.

A salient question is where can future team training research best draw its instructional methods? Fortunately, several cumulative efforts of existing theory in the team literature have been conducted. One of the most recent efforts is by Bell, Kozlowski, and Blawath (2012) who reviewed and integrated numerous theoretical models that describe team learning, adaptation, and performance. In doing so, these authors emphasized the importance of conceptualizing team learning as multilevel, dynamic, and emergent in nature, and go on to articulate the various factors that are thought to underlie team and individual learning in team settings. These factors include team learning processes (e.g., regulation), team emergent states (e.g., cohesion), and team knowledge representations (e.g., team mental models). The comprehensiveness of this theoretical integration makes Bell et al.'s work both a perfect and valuable departure point for future team training research. However, as we noted earlier, research must go beyond testing whether the proposed mechanisms of the models summarized by Bell and colleagues function as theoretically predicted, but also include tests of the kinds of instructional techniques that can ultimately affect these proposed factors. As an illustration, these authors note the need for research that examines the implications for collective knowledge on team performance. Here, even by adding the simple question of which techniques can be effectively brought to bear to inculcate collective knowledge during team training (or when examining any of the numerous recommendations offered by these authors) would represent a substantial move in the right direction for team training research.

Future research should extend investigations to other individual-level instructional methods for their potential application and integration in team training. For example, there is a wealth of evidence for the effectiveness of behavioral modeling on individual learning and the transfer of learning (Taylor, Russ-Eft, & Chan, 2005). The same can be said of error management training (Keith & Frese, 2008). Both techniques seem particularly relevant to many of the competencies required for effective teamwork (e.g., cooperation, conflict management, mutual performance monitoring, and coordination) as well as instructionally congruent with tactics commonly used in team training to boost both team-work and task work (e.g., CRM training, cross-training). Indeed, there is some evidence from the health care domain that suggests the effectiveness of including error management components within team training designs (Deering et al., 2011; Morey et al., 2002). Thus, research that examines how best to integrate these techniques into team training designs, including the degree to which such designs focus on aspects of teamwork or task work or both influence training effectiveness, represents an important path to pursue.

In addition to behavior modeling and error management, incorporating self-regulation tactics seems particularly valuable to team training. The positive effects of self-regulation on individual-level learning are well documented (Beier & Kanfer, 2010), as are the benefits of self-regulatory and metacognitive interventions (de Boer, Donker-Bergstra, & Kostons, 2013; Sitzmann & Ely, 2011). Self-regulation is at least as, perhaps even more, pertinent during team training because individuals must not only monitor how the team is learning as a unit, but also how they are learning as individuals in team training (Ellington & Dierdorff, 2014). This implies a dual-process requirement whereby individuals need to be aware of their own learning process, the team's process, and how these processes might interrelate. On one hand, because the personal resources needed for self-regulation are finite or limited, team training contexts might further tax these resources and make self-regulation in team training somehow more difficult. On the other hand, team training could reflect a context that amplifies the positive effects of self-regulation on learning for the reasons noted in the preceding text. Research that addresses these kinds of issues could provide conceptual clarification and reveal the utility of self-regulation interventions in team training. Moreover, such research would be well served to examine more specific components that reflect self-regulated learning, including self-observation, practice behaviors, goal setting, and emotional reactions to goal progress (see Bell & Kozlowski, 2010).

Related to the general notion of self-focused awareness and attention, scholarship has increased regarding the potential benefits of "mindfulness" – defined as present-centered attention and awareness (Brown & Ryan, 2003). In a recent literature review, Good and colleagues (2016) suggested that mindfulness holds relevance in team-based contexts in general and team training in particular because mindfulness is thought to promote relational processes, which are aligned with the social processes that underlie all team functioning. Studies in health care, for example, have shown positive benefits of mindfulness interventions on teamwork processes in therapeutic treatment teams, such as active listening and collaboration (e.g., Singh et al., 2006). Other research using student teams has found mindfulness inductions to increase cohesion and collective performance (Cleirigh & Greaney, 2014). An additional implication for mindfulness in team training might be found in its potential to foster situational awareness among a team's members. Because situational awareness has been proffered as important to team processes (Cooke, Stout, & Salas, 2001), boosting situational awareness among team members might lead to increases in team training transfer due to enhanced performance monitoring and adjustment as well as coordination behaviors in a team.

Pertinent inquires along the lines of those discussed previously not only include whether tactics such as behavior modeling, error management, self-regulation, and mindfulness make team training more effective when they are embedded, but also how to best integrate these components with other instructional methods frequently used in team training. For instance, should such interventions emphasize more general teamwork components, more team-specific task work components, or both (see Cannon-Bowers et al., 1995)? Does the location or placement (early or late) of these interventions matter to effectiveness? What are the potential trade-offs of such individual-level interventions on overall team learning outcomes? How do these interventions align with other forms of team training (e.g., cross-training, communication)? Finally, given the evidence that teamwork processes more generally encompass transition, action, and interpersonal factors (LePine et al., 2008), linking specific tactics to these distinct teamwork processes should provide theoretical insight as well as diagnostic information to improve the design of team training.

It is important to note that any future research seeking to establish linkages between specific instructional methods and various learning outcomes of team training must strive to choose methods that are theoretically congruent with the targeted learning outcome. One obvious way to accomplish this consistency would be to consider whether the learning outcome is compilational (e.g., team transactive memory) or compositional (e.g., team mental models), as well as considering whether it is a process-oriented, emergent state, or performance-based outcome. The value here is that considering theoretical congruence will inform the kinds of methods to bring to bear (e.g., those more cognitive, emotional, or behavioral in nature), the levels at which one would expect results (e.g., individual learning, team learning, or both), as well as how to best implement the chosen methods within team training designs.

Moving Beyond the Intervention Environment

Perhaps one of the largest gaps in the extant repository of research relates to examinations of the transfer of team training. The scarcity of transfer studies is somewhat surprising when one considers the volume of training evaluation research that has accumulated for team training. The meta-analysis by Salas et al. (2008), for example, did not examine transfer outcomes of team training, suggesting an insufficient number of available studies. A more recent meta-analysis by Delise et al. (2010) was able to examine transfer outcomes, finding favorable overall effects for team training transfer ($d = .68$, $k = 11$). However, these authors also noted that only 26% of the studies in their sample included measures of transfer, representing only about 15% of the total cumulated effect sizes. A similar dearth of transfer examination occurs in the health care domain where team training research has grown to be quite prevalent. For instance, in their narrative review, Weaver et al. (2014) found that less than half of existing studies (42%) measured outcomes longer than six months posttraining.

Training without transfer beyond the intervention environment ultimately adds very little value to organizations. Thus, the need for additional research on the transfer of team training simply cannot be overstated. Primary questions remain to be addressed about the longevity of team training effects, methods to promote maintenance and application of acquired competencies (e.g., retraining, dedicated practice), as well as the transportability of team training to the multiple teams in which individuals eventually find themselves as members. Still further, a more expansive set of transfer metrics would be beneficial for future research to incorporate. For example, transfer studies using measures that are sensitive to "cycle time" have been recommended in the broader training literature (Aguinis & Kraiger, 2009). In team training, these would include a measurement focus on capturing time-to-proficiency as well as longitudinal examinations of team performance trajectories within the transfer environment. This latter type of investigation would be especially valuable because it would allow empirical questions to move beyond – "does team training transfer" – to questions about the speed, decay, and sustainability of transfer, as well as allow for more precise isolation of factors that promote or attenuate team performance trajectories or "transfer curves."

It is important to point out that integrating factors that might contribute to effective team training transfer is consistent with calls from the general training literature as well (e.g., Grossman & Salas, 2010). Findings from a meta-analysis of individual training transfer by Blume et al. (2010) suggest that factors such as pretraining self-efficacy, motivation, and the work environment (e.g., social support) would be key influences to examine, as each of these showed stronger relationships to transfer for "open skills" (where team training content would be relevant). Many of these variables have analogs at the team level, such as team efficacy, and others could be operationalized as compositional variables when investigating their influences on team training transfer, such as overall levels of motivation or social support in teams. Other chapters in the current handbook further point to potentially valuable factors to examine (e.g., see chapters by Huang, Ran, & Blume [Chapter 4] and Tews & Burke-Smalley [Chapter 9]).

Finally, because contemporary teams may be part of larger "multiteam systems" (Zaccaro, Marks, & DeChurch, 2011), external factors linked to these systems such as superordinate goals, between-team interdependence, shared expertise, and task redundancy could be particularly important in the transfer of team training. Related to suprateam factors, training scholars have also argued for the importance of moving beyond learning transfer to the performance context (i.e., horizontal transfer), but also considering the vertical transfer of training, which refers to the upward propagation of training consequences across levels of the organization (Kozlowski et al., 2000). Others have noted the potential role that social network ties between teams ("team networks") might play in promoting vertical transfer across an organization (Kozlowski, Chao, & Jensen, 2010). These concepts raise a host of interesting questions that can inform team training practice to increase effectiveness and efficiency. For example, when can we train one person and reap benefits that extend to the entire team? How well does team training generalize when some members move to other teams that have not received formal training? When must we train the entire intact team? How can we best train multiple teams during team training and how does this learning impact the broader multiteam system in an organization?

Meeting the New Reality of Teams

As we noted earlier, the nature of teams in today's organizations has changed along several dimensions, including more fluid membership, greater use of technology, more geographic dispersion, and increased team member diversity. One implication of these shifts is the need to address how learning transfers "downward" to individuals participating in team training. That is, in addition to examining the vertical transfer of team training to broader multiteam systems discussed in the preceding text, a key question deals with what mechanisms influence the extent to which specific individuals acquire the competencies inculcated during team training. Another question is to what extent is team training transportable from team to team, as individuals will inevitably be members of multiple teams during their work careers (Tannenbaum et al., 2012). At first blush, these may seem like rhetorical questions; however, it is important to recognize three key points. First, the vast majority of team training is centrally focused on fostering and assessing team-level outcomes. This makes sense because improving team-level processes and outcomes is the *sine qua non* of team training. Second, effectively performing teams require effectively performing individuals in those teams (Ellis et al., 2003). In other words, team functioning begins with individuals but ends with team-level consequences. Third, team training need not be restricted only to intact teams. In fact, individuals often receive training on teamwork competencies while in temporary teams, such as those formed during leadership development programs or those used in action learning settings. The important ramification is that it would seem paramount that *each* individual acquires the teamwork competence and subsequently transfer it back to his or her own team, or transport it to a new team. Yet at the same time, other research has indicted that particular members can hold more influence on team functioning and performance than other team members (Humphrey, Morgeson, & Mannor, 2009; Raver, Ehrhart, & Chadwick, 2012). This finding suggests that training certain central members of a team (e.g., team leaders) or those occupying certain roles in a team (e.g., "strategic core"; Humphrey et al., 2009) might be particularly effective.

Recognizing these points reveals several valuable areas to examine in future research. For example, multilevel investigations of team training are much needed, where the effects of team-level factors on individual-level acquisition of team training content are the focus of study. Likewise, examinations are needed that study the effects of how training a single individual might influence team-level outcomes, such as training team leaders who likely have more power to prompt learning monitoring and regulation in teams (Kozlowski et al., 2010). In this regard, Mathieu and Tesluk (2010) suggest that multilevel training research would benefit by applying a "bracketing" framework (Hackman, 2003) whereby variables either a level above or below the focal variable are incorporated into research designs. Indeed, higher-level influences from team composition variables on individual learning in team training have already found support (e.g., average goal orientations in teams; Dierdorff & Ellington, 2012), suggesting value for future research efforts. Potentially useful composition variables would also include those that relate to dynamic team composition, such as the rapidity or proportion of membership turnover, turnover of specific roles (e.g., team leaders), changes in membership diversity, role clarity, and so forth. Compilation variables are also pertinent for future research and could include team-level factors such as cohesion, team identity, conflict, group potency, and team efficacy. These compilation variables are recognized as important to overall team functioning and are likely to shape the nature of intrateam interpersonal interactions that can facilitate or inhibit the flow of information and collaborative learning. The central point here is that, whereas we know a great deal about individual learning, we know far less about how individuals learn while in team training and the effects of this individual-level learning on team-level outcomes and vice versa.

In addition to multilevel examinations in formal team training settings, the fluidity of team membership further implicates the value of investigating informal mechanisms by which teams collectively, and team members individually, acquire knowledge and skills related to teamwork. Teams are known to create salient contexts that exert top-down influences on learning and behavior (Klimoski, 2012; Porter, 2008). This suggests that team-level factors are very likely to shape how, when, and how much informal learning occurs as well as its effectiveness. For example, the recognition of learning opportunities, social support and encouragement from peers and supervisors, feedback orientation, and levels of self-awareness have been suggested as important variables in the informal learning process (Tannenbaum et al., 2010). Previous research has found tools such as after-action reviews promote team learning (Smith-Jentsch et al., 2008), suggesting that performance monitoring and adjustment processes could be key ways that teams engage in informal learning. Others have noted the need for research that investigates the emergence of informal learning in teams and how individual and team regulation shapes this emergence (Kozlowski et al., 2010). We would further add that future studies are needed to test the effectiveness of formal team training interventions specifically designed to facilitate informal learning processes in teams (i.e., teaching teams to engage informal learning). Moreover, research that investigates how informal learning shapes individual learning and how this individual-level learning can be transported to other teams would be important as well.

Finally, the use of geographically dispersed or virtual teams by contemporary organizations is well documented, and some training research has begun to examine learning and performance in these teams (e.g., Rentsch et al., 2014). Put bluntly, however, we need substantially more empirical focus in this area if the team training literature is to keep pace with the increasing prevalence of these team structures. Future research is needed even on primary questions such as the effectiveness of delivering team training *within* virtual environments in general (as is a likely occurrence with such teams), as well as empirical evaluations of different team training tactics to inculcate teamwork competencies of these teams in particular. For example, common challenges facing geographically dispersed or virtual teams include issues of interpersonal trust and high-quality communication (Martins, Gilson, & Maynard, 2004). In addition, research has found that the capacities to build transactive memory systems and engage in preparation activities are associated with the effectiveness of virtual teams (Maynard et al., 2012). The relevance for team training is that these kinds of factors are among the outcomes that frequently fall under the purview of team training; yet, what is needed is research that examines the utility of using team training to instruct these types of outcomes in distributed teams.

Geographically dispersed or virtual teams also heavily rely on communication and collaborative technologies. Thus, future research along the lines of research by Kirkman and colleagues (Kirkman et al., 2006) that examines the use of these technologies as a part of team training, as well as the instructional focus of team training would be especially valuable. Because competencies such as cooperation and coordination are common to team training in general, studies that investigate how these competencies relate to and are impacted by communication technology seem especially pertinent. For example, are the knowledge and skills that reflect cooperation and coordination substantially different in face-to-face team training as compared to team training infusing these technologies? If yes, how are these best trained? What aspects can collaborative technology effectively replace when compared to more face-to-face and interpersonally oriented team training? Moreover, research has found factors such as psychological safety and empowerment can boost the positive effects of communication technology on team functioning (Kirkman et al., 2004; Kirkman et al., 2013). In this sense, future team training research on how to effectively train the use of the technology in teams and the factors that facilitate the benefits of this technology hold significant practical value, especially, considering that most existing research on dispersed or virtual teams tends to treat technology use as a predictor or moderator of team performance as opposed to an outcome of an instructional intervention like team training.

Summary

The science of team training has grown into a considerable body of work that offers convincing evidence for the benefits of instructional interventions that develop the essential knowledge, skills, and attitudes that underlie effective team functioning. As we sought to articulate in this chapter, the general question of whether team training results in favorable outcomes has been addressed, and thus now is the time to turn our focus to why and how team training reaps such outcomes. Shifts in the contemporary world of work have created a confluence of influences that make the need for expansive and deeper investigations of team training even more salient to both science and practice. New team structures, contexts, tools, and demands dramatically increase the importance of being able to more quickly and effectively develop collections of individuals into highly functioning teams. Future team training scholarship that builds empirical evidence of when and how to use different tactics to foster different learning outcomes of team training, both for teams as a unit and the individual team members that comprise the unit, holds the promise to fill a crucial gap in the current literature. So too are studies designed to uncover the various factors that facilitate the application and maintenance of team training consequences over time and situations; especially the situations resulting from the increased fluidity of team membership, growing use of communication and collaborative technology, and prevalence of geographically dispersed teams. In short, now that we know team training works, we must begin the more challenging yet compelling work of ascertaining the conditions that improve its effectiveness.

References

Aguinis, H., and Kraiger, K. 2009. Benefits of training and development for individuals and teams, organizations, and society. *Annual Review of Psychology* 60: 451–474.

Bell, S. T. 2007. Deep-level composition variables as predictors of team performance: A meta-analysis. *Journal of Applied Psychology* 92: 595–615.

Bell, B. S., Kozlowski, S. W. J., and Blawath, S. 2012. Team learning: A theoretical integration and review. In S. Kozlowski, ed., *The Oxford Handbook of Organizational Psychology* 2: 859–909. New York: Oxford University Press.

Blume, B. D., Ford, J. K., Baldwin, T. T., and Huang, J. L. 2010. Transfer of training: A meta-analytic review. *Journal of Management* 36: 1065–1105.

Brown, K. W., and Ryan, R. M. 2003. The benefits of being present: Mindfulness and its role in psychological wellbeing. *Journal of Personality and Social Psychology* 84: 822–848.

Cannon-Bowers, J. A., Tannenbaum, S. I., Salas, E., and Volpe, C. E. 1995. Defining competencies and establishing team training requirements. In R. A. Guzzo and E. Salas, eds., *Team Effectiveness and Decision-making in Organizations*, 333–338. San Francisco: Jossey Bass.

Clay-Williams, R., McIntosh, C. A., Kerridge, R., and Braithwaite, J. 2013. Classroom and simulation team training: A randomized controlled trial. *International Journal for Quality in Health Care* 25: 314–321.

Cleirigh, D. O., and Greaney, J. 2014. Mindfulness and group performance: An exploratory investigation into the effects of brief mindfulness intervention on group task performance. *Mindfulness* 6: 601–609.

Combs, J., Liu, Y., Hall, A., and Ketchen, D. 2006. How much do high-performance work practices matter? A meta-analysis of their effects on organizational performance. *Personnel Psychology* 59: 501–528.

Cooke, N. J., Stout, R., and Salas, E. 2001. A knowledge elicitation approach to the measurement of team situation awareness. In M. McNeese, M. Endsley, and E. Salas, eds., *New Trends in Cooperative Activities: System Dynamics in Complex Settings*, 114–139. Santa Monica, CA: Human Factors and Ergonomics Society.

Davidovitch, L., Parush, A., and Shtub, A. 2010. Simulator-based team training to share resources in a matrix structure organization. *IEEE Transactions on Engineering Management* 57: 288–300.

deBoer, H., Donker-Bergstra, A. S., and Kostons, D. D. N. M. 2013. *Effective Strategies for Self-regulated Learning: A Meta-analysis*. Groningen, Netherlands: GION.

Deering S., Rosen M. A, Ludi V., Munroe, M., Pocrnich, A., Laky, C., and Napolitano, P. G. 2011. On the front lines of patient safety: implementation and evaluation of team training in Iraq. *Joint Commission Journal on Quality and Patient Safety* 37: 350–356.

Delise, L. A., Gorman, C. A., Brooks, A. M., Rentsch, J. R., and Steele-Johnson, D. 2010. The effects of team training on team outcomes: A meta-analysis. *Performance Improvement Quarterly* 22: 53–80.

Denson, R. W. 1981. *Team Training: Literature Review and Annotated Bibliography (Final Rep. AFHRL-TR-80-40)*. Brooks Air Force Base, TX: HQ Air Force Human Resources Laboratory.

Devine, D. J., Clayton, L. D., Philips, J. L., Dunford, B. B., and Melner, S. B. 1999. Teams in organizations: Prevalence, characteristics and effectiveness. *Small Group Research* 30: 678–711.

Dierdorff, E. C., and Ellington, J. K. 2012. Members matter in team training: Multilevel and longitudinal relationships between goal orientation, self-regulation, and team outcomes. *Personnel Psychology* 65: 661–703.

Dyer, J. L. 1984. Team research and team training: A state-of-the-art review. In F. A. Muckier, ed., *Human Factors Review*, 285–323. Santa Monica, CA: Human Factors Society.

Ellington, J. K., and Dierdorff, E. C. 2014. Individual learning in team training: Self-regulation and team context effects. *Small Group Research* 45: 37–67. doi: 10.1177/1046496413511670

Ellis, A. P. J., Bell, B. S., Ployhart, R. E., Hollenbeck, J. R., and Ilgen, D. R. 2005. An evaluation of generic teamwork skills training with action teams: Effects on cognitive and skill-based outcomes. *Personnel Psychology* 58: 641–672.

Ellis, A. P. J., Hollenbeck, J. R., Ilgen, D. R., Porter, C. O. L. H., West, B. J., and Moon, H. 2003. Team learning: Collectively connecting the dots. *Journal of Applied Psychology* 88: 821–835.

Ellis, A. P. J., and Pearsall, M. J. 2011. Reducing the negative effects of stress in teams through cross-training: A job demands-resources model. *Group Dynamics: Theory, Research, and Practice* 15: 16–31.

Espevik, R., Johnsen, B. H., and Eid, J. 2011. Outcomes of shared mental models of team members in cross training and high-intensity simulations. *Journal of Cognitive Engineering and Decision Making* 5: 352–377.

Fiore, S. M., and Schooler, J. W. 2004. Process mapping and shared cognition: Teamwork and the development of shared problem models. In E. Salas and S. Fiore, eds., *Team Cognition: Understanding the Factors That Drive Process and Performance*, 133–152. Washington, DC: American Psychological Association.

Good, D., Lyddy, C. J., Glomb, T. M., Bono, J. E., Brown, K. W., Duffy, M. K., Baer, R. A., Brewer, J. A., and Lazar, S. W. 2016. Contemplating mindfulness at work: An Integrative review. *Journal of Management* 42: 114–142.

Gorman, J. C., Cooke, N. J., and Amazeen, P. G. 2010. Training adaptive teams. *Human Factors* 52: 295–307.

Hackman, J. R. 2003. Learning more from crossing levels: Evidence from airplanes, orchestras, and hospitals. *Journal of Organizational Behavior* 24: 1–18.

Humphrey, S. E., Morgeson, F. P., and Mannor, M. J. 2009. Developing a theory of the strategic core of teams: The contribution of core and non-core roles to team performance. *Journal of Applied Psychology* 94: 48–61.

Ilgen, D. R., Hollenbeck, J. R., Johnson, M., and Jundt, D. 2005. Teams in organizations: From input-process-output models to IMOI models. *Annual Review of Psychology* 56: 517–543.

Keith, N., and Frese, M. 2008. Effectiveness of error management training: A meta-analysis. *Journal of Applied Psychology* 93: 59–69.

Klein, C., DiazGranados, D., Salas, E., Le, H., Burke, C. S., Lyons, R., and Goodwin, G. F. 2009. Does team building work? *Small Group Research* 40: 181–222.

Klimoski, R. 2012. Context matters. *Industrial and Organizational Psychology* 5: 28–31.

Kirkman, B. L., Cordery, J. L., Mathieu, J. E., Rosen, B., and Kukenberger, M. 2013. Global organizational communities of practice: The effects of nationality diversity, psychological safety, and media richness on community performance. *Human Relations* 66: 333–362.

Kirkman, B. L., and Mathieu, J. E. 2005. The dimensions and antecedents of team virtuality. *Journal of Management* 31: 700–718.

Kirkman, B. L., Rosen, B., Tesluk, P. E., and Gibson, C. B. 2004. The impact of team empowerment on virtual team performance: the moderating role of face-to-face interaction. *Academy of Management Journal* 47: 175–192.

Kirkman, B. L., Rosen, B., Tesluk, P. E., and Gibson, C. B. 2006. Enhancing the transfer of computer-assisted training proficiency in geographically distributed teams. *Journal of Applied Psychology* 91: 706–716.

Koutantji, M., McCulloch, P., Undre, S., Gautama, S., Cunniffe, S., Sevdalis, N., … Darzi, A. 2008. Is team training in briefings for surgical teams feasible in simulation? *Cognition, Technology & Work* 10: 275–285.

Kozlowski, S. W. J., Brown, K. G., Weissbein, D., Cannon-Bowers, J., and Salas, E. 2000. A multilevel approach to training effectiveness: Enhancing horizontal and vertical transfer. In K. Klein and S. W. J. Kozlowski, eds., *Multilevel Theory, Research and Methods in Organizations*, 157–210. San Francisco, CA: Jossey-Bass.

Kozlowski, S. W. J., Chao, G. T., and Jensen, J. M. 2010. Building an infrastructure for organizational learning: A multilevel approach. In S. W. J. Kozlowski and E. Salas, eds., *Learning, Training, and Development in Organizations*, 363–403. New York: Taylor & Francis Group.

Kozlowski, S. W. J., Gully, S. M., Nason, E. R., and Smith, E. M. 1999. Developing adaptive teams: A theory of compilation and performance across levels and time. In D. R. Ilgen and E. D. Pulakos, eds., *The Changing Nature of Work Performance: Implications for Staffing, Personnel Actions, and Development*, 240–292. San Francisco, CA: Jossey-Bass.

Kraiger, K., Ford, J. K., and Salas, E. 1993. Application of cognitive, skill-based, and affective theories of learning outcomes to new methods of training evaluation. *Journal of Applied Psychology* 78: 311–328.

LePine, J. A., Piccolo, R. F., Jackson, C. L., Mathieu, J. E., and Saul, J. R. 2008. A meta-analysis of teamwork processes: Tests of a multidimensional model and relationships with team effectiveness criteria. *Personnel Psychology* 61: 273–307.

Marquardt, N., Robelski, S., and Hoeger, R. 2010. Crew resource management training within the automotive industry: Does it work? *Human Factors* 52: 308–315.

Martínez-Moreno, E., Zornoza, A., Orengo, V., and Thompson, L. F. 2014. The effects of team self-guided training on conflict management in virtual teams. *Group Decision and Negotiation* 24(5): 1–19.

Martins, L. L., Gilson, L. L., and Maynard, M. T. 2004. Virtual teams: What do we know and where do we go from here? *Journal of Management* 30: 805–835.

Martins, L. L., and Shalley, C. E. 2011. Creativity in virtual work effects of demographic differences. *Small Group Research* 42: 536–561.

Mathieu, J. E., Maynard, M. T., Rapp, T., and Gilson, L. 2008. Team effectiveness 1997-2007: A review of recent advancements and a glimpse into the future. *Journal of Management* 34: 410–476.

Mathieu, J. E., and Tesluk, P. E. 2010. A multilevel perspective on training and development effectiveness. In S. W. J. Kozlowski and E. Salas, eds., *Learning, Training, and Development in Organizations*, 405–442. New York, NY: Routledge.

Maynard, T., Mathieu, J. E., Gilson, L., and Rapp, T. 2012. Something(s) old and something(s) new: Modeling drivers of global virtual team effectiveness. *Journal of Organizational Behavior* 33: 342–365.

Morey, J. C., Simon, R., Jay, G. D., Wears, R. L., Salisbury, M., Dukes, K. A., and Berns, S. D. 2002. Error reduction and performance improvement in the emergency department through formal teamwork training: Evaluation results of the MedTeams project. *Health Services Research* 37: 1553–1581.

O'Leary, M. B., and Cummings, J. N. 2007. The spatial, temporal, and configurational characteristics of geographic dispersion in teams. *Management Information Science Quarterly* 31: 433–452.

Porter, C. O. L. H. 2008. A multilevel, multiconceptualization perspective of goal orientation in teams. In V. I. Sessa and M. London, eds., *Work group Learning: Understanding, Improving, and Assessing How Groups Learn in Organizations*, 149–173. New York: Lawrence Erlbaum.

Rapp, T. L., and Mathieu, J. E. 2007. Evaluating an individually self-administered generic teamwork skills training program across time and levels. *Small Group Research* 38: 532–555.

Raver, J., Ehrhart, M. G., and Chadwick, I. C. 2012. The emergence of team helping norms: Foundations within members' attributes and behavior. *Journal of Organizational Behavior* 33: 616–637.

Rentsch, J. R., Delise, L. A., Mello, A. L., and Staniewicz, M. J. 2014. The integrative team knowledge building training strategy in distributed problem-solving teams. *Small Group Research* 45: 568–591.

Rentsch, J. R., Delise, L. A., Salas, E., and Letsky, M. P. 2010. Facilitating knowledge building in teams: Can a new team training strategy help? *Small Group Research* 41: 505–523.

Rosen, B., Furst, S., and Blackburn, R. 2006. Training for virtual teams: An investigation of current practices and future needs. *Human Resource Management* 45: 229–247.

Salas, E., and Cannon-Bowers, J. A. 1997. Methods, tools, and strategies for team training. In M. A. Quiñones and A. Ehrenstein, eds., *Training for a Rapidly Changing Workplace*, 249–279. Washington, DC: American Psychological Association.

Salas, E., DiazGranados, D., Klein, C., Burke, C. S., Stagl, K. C., Goodwin, G. F., and Halpin, S. M. 2008. Does team training improve team performance? A meta-analysis. *Human Factors* 50: 903–933.

Salas, E., Dickinson, T. L., Converse, S. A., and Tannenbaum, S. I. 1992. Toward an understanding of team performance and training. In R. W. Swezey and E. Salas, eds., *Teams: Their Training and Performance*, 3–29. Norwood, NJ: Ablex.

Salas, E., Nichols, D. R., and Driskell, J. E. 2007. Testing three team training strategies in intact teams: A meta-analysis. *Small Group Research* 38: 471–488.

Salas, E., Rozell, D., Mullen, B., and Driskell, J. E. 1999. The effect of team building on performance. *Small Group Research* 30: 309–329.

Salas, E., Stagl, K. C., and Burke, C. S. 2004. 25 years of team effectiveness in organizations: Research themes and emerging needs. In C. L. Cooper and I. T. Robertson, eds., *International Review of Industrial and Organizational Psychology*, 47–91. New York: Wiley.

Salas, E., Tannenbaum, S. I., Kraiger, K., and Smith-Jentsch, K. A. 2012. The science of training and development in organizations: What matters in practice. *Psychological Science in the Public Interest* 13: 74–101.

Singh, N. N., Singh, S. D., Sabaawi, M., Myers, R. E., and Wahler, R. G. 2006. Enhancing treatment team process through mindfulness-based mentoring in an inpatient psychiatric hospital. *Behavior Modification* 30: 423–441.

Sitzmann, T., and Ely, K. 2011. A meta-analysis of self-regulated learning in work-related training and educational attainment: What we know and where we need to go. *Psychological Bulletin* 137: 421–442.

Smith-Jentsch, K. A., Cannon-Bowers, J. A., Tannenbaum, S. I., and Salas, E. 2008. Guided team self-correction: Impacts on team mental models, processes, and effectiveness. *Journal of Small Group Research* 39: 303–327.

Stagl, K. C., Salas, E., Rosen, M. A., Priest, H. A., Burke, C. S., Goodwin, G. F., et al. 2007. Distributed team performance: A multilevel review of distribution, demography, and decision making. *Research in Multi-Level Issues* 6: 11–58.

Tannenbaum, S. I., Beard, R. L., McNall, L. A., and Salas, E. 2010. Informal learning and development in organizations. In S. W. J. Kozlowski and E. Salas, eds., *Learning, Training, and Development in Organizations*, 303–332. New York, NY: Routledge.

Tannenbaum, S. I., Beard, R. L., and Salas, E. 1992. Team building and its influence on team effectiveness: An examination of conceptual and empirical developments. In K. Kelley, ed., *Issues, Theory, and Research in Industrial/Organizational Psychology*, 117–153. Amsterdam: North-Holland.

Tannenbaum, S. I., Mathieu, J. E., Salas, E., and Cohen, D. 2012. Teams are changing: Are research and practice evolving fast enough? *Industrial and Organizational Psychology: Perspectives on Science and Practice* 5: 2–24. doi:10.1111/j.1754- 9434.2011.01396.x

Taylor, P. J., Russ-Eft, D. F., and Chan, D. W. L. 2005. A meta-analytic review of behavior modeling training. *Journal of Applied Psychology* 90: 692–709.

Thompson, L. L. 2008. *Making the Team: A Guide for Managers*, 3rd ed. New Jersey: Pearson Prentice Hall.

Weaver, S. J., Dy, S. M., and Rosen, M. A. 2014. Team-training in healthcare: A narrative synthesis of the literature. *BMJ Quality & Safety* 23: 359–372.

Zaccaro, S., Marks, M., and DeChurch, L. 2011. *Multiteam Systems: An Organizational Form for Dynamic and Complex Environments*. New York: Routledge Academic.

18 Developing Cultural Intelligence

Jana L. Raver and Linn Van Dyne

It has become nearly axiomatic, that nations are globally interdependent and doing business across national and cultural borders is the norm rather than the exception. Global trade has increased steadily, and the total value of global imports and exports across nations now accounts for more than 50% of the world's GDP (World Bank, 2014). There are more than 82,000 multinational corporations (MNCs) with 810,000 subsidiaries distributed globally, with nearly 71 million foreign affiliates employed by these MNCs (UNCTAD, 2008; 2014). Even for employees whose jobs do not require cross-border interactions, the likelihood of interacting with culturally dissimilar co-workers continues to rise. There are 232 million international migrants – a 150% increase since 1990 (United Nations, 2013). The world has not only grown smaller, but has grown more interdependent. As a result, there is a critical business need for leaders and employees who can handle the complexities of intercultural interactions. This is where *cultural intelligence* (CQ) – the capability to function effectively in intercultural contexts (Earley & Ang, 2003) – plays an essential role.

CQ is a relative newcomer to the research on intercultural competence, but theory, research, and practice on CQ have evolved rapidly. From its theoretical beginnings as a unique form of intelligence (Earley & Ang, 2003), to the development of the cultural intelligence scale (CQS) with predictive validity (Ang et al., 2007), to the accumulation of dozens of studies documenting the benefits of CQ for intercultural adjustment, performance, leadership, team trust, and other outcomes (Ang, Van Dyne, & Rockstuhl, 2015), scholarship on CQ has flourished. Practitioners have also dedicated considerable attention to implementing the CQ framework in work and educational contexts, with the support of science-to-practice translations (Livermore, 2010; Livermore & Van Dyne, 2015) and teaching resources (e.g., The Cultural Intelligence Center, http://www.culturalq.com). An active global community of CQ facilitators has been certified by the Cultural Intelligence Center, and these facilitators are putting CQ principles into practice through training workshops, educational programs, and individual coaching.

This chapter focuses on the nexus of CQ research and CQ training. Some people have higher intercultural competence than others, but CQ is a malleable form of intelligence that can be developed through training, travel, and exposure to different cultural contexts (Ang et al., 2015). As such, scientists and practitioners both have a keen interest in discovering and documenting the ways in which CQ may be developed. This chapter provides a critical and integrative review of the ways that organizations may systematically increase employee CQ through training and development activities. Many CQ training and development studies have accumulated in the past few years, but the field lacks a synthesis and evaluation of this emerging body of research. In response, we offer the current chapter with the goal of advancing both the science and the practice of developing CQ.

In what follows, we begin with a brief review of the CQ construct and the key findings with regard to its benefits for individuals and organizations. We then discuss the broader intercultural training literature to position the development of CQ within the larger context of increasing intercultural competence. The bulk of the chapter is dedicated to reviewing specific studies on the development of CQ. We organize the studies based upon their research design and intervention approach (i.e., training vs. intercultural experience). We conclude the chapter with recommendations for future scholarship on developing CQ.

Overview of Cultural Intelligence and Its Importance

Research on intercultural competence has been accumulating for decades along several divergent paths. *Intercultural competence* has been defined broadly as "the ability to think and act in interculturally appropriate ways" (Hammer, Bennett, & Wiseman, 2003: 422) or more specifically as "an individual's effectiveness in drawing upon a set of knowledge, skills, and personal attributes in order to work successfully with people from different national cultural backgrounds at home or abroad" (Johnson, Lenartowicz, & Apud, 2006: 530). Leung, Ang, and Tan's (2014) review of the intercultural competence literature noted more than 30 intercultural competence models and more than 300 personal characteristics as sources of intercultural competence.

Due to the sheer number of intercultural competence constructs and studies, much of this work has been fragmented – with conflicting conceptualizations of the phenomenon (Leung et al., 2014) and the lack of a theoretical foundation for some studies (see Ang et al., 2007 for a discussion of this problem). To date, most intercultural competence research has adopted an individual-difference perspective and conceptualized competence as personal traits (e.g., open-mindedness, cognitive complexity). A second stream of research has conceptualized intercultural competence as intercultural attitudes and worldviews (e.g., ethnocentric-ethnorelative worldviews, cosmopolitan outlook). A third and final stream of research has conceptualized intercultural competence as a set of intercultural capabilities (i.e., knowledge, skills, and abilities that a person can use to be effective in culturally diverse or intercultural contexts). CQ fits within this latter stream and is thus distinct from the individual-difference and attitudinal traditions.

Conceptualizing Cultural Intelligence

CQ has been conceptualized as a malleable set of intercultural capabilities that reflect the degree to which an individual is able to function effectively in intercultural contexts (Ang & Van Dyne, 2008; Earley & Ang, 2003). It is a multidimensional construct consisting of four interrelated capabilities, each with subdimensions (Van Dyne et al., 2012). First, *motivational CQ* is the ability to direct and sustain effort toward functioning in intercultural situations. It is based upon the expectancy-value theory of motivation (Eccles & Wigfield, 2002) and includes the subdimensions of self-efficacy, intrinsic motivation, and extrinsic motivation. When sojourners have high motivational CQ, they have confidence in their ability to function effectively in diverse settings. Second, *cognitive CQ* is knowledge about cultures and cultural differences, including both culture-general and culture-specific knowledge such as awareness of norms, practices, and social systems in different cultures. Third, *metacognitive CQ,* sometimes referred to as "thinking about thinking," is the ability to acquire, assess, and understand cultural knowledge. It is the capability to plan for cultural interactions, maintain awareness of cultural differences as they occur, and check/revise assumptions about different cultures. Metacognitive CQ allows individuals to have some degree of control over their own thought processes about cultural differences. Finally, *behavioral CQ* is the ability to exhibit flexibility in verbal behaviors, nonverbal behaviors, and speech acts when adapting to other cultural contexts.

Overall, CQ is represented by these four capabilities and their subdimensions. Empirical data, however, shows that the antecedents and consequences of CQ often differ across the four dimensions (Ang et al., 2015). As a consequence, we highlight the need for additional research and training on the four capabilities because this should provide more insights than research on the overall construct.

Although research on CQ is relatively new, it has expanded rapidly over the last decade and has become the most prominent framework for studying intercultural competence. Gelfand, Imai, and Fehr (2008) summarized reasons for this growth and prominence. First, CQ offers a parsimonious approach because it focuses on four dimensions that represent the relevant elements of competence at a higher, more abstract level, rather than at a more specific level. Second, it offers theoretical synthesis because it captures the multifaceted nature of intercultural competence in a cohesive manner that allows incorporation of findings from earlier models of intercultural capabilities. Third, it offers theoretical precision because it differentiates motivation, cognition, metacognition, and behavior and it excludes factors that are not capabilities (e.g., personality, values). As a result, CQ has been useful for "construct clean-up."

Additionally, Matsumoto and Hwang's (2013) rigorous review of measures of cross-cultural competence concluded that many scales lack validity and have unstable factor structures. In contrast, they concluded that CQ has a stable factor structure and there is "considerable evidence for the concurrent and predictive ecological validity" of CQ with samples from multiple cultures.

CQ also has relevance at different levels of analysis. Research has begun to go beyond the individual level (Ang et al., 2007) and consider CQ in groups and teams (e.g., additive CQ and leader's CQ; Adair, Hideg, & Spence, 2013; Chen & Lin, 2013; Erez et al., 2013; Moynihan, Peterson, & Earley, 2006; Rockstuhl & Ng, 2008; Shokef & Erez, 2008), at the organizational level (e.g., processes for cultural knowledge integration; Ang & Inkpen, 2008; Moon, 2010), and even in interorganizational social networks (e.g., network heterophily; Gjertsen et al., 2010). CQ is also useful in multilevel and cross-level research (Chen, Liu, & Portnoy, 2012; Groves & Feyerherm, 2011).

Nomological Network of Cultural Intelligence

The theoretical framework offered by CQ has reinvigorated intercultural competence research, as evidenced by dozens of studies that have documented positive outcomes of CQ. A full review of the CQ research literature is outside the scope of this chapter, and so we encourage interested readers to see Ang et al. (2015); Ng, Van Dyne, and Ang (2012); or Leung et al. (2014). For our purposes, it is important to note that the 20-item CQS initially developed and validated by Ang and colleagues (2007) has been extensively cross-validated in additional contexts, with results supporting the four-factor structure and demonstrating high reliability and predictive validity across multinational samples (e.g., Shannon & Begley, 2008; Shokef & Erez, 2008) in addition to country-specific studies (e.g., Imai & Gelfand, 2010; Moon, 2010; Sahin et al., 2013).

Research consistently supports the importance of CQ as an intercultural capability that fosters personal and professional effectiveness in culturally diverse contexts. For example, CQ is positively related to intercultural adjustment (Malek & Budwar, 2013), psychological well-being (Ward, Wilson, & Fischer, 2011), intercultural cooperation (Mor, Morris, & Joh, 2013), and performance (e.g., Chen et al., 2010; Chen et al., 2012). CQ uniquely predicts trust development in intercultural contexts, even after controlling for cognitive ability, personality, international experience, and demographics (Chua, Morris, & Mor, 2012; Rockstuhl et al., 2010). CQ also predicts leadership effectiveness in cross-border contexts, after accounting for general mental ability and emotional intelligence (Rockstuhl et al., 2011).

To date, most CQ research has focused on consequences of CQ, with less attention to predictors of CQ and how it may be developed. Nevertheless, there is some conceptualization and research on antecedents. Ang and Van Dyne (2008) advanced a CQ nomological network wherein CQ is predicted by individual characteristics (e.g., personality, values) and activities (e.g., cross-cultural experience) and predicts intercultural effectiveness (see also Leung et al., 2014). Research is beginning to validate components of this model. For example, CQ mediates the effects of the personality characteristic of openness to experience on adaptive performance of exchange students (Oolders, Chernyshenko, & Stark, 2008) and on job performance of expatriates (Sri Ramalu, Shamsudin, & Subramaniam, 2012). Moreover, prior intercultural contact predicts international leadership potential through its mediated effects on observer-rated CQ (Kim & Van Dyne, 2012). Although personality and prior intercultural experience act as antecedents to CQ, they are not the only ways to develop CQ. Next we consider the intercultural training literature as an important approach for systematically increasing CQ based on developmental interventions.

Intercultural Training Foundations

To provide a broader context for understanding different approaches to CQ training, we begin with an overview of research on intercultural training. We focus on *intercultural training,* defined as "the educative processes used to improve intercultural learning via the development of cognitive, affective, and behavioral competencies needed for successful interactions in diverse cultures" (Littrell et al., 2006: 356). To bridge our review with prior work on expatriate training, we use the terms *cross-cultural training* and *intercultural training* interchangeably. Nevertheless, we note the current shift toward using the term *intercultural training* because many intercultural (and cross-cultural) interactions take place within one's home country and many workplace interactions are culturally diverse (e.g., they often include people from more than two cultures). As such, developing intercultural competencies can be beneficial for everyone, not just expatriates or members of global virtual teams.

Intercultural Training Theory and Methods

While challenges related to intercultural adaptation and effectiveness have existed since antiquity, the modern field of intercultural training began as a result of the ethnocentric atrocities that occurred during World War II. In the subsequent decades, governmental programs emphasized intercultural contact (e.g., Peace Corps), and this increased public and academic interest in the challenges of intercultural adjustment and intercultural understanding (Bhawuk & Brislin, 2000; Furnham & Bochner, 1986). In the 1950s and 1960s, attention focused on understanding the processes of intercultural adjustment and the implications for development of training programs.

Oberg's (1960) notion of *culture shock*, which refers to the distress – including anxiety and psychosomatic symptoms – experienced by sojourners when their familiar symbols and patterns of interaction are removed (Furnham & Bochner, 1986), was an important advancement in this area. There is substantial theory and evidence documenting the stress that sojourners may experience as they attempt to acculturate to a new context (e.g., Berry, 1989; Berry & Sam, 1997; Furnham & Bochner, 1986). Another development in the early literature was the *U-curve of adjustment* (Church, 1982; see also Bhawuk & Brislin, 2000). According to this model, sojourners start with a high level of excitement, but their enthusiasm abates as they experience feelings of displacement and unmet expectations (i.e., culture shock). After a period of time, sojourners recover and begin to adjust successfully to the culture. Although empirical tests of this model have not fully corroborated its validity (Dinges & Baldwin, 1996), the U-curve model is a useful heuristic that can help sojourners anticipate some of the challenges and stages of adjustment. Culture shock and the U-curve of adjustment became the foundation of training programs aimed at reducing the period that sojourners experienced culture shock and increasing their potential for successful adaptation; they are still taught in intercultural training programs today (Littrell et al., 2006).

Training methods and content evolved through the 1980s and 1990s, when organizational and academic interest in intercultural training increased dramatically due to the increased frequency of international business travel. Early training methods provided *didactic*, classroom-based, training (i.e., factual information about the target country). Didactic training remains an important component of many intercultural training programs, but it has inherent limitations (Brislin & Horvath, 1997) including the difficulties of recalling information presented in an abstract manner with little direct application to behavior (Furnham & Bochner, 1986).

During this period, researchers and practitioners also sought to develop training methods that would be more directly applicable. One advancement was the recognition that sojourners integrate into a new culture more effectively if they understand *why* people behave the way they do. *Attribution training* was developed to teach trainees how to make attributions for others' behaviors that are consistent with explanations provided by members of the target culture. This consistency of attributions is termed isomorphic attributions (Fiedler, Mitchell, & Triandis, 1971). Training programs on isomorphic attributions typically use a technique called the culture assimilator, in which trainees are presented with critical incidents and must choose the best explanation for an actor's behavior in a specific culture (Cushner & Brislin, 1996; see also Bhawuk, 1998). Attribution training with the culture assimilator method provides benefits for sojourner's intercultural competencies but more so for cognitive outcomes than for affective or behavioral outcomes (Albert, 1983; Harrison, 1993). Another method that developed in the 1980s and is still popular today is *cultural awareness training.* In this approach, trainees gain an awareness of their own cultural assumptions and are trained to question their own assumptions. As a result, they become sensitized to cultural differences (Gudykunst, Buzley, & Hammer, 1996).

Although each of the preceding intercultural training methods is still used, scholars today emphasize the value of *experiential training*, consistent with broader trends in the organizational learning literature (Noe, Clarke, & Klein, 2013). There are different approaches to experiential learning. One popular model is based on the experiential learning theory (ELT) developed by Kolb (1984). This model emphasizes a continuous process of learning that includes four stages: concrete experiences, reflective observation, abstract conceptualization, and active experimentation. The key assumption of ELT is that the four types of active involvement (experiencing, processing, developing mental models, and testing assumptions) are all required for effective experiential learning. People differ in their natural tendencies to use the four techniques and can start with any of the four processes, but they gain the most when they use all four approaches (Kolb & Kolb, 2005).

Experiential training focuses upon developing skills for working effectively with members of the target culture. It includes active techniques such as role-plays, simulations, and look-see visits (Kealey & Protheroe, 1996; Morris & Robie, 2001). The emphasis is on being fully engaged and actively involved in activities with direct relevance to functioning in the new cultural context. This shift toward experiential learning and experiential training is consistent with Black and Mendenhall's (1990) influential *social learning theory* of cross-cultural training. This theory posits that people learn appropriate intercultural behavior through modeling processes, cognitive attention and retention, as well as behavioral enactment such as reproduction of behaviors (practice) and reinforcement of behaviors with incentives. Based on the higher involvement and engagement associated with experiential learning and experiential training (compared to didactic classroom training), Black and Mendenhall argued that experiential approaches are more effective at increasing intercultural skills.

Benefits of Intercultural Training

Reviews of the intercultural training literature support the benefits of intercultural training across training methods. Black and Mendenhall (1990) demonstrated the benefits of cross-cultural training for personal and cognitive skill development. Morris and Robie's (2001) meta-analysis reported positive relationships for intercultural training with expatriates' intercultural adjustment ($\rho = 0.12$, $p < .05$) and performance ($\rho = .23$, $p < .05$). Littrell and colleagues' (2006) narrative review of the cross-cultural training literature concluded that cross-cultural training is effective because it helps foster self-maintenance, interpersonal, and cognitive skills, which are all important for success in a new culture (see also Deshpande & Viswesvaran, 1992).

Despite the documented benefits of intercultural training, organizations too often focus on country-specific training for soon-to-be expatriates and some regard intercultural training with skepticism (Black & Mendenhall, 1990). For example, Livermore and Van Dyne (2015: 14) noted that "[t]eam members often approach diversity training apathetically, going through the motions just because it is required." With the advent of CQ and the rigorous statistical evidence that CQ predicts adjustment, decision making, and performance in *many* culturally diverse contexts, intercultural training clearly has relevance to all employees.

Development of Cultural Intelligence: Review of the Current Evidence

We conducted a comprehensive literature review to uncover research publications that have focused on training and development interventions that may systematically increase employee's CQ. We cast a wide net, aiming to capture all publications that have focused on CQ as the intercultural competence of interest (i.e., excluding individual traits and individual attitudes), regardless of the training or development method, study methodology, study context, or sample. Our initial search revealed some literature reviews and conceptual articles about development of CQ that did not report empirical results. After excluding nonempirical papers, we examined 28 published articles and chapters that reported results on the extent to which specific training or development activities predicted CQ. In what follows, we begin by providing an overview of major observations and trends across this full set of papers, and we then delve into specific findings from these studies in greater detail in subsequent sections on: (1) CQ training interventions, and (2) intercultural experience interventions. Table 18.1 summarizes key features of the studies.

Trends in Research on Development of Cultural Intelligence

Sample Characteristics

As indicated by the information in the second column of Table 18.1, most CQ intervention studies relied upon student samples, albeit many of the students were in professional programs (e.g., MBA, executive programs). Only one training program focused on a professional context where employees were preparing for expatriate assignments (Rehg, Gundlach, & Grigorian, 2012). This contrasts with the cross-cultural training literature, which traditionally focused on training expatriates (e.g., Littrell et al., 2006). The use of student samples is not surprising given the novelty of CQ training and the importance of training interventions within cross-cultural management (CCM) or psychology courses. Nevertheless, this may influence generalizability and the concomitant recommendations for CQ program design.

Research Design

More than half ($n = 16$) of the studies employed quasi-experimental, repeated-measures designs with a pre- and postintervention CQ survey. This study design is more appropriate than correlational designs for drawing conclusions about increases in CQ that may result from training or development interventions and so we emphasize these studies in our review. We note, however, that only four of these studies included a matched-sample control group and none used random assignment.

Ten studies in Table 18.1 used correlational field survey designs where participants reported their experiences during a CQ training program ($n = 1$) or their prior intercultural experiences ($n = 9$) and this information was used as independent variables. Although correlational designs do not provide a strong foundation for drawing conclusions about change, they still offer insights about the development of CQ so we have retained them in our review. Importantly, researchers who used correlational field survey designs were more likely to access employees in professional contexts (e.g., Gupta et al., 2013). As a result, the combination of correlational and more controlled quasi-experimental student

Table 18.1 *Summary of the research evidence on developing cultural intelligence*

Study	Sample	Research Design	Independent Variables	Training or Development Program Content	Summary of Findings
1. Bücker & Korzilius (2015)	66 students in France and the Netherlands, plus 15 control groups students in the Netherlands	Quasi-experimental, pre-post intervention repeated measures, with matched samples control	Training program (classroom based)	Ecotonos simulation, a behavioral role play	Metacognitive, motivational, and behavioral CQ increased after training for the treatment group. Compared to the control group's CQ score gains, the treatment group's CQ score gains were only significantly better for metacognitive CQ.
2. Crowne (2008)	140 U.S. participants in a convenience sample (mostly adult students)	Field survey, cross-sectional	International experience (self-reported)	N/A	The number of countries visited was positively related to each dimension of CQ, but results differed as a function of whether these visits were for employment, education, vacation, or other purposes.
3. Eisenberg et al. (2013)	*Study 1*: 289 students in Austrian university *Study 2*: 150 students in international management master's program plus 40 control group students	Quasi-experimental, pre-post intervention repeated measures (*Study 1*) with matched samples control (*Study 2*)	Training program (CCM course), international experience	2.5-day CCM course with 60% didactic, 40% experiential and self-awareness	*Study 1*: Only cognitive and metacognitive CQ improved after CCM course. International experience predicted all dimensions except behavioral CQ more strongly at time 1. *Study 2*: Cognitive, metacognitive, and motivational CQ improved after CCM course. The control group showed no improvements. International experience predicted time 1 CQ but not time 2.

(*cont.*)

415

Table 18.1 (*cont.*)

Study	Sample	Research Design	Independent Variables	Training or Development Program Content	Summary of Findings
4. Engle & Crowne (2014)	105 students in U.S. university, plus 30 control group students	Quasi-experimental, pre-post intervention repeated measures with matched samples control	Cross-cultural sojourn, prior intercultural experience	7–14 day study abroad program for community service	All CQ dimensions increased significantly after the study abroad experience. For the control group, there were no significant changes in CQ. Prior intercultural experience was unrelated to CQ and changes in it.
5. Erez et al. (2013)	1,221 MBA and graduate students across 12 nations	Quasi-experimental, pre-post intervention repeated measures; multilevel (individuals nested in teams)	Training experience (multicultural virtual team project), team trust	Four-week multicultural virtual team project with self-awareness and experiential components; embedded within global management courses	Training experience increased overall CQ (no subscales were reported). Participants working in teams with high trust evidenced further benefits of training. Improvements in CQ were stable over six months.
6. Fischer (2011)	49 students in New Zealand university	Quasi-experimental, pre-post intervention repeated measures	Training program (in org. psychology course), cultural essentialism beliefs, open-mindedness, minority status	Five weeks of course with a mix of didactic and experiential components	No direct increase in any CQ dimension as a function of training. Open-mindedness moderated training's effectiveness: only open-minded students evidenced increased motivational CQ. Motivation and metacognitive CQ were higher for minority students.

Study	Sample	Method	Variable	Intervention	Findings
7. Gertsen & Soderberg (2010)	Four interviews of Danish expatriates in MNCs	Qualitative: Narrative interviews were examined in depth	Expatriate experience	Differs for each expatriate	Narration provides a context for developing metacognitive CQ but does not guarantee it. Events must be perceived and lead to reflection for learning to occur. They suggest narrative therapy may be beneficial to incorporate into CQ training programs.
8. Gupta et al. (2013)	233 Indian expatriates working in Europe or the United States	Field survey, cross-sectional	International experience (self-reported), expatriate training (self-reported), self-monitoring	N/A	Prior international experience was unrelated to all CQ dimensions. Expatriate training was only positively related to motivational CQ. Self-monitoring was positively related to cognitive, motivational, and behavioral CQ.
9. Hodges et al. (2011)	172 textile and apparel students in Thailand, Australia, and Russia	Quasi-experimental, pre-post intervention repeated measures, with open-ended questions	Training program	Eight didactic, web-based, customized learning modules for textile and apparel industry	Cognitive and metacognitive CQ increased after training. Qualitative results highlighted the importance of being open-minded to diverse perspectives, career preparation, and learning as an ongoing process.
10. Kim & Van Dyne (2012)	*Sample 1*: 441 adult participants in a development program *Sample 2*: 181 matched employee-observer pairs	Field survey, cross-sectional	International experience (self-reported)	N/A	Prior intercultural contact predicted self-reported (Study 1) and observer-reported (Study 2) overall CQ for U.S.-born majority group members, but overall CQ was uniformly high for those born in other countries (no dimensions reported).

(cont.)

Table 18.1 (*cont.*)

Study	Sample	Research Design	Independent Variables	Training or Development Program Content	Summary of Findings
11. Li et al. (2013)	294 international business executives	Field survey, cross-sectional	International experience (self-reported)	N/A	Length of international experience was positively related to overall CQ (no dimensions reported). The relationship length of experience and CQ was qualified by divergent learning style.
12. MacNab & Worthley (2012)	Over 370 managers and management students	Field survey, time-lagged	International experience (self-reported), general self-efficacy	N/A	There was no relationship between any type of international experience (travel, work, management) and CQ. General self-efficacy was positively related to CQ.
13. MacNab (2012)	373 management education professionals in Australian and American universities	Quasi-experimental, pre-post intervention repeated measures	Training program	Eight-week CQ training program, heavily experiential (7-stages) with some didactic and self-awareness elements	Metacognitive, motivational, and behavioral CQ increased after training. Cognitive CQ was not assessed in the study.
14. MacNab et al. (2012)	373 business students in Australian and American universities	Field survey, cross-sectional	International experience (self-reported), general self-efficacy	N/A	Experience with high-quality intercultural contacts (i.e., contact theory; characterized by equal status, common ground, meaningful individual contact, and support of authority) was positively related to overall CQ (no subscales reported). General self-efficacy was positively related to CQ.

	Sample	Method	Variables	Training	Findings
15. Moon, Choi, & Jung (2012)	190 Korean expatriates currently on assignment overseas	Field survey, cross-sectional	Training exposure before departure (self-reported), International experience (self-reported)	N/A	Comprehensiveness of predeparture training was positively related to all CQ dimensions. Prior international nonwork experience predicted all CQ dimensions, but prior international work experience only predicted cognitive and metacognitive CQ.
16. Pless, Maak, & Stahl (2011)	70 participants in a service-learning program engaged with cross-sector partnerships in developing countries	Qualitative: Interviews were content-analyzed for learning narratives	Cross-cultural sojourn with experiential training elements	4.5-month, six-phase service learning program, aimed at fostering leadership development	All of the program participants evidenced CQ learning, with the highest learning for culture-general knowledge. Learning processes occurred at cognitive, behavioral, and affective levels and included resolving paradoxes, constructing a new view of oneself in the world, and making sense of one's emotions while on assignment.
17. Ramsey & Lorenz (2016)	152 MBA students in United States plus 129 control group students	Quasi-experimental, pre-post intervention repeated measures, with matched samples control	Training program (CCM course)	Course included textbook readings on international management and current event discussions	Overall CQ increased after the CCM course (no subscales reported). Increased CQ predicted satisfaction with CCM studies.
18. Rehg et al. (2012)	110 U.S. government contracting trainees	Quasi-experimental, pre-post intervention repeated measures	Training program, specific self-efficacy	Nine-day training course with didactic method; content predominantly focused on laws, regulations, and contracting procedures	Cognitive and motivational CQ increased after training. Metacognitive CQ was not assessed. Specific self-efficacy predicted all three CQ dimensions at time 2.

(cont.)

419

Table 18.1 (*cont.*)

Study	Sample	Research Design	Independent Variables	Training or Development Program Content	Summary of Findings
19. Reichard et al. (2014)	130 organizational leaders from United States; 55 administrative staff members from South African university	Quasi-experimental, pre-post intervention repeated measures	Training program on cross-cultural psychological capital (PsyCap)	Two-hour cross-cultural PsyCap training session, with self-awareness, experiential, and didactic components	CQ total increased after PsyCap training program (no subscales reported). Increases in CQ remained stable two months after training program.
20. Reichard et al. (2015)	133 employees from 14 organizations in California (U.S.)	Quasi-experimental, pre-post intervention repeated measures	Training program (classroom based)	Cultural trigger events and self-awareness; psychological and social resources (four hours in classroom)	Metacognitive and behavioral CQ increased after training. Cognitive and motivational CQ did not. Ethnocentrism scores were also significantly reduced.
21. Rosenblatt et al. (2013)	212 Australian students in a cross-cultural management course	Quasi-experimental, pre-post intervention repeated measures	Cross-cultural contact experiences, perception of optimal contact, expectancy disconfirmation	6–8 week intervention to foster more positive intercultural contact experiences	CQ improvements were operationalized by a difference score (CQ development). CQ development was positive on average, showing upward change. Perceptions of optimal contact were not directly related to CQ development, but were mediated by expectancy disconfirmation, which positively predicted all CQ dimensions.

	Sample	Method	Predictor/Variables	Training intervention	Findings
22. Shannon & Begley (2008)	245 business students	Field survey, time-lagged (two points)	International experience (self-reported), language acquisition, diversity of social contacts	N/A	International experience was positively related to motivational CQ, but not to any other dimension. Language acquisition was positively related to cognitive CQ. Diversity of social contacts was unrelated to all CQ dimensions.
23. Shokef & Erez (2008)	191 MBA students working in multicultural teams	Quasi-experimental, pre-post intervention repeated measures	Training experience (multicultural virtual team project)	Four-week multicultural virtual team project with self-awareness and experiential components; embedded within global management courses	Metacognitive, motivational, and behavioral CQ increased after exposure to the multicultural virtual team project. Cognitive CQ did not increase. Global identity also increased. (*NOTE:* this sample is also included within Erez et al., 2013)
24. Tarique & Takeuchi (2008)	212 undergraduate management students at U.S. university	Field survey, time-lagged (two points)	International nonwork experience (self-reported; number and length)	N/A	The number of international nonwork experiences was positively related to all dimensions of CQ. The length of international nonwork experiences was positively related metacognitive and cognitive CQ.
25. Tay et al. (2008)	70 business travelers working in multinational corporations	Field survey, cross-sectional	International experience, need for control	N/A	Business travelers' multicultural experiences were positively related to cognitive CQ only. Need for control was positively related to all four CQ dimensions, and it further qualified CQ relationships.

(cont.)

Table 18.1 (*cont.*)

Study	Sample	Research Design	Independent Variables	Training or Development Program Content	Summary of Findings
26. Van Dyne et al. (2008)	204 Singaporean students	Quasi-experimental, pre-post intervention repeated measures	Training program (international management course)	Course included didactic and experiential components	The CQS evidenced measurement invariance across time. Cognitive CQ and behavioral CQ increased significantly as a function of course training. Metacognitive and motivational CQ did not increase.
27. Varela & Gatlin-Watts (2014)	84 U.S. business students participating in an exchange program	Quasi-experimental, pre-post intervention repeated measures	Cross-cultural sojourn, personality, cognitive ability, cultural distance, length of sojourn	Academic semester abroad program in Mexico or French-speaking Canada (average of 65 days)	Cognitive and metacognitive CQ increased after study abroad; motivational and behavioral CQ did not. Openness to experience (intellect) predicted metacognitive CQ development but cognitive ability predicted cognitive CQ development. Results were qualified by cultural distance and length of sojourn.
28. Wood & St. Peters (2014)	42 working professionals in a U.S. MBA program	Quasi-experimental, pre-post intervention repeated measures	Cross-cultural sojourn	11–12 day cross-cultural study tour	Cognitive, metacognitive, and motivational CQ all increased significantly after the study tour; behavioral CQ did not.

sample studies provides a nice balance. Additionally, our database included two qualitative, interview-based investigations of development of CQ that we also review in the following text.

Before moving on, we note that there are currently no published studies on the development of CQ that meet all of the recommendations for methodological rigor outlined in prior cross-cultural training reviews (i.e., control groups, pre-post design, random assignment, longitudinal measures; Kealey & Protheroe, 1996; Littrell et al., 2006). We return to this issue in the discussion of future research.

Predictors of Development of Cultural Intelligence

Regarding independent variables, the quasi-experimental studies can be further divided into those that examined training program delivery as the primary treatment variable ($n = 12$) versus those that examined cross-cultural sojourn experience as the treatment variable ($n = 4$). The correlational studies showed a similar divide but only one study focused on participant's reports of their experiences during a CQ training program (i.e., Moon, Choi, & Jung, 2012); all remaining correlational studies focused on participants' reports of international experience. This contrast between formal training and intercultural experience appears to reflect divergent assumptions about the best approaches for increasing CQ. Importantly, our analysis reveals that there is surprisingly little cross-fertilization between these streams of research. One exception is Pless, Maak, and Stahl's (2011) examination of a service-learning program, which included both experiential training and a cross-cultural sojourn.

Training or Development Program Content

The third column in Table 18.1 summarizes the research design and content of the study's training or development program. Consistent with the multifaceted nature of CQ (e.g., motivational, cognitive, metacognitive, and behavioral components), programs have used multifaceted training methods to enhance CQ. Overall, blended learning is the norm for CQ training, such that most programs included didactic and experiential components, and some also included a self-awareness component. Although most papers did not refer explicitly to self-awareness training, a few studies described fostering self-awareness as part of the program delivery (e.g., Erez et al., 2013; MacNab, 2012; Reichard, Dollwet, & Louw-Potgieter, 2014). In sum, these studies show that experiential, multifaceted learning approaches are the norm for development of CQ. We view this as a positive trend. We next describe the designs and findings of specific training intervention studies – starting with quasi-experimental research, followed by correlational research.

Key Findings on Cultural Intelligence Training Interventions

Quasi-Experimental Cultural Intelligence Training Research

The earliest evidence documenting that CQ could be developed through training was published as part of Van Dyne, Ang, and Koh's (2008) validation of the

CQS. They reported results of a four-month, time-lagged study of students in an international management course that emphasized cognitive instruction on cultural values and behavioral role-playing exercises. Results demonstrated longitudinal measurement invariance of the CQS and showed significant increases in cognitive and behavioral CQ.

Fischer's (2011) subsequent quasi-experimental study on CQ training found only modest support for the possibility that CQ could be developed. This study used lectures, self-awareness, experiential exercises (BAFA BAFA: Shirts, 1977), and behavioral modification training (Excell: Mak et al., 1999) across five weeks in a New Zealand organizational psychology course. Despite the strengths of this multifaceted approach, results showed CQ scores did not increase, and cognitive CQ was significantly lower at T2. Fischer (2011) suggested that the decrease in cognitive CQ could be based on moving from "unconscious incompetence" (i.e., being unaware) to "conscious incompetence" (i.e., being aware that their cultural competence was low) based on Bhawuk's (1998) stages of intercultural development. Students with higher open-mindedness (assessed through the Multicultural Personality Questionnaire; van der Zee & Van Oudenhoven, 2000) showed significant improvements in motivational CQ, indicating that some people are more likely to benefit from training programs than others.

Hodges and colleagues (2011) used a CQ training program with eight, web-based didactic training modules that covered topics from global sourcing and competitive positioning to intercultural communication – specifically tailored to textile and apparel industry professionals. The training modules were embedded within courses at three U.S. universities and resulted in significant increases in cognitive and metacognitive CQ, but not behavioral or motivational CQ.

Rehg and colleagues (2012) conducted the only study we located on employee CQ training aimed at improving execution of job duties. This study examined CQ training for civilian contractors for the U.S. government who would be executing governmental contracts overseas. The training program was entirely lecture based, and emphasized factual information about cultural values, how culture affects behavior, and specific cultural knowledge about Iraq. Results demonstrated that cognitive and behavioral CQ improved after training, but motivational CQ did not. Metacognitive CQ was not measured. Results also showed that task-specific self-efficacy increased as a function of training and predicted the three dimensions of CQ at time 2.

MacNab (2012) drew on Kolb's (1984) ELT to argue that direct experiences coupled with reflection and cumulative knowledge building are superior to information-only training approaches. He designed a CQ education program that mapped onto Cushner and Brislin's (1996) five-step learning process (i.e., developing awareness, fostering experience, internalization, communication, and social sharing). A sample of 373 management professionals completed the training program (about eight weeks), and the results demonstrated significant improvements in metacognitive, motivational, and behavioral CQ; cognitive CQ was not assessed in this study.

Eisenberg and colleagues' (2013) quasi-experimental research offered two studies where the second study included a matched-sample control group. Drawing on Earley and Peterson (2004), they argued that course-based training is more likely to influence cognitive and metacognitive CQ (the "mental dimensions") than motivational or behavioral CQ. The Study 1 training intervention was an intensive 2.5 day CCM course delivered to Austrian students about to study abroad. As predicted, results demonstrated that cognitive and metacognitive CQ improved after training, whereas motivational and behavioral CQ did not. The Study 2 training intervention was a more involved CCM course delivered over an average of eight weeks to Masters of International Management students at partner universities in six countries. Again, cognitive and metacognitive CQ improved. Additionally, motivational CQ also increased significantly. There were no significant changes in behavioral CQ. For the control group, none of the CQ dimensions significantly changed. Analyses also demonstrated that prior international experience predicted CQ scores at time 1, but this relationship disappeared at time 2, suggesting that the CCM course acted as an "equalizer" that increased CQ of trainees who had little prior intercultural experience.

Erez and colleagues (2013) reported results of a unique study of intercultural training and CQ within the context of a multicultural virtual team project, and Shokof and Erez (2008) provided preliminary results of this multiyear study. Participants were 1,221 graduate students in global management courses distributed across 12 nations who participated in a four-week, three-phrase program (getting to know each other, a virtual team project, and postproject wrap-up). Overall CQ improved as a function of the training experience (no subscales were reported), and CQ was further enhanced when participants worked in teams with high levels of trust. A subsample of participants ($n = 121$) also completed a six-month follow-up survey to assess the stability of CQ improvements and showed that the gains in CQ did not decrease after six months. These results are consistent with early arguments by Moynihan and colleagues (2006) that working in multinational teams provides a rich experiential context to grown one's CQ.

A quasi-experimental study by Reichard and colleagues (2014) offered a distinct approach to intercultural training. This program was designed to increase participants' psychological capital (PsyCap), defined as the positive psychological states of efficacy, hope, optimism, and resilience (Luthans, Youssef, & Avolio, 2007). The program included two-hour training sessions for professionals in the United States and South Africa aimed at increasing self-awareness, reframing past events, and identifying strategies for intercultural success. The training increased overall CQ (no subscales were reported) and that these increases remained stable for two months after the program.

A subsequent study by Reichard and colleagues (2015) built upon this foundation by developing a training program to foster employees' psychological and social resources based upon cultural trigger events (i.e., discrete cultural occurrences that are often negative in nature). Their first study developed cultural trigger event scenarios based upon thematic analysis, and their second study was a quasi-experimental exploration of whether employees who underwent classroom training on trigger events would evidence increased CQ. Results showed that metacognitive and behavioral CQ increased after training, whereas cognitive and motivational CQ did not. Results also showed reduced levels of ethnocentrism for participants.

Bücker and Korzilius (2015) assessed the extent to which a cross-cultural behavioral role-play simulation (Ecotonos) improved CQ amongst international management students. Their quasi-experimental design included a matched-samples control group. This experiential training program showed significant improvements for metacognitive, motivational, and behavioral CQ after training for the treatment group; and no significant change in cognitive CQ. CQ also increased in the control group, and results showed a significantly greater increase in metacognitive CQ for the treatment group compared to the control group.

Finally, a recent study by Ramsey and Lorenz (2016) employed a quasi-experimental, matched-samples control design to explore improvements in overall CQ (no subscales) for MBA students in a CCM course. The treatment in this study was the international management textbook readings along with discussions of current events so the training was largely didactic. Results showed significant improvements in total CQ for the treatment group at time 2, and as expected, no significant change in CQ scores for the control group.

Correlational Cultural Intelligence Training Research

Whereas the prior section focused on studies that used pre- and posttraining interventions and assessed changes in CQ, another study used a correlational design. Specifically, Moon and colleagues (2012) surveyed Korean expatriates about their prior intercultural experience and predeparture intercultural training (length and comprehensiveness) to determine whether training was linked to CQ. Their sample is unique because it is the only CQ training study that focused on expatriates currently on assignment. The results of this cross-sectional, self-reported survey demonstrated a positive relationship between previous international *nonwork* experience and all dimensions of CQ. Interestingly, previous international *work* experience was positively related to cognitive and metacognitive CQ, but not to motivational or behavioral CQ. Expatriates who had more comprehensive intercultural training programs before departure reported significantly higher CQ on all dimensions. Finally, these results were qualified by mastery and performance avoidance goal orientations, such that comprehensive predeparture intercultural training was more likely to predict CQ for those with a mastery-goal orientation and less likely to predict CQ for those with a performance-avoid orientation. This provides important evidence that individual differences function as boundary conditions for the effectiveness of training.

Cultural Intelligence Training Research Summary

Despite some early concerns about whether training interventions could predict CQ improvements (Fischer, 2011), the bulk of the evidence has demonstrated that a variety of intercultural training interventions increase CQ.

These interventions include fully didactic (Rehg et al., 2012), fully experiential (MacNab, 2012), and blended approaches (Erez et al., 2013), and all of these approaches predicted increased CQ.

Overall, the training benefits are stronger for cognitive and metacognitive CQ, consistent with Eisenberg and colleagues' (2013) arguments, but this observation must be qualified based upon the limited number of studies and the studies that do not report separate results for the four CQ dimensions (e.g., Erez et al., 2013; MacNab, 2012; Ramsey & Lorenz, 2016; Rehg et al., 2012; Reichard et al., 2014). We now turn our attention to intercultural experience as a way to enhance CQ.

Key Findings on Intercultural Experience and Cultural Intelligence

Quasi-Experimental Intercultural Experience Research

Although the idea that intercultural experience can help to foster CQ is not new, quasi-experimental research that directly tests this proposition has only recently emerged. Rosenblatt, Worthley, and MacNab (2013) were the first to employ a pre- and posttest design to examine predictors of development of CQ (i.e., changes in CQ from time 1 to time 2). This research occurred in the context of an intercultural education program in Australia but the intervention encouraged participants to seek out and experience intercultural interactions with a novel cultural group. When intercultural experiences were perceived as upholding Allport's (1954) principles of optimal contact (e.g., equal status among participants, personalized contact, common goals, authority support), participants reported higher expectancy disconfirmation (e.g., stereotype violations). Higher expectancy disconfirmation subsequently predicted improvements on all four dimensions of CQ.

Three additional studies provide more direct assessments of changes in CQ as a function of cross-cultural sojourn experience. Wood and St. Peters (2014) assessed results of a short (11–12 day) cross-cultural study tour for professionals in a U.S. MBA program. Their results demonstrated that cognitive, metacognitive, and motivational CQ increased after the sojourn, but behavioral CQ did not increase.

Varela and Gatlin-Watts (2014) studied the effects of a semester-long study abroad program on increases in CQ for U.S. undergraduates. They also considered whether development of CQ was influenced by personality (conscientiousness, openness to experience, extraversion) and/or cognitive ability, as well the roles of cultural distance and length of the sojourn as moderators. Their results showed that cognitive and metacognitive CQ increased after the cross-cultural sojourn. Openness to experience (intellect dimension) was positively related to increases in metacognitive CQ, and cognitive ability was positively related to increases in cognitive CQ. These relationships were further qualified by cultural distance and length of the sojourn. The authors emphasized richness and depth of cultural experiences as determinants of deep-level learning, suggesting that many study abroad programs increase cognitive and metacognitive CQ because much of the learning is knowledge based and not based on deep-level reflection and practice (see also Pless & colleagues, 2011, and the following text).

A final quasi-experimental cross-cultural sojourn study by Engle and Crowne (2014) used a more rigorous methodological design, with a matched samples control group, to assess the degree to which a short international experience may foster increases in CQ. Their sample was 105 U.S. students travelling abroad for a short (7–14 day) community service project. Thus, this study provides a relatively strict test of whether CQ can be enhanced based on a short-term international experience. Importantly, results demonstrated that all four dimensions of CQ increased for the study abroad group, but there were no significant changes in CQ for those in the control group. Overall, these studies show the promising potential of developing CQ through both short- and long-term international experience interventions, with especially strong effects for cognitive and metacognitive CQ.

Correlational Intercultural Experience Research

The earliest research aimed at understanding development of CQ used correlational field survey designs to assess the relationship between international experience and CQ. Shannon and Begley (2008) reported a positive relationship between prior international experience and motivational CQ, but not for the other dimensions of CQ. Tarique and Takeuchi (2008) reported that the overall number of international nonwork experiences was positively related to all four dimensions of CQ, but that total length of exposure was positively related to metacognitive and cognitive CQ. Tay, Westman, and Chia (2008) focused on the multicultural experiences of short-term business travelers and reported that multicultural experiences were positively related to cognitive CQ. Additionally, need for control was positively related to all CQ dimensions. These studies suggest the importance of additional research that considers boundary conditions that explain when international experiences does and does not predict specific dimensions of CQ.

Additional studies offer correlational evidence for the relationship between international experience and CQ – with only two studies (Gupta et al., 2013; MacNab & Worthley, 2012) reporting nonsignificant relationships. Crowne (2008) investigated three types of intercultural experience (e.g., work, vacation, and education) and showed that some type of intercultural experience predicted each dimension of CQ but that the relationships differed across types of experience. MacNab, Brislin, and Worthley (2013) hypothesized and found that higher-quality intercultural contact experiences (as defined by contact theory; Allport, 1954) were positively associated with CQ. Kim and Van Dyne (2012) demonstrated that intercultural contact predicted observer-rated CQ for those with majority status (those born in the United States), but the level of CQ was uniformly high for those born in another country. Finally, Li, Mobley, and Kelly (2013) reported that the relationship between an executive's length of global experience and CQ depended upon whether they had a divergent learning style (i.e., the extent to which they prioritized concrete experience and reflective observation).

Intercultural Experience Research Summary

As the preceding research demonstrates, intercultural experience is an alternative to CQ training because international experience is another way in which to foster increases in CQ. To date, the most rigorous studies on intercultural experience have shown the strongest results for metacognitive and cognitive CQ. Nevertheless, evidence from a handful of other studies shows that international experience predicts all four dimensions of CQ, as well as overall CQ. The depth and richness of intercultural experience seem to play a role in whether CQ improves, but few quantitative studies provide sufficient detail on the nature of the intercultural sojourn experience to discern the characteristics of programs and experiences that matter most. We now turn to two studies that provide depth and richness to our understanding of learning processes during intercultural encounters.

Key Findings from Narrative Research on Cultural Intelligence

Two qualitative studies have explored the cultural learning process by delving into rich reports of participant's experiences. Gertsen and Søderberg (2010) presented four in-depth cases that explored narratives of how expatriates understood and constructed cultural encounters, and how this process is linked to metacognitive CQ. They described how specific encounters elicited emotions and challenged existing understandings and triggered sense-making processes that fostered new learning and development of CQ. Overall, Gersten and Søderberg argued that the narrative approach should be particularly useful for illuminating expatriate's experiences during cultural encounters and how these experiences enable them to practice and further develop their CQ.

Pless and colleagues (2011) used a different qualitative approach and focused on interviews from 70 participants in a large-scale service learning project called "Project Ulysses." Project Ulysses is part of PricewaterhouseCooper's (PwC) global talent development program, and has the goal of promoting responsible leadership within PwC's global network of firms and developing well-rounded leaders through service learning. The six-phase program involves nomination, preparation (two months), induction (weeklong training), a field assignment (two months), debriefing (weeklong review), and networking after the program. Pless and colleagues (2011) described the program's foundations within ELT (Kolb, 1984) and emphasized the importance of a multifaceted range of opportunities that facilitate deep-level learning. Based upon the interview results, all program participants evidenced CQ learning, with the highest learning for culture-general knowledge. Learning processes occurred at cognitive, behavioral, and affective levels and included resolving paradoxes, constructing a new view of oneself in the world, and making sense of personal emotions while on assignment. The richness and depth of the Project Ulysses program, coupled with providing participants with support and expectations for ongoing cultural learning, make this program a model for future programs on development of CQ. Indeed, intercultural service learning programs for corporate leaders are becoming increasing popular, including programs at IBM, Cigna, and GlaxoSmithKlein (Caligiuri, Mencin, & Jiang, 2013; Chong & Fleming, 2014; Maas, 2015). Supporting these programs with effective CQ training is an important future direction.

Development of Cultural Intelligence: Suggested Avenues for Future Research

Research on developing CQ has come a long way in a very short time frame. In the few years since the first development of CQ study, the field has already accumulated 28 studies, including 16 quasi-experimental, repeated-measures studies that documented changes in CQ based on pre- and postintervention assessments. The research summarized in Table 18.1 evidences substantial diversity of approaches for developing CQ and provides additional information on the degree to which various training interventions and intercultural experiences foster improvements in CQ.

In total, the evidence provides a resounding "yes" to the question of whether CQ can be developed. With this firm foundation, scholars can now shift their attention to more rigorous designs, more nuanced questions about developing specific dimensions of CQ, transfer of training, and boundary conditions that qualify these relationships. In the next section, we offer ideas on especially promising avenues for future research.

Increasing Methodological Rigor and Sample Diversity

We recognize the challenges of conducting research on the development of intercultural competence and implementing intercultural, longitudinal research designs (Gelfand, Raver, & Ehrhart, 2002). Nonetheless, we agree with prior critiques of the intercultural training literature (Kealey & Protheroe, 1996; Littrell et al., 2006) that it is important for researchers to use more rigorous designs. The trend toward using matched-samples control groups (Bücker & Korzilius, 2015; Eisenberg et al., 2013; Engle & Crowne, 2014; Ramsey & Lorenz, 2016) is a positive development, as is the use of longitudinal assessments of increases in CQ (Erez et al., 2013; Reichard et al., 2014). These research designs need to become the norm for studies that aim to quantify the effects of CQ development.

Where possible (e.g., student training programs), it is also necessary to use random assignment of participants into treatment and control groups to establish whether CQ may be developed for participants who do not self-select into cross-cultural programs. Interestingly, the only study that showed minimal benefits of CQ training used students who did not self-select into cultural training (Fischer, 2011). The other studies examined the development of CQ in samples who were likely already motivated to learn about cultural differences (e.g., those who enrolled in CCM courses or signed up for a cross-cultural sojourn). It is important for future research to establish whether CQ interventions are equally effective for those who do not self-select into these programs. Delayed treatment control groups may be a viable option for eventually delivering training to all program participants while meeting the standards of rigorous experimental design.

More research is also needed on working adults in employment contexts. Traditionally, the intercultural training literature has focused on expatriates (Littrell et al., 2006), and yet this population is strikingly underrepresented in the studies we have reviewed. It is possible that results with nonstudent samples will be even stronger (Despande, Joseph, & Viswesvaran, 1994). However, it is also possible that the nature of these training programs will differ (e.g., shorter, more didactic; e.g., Reichard et al., 2015), thereby affecting the potential benefits of developing CQ interventions.

Matching Dimensions of Cultural Intelligence to Development Methods

We also need research on why and how CQ training differentially influences specific dimensions of CQ. Our summary of existing research suggests that the effects of CQ training and cross-cultural experience are stronger for cognitive and metacognitive CQ, followed by motivational CQ, with the least gains seen for behavioral CQ. The reason for these differences is not entirely clear but they are consistent with findings from the broader training literature. Meta-analytic evidence on training interventions has shown that effect sizes for behavioral change tend to be smaller than those for cognitive change (Arthur et al., 2003). The difficulty of eliciting behavioral and results-focused improvements may be due to situational constraints that discourage the transfer of training. Nonetheless, it is promising that two recent CQ training studies (Bücker & Korzilius, 2015; Reichard et al., 2015) did elicit improvement in behavioral CQ. One topic for future research is to investigate whether participants' motivational or behavioral CQ is more likely to increase based on experiential (simulation) training and/or a combination of experiential training and sojourner experiences such as described by Pless and colleagues (2011), especially if coupled with a supportive transfer environment.

The broader training literature has also documented stronger links between parallel training methods and outcomes (Arthur et al., 2003). For example, cognitive change occurs after attributional or cognitive training methods (Bhawuk, 1998) whereas behavioral change occurs after behavior modification (Mak & Buckingham, 2007) and behavioral modeling training (Taylor, Russ-Eft, & Chan, 2005). We encourage scholars to specify the didactic, self-awareness, attributional, and/or experiential elements of their interventions and to investigate theoretically matched CQ outcomes. It will be beneficial to draw from theory in the organizational training literature (e.g., Taylor et al., 2005) to specify the ways in which learning outcomes are matched to the specific training method.

Transferring Cultural Intelligence Gains to Subsequent Outcomes

We found no studies that linked developmental interventions (e.g., training, experience) with indicators of intercultural effectiveness. Exploring more complex, mediated models is an important future direction. As noted by scholars in the broader industrial-organizational literature on training, the field needs to separate training outcomes from transfer outcomes (Blume et al., 2010). Thus, increases in CQ do not necessarily equal better acculturation or intercultural effectiveness.

Additionally, the organizational training literature has emphasized the importance of the learning context and transfer of training (Aguinis & Kraiger, 2009), yet this is not true of the intercultural training literature. We suggest the value of theoretically based studies on the transfer of CQ gains to subsequent indicators of intercultural effectiveness (e.g., acculturation in new cultural contexts, global leadership potential, and global leader effectiveness).

One promising theory drew on ELT to propose that concrete international experience, reflective observation, abstract conceptualization, and active experimentation are foundations for global leadership development (Ng, Van Dyne, & Ang, 2009). This theoretical model positioned CQ as an exogenous factor, but it also may mutually reinforce international experience, such that both CQ and intercultural experience influence global leadership self-efficacy, accuracy of mental models, flexible styles, and global leader effectiveness. Research testing propositions from this model is strongly encouraged.

Considering Individual and Cultural Boundary Conditions

Research has begun to provide some evidence for boundary conditions that qualify relationships predicting the development of CQ, especially with regard to individual differences (e.g., open-mindedness, divergent learning style, goal orientation; Fischer, 2011; Li et al., 2013; Moon et al., 2012). These studies shed light on why some people are better or less able to benefit from interventions designed to develop CQ, but there is much more work to be done.

In addition to investigating other individual characteristics, it is also likely that cultural background of participants matters. For example, research has demonstrated that culture of the participant interacts with type of training to impact outcomes (Earley, 1994; Triandis, Brislin, & Hui, 1988), and yet intercultural training has proceeded as if training methods and benefits are equally appropriate across cultures. It is possible, for example, that participants from high power distance cultures may react more favorably and learn more from didactic, classroom-based training, whereas those from low power distance cultures may benefit less. Similarly, training participants from loose cultures (Gelfand, Nishii, & Raver, 2005) may be more open to divergent perspectives and thus may more quickly benefit from attribution training, compared to participants from tight cultures. Thus, future research on culturally intelligent ways to conduct training should consider ways to adapt the content and delivery to be culturally appropriate. Finally, it would be valuable to incorporate scholarship on cultural differences in thinking and learning styles into the design of training programs.

Conclusion

Research on the development of CQ has only recently emerged, and yet scholars have very quickly developed an impressive array of studies that document the gains in CQ that result from training interventions and intercultural experience programs. Thus, it is no longer a question of whether CQ may be developed. Instead, the evidence is clear: Positive changes in CQ occur as a function of systematic interventions, particularly for cognitive and metacognitive CQ. Given this strong foundation, future research should now shift toward understanding how the specific dimensions of CQ may be enhanced by domain-matched development methods, what subsequent outcomes occur as a function of CQ training and experience, and how individual and cultural boundary conditions influence training effectiveness. This stream of research has come a long way and there are many more opportunities for future research on developing CQ and the subsequent transfer of training.

References

Adair, W. L., Hideg, I., and Spence, J. R. 2013. The culturally intelligent team: The impact of team cultural intelligence and cultural heterogeneity on team shared values. *Journal of Cross-Cultural Psychology* 44: 941–962.

Aguinis, H., and Kraiger, K. 2009. Benefits of training and development for individuals, teams, organizations, and society. *Annual Review of Psychology* 60: 451–74.

Albert, R. D. 1983. The intercultural sensitizer or culture assimilator: A cognitive approach. In D. Landis and R.W. Brislin, eds., *Handbook of Intercultural Training*, 2: 186–217. New York: Pergamon.

Allport, G. 1954. *The Nature of Prejudice*. Reading, MA: Addison Wesley.

Ang, S., and Inkpen, A. C. 2008. Cultural intelligence and offshore outsourcing success: A framework of firm-level intercultural capability. *Decision Sciences* 39: 33–358.

Ang, S., and Van Dyne, L., 2008. Conceptualization of cultural intelligence: Definition, distinctiveness, and nomological network. In S. Ang, and L. Van Dyne, eds., *Handbook on Cultural Intelligence: Theory, Measurement and Applications*, 3–15. Armonk, NY: M. E. Sharpe.

Ang, S., and Van Dyne, L., eds. 2008. *Handbook on Cultural Intelligence: Theory, Measurement and Applications*. Armonk, NY: M. E. Sharpe.

Ang., S., Van Dyne, L., and Rockstuhl, T. 2015. Cultural intelligence: Origins, conceptualization, evolution, and methodological diversity. In M. Gelfand, C. Y. Chiu, and Y. Y. Hong, eds., *Advances in Culture and Psychology*, 5: 273–323. New York: Oxford University Press.

Ang, S., Van Dyne, L., Koh, C., Ng, K. Y., Templer, K. J., Tay, C., and Chandrasekar, N. A. 2007. Cultural intelligence: Its measurement and effects on cultural judgment and decision making, cultural adaptation and task performance. *Management and Organization Review* 3: 335–371.

Arthur, W., Jr., Bennett, W., Jr., Edens, P. S., and Bell, S. T. 2003. Effectiveness of training in organizations: A meta-analysis of design and evaluation features. *Journal of Applied Psychology* 88: 234–245.

Berry, J. W. 1989. Psychology of acculturation. In J. Brown, ed., *Cross-cultural Perspectives: Nebraska Symposium on Motivation*, 201–234. Lincoln: University of Nebraska Press.

Berry, J. W., and Sam, D. L. 1997. Acculturation and adaptation. In J. W. Berry, Y. H. Poortinga, and J. Pandey, eds., *Handbook of Cross-cultural Psychology*, 2nd ed., 291–326. Needham Heights, MA: Allyn and Bacon.

Bhawuk, D. P. S. 1998. The role of culture theory in cross-cultural training: A multi-method study of culture specific, culture-general, and culture theory based assimilators. *Journal of Cross-Cultural Psychology* 295: 630–655.

Bhawuk, D. P. S., and Brislin, R. W. 2000. Cross-cultural training: A review. *Applied Psychology: An International Review* 491: 162–191.

Black, J. S., and Mendenhall, M. 1990. Cross-cultural training effectiveness: A review and a theoretical framework for future research. *Academy of Management Review* 151: 113–136.

Blume, B. D., Ford, J. K., Baldwin, T. T., and Huang, J. L. 2010. Transfer of training: A meta-analytic review. *Journal of Management* 36: 1065–1105.

Brislin, R. W., and Horvath, A. 1997. Cross-cultural training and multicultural education. In J. W. Berry, Y. H. Poortinga, and J. Pandey, eds., *Handbook of Cross-cultural Psychology*, 2nd ed., 327–369. Needham Heights, MA: Allyn and Bacon.

Bücker, J. J. L. E., and Korzilius, H. 2015. Developing cultural intelligence: Assessing the effects of the Ecotonos cultural simulation game for international business students. *The International Journal of Human Resource Management* 26: 1995–2014.

Caligiuri, P., Mencin, A., and Jiang, K. 2013. Win-win-win: The influence of company-sponsored volunteerism programs on employees, NGOs and business units. *Personnel Psychology* 66: 825–860.

Chen, M. L., and Lin, C. P. 2013. Assessing the effects of cultural intelligence on team knowledge sharing from a socio-cognitive perspective. *Human Resources Management* 52: 675–695.

Chen, X. P., Liu, D., and Portnoy, R. 2012. A multilevel investigation of motivational cultural intelligence, organizational diversity climate, and cultural sales: Evidence from U.S. real estate firms. *Journal of Applied Psychology* 97: 93–106.

Chen, G., Kirkman, B. L., Kim, K., Farh, C. I. C., and Tangirala, S. 2010. When does cross-cultural motivation enhance expatriate effectiveness? A multilevel investigation of the moderating roles of subsidiary support and cultural distance. *Academy of Management Journal* 53: 1110–1130.

Chong., R., and Fleming, M. 2014. Why IBM gives top employees a month to do service abroad. *Harvard Business Review*. November 5. https://hbr.org/2014/11/why-ibm-gives-top-employees-a-month-to-do-service-abroad (accessed February 1, 2016).

Chua, R. Y. J., Morris, M. W., and Mor, S. 2012. Collaborating across cultures: Cultural metacognition and affect-based trust in creative collaboration. *Organizational Behavior and Human Decision Processes* 118: 116–131.

Church, A. 1982. Sojourner adjustment. *Psychological Bulletin* 91: 540–572.

Crowne, K. A. 2008. What leads to cultural intelligence? *Business Horizons* 515: 391–399.

Cushner, K., and Brislin, R. W. 1996. *Intercultural Interactions: A Practical Guide*, 2nd ed. Thousand Oaks, CA: Sage.

Deshpande, S. P., and Viswesvaran, C. 1992. Is cross-cultural training of expatriate managers effective: A meta analysis. *International Journal of Intercultural Relations* 163: 295–310.

Deshpande, S. P, Joseph, J., and Viswesvaran, C. 1994. Does use of student samples affect results of studies in cross-cultural training? A meta-analysis. *Psychological Reports* 743: 779–785.

Dinges, N. G., and Baldwin, K. D. 1996. Intercultural competence: A research perspective. In D. Landis and R. S. Bhagat, eds., *Handbook of Intercultural Training*, 2nd ed., 106–123. Thousand Oaks, CA: Sage.

Earley, P. C. 1994. Self or group? Cultural effects of training on self-efficacy and performance. *Administrative Science Quarterly* 391: 89–117.

Earley, P. C., and Ang, S. 2003. *Cultural Intelligence: Individual Interactions across Cultures.* Palo Alto, CA: Stanford University Press.

Earley, P. C., and Peterson, R. S. 2004. The elusive cultural chameleon: Cultural intelligence as a new approach to intercultural training for the global manager. *Academy of Management Learning and Education* 3: 100–115.

Eccles, J. S., and Wigfield, A. 2002. Motivational beliefs, values, and goals. *Annual Review of Psychology* 53: 109–132.

Eisenberg, J., Lee, H., Bruck, F., Brenner, B., Claes, M., Mironski, J., and Bell, R. 2013. Can business schools make students culturally competent? Effects of cross-cultural management courses on cultural intelligence. *Academy of Management Learning and Education* 124: 603–621.

Engle, R. L., and Crowne, K. A. 2014. The impact of international experience on cultural intelligence: An application of contact theory in a structured short-term programme. *Human Resource Development International* 171: 30–46.

Erez, M., Lisak, A., Harush, R., Glikson, E., Nouri, R., and Shokef, E. 2013. Going global: Developing management students' cultural intelligence and global identity in culturally diverse virtual teams. *Academy of Management Learning and Education* 123: 330–355. doi:10.5465/amle.2012.0200

Fiedler, F. E., Mitchell, T., and Triandis, H. C. 1971. The cultural assimilator: An approach to cross cultural training. *Journal of Applied Psychology* 55: 95–102.

Fischer, R. 2011. Cross-cultural training effects on cultural essentialism beliefs and cultural intelligence. *International Journal of Intercultural Relations* 356: 767–775.

Furnham, A., and Bochner, S. 1986. *Culture Shock: Psychological Reactions to Unfamiliar Environments.* London: Methuen.

Gelfand, M. J., Imai, L., and Fehr, R. 2008. Thinking intelligently about cultural intelligence: The road ahead. In S. Ang and L. Van Dyne, eds., *Handbook of Cultural Intelligence: Theory, Measurement, and Applications*, 375–387. New York: M. E. Sharpe.

Gelfand, M. J., Nishii, L. H., and Raver, J. L. 2006. On the nature and importance of cultural tightness-looseness. *Journal of Applied Psychology* 91(6): 1225–1244.

Gelfand, M. J., Raver, J. L., and Ehrhart, K. H. 2002. Methodological issues in cross-cultural organizational research. In S. G. Rogelberg, ed., *Handbook of Research Methods in Industrial and Organizational Psychology*, 216–246. Malden, MA: Blackwell.

Gertsen, M. C., and Søderberg, A. 2010. Expatriate stories about cultural encounters: A narrative approach to cultural learning processes in multinational companies. *Scandinavian Journal of Management* 263: 248–257.

Gjertsen, T., Torp, A. M., Tan M. L., and Koh, C. 2010. The impact of cultural intelligence on homophily in intra-organizational multinational networks. Presented at the 70th Annual Meeting of the Academy of Management, August. Montreal, Canada.

Groves, K., and Feyerherm, A. 2011. Leader cultural intelligence in context: Testing the moderating effects of team cultural diversity on leader and team performance. *Group and Organization Management* 36: 535–566.

Gudykunst, W. B., Buzley, R. M., and Hammer, M. R. 1996. Designing intercultural training. In D. Landis and R. S. Bhagat, eds., *Handbook of Intercultural Training*, 2nd ed., 61–80. Thousand Oaks, CA: Sage.

Gupta, B., Singh, D., Jandhyala, K., and Bhatt, S. 2013. Self-monitoring, cultural training and prior international work experience as predictors of cultural intelligence – A study of Indian expatriates. *Organizations and Markets in Emerging Economies* 41: 56–71.

Hammer, M. R., Bennett, M. J., and Wiseman, R. 2003. Measuring intercultural sensitivity: The intercultural development inventory. *International Journal of Intercultural Relationships* 27: 421–443.

Harrison, J. K. 1993. Individual and combined effects of behavior modeling and the cultural assimilator in cross-cultural management training. *Journal of Applied Psychology* 77(6): 952–962.

Hodges, N., Watchravesringkan, K., Karpova, E., Hegland, J., O'Neal, G., and Kadolph, S. 2011. Collaborative development of textile and apparel curriculum designed to foster students' global competence. *Family and Consumer Sciences Research Journal* 39(4): 325–338.

Imai, L., and Gelfand, M. J. 2010. The culturally intelligent negotiator: The impact of cultural intelligence CQ on negotiation sequences and outcomes. *Organizational Behavior and Human Decision Processes* 112: 83–98.

Johnson, J. P., Lenartowicz, T., and Apud, S. 2006. Cross-cultural competence in international business: Toward a definition and a model. *Journal of International Business Studies* 37: 525–543.

Kealey, D. J., and Protheroe, D. R. 1996. The effectiveness of cross-cultural training for expatriates: An assessment of the literature on the issue. *International Journal of Intercultural Relations* 20: 141–165.

Kim, Y. J., and Van Dyne, L. 2012. Cultural intelligence and international leadership potential: The importance of contact for members of the majority. *Applied Psychology: An International Review* 61: 272–294.

Kolb, D. A. 1984. *Experiential Learning: Experience as the Source of Learning and Development*. Englewood Cliffs, NJ: Prentice-Hall.

Kolb, A. Y., and Kolb, D. A. 2005. Learning styles and learning spaces: Enhancing experiential learning in higher education. *Academy of Management Learning and Education* 4: 193–212.

Leung, K., Ang, S., and Tan, M. L. 2014. Intercultural competence. *Annual Review of Organizational Psychology and Organizational Behavior* 1: 489–519.

Li, M., Mobley, W. H., and Kelly, A. 2013. When do global leaders learn best to develop cultural intelligence? An investigation of the moderating role of experiential learning style. *Academy of Management Learning and Education* 12(1): 32–50.

Littrell, L. N., Salas, E., Hess, H. P., Paley, M., and Riedel, S. 2006. Expatriate preparation: A critical analysis of 25 years of cross-cultural training research. *Human Resource Development Review* 5: 355–388.

Livermore, D. 2010. *Leading with Cultural Intelligence: The New Secret to Success.* New York: American Management Association.

Livermore, D., and Van Dyne, L. 2015. *Cultural Intelligence: The Essential Intelligence for the 21st Century.* SHRM Foundation Effective Practice Guideline Series. Alexandria, VA: SHRM.

Luthans, F., Youssef, C. M., and Avolio, B. J. 2007. *Psychological Capital: Developing the Human Competitive Edge.* New York: Oxford University Press.

Maas, S. 2015. Northeastern program connects corporations with NGOs. *Boston Globe.* May 14. https://www.bostonglobe.com/business/2015/05/14/northeastern-program-connects-corporations-with-ngos-developing-nations/WR6plnMpfLC4UUlYPRVl7H/story.html (accessed February 1, 2016).

MacNab, B. R. 2012. An experiential approach to cultural intelligence education. *Journal of Management Education* 36(1): 66–94.

MacNab, B. R., and Worthley, R. 2012. Individual characteristics as predictors of cultural intelligence development: The relevance of self-efficacy. *International Journal of Intercultural Relations* 36(1): 62–71.

MacNab, B., Brislin, R., and Worthley, R. 2012. Experiential cultural intelligence development: Context and individual attributes. *The International Journal of Human Resource Management* 23(7): 1320–1341.

Mak, A. S., and Buckingham, K. 2007. Beyond communication courses: Are there benefits in adding skills-based EXCELL™ sociocultural training? *International Journal of Intercultural Relations* 31(3): 277–291.

Mak, A. S., Barker, M., Logan, G., and Millman, L. 1999. Benefits of cultural diversity for international and local students: Contributions from an experiential social learning program the EXCELL Program. In D. Davis and A. Olsen, eds., *International Education: The Professional Edge*, 63–76. Sydney, Australia: IDP Education.

Malek, M. A., and Budhwar P. 2013. Cultural intelligence as a predictor of expatriate adjustment and performance in Malaysia. *Journal of World Business* 48: 222–231.

Matsumoto, D., and Hwang, H. C. 2013. Assessing cross-cultural competence: A review of available tests. *Journal of Cross-Cultural Psychology* 44: 849–873.

Moon, H. K., Choi, B. K., and Jung, J. S. 2012. Previous international experience, cross-cultural training, and expatriates' cross-cultural adjustment: Effects of cultural intelligence and goal orientation. *Human Resource Development Quarterly* 23: 285–330.

Moon, T. 2010. Organizational cultural intelligence: Dynamic capability perspective. *Group and Organization Management* 35: 456–493.

Mor, S., Morris, M., and Joh, J. 2013. Identifying and training adaptive cross-cultural management skills: The crucial role of cultural metacognition. *Academy of Management Learning and Education* 12: 453–475.

Morris, M. A., and Robie, C. 2001. A meta-analysis of the effects of cross-cultural training on expatriate performance and adjustment. *International Journal of Training and Development* 5: 112–125.

Moynihan, L. M., Peterson, R. S., and Earley, P. C. 2006. In E. A. Mannix, M. Neale, and Y. Chen, eds., *Research on Managing Groups and Teams,* 9: 299–323. Oxford: Elsevier.

Ng, K. Y., Van Dyne, L., and Ang, S. 2009. From experience to experiential learning: Cultural intelligence as a learning capability for global leader development. *Academy of Management Learning and Education* 8: 511–526.

Ng, K. Y., Van Dyne, L., and Ang, S. 2012. Cultural intelligence: A review, reflections, and recommendations for future research. In A. M. Ryan, F. T. Leong, and F. L. Oswald, eds., *Conducting Multinational Research: Applying Organizational Psychology in the Workplace*, 29–58. Washington, DC: American Psychological Association.

Noe, R. A., Clarke, A. D. M., and Klein, H. J. 2013. Learning in the twenty-first century workplace. *Annual Review of Organizational Psychology and Organizational Behavior* 1: 245–275.

Oberg, K. 1960. Culture shock: Adjustment to new cultural environments. *Practical Anthropology* 7: 177–182.

Oolders, T., Chernyshenko, O. S., and Stark, S. 2008. Cultural intelligence as a mediator of relationships between openness to experience and adaptive performance. In S. Ang and L. Van Dyne, eds., *Handbook of Cultural Intelligence: Theory, Measurement, and Applications*, 145–158. New York: M. E. Sharpe.

Pless, N. M., Maak, T., and Stahl, G. K. 2011. Developing responsible global leaders through international service-learning programs: The Ulysses experience. *Academy of Management Learning and Education* 10: 237–260.

Ramsey, J. R., and Lorenz, M. P. 2016. Exploring the impact of cross-cultural management education on cultural intelligence, student satisfaction, and commitment. *Academy of Management Learning and Education* 15: 79–99.

Rehg, M. T., Gundlach, M. J., and Grigorian, R. A. 2012. Examining the influence of cross-cultural training on cultural intelligence and specific self-efficacy. *Cross Cultural Management* 19(2): 215–232.

Reichard, R. J., Dollwet, M., and Louw-Potgieter, J. 2014. Development of cross-cultural psychological capital and its relationship with cultural intelligence and ethnocentrism. *Journal of Leadership and Organizational Studies* 21(2): 150–164.

Reichard, R. J., Serrano, S. A., Condren, M., Wilder, N., Dollwet, M., and Wang, W. 2015. Engagement in cultural trigger events in the development of cultural competence. *Academy of Management Learning and Education* 14: 461–481.

Rockstuhl, T., and Ng, K. Y. 2008. The effects of cultural intelligence on interpersonal trust in multi-cultural teams. In S. Ang and L. Van Dyne, eds., *Handbook of Cultural Intelligence: Theory, Measurement and Applications*, 206–220. Armonk, NY: ME Sharpe.

Rockstuhl, T., Ng, K. Y., Ang, S., and Van Dyne, L. 2010. CQ and trust development between culturally diverse team members. Paper presented at Academy of Management Annual Meeting, August. Montreal, Canada.

Rockstuhl, T., Seiler, S., Ang, S., Van Dyne, L., and Annen, H. 2011. Beyond general intelligence IQ and emotional intelligence EQ: The role of cultural intelligence CQ on cross-border leadership effectiveness in a globalized world. *Journal of Social Issues* 67: 825–840.

Rosenblatt, V., Worthley, R., and MacNab, B. 2013. From contact to development in experiential cultural intelligence education: The mediating influence of expectancy disconfirmation. *Academy of Management Learning and Education* 12(3): 356–379.

Sahin, F., Gurbuz, S., Kokswal, O, and Ercan, U. 2013. Measuring cultural intelligence in the Turkish context. *International Journal of Selection and Assessment* 21: 135–144.

Shannon, L. M., and Begley, T. M. 2008. Antecedents of the four factor model of cultural intelligence. In S. Ang and L. Van Dyne, eds., *Handbook of Cultural Intelligence: Theory, Measurement, and Applications*, 41–55. Armonk, NY: M. E. Sharpe.

Shirts, R. G. 1977. *BAFA, BAFA: A Cross-culture Simulation*. Del Mar, CA: Simile II.

Shokef, E., and Erez, M. 2008. Cultural intelligence and global identity in multicultural teams. In S. Ang and L. Van Dyne, eds., *Handbook of Cultural Intelligence: Theory, Measurement, and Applications*, 177–191. Armonk, NY: M. E. Sharpe.

Sri Ramalu, S., Shamsudin, F. M., and Subramaniam, C. 2012. The mediating effect of cultural intelligence on the relationship between openness personality and job performance among expatriates on international assignments. *International Business Management* 6: 601–610.

Tarique, I., and Takeuchi, R. 2008. Developing cultural intelligence: The roles of international nonwork experience. In S. Ang and L. Van Dyne, eds., *Handbook of Cultural Intelligence: Theory, Measurement, and Applications*, 56–70. New York: M. E. Sharpe.

Tay, C., Westman, M., and Chia, A. 2008. Antecedents and consequences of cultural intelligence among short-term business travelers. In S. Ang and L. Van Dyne, eds., *Handbook of Cultural Intelligence: Theory, Measurement, and Applications*, 126–144. New York: M. E. Sharpe.

Taylor, P. J., Russ-Eft, D. F., and Chan, D. W. 2005. A meta-analytic review of behavior modeling training. *Journal of Applied Psychology* 90: 692–709.

Triandis, H. C., Brislin, R., and Hui, C. H. 1988. Cross-cultural training across the individualism-collectivism divide. *International Journal of Intercultural Relations* 12: 269–289.

United Nations. 2013. World migration in figures: A joint contribution by UN-DESA and the OECD to the United Nations High-Level Dialogue on Migration and Development. www.oecd.org/els/mig/World-Migration-in-Figures.pdf (accessed March 20, 2015).

United Nations Conference on Trade and Development. 2008. *World Investment Report 2008*. http://unctad.org/en/Docs/wir2008_en.pdf (accessed April 6, 2015).

United Nations Conference on Trade and Development. 2014. *World Investment Report 2014*. http://unctad.org/en/PublicationsLibrary/wir2014_en.pdf (accessed April 6, 2015.

Van der Zee, K. I., and Van Oudenhoven, J. P. 2000. The Multicultural Personality Questionnaire: A multidimensional instrument of multicultural effectiveness. *European Journal of Personality* 14: 291–309.

Van Dyne, L., Ang, S., and Koh, C. 2008. Development and validation of the CQS: The cultural intelligence scale. In S. Ang, and L. Van Dyne, eds., *Handbook on Cultural Intelligence: Theory, Measurement and Applications*, 16–38. Armonk, NY: M.E. Sharpe.

Van Dyne, L., Ang, S., Ng, K.-Y., Rockstuhl, T., Tan, M.L., and Koh, C. 2012. Sub-dimensions of the four factor model of cultural intelligence: Expanding the conceptualization and measurement of cultural intelligence CQ. *Social and Personal Psychology: Compass* 6(4): 295–313.

Varela, O. E., and Gatlin-Watts, R. 2014. The development of the global manager: An empirical study on the role of academic sojourns. *Academy of Management Learning and Education* 13: 187–207.

Ward, C., Wilson, J., and Fischer, R. 2011. Assessing the predictive validity of cultural intelligence over time. *Personality and Individual Differences* 51: 138–142.

Wood, E. D., and St. Peters, H. Y. Z. 2014. Short-term cross-cultural study tours: Impact on cultural intelligence. *The International Journal of Human Resource Management* 25: 558–570.

The World Bank. 2014. *World Development Indicators: Structure of Demand.* http://wdi .worldbank.org/table/4.8 (accessed March 20, 2015).

19 Implications of Positive Organizational Behavior and Psychological Capital for Learning and Training Effectiveness

Alan M. Saks and Jamie A. Gruman

Training is an important component of strategic human resources management and high-performance work systems (Combs et al., 2006). There is strong evidence that training has a positive effect on trainee learning and performance (Arthur, Bennett, Edens, and Bell, 2003) and can also promote career success (Burke & McKeen, 1994; Koen, Klehe, & Van Vianen, 2012). Training can also have a positive effect on human resource outcomes, organizational performance, and financial outcomes (Tharenou, Saks, & Moore, 2007) and has been found to be more strongly related to organization productivity than operational management practices such as advanced manufacturing technology (Birdi et al., 2008). Thus, training and development benefits individuals, teams, organizations, and society (Aguinis & Kraiger, 2009).

Given the potential benefits of training, an important concern of researchers and practitioners is how to facilitate trainee learning and improve the effectiveness of training programs. For decades, the primary approach to training has involved the development of human capital and more recently, social capital (Brown & Van Buren, 2007). However, with the increasing evidence that positive organizational behavior (POB) and psychological capital (PsyCap) have positive implications for employee attitudes, behavior, and performance (Avey et al., 2011) along with research evidence that training interventions can develop individuals' PsyCap (Luthans, Avey, Avolio, & Peterson, 2010), there exists the potential to make training programs more effective by developing the PsyCap of trainees. In other words, PsyCap along with human and social capital might be considered direct outcomes of training which might then lead to and facilitate learning and other training outcomes.

In this chapter, we argue that POB provides a new perspective and approach to trainee learning and training effectiveness. In particular, we describe how POB and PsyCap can be incorporated into all stages of the training process (i.e., needs analysis, design, transfer, and evaluation) thereby expanding existing frameworks for training research and practice.

The chapter is organized into five sections. First, we briefly review research on training effectiveness and highlight the need for new ways to make training programs more effective. Second, we discuss positive psychology and POB with particular emphasis on PsyCap and interventions to facilitate its development. Third, we discuss the implications of PsyCap for all stages of the training process. Fourth, we discuss the implications of a PsyCap perspective for training research and practice. In the last section of the chapter we discuss how POB and PsyCap can expand and contribute to our understanding of the training process and training effectiveness.

Training Effectiveness

There is considerable empirical evidence that attests to the effectiveness of training programs. For example, a meta-analysis of training found effect sizes of .60 to .63 for reaction, learning, behavior, and results criteria (Arthur et al., 2003). However, within-study analyses indicated a substantial decline in effect sizes from learning to behavior and results criteria which suggests that training is not as effective for behavior and results criteria as it is for learning.

While it is noteworthy that research has found that training has positive effects on training outcomes, even more important is an understanding of what makes training programs effective. For example, Arthur et al. (2003) found that the effectiveness of training varies as a function of the delivery method and the skill or task being trained. Training research has identified many other factors that contribute to training effectiveness such as individual differences, instructional strategies, and transfer of training strategies.

Individual Differences

Individual differences or trainee characteristics have been found to be strongly predictive of training outcomes. Among the individual differences that have been found to predict training outcomes, cognitive ability, motivation to learn, self-efficacy, personality, and goal orientation have been found to be especially important. Cognitive ability has been found to be a strong predictor of training success across a wide variety of jobs (Colquitt, LePine, & Noe, 2000). In their meta-analysis, Colquitt et al. (2000) found that cognitive ability was strongly related to declarative knowledge, skill acquisition, and transfer.

Motivation to learn or training motivation refers to "the direction, intensity, and persistence of learning-directed behavior in training contexts" (Colquitt et al., 2000: 678). Colquitt et al. (2000) found that motivation to learn is positively related to declarative knowledge, skill acquisition, reactions, posttraining self-efficacy; and transfer and motivation to learn is predicted by individual characteristics (e.g., locus of control), job/career variables (e.g., job involvement), and situational factors (e.g., supervisor support).

Self-efficacy has also consistently been found to be related to training outcomes including learning, on-the-job behavior, and performance. For example, Colquitt et al. (2000) found that pretraining self-efficacy was positively related to declarative knowledge, skill acquisition, transfer, and job performance and posttraining self-efficacy was positively related to transfer independent of skill acquisition.

Personality has also been found to be related to training outcomes. For example, in their meta-analysis of training motivation, Colquitt et al. (2000) found that locus of control was related to declarative knowledge and transfer, however, conscientiousness was only related to motivation to learn.

Finally, there is also some evidence that a learning goal orientation is positively related to learning and performance outcomes. A meta-analysis of goal orientation found that both trait and state learning goal orientation are positively related to several proximal and distal consequences. With respect to proximal consequences, trait learning goal orientation was positively related to self-efficacy, self-set goal level, learning strategies, and feedback seeking, and negatively related to state anxiety. In terms of distal consequences, trait learning goal orientation was positively related to learning, academic performance, and job performance and state learning goal orientation related positively to learning and job performance. In addition, goal orientation explained significant incremental variance in job performance above cognitive ability and the Big Five personality dimensions, which was largely due to learning goal orientation (Payne, Youngcourt, & Beaubien, 2007).

Thus, to date, a handful of individual difference variables have been found to predict learning and training outcomes. However, some of these are stable individual differences (e.g., cognitive ability) that cannot be changed or modified. Thus, there are only a handful of modifiable individual differences that can be changed to improve a training program's effectiveness: self-efficacy, motivation to learn, and state learning goal orientation. Trainers can improve learning and training outcomes by increasing trainees' motivation to learn and self-efficacy and by having trainees set learning goals.

Instructional Strategies

Most of what is known about training program effectiveness involves learning principles and instructional strategies. As defined by Salas, Tannenbaum, Kraiger, and Smith-Jentsch (2012), instructional strategies refer to the "tools, methods, and context that are combined and integrated to create a delivery approach" (85). General learning principles such as task sequencing and overlearning have been known for decades and tend to be associated with improved learning and retention (Baldwin & Ford, 1988).

Two of the most important instructional strategies for learning and training effectiveness are practice and feedback (Salas et al., 2012). Furthermore, practice is most effective when it is accompanied with timely, constructive, and diagnostic feedback (Salas et al., 2012). Sitzmann et al. (2006) found that web-based instruction (WBI) is more effective than classroom instruction (CI) for teaching declarative knowledge when WBI includes practice and feedback. When both WBI and CI include practice and feedback, they are equally effective. Thus, practice and feedback are key factors for the effectiveness of both types of training and more important than the media used to deliver training. Thus, instructional methods are the primary factors that determine trainee learning not the media used to deliver the training content (Brown & Sitzmann, 2011; Clark, 1994).

With respect to training methods, it has long been known that behavior modeling training (BMT), in which trainees observe and then imitate behaviors performed by a model, is one of the most effective methods for learning interpersonal and supervisory skills (Taylor, Russ-Eft, & Chan, 2005). A meta-analysis of BMT found that it had positive effects on declarative and procedural knowledge, as well as attitudes, behavior, and results although the effects were larger for learning outcomes than behavior and results (Taylor et al., 2005). Furthermore, several factors were found to increase the effects of BMT on learning and job behavior (e.g., presenting learning points, use of negative and positive models).

Simulations (working representations of reality that provide trainees with structured opportunities to practice job-relevant skills) have also been found to be effective for enhancing learning and improving performance (Salas et al., 2012). In a meta-analysis of computer-based simulation games, Sitzmann (2011) found that compared to a control group, simulation games resulted in higher declarative and procedural knowledge, as well as higher posttraining self-efficacy and retention, and simulation games were more effective than other instructional methods (i.e., lecture and discussion).

In recent years, error management training that explicitly encourages trainees to make errors during training and to learn from them, has received considerable attention (Keith & Frese, 2008). A meta-analysis found that error management training results in more positive training outcomes than training that does not encourage trainees to make errors during training (Keith & Frese, 2008). Furthermore, error training was found to be more effective for posttraining task performance than within-training task performance, and more effective for adaptive tasks than analogical tasks. It should be noted that none of the studies in the meta-analysis measured on-the-job performance.

There is also some evidence that setting a training goal that emphasizes learning the training material (a mastery or learning training goal) rather than a training goal for high levels of performance (a performance training goal) can improve training outcomes especially for complex tasks (Kozlowski et al., 2001). Kozlowski et al. (2001) found that a mastery training goal was positively related to knowledge structure coherence and self-efficacy, which were subsequently related to adaptive performance.

Finally, several studies have examined the effects of prompting self-regulation on trainee learning that involves asking trainees reflective questions during training to stimulate self-regulatory processes such as self-monitoring and self-evaluation (Sitzmann & Ely, 2010). Self-regulation prompts encourage trainees to engage in self-regulatory activities during training by asking them if they have set goals, if they are using effective strategies, and if they are making progress toward their goals (Sitzmann et al., 2009). Prompting self-regulation has been found to have positive effects on declarative and procedural knowledge as well as performance (Sitzmann et al., 2009; Sitzmann & Ely, 2010).

Transfer of Training Strategies

Although training is primarily focused on learning outcomes, learning alone is seldom the main objective of training. Rather, a key indicator of training effectiveness is the transfer of training or the extent to which knowledge and skills learned in training are used on the job and result in meaningful changes in job performance (Blume et al., 2010). Early research on transfer focused on several learning principles such as identical elements, general principles, stimulus variability, and conditions of practice (e.g., feedback; Baldwin & Ford, 1988). Most of this research was conducted in the laboratory and involved memory and motor tasks. Learning principles have been found to improve learning and immediate retention of the training material (Baldwin & Ford, 1988). Transfer research has also explored individual differences, work environment characteristics, and posttraining interventions.

Many of the individual difference variables described earlier (e.g., self-efficacy, motivation to learn) have been linked to transfer of training. In their meta-analysis, Blume et al. (2010) found that the trainee characteristics with the strongest relationships were cognitive ability and conscientiousness, while neuroticism, pretraining and posttraining self-efficacy, motivation to learn, and a learning goal orientation had small to moderate relationships with transfer. Furthermore, of all the predictor variables included in their meta-analysis, cognitive ability had the largest relationship with transfer.

Posttraining work environment factors, such as opportunities to practice and supervisor support have also been a focus of transfer research. For example, trainees have been found to be more likely to transfer when they are provided with opportunities to practice (Ford et al., 1992). A meta-analysis of the transfer of management training found that transfer was greater for training programs that included opportunities for managers to practice newly learned skills (Taylor et al., 2009).

Other important work environment factors that influence transfer include the transfer climate and an organization's learning culture. A positive transfer climate and a continuous learning culture have been found to be positively related to training outcomes (Rouiller & Goldstein, 1993; Tracey, Tannenbaum, & Kavanagh, 1995). In their meta-analysis, Blume et al. (2010) found that work environment factors had the strongest relationship with transfer, which was primarily due to the transfer climate followed by support. Furthermore, supervisor support had a stronger relationship with transfer than peer support. Overall, the situational variables were just as strongly related to transfer as trainee characteristics.

Finally, transfer research has often investigated the effects of posttraining transfer interventions that can be added at the end of a training program to prepare trainees to transfer newly acquired knowledge and skills. One of the most researched is relapse prevention (RP) in which trainees identify and prepare for high-risk situations that might prevent transfer (Hutchins & Burke, 2006). Hutchins and Burke (2006) reviewed the research on RP and found that several factors have contributed to mixed and inconsistent results for its effectiveness. Blume et al. (2010) found that the effects of transfer interventions were small to moderate.

Thus, while several factors have been found to predict the transfer of training, it is important to point out that Blume et al. (2010) found same-source and same-measurement-context (SS/SMC) bias inflated the observed relationships between predictors and transfer outcomes. In fact, when SS/SMC was controlled there were few strong predictor relationships with transfer. This led the authors to conclude that "although there are some significant relationships across studies, there are surprisingly few consistently strong individual predictors of transfer" (90). As a result, they suggested that the most promising approach to improve transfer of training is to increase trainee motivation and induce high levels of support in the work environment. They also suggested that transfer of training will be more likely if a training program increases trainees' posttraining knowledge and self-efficacy.

Summary

Although we have learned a great deal about the factors associated with training outcomes and how to make training programs more effective, the practical implications that stem from the extant literature are limited. This is because many of the results pertain more to learning than behavior or job performance; there are only a few individual differences that can be modified, and the two strongest predictors of transfer of training are stable individual differences that cannot be changed (i.e., cognitive ability and conscientiousness); there have not been many new developments when it comes to the design of training programs; and most of the strategies that are effective for improving the transfer of training take place after a training program in the work environment (e.g., opportunities to practice, transfer climate, supervisor support). Thus, there remains much to learn about how to improve the effectiveness of training programs when it comes to behavior, transfer, and performance criteria. We believe that the research and literature on POB and PsyCap have much to offer in this regard. Therefore, in the next section we discuss research on POB and PsyCap with the objective of developing a new perspective and approach to the training process and training effectiveness.

Positive Organizational Behavior and Psychological Capital

Building on the growth of positive psychology (Seligman & Csikszentmihalyi, 2000), many organizational scholars have turned their attention to positive organizational research, theory, and practice. This new positive approach to work settings has culminated in three interrelated scholarly areas: positive organizational psychology, positive organizational scholarship, and POB (Donaldson & Ko, 2010). Positive organizational psychology broadens the general definition of *positive psychology* to work contexts and focuses on positive subjective experiences and traits at work and associated positive institutions (Donaldson & Ko, 2010: 178). Positive organizational scholarship examines "positive deviance, or the way in which organizations and their members flourish and prosper in especially favorable ways" (Cameron & Caza, 2004: 731). POB, unlike the other two areas, doesn't concern itself with organization-level issues. Specifically, POB is "the study and application of positively oriented human resource strengths and psychological capacities that can be measured, developed, and effectively managed for performance improvement in today's workplace" (Luthans 2002a: 59).

The original work on POB considered a number of constructs, such as well-being and emotional intelligence, which satisfied the criteria Luthans (2002a; 2002b) established for defining a POB construct, including the need for constructs to be open to development. However, research on POB quickly coalesced around a specific multidimensional construct known as PsyCap. PsyCap is defined as:

> an individual's positive psychological state of development and is characterized by: 1) having confidence (self-efficacy) to take on and put in the necessary effort to succeed at challenging tasks; 2) making a positive attribution (optimism) about succeeding now and in the future; 3) persevering towards goals and, when necessary, redirecting paths to goals (hope) in order to succeed; and 4) when beset by problems and adversity, sustaining and bouncing back and even beyond (resiliency) to attain success. (Luthans, Youssef, & Avolio, 2007: 3)

Dimensions of PsyCap

Luthans et al. (2007) suggest that PsyCap represents an employee's "positive appraisal of circumstances and probability for success based on motivated effort and perseverance" (550). As suggested in the preceding definition, PsyCap is a higher-order construct comprised of four constituent components: hope, self-efficacy, resiliency, and optimism (Luthans et al., 2007).

Hope

Based on the work of Snyder (e.g., Snyder, 1995), *hope* is a defined as "a cognitive or thinking state in which an individual is capable of setting realistic but challenging goals and expectations and then reaching out for those aims through self-directed determination, energy, and perception of internalized control" (Luthans et al., 2007: 66). Hope has two components: the perceived ability to generate workable routes to desired goals (pathways thinking) and the will-power or energy to work toward those goals (agency thinking; Snyder, 1995). Hope has been shown to be positively associated with a number of work outcomes including retention, job satisfaction, job performance, and profitability (Peterson & Byron, 2008; Peterson & Luthans, 2003).

Optimism

Optimism involves having positive outcome expectancies and/or making positive causal attributions for events (Luthans, 2002a). Such causal attributions or explanatory styles, involve making external, unstable, specific attributions for negative events, and the opposite pattern of attributions for positive events (Luthans, 2002a; Peterson & Seligman, 1984). Optimism has been shown to be positively associated with job attitudes and job performance, and negatively associated with burnout and turnover (Kluemper, Little, & DeGroot, 2009; Seligman & Shulman, 1986).

Self-Efficacy

Building on Bandura's (1997) work, *self-efficacy* refers to "an individual's conviction (or confidence) about his or her abilities to mobilize the motivation, cognitive resources, and courses of action needed to successfully execute a specific task within a given context" (Stajkovic & Luthans, 1998a: 66). Self-efficacy is positively associated with work attitudes, learning, creativity, leadership effectiveness (Luthans & Youssef, 2007), and job performance (Stajkovic & Luthans, 1998b). Of the four PsyCap constructs, only self-efficacy has been included in training research. As indicated earlier, in the training literature self-efficacy has been found to be positively related to declarative knowledge, skill acquisition, transfer, and job performance (Blume et al., 2010; Colquitt et al., 2000).

Resiliency

Resiliency is the "capacity to rebound, to 'bounce back' from adversity, uncertainty, conflict, failure, or even positive change, progress, and increased responsibility" (Luthans, 2002b: 702). As suggested in this definition, resiliency involves not only maintaining adjustment in the face of difficulty, but also when confronted by positive events such as promotions, and the will to move beyond one's equilibrium point (Luthans et al., 2007). Resiliency has been shown to be negatively related to appraisals of threat and cardiovascular reactivity (Tugade & Fredrickson, 2004), perceived stress (Smith et al., 2010), and emotional exhaustion (Manzano García & Ayala Calvo, 2012).

PsyCap and Work Outcomes

PsyCap is conceptualized as a major determinant of behavior and performance in organizations. Peterson et al. (2011) argue that PsyCap is "critical to human motivation, cognitive processing, striving for success, and resulting performance in the workplace" (429). There are at least two reasons it is considered so critical. The first reason is that unlike more limited constructs with more circumscribed effects, PsyCap influences work outcomes through a comprehensive set of mechanisms including cognitive, affective, conative, and social (Youssef & Luthans, 2013). The cognitive mechanism enables positive appraisals of current and future situations that can impact motivation and productivity. The affective mechanism involves the experience of positive emotions that have been shown to broaden thought-action repertoires and build resources (Fredrickson, 2001). The conative mechanism, which involves deliberate, goal-oriented and proactive behavior, induces employees to initiate action toward important goals. Finally, the social mechanism involves PsyCap's ability to intensify the impact of social relationships in producing valued outcomes. The combined effect of these mechanisms makes PsyCap a potent source of leverage for achieving work outcomes, including those related to training.

The second, related, reason is that there is evidence to suggest that PsyCap has a stronger and more consistent relationship with organizational outcomes than the individual constructs that comprise it (Luthans et al., 2005; Luthans et al., 2007). It is suggested that this occurs because although each individual component of PsyCap has unique cognitive and motivational processes, when combined into the higher-order PsyCap construct these processes are mutually enhanced (Luthans et al., 2007). In essence, the PsyCap whole is greater than the sum of its constituent parts (Luthans et al., 2006).

There is now growing evidence demonstrating that PsyCap is positively associated with numerous valued outcomes in organizations and a growing amount of research demonstrating its mediating and moderating effects on such outcomes. A meta-analysis (Avey et al., 2011) found that PsyCap has significant correlations with work outcomes such as job satisfaction (corrected $r = .54$, $p < .05$), organizational commitment (corrected $r = .48$, $p < .05$), turnover intentions (corrected $r = -.32$, $p < .05$), and stress and anxiety (corrected $r = -.29$, $p < .05$), and correlates significantly with behaviors such as organizational citizenship behaviors (corrected $r = .45$, $p < .05$), and employee performance (corrected $r = .26$, $p < .05$).

Using a multiple-indicator latent growth modelling approach, Peterson et al. (2011) demonstrated that not only is PsyCap associated with supervisor-rated performance and sales revenue, but that intraindividual variability in PsyCap parallels changes in these two outcomes. The symmetric association between PsyCap and performance outcomes likely occurs because changes in the mechanisms postulated to account for PsyCap's effects covary with changes in the level of the construct. Consistent with this idea, a cross-lagged panel analysis suggested that the direction of causality between PsyCap and performance outcomes is unidirectional with the former producing changes in the latter (Peterson et al., 2011). Attesting to its additive value, PsyCap has also been shown to offer incremental prediction of attitudinal and behavioral criteria over and above that provided by more established constructs such as personality, core-self-evaluations, person-job, and person-organization fit (Avey, Luthans, & Youssef, 2010).

Although most PsyCap research has been conducted at the individual level, there is a growing amount of evidence that collective PsyCap positively influences group performance. In a sample of retail store employees, Clapp-Smith, Vogelgesang, and Avey (2009) found that the collective PsyCap of followers was positively related to sales growth performance through trust in management. Similarly, Peterson and Zhang (2011) demonstrated that the collective PsyCap of top management teams was related to the performance of their business units.

PsyCap has also been shown to have mediating effects. For example, PsyCap has been shown to fully mediate the relationship between a supportive organizational climate and employee performance (Luthans et al., 2008). Wang et al. (2012) found that PsyCap partially mediates the relationship between work-family conflict and burnout among female doctors. PsyCap has also been found to mediate the relationship between authentic leadership and creativity (Rego et al., 2012), and between transformational leadership and both in-role performance and organizational citizenship behaviors (Gooty et al., 2009).

Recently, moderating effects of PsyCap have also been observed. For example, the relationship between authentic leadership and follower job performance has been shown to be stronger among employees with low rather than high PsyCap levels (Wang et al., 2014). Similarly, Abbas et al. (2014) demonstrated that the relationship between perceptions of organizational politics, on the one hand, and job satisfaction and job performance, on the other hand, were moderated by PsyCap such that the negative relationships were stronger when PsyCap was low.

In summary, there is now substantial evidence underscoring the legitimacy and value of PsyCap as an organizational construct. For our purposes, it behooves us to consider whether and how PsyCap can be developed and leveraged to make training programs more effective. Toward this end, in the next section we discuss how PsyCap can be developed.

Developing Psychological Capital

As noted previously, one criterion for including variables within POB is that they be malleable (Luthans 2002a; 2002b). This malleability has been demonstrated by Peterson et al. (2011) who found that employees' PsyCap levels naturally change over time. In general, PsyCap is thought to demonstrate moderate mutability in that it displays more stability than states such as emotions, but less stability than traits such as personality or intelligence (Luthans et al., 2007). PsyCap is therefore considered statelike (Luthans et al., 2007) and subject to development. Luthans and his colleagues have shown that PsyCap levels can indeed be increased through training interventions (Luthans et al., 2006; Luthans, Avey, & Patera, 2008; Luthans et al., 2010), a process referred to as PsyCap intervention (PCI: Luthans et al., 2006).

Table 19.1 *Strategies for developing trainees' psychological capital*

PsyCap Variable	PsyCap Intervention Strategies	Instructional Strategies	Transfer of Training Strategies
Hope	Goal setting	Mastery training goal	Transfer goal setting
	Pathways planning	Self-regulation prompts	Supervisor support
	Obstacle planning		
	Resources audit		
Optimism	Increasing positive expectations	Mastery training goal	Transfer goal setting
	Challenging negative expectations	Error management instructions	Supervisor support
	Fostering internal attributions of success	Self-regulation prompts	
Self-Efficacy	Task mastery	Mastery training goal	Transfer goal setting
	Modeling	Behavioral modeling training	RP
	Social persuasion		Supervisor support
	Physiological arousal		
Resiliency	Build sense of ability to exert influence	Realistic training preview	Realistic training preview
	Resources audit	RTTS	RTTS
	Planning to avoid/mitigate obstacles	Error management training	RP
	Cultivate resilient thoughts		Supervisor support

Interventions to Develop PsyCap Dimensions

Table 19.1 indicates how trainees' PsyCap can be developed using PsyCap interventions as well as instructional strategies and transfer of training strategies from the training literature that we discuss later in the chapter. PCI is a form of training that targets the individual components of PsyCap. This training is based on prior conceptual and empirical work addressing how each individual component can be developed. It should be noted, however, that efforts to develop each component of PsyCap can also produce salutary influences on levels of the other components. This is because the individual components of PsyCap operate synergistically. As noted by Peterson et al. (2011), if one component of PsyCap is affected (e.g., self-efficacy) the others (e.g., hope, optimism, resiliency) will also likely be affected. Therefore, although based on techniques that build each component of PsyCap individually, the PCI produces interactive benefits that foster the development of PsyCap as a whole.

Developing Hope

Hope is developed based on a goal-orientation framework comprised of goal design, generating pathways to goals, overcoming obstacles, and fostering agency (Luthans et al., 2006). Participants practice developing specific, challenging work-related goals that foster agency. These goals should be person-ally valuable, have concrete start and end points, involve approach (as opposed to avoidance) goals, and involve subgoals (Luthans et al., 2006). Participants also generate multiple pathways to the goals they identify, consider obstacles to those goals, and plan how to address these obstacles. Participants then discuss their ideas in groups, which provide an opportunity to receive, and provide oth-ers with, input into alternative pathways to the goals that have been chosen, and methods for dealing with the obstacles identified. Participants also con-sider the resources needed to pursue the various pathways (i.e., resources audit). Throughout the PCI the facilitator encourages positive "self-talk" and empha-sizes transferability to the job (Luthans et al., 2006).

Developing Optimism

Optimism is similarly influenced by the goal exercise. The tactics that gener-ate hope correspondingly build optimism by stimulating internal attributions for success and positive future expectations (Luthans, 2012). Generating path-ways to important goals and developing confidence to overcome impediments to goals generates positive expectations. Put another way, participants challenge negative expectations that goals will not be attained by generating pathways to their goals and devising ways to overcome obstacles. The processes that build self-efficacy discussed in the following text, which build on an expectancy-value orientation and a positive explanatory style, also build optimism (Luthans et al., 2006). Additionally, group feedback fosters positive expectations as participants interact with others who are likewise expecting and planning for success. Optimism rises as participants' expectations for success rise (Luthans et al., 2007).

Developing Self-Efficacy

Self-efficacy is developed through all the sources Bandura (1977) suggests promote self-efficacy: performance accomplishment (task mastery), vicarious experience (modeling), verbal (social) persuasion, and emotional (psychologi-cal) arousal. These sources of efficacy are incorporated within the goal exercise designed to generate hope (Luthans et al., 2006). Task mastery for developing and implementing goals is accomplished by establishing goals and subgoals, thinking through how they can be accomplished, and explaining these ideas to the group. Vicarious learning occurs as participants hear others, who serve as role models, and discuss goal formulation and accomplishment. The validation of schedules and timelines produced by these discussions, in addition to social persuasion by the facilitator and group members, fosters positive expectations for success.

Developing Resiliency

The development of resiliency has been accomplished with two general approaches. One approach builds on the work of Masten (2001) and focuses on building resiliency by positively affecting participants' perception of their ability to exert influence (Luthans et al., 2006; Luthans et al., 2008). Participants are asked to identify a personal setback at work and write down their initial reactions to it. The facilitator then works with participants to understand where they can exert influence, where they cannot, and their realistic options. Participants are then asked to practice this staunch view of reality, individually and in groups, by thinking about other personal setbacks or the goals established in the initial goal exercise. This process also impacts the development of realistic optimism.

The second approach focuses on the assets and resources, such as skills and social capital, that participants have available for achieving their goals (Luthans et al., 2007; Luthans et al., 2010). Participants create a list of such resources (i.e., resources audit) that they share with the group to uncover further potential assets, and are then urged to take advantage of the resources identified. Participants again anticipate obstacles to achieving their goals, but this time they focus on avoiding the obstacles or mitigating their effects. Additionally, the facilitator helps participants become aware of the positive and negative thoughts they have when facing hardships, and encourages them to select resilient thoughts by considering the resources they have available, and the methods for avoiding/mitigating these hardships.

Research on PsyCap Development

The PCI has been applied in short, micro-interventions lasting from one to three hours (Luthans et al., 2006; Luthans et al., 2010) and has taken the form of traditional face-to-face (e.g., Luthans et al., 2010) and online training (Luthans et al., 2008). In their initial report on the effectiveness of the PCI, Luthans et al. (2006) reported that a one-hour PCI micro-intervention with management students, and a two-hour PCI with practicing managers, each significantly increased PsyCap by approximately 3%. They also reported that PsyCap increased significantly after a 2.5-hour PCI session with employees in a high-tech manufacturing firm, but not to the same degree. Luthans et al. (2008) investigated the effectiveness of an online PCI comprised of two 45-minute sessions two weeks apart. Controlling for pretraining PsyCap scores and several other covariates, Luthans et al. (2008) found that compared to a control condition, participants in the PCI experienced a significant increase in PsyCap scores.

Recent research has demonstrated that not only can PsyCap be developed generally, but the PCI can be tailored to address specific work demands or training goals. For example, Reichard, Dollwet, and Louw-Potgieter (2014) developed and tested a training program designed to develop cross-cultural PsyCap in U.S. and African working adults. Cross-cultural PsyCap refers to one's confidence, hope, optimism, and resiliency specifically within cross-cultural interactions (Dollwet & Reichard, 2014). Reichard et al. (2014) found that training increased cross-cultural PsyCap levels and increased participants' cultural intelligence and positive emotions, and decreased ethnocentrism. Similarly, Luthans, Luthans, and Avey (2014) demonstrated that relative to a control group, a two-hour PCI focused on increasing students' academic PsyCap resulted in higher academic PsyCap scores, although the training produced the same results for general (nonacademic) PsyCap.

In considering whether PsyCap training will transfer to the work environment it is necessary to consider the work context. As noted by Peterson et al. (2011), the extent to which employees' levels of PsyCap increase or decrease is affected by the work context, such as the organizational climate, the availability of social support, and leadership. In two studies, Avey (2014) found that PsyCap was predicted by contextual antecedents including authentic leadership, ethical leadership, and empowering leadership (leadership category), and task complexity (job design category). Similarly, in a review of the PsyCap literature, Newman et al. (2014) reported that PsyCap is enhanced by workplace support and buddying, and is reduced by stressful work environments and work-family conflict. Such contextual factors are also likely to influence the degree to which training that includes PsyCap components transfers to work behavior.

In summary, research has shown that PsyCap can be developed using traditional face-to-face and online training interventions and PCIs can be tailored to specific work situations and training goals. With this in mind, we now turn to a consideration of the development of PsyCap for learning and training program effectiveness.

Implications of PsyCap for Learning and Training

The growing literature on PsyCap has much to offer the science and practice of training. All four of the PsyCap variables have implications for learning and transfer. For example, within the context of training, *hope* refers to trainees' perception that they can generate workable routes to learning and transfer goals (pathways thinking) and the willpower or energy to work toward those goals (agency thinking). *Optimism* refers to trainees having positive outcome expectancies for learning and applying the training content and making positive causal attributions for their learning and transfer outcomes.

Self-efficacy refers to trainees' confidence about their abilities to mobilize the motivation, cognitive resources, and courses of action needed to successfully learn and apply the training material. *Resiliency* in training refers to trainees' capacity to rebound and "bounce back" from learning and transfer difficulties, errors, and failures. Thus, all four PsyCap variables can be linked to trainee learning and transfer. We know that PsyCap is related to numerous work outcomes and it is very likely to be related to training outcomes. In other words, trainees with high optimism, hope, self-efficacy, and resiliency are more likely to learn training content and to transfer what they learn on the job.

In this section, we describe the implications of PsyCap for training and development with particular emphasis on making training programs more effective. Our main proposition is that training programs should be designed to develop trainees' PsyCap. In fact, as already indicated, self-efficacy has been found to

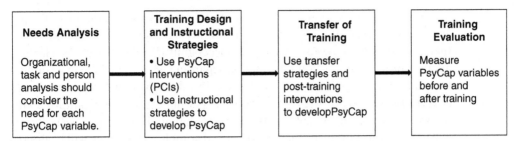

Figure 19.1. *A psychological capital model of the training and development process.*

be an important variable in training research and a strong predictor of learning and transfer outcomes (Blume et al., 2010; Colquitt et al., 2000).

In effect, what we are suggesting is that regardless of the content and objectives, training programs should be designed to develop trainees' optimism, hope, self-efficacy, and resiliency for learning and transfer. At the same time, we recognize that not all the PsyCap variables will be important for all training programs or in need of development. Thus, our focus is on the development of each PsyCap variable rather than PsyCap in the aggregate although as indicated earlier, the development of each component of PsyCap will produce salutary influences on the other components because the individual components operate synergistically.

As shown in Figure 19.1, our position is that PsyCap be integrated and embedded into the training and development process beginning with needs analysis and ending with training evaluation. In the remainder of this section, we describe how PsyCap can be incorporated into the training process with respect to needs analysis, training design (through instructional strategies), transfer of training strategies, and training evaluation.

Needs Analysis

As the first step in the training process, a needs analysis can determine which of the PsyCap constructs will be important for a training program's success and should be designed into the training program. Each level of the needs analysis process (organizational, task, and person analysis) will provide important information about the need for each PsyCap construct. For example, a key part of an organizational analysis is to determine if the environment will support the training or what Salas et al. (2012) refer to as *environmental readiness*. This also helps to identify any obstacles to the success of a training program so that they can be removed or plans can be made to address them during or after training. One way to address potential obstacles to training success is to develop trainees' PsyCap. For example, if the training will be especially difficult to apply on the job or if the work environment is not very supportive of the training it will be important to develop trainees' self-efficacy and resiliency for applying it on the job.

A task analysis is conducted to identify the critical work functions of a job as well as the task requirements and the knowledge, sklls, and abilities (KSAs) that are necessary to perform each task successfully (Salas et al., 2012). The task analysis provides important information regarding what to include in a training program and the performance standards. In addition, a task analysis should also consider which of the PsyCap constructs will be most important for learning the KSAs and being able to use them on the job. For example, self-efficacy will be important for tasks that are novel and complex. Resiliency will be important for tasks that are difficult to learn and/or apply in the work environment. Optimism and hope will be important for tasks that require persistence to learn and transfer.

A person analysis helps to identify who is lacking the KSAs for the tasks identified in the task analysis and therefore who needs training. However, a person analysis can also identify characteristics of trainees that are important for training success such as motivation to learn (Salas et al., 2012). With respect to PsyCap, a new component of a person analysis is to measure the PsyCap of trainees to identify those who are low on the PsyCap constructs that have been identified in the organization and task analysis as important for learning and using the trained KSAs on the job. Thus, a person analysis will not only identify trainees who need training but also those who should have one or more components of their PsyCap developed during the training to facilitate their learning and transfer.

In summary, needs analysis can be expanded to consider the relevance of each of the PsyCap constructs for learning training content and applying it in the work environment. This sets the stage for the design of training programs that develop one or more of the PsyCap constructs to facilitate learning and transfer outcomes.

Training Design and Instructional Strategies

A PsyCap approach to training design means that training programs should be designed with instructional strategies to facilitate the development of trainees' PsyCap. The instructional strategies will depend on the PsyCap variables that are most in need of development for a particular training program as per the needs analysis. As described in the following text, the interventions used to develop PsyCap discussed earlier (PCIs, see Table 19.1) can be used in training. In addition, as shown in Table 19.1, instructional strategies for training design can also be used to develop trainees' PsyCap.

Hope

As indicated earlier, the development of hope in PsyCap research involves goal setting. As an instructional strategy for a particular training program, the goal-setting process should focus on the training program content and objectives, as well as the expected learning outcomes. Along these lines, the training program should begin with a review of the training content and objectives followed by a goal-setting exercise in which trainees set specific and challenging goals for learning the training content and achieving the training objectives. Thus, the emphasis here should be a mastery or learning goal that is aligned with the training program content and objectives. Trainees should also identify obstacles to their goals and develop plans to overcome them. Trainees should discuss their goals in groups along with alternative pathways to achieving them and methods for overcoming learning obstacles.

Self-regulation prompting might also be an effective strategy for the development of hope. This is because self-regulation prompts encourage self-regulatory activities such as goal setting, developing plans for reaching one's goals, the identification of obstacles that might prevent one from achieving their learning goals, and the identification of strategies to maximize progress toward one's goals (Sitzmann et al., 2009).

Optimism

The goal-setting process for hope can also be used to develop optimism. The difference is that the development of optimism involves creating high expectations of success in the training program and an emphasis on making internal attributions for training success. In terms of the type of goal, mastery or learning goals are also likely to facilitate the development of optimism. Mastery goals focus the trainee on knowledge and skills and prompt a self-regulatory process toward learning objectives that leads to learning key task concepts and task relations (Kozlowski et al., 2001). As a result, trainees are more likely to generate multiple pathways to their goals and to overcome obstacles. Mastery goals are also likely to facilitate the development of optimism because they provide trainees with opportunities to engage in self-regulation and inform trainees that their skills are malleable and that errors provide opportunities for leaning (Kozlowski et al., 2001). As a result, trainees will be more likely to make positive causal attributions for their learning.

In addition to mastery goals, optimism can also be facilitated with error management instructions that inform trainees that making mistakes is acceptable and even expected. Error management instructions have been found to be beneficial even without error management training (Carter & Beier, 2010). With respect to optimism, error management instructions are likely to mitigate internal attributions for failure and lead to more positive expectations for learning and training success.

Self-regulation prompting might also be an effective strategy for the development of optimism. This is because self-regulation prompts remind trainees that their learning and success is under their control (Sitzmann & Ely, 2010). Thus, self-regulation prompts are likely to result in multiple pathways toward goal attainment, and because trainees have control over their learning they will be more inclined to make internal attributions for goal accomplishment and learning outcomes.

Self-Efficacy.

As indicated earlier, self-efficacy is the only PsyCap variable that has been extensively studied in the training literature. The development of trainee self-efficacy generally involves incorporating the sources of self-efficacy information in the design of a training program. In terms of instructional strategies, mastery goals can be used to increase self-efficacy. As noted by Kozlowski et al. (2001), mastery goals should enhance self-efficacy because they are an indicator of perceived competency and motivational resiliency. They found that mastery goals were associated with the development of self-perceived capability to deal with task challenges.

Behavioral modeling training can also be used to develop trainee self-efficacy. In fact, Bandura's (1977) social learning theory is the foundation of BMT with its emphasis on vicarious learning. Besides the use of a model exhibiting the desired behavior (vicarious learning), BMT also provides the other sources of self-efficacy information for trainees (task mastery through opportunities to practice, verbal persuasion through feedback and reinforcement, and low physiological arousal by providing a safe environment to practice the behavior). BMT has been found to be an effective instructional method for developing trainees' self-efficacy (Gist, Schwoerer, & Rosen, 1989). According to Gist et al. (1989), behavioral modeling is effective because it operates through self-efficacy to influence performance.

Resiliency

In the training literature, there are three instructional strategies that might be effective for developing trainees' resiliency: realistic training previews, realistic orientation programs for new employee stress or ROPES, and error management training.

The first approach is to provide trainees with a realistic training preview at the start of a training program to provide them with a realistic and accurate view of what to expect in the training program and the expected outcomes. Hicks and Klimoski (1987) found that trainees who received a realistic training preview for a training workshop on performance reviews and interviewing were more likely to believe that the training program was appropriate for them and that they would profit from it, were more committed to their decision to attend the training, and were more motivated to learn than trainees who received a traditional announcement about the training program. Like realistic job previews, a realistic training preview should lead to more realistic expectations of a training program, which should lead to more positive training outcomes. A study by Tannenbaum et al. (1991) found that military trainees whose expectations for training were met (what the authors called *training fulfillment*) had higher organizational commitment, training motivation, and self-efficacy.

A second approach involves the use of ROPES, which can be easily adapted for trainees (*realistic training programs for trainee stress* or RTTS). ROPES teach coping skills for the most important stressors that newcomers (trainees) will encounter in their job (during training). The basic principles for the design of ROPES are the following: (1) realistic information that forewarns newcomers (trainees) about typical disappointments to expect and possible adjustment (learning) problems, as well as how to cope by setting goals and taking action; (2) general support and reassurance; (3) BMT (use models to show coping skills, discuss the model's actions, include behavioral rehearsal with feedback); (4) self-control of thoughts and feelings; and (5) specific stressors targeted to newcomers (trainees) (Wanous & Reichers, 2000).

Although it has not been tested, ROPES hold much promise for developing trainee learning resiliency as it provides individuals with emotion-focused and problem-focused coping skills that will be useful for recovering from difficulties and setbacks during a training program. Additionally, the coping skills developed during ROPES are conceptually similar to the instrumental and palliative coping skills developed through stress inoculation training, which is designed to help people better handle stressors (Meichenbaum & Deffenbacher, 1988).

Fan and Wanous (2008) compared a ROPES intervention to a more traditional orientation program in a sample of 72 new graduate students from Asia attending a large university in the United States. A ROPES intervention was designed to teach international students how to cope with three major entry stressors: the fast pace of the academic quarter system (the university has three quarters vs. two semesters), language difficulties, and social interaction difficulties. Students were randomly assigned to receive the ROPES intervention or a more traditional three-hour orientation session that focused on students' immediate concerns, such as how to keep legal status in the United States, personal safety issues, and how to connect a home phone. Students in the experimental condition received a shorter version of the traditional orientation program plus ROPES.

The results indicated that the ROPES participants reported lower preentry expectations at the end of the orientation program as well as lower stress and higher academic and interaction adjustment six and nine months after the program. The positive effects of ROPES became stronger over time. Furthermore, stress mediated the effect of the ROPES intervention on academic and interaction adjustment.

When used for training, a trainer can employ each of the ROPES principles throughout a training program. For example, when introducing the training program and its objectives to trainees, the trainer can provide realistic information that forewarns trainees about any difficulties to expect during the training program and how to cope with them. The trainer might also instruct trainees on how to control their thoughts and feelings. During the training program the trainer should provide trainees with support and reassurance and use behavior modeling and provide opportunities for behavioral rehearsal along with feedback.

A third approach for developing trainees' resiliency is error management training. As indicated earlier, error management training encourages trainees to make errors and to learn from them (Keith & Frese, 2008). Trainees work independently on difficult training tasks and are provided with only minimal guidance and information on how to solve training tasks. As a result, trainees make errors that they must learn from and then try other solutions. In effect, trainees must bounce back from their errors and soldier on so to speak to find the right solution. This process of making errors and recovering from them is expected to develop trainees' resiliency, which might also be a key factor for the effects of error management training on learning and task performance.

Transfer of Training Strategies

Although Blume et al. (2010) found that the effects of transfer interventions on transfer were small to moderate, transfer interventions might be more effective if they are designed to develop trainees' PsyCap. As indicated earlier, only a few individual difference variables that are susceptible to change have been found to predict transfer of training (e.g., self-efficacy, training motivation) and many of the strategies for improving transfer take place in the work environment after training (e.g., opportunities to practice, transfer climate, supervisor support). Therefore, in addition to self-efficacy, transfer of training strategies should focus on the development of trainees' hope, optimism, and resiliency for transfer.

Some of the instructional strategies discussed in the previous section can also be used as a transfer strategy. The difference is that the focus shifts from learning during training to on-the-job behavior and performance in the work environment.

To develop hope, optimism, and self-efficacy goal setting should involve goals for using the training content on-the-job or transfer goals. Goal-setting interventions should focus on multiple pathways to achieve transfer goals, consideration of obstacles to transfer goals, and the development of a plan to deal with obstacles to goal achievement. As indicated earlier, the effect of BMT on job behavior was greater in studies that had trainees set goals for how they will apply their new skills on the job (Taylor et al., 2005).

Although research on RP has been mixed (Hutchins & Burke, 2006) and Blume et al. (2010) found that the effects of transfer interventions were small to moderate, RP might be more effective if the focus is on the development of trainees' self-efficacy and resiliency for transfer. Because RP prepares trainees to anticipate and cope with high-risk situations to overcome transfer obstacles and barriers, it is an ideal intervention to develop trainee self-efficacy and resiliency for transfer. In fact, the original conception of RP is to enhance trainees' self-efficacy for using and maintaining trained skills (Hutchins & Burke, 2006). Thus, RP might have direct positive effects on trainee self-efficacy and resiliency, which will in turn lead to greater transfer. Thus, RP interventions should be designed with particular attention on the four sources of self-efficacy development.

Realistic training previews as well as RTTS can also be used at the end of a training program as a posttraining intervention to develop trainee resiliency for transfer. The focus now shifts from learning the training material to transfer. Thus, trainees will develop realistic expectations about transfer and they will learn emotion-focused and problem-focused coping skills for the potential transfer obstacles they might encounter on the job.

Finally, as noted earlier, factors in work environment such as the transfer climate and supervisor support are important determinants of transfer. Similarly, research on PsyCap has found that it is influenced by contextual factors such as authentic leadership, ethical leadership, and empowering leadership as well as workplace support. Therefore, supervisors should be encouraged to support trainees by developing their hope, optimism, self-efficacy, and resiliency for transfer.

In addition, there is some research suggesting that the development of PsyCap during training might influence employees' perceptions of the transfer climate and encourage transfer. In two studies, Bergheim et al. (2013) demonstrated that employees' levels of PsyCap influenced their perceptions of climate, in this case, safety climate. These results suggest the possibility that training programs that focus on developing the components of PsyCap and activate the mechanisms through which it operates, may encourage training transfer by improving employees' perceptions of the transfer climate. Employees who are more hopeful, optimistic, confident, and resilient may perceive opportunities, resources, and support in the transfer environment that those who are low on these constructs overlook or interpret differently.

Thus, while the training literature considers supervisor supportive behaviors in terms of encouragement, positive feedback, and involvement in training (Burke & Hutchins, 2007), we believe this can be extended to involve behaviors that are aimed at the development of trainees' PsyCap for transfer.

Training Evaluation

A PsyCap approach to training has several implications for training evaluation. First, training programs should include the measurement of PsyCap as part of training evaluation. In particular, the PsyCap variables should be measured before a training program as well as immediately after and at some point on the job. It is worth noting that Kraiger, Ford, and Salas's (1993) affective evaluation dimension of their multidimensional evaluation model includes self-efficacy. Thus, an extension of the Kraiger et al. (1993) model is to include hope, optimism, and resiliency in addition to self-efficacy and to make PsyCap a distinct dimension of training evaluation.

Second, the measurement of PsyCap provides a new set of criteria for formative evaluation, which is important for understanding why a training program did or did not have an effect on training outcomes and has often been neglected in training evaluation relative to summative evaluations (Brown & Gerhardt, 2002). Given that formative evaluation is necessary for identifying the critical components for training success, adding PsyCap to existing models of formative evaluation contributes to the expansion of existing models by adding additional criteria that are important for training effectiveness (Brown & Gerhardt, 2002). In addition, PsyCap evaluation makes it possible to examine the mediating mechanisms for the effects of a training program on learning and transfer outcomes.

Summary

In this section, we have described the implications of PsyCap for the training and development process. It is our contention that training programs can be more effective for trainee learning and transfer if they include strategies and interventions to develop trainees' PsyCap for learning and transfer of training.

Implications for Training Research and Practice

A PsyCap approach to training offers many new directions for training research. For starters, training researchers might begin to include measures of the PsyCap variables in their training research. Ideally, PsyCap should be measured before and after a training program to identify any changes as a result of the training. The relationship between the PsyCap constructs and training outcomes such as declarative and procedural knowledge, skill acquisition, motivation to learn, and transfer should also be investigated. We have suggested that the PsyCap variables will predict learning and transfer outcomes. However, to date we only know that this is the case for self-efficacy. Thus, future research is needed to test relationships between the other PsyCap constructs and training outcomes. In addition, given that PsyCap has been positively linked to job attitudes, psychological well-being, and lower job stress and anxiety (Avey et al., 2011), these variables should also be considered in future training research as the benefits of trainee PsyCap might extend beyond traditional learning and training outcomes.

A second avenue for future research is to test the instructional design strategies we have suggested for developing each of the PsyCap variables. Although some of these strategies have been used to develop PsyCap, they have not been tested within the context of specific training programs for the purpose of developing each of the PsyCap variables for learning training content. It is possible that some of the interventions will be effective for more than one PsyCap variable. However, it remains for future research to identify those strategies and interventions that are most effective for developing each of the PsyCap variables during training.

Future research might also test the transfer strategies for developing each of the PsyCap constructs for transfer as well as posttraining transfer interventions such as goal setting and RP. While previous research has found these interventions to be effective for strengthening trainees' self-efficacy (Hutchins & Burke, 2006), we do not know if they will also strengthen trainees' hope, optimism, and resiliency for transfer. It is possible that transfer interventions such as RP and goal setting will be more effective if they are designed specifically to develop trainees' PsyCap. This might require some modifications to existing approaches.

For example, goal-setting interventions might go beyond a discussion of the goal-setting process and setting goals (Richman-Hirsch, 2001) and include a discussion of multiple pathways to achieve transfer goals, consideration of obstacles to transfer goals, and the development of a plan to deal with obstacles to goal achievement. RP interventions might go beyond a consideration of high-risk situations and coping responses to also consider the importance of internal attributions for success and positive expectations for transfer, as well as a consideration of the resources that trainees can access to help them overcome transfer obstacles. Trainees might also be asked to identify the difficulties they have had with transfer in the past and what they can learn from their experiences to develop a training transfer plan.

In addition to research on the effects of PsyCap on learning and training outcomes, future research might also consider the role of PsyCap as a mediating and moderating variable for the effects of training. As indicated earlier, several studies have shown that PsyCap has mediating effects and self-efficacy has been shown to mediate the effects of training on training outcomes (Saks, 1995). Thus, it is possible that the PsyCap variables will mediate the effects of training on training outcomes. In addition, PsyCap might also moderate the effects of training on training outcomes. As indicated earlier, PsyCap has been found to moderate the effects of authentic leadership on follower job performance as well as perceptions of organizational politics on job satisfaction and job performance. In addition, several studies have found that self-efficacy moderates the effect of training (Saks, 1995). Thus, it is possible that the effectiveness of training programs might depend in part on trainees' levels of optimism, hope, self-efficacy, and resiliency.

Finally, future research is needed to determine which PsyCap variables are most malleable during training and most important in terms of particular types of training programs and skills (e.g., interpersonal vs. technical skills) as well as for different trainees (e.g., low vs. high cognitive ability). In addition, research is also needed to determine which PsyCap constructs are most strongly related to training outcomes. For example, some PsyCap variables might be strongly related to particular training outcomes (e.g., declarative knowledge vs. transfer).

A PsyCap approach to training also has implications for practice. As we have indicated, every stage of the training process from needs analysis to training evaluation can be approached from a PsyCap perspective. Thus, when conducting a needs analysis trainers should consider the relevance of PsyCap for learning and transfer; when designing training programs they should include instructional strategies that will help to develop trainees' PsyCap for learning; transfer strategies can be used to strengthen trainees PsyCap for transfer; and the evaluation of training should include the measurement of trainee PsyCap before and after training programs. PsyCap measures are relatively short, making them easy to include in existing training evaluation forms.

Another implication for practice is that PsyCap training and transfer may be enhanced by including tactics that address participants' emotions in addition to their cognitions. The existing PCI is heavily focused on cognitive tactics such as goal setting, conceptualizing alternative pathways to goals, and auditing one's availability of resources. However, hope, optimism, self-efficacy, and resiliency might be effectively developed by focusing on emotional tactics. Indeed, a primary way to boost self-efficacy is by minimizing aversive physiological arousal in challenging circumstances (Bandura, 1977).

PCI training should reduce or eliminate negative emotions and promote positive emotions. Fostering positive emotions during training can not only serve as a signal of competence for trainees, but also may assist in furthering the objectives of the more cognitively oriented aspects of training. As suggested earlier, the broaden-and-build theory of positive emotions suggests that positive emotions such as interest and pride broaden people's thought-action repertoires, widening the range of thoughts and actions considered, and building personal resources that endure beyond the precipitating, ephemeral emotional states (Fredrickson, 2001). PCI training that includes tactics specifically designed to induce positive emotions may thus ameliorate training by expanding the alternatives considered during training exercises, and enhance transfer by enriching perceptions of talent and proficiency.

Conclusion

Although we have learned a great deal about the science and practice of training over the last several decades, when it comes to making training programs more effective there is still much to learn. In this chapter, we have proposed a PsyCap approach to training that provides researchers and practitioners many new ideas for improving training.

First, PsyCap offers four individual difference variables that have been shown to be related to a variety of work outcomes. What's more, unlike other variables that are related to training outcomes but are stable individual differences that cannot be modified (e.g., cognitive ability), all four PsyCap variables can be developed.

Second, a PsyCap approach to training has implications for the design of training programs. This means that trainers and practitioners now have new strategies to incorporate into training programs to make them more effective for trainee learning and retention.

Third, PsyCap provides new strategies for improving the transfer of training without having to rely on the work environment and factors outside of the control of trainees and trainers. That is, training programs can now include transfer strategies to develop trainees' PsyCap so that they will be more likely to apply what they learn in training on the job.

Fourth, PsyCap represents a potentially important mediating variable for training effectiveness that can explain the effects of training programs on training outcomes.

Fifth, PsyCap represents a set of potential moderating variables that might result in aptitude-treatment-interactions. In other words, the effect of some training programs and/or instructional methods on training outcomes might depend on trainees' standing on one or more of the PsyCap constructs.

Sixth, PsyCap represents additional variables to consider when evaluating training programs. Thus, the effectiveness of a training program might be judged in part on the extent to which trainees have developed high levels of PsyCap.

Seventh, PsyCap compliments the more traditional approach to training that focuses mostly on the development of human capital and more recent approaches that link training to the development of trainees' social capital (Brown & Van Buren, 2007). In other words, training programs should focus on the development of trainees' human capital, social capital, and PsyCap.

Finally, it is worth noting that in their annual review, Aguinis and Kraiger (2009) stated that "training in work organizations is an area of applied psychological research that is particularly well suited for making a clear contribution to the enhancement of human well-being and performance in organizational and work settings as well as in society in general" (452). Given that PsyCap is associated with psychological health and well-being (Avey et al., 2011), it is our contention that training programs that are designed to develop trainees' PsyCap will not only make training programs more effective, but will also contribute to the health and psychological well-being of individuals and organizations.

In conclusion, the effectiveness of training programs is very much a function of trainee characteristics and the way a training program is designed. PsyCap provides a new way to integrate both by designing training programs that strengthen trainees' PsyCap. Given that PsyCap is strongly related to work attitudes, behavior, and performance, it is highly likely to also be related to training outcomes. Thus, developing trainees' PsyCap holds great promise for making training programs more effective.

References

Abbas, M., Raja, U., Darr, W., and Bouckenooghe, D. 2014. Combined effects of perceived politics and psychological capital on job satisfaction, turnover intentions, and performance. *Journal of Management* 40: 1813–1830.

Aguinis, H., and Kraiger, K. 2009. Benefits of training and development for individuals and teams, organizations, and society. *Annual Review of Psychology* 60: 451–474.

Arthur, W., Jr., Bennett, W., Jr., Edens, P. S., and Bell, S. T. 2003. Effectiveness of training in organizations: A meta-analysis of design and evaluation features. *Journal of Applied Psychology* 88: 234–245.

Avey, J. B. 2014. The left side of psychological capital: New evidence on the antecedents of PsyCap. *Journal of Leadership and Organizational Studies* 21: 141–149.

Avey, J. B., Luthans, F., and Youssef, C. M. 2010. The additive value of positive psychological capital in predicting work attitudes. *Journal of Management* 36: 430–452.

Avey, J. B., Reichard, R. J., Luthans, F., and Mhatre, K. H. 2011. Meta-analysis of the impact of positive psychological capital on employee attitudes, behaviors, and performance. *Human Resource Development Quarterly* 22: 127–152.

Baldwin, T. T., and Ford, K. J. 1988. Transfer of training: A review and directions for future research. *Personnel Psychology* 41: 63–105.

Bandura, A. 1977. Self-efficacy: Toward a unifying theory of behavioral change. *Psychological Review* 84: 191–215.

Bandura, A. 1997. *Self-efficacy: The Exercise of Control.* New York: Freeman.

Bergheim, K., Eid, J., Hystad, S. W., Nielsen, M. B., Mearns, K., Larsson, G., and Luthans, B. 2013. The role of psychological capital in perception of safety climate among air traffic controllers. *Journal of Leadership and Organizational Studies* 20: 232–241.

Birdi, K., Clegg, C., Patterson, M., Robinson, A., Stride, C. B., Wall, T. D., and Wood, S. J. 2008. The impact of human resource and operational management practices on company productivity: A longitudinal study. *Personnel Psychology* 61: 467–501.

Blume, B. D., Ford, J. K., Baldwin, T. T., and Huang, J. L. 2010. Transfer of training: A meta-analytic review. *Journal of Management* 36: 1065–1105.

Brown, K. G., and Gerhardt, M. W. 2002. Formative evaluation: An integrative practice model and case study. *Personnel Psychology* 55: 951–983.

Brown, K. G., and Sitzmann, T. 2011. Training and employee development for improved performance. In S. Zedeck, ed., *Handbook of Industrial and Organizational Psychology*, 2: 469–503. Washington, DC: American Psychological Association.

Brown, K. G., and Van Buren, M. 2007. Applying a social capital perspective to evaluation of distance training. In S. M. Fiore and E. Salas, eds., *Toward a Science of Distributed Learning*, 41–63. Washington, DC: American Psychological Association.

Burke, L. A., and Hutchins, H. M. 2007. Training transfer: An integrative literature review. *Human Resource Development Review* 6: 263–296.

Burke, R. J., and McKeen, C. A. 1994. Training and development activities and career success of managerial and professional women. *Journal of Management Development* 13: 53–63.

Cameron, K. S., and Caza, A. 2004. Introduction: Contributions to the discipline of positive organizational scholarship. *American Behavioral Scientist* 47: 731–739.

Carter, M., and Beier, M. E. 2010. The effectiveness of error management training with working-aged adults. *Personnel Psychology* 63: 641–675.

Clapp-Smith, R., Vogelgesang, G. R., and Avey, J. B. 2009. Authentic leadership and positive psychological capital: The mediating role of trust at the group level of analysis. *Journal of Leadership and Organizational Studies* 15: 227–240.

Clark, R. E. 1994. Media will never influence learning. *Educational Technology Research and Development* 42: 21–29.

Colquitt, J. A., LePine, J. A., and Noe, R. A. 2000. Toward an integrative theory of training motivation: A meta-analytic path analysis of 20 years of research. *Journal of Applied Psychology* 85: 678–707.

Combs, J., Liu, Y., Hall, A., and Ketchen, D. 2006. How much do high-performance work practices matter? A meta-analysis of their effects on organizational performance. *Personnel Psychology* 59: 501–528.

Dollwet, M., and Reichard, R. J. 2014. Assessing cross-cultural skills: Validation of a new measure of cross-cultural psychological capital. *International Journal of Human Resource Management* 25: 1669–1696.

Donaldson, S. I., and Ko, I. 2010. Positive organizational psychology, behavior and scholarship: A review of the emerging literature and evidence base. *The Journal of Positive Psychology* 5: 177–191.

Fan, J., and Wanous, J. P. 2008. Organizational and cultural entry: A new type of orientation program for multiple boundary crossings. *Journal of Applied Psychology* 93: 1390–1400.

Ford, J. K., Quiñones, M., Sego, D., and Sorra, J. 1992. Factors affecting the opportunity to perform trained tasks on the job. *Personnel Psychology* 45: 511–527.

Fredrickson, B. L. 2001. The role of positive emotions in positive psychology: The broaden-and-build theory of positive emotions. *American Psychologist* 56: 218–226.

Gist, M. E., Schwoerer, C., and Rosen, B. 1989. Effects of alternative training methods on self-efficacy and performance in computer software training. *Journal of Applied Psychology* 74: 884–891.

Gooty, J., Gavin, M., Johnson, P. D., Frazier, M. L., and Snow, D. B. 2009. In the eyes of the beholder: Transformational leadership, positive psychological capital, and performance. *Journal of Leadership and Organizational Studies* 15: 353–367.

Hicks, W. D., and Klimoski, R. J. 1987. Entry into training programs and its effects on training outcomes: A field experiment. *Academy of Management Journal* 30: 542–552.

Hutchins, H. M. and Burke, L. A. 2006. Has relapse prevention received a fair shake? A review and implications for future transfer research. *Human Resource Development Review* 5: 8–24.

Keith, N., and Frese, M. 2008. Effectiveness of error management training: A meta-analysis. *Journal of Applied Psychology* 93: 59–69.

Kluemper, D. H., Little, L. M., and DeGroot, T. 2009. State or trait: Effects of state optimism on job-related outcomes. *Journal of Organizational Behavior* 30: 209–231.

Koen, J., Klehe, U-C., and Van Vianen, A. E. M. 2012. Training career adaptability to facilitate a successful school-to-work transition. *Journal of Vocational Behavior* 81: 395–408.

Kozlowski, S. W. J., Gully, S. M., Brown, K. G., Salas, E., Smith, E. M., and Nason, E. R. 2001. Effects of training goals and goal orientation traits on multidimensional training outcomes and performance adaptability. *Organizational Behavior and Human Decision Processes* 85: 1–31.

Kraiger, K., Ford, J. K., and Salas, E. 1993. Application of cognitive, skill-based, and affective theories of learning outcomes to new methods of training evaluation. *Journal of Applied Psychology* 78: 311–328.

Luthans, B. C., Luthans, K. W., and Avey, J. B. 2014. Building the leaders of tomorrow: The development of academic psychological capital. *Journal of Leadership and Organizational Studies* 21: 191–199.

Luthans, F. 2002a. Positive organizational behavior: Developing and managing psychological strengths. *Academy of Management Executive* 16: 57–72.

Luthans, F. 2002b. The need for and meaning of positive organizational behavior. *Journal of Organizational Behavior* 23: 695–706.

Luthans, F. 2012. Psychological capital: Implications for HRD, retrospective analysis, and future directions. *Human Resource Development Quarterly* 23: 1–8.

Luthans, F., and Youssef, C. M. 2007. Emerging positive organizational behavior. *Journal of Management* 33: 321–349.

Luthans, F., Avey, J. B., and Patera, J. L. 2008. Experimental analysis of a web-based training intervention to develop positive psychological capital. *Academy of Management Learning and Education* 7: 209–221.

Luthans, F., Youssef, C. M., and Avolio, B. J. 2007. *Psychological Capital: Developing the Human Competitive Edge*. Oxford: Oxford University Press.

Luthans, F., Avey, J. B., Avolio, B. J., and Peterson, S. J. 2010. The development and resulting performance impact of positive psychological capital. *Human Resource Development Quarterly* 21: 41–67.

Luthans, F., Avoilo, B. J., Avey, J. B., and Norman, S. M. 2007. Positive psychological capital: Measurement and relationship with performance and satisfaction. *Personnel Psychology* 60: 541–572.

Luthans, F., Avolio, B. J., Walumbwa, F. O., and Li, W. 2005. The psychological capital of Chinese workers: Exploring the relationship with performance. *Management and Organization Review* 1: 249–271.

Luthans, F., Norman, S. M., Avolio, B. J., and Avey, J. B. 2008. The mediating role of psychological capital in the supportive organizational climate – employee performance relationship. *Journal of Organizational Behavior* 29: 219–238.

Luthans, F., Avey, J. B., Avolio, B. J., Norman, S, M., and Combs, G. M. 2006. Psychological capital development: Toward a micro-intervention. *Journal of Organizational Behavior* 27: 387–393.

Newman, A., Ucbasaran, D., Zhu, F., and Hirst, G. 2014. Psychological capital: A review and synthesis. *Journal of Organizational Behavior* 35: S120 – S138.

Manzano García, G., and Ayala Calvo, J. C. 2012. Emotional exhaustion of nursing staff: Influence of emotional annoyance and resilience. *International Nursing Review* 59: 101–107.

Masten, A. S. 2001. Ordinary magic: Resilience processes in development. *American Psychologist* 56: 227–239.

Meichenbaum, D. H., and Deffenbacher, J. L. 1988. Stress inoculation training. *The Counseling Psychologist* 16: 69–90.

Payne, S. C., Youngcourt, S. S., and Beaubien, J. M. 2007. A meta-analytic examination of the goal orientation nomological net. *Journal of Applied Psychology* 92: 128–150.

Peterson, C., and Seligman, M. E. P. 1984. Causal explanations as a risk factor for depression: Theory and evidence. *Psychological Review* 91: 347–374.

Peterson, S. J., and Byron, K. 2008. Exploring the role of hope in job performance: Results from four studies. *Journal of Organizational Behavior* 29: 785–803.

Peterson, S. J., and Luthans, F. 2003. The positive impact and development of hopeful leaders. *Leadership and Organization Development Journal* 24: 26–31.

Peterson, S. J., and Zhang, Z. 2011. Examining the relationships between top management team psychological characteristics, transformational leadership, and business unit performance. In M. A. Carpenter, ed., *Handbook of Top Management Team Research*, 127–149. Northampton, MA: Edward Elgar.

Peterson, S. J., Luthans, F., Avolio, B. J., Walumbwa, F. O., and Zhang, Z. 2011. Psychological capital and employee performance: A latent growth modelling approach. *Personnel Psychology* 64: 427–450.

Rego, A., Sousa, F., Marques, C., and Pina e Cunha, M. 2012. Authentic leadership promoting employees' psychological capital and creativity. *Journal of Business Research* 65: 429–437

Reichard, R. J., Dollwet M., and Louw-Potgieter, J. 2014. Development of cross-cultural psychological capital and its relationship with cultural intelligence and ethnocentrism. *Journal of Leadership and Organizational Studies* 21: 150–164.

Richman-Hirsch, W. L. 2001. Posttraining interventions to enhance transfer: The moderating effects of work environments. *Human Resource Development Quarterly* 12: 105–120.

Rouiller, J. Z., and Goldstein, I. L. 1993. The relationship between organizational transfer climate and positive transfer of training. *Human Resources Development Quarterly* 4: 377–390.

Saks, A. M. 1995. Longitudinal field investigation of the moderating and mediating effects of self-efficacy on the relationship between training and newcomer adjustment. *Journal of Applied Psychology* 80: 211–225.

Salas, E., Tannenbaum, S. I., Kraiger, K., and Smith-Jentsch, K. A. 2012. The science of training and development in organizations: What matters in practice. *Psychological Science in the Public Interest* 13: 74–101.

Seligman, M. E. P., and Csikszentmihalyi, M. 2000. Positive Psychology: An introduction. *American Psychologist* 55: 5–14.

Seligman, M. E. P., and Shulman, P. 1986. Explanatory style as a predictor of productivity and quitting among life insurance sales agents. *Journal of Personality and Social Psychology* 50: 832–838.

Smith, B. W., Tooley, E. M., Christopher, P. J., and Kay, V. S. 2010. Resilience as the ability to bounce back from stress: A neglected personal resource? *The Journal of Positive Psychology* 5: 166–176.

Sitzmann, T. 2011. A meta-analytic examination of the instructional effectiveness of computer-based simulation games. *Personnel Psychology* 64: 489–528.

Sitzmann, T., and Ely, K. 2010. Sometimes you need a reminder: The effects of prompting self-regulation on regulatory processes, learning, and attrition. *Journal of Applied Psychology* 95: 132–144.

Sitzmann, T., Bell, B. S., Kraiger, K., and Kanar, A. M. 2009. A multilevel analysis of the effect of prompting self-regulation in technology-delivered instruction. *Personnel Psychology* 62: 697–734.

Sitzmann, T., Kraiger, K., Stewart, D., and Wisher, R. 2006. The comparative effectiveness of web-based and classroom instruction: A meta-analysis. *Personnel Psychology* 59: 623–664.

Snyder, C. R. 1995. Conceptualizing, measuring and nurturing hope. *Journal of Counseling and Development* 73: 355–360.

Stajkovic, A. D., and Luthans, F. 1998a. Social cognitive theory and self-efficacy: Going beyond traditional motivational and behavioral approaches. *Organizational Dynamics* 26: 62–74.

Stajkovic, A. D., and Luthans, F. 1998b. Self-efficacy and work-related performance: A meta-analysis. *Psychological Bulletin* 124: 240–261.

Tannenbaum, S. I., Mathieu, J. E., Salas, E., and Cannon-Bowers, J. A. 1991. Meeting trainees' expectations: The influence of training fulfillment on the development of commitment, self-efficacy, and motivation. *Journal of Applied Psychology* 76: 759–769.

Taylor, P. J., Russ-Eft, D. F., and Chan, D. W. L. 2005. A meta-analytic review of behavior modeling training. *Journal of Applied Psychology* 90: 692–709.

Taylor, P. J., Russ-Eft, D. F., and Taylor, H. 2009. Transfer of management training from alternative perspectives. *Journal of Applied Psychology* 94: 104–121.

Tharenou, P., Saks, A., and Moore, C. 2007. A review and critique of research on training and organizational-level outcomes. *Human Resource Management Review* 17: 251–273.

Tracey, J. B., Tannenbaum, S. I., and Kavanagh, M. J. 1995. Applying trained skills on the job: The importance of the work environment. *Journal of Applied Psychology* 80: 239–252.

Tugade, M. M., and Fredrickson, B. L. 2004. Resilient individuals use positive emotions to bounce back from negative emotional experiences. *Journal of Personality and Social Psychology* 86: 320–333.

Wang, H., Sui, Y., Luthans, F., Wang, D., and Wu, Y. 2014. Impact of authentic leadership on performance: Role of followers' positive psychological capital and relational processes. *Journal of Organizational Behavior* 35: 5–21.

Wang, Y., Liu, L., Wang, J., and Wang, L. 2012. Work-family conflict and burnout among Chinese doctors: The mediating role of psychological capital. *Journal of Occupational Health* 54: 232–240.

Wanous, J. P., and Reichers, A. E. 2000. New employee orientation programs. *Human Resource Management Review* 10: 435–451.

Youssef, C. M., and Luthans, F. 2013. Managing psychological capital in organizations: Cognitive, affective, conative, and social mechanisms of happiness. In S. David, I Boniwell, and C. Ayers, eds., *The Oxford Handbook of Happiness*, 751–766. Oxford: Oxford University Press.

20 Rings of Fire

Training for Systems Thinking and Broadened Impact

Anders Dysvik, Arne Carlsen, and Miha Škerlavaj

What is the impact of training and development activities at work? In this chapter we argue that such a question should not only be an academic concern but also one that gets built into all decisions about training. Building an understanding of impact into training means more than measuring effects and basing training on evidence (Pfeffer & Sutton, 2006b). It means moving toward a systemic approach where employees get a holistic sense of the totalities they are operating within and are attuned to acquire and understand feedback from those totalities from their performance at work. We write *totalities* in plural because *impact* must be seen with at least three sets of realms. These are realms that are partly overlapping but each have their own sets of concerns and implications for training: the realm of business impact, the realm of beneficiary impact, and the realm of societal impact (see Figure 20.1). With the term *beneficiary impact* we do not refer to the impact for trainees but rather for the people benefitting from the increased skills of the trainees, in particular end users of trained employees' work as well as their colleagues.

Employee training and development, defined as a systematic approach to learning and development to improve individual, team, and organizational effectiveness (Kraiger & Ford, 2007), is a widespread human resource practice. Training and development interventions vary greatly in terms of content and scope from basic skill acquisition programs to complex programs, such as diversity training and leadership development. Despite the variety of interventions, the literature on training and development is supportive of a range of beneficial outcomes following training participation, such as individual knowledge and skill acquisition, individual performance (Arthur et al., 2003; Colquitt, LePine, & Noe, 2000), and organizational performance (Aguinis & Kraiger, 2009; Tharenou, Saks, & Moore, 2007).

The field of training and development research has gradually evolved. Initially, training and development research focused on isolated and specific activities (e.g., needs assessment, training objectives, evaluation criteria, and training transfer) and used the traditional instructional design model (Gagné, Briggs, & Wager, 1992) to explain how training leads to beneficial employee outcomes. As noted by Noe et al. (2010), a shortcoming of this tradition is that it is predominantly technical and instructor focused. Furthermore, this approach fails to integrate training with all the activities employees perform when at work. This is important because events prior to, during, and after training influence

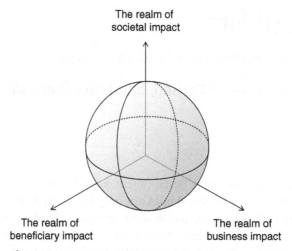

Figure 20.1. *Training for systems thinking along three realms to broaden impact.*

the outcomes of training interventions (Blume et al., 2010; Mesmer-Magnus & Viswesvaran, 2010). The results from these meta-analyses on training transfer and pretraining interventions show, among other things, that the process of ensuring beneficial individual outcomes from training and development initiatives is embedded in a wider context. Therefore, there may be additional benefits for training research and practitioners in conceptualizing the trainee and the training as embedded within a particular set of systems. Recognizing this requires systems thinking, but the benefits for training on individuals, organizations, and the wider business environment may be substantial when systems thinking is alive and present.

The purpose of our chapter is to investigate how training can contribute to development of systems thinking of trainees as seen through three lenses of building impact: the realm of business impact, the realm beneficiary impact, and the realm of societal impact. Knowledge creation is socially constructed through the development of shared meaning between employees participating in training, their trainers, and their respective colleagues and beneficiaries during and after training program completion. This implies a need for training advocates and training research to focus on conditions that enable the training participant to be active and integrate new knowledge into existing knowledge structures (Bell & Kozlowski, 2008) while recognizing the socially embeddedness of training (Noe, Clarke, & Klein, 2014). In short, training should be aligned and integrated with the core drivers for organizational performance, and provide employees with a holistic and systemic understanding to act autonomously and proactively in applying relevant training content when deemed relevant.

Prior work on systems thinking in training has identified two essential processes for training effectiveness, namely horizontal and vertical transfer (Kozlowski et al., 2000). *Horizontal transfer* refers to the critical process of ensuring that individuals acquire the knowledge and skills during training and actually make use of training content after training completion to improve individual performance. *Vertical transfer* implies that employees jointly contribute to increased unit or organizational performance based on coordinated and recognized standards at the organizational level. While both of these processes are clearly important for understanding how training influences organizational outcomes (Kozlowski et al., 2000), empirical research embracing a systems approach to training remains to the best of our knowledge limited. Brinkerhoff and Gill (1994) suggested a paradigm that organizes the principles and processes of an emerging human resource development paradigm requiring "training to be everyone's business." They established four basic principles that follow from the new Human Resource Development (HRD) paradigm: strengthen the linkage of training results to critical business goals; maintain a strong customer service focus; integrate training efforts into a total performance improvement system; and use measurement and feedback to continuously improve the process of learning and change.

We acknowledge the approach of Brinkerhoff and Gill (1994) – and related approaches in organizational learning (Jackson, 2003; Senge & Sterman, 1992) and knowledge management (Rubenstein-Montano et al., 2001) – as important foundations. However, we also see the need for further theoretical and empirical development, including the incorporation of systemic approaches in more recent research traditions. The call for a more integrated approach is also echoed in the literature of strategic Human Resource Management (HRM) (Chadwick, 2010) where it is emphasized that more fine-grained theorizing and empirical analyses are warranted to unveil the benefits of internally consistent HRM. That is, research is needed to understand the extent to which effects of one human resource practice such as training is contingent upon alignment with other human resource practices.

Systems thinking emerged as a criticism to reductionist view on organizations, at first as generalized system theory (von Bertalanffy, 1956) and later system thinking (Emery, 1969). Emery (1969) saw organizations as complex systems made up of interrelated parts most usefully studied as a whole. Systems' thinking was enthusiastically taken up as the basis of a new form of social theory. Brinkerhoff and Gill suggested a form of systems thinking that is primarily directed at the realm of business – a realm where the tradition of design thinking (Dunne & Martin, 2006; Martin, 2009; Seidel & Fixson, 2013) has set a new agenda for holistic approaches to innovation and learning in organizations. Furthermore, research traditions within such fields as corporate social responsibility (CSR) (Aguinis & Glavas, 2012; Sharma, Sharma, & Devi, 2011), care and compassion (Rynes et al., 2012), high-quality connections (Stephens, Heaphy, & Dutton, 2012), and prosocial behavior (Grant, 2007; 2013) has extended new horizons for what it means to think in systemic ways and to have an impact in organizations. Training should thus not just be seen as addressing matters of impact in the realm of business and competitive landscape, whether considered operational excellence or developmental vitality. Two relational realms deserve consideration – the microrelational realm of impact on (direct) beneficiaries and the macrorelational realm of societal impact (with indirect beneficiaries). We thus contribute to a system thinking training by developing and illustrating a framework where we deepen, reorient, and expand systemic approaches along three sets of systemic realms: the realm of business, the realms of beneficiaries, and the societal realm. We reason from three main sets of contrasting empirical examples.

Case Settings and Method

The primary form of reasoning in this chapter is deductive in the sense that we start from theories of systemic thinking in each of the three realms of impact and then illustrate, ground, and further develop our argument through three cases. The three cases are Southwest Airlines; the Zingerman's community of small food-related businesses in Ann Arbor, Michigan; and the exploration units of a major oil company that we call Explore.[1] These empirical settings are purposively sampled (Huberman & Miles, 1994) because they contrast on several dimensions of importance to system thinking training, such as types of value creation activities, knowledge base of personnel, frequency of beneficiary interaction, and framing of societal contribution.

For Southwest Airlines we rely on secondary data – as a substantial number of case descriptions (Heskett & Sasser, 2010; John, Ananthi, & Syed, 2008; O'Reilly & Pfeffer, 1995), research papers (Bunz & Maes, 1998; Kuvaas & Dysvik, 2012), and books (Collins & Hansen, 2011; Gittell, 2003; O'Reilly & Pfeffer, 2000) have been written about the company and its training and development practices. For Zingerman's we rely on three case descriptions (Baker, 2013a; 2013b; Smerek & Baker, 2010), a tale from one of the founders (Weinzweig, 2003), and personal observations by one of the authors as customer over a six-month period. For Explore we base our reasoning on a sustained action research engagement by one of the authors over eight years, partly documented in a recent book (Carlsen, Clegg, & Gjersvik, 2012). The research engagement involved more than 100 interviews and 12 facilitated sense-making events where researchers and practitioners discussed preliminary findings. The project had a primary purpose of investigating creativity in hydrocarbon exploration but also involved repeated discussion and interventions with staff responsible for training engineers engaged in oil and gas exploration.

The variation in the three cases makes them well suited to constant comparison in grounded theory building (Suddaby, 2006). It is nevertheless important to note that we use the three settings not as evidence of a renewed framework or in a normative sense. Rather, they are used as reasoning devices that help us explore the dimensions of systems thinking training and detail a new research agenda. The cases vary in the extent to which they shed light on each of the proposed realms of impact. Other empirical examples are drawn upon and used selectively.

Training for Systems Thinking – a Framework

We define *systems thinking training* as efforts of training and development activities in organizations that set out to bring systemic understanding to people – whether managers or employees – in ways that make them more capable of acquiring and using feedback from the totalities they are operating within to understand the impact of their actions and act in more fruitful ways. We suggest three sets of overlapping totalities deserve attention for training: (1) the realm of business including the operational and developmental systems, (2) the intersubjective and microrelational realm of immediate internal and external beneficiaries, and (3) the macrorelational societal realm, including impact for nearby and more distant communities. See Table 20.1 for an analytical framework with definitions of these realms.

The Business Realm

There are several streams of training-related literature that speak to the importance of having participants in training acquire systemic understanding in business operations. The tradition of experiential learning (Kolb, 1984; Kolb & Kolb, 2005) laid the premise for thinking about how to integrate one's ongoing experiences at work with efforts of collecting performance data, reflecting and developing more precise language for understanding the impact of one's actions and adjust the course accordingly. This tradition of research has more recently been paralleled by evidence-based approaches to managing and developing organizations (Michie & West, 2004; Pfeffer & Sutton, 2006a), though mostly applied in the health services (Michie & West, 2004; Rousseau, 2006). Open book management (Mouritsen, Hansen, & Hansen, 2001) with extensive sharing of financial and performance information to all parts of the organization, draws from both these sets of literatures (Pfeffer, 1998; Pfeffer & Sutton, 2006b).

Another and more direct descendant (Beckman & Barry, 2007) of experiential learning is the tradition of design thinking (Martin, 2009; Rylander, 2009). Design thinking typically sets out to use integrative approaches to solve complex challenges in a way that addresses user feasibility, technical/competence feasibility, and business feasibility (Brown, 2008). Design thinking is a broad field of practice more than a clearly defined field of research. There has been repeated calls for uptake of design thinking in education and project-based learning (Dunne & Martin, 2006; Dym et al., 2005), but as far as we know the tradition has received little attention in research on training design.

So what could systems thinking in the business realm mean for training? The cases prepared on Zingerman's community of businesses by Wayne Baker and colleagues at University of Michigan (Baker, 2013a; 2013b; Smerek & Baker, 2010) are indicative of the potential for enhancing training with systemic understanding as a main target. Waiters or other frontline service personnel at Zingerman's are known to be able – and quite enthusiastic about – giving

Table 20.1 *A framework for systems thinking training*

Realm of Impact	Description	Chief Concerns for Training
Business Realm	The operational production system of the organization as well as the system of developing new products, services, and practices. This realm also includes understanding of the objectives and vision of the organization as well as its position in the larger competitive and regulatory institutional landscape.	Enabling better decision making and task execution in everyday work through providing people with a shared, detailed, and comprehensive understanding of how (their part of) the organization performs and contributes to progress in core value-creating activities. Enabling people to better take part in and help integrate development activities across disciplines and organizational units to meet unique user needs.
Beneficiary Realm	The interpersonal system of interactional and reciprocity dynamics with internal beneficiaries and proximal external beneficiaries. This is a microrelational realm of understanding one's impact on singular others.	Enabling the ability to take the perspective of others and understand the effect of one's behavior on in everyday interactions; enabling more energizing behavior and stimulating giving behavior with internal and external beneficiaries through increased awareness of how one's actions affect others.
Societal Realm	The macrorelational realm consisting of the larger institutional field, communities and potentially global societal consequences that work in the organizations has consequences for and is shaped by. This macrorelational realm includes distant and future beneficiaries.	Enabling to understand larger societal impact of one's work and act on such understanding to facilitate integration of practices for achieving sustainability, citizenship behavior, and community development with both production and new business development.

articulated and spontaneous accounts of the company's vision, values, strategies, or finances to customers. The firm's mission and vision were often summarized as building shared commitment to a triple bottom line of: (1) great food, (2) great service, and (3) great finance (Baker, 2013a). The mission is followed up by deliberate installment of holistic understanding in all employees with extensive sharing of performance data, practices for participation in strategy discussion, and a broad-based ownership program (Baker, 2013b). A key practice is a weekly "huddle" built on principles of open-book finance with joint sharing and discussions over past and forecasted performance data visualized on big white boards (Smerek & Baker, 2010). The event involves all available employees, who take turns facilitating and keeping metrics updated between events. Participation from newcomers is particularly emphasized.

Zingerman's training practices also include: (1) a new employee introduction course taught by the two founders of the firm: "New employee orientation is the last thing Ari and I would have ever considered delegating or outsourcing" (Baker, 2013a: 13); (2) extensive in-house training at the "University of Zingerman's" where employees are requested to attend a series of orientation courses and also can earn training certificates and associate, bachelor, and more advance degrees; (3) all managers are expected to spend two hours of formal study every week and all leaders are expected to provide at least one hour of formal teaching every month in this setting; and (4) informal learning takes place on the job with regular food-tasting sessions where employees learn about new products and potential suppliers.

The training practices at Zingerman's, and the broader outlook on participation and ownership, have several parallels at Southwest Airlines. Just as with Zingerman's, airline personnel at Southwest Airlines are trained to "go the extra mile" and use their common sense when facing unique situations with passengers. Systemic understanding is central to ensuring that autonomy yields exceptional service.

To reduce unnecessary red tape, Southwest does not have a formal performance management system. The focus is on the core of their business, ensuring fast turnaround and providing excellent customer service. Southwest conducts most if not all training in-house with extensive use of experiential learning and a large degree of participation of leaders in training activities, including introductory courses for newcomers. For new training initiatives, leaders undergo training first to signal the importance of participation and to be familiar with the content that their employees will learn.

Given the emphasis on employee competence in Southwest, continuous training of its employees is essential. As noted by O'Reilly and Pfeffer: "The emphasis is on performing operations better, faster, and cheaper, understanding other people's jobs; delivering outstanding customer service; and keeping the culture alive and well (O'Reilly & Pfeffer, 2000: 39). The essentials of Southwest culture are the focus for their introductory courses for all employees where the emphasis is on two of the cornerstones of the business model: relational coordination and excellent customer service. Flight attendants go through extensive training where much of the training focuses on customer service. All training also underpins how to work in teams and cross-functionally. It is key to handling the mutual interdependence of achieving aircraft turnaround within the allocated time, where flight attendants, gate agents, and pilots help each other. Training is almost 100% run by internal resources, to make the content tailor-made and relevant for the participants. Continuously, new training programs are designed when needs emerge, with managers undergoing training along with their peers. Last, but not least, special events such as Front Line forums are set together, where tenured employees discuss the progress of the company, whether train-ing is beneficial, and what needs to be done to maintain the company culture (O'Reilly & Pfeffer, 2000).

The empirical grounding in evidence also extends to employee development efforts. Collins and Hansen (2011) have coined such grounding "empirical cre-ativity," using Southwest Airlines as one of their cases. A good example here is the development work on changing boarding practices (Heskett & Sasser, 2010). In an experiment in 2007 in San Diego, passengers were for the first time allowed to reserve their seats in advance. The actual boarding processes were filmed and the passengers were interviewed about their experience. Southwest found that customers preferred its open seating by two to one and that the assigned seating slowed the boarding process by four to six minutes. As a result of this experiment, management decided to maintain open seating but began allowing passengers to "reserve" places in the waiting line (Heskett & Sasser, 2010: 7–8) What we see here is a form of evidence-based practice development where members of the organization gather evidence of customer preferences and/or the working of practices (e.g., like boarding), perform small experiments on these practices, and redesign them accordingly. It is a form of development activity where training and improvement efforts may blend, that is cyclical and participative, and that starts with observations in the field.

Like at Zingerman's frontline employees at Southwest Airlines are noted for being articulate about vision and strategy, "Nothing about nurturing the culture at Southwest Airlines is casual. The result? Southwest people – even at the low-est part of the employee food chain – are extraordinarily articulate about the essence of the Southwest vision" (O'Reilly, 1995: 7).

At Explore, training for systems thinking takes two major forms. First, there is cross-disciplinary training. Geoscientists who explore for oil and gas face inevi-table needs for combining information from many different sources and disci-plines to: (1) develop geological prospects for where oil and gas can be found, (2) communicate these prospects to internal and internal stakeholders in a way that is system competent (e.g., knowing the larger basin in which they are placed, the position and strategies of this basin as well as competing prospects within and outside the basin), and (3) integrate efforts to bring prospects closer to matura-tion. Senior explorers in charge of training and mentoring activities talk about the necessity of investing in t-shaped (breadth and depth) competence building (Barile et al., 2012) to facilitate cross-disciplinary combination. For example, a specialist in sedimentology, having depth, may need to invest up to five years of his or her career into work activities that provide on-the-job training in comple-mentary disciplines, thus acquiring breadth, including the business of oil field development.

Second, systems thinking at Explore is also nurtured through on-the job training in projects. Successful exploration projects and task forces typically rely on extensive mobilization practices with regard to facilitating open discussions of objectives, plans, and commitments in the early phases, seeding the ground for not only enrollment of people but also holistic understanding and autonomy in the project. Senior exploration managers also frequently talk about the need to nurture and grow people who can become integrators in terms of being ready to assume responsibility for the total development of prospects all the way to drilling. A tale from one successful exploration manager about his own growth as a threshold experience is illustrative:

> Those first three years, I delivered specialized services, right. So you care about that little piece there and let go of everything else.... But when it gets to the point that you are investing in a hundred million dollars to drill a well, then you need to be accountable and proper and document things in a much wider scope – and approach the larger, total picture … it takes insanely much to realize an idea, and that is what you get to see, how hard it is to convince everyone around you that this is a good idea, and that you are allowed to use X million dollars to test your idea. And that means you are really beginning to become interested in the totality.

Developing people with such integrator capabilities is recognized as important at Explore. Managers and current integrators believe that the main way to accomplish this is with on-the-job learning, where employees take on responsibility for real-life projects. Such learning is increasingly coupled with systematic efforts of coaching and joint reflection in formalized training arrangements at the internal Exploration Academy.

A particularly interesting feature of training for system understanding at Explore is the role of the visual. Explorers seldom see or touch the material realities they work with, and interpretive complexity amongst masses of data presents a real danger for fragmentation of work. Newcomer specialists who are delivering small analytics into large projects often voice concerns about such fragmentation and alienation. By contrast, well-working exploration teams typically have arrangements that parallel the huddle at Zingerman's: There are visual sensemaking sessions within projects that place data and maps into larger regional wholes and there are (less frequent) visual delivery schedules and prospect inventories across prospects. The visual becomes the basis for seeing progress in work (Amabile & Kramer, 2011) and for relational coordination (Bechky, 2003; Seidel & Fixson, 2013; Seidel & O'Mahony, 2014), training that literally allow newcomers to see how their work fits into and affects the larger landscape of deliverables. So far such schemes are more part of learning-oriented work practice than training per se.

The Beneficiary Realm

The beneficiary realm of making an impact with training consist of the interpersonal system of interactional and reciprocity dynamics with internal beneficiaries and proximal external beneficiaries. The perceived importance of this realm has grown along with increasing awareness of the importance of prosocial behavior (Grant, 2007), high-quality connections (Stephens et al., 2012), and increased attention to relational being at work (Dutton & Ragins, 2007; Gergen, 2009; Sennett, 2012). Brown and van Buren (2007) suggest that training involving employee-helping behavior will develop stronger reciprocity norms in organization. More specifically, work on generalized reciprocity and giving behavior show how performance is boosted by being aware of the consequences of one's action in terms of making a difference to others (Grant, 2013; Grant & Berry, 2011).

Much of this theorizing takes an implicit systemic view in the sense that training for one's perspective taking (Buell, Kim, & Tsay, 2014; Galinsky et al., 2008; Hoever et al., 2012) is seen as key to connect, read feedback from immediate others, and perform well (e.g., in terms of social processes such as creativity or negotiations). Galinsky et al. (2008) highlight the importance of perspective taking for negotiation outcomes as well as it's differential effect vis-à-vis empathy. While perspective taking was beneficial for negotiation outcomes, empathy was not. Grant (2008) convincingly demonstrated how exposure to primary beneficiary of call center operators' work and psychological mechanism of perspective taking stimulates individual creativity, effort, and funds raised. Hoever et al. (2012) conducted a series of experiments to show that diversity only breeds team creativity when supported by perspective taking.

In the high-quality connections literature (Dutton, 2003; Dutton & Heaphy, 2003; Stephens et al., 2012) the microdynamics of seeing others, listening to others, and being genuine in relation to others all presupposes ability to understand the effect one has on others. Being able to form high-quality connections is an intersubjective systemic skill in the relational realm. The systemic quality is particularly well qualified by the work of Esa Saarinen and colleagues (Luoma, Hämäläinen, & Saarinen, 2008; Saarinen & Hämäläinen, 2010) who talks about systems intelligence as a broadened version of emotional and social intelligence. As defined by Hämäläinen and Saarinen (2006: 191), "A subject acting with systems intelligence engages successfully and productively with the holistic feedback mechanisms of her environment. She perceives herself as part of a whole, the influence of the whole upon herself as well as her own influence upon the whole." The wholes that Hämäläinen and Saarinen (2006: 191) are particularly concerned with are the relational ones, for example what they call interpersonal "systems of holding back" (Hämäläinen and Saarinen 2006: 196–198). Couples may stop doing small gestures of love and people at work may stop trying to do the small positive behaviors that make others thrive, and make a difference to customers because of lack of sensitivity and unchecked assumption about others. We risk being trapped into negative behavioral dynamics because of lack of systems intelligence.

Finally, the beneficiary realm has been further accentuated by a stream of research on help-seeking and help-giving behavior (Amabile, Fisher, & Pillemer, 2014; Brooks, Gino, & Schweitzer, 2015; Cerne et al., 2013; Fisher, Pillemer, & Amabile, 2014; Grodal, Nelson, & Siino, 2015; Hargadon & Bechky, 2006; Shapiro, 2013). For example, being system competent in an organization like the design firm IDEO presupposes learning about and acting upon expectations for actively seeking help for complex problem solving outside one's project team (Amabile et al., 2014). Other examples of organizations that systematically nurture help-seeking and help-giving behaviors at work include Google and ConocoPhilips where peer-to-peer appreciation is used to signal benefits and collaborative systems offers a means to giving and receiving help. Addressing overwhelming fear of losing face or exposing oneself for vulnerability while asking for help, Brooks, Gino et al. (2015) have recently found that asking for help actually increased perceptions of help seekers' competence (especially if problems were seen as tough and person asked was an expert in the field). Knowing where, when, and how to ask for help and being able to offer help in return should be part of the agenda for training.

Training that addresses the beneficiary systemic realm is well exemplified at Zingerman's. Its importance is shown clearly by the founders who championed an explicitly giving-oriented culture with emphasis on trust and care. Several parts of the vision statement and the guiding principles allude to the importance of this realm. Examples include (Baker, 2013a: 4): "Showing love and care in all our actions. To enrich as many lives as we possibly can" (from the mission statement) and "Strong relationships! Successful working relationships are an essential component of our health and success as a business" (from the guiding principles statement). In terms of human resource and management practices, examples of beneficiary-related training arrangements include (Baker, 2013a; 2013b): (1) teaching relational skills of servant leadership as core to giving great service and handling complaints; (2) instituting a concept called "positive energy" in which all employees should strive to have professional fun and a positive attitude; (3) fostering open communication with inviting newcomers and others to partner meetings and ensuring key decisions are made in face-to-face meetings with consensus; (4) practices for publicly giving appreciation of co-workers at the end of meetings, expressing gratitude to co-workers for specific actions in the monthly newsletter, and giving formal and public awards for actions qualifying for the "x-tra mile files" and "service stars"; (5) teaching a process known as "caring confrontation" in which employees are told to handle work concerns in a direct and respectful manner; and (6) letting employees fill out donation request forms for charity contributions to recipient organizations in the local community.

Again, several of these ways of thinking about training are mirrored at Southwest Airlines in terms of purposively emphasizing and investing in relations as the major basis of competitive advantage and employee well-being (Gittell, 2001). Like at Zingerman's, the company was set up with an egalitarian family-like culture emphasizing deeply meaningful work. Relational competence is continually emphasized not just in training, but in recruitment and leadership practices as well (O'Reilly & Pfeffer, 1995).

Indeed, Judy Gittell's in-depth studies claimed that relational coordination – as in the fast turnaround processes – is a major explanation of the company's competitive advantage (Gittell, 2000; 2006). Such relational coordination, according to Gittell, resides in shared goals, shared knowledge, and mutual respect, factors that in turn promote more frequent, timely, and joint communication on crucial issues. From the early days, relational practices at Southwest

Airlines included (O'Reilly & Pfeffer, 1995): (1) celebrating a fun-loving culture with serious attention to parties and celebrations; (2) empowering employees to make on-the-spot commonsense decisions to provide customer service, and celebration of examples of helping customers in need; (3) cherishing the customer centric by arranging a "day in the field" program for officers and directors and staffing the human resource department with people with frontline experience only; (4) allowing peer recruiting to better screen for value fit, positive attitudes, and ability to do team work; and (5) appreciating peer-to-peer and cross-function contributions as well as positively deviant customer service experiences. Compared to Zingerman's, people at Southwest Airlines seem to be more conscious about the value of beneficiary contact practices for creating, gathering, and using stories of positively deviant services. Employees of the company were famous for rapping or singing security announcements and freely using other opportunities to provide unexpected entertainment for passengers. Even turning down people in recruitment in a gracefully and respectful manner seems to have been a means to create positively deviant beneficiary service (O'Reilly & Pfeffer, 1995).

Moving on to Explore, we can say that relational practices have, quite unlike the two other case companies, traditionally not been a major concern in training or team development. Technical concerns and subjects are prioritized and there is little local language for relations that are enlivening and mutually rewarding. Interaction with direct outside beneficiaries is not a part of everyday work. There are no immediate external beneficiaries (as opposed to anonymous energy users) of exploration to interact with except family and other local community members for whom an eventual discovery could mean more investments and high-paying jobs in their area.

Nevertheless, the relational dimension that appears crucial in hydrocarbon exploration activities at Explore is the ability to maneuver in a landscape of specialists and knowing how other specialists or integrators may benefit from one's work. Finding good ways of asking for help and offering help is of major importance to move prospects further up the line, as there is no such thing as single-person prospect development. Training schemes are giving increased attention to practices for giving appreciation within and across departments. Furthermore, while the organization has for a long time staged peer-review and peer-assist sessions, the generative, energizing and connective aspects of such sessions are now being recognized along with technical matters.

A qualitative study of knowledge creation in one exploration unit and a consulting firm found that high-quality connections played a major role in projects considered particularly fruitful (Aarrestad, Brøndbo, & Carlsen, 2015). In short, explorers experience being more productive and alive in knowledge creation when there is room for more emotionally intense and overlapping interactions, when an open-ended and respectful questioning expands reciprocity in interactions, and when connectivity is helped by the sensory richness of proximity and more use of visuals and tangibles in synchronous interactions. The use of visuals and tangibles in relating is more accentuated in Explore than at

Southwest and Zingerman's, probably due to the complexity of work with need for knowledge cocreation and coordination between many subdisciplines. When transcending knowledge differences (Majchrzak, More, & Faraj, 2012) and encouraging seeking and providing help, active use of visual boundary objects seems to be necessary.

The Societal Realm

Beyond the business realm and beyond the realm of internal and proximal external beneficiaries are larger societal wholes – be they environmental, human-rights related, matters of regional social economic growth, or ethical concerns – that people's work in organizations may influence. Ultimately, this societal realm, or realms in plural to be more precise, can be seen as a set of CSRs that are immanent in work in ways people are not aware of normally. The consequences of CSR for training at work is a topic that transcends levels of analysis, and for which there is little current knowledge (Aguinis & Glavas, 2012). We know little about how concrete activities within human resource management and training impact CSR (Sharma et al., 2011). Our discussion here is thus tentative. We open for consideration of larger questions than we can hope to answer: Are there systemic realms of a societal nature that training in organizations could target and, if so, how?

Returning briefly to our three cases, the answer to the first part of this question must be a clear "yes." This is easiest to see in the case of Zingerman's community of businesses. The founders of the firm appear to have been successful in integrating new business development and ownership with an agenda of local community development in Ann Arbor and Washtenaw County, as well as sustainability and food justice. One of the guiding principles of the business taught to all employees is that Zingerman's should be "an active part of the community. We believe that a business has an obligation to give back to the community of which it is a part" (Baker, 2013a: 4). The owners of the firm have declined several offers to sell or expand upon the brand to other cities and emphasize engaging employees in development of local workplaces and healthy, sustainable food from local suppliers. The community agenda includes the founding of the Food Gatherers, an independent not-for-profit food rescue program and food bank that in 2011 delivered nearly 12,000 meals a day to nearly 44,000 residents of Washtenaw County. Employees handle up to a dozen requests for food donations every day, based on a standardized form given out in all service outlets. Ten percent of the profit posttax is donated to the community as cash. Other initiatives for achieving zero carbon footprints and maintaining "thriveable wages" give further credit to Zingerman's efforts for making social contributions.

For Southwest Airlines, the clearest systemic societal realm here seems to be workplace democracy. While democracy at work may have several limits as a form of governance (Kerr, 2004), there is little doubt that Southwest Airlines was an industry pioneer in promoting organizational practices – including training, ownership, collaboration, and labor relations – that were considered participative and in promotion of better and more meaningful and egalitarian places to work. The organization seem to have been infused with a societal mission (O'Reilly & Pfeffer, 1995) of showing the possibility of creating a workplace where people can find deep meaning, bring their whole self to work, and do well when doing good – a "level five ambition" (Collins & Hansen, 2011). Systems thinking in this regard would be more than merely knowing the internal practices well. Employees' credibility as spokespersons and exemplars of the pioneering quest would require knowledge of the larger discourses of workplace democracy, including knowledge of institutional arrangements concerning democracy and labor collaboration in the aviation industry and other service sectors.

At Explore, the need for systems thinking in the societal realm is evident in many parts of exploration: (1) regional socioeconomic consequences of locating discovery activities and concept decisions with regard to infrastructure for exploiting resources and transport oil and gas (reflected in training arrangements for analysts); (2) safety and environmental consequences of exploration practices, including, for example, the need for emergency preparations regarding oil spills along the coast, something that also affects ship traffic (a key part of the security training for drilling personnel and engineers involved in planning and project management); and (3) sociopolitical impact of international exploration activities, in particular in Third World areas in terms of building institutional capabilities and contributing to democratic development (part of training arrangements for all personnel going abroad, increasing in scope and depth with length of stay and role. Additionally, there are obvious larger environmental and geopolitical issues tied to long-term sustainable energy supply, though this has not been a concern for training so far.

In summary, training for systems thinking in the societal realm may potentially cover a large and varied set of societal systems, depending on nature of value creating activities and the environments they meet. Even a cursory look reveals that training to help employees meet such concerns is complex in various ways, many of them mainly targeted to mid-level managers and project leaders.

Implications for Future Research

We have suggested a training framework for systems thinking in organizations and developed it through exploring three realms of creating impact. We started from renewed attention to holistic thinking and impact orientation in research traditions such as design thinking and prosocial behavior and used three cases as reasoning devices. Looking across the reasoning in the three realms of our suggested framework, we end up with three sets of insights that both summarize what we have learned and conjure implications for future research: (1) fostering interdependent autonomy, (2) getting visual with perspective taking and transparency, and (3) creating embedded training arrangements.

Fostering Interdependent Autonomy and Becoming Systems Competent

Job autonomy appears to be one of the essential tenets for integrating training and systems thinking. Job autonomy – or the extent to which a job allows freedom, independence, and discretion to schedule work, make decisions, and choose the methods used to perform tasks (Morgeson & Humphrey, 2006) – is a cornerstone in contemporary work-design theories and is convincingly related to a number of employee outcomes focal to training, such as increased work performance, organizational commitment, and helping behaviors, as well as reduced stress and turnover (Humphrey, Nahrgang, & Morgeson, 2007). In our cases, we have seen that autonomy is both given and expected in the sense that people are brought into roles and organizational arrangements where they are provided knowledge and leeway to make decisions and initiate actions that have impact – whether that means servicing a customer or bringing a hydrocarbon prospect closer to drilling.

One could probably flag *systems thinking* as a label for a very different organizational philosophy in which people were trained to follow prescribed behaviors based on organizational structure and mechanisms. Such a control version of systems thinking is not the situation in any of our cases. Rather, what we see is the nurturing of proactive behaviors in which people are encouraged to produce fast and fruitful responses from a different part of their working environment and acquire the needed information to do so. This requires interdependent autonomy in which each node carries responsibility for aligning actions in a system-consistent manner. Autonomy is thus accentuated as both an outcome and contingency of systems thinking and, for some (like the exploration project leader), the challenge of a new role may provide the threshold experience to grow into a fully autonomous and system competent actor.

Further research would be needed to understand the development trajectories of individuals who are growing to become system competent in this manner and shape their work-related identity accordingly. We know little about the formative experiences; training arrangements set people on the pathways of becoming integrators, givers, or socially responsible. There is a rich tradition of research within narrative psychology that qualifies how individuals tend to grow into becoming more generative and increasingly contribute to both proximal and distant beneficiaries as they pass mid-life (e.g., McAdams & Guo, 2015). We may speculate that this type of life motive amounts to the equivalence of becoming more system competent along the beneficiary and societal realms. But we know of no research on training that tries to investigate such growth trajectories.

Furthermore, other cases would be needed to understand variations of systems thinking, autonomy, and individual growth trajectories across industries. For a fast-paced software development environment like for example Spotify,[2] it seems that autonomy represents a necessity to answer demands for agile development activities of new services and upgrades, in addition to rapid responses to customers' demands. Development activities, from programming to systems design to service development, are done in parallel and in response to multiple real-time scenarios. Such activities involve many small and large decisions for which formal coordination and control must be limited. Here autonomy necessitates high levels of systems understanding in the sense of being able to see how one's work relates to work together within and across developments teams and to the larger portfolio of services as seen by users. Growth of the organization and broadening of service offers may pose further challenges. Initial evidence for this proposition was recently found by Dysvik, Kuvaas, and Buch (2016) who observed a positive relationship between perceived investment in employee development and taking charge behavior for employees with high levels of job autonomy. In other words, investments in developing employees competence needs to be accompanied by the everyday perception of having the leeway to make use of acquired knowledge and skills, in line with our systems thinking approach.

Getting Visual with Perspective Taking and Transparency

Training for systems thinking means institutionalizing practices for perspective taking and creating transparency, both of which underpin interdependent autonomy. A striking feature of these practices is their visual and physical character. Key to the huddle and open-book management at Zingerman's is the large whiteboard as a shared visual resource for providing overview of key financial metrics and forecasts. This organization also emphasizes making beneficiary stories visible in internal pamphlets and other graphic boundary objects to communicate awards for going the "X-tra mile." At Explore, the extensive use of large maps, seismic charts, and well logs in shared office space is regarded key to fostering collaboration in exploration, in particular with regard to involving newcomers. Visuals become central to a way to transcend knowledge boundaries (Majchrzak et al., 2012) and create shared imaginings, literally seeing how one makes a difference to colleagues in their knowledge creation. We also note that several of the training arrangements at Southwest Airlines, such as "a day in the field," or joint work on turnarounds and luggage handling, presupposes physical proximity in relational coordination.

A growing body of literature on the role of visuals in perspective taking and transparency is promising. It is pointing toward several impactful training interventions. For example, visualizing the end user has a significant effect on the task performance. In the health care sector, a group of Israeli radiologists (Turner et al., 2008) conducted an experiment on the task of diagnosing computed tomography (CT) exams from patients. It is a striking finding that attaching patient photo next to the CT exam improved diagnostic accuracy by 46% and that almost 80% of the key results came about only when the radiologists saw the patient's photograph. Similarly, Buell et al. (2014), show that restaurant chefs who saw their customers made them make (objectively) more tasty food and achieve 10% higher customer satisfaction through feelings of appreciation and meaningfulness. When both customers and cooks were able to see one another (without speaking to each other), the customer satisfaction increased by 17.3% and speed of service delivery increased by 13.2%. In a series of different settings, from call center operators to firemen, Adam Grant and colleagues report even more impactful evidence of triggering prosocial motivation through perspective taking on creativity (Grant & Berry, 2011), persistence, performance, and productivity (Grant & Sumanth, 2009). Training for perspective taking, including visualizing, is thus a powerful driver of system thinking at work.

There is a strong research agenda for the systematic focus on perspective taking and visualizing as essential ingredients of integrated training systems – "systems predicated on influencing organizational effectiveness" (Kozlowski et al., 2000: 203). Future research should span across multiple levels of analysis to help understand the role of perspective taking in facilitating training contexts and processes for broader impact and vertical transfer of training. For example, as far as we know, little research exists about systematic collection and display of end-user testimonials, or other reminder of beneficiaries, for training purposes.

Following the visual and material turn in organization studies (Ashcraft, Kuhn, & Cooren, 2009; Meyer et al., 2013) there is also a broader agenda for studying the use of tangibles and work space in training arrangements. The promise here is that use of visuals will help build transparency, aid coordination, and foster better collaboration (de Vaujany & Mitev, 2013; Doorley & Witthoft, 2011). One example is the use of huddles, like at Zingerman's. There is some research on huddles (Provost et al., 2014; Quinn & Bunderson, 2013), but not regarding the role of the particular visuals being used or the effect and relevance for training.

Creating Embedded Training Arrangements

The cases we have looked at here all confirm and extend the importance of internally consistent human resource practices, that is, the effect of one human resource practice such as training is contingent upon the wider organizational context including other human resource practices, job design features, and managerial styles. For example, Kraimer et al. (2011) found that while employees may be satisfied with their developmental opportunities, a lack of career opportunities may make them more likely to leave the company and work less effective while they remain. In contrast, a systems approach to training would imply ensuring both horizontal and vertical processes ensuring that employees are allowed to make use of acquired knowledge and skills through horizontal transfer within roles that develop as their understanding of their role embedded in the wider organizational context increases through vertical transfer (Kozlowski et al., 2000). In addition, Blume et al. (2010) found that perceived support from the work environment fosters training transfer. Thus, support from both colleagues (Chiaburu & Harrison, 2008) and supervisors (Eisenberger et al., 2002) is important for systems thinking toward training to be sustainable over time because a lack of support could lead to less transfer and consequently less systems thinking. This is most evident at Southwest Airlines and Zingerman's where core values, service concepts, ownership models, and recruitment all shape and are shaped by training arrangements.

Training with a systems perspective is not always defined strictly as training but may be a mix of embedded and interrelated organizational practices. In line with such a trend, an increasing number of organizations worldwide are adopting so called 70:20:10 learning strategy implementations (Jennings, 2013; Lombardo & Eichinger, 1996), where the emphasis on the time, effort, and money spent on training is on the informal learning part, mostly through experiential learning (70%) and relationships (20%), whereas merely 10% of training investments are devoted to formal and traditional learning activities (Lombardo & Eichinger, 1996). This underlines our call for a shift in how training providers understand training and development as broadening impact, whether for business, beneficiaries, and society.

Conclusion

By emphasizing three distinct, yet related realms (business, beneficiary, societal) for training impact we have attempted to extend prior work on systems thinking in training. First, we have extended previous work on horizontal transfer to argue that training should not only be used as a means to improve in-role performance of employees but to serve beneficial outcomes within a wider set of realms. Second, we align with ideas of vertical transfer to ensure that the efforts and contributions made by employees form coordinated patterns aimed at achieving recognized standards. The cases described in this chapter illustrate organizations succeeding more than they fail in facilitating such processes. One of the contingencies that seem essential for establishing and maintaining a broadening of impact is autonomy because employees embedded in such systems work harder being more involved and committed owing to having more say in their work, smarter because they are encouraged to continuously develop their competence, and more responsible because there are actually empowered to do so (Pfeffer & Veiga, 1999: 40). While such a contention looks relatively straightforward, developing people to become system competent, implementing a system thinking approach in training, and making it work are not. The promise we take from the empirical evidence presented in our three cases is however clear: It is possible and beneficial to train people in organizations for systems thinking and broadening of impact. When at its best, such training may produce rings of fire that make both people and organizations thrive.

Notes

1 *Explore* is short for the exploration units of an integrated oil company. In these units, a variety of geoscientists (engineers trained in disciplines like sedimentology, petrochemics, geophysics, and geology) work to identity prospects for where oil and gas

can be found. This work requires an ability to imagine processes that took place hundreds of millions of years ago based on synthesis of data that are always incomplete, from well logs, seismic images, and rock samples. Exploration can take place close to proven oil fields as well as in frontier basins.

2 Based on group interview and site visit in October 22, 2014.

References

Aarrestad, M., Brøndbo, M. T., and Carlsen, A. 2015. When stakes are high and guards are low: High-quality connections in knowledge creation. *Knowledge and Process Management* 22(2): 88–98.

Aguinis, H., and Glavas, A. 2012. What we know and don't know about corporate social responsibility a review and research agenda. *Journal of Management* 38(4): 932–968.

Aguinis, H., and Kraiger, K. 2009. Benefits of training and development for individuals and teams, organizations, and society, *Annual Review of Psychology*, 60: 451–474.

Amabile, T., and Kramer, S. 2011. *The Progress Principle: Using Small Wins to Ignite Joy, Engagement, and Creativity at Work*. Boston: Harvard Business School Publishing.

Amabile, T., Fisher, C. M., and Pillemer, J. 2014. IDEO's culture of helping. *Harvard Business Review* 92(1): 54–61.

Arthur, W., Bennett, W., Edens, P. S., and Bell, S. T. 2003. Effectiveness of training in organizations: A meta-analysis of design and evaluation features. *Journal of Applied Psychology* 88(2): 234–245.

Ashcraft, K. L., Kuhn, T. R., and Cooren, F. 2009. Constitutional amendments: "Materializing" organizational communication. *Academy of Management Annals* 3: 1–64.

Baker, W. E. 2013a. *Zingerman's Community of Businesses: A Recipe for Building a Positive Business*. Ann Arbor: GlobalLens.

Baker, W. E. 2013b. *Zingerman's: Broad-Based Ownership, Governance, and Sustainability*. Ann Arbor: GlobalLens.

Barile, S., Franco, G., Nota, G., and Saviano, M. 2012. Structure and dynamics of a "T-shaped" knowledge: From individuals to cooperating communities of practice. *Service Science* 4(2): 161–180.

Bechky, B. A. 2003. Sharing meaning across occupational communities: The transformation of understanding on a production floor. *Organization Science* 14(3): 312–330.

Beckman, S. L., and Barry, M. 2007. Innovation as a learning process: Embedding design thinking. *California Management Review* 50(1): 25.

Bell, B. S., and Kozlowski, S. W. J. 2008. Active learning: Effects of core training design elements on self-regulatory processes, learning and adaptability. *Journal of Applied Psychology* 93(2): 296–316.

Blume, B. D., Ford, J. K., Baldwin, T. T., and Huang, J. L. 2010. Transfer of training: A meta-analytic review. *Journal of Management* 36(4): 1065–1105.

Brinkerhoff, R. O., and Gill, S. J. 1994. *The Learning Alliance: Systems Thinking in Human Resource Development*. San Francisco, CA: Jossey-Bass.

Brooks, A. W., Gino F., and Schweitzer, M. E. 2015. Smart people ask for (my) advice: Seeking advice boosts perceptions of competence. *Management Science* 61(6):1421–1435.

Brown, K. G., and van Buren, M. E. 2007. *Applying a Social Capital Perspective to the Evaluation of Distance Training.* In S. M. Fiore and E. Salas, eds., *Toward a Science of Distributed Learning,* 41–63. Washington, DC: American Psychological Association.

Brown, T. 2008. Design thinking. *Harvard Business Review* 86(6): 84.

Buell, R. W., Kim, T., and Tsay, C.-J. 2014. Cooks make tastier food when they can see their customers. *Harvard Business Review* (November): 37–38.

Bunz, U. K., and Maes, J. D. 1998. Learning excellence: Southwest Airlines' approach. *Managing Service Quality* 8(3): 163–169.

Carlsen, A., Clegg, S., and Gjersvik, R., eds. 2012. *Idea Work: Lessons of the Extraordinary in Everyday Creativity.* Oslo: Cappelen Damm.

Cerne, M., Nerstad, C., Dysvik, A., and Škerlavaj, M. 2013. What goes around comes around: Knowledge hiding, perceived motivational climate, and creativity. *Academy of Management Journal* 57(1): 172–192.

Chadwick, C. 2010. Theoretic insights on the nature of performance synergies in human resource systems: Toward greater precision. *Human Resource Management Review* 20: 85–101.

Chiaburu, D. S., and Harrison, D. A. 2008. Do peers make the place? Conceptual synthesis and meta-analysis of coworker effects on perceptions, attitudes, OCBs, and performance. *Journal of Applied Psychology* 93(5): 1082–1103.

Collins, J., and Hansen, M. T. 2011. *Great by Choice: Uncertainty, Chaos and Luck-Why Some Thrive Despite Them All.* New York: Random House.

Colquitt, J. A., LePine, J. A., and Noe, R. A. 2000. Toward an integrative theory of training motivation: A meta-analytic path analysis of 20 years of research. *Journal of Applied Psychology* 85(5): 678–707.

de Vaujany, F.-X., and Mitev, N. 2013. *Materiality and Space: Organizations, Artefacts and Practices.* Basingstoke, UK: Palgrave Macmillan.

Doorley, S., and Witthoft, S. 2011. *Make Space: How to Set the Stage for Creative Collaboration.* New York: John Wiley and Sons.

Dunne, D., and Martin, R. 2006. Design thinking and how it will change management education: An interview and discussion. *Academy of Management Learning and Education* 5(4): 512–523.

Dutton, J. E. 2003. *Energize Your Workplace: How to Create and Sustain High-Quality Connections at Work.* San Francisco, CA: Jossey-Bass.

Dutton, J. E., and Heaphy, E. 2003. The power of high quality connections. In K. Cameron, J. E. Dutton, and R. E. Quinn, eds., *Positive Organizational Scholarship,* 263–278. New York: Lawrence Erlbaum Associates.

Dutton, J. E., and Ragins, B. R., eds. 2007. *Exploring Positive Relationships at Work: Building a Theoretical and Research Foundation.* Mahwah, NJ: Lawrence Erlbaum.

Dym, C. L., Agogino, A. M., Eris, O., Frey, D. D., and Leifer, L. J. 2005. Engineering design thinking, teaching, and learning. *Journal of Engineering Education* 94(1): 103–120.

Dysvik, A., Kuvaas, B., and Buch, R. 2016. Perceived investment in employee development and taking charge. *Journal of Managerial Psychology* 31(1): 50–60.

Eisenberger, R., Stinglhamber, F., Vandenberghe, C., Sucharski, I. L., and Rhoades, L. 2002. Perceived supervisor support: Contributions to perceived organizational support and employee retention. *Journal of Applied Psychology* 87(3): 565–573.

Emery, F. E. 1969. *Systems Thinking.* Harmondsworth, UK: Penguin Books.

Fisher, C. M., Pillemer, J., and Amabile, T. M. 2014. *Helping You Help Me: The Role of Diagnostic (In) congruence in the Helping Process within Organizations.* Cambridge, MA: Harvard Business School.

Gagné, R. M., Briggs, L.-J., and Wager, W. W. 1992. *Principles of Instructional Design.* Fort Worth, TX: Harcourt Brace Jovanovich.

Galinsky, A. D., Maddux, W. W., Gilin, D., and White, J. B. 2008. Why It Pays to Get Inside the Head of Your Opponent: The Differential Effects of Perspective Taking and Empathy in Negotiations. *Psychological Science* 19(4): 378–384.

Gergen, K. J. 2009. *Relational Being: Beyond Self and Community.* Oxford: Oxford University Press.

Gittell, J. H. 2001. Investing in relationships. *Harvard Business Review* 79(6): 28–30.

Gittell, J. H. 2003. *The Southwest Airlines Way: Using the Power of Relationships to Achieve High Performance.* New York: McGraw-Hill.

Gittell, J. H. 2000. Paradox of coordination and control. *California Management Review* 42(3):101–117.

Gittell, J. H. 2006. Relational coordination: Coordinating work through relationships of shared goals, shared knowledge and mutual respect. In O. Kyriakidou and M. Ozbilgin, eds., *Relational Perspectives in Organizational Studies: A Research Companion,* 74–94, Cheltenham, UK: Edward Elgar.

Grant, A. M. 2007. Relational job design and the motivation to make a prosocial difference. *Academy of Management Review* 32(2): 393–417.

Grant, A. M. 2008. Does intrinsic motivation fuel the prosocial fire? Motivational synergy in predicting persistence, performance, and productivity. *Journal of Applied Psychology* 93(1): 48–58.

Grant, A. M. 2013. *Give and Take: A Revolutionary Approach to Success.* New York: Penguin.

Grant, A. M., and Berry, J. W. 2011. The necessity of others is the mother of invention: Intrinsic and prosocial motivations, perspective taking, and creativity. *Academy of Management Journal* 54(1): 73–96.

Grant, A. M., and Sumanth, J. J. 2009. Mission possible: The performance of prosocially motivated employees depends on manager trustworthiness. *Journal of Applied Psychology* 94: 927–944.

Grodal, S., Nelson, A., and Siino, R. 2015. Help-seeking and help-giving as an organizational routine: Continual engagement in innovative work. *Academy of Management Journal* 58(1): 136–168.

Hämäläinen, R. P., and Saarinen, E. 2006. Systems intelligence: A key competence in human action and organizational life. *Reflections. The Sol Journal on Knowledge, Learning and Change* 7(4): 17–28.

Hargadon, A. B., and Bechky, B. A. 2006. When collections of creatives become creative collectives: A field study of problem solving at work. *Organization Science* 17(4): 484–500.

Heskett, J. L., and Sasser, W. E. 2010. Southwest Airlines: In a different world. Harvard Business School Case 910-419. Boston, MA: Harvard Business School Publishing (Revised 2013).

Hoever, I., van Knippenberg, D., van Ginkel, W., and Barkema, H. 2012. Fostering team creativity: Perspective taking as key to unlocking diversity's potential. *Journal of Applied Psychology* 97(5): 982–996.

Huberman, A. M., and Miles, M. B. 1994. *Qualitative Data Analysis: An Expanded Sourcebook*. Thousand Oaks, CA: Sage.

Humphrey, S. E., Nahrgang, J. D., and Morgeson, F. P. 2007. Integrating motivational, social and contextual work design features: A meta-analytic summary and theoretical extension of the work design literature. *Journal of Applied Psychology* 92(5): 1332–1356.

Jackson, M. C. 2003. *Systems Thinking: Creative Holism for Managers*. Chichester, UK: John Wiley & Sons.

Jennings, C. 2013. 70:20:10 Framework Explained. Surrey Hills, Victoria, Australia: 70:20:10 Forum Pty Ltd.

John, D., Ananthi, R., and Syed, A. 2008. *Innovate HR Practices at Southwest: Can It Be Sustained?* Hyderabad, India: IBS Research Center.

Kerr, J. L. 2004. The limits of organizational democracy. *The Academy of Management Executive* 18(3): 81–95.

Kolb, A. Y., and Kolb, D. A. 2005. Learning styles and learning spaces: Enhancing experiential learning in higher education. *Academy of Management Learning and Education* 4(2): 193–212.

Kolb, D. A. 1984. *Experiential Learning: Experience as the Source of Learning and Development*. Englewood Cliffs, NJ: Prentice-Hall.

Kozlowski, S. W. J., Brown, K. G., Weissbein, D., Cannon-Bowers, J., and Salas, E. 2000. A multilevel approach to training effectiveness. In K. J. Klein and S. W. J. Kozlowski, eds., *Multilevel Theory, Research and Methods in Organizations*, 157–210. San Francisco, CA: Jossey-Bass.

Kraiger, K., and Ford, J. K. 2007. The expanding role of workplace training: Themes and trends influencing training research and practice. In L. L. Koppes, ed., *Historical Perspectives in Industrial and Organizational Psychology*, 281–309. Mahwah, NJ: Lawrence Erlbaum Associates.

Kraimer, M. L., Seibert, S. E., Wayne, S. J., Liden, R. C., and Bravo, J. 2011. Antecedents and outcomes of organizational support for development: The critical role of career opportunities. *Journal of Applied Psychology* 96(3): 485–500.

Kuvaas, B., and Dysvik, A. 2012. Comparing internally consistent HR at the airport express train, Oslo, Norway, and Southwest Airlines, Dallas, TX, USA. In J. C. Hayton, M. Biron, L. Castro Christiansen, and B. Kuvaas, eds., *Global Human Resource Management Casebook*, 101–111. London: Routledge.

Lombardo, M. M., and Eichinger, R. W. 1996. *The Career Architect Development Planner*. Minneapolis, MN: Lominger.

Luoma, J., Hämäläinen, R. P., and Saarinen, E. 2008. Perspectives on team dynamics: Meta learning and systems intelligence. *Systems Research and Behavioral Science* 25(6): 757–767.

Majchrzak, A., More, P. H. B., and Faraj, S. 2012. Transcending knowledge differences in cross-functional teams. *Organization Science* 23(4): 951–970.

Martin, R. L. 2009. *The Design of Business: Why Design Thinking Is the Next Competitive Advantage*. Cambridge, MA: Harvard Business Press.

McAdams, D. P., and Guo, J. 2015. Narrating the generative life. *Psychological Science* 26(4): 475–483.

Mesmer-Magnus, J., and Viswesvaran, C. 2010. The role of pre-interventions in learning: A meta-analysis and integrative review. *Human Resource Management Review* 20: 261–282.

Meyer, R. E., Höllerer, M. A., Jancsary, D., and van Leeuwen, T. 2013. The visual dimension in organizing, organization, and organization research: Core ideas, current developments, and promising avenues. *Academy of Management Annals* 7: 489–555.

Michie, S., and West, M. A. 2004. Managing people and performance: An evidence based framework applied to health service organizations. *International Journal of Management Reviews* 5(2): 91–111.

Morgeson, F. P., and Humphrey, S. E. 2006. The work design questionnaire (WDQ): Developing and validating a comprehensive measure for assessing job design and the nature of work. *Journal of Applied Psychology* 91(6): 1321–1339.

Mouritsen, J., Hansen, A., and Hansen, C. Ø. 2001. Inter-organizational controls and organizational competencies: Episodes around target cost management/functional analysis and open book accounting. *Management Accounting Research* 12(2): 221–244.

Noe, R. A., Clarke, A. D. M., and Klein, H. J. 2014. Learning in the twenty-first century workplace. *Annual Review of Organizational Psychology and Organizational Behavior* 1: 245–275.

Noe, R. A., Tews, M. J., and McConnell Dachner, A. 2010. Learner engagement: A new perspective for enhancing our understanding of learner motivation and workplace learning. *Academy of Management Annals* 4: 279–315.

O'Reilly, C. 1995. *Southwest Airlines (B): Using Human Resources for Competitive Advantage*. Stanford GSC Case No. HR1B. Palo Alto, CA: Stanford University Graduate School of Business (Revised 2006).

O'Reilly, C. A., and Pfeffer, J. 1995. *Southwest Airlines: Using Human Resources for Competitive Advantage*. Stanford GSC Case No. HR1A. Palo Alto, CA: Stanford University Graduate School of Business.

O'Reilly, C. A., and Pfeffer, J. 2000. *Hidden Value: How Great Companies Achieve Extraordinary Results with Ordinary People*. Boston, MA: Harvard Business Press.

Pfeffer, J. 1998. Seven practices of successful organizations. *California Management Review* 40(2): 96–124.

Pfeffer, J., and Sutton, R. I. 2006a. Evidence-based management. *Harvard Business Review* 84(1): 62.

Pfeffer, J., and Sutton, R. I. 2006b. *Hard Facts, Dangerous Half-Truths, and Total Nonsense: Profiting from Evidence-Based Management*. Boston: Harvard Business School Press.

Pfeffer, J., and Veiga, J. F. 1999. Putting people first for organizational success. *Academy of Management Executive* 13(2): 37–48.

Provost, S. M., Lanham, H. J., Leykum, L. K., McDaniel Jr, R. R., and Pugh, J. 2014. Health care huddles: Managing complexity to achieve high reliability. *Healthcare Management Review* 40(1): 2–12.

Quinn, R. W., and Bunderson, J. S. 2013. Could we huddle on this project? Participant learning in newsroom conversations. *Journal of Management* 42(2): 386–418.

Rousseau, D. M. 2006. Is there such a thing as "evidence-based management"? *Academy of Management Review* 31(2): 256–269.

Rubenstein-Montano, B., Liebowitz, J., Buchwalter, J., McCaw, D., Newman, B., and Rebeck, K. 2001. A systems thinking framework for knowledge management. *Decision Support Systems* 31(1): 5–16.

Rylander, A. 2009. Design thinking as knowledge work: Epistemological foundations and practical implications. *Design Management Journal* 4(1): 7–19.

Rynes, S. L., Bartunek, J. M., Dutton, J. E., and Margolis, J. D. 2012. Care and compassion through an organizational lens: Opening up new possibilities. *Academy of Management Review* 37(4): 503–523.

Saarinen, E., and Hämäläinen, R. P. 2010. The originality of systems intelligence. *Essays on Systems Intelligence*: 9–28.

Seidel, V. P., and Fixson, S. K. 2013. Adopting design thinking in novice multidisciplinary teams: The application and limits of design methods and reflexive practices. *Journal of Product Innovation Management* 30(S1): 19–33.

Seidel, V. P., and O'Mahony, S. 2014. Managing the repertoire: Stories, metaphors, prototypes, and concept coherence in product innovation. *Organization Science* 25(3): 691–712.

Senge, P. M., and Sterman, J. D. 1992. Systems thinking and organizational learning: Acting locally and thinking globally in the organization of the future. *European Journal of Operational Research* 59(1): 137–150.

Sennett, R. 2012. *Together: The Rituals, Pleasures and Politics of Cooperation*. New Haven, CT: Yale University Press.

Shapiro, B. 2013. Cooperation, collaboration and help-seeking in small group work: Investigating learning engagement "through a sea of talk." 1st Annual Collaborating for Learning Conference. Calgary: University of Calgary.

Sharma, S., Sharma, J., and Devi, A. 2011. Corporate social responsibility: The key role of human resource management. *Business Intelligence Journal* 2(1): 205–213.

Smerek, R., and Baker, W. E. 2010. *Open Book Finance*: 22. Ann Arbor: GlobalLens.

Stephens, J. P., Heaphy, E., and Dutton, J. E. 2012. High quality connections. In K. Cameron and G. Spreitzer, eds., *The Oxford Handbook of Positive Organizational Scholarship*, 385–399. New York: Oxford University Press.

Suddaby, R. 2006. From the editors: What grounded theory is not. *Academy of Management Journal* 49(4): 633–642.

Tharenou, P., Saks, A. M., and Moore, C. 2007. A review and critique of research on training and organization level outcomes. *Human Resource Management Review* 17(3): 251–273.

Turner, Y., Silberman, S., Joffe, S., and Hadas-Halpern, I. 2008. The effect of adding a patient's photograph to the radiographic examination. Annual Meeting of the Radiological Society of North America.

von Bertalanffy, L. 1956. *General Systems Theory*. New York: George Braziller.

Weinzweig, A. 2003. *Zingerman's Guide to Good Eating: How to Choose the Best Bread, Cheeses, Olive Oil, Pasta, Chocolate, and Much More*. New York: Houghton Mifflin Harcourt.

21 Rockstar vs. Ringmaster

Balancing Complementary Teaching Roles to Develop Management Skills

Peter A. Heslin, Geoff Mortimore, and Lauren A. Keating

Business school professors are under pressure. With students increasingly being viewed as customers who need to be "satisfied," student evaluations are more and more consequential in determining contract renewal, tenure, and promotion decisions. Websites such as www.ratemyprofessors.com – enabling students to share unvarnished critiques of their instructors – up the ante. The proliferation of business school rankings taking account of "teaching quality" is creating a further institutional imperative for professors to strive to be stellar teachers, as well as top researchers. What are management instructors[1] who want to improve their teaching to do?

Novice educators often focus on developing "great" lectures, accompanied by compelling slides and anecdotes. However, theory and research regarding how adults learn (Knowles, 1978; Knowles, Holton, & Swanson, 2011), the nature of the managerial role (Benjamin & O'Reilly, 2011; Mintzberg, 2004), and how knowledge structures are constructed and applied (Anderson, 1982; Duffy & Jonassen, 1992) have converged in raising serious concerns about the value of lecturing. Resulting discussions of effective management education routinely shun lectures and laud the merits of participative and collaborative processes for fostering student learning. This trend is neatly captured by King's (1993) popular distinction between the expository *sage on the stage* (henceforth, "sage") and the facilitative *guide on the side* (henceforth, "guide") teaching roles, as well as by Mintzberg's (2004) scathing evaluation of management education within business schools (see also Pfeffer & Fong, 2002).

The purpose of this chapter is to highlight some inherent limitations of King's teaching roles, viewed as proxies for the broad distinction between *expository* versus *facilitative* modes of teaching, as well as contextual contingencies indicating when each mode would be most suitable. We thus aim to restore balance to this literature by drawing attention to instances when an expository mode of teaching – exemplified by, though not limited to, episodes of lecturing – may be pedagogically useful and indeed preferable to facilitative methods, as well as vice versa.

After we identify features of the sage and guide metaphors that limit their applicability and obscure the potential positive impact of both expository and facilitative teaching, we propose the alternative metaphors of teaching as a *rockstar* and *ringmaster*, to distinguish how instructors conceptualize and conduct their teaching.[2] We develop these prototypical teaching roles into what we hope will provide a practically useful tool for management educators to reflect upon and improve their teaching effectiveness. This tool may first be used to review the extent to which one holds the assumptions associated with expository versus facilitative teaching, as encapsulated in rockstar versus ringmaster teaching roles. It may also be applied to evaluate the nature and alignment between one's assumptions and how one *actually* goes about preparing and delivering a management class or workshop. These reflexive processes will ultimately help management educators discern a wider range of deliberate choices in conceptualizing, designing, and delivering their teaching.

We pursue this agenda by first briefly reviewing some of the critiques of traditional management lectures that have echoed King (1993) in advocating the pedagogical virtues of facilitative, relative to expository teaching. We then outline the nature of the *sage on the stage* and *guide on the side* teaching roles, together with some of their connotations that limit their applicability and usefulness. Next we introduce the alternative teaching roles of rockstar and ringmaster, before discussing some contextual contingencies that influence the usefulness of these expository and facilitative teaching roles for fostering students' learning. We then discuss how instructors might strive to balance the rockstar and ringmaster roles, as well as suggest how institutions may support or impede them in doing so. We conclude by outlining some avenues for research regarding the potential utility of our model for studying and cultivating exemplary management teaching.

Critiques of Traditional Lectures

During the early years of formal management education (c. 1950s–1980s), students were often largely viewed as essentially empty vessels into which instructors poured their insights. Careful listening, voracious note taking, and memorization preceded standardized examinations during which students reproduced what they had learned. This passive, transmittal model of learning has been widely criticized as unlikely to prepare management students for a complex world in which they will be expected to think independently, pose and solve complex problems, and generally produce – rather than (merely) reproduce – useful knowledge, insights, and decisions that are precursors to effective managerial action (Benjamin & O'Reilly, 2011; Mintzberg, 2004; Pfeffer & Fong, 2002).

In contrast to this passive model, adult learning theory (Knowles, 1978; Knowles et al., 2011) emphasizes that adults learn best from the analysis of their experiences, when they appreciate the purpose of what they are learning, when enabled to be self-directed, and when the content of the learning allows them to more effectively deal with their real-life challenges. In essence, adult learning theory underscores how effective adult education begins and deals with students where they are, as opposed to giving precedence to the material the instructor perceives the need to cover. Thus, traditional lecture-based management classes are often deemed deficient at meeting the needs of adult learners.

Pfeffer and Fong (2002) argue that taking management classes yields little discernible impact on students' learning or careers for a host of reasons, including too much emphasis on lecturing about analytical frameworks and not enough emphasis on processes to develop interpersonal and communication skills (see also Benjamin & O'Reilly, 2011). Mintzberg (2004) argues that the intuition, judgment, and wisdom needed to manage effectively are less likely to be developed by listening to lectures than by having management students actively apply course concepts to address real-life managerial challenges.

This call to focus on students' experience and reflection, by spending more time facilitating than lecturing, is consistent with some prominent pedagogical developments within educational psychology. For instance, drawing on the work of Piaget (1977) and Vygotsky (1986), the constructivist theory of learning (Duffy & Jonassen, 1992; Schunk, 2012) suggests that learning requires self-organization and invention by allowing students to raise their own questions, generate their own hypotheses, test out their viability, and defend them in communities of discourse and practice.

Sage on the Stage vs. Guide on the Side

Based on constructivist theory, King (1993: 30) reconceptualized the traditional role of an instructor along the following lines:

> The professor, instead of being the "sage on the stage," functions as a "guide on the side," facilitating learning in less directive ways.... Essentially, the professor's role is to facilitate students' interaction with the material and with each other in their knowledge-producing endeavor.

To help instructors function as a guide, King (1993) outlines a set of teaching activities. These include having students use the material presented to critique a common practice, or working in pairs to generate questions about the course material, perhaps by completing a set of generic questions such as "What is the main idea of ... ?", "Explain why ... ?", and "How would I use ... to ...?" (King, 1993: 32). Students are then instructed to attempt to answer each other's questions or to collaborate with their classmates to find answers to them. Based on the premise that students often only engage in active learning when prompted to do so, King (1993) proposes that instructors should have students engage in a suitable active learning exercise for each major course concept or principle.

King (1993) offers no advice for being an effective sage.

The insights regarding the limitations of lectures and the merits of facilitated learning noted by King (1993) have been widely echoed within the management education literature (e.g., Benjamin & O'Reilly, 2011; Mintzberg, 2004; Pfeffer & Fong, 2002). Indeed, virtually every identified citation of King (1993) references the expository sage role in a pejorative tone and lauds the facilitative guide role. For instance, Webber and Johnston (2000: 391) note that:

> the King view of teaching and learning is valid and in line with students' own experiences, i.e., active, information seeking, constructivist approaches make

for better understanding and retention, while passive listening to lecturers (although easier) results in boredom, exam cramming, and poor retention.

This bias against lecturing is problematic insofar as it downplays some of the potentially useful pedagogical functions of expository teaching. While lectures are no longer needed for merely transmitting information, they can be fruitfully used to inspire students to appreciate the value and scope for applying evidence-based principles, concepts, best practices, and considering relevant contingencies for addressing management challenges; providing an update on late breaking news that is yet to appear in any published source; and synthesizing insights from various sources and illuminating their implications. As Iphofen (1997) noted, "[T]here is nothing like the lecture for developing the grand view, for conveying the sense of conceptual breakthrough, for inspiring enthusiasm, or for observing the trained mind in action." Given these important pedagogical functions, claims that the *lecture is dead* seem overplayed.

Although the vivid sage and guide metaphors help underscore the limitations of exposition, they also depict lecturing in a manner that is easy to dismiss. For instance, the *Oxford Dictionary and Thesaurus* (1996, synonym section) suggests that the word *sage* connotes "wise man, elder, doyen." The elite status and almost omniscient posture associated with a sage suggests a substantial power differential that can impede sages' perceived accessibility and students' openness to learn from them (Schein, 1969; 2009). Students seeking excitement in their classes might be underwhelmed by instructors enacting the stereotypically solemn, esoteric, and/or self-absorbed connotations of a sage, who is somewhat detached and unconcerned by immediate worldly concerns. Such features of the sage metaphor have likely contributed to the potential merits of expository teaching often being either overlooked or disparaged.

The metaphor of teaching as a guide is also limited. Specifically, the "guide on the side" portrays instructors as relatively subdued, passive, and out of the spotlight: characteristics that are potentially ineffectual in the context of management students who expect their instructors to be energetic (Bain, 2004) and entertaining (Gosling & Mintzberg, 2006). The metaphor of a guide does not really conjure images of the possibility for a more captivating and dynamic way of playing a facilitative teaching role.

To reinvigorate the legitimacy of expository teaching in a manner that avoids the negative associations with the role of *sage*, as well as to depict a more energetic and compelling way of playing the facilitative *guide* role, we propose the alternative expository and facilitative teaching roles of rockstar and ringmaster.

The Rockstar and the Ringmaster

When beginning an academic job, one of us was advised by his new Department Chair that when teaching, "You need to be Johnny Carson." Popular instructors are routinely applauded for being a "rockstar in the classroom." It is nonetheless with some ambivalence that we have incorporated the rockstar concept into our model. This is because rockstars are renowned for drawing attention to themselves and what they have to offer, in a manner reminiscent of the *sage on the stage* (King, 1993), that does not necessarily serve instructors or students well. By contrast, rockstars typically act like charismatic characters who have thought through what they want their audience to experience. Granted that students seem eager to learn from instructors who have a compelling personal and professional impact (Bain, 2004), we believe that it can sometimes be useful for instructors to exhibit characteristics of a prototypical teaching rockstar, as outlined in Figure 21.1.[3]

Given that underlying assumptions guide people's thoughts and behavior (Argyris, 1990; Schein, 1992), we depict the rockstar and ringmaster roles in Figure 21.1 in terms of a range of contrasting assumptions and foci of action, each of which have pedagogical merit depending upon relevant contingencies discussed later in this chapter.

Underlying Assumptions

Instructor Purpose

The prime purpose of teaching, from a *rockstar* perspective, is for the instructor to persuasively convey to students relevant concepts, principles, evidence, and examples. Such assumptions readily cue instructors to embark on a mission to set the scene, provide an overview, elucidate evidence-based principles, and illustrate how to apply them. An instructor in the role of a rockstar assumes that effective teaching involves putting on a compelling performance that motivates and edifies their audience. This is understandable given how, as Gosling and Mintzberg's (2006: 425) critique observed:

> Business schools proudly show off their arched amphitheatres, while their professors prepare for their performances like actors stepping out on a stage. And no wonder – they are in the spotlight; the quality of the education seems to depend on their ability to entertain their audience.

Regardless of whether they recognize or enjoy it, when instructors conceive of their teaching as requiring a rockstar performance they view the spotlight within a classroom as squarely focused on them.

When teaching as a ringmaster, the real "show" only begins when instructors start actively redirecting the spotlight around the room for the purpose of drawing out, positively reinforcing, and building student's energy, knowledge, experiences, concerns, and skills regarding the topic at hand. Core ringmaster teaching purposes are to bring concepts alive by connecting them with students' current challenges and to empower students by increasing what they can do through the application of course concepts. The hallmark of great teaching, from a ringmaster perspective, is when students actively engage with the concepts and each other in a manner that leaves them inspired to explore, consider, and/or do things they could or would not have done before taking the class.

Figure 21.1. Prototypical rockstar and ringmaster teaching roles.

	ROCKSTAR 100%	50/50	RINGMASTER 100%
Instructor Purpose	To convey knowledge & compelling experiences To showcase what the instructor can do To explicate fundamental principles		To draw out knowledge and experiences To increase what students can do To foster deep learning
Prime Sources of Useful Knowledge	Academic theory/research Examples shared by instructor Insights imparted through content delivery Competition to have the most robust ideas Information flow: Instructor → students		Students' experiences and insights Examples generated by the class Insights created through concept application Collaboration to discover valid/useful ideas Information flow: Student ↔ Instructor ↔ Student
Students' Impetus to Learn	Excitement from instructor's performance Instructor's wisdom & wit Exposure to what the instructor knows & can do		Excitement from lively exchanges Student interaction & peer coaching Students developing what they know & can do
Preparation	Search literature to update evidence Clarify knowledge/skills to be imparted Prepare many impactful slides & illustrations Rehearse key statements for precise delivery Fire oneself up for maximum positive impact		Fine-tune methods of eliciting engagement Clarify learning processes & activity instructions Prepare minimal slides, mainly as signposts Develop thought-provoking questions Cultivate one's openness to emergent insights
Strategies and Tactics	To edify & entertain To make impressive, validated statements To highlight evidence-based principles To showcase robust methods & solutions To illustrate the path to correct answers To provide clarity & closure		To elicit relevant contributions & collaboration To ask insightful questions To unearth & build on students' insights To invite the generation of alternatives To stimulate curiosity about possibilities To model engaging with diverse perspectives

Underlying Assumptions: Instructor Purpose, Prime Sources of Useful Knowledge, Students' Impetus to Learn

Foci of Action: Preparation, Strategies and Tactics

Prime Sources of Useful Knowledge

The archetypical rockstar assumes that the key font of valid and useful knowledge is the academic theory and research revealed in journal articles, textbooks, and other assigned readings, as well as their carefully prepared lectures and examples. The prime communication flow, during moments of rockstar teaching, is from the instructor to the students.

When students speak, positivist assumptions that certain perspectives are superior to others, as determined by the degree of support they have received by the relevant scholarly literature, can create competition about who possesses the most robust arguments. Such intellectual battles are often dramatic and exciting, though if taken to an extreme may demoralize some students (Dean & Jolly, 2012). Nonetheless, given how frequently intuition, biases, and "common sense" result in flawed managerial thinking and action (Pfeffer & Sutton, 2006), compelling rockstar performances have an important role to play in building awareness and interest in understanding and applying evidence-based principles and best practices (Charlier, Brown, & Rynes, 2011; Rousseau, 2006; Rubin & Dierdorff, 2011).

Adopting a ringmaster role does not involve shunning academic theory and research. However, theory and research are considered relatively sterile and impotent until brought to life by being actively probed, pondered, and infused by students into challenges they care about (Mintzberg, 2004; Pfeffer & Fong, 2002). The ringmaster role embodies the constructivist pedagogical assumption that learning occurs when new perspectives and concepts are applied to prior assumptions, experiences, and agenda to create fresh knowledge structures and skills (Schunk, 2012). Beyond the insights and implications of scholarly theory and research, ringmasters also emphasize the epistemological and pedagogical value of students' insights and experiences. When a ringmaster is in action, communication flows not only back and forth between the instructor and students, but also between students (see Figure 21.1).

Students' Impetus to Learn

Perhaps prompted by students who relish and appreciate being entertained by their management instructor (Bain, 2004; Gosling & Mintzberg, 2006), rockstars presume that students will be most motivated to learn from classes in which concepts are conveyed through an inspiring pedagogical performance. Such assumptions imply that instructors need to draw upon not only their scholarly insights about current theory, evidence, and applications (Wren, Halbesleben, & Buckley, 2007), but also all the wit, charisma, and charm they can muster. Resulting engagement with instructors' exposition of course concepts may inspire and enable student learning. In short, when instructors conceive of their teaching as requiring them to put on an impressive show that inspires and motivates students, they prime themselves to assume a rockstar teaching role.

As at the circus, teaching as a ringmaster also puts oneself at the center of attention, though largely in the service of preparing, coordinating, and reinforcing the activities, performances, and exchanges between others in the "tent" – in this case, management students as they actively apply course concepts. Consequent lively exchanges are aimed at discovering, reinforcing, and expanding what students know and can do (see Figure 21.1).

Foci of Action

Preparation

As depicted in Figure 21.1, rockstar assumptions readily cue a methodical approach to class preparation. Potential ingredients include surveying the relevant literature to ensure that the latest theoretical and empirical insights will be conveyed. Lecture slides are often constructed to help students stay on the same page as the instructor as the exposition unfolds. Ideally such slides include limited text and numerous large, evocative photos to elicit memories, stereotypes, prototypes, attitudes, or relevant emotions (Reynolds, 2008). Captivating teaching materials such as vivid war stories, compelling testimonials, interesting film clips, and slick videos are collected to vividly depict the key points the instructor wants to make in an ideally entertaining manner. Preparing to teach as a rockstar might also include fine-tuning and rehearsing key transition statements and conclusions, as well as firing oneself up to have a captivating personal impact on the audience.

Four interrelated ways that instructors might fruitfully work to increase their impact in the rockstar role are as follows. First, they could develop their knowledge and skill at applying relevant principles for framing and presenting course concepts in a "sticky" manner (Heath & Heath, 2007). Second, instructors might follow the advice of Anderson (2013: 121) regarding "how to give a killer presentation" (i.e., by crisply framing one's story, planning the delivery, and developing one's stage presence) and avoid common oratorical mistakes (i.e., excessive framing, busy slides, and using unnecessary jargon). Third, aspiring rockstars might learn to craft and present stories in a way that fits their objective in telling the story (Denning, 2004), using the classic structure suggested by Aristotle; that is, presenting a protagonist the listener cares about, a catalyst that compels the protagonist to take action, trials and tribulations, a turning point, and a resolution wherein the protagonist either "succeeds magnificently or fails tragically" (Ibarra & Lineback, 2005: 67). Finally, given that charisma can be developed though techniques such as observing movies featuring great orators, practicing animated speaking, facial expressions and gestures, as well as using metaphors, anecdotes, and expressions of moral conviction (Antonakis, Fenley, & Liechti, 2011; 2012), instructors may work to master the hallmarks of great oratory.

When preparing to play the role of a ringmaster, instructors aim to design learning processes that facilitate active learning. This typically involves developing thought-provoking questions and thinking through the processes that will be deployed to get students to deeply engage with the course concepts and each other. Such processes can include self-assessments, pair and share, small-group discussions, peer interviews, peer coaching, debates, role plays, and student reports to the class. Because such processes are time consuming and can get "out of control," considerable thought is needed to design them in a manner that keeps students focused on working toward meeting the course objectives and enables class to still conclude smoothly and on time. In this way, playing the ringmaster role might involve preparing minimal slides as signposts to guide student learning and participation in class activities.

Effectively enacting the ringmaster role requires that instructors have a socio-emotional mind-set that is genuinely open to and interested in student contributions. Broaden and build theory (Fredrickson, 2001) highlights how positive emotions (e.g., interest, gratitude, and joy) serve to broaden people's thinking and openness to consider and build upon divergent possibilities, in contrast to the narrower and more myopic focus of attention associated with negative emotions. Instructors' degree of positivity and their openness, which can readily "infect" students and thereby foster learning, can be increased using techniques identified by Fredrickson (2001; 2009) and outlined in the discussion section.

In summary, when preparing to teach as a rockstar, instructors fine-tune precisely *what* they will teach their students and *how* they will express their key messages in an inspiring, compelling, and memorable fashion. Gearing up to teach as a ringmaster involves more focus on honing relevant learning processes (Schein, 1969; 2009; Schunk, 2012; Schwarz 2002; Schwarz et al., 2005) and priming oneself into a mind-set that is truly curious about and receptive to students' contributions to the class (see Figure 21.1).

Strategies and Tactics

How instructors teach stems from the focus of their class preparation initiatives, as well as their assumptions about an instructor's purpose as a teacher, the key sources of useful/valid knowledge, and students' impetus to learn (see Figure 21.1). In rockstar mode, instructors may enthusiastically perform in accordance with a script designed to edify and entertain students with impressive, vivid, validated statements and anecdotes that highlight the field's established knowledge and best practices. Such performances can clarify, contextualize, and instill passion to apply course concepts and principles. Compelling video clips, recorded interviews, news feeds, and social media may be incorporated into the multimedia presentation. In short, instructors performing as rockstars reveal their notable experiences and wit as they highlight evidence-based principles, illuminate robust methods and solutions, illustrate the path to correct answers, captivate the crowd with vivid examples, and ensure that the class ends with a bang!

Teaching as a ringmaster involves having a more emergent and interactive agenda. It is also marked by greater awareness of how one's technical preparation, psychological mind-set, role modeling, and process facilitation interact to affect students' engagement with grasping, critiquing, and applying the course content. Attempts to elicit thoughtful contributions and foster productive collaborations are made by modeling the spirit of curiosity and openness that instructors want students to have toward the course content and each other's views on it. Deficiencies in student inputs are ideally noted with sensitivity to the status imbalance between instructors and students (Schein, 1969; 2009) by trying to focus and build on the merits of student contributions. Ringmasters not only pose insightful questions, but also invite students to generate alternative perspectives regarding the focal topic and engage with each other's perspectives. Controversies in the field are highlighted in a manner that mirrors the pluralism of management scholarship (Colquitt & Zapata-Phelan, 2007), with the objective of encouraging continued engagement with diverse perspectives and stimulating curiosity about possible solutions that may be applied within the workplace (see Figure 21.1).

Contingencies of Rockstar and Ringmaster Teaching

The relative merits of content exposition and process facilitation, as embodied in the rockstar and ringmaster teaching roles, respectively, depend on a range of contextual considerations such as cultural context, institutional context, program culture, facilities, class size, class time, student openness, and student knowledge/experience. It is important to underscore that these contingencies are presented as relatively stark contrasts for illustrative purposes. Many teaching contexts will undoubtedly represent a blend of these factors.

Cultural Context

In relatively high power distance cultural contexts, as typically observed in countries such as China and Malaysia (Hofstede, 2001; Taras, Steel, & Kirkman, 2012), instructors are put on a pedestal and students expect to be given "correct" answers. Learning is believed to stem from the transfer of knowledge from a wise teacher – deemed by Confucius to be the most respected role within society (Hofstede, 1986) – to presumably naïve students. In higher power distance contexts, a ringmaster teaching style could thus be culturally incongruent. Students' resulting threat rigidity (Staw, Sandelands, & Dutton, 1981) may diminish the effectiveness of ringmaster strategies that work well in relatively low power distance contexts (e.g., Australia and the United States; Hofstede, 2001; Taras et al., 2012).

Similarly, Moloney and Xu (2012) discuss how Chinese language learning in Australian schools is impeded by instructors holding culturally incongruent traditional Confucian schema, with assumptions about a hierarchical relationship between teacher and student, and about education involving knowledge transmission rather than a process in which students actively participate. While a strong focus on exposition of received knowledge tends to be shunned within lower power distance contexts by students who are frustrated by the cultural incongruence of not being actively engaged in shaping the process and content of their learning, it may thus play a larger role in effective teaching amidst higher levels of power distance.

Institutional Context

Research-intensive universities that emphasize creating and explaining empirically verified knowledge may expect instructors to play predominantly rockstar roles, delivering content-driven lectures that showcase cutting-edge scholarly work. In prototypically teaching-oriented institutions that give precedence to collaborative learning and knowledge creation, there may be a greater focus on developing, refining, and using ringmaster teaching pedagogies.

Perceived imperatives for courses to cover certain content, as required by accreditation bodies such as AACSB, EQUIS, and AMBA, may represent another institutional cue to engage in rockstar exposition to present that content. However, the AACSB 2012 accrediting standards also argue that "passive learning should not be the sole, or primary, model of collegiate business education" (31), thereby cuing more ringmaster-style teaching. The latter is enabled by online technological developments that have increased the ease of assigning readings, cases, and videos that are discussed and applied to experiential activities within a flipped class format.

Program Culture

Within a given business school, programs can vary substantially in the expectations they place on students to prepare for class through activities such as reading articles and preparing their response to case studies. When students are well prepared in these ways, there is a foundation for using facilitated approaches such as the case method, discussions, and experiential activities to deepen students' ability to apply concepts. Rockstar teaching might be more suitable within programs where students are typically less willing and/or able to seriously prepare for class, such as attending noncredit management training.

Facilities

Facilitated classes are aided by flat rooms that enable flexible seating arrangements (e.g., conference rounds and chairs arranged in a horseshoe shape) whereby students face and directly address each other, rather than primarily just the instructor. Chairs that are fixed, front-facing, and/or on a raked floor tend to set the stage for the performance of a rockstar presenter.

Impactful rockstar teaching can be supported by easily adjustable lights, high-quality audio-visual equipment, and/or high-speed Internet access that enables the streaming of videos, video conferences, or analysis of real-time data. Such technology is less important when engaging in ringmaster teaching.

Class Size

With a large number of students, a rockstar mode of instruction may be more viable for fostering learning. While students can have guided discussions in pairs even within massive classes, such contexts constrain the proportion of students who can hear and respond to each other, or be called upon to contribute to an interactive learning process. Smaller class sizes enable instructors to orchestrate live contributions, critiques, peer coaching (whereby participants learn from coaching, being coached, and observing coaching dynamics), as well as the exchange between students who discuss, voice, and respond to the ideas that are presented by other students from around the room.

Class Time

While it is well established that students learn more deeply when they are led to reflect on the relevance of managerial concepts to their personal experiences and challenges (Knowles et al., 2011), doing so can be quite time consuming (Hativa, 2000). In situations in which time is particularly limited, a clear and compelling presentation of relevant concepts and procedures may be more applicable than hurriedly eliciting and superficially engaging with students' perspectives.

Student Openness

Classes with a preponderance of students with a high learning goal orientation (VandeWalle, 1997), who are willing to incur frustrations and setbacks in the service of learning, might be particularly open to the dynamics of a facilitated classroom wherein students are called upon to make public, on-the-spot contributions. Students with a high performance-avoid goal orientation (VandeWalle, 1997; i.e., a concern to avoid exposing an ability deficit by providing a "wrong" answer) may feel threatened by being publicly probed and prefer the lower accountability associated with rockstar pedagogies where the instructor delivers most of the content. Similarly, when students have a high need for closure (Kruglanski & Webster, 1996), they might prefer content-driven classes where instructors impart established knowledge and "correct" answers, rather than stimulate debate regarding possible alternatives. Given their higher tolerance for ambiguity, students with a low need for closure may prefer and learn particularly well from ringmaster teaching that encourages them to generate and engage with diverse perspectives.

Student Knowledge/Experience

When students have little if any knowledge or experience regarding class topics, they may benefit most from a compelling presentation of key concepts and illustrative examples. In contrast, more experienced students – and especially practicing managers – tend to relish facilitated opportunities to publicly recount, hear, and analyze illustrative war stories from their organizational lives. For such students, a predominantly rockstar mode of instruction is often deemed less engaging and useful than a facilitated approach (Knowles et al., 2011; Mintzberg, 2004).

When challenging students to move out of their comfort zones, given their culture and personality, it can be prudent to manage the risk of "losing" students or indeed a whole class because of having pushed them too far. This may be done by deliberately striking a balance between creating comfortable and uncomfortable learning experiences for students, in light of all the previously mentioned contingencies.

Discussion

> Since the turn of the century, educators have periodically mounted determined campaigns to replace the lecture with what they perceived as better forms of teaching Hativa (2000: 78).

King's (1993) metaphors of teaching as a guide on the side, rather than a sage on the stage, as well as subsequent popular critiques of management education (Mintzberg, 2004; Pfeffer & Fong, 2002), vividly depict the imperative for management education to actively engage students in an interactive learning process. The applicability and value of King's (1993) metaphors are nonetheless limited in ways that we have sought to address by developing the alternative metaphors of teaching as a rockstar and ringmaster. For instance, we have depicted the rockstar role as more energetic, charismatic, and engaging than the staid, esoteric, and unilateral connotations of the sage on the stage, thus making it likely to be more relevant to management student demands for classes that are vibrant and entertaining (Bain, 2004; Gosling & Mintzberg, 2006). We have illuminated the valuable pedagogical functions of both the ringmaster and rockstar modes of teaching, as well as suggested underlying assumptions likely to cue instructors to engage in more rockstar- versus ringmaster-related teaching initiatives. Unearthing such assumptions may yield valuable insights into why instructors teach as they do, as well as provide potential points of leverage for fine-tuning their teaching and effectiveness, given the learning objectives and their teaching context.

We have highlighted resources for developing one's teaching as a more effective rockstar (Anderson, 2013; Antonakis et al., 2012; Denning, 2004; Heath & Heath, 2007; Ibarra & Lineback, 2005; Pepper, 2004) *and* ringmaster (Schein, 1969, 2009; Schunk, 2012; Schwarz, 2002; Schwarz et al., 2005). Finally, to help rectify the bias in the management education literature in favor of ringmaster over rockstar teaching methods, we have outlined a range of contextual contingencies when rockstar and ringmaster teaching methods might each be most appropriate.

In the following sections, we further discuss how to balance the rockstar and ringmaster teaching roles, as well as how our model may serve as a tool for self-reflection, analysis, and fine-tuning one's assumptions and foci of action in designing, delivering, and reviewing a management class one has delivered. We then discuss how instructors might enhance their capacity to flexibly enact and coordinate their use of the rockstar and ringmaster roles by fostering their positivity and mindfulness, as well as managing any underlying competing commitments. We conclude by discussing implications for business schools, training within organizations, and future research on the application of teaching roles within effective management education and training.

Finding the Right Balance

It is important to underscore the complementarity of the rockstar and ringmaster roles. Both roles are potentially valuable and either could be problematic if overplayed. A strong emphasis on the rockstar role may (or may not) be entertaining and risk exacerbating the status differential between instructors and students (Schein, 1969; 2009), losing students' attention, and not stimulating the deep learning and skill development that can occur when students are led to apply concepts to personally meaningful experiences (Mintzberg, 2004; Pfeffer & Sutton, 2006).

An overemphasis on the ringmaster role, by contrast, risks students not being adequately exposed to relevant developments in management theory and research (Wren et al., 2007), as well as evidence-based best practices (Pfeffer, & Sutton, 2006; Rynes, Giluk, & Brown, 2007) – an imperative that is currently being explicitly addressed in scarcely a quarter of the required management courses in U.S.-based MBA programs (Charlier et al., 2011). When taken to the extreme, a ringmaster role runs the risk of reducing an academically grounded course to a reflective practice session in which students share their experiences and help each other resolve their management challenges, without learning to apply evidence-based course concepts.

We thus need more and better ringmaster *and* rockstar performances. Just as truly helping others involves mindfully shifting back and forth between the roles of "expert" and "process consultant" (Schein, 1969; 2009), effective management education likely reflects an artful blend and execution of rockstar and ringmaster teaching. How much of the rockstar or ringmaster roles instructors should enact within a given instance will depend on a range of contextual factors like those we discussed earlier, as well as instructors' identity, default style, and level of competence at enacting each role. For instance, heroic attempts at a radical and sudden shift to a teaching role well beyond one's comfort zone, without adequate planning and preparation, may be perceived as inauthentic and ineffective, and students may withdraw (psychologically if not physically) from the course.

Developing Teaching Effectiveness

Our contrast between rockstar and ringmaster roles could be applied by instructors to decide how to balance these roles for a forthcoming class, given class objectives and relevant contextual contingencies. Instructors could try representing – with a small dot – where on each continuum in Figure 21.1, from "100% Instructor as Rockstar" to "100% Instructor as Ringmaster," they plan to function within a given class or within a module with a given learning objective. Such ratings could serve as a valuable point of reference for designing, evaluating, and refining class plans. For example, instructors might complete Figure 21.1 in a manner that implies an intention to play a predominantly ringmaster role, yet *still* habitually produce so many detailed slides and anecdotes that it takes much of the available class time to adequately work through them, thereby leaving little time for teaching as a ringmaster. Realizing this disconnect could prompt such instructors to substantially prune back their class content and related slides to increase the scope to fully embrace the ringmaster role.

During class, if a facilitated segment seems to have drifted toward consensus around conclusions that are contrary to what robust empirical research has found, a savvy instructor might spontaneously pivot into a rockstar mode to deliver a statement of relevant research findings. Similarly, if students appear relatively disengaged and drowsy in response to an extended rockstar segment of a management class, a ringmaster-like impromptu activity requiring focused input from students may reinvigorate them.

Following class, Figure 21.1 could also be used to analyze the teaching role assumptions and strategies that one actually manifested within a class, based on self-assessment from memory, video analysis, peer and/or student feedback. Such postclass debriefs could highlight not only the extent to which one was on target or deviated from one's planned trade-offs between the rockstar- and ringmaster-related assumptions and actions, but also illuminate issues such as: *What facets of the rockstar and ringmaster roles were played particularly well? Which felt most right? Which seemed to foster the engagement of the class? Which fell flat? Which role facets might have fruitfully been played more often, less often, or differently?* We anticipate that answering such questions – ideally working with a peer coach (Parker, Hall, & Kram, 2008) – could provide invigorating jolts of self-appreciation (Spreitzer, 2006) for what is working well in one's classes, as well as highlighting specific opportunities for reflection and improvement.

A Potential Reality Check

Self-assessment of one's teaching assumptions and foci of action using Figure 21.1, even aside from a particular management class or workshop, can provide the starting point for profound self-reflection and discussion. For instance, when we had highly experienced executive educator colleagues complete Figure 21.1 during a teaching development workshop, they consistently revealed assumptions highly associated with the ringmaster role. Subsequent peer discussion cued queries about the extent to which these instructors actually manifested those ringmaster-related assumptions in how they led their sessions. Friendly jesting arose about the frequency and zeal with which some of these instructors – who proudly label themselves as "facilitators" – routinely held the limelight with extended periods of exposition and colorful anecdotes. This prompted sobering yet subsequently applauded insights about gaps between their *espoused* and *enacted* theories (Argyris, 1990) of effective executive education. A few participants anecdotally reported subsequently reevaluating some of their long-held pedagogical assumptions, identity, and approaches.

Priming Oneself to Enact and Balance the Rockstar and Ringmaster Roles

A challenge for management instructors, mirroring that of practicing managers (Gosling & Mintzberg, 2003), is to simultaneously work with the contrasting yet complementary rockstar and ringmaster roles. We suspect that stellar instructors move flexibly between these roles as the occasion demands. Rather than acting on the basis of predetermined behavioral recipes, instructors might instead psychologically warm up to an intended blend of rockstar and ringmaster roles, to provide a platform from which they can respond creatively and spontaneously to the teaching and learning needs and opportunities that arise within their class (Brown et al., 2013). Three promising levers for psychologically preparing to enact and juggle a broader range of teaching repertoires are positivity, mindfulness, and competing commitments.

Positivity

There is substantial evidence that positive emotions (e.g., joy, gratitude, pride) increase mental agility (Fredrickson & Branigan, 2005), recovery from negative emotional experiences (Tugade & Fredrickson, 2004), and the quality of interpersonal interactions (Fredrickson, 2009). Earlier, we discussed how positivity fosters openness to students' ideas, which is an inherent facet of teaching as a ringmaster.

Akin to the energy and charisma of great rockstars, positivity also plays an important role in pulling off a rousing rockstar teaching performance, as well as having the flexibility to seamlessly alternate between rockstar and ringmaster roles. Instructors wanting to cultivate their positivity may thus profit from experimenting with the extensive array of proven initiatives for generating positive emotions within oneself. These include readily usable protocols to find meaning, relish goodness, count your blessings, connect with others and/or connect with nature (see Fredrickson, 2009 for details).

Mindfulness

Transitioning fruitfully between the rockstar and ringmaster roles likely also requires mindfulness (Langer, 1997) – instructors' real-time self-awareness of the assumptions and intentions that influence their teaching practice, as well as nonjudgmental awareness of what transpires within their classrooms and themselves. For instance, it can be easy to be drawn into the rockstar role and present content for too long, when the class would benefit from being actively drawn into the learning process by a ringmaster intervention. In a similar vein, when teaching as a ringmaster, one may focus too much on designing and facilitating activities that create a strong buzz of student interaction, excitement, and enjoyment, though not provide students with sufficient conceptual scaffolding and connections to relevant empirical research and best practices.

Instructors' self-awareness at critical points of choice in designing and conducting a class might provide the insight and impetus to change gear and move into a different role, or to play a given role differently. For example, mindfulness might enable an instructor to notice when the class could profit from hearing a more rockstar-like spontaneous statement of relevant theory or research findings. Alternatively, instructors might notice that they are too engrossed in a rockstar mode by becoming aware that they are pouring much more energy into a class than their students. This awareness could prompt spontaneously pivoting to a more ringmaster-like approach to generate and draw more energy from the students and the dynamics of the group.

Mindfulness of one's assumptions, intent, and actions as a management instructor may be developed by reflecting upon and discussing one's intentions and reality regarding the continua identified in Figure 21.1. Other valuable insights for fostering one's mindful engagement and learning are outlined by Langer (1997), as well as Heslin and Keating (in press, 2017).

Competing Commitments

One's freedom to move into a relatively underdeveloped teaching role may be increased by reflecting on the reasons for one's attachment to an alternative role. Kegan and Lahey's (2001; 2009) model of competing commitments could prove helpful in this reflection. Imagine an instructor who aspires to play a stronger ringmaster role, though keeps acting predominantly in a manner characteristic of a teaching rockstar. A competing commitments analysis would entail such instructors focusing on uncovering the things they value and perhaps cherish (e.g., appearing in control, being the expert, and/or being on time) that compete with their intentions to teach in more of a ringmaster mode. Alternatively, those aiming to strengthen their rockstar repertoire may be constrained from doing so by underlying commitments to not being perceived as intellectually arrogant, domineering, or overwhelming.

Competing commitments are often held in place by unconscious assumptions about the painful consequences (e.g., feeling anxious, vulnerable, not oneself, or lost) that would ensue from compromising one's deeply held values (e.g., to be in control), for instance, by sharing control of the class agenda with students. Kegan and Lahey's (2001; 2009) five-step competing commitments protocol provides a sophisticated and powerful process for surfacing, analyzing, and ultimately transcending values-based, internalized impediments to making intended changes in one's mental and behavioral modus operandi. This protocol might be useful for those seeking to expand the ease with which they can authentically adopt the full spectrum of the rockstar and ringmaster teaching roles.

Implications for Business Schools

Business school deans and other administrators who mindlessly declare that instructors should abandon sagelike lecturing in favor of guidelike facilitation need to think again! Management instructors – especially those in the early stage of their teaching career – might respond to such declarations by being reluctant to incorporate rockstar elements into their management classes, even when doing so fits other relevant contextual contingencies such as those we discussed.

Reluctance to develop one's rockstar skills or ambivalence about exercising them could undermine instructors' capacity to authentically deliver the exciting and impactful classes that many students prefer, as well as the valuable injection of relevant evidence-based theory and research findings into management class discussions (Charlier et al., 2011; Rousseau, 2006). Regarding our opening conjecture about whether professors should largely cease "professing" to their students, use of our model will ideally liberate instructors to teach in whatever manner best serves their learning objectives and teaching context, unconstrained by a hyperbolic mantra that effective management education largely eschews exposition.

Business schools might support (or impede) the effective enactment of the rockstar and ringmaster roles using the program context and facilities, such as room design, flexible furniture, and technological infrastructure, they (fail to) provide. Institutions could support ringmaster teaching by developing program cultures in which students receive consistent messages about the imperative to engage in reading, case preparation, and whatever else is assigned for being fully prepared for class. They might support rockstar teaching by providing state-of-the art technology and encouraging instructors to deliver lectures that showcase their areas of academic expertise. Given the value of infusing students with enthusiasm for evidence-based management principles (Charlier et al., 2011; Pfeffer & Sutton, 2006; Rousseau, 2006), as well as facilitating active learning within management classrooms (Mintzberg, 2004), we recommend that business schools actively support both rockstar and ringmaster teaching.

Our model will hopefully contribute to the work of business school administrators who increasingly recognize that managerial education can succeed only if managerial educators are both content and process experts (Brown et al., 2013; Mintzberg, 2004; Pfeffer & Fong, 2002). One feature of a model community of practice (Wenger, McDermott, & Snyder, 2002) for managerial educators to hone their skills at performing and balancing the rockstar and ringmaster roles might be a local, informal forum for sharing stories, resources, and best practices for enacting the rockstar and ringmaster roles. Related options would be to workshop stimulus readings (e.g., Anderson, 2013; Antonakis et al., 2012; Ibarra & Lineback, 2005; Schein, 2009; Schwarz et al., 2005) or organize peer observations, feedback, and mentoring centered on developing the assumptions, identity, dispositions, and skills associated with being a compelling expounding rockstar and facilitating ringmaster. Finally, faculty should be recognized and rewarded for actively and systematically experimenting with opportunities for expanding their repertoire and effectiveness (Brown et al., 2013) at enacting the rockstar and ringmaster roles.

Implications for Training within Organizations

Compared to instructors in business schools, professional trainers are typically concerned with the development of more specifically defined competencies, and with competencies across a wider range of professional domains (e.g., technical, legal, information technology, mechanical, safety, design, and operational). Nonetheless, trainers have the same choice between rockstar and ringmaster pedagogies, and the same challenge of selecting the rockstar or ringmaster assumptions and foci of action that best fit the prevailing training context and learning objectives.

Imagine a highly experienced trainer who has for many years successfully provided safety training to cohorts of new hires using a largely rockstar mode, but is now asked to train future safety trainers who require greater depth in the same safety protocols. The revised teaching purpose (i.e., to prepare the trainees to clarify, explain, demonstrate, and defend safety protocols) involves a shift to the right on Figure 21.1 and calls for more of a ringmaster approach. The related foci of action in Figure 21.1 may guide this trainer to think through the implications, opportunities, and challenges – such as regarding prereading, seating arrangements, exercises, discussions, role plays, information flow, and training evaluation criteria – to best meet the new training objectives within their altered training context.

Alternatively, a proud, longtime provider of highly facilitated training to groups of 20–30 trainees who was called upon to provide similar training to a group of 300 may productively recognize that the substantially increased "class" size may call for a more rockstar mode. Review of the underlying assumptions and foci of action associated with the rockstar mode might help such a trainer in two ways: first, to avoid the trap of habitually trying to facilitate discussions and activities in a manner that are less suited to the new, larger context; and second, to reimagine how to most effectively conceptualize and deliver their content within this new context. Realizing that sometimes people have attended a session to hear from an expert, rather than talk among themselves, may help motivate diehard ringmasters to more seriously consider stepping into the rockstar role in instances when doing so fits with the context.

While the objectives of educators and trainers may thus differ on dimensions such as the breadth, focus, and concreteness of what they aim to convey to their students and trainees, respectively, our distinction between the rockstar and ringmaster roles may nonetheless be applied to guide the conceptualization, delivery, and evaluation of effective training within organizations. We thus suggest that the research avenues outlined next may be productively pursued within both educational and training contexts.

Research Implications

Our model suggests three broad avenues for research. First, we have proposed that reflecting on how one has completed Figure 21.1, together with relevant contingencies, might enable improving one's teaching effectiveness. Research is needed regarding whether such initiatives, as well as the other applications we have outlined, do indeed lead to more effective teaching. Such research might examine differences between pre- and postintervention ratings of teaching effectiveness, as ideally indicated not just by student satisfaction ratings and changes in students' knowledge and what they can do (skills), but also affective outcomes such as changes in their motivation, attitudes, and identity that influence whether they will autonomously and proactively apply what they have learned in future, real-world contexts (Kraiger, Ford, & Salas, 1993). Other teaching effectiveness criteria such as student comments, peer ratings, and comments, as well as (video-based) self-analysis, may enable fine-grained assessment of the effectiveness with which instructors enact the rockstar and ringmaster roles.

Second, Figure 21.1 could serve as a useful conceptual foundation for studying how exemplary instructors technically, mentally, and emotionally prepare to teach, as well as how they frame and deal with the most challenging points of choice they encounter in the process of enacting the rockstar and ringmaster roles.

Finally, perhaps the quality with which teaching roles are enacted is more important than what position one adopts along each of our dimensions. For instance, the effectiveness of rockstar performance might be judged in terms of the extent to which content is delivered with charisma (Antonakis et al., 2011; 2012) and effective storytelling (Denning, 2004; Ibarra & Lineback, 2005), while ringmaster performances may be judged by the precise application of robust process facilitation principles (Schein, 1969; 2009; Schunk, 2012; Schwarz, 2002; Schwarz et al., 2005) and the quality of student contributions they elicit. Research is needed on the relative contributions to teaching effectiveness of the appropriateness of teaching roles adopted, given relevant contingencies, versus how well they are enacted. Overall, research along the lines we have just outlined may illuminate whether and how our model of rockstar and ringmaster roles can ultimately help improve the teaching of those who strive to apply it.

Conclusion

The rockstar and ringmaster metaphors will not work for everyone. Nonetheless, with the widespread critiques and challenges to management education, now more than ever instructors need to consider how they can add value in the classroom. Contrary to the notion that "lecturing" is synonymous with ineffective teaching, we have shown that there are instances when both rockstar and ringmaster teaching roles are valuable for fostering student learning. Our model of complementary rockstar and ringmaster roles will hopefully destigmatize both moments of rockstar teaching, as well as instructors who work to increase their capacity to deliver them with high positive impact on students' learning, when doing so fits the prevailing pedagogical purpose and context. Given that both teaching roles involve skills that can be readily developed, we hope our model provides a valuable resource for instructors to reflect upon their assumptions and default approach to teaching, before systematically experimenting with a broader range of relevant options for delivering impactful and valuable instruction.

Notes

1 In this chapter, we use the term *instructors* in a generic sense that includes all professors, lecturers, adjuncts, and others who assume primary responsibility for teaching.
2 For the sake of explanatory convenience, we subsequently refer to the collection of assumptions and foci of action associated with the rockstar and ringmaster teaching metaphors as simply "roles."
3 The sets of assumptions and foci of action that characterize teaching as a *rockstar* or *ringmaster* are not intended to provide a model that could be (mis)used to typecast particular individuals as either a typical *rockstar* or *ringmaster* teacher. Doing this would be invalid insofar as all instructors are multifaceted beings who to some extent manifest elements of both teaching roles. In other words, no instructor is – or should strive to be – a pure *ringmaster* or *rockstar*. Rather, our intention in developing Figure 21.1 is to highlight what we believe is a fairly coherent set of assumptions and foci that instructors might fruitfully trade-off against each other.

References

Anderson, C. 2013. How to give a killer presentation: Lessons from TED. *Harvard Business Review*, June: 121–125.

Anderson, J. R. 1982. Acquisition of cognitive skill. *Psychological Review* 89: 369–406.

Antonakis, J., Fenley, M., and Liechti, S. 2011. Can charisma be taught? Tests of two interventions. *Academy of Management Learning and Education* 10: 374–396.

Antonakis, J., Fenley, M., and Liechti, S. 2012. Learning charisma. Transform yourself into the person others want to follow. *Harvard Business Review*, June: 127–30.

Argyris, C. 1990. *Overcoming Organizational Defenses: Facilitating Organizational Learning*. Boston: Allyn and Bacon.

Bain, K. 2004. *What the Best College Teachers Do*. Cambridge, MA: Harvard University Press.

Benjamin, B., and O'Reilly, C. 2011. Becoming a leader: Early career challenges faced by MBA graduates. *Academy of Management Learning and Education* 10: 452–472.

Brown, K. G., Arbaugh, J. B., Hrivnak, G., and Kenworthy, A. 2013. Overlooked and unappreciated: What research tells us about how teaching must change. In B. Holtom and E. Dierdorff, eds., *Disrupt or Be Disrupted: Evidence-Based Strategies for Graduate Management Education*, 219–258. Hoboken, NJ: Wiley and Sons.

Charlier, S. D., Brown, K. G., and Rynes, S. L. 2011. Teaching evidence-based management in MBA programs: What evidence is there? *Academy of Management Learning and Education* 10: 222–236.

Colquitt, J. A., and Zapata-Phelan, C. P. 2007. Trends in theory building and theory testing: A five-decade study of the Academy of Management Journal. *Academy of Management Journal* 50: 1281–1303.

Dean, K. L., and Jolly, J. P. 2012. Student identity, disengagement, and learning. *Academy of Management Learning and Education* 11: 228–243.

Denning, S. 2004. Telling tales. *Harvard Business Review*, May: 122–129.

Duffy, T. M. and Jonassen, D., eds. 1992. *Constructivism and the Technology of Instruction: A Conversation*. Hillsdale, NJ: Lawrence Erlbaum Associates.

Fredrickson, B. L. 2001. The role of positive emotions in positive psychology: The broaden-and-build theory of positive emotions. *American Psychologist* 56: 218–226.

Fredrickson, B. L. 2009. *Positivity*. New York: Crown Publishers.

Fredrickson, B. L., and Branigan, C. 2005. Positive emotions broaden the scope of attention and thought-action repertoires. *Cognition and Emotion* 19: 313–332.

Gosling, J., and Mintzberg, H. 2003. The five minds of a manager. *Harvard Business Review*, November: 54–63.

Gosling, J., and Mintzberg, H. 2006. Management education as if both matter. *Management Learning* 37: 419–428.

Hativa, N. 2000. *Teaching for Effective Learning in Higher Education*. Dordrecht, The Netherlands: Kluwer Academic Publishers.

Heath, C., and Heath, D. 2007. *Made to Stick: Why Some Ideas Survive and Others Die*. New York: Random House.

Heslin, P. A., and Keating, L. A. (2017). In learning mode? The role of mindsets in derailing and enabling experiential leadership development. *The Leadership Quarterly* 28(3): 367–384.

Hofstede, G. 1986. Cultural differences in teaching and learning. *International Journal of Intercultural Relations* 10: 301–320.

Hofstede, G. 2001. *Cultures Consequences: Comparing Values, Behaviors, Institutions and Organizations across Nations*, 2nd ed. Thousand Oaks, CA: Sage.

Ibarra, H., and Lineback, K. 2005. What's your story? *Harvard Business Review*, January: 64–71.

Iphofen, R. 1997. Long live the lecture. http://www.timeshighereducation.co.uk/103747.article (accessed April 21, 2015).

Kegan, R., and Lahey, L. L. 2001. The real reason people won't change. *Harvard Business Review*, November: 85–92.

Kegan, R., and Lahey, L. L. 2009. *Immunity to Change: How to Overcome It and Unlock the Potential in Yourself and Your Organization*. Boston: Harvard Business School Press.

King, A. 1993. Making a transition from "Sage on the Stage" to "Guide on the Side." *College Teaching* 41: 30–35.

Knowles, M. S. 1978. *The Adult Learner: A Neglected Species*, 2nd ed. Houston, TX: Gulf Publishing.

Knowles, M. S., Holton III, E. F., and Swanson, R. A. 2011. *The Adult Learner*. 7th ed. Oxford: Butterworth-Heinemann.

Kraiger, K., Ford, J. K., and Salas, E. 1993. Application of cognitive, skill-based, and affective theories of learning outcomes to new methods of training evaluation. *Journal of Applied Psychology* 78(2): 311–328.

Kruglanski, A. W., and Webster, D. M. 1996. Motivated closing of the mind: "Seizing" and "freezing." *Psychological Review* 103: 263–283.

Langer, E. J. 1997. *The Power of Mindful Learning*. Cambridge, MA: Da Capo Press.

Mintzberg, H. 2004. *Managers, Not MBAs: A Hard Look at the Soft Practice of Managing and Management*. San Francisco: Berrett-Koehler.

Moloney, R., and Xu, H. 2012. We are not teaching Chinese kids in Chinese context, we are teaching Australian kids: Mapping the beliefs of teachers of Chinese language in Australian schools. Proceedings of CLaSIC 2012.

Oxford Dictionary and Thesaurus: American Edition. 1996. New York: Oxford University Press.

Parker, P., Hall, D. T., and Kram, K. E. 2008. Peer coaching: A relational process for accelerating career learning. *Academy of Management Learning and Education* 7: 487–503.

Pepper, B. 2004. *Voice in Action.* [DVD] Annandale, NSW: Currency Press.

Pfeffer, J., and Fong, C. T. 2002. The end of business schools? Less success than meets the eye. *Academy of Management Learning and Education* 1: 78–95.

Pfeffer, J., and Sutton, R. I. 2006. *Hard Facts, Dangerous Half-truths, and Total Nonsense: Profiting from Evidence-Based Management.* Cambridge, MA: Harvard Business School Press.

Piaget, J. 1977. *The Development of Thought: Equilibration of Cognitive Structures.* New York: Viking.

Reynolds, G. 2008. *Presentation Zen: Simple Ideas on Presentation Design and Delivery.* Berkeley, CA: New Riders.

Rousseau, D. M. 2006. Is there such a thing as evidence-based management? *Academy of Management Review* 31: 256–269.

Rubin R. S., and Dierdorff, E. C. 2011. On the road to Abilene: Time to manage agreement about MBA curricular relevance. *Academy of Management Learning and Education* 10: 148–161.

Rynes, S. L., Giluk, T. L., and Brown, K. G. 2007. The very separate worlds of academic and practitioner periodicals in human resource management: Implications for evidence-based management. *Academy of Management Journal* 50: 987–1008.

Schein, E. H. 1969. *Process Consultation.* Reading, MA. Addison-Wesley.

Schein, E. H. 1992. *Organizational Culture and Leadership*, 2nd ed. San Francisco: Jossey-Bass.

Schein, E. H. 2009. *Helping.* San Francisco: Berrett-Koehler.

Schunk, D. H. 2012. *Learning Theories: An Educational Perspective*, 6th ed. Boston: Allyn and Bacon.

Schwarz, R. 2002. *The Skilled Facilitator*, 2nd ed. San Francisco: Jossey-Bass.

Schwarz, R., Davidson, A., Carlson, P., and McKinney, S. 2005. *The Skilled Facilitator Field Book.* San Francisco: Jossey-Bass.

Spreitzer, G. M. 2006. Leadership development lessons from positive organizational studies. *Organizational Dynamics* 35: 305–315.

Staw, B. M., Sandelands, L. E., and Dutton, J. E. 1981. Threat rigidity effects in organizational behavior: A multilevel analysis. *Administrative Science Quarterly* 26: 501–524.

Taras, V., Steel, P., and Kirkman, B. L. 2012. Improving national cultural indices using a longitudinal meta-analysis of Hofstede's dimensions. *Journal of World Business* 47: 329–341.

Tugade, M. M., and Fredrickson, B. L. 2004. Resilient individuals use positive emotions to bounce back from negative emotional experiences. *Journal of Personality and Social Psychology* 86: 320–333.

VandeWalle, D. 1997. Development and validation of a work domain goal orientation instrument. *Educational and Psychological Measurement* 57: 995–1015.

Vygotsky, L. 1986. *Thought and Language*. Cambridge, MA: MIT Press.

Webber, S., and Johnston, B. 2000. Conceptions of information literacy: New perspectives and implications. *Journal of Information Science* 26: 381–397.

Wenger, E. C., McDermott, R., and Snyder, W. C. 2002. *Cultivating Communities of Practice: A Guide to Managing Knowledge*. Boston: Harvard Business.

Wren, D. A., Halbesleben, J. B., and Buckley, M. 2007. The theory-application balance in management pedagogy: A longitudinal update. *Academy of Management Learning and Education* 6: 484–492.

PART V

Workplace Learning from Other Lenses

22 Training from the Perspective of Human Resource Development and Industrial-Organizational Psychology

Common Pasts, Parallel Paths – Going Where?

Jon M. Werner

In this chapter, training and development is examined from the perspectives of the related academics disciplines of human resource development (HRD) and industrial-organizational (I-O) psychology. Past and present perspectives are provided, with the goal of demonstrating that, despite common heritage, parallel paths – if not parallel universes – can be seen concerning published work on training and development. Connections are made to the three largest professional associations for academics interested in training and development, that is, the Academy of Human Resource Development (AHRD), the Society for Industrial and Organizational Psychology (SIOP), and the Human Resources and Management Education and Development Divisions of the Academy of Management (AOM). Similar to what Aguinis, Bradley, and Brodersen (2014) found concerning the increase of I-O psychologists working in business schools, there is an increase in the number of AHRD-affiliated individuals with academic appointments in schools of business. Finally, the prospects for more intertwined academic study of training and development, as well as work-based practice, are presented.

As an undergraduate psychology major at Michigan State University in the 1970s, I took a training and development course from a "grizzled training veteran" named Frederick Wickert (see Schmitt & Ford, 2014). Wickert had taught around the world, helped to found the I-O psychology program at Michigan State, and required his undergraduate students to train another person to do some sort of physical task (I taught someone how to show a film using a movie projector, i.e., a full-sized movie reel using a dedicated projector). I later obtained an MBA and a PhD in organizational behavior, and never lost my interest in the "applied" topic of training and development. My writing on HRD has been strongly shaped by research from I-O psychology, management, and HRD perspectives (Werner & DeSimone, 2012). As a side note, I was privileged to be exposed to nine present SIOP Fellows who were at Michigan State while I was there (Georgia Chao, J. Kevin Ford, John Hollenbeck, Daniel Ilgen, Ellen Kossek, Steve Kozlowski, Neil Schmitt, Ben Schneider, and Kenneth Wexley).

As a co-editor of *Human Resource Development Quarterly*, I can address how the academic disciplines of I-O psychology and HRD view and address the topic of training and development.

Snippets from the Past – More Commonality Than Might Be Expected

The training of individuals by others has occurred as long as there have been humans on the earth. The first biblical reference to training occurs in Genesis, where the patriarch Abram (Abraham) learns that his nephew Lot and those connected to Lot had been taken captive. It is recorded that Abram led his 318 "trained men" to find and reclaim these individuals (Genesis 14:14). Swanson and Holton (2009) provide an extended coverage of the history of training and development, with examples of parents training their children, apprentices learning skills from those more skilled, to the development of artisans and craft guilds in the Middle Ages, particularly in Europe.

In U.S. history, apprenticeships were used for training purposes, in addition to considerable "manual training," often for those not able to engage in more traditional or "classical" education. Beginning with the Morrill Act in 1862, federal support for "land grant universities" fueled a broadening of subjects taught at public universities, and a subsequent increase in the number of individuals attending college and attaining degrees. A growing focus on vocational education took place in the latter half of the nineteenth century as well.

The enormous impact of both world wars on the field of training and development can hardly be overstated. In 1913, individuals such as Channing Dooley at Standard Oil and J. Walter Dietz at Western Electric began increased efforts to focus on business and training needs (Swanson & Holton, 2009). Dooley was then hired by the U.S. government to spearhead army needs for trade skills to support World War I. In 1940, the U.S. government created the Training Within Industry Service (TWI) with Dooley as its leader. With the need for training in both the military and industry, TWI had remarkable influence and success in assisting supervisors with the training of their employees. More than 1.6 million workers are estimated to have completed TWI programs from 1940 to 1945, and TWI is considered the roots of the modern quality movement (Dinero, 2005). In 1943, an organization was formed with the original name of the American Society for Training Directors (ASTD) – now called the Association for Talent Development (About ATD, 2015). Around the same time (1945), Division 14 of the American Psychological Association was formed, with a major focus on "applied" psychological topics, such as selection, training, and appraisal (Koppes, n.d.).

From this brief historical review, the common background for the fields of I-O psychology and HRD can be seen. Despite this common heritage, the fields of I-O and HRD point to different "starting points" for their respective histories. Applied or industrial psychology traces its roots to the founding of the American Psychological Association (APA) in 1892, then to the creation of Division 14 of the APA in 1945, and the subsequent renaming of this division as the SIOP in 1982 (Benjamin, 1997; Koppes, 1997). As discussed in the following text, HRD as a term for a field of study and practice traces its roots to the late 1970s and early 1980s. The respective histories are expanded in the next sections.

Back to the Present, Part 1: HRD's Take on Training

As noted, major historical events for HRD include World War II, the TWI, and the founding of ASTD – all occurring in the 1940s. Three other significant events include Donald Kirkpatrick publishing his four-level evaluation framework in 1959, the founding of the National Society for Programmed Instruction in 1962 (now the International Society for Performance Improvement), and the publication of Developing Human Resources by Leonard Nadler in 1970 (Kirkpatrick, 1959; Nadler, 1970; Swanson & Holton, 2009).

Nadler (1970: 3) described HRD as "a series of organized activities conducted within a specified time and designed to produce behavioral change." In addition to Nadler, the ASTD organization promoted use of the term *HRD*, and in an ASTD-sponsored study, Pat McLagan (1989) presented HRD as having three primary parts: training and development, career development, and organization development. This change was conveyed as an expansion from the original focus on training, particularly as conducted in a classroom. In 2004, a "new learning and performance wheel" was developed (Davis, Naughton, & Rothwell, 2004), which expanded the three areas from McLagan's study to include human resource management and other business functions.

More recently, these HRD topics were refined again, with a new list of 10 HRD competencies (Arneson, Rothwell, & Naughton, 2013): performance improvement, instructional design, training delivery, learning technologies, evaluating learning impact, managing learning programs, integrated talent management, coaching, knowledge management, and change management (Arneson et al., 2013). It is worth noting that the earlier emphasis on training and development, career development, and organization development can be seen still in this most recent iteration.

In May 2014, ASTD changed its name from the American Society for Training and Development to the Association for Talent Development, or ATD. ATD remains the primary professional organization for training practitioners, with nearly 40,000 members worldwide (ASTD, 2014). Their major periodical is the monthly publication now called *TD*, for talent development. This is a deliberate organizational rebranding with the goal of expanding their focus beyond training and development. One of the current ATD communities of practice is the Science of Learning Community; there is also a Higher Education Community for faculty, students, and practitioners (Communities of Practice, 2015).

The AHRD was founded in 1993, and is largely an offshoot of the former Professor's Network at ASTD (Swanson & Holton, 2009). Dooley (2004) describes the perceived tension between the strong practice-focus of ASTD/ ATD, and the strong research focus of AHRD. In many ways, this dynamic between ATD and AHRD is similar to what the Society for Human Resource Management (SHRM) experiences with both SIOP and the Academy of Management. Currently, one of the larger Special Interest Groups in AHRD is the Scholar-Practitioner SIG, which recently awarded their Scholar Practitioner Award to Gosser and Cumberland (2014) for their study of employee and customer satisfaction in the restaurant industry.

As a relatively young field of study, HRD has gone through numerous efforts to define itself, and to distinguish itself from other related topic areas such as human resource management and psychology (Swanson & Holton, 2009; Werner, 2014). As HRDQ editor, Tim Hatcher (2006) challenged the field to better define HRD, and to continue to expand HRD theory, research, and practice. Hamlin & Stewart (2011) summarized 24 different definitions of HRD. Wang et al. (2015) defined HRD as "a process of shaping individuals' values and beliefs and instilling required knowledge, skills, competencies, and attitudes through learning interventions to support the performance and sustainability of the host system."

A recent edited volume on HRD (Poell, Rocco, & Roth, 2014), opens with the following chapters under the heading origins of the field: history, status, and future of HRD (Lee, 2014), andragogy (Kessels, 2014), adult learning (Illeris, 2014), technical and vocational learning (Billett, 2014), and continuing professional education, development, and learning (Daley & Cervero, 2014). Subsequent chapters address "adjacent and related fields," that is, organization development, career development, labor unions, human resource management, and performance improvement. Together, these 10 chapters portray major topic areas in HRD and establish related fields of study to include labor and human resource management, but not I-O psychology.

Back to the Present, Part 2: I-O Psychology's Take on Training

As noted, both world wars had an enormous impact on the growth of applied (I-O) psychology, particularly in terms of testing (Farr, 1997; Levy, 2009). In addition to a strong focus on selection, evaluation, and appraisal, I-O psychologists increasingly focused on training and development, especially after World War II. However, it was not until 1971 that John Campbell wrote the seminal training-focused *Annual Review of Psychology* chapter, entitled "Personnel Training and Development." Topics covered by Campbell included learning principles, the importance of trainee attitudes and motivation, behavior modification and modeling, and the need to address individual trainee differences. Campbell covered many training techniques, and provided extensive coverage of training evaluation. Campbell's scathing critique bears repeating:

By and large, the training and development literature is voluminous, nonempirical, nontheoretical, poorly written, and dull.... it is faddish to an extreme. The fads center around the introduction of new techniques and follow a characteristic pattern. A new technique appears on the horizon and develops a large stable of advocates who first describe its "successful" use in a number of situations. A second wave of advocates busy themselves trying out numerous modifications of the basic technique. A few empirical studies may be carried out to demonstrate that the method "works." Then the inevitable backlash sets in and a few vocal opponents begin to criticize the usefulness of the technique, most often in the absence of data. Such criticisms typically have very little effect. What does have an effect is the appearance of another new technique and a repetition of the same cycle. (Campbell, 1971: 565–566)

Since Campbell, there have been seven other *Annual Review* chapters on this topic (Aguinis & Kraiger, 2009; Goldstein, 1980; Heller & Clark, 1976; Latham, 1988; Salas & Cannon-Bowers, 2001; Tannenbaum & Yukl, 1992; Wexley, 1984). Goldstein (1980) and Wexley (1984) expressed dismay about the state of the training literature. Latham (1988) was the first to express more optimism. A summary of dominant themes in these reviews, through Tannenbaum and Yukl (1992), can be seen in Table 22.1. A few items appear odd today, for example, "television" as a means of presenting training, or lumping under "special issues" the following disparate topics: the disadvantaged, hard-core unemployed, women, the aged, and police. Despite these quirks, this basic framework has defined the primary approach to training and development that has been followed by writers in I-O psychology and management since the 1980s (Goldstein & Ford, 2002; Kraiger, 2002; Noe, 2013; Salas & Kozlowski, 2009; Swanson & Holton, 2009; Werner, 2017; Wexley & Latham, 2001).

Early training texts written by I-O psychologists are noteworthy. First, Goldstein's (1974) book, *Training: Program Development and Evaluation*, emphasized needs assessment, training, and evaluation issues, including learning principles and training transfer. Fully one-third of the book emphasizes measurement-related issues. Goldstein paid relatively less attention to instructional techniques and "special approaches," such as the hard-core unemployed and training for second careers. Second, Wexley and Latham (1981) followed a similar systems approach, though with more extensive coverage of various training methods and management development techniques. Wexley and Latham (1981) concluded their book with "special concerns," including the disadvantaged, police, and safety and health training.

From this brief coverage, the strong I-O focus on measurement, design, and evaluation is evident. Particular emphasis has been placed on topics such as learning principles, training transfer, and rater training. Even with the common heritage for both HRD and I-O psychology, and the same societal forces increasing interest in training and development, the fields proceeded in different ways. Since the 1970s, HRD broadened its focus to include other interventions, including career and organization development, coaching, and more recently to "talent management" – a still elusive construct (Collings, 2014). In contrast, I-O psychologists until relatively recently have remained more narrowly focused

Table 22.1 *Dominant themes in early* Annual Review of Psychology *chapters*

A. Systems theory/approach
   1. Needs assessment: organizational, task, and person analysis
   2. Instructional design
      • Maximizing trainee learning
      • From learning principles to task design
      • Need to focus on behaviors, transfer
      • Importance of individual differences (aptitude-treatment interaction)
      • Motivation, attitudes
   3. Delivery/techniques
   a. Approaches:
      • Programmed instruction/computer-assisted instruction
      • Television
      • Modeling
      • Simulation
   b. Topics:
      • Basic/job skills
      • Orientation/socialization
      • Sales training
      • Team training
      • Rater training
      • Career development
      • Sensitivity training
      • Management/leadership development
      • Organization development
      • Cross-cultural training
      • Legal/fair employment
      • Special needs/issues: disadvantaged, hard-core unemployed, women, aged, police
   4. Evaluation
   a. Methodology/design
   b. Criterion issues
B. Progress, or lack of progress, in both research and practice

---

on training and development, with a central emphasis on measurement (both assessment and evaluation), and strong quantitative research. The next section will examine these issues and differences in more detail.

I-O (SIOP) and HRD (AHRD): Parallel Universes?

In the latest *Annual Review of Psychology* article, Aguinis and Kraiger (2009) described many potential benefits of training and development, for individuals, teams, organizations, and society. Well-conducted research from multiple disciplines was highlighted to demonstrate these benefits and, though optimistic, Aquinis and Kraiger (2009) also emphasized the need for more research, especially from a multidisciplinary perspective. Cascio and Aguinis

(2008: 1062) included training and development as a "central" topic in I-O psychology. Despite this statement, they found that, from 1963 to 2007, the number of articles narrowly focused on training averaged only 6.3% of all *Personnel Psychology* (PP) articles, and 3.6% of all *Journal of Applied Psychology* (JAP) articles. They also found that training-related articles in these journals peaked from 1988 to 1992. Next, current efforts to study training and development are addressed, particularly as this relates to SIOP, AHRD, and the top journals for both I-O psychology and HRD. Original research is presented concerning the degree of past and present overlap between I-O psychology and HRD research.

I-O and SIOP

The two top I-O journals are JAP and PP (Aguinis et al., 2014). The JAP is published by the American Psychological Association, and began publication in 1917. It has an impact factor of 4.37 (American Psychological Association, 2015). In 2014, it received 941 new manuscripts (Wood, 2015), and published 83 articles. PP began publication in 1948, and has an impact factor of 4.54 (Personnel Psychology, 2015). In 2014, it received 286 new manuscripts (Bell, 2015), and published 26 articles. Neither journal is directly affiliated with SIOP, though the vast majority of those involved with these two journals are also SIOP members. SIOP describes itself as "the premiere membership organization for those practicing and teaching I-O psychology" (Cortina, 2014). SIOP has more than 8,000 members; as of June 2015, this includes 3,911 student affiliates (SIOP Membership Services, 2015). This is a significant increase in membership from 2000, when there were roughly 4,500 members, which included 1,703 student affiliates (Silzer & Parson, 2013). The highest distinction offered in SIOP is the "Fellow," for individuals who have made outstanding contributions to the field. As of this writing, 325 individuals are current SIOP Fellows (Announcement of New SIOP Fellows, 2015; SIOP Fellows, 2014).

HRD and AHRD

As mentioned, the AHRD is a professional organization primarily for academics (with some graduate students and a smaller number of practitioners) who specialize in HRD. Their vision statement is "Leading human resource development through research" (About AHRD, 2015). In January 2015, AHRD had 509 members (this included 173 student members). This is down from a high of 723 members in 2010 (Jacobs, 2016). AHRD has four affiliated journals: *Human Resource Development Quarterly* (HRDQ), *Human Resource Development Review* (HRDR), *Human Resource Development International* (HRDI), and *Advances in Developing Human Resources* (ADHR). HRDQ is the oldest of these four journals, having celebrated its twenty-fifth anniversary in 2014 (Ellinger, 2014). HRDQ was the first AHRD journal to be listed in the Social Science Citation Index (impact factor = .854). In 2014, HRDQ received 195 new manuscripts, and published 21 articles (HRDQ, 2015). HRDI began

Table 22.2 *Members of the HRD Scholar Hall of Fame*

Channing R. Dooley, 1993, Training Within Industry (engineering)
Malcolm S. Knowles, 1994, adult learning (education)
Lillian M. Gilbreth, 1995, human aspects of management (psychology)
Kurt Lewin, 1996, change theory (psychology)
B. F. Skinner, 1997, teaching machines (psychology)
Donald E. Super, 1998, career development (psychology)
Robert M. Gagné, 1999, instructional design; conditions of learning (psychology)
Gary S. Becker, 2000, human capital (economics)
Leonard Nadler, 2001, foundations of HRD (education)
John C. Flanagan, 2002, critical incident technique (psychology)
Richard A. Swanson, 2004, HRD research (education)
Gary N. McLean, 2006, internationalization (education)
Karen E. Watkins, 2013, adult learning; learning organizations (education)

Source: http://www.ahrd.org/?hall_of_fame_2#2015 (accessed June 18, 2015).

publication in 1998, ADHR began publication in 1999, and HRDR began publication in 2002. HRDR got listed in the SSCI in 2014 (Jacobs, 2016).

The two highest distinctions in AHRD are the "HRD Scholar Hall of Fame," and the "HRD Scholar Award." Between 1993 and 2014, 13 individuals have been inducted into the HRD Scholar Hall of Fame (See Table 22.2). Five of these individuals have backgrounds in education, six in psychology, and one each from engineering and economics. Similar to Table 22.1, Table 22.2 suggests considerable common heritage between I-O psychology and HRD.

Examining Overlap between SIOP and AHRD

The majority of SIOP members have educational backgrounds in I-O psychology, though many have backgrounds in management or industrial relations. Conversely, as will be demonstrated in the following text, the greatest number of academic members of AHRD have backgrounds in education. In looking at current SIOP Fellows, Allen Church, an organization development expert at Pepsico, is the only SIOP Fellow (out of 325) who is also an AHRD member.

Of the 19 recipients of AHRD's "HRD Scholar Award," most have backgrounds in education. The only current SIOP Fellow to receive the "HRD Scholar Award" is management professor Todd Maurer of Georgia State University, who won the award in 2003 (Outstanding HRD Scholar Award, 2015). So, despite the overlapping interest in training and development, career development, and organization development (McLagan, 1989), there is virtually no overlap between SIOP Fellows and scholarly recognition by AHRD.

A further question is whether SIOP Fellows publish in HRDQ, the original AHRD journal. Looking at the past decade (i.e., 2005–2014), there were 261 articles published in HRDQ, excluding book reviews. An author search revealed that 13 of these articles, or 5.6%, had a SIOP Fellow as an author or co-author. These individuals are Tammy Allen (2006), Bruce Avolio (2010), Bradford Bell (2007), J. Kevin Ford (2007), Jonathon Halbesleben (2013), Kurt Kraiger (2014), Carol Kulik (2010), Todd Maurer (2010), Ray Noe (2013), Daniel Newman (2011), Miguel Quiñones (2005), Eduardo Salas (2005), and Scott Tannenbaum (2005; 2006).

The top research award for HRDQ is the Richard A. Swanson Research Award, given out to the article from each volume deemed to have made the most significant contribution to HRD. Twenty-five articles have been selected to date (Richard A. Swanson Research Excellence Award, 2015). Fifty-six names are cited on this list, and this covers 50 individuals (six individuals won the award twice, i.e., Timothy Baldwin, Reid Bates, Caroline D'Abate, Erik Eddy, Andrea Ellinger, and Elwood Holton III). Five current SIOP Fellows have won this award (11% of all winners, i.e., Bruce Avolio, Allen Church, Irwin Goldstein, Scott Tannenbaum, and Kenneth Wexley). By comparison, nine current HRDQ editors or editorial board members have won the Swanson Award (19% of all winners, i.e., Reid Bates, Laura Bierema, Shani Carter, Toby Egan, Andrea Ellinger, Ronald Jacobs, Thomas Reio, Wendy Ruona, and Jon Werner). It is not surprising that past Swanson Award winners are heavily represented on the current HRDQ board. It is noteworthy that SIOP Fellows have done well in winning this award, especially considering the relatively low number of articles they have published in HRDQ.

Looking at who publishes most frequently in HRDQ, the individuals selected as Outstanding HRD Scholars published 48 articles in HRDQ during this 10-year period, and this constitutes 18.4% of all articles published. From this group, the top seven contributors, by number of publications, are Darlene Russ-Eft (7 articles), Elwood Holton III (6), Ronald Jacobs (6), Gary McLean (6), Reid Bates (5), and Andrea Ellinger (5). Of this group, only Russ-Eft is a member of SIOP.

Another query concerns publications in HRDQ by the current HRDQ editors and editorial board (6 editors, and 49 board members). From 2005 to 2014, the editors published 16 times (11 unique articles, including editorials), and the rest of the board published 73 times in 68 separate articles (25.7% of articles published in HRDQ). This constitutes a total of 89 times these names appear as an author/co-author in HRDQ. Combining the numbers for the editors and board members leads to 79 unique articles, or 30.3% of all articles published in HRDQ in the past decade.

Looking at all four AHRD-affiliated journals, another question concerns who publishes most frequently across all four AHRD journals. There are 21 individuals who have published the most articles in these four journals (see Table 22.3). The top nine on this list are Gary McLean (44 articles), Thomas Reio (24), Thomas Garavan (22), Toby Egan (18), Julia Storberg-Walker (17), Jia Wang (16), Elwood Holton III (14), Darlene Russ-Eft (14), and Darren C. Short (14). These individuals are active in AHRD. An online search on

Table 22.3 *"Top 21" HRD scholars, by ten-year count, in four AHRD journals*

Name	Total articles
Gary N. McLean	44
Thomas G. Reio	24
Thomas N. Garavan	22
Toby M. Egan	18
Julia Storberg-Walker	17
Jia Wang	16
Elwood F. Holton III	14
Darlene Russ-Eft	14
Darren C. Short	14
Kim F. Nimon	13
Richard A. Swanson	13
Robert G. Hamlin	12
Richard Torraco	12
Andrea D. Ellinger	11
David McGuire	11
Michael Lane Morris	11
Sally Sambrook	11
Ronald L. Jacobs	10
Susan A. Lynham	10
Rob F. Poell	10
Baiyin Yang	9

Notes. Count of articles (including editorials) published in HRDQ, HRDR, HRDI, and ADHR, from 2005 to 2014. Includes Outstanding HRD Scholar Award winners, current HRDQ editors, and HRDQ editorial board members. Source: Searches using EBSCOHost and Sage Premiere, June 2015.

June 15, 2015, followed up by an e-mail query to the authors, found that Thomas Garavan, Kim Nimon, Thomas Reio, and Darlene Russ-Eft are current SIOP members, and Toby Egan and Richard Torraco are former SIOP members.

Another question is whether recognized HRD scholars publish in JAP and PP. The answer here is rather stark: not much! Of those honored in the HRD Hall of Fame, only John Flanagan published two articles in PP. Of the 19 Outstanding HRD Scholars, Todd Maurer was the most prolific publisher in these two journals (eight articles in JAP, and four in PP). In addition, Darlene Russ-Eft published two articles in JAP. Of these three, only Russ-Eft has been actively involved in the AHRD.

Finally, looking at current HRDQ editors and board members, it can be asked whether they have published in JAP or PP. The answer here is more. The list of publications in these two journals is shown in Table 22.4. These individuals have published 17 articles to date in JAP, and six articles in PP.

Table 22.4 *Current HRDQ editors and board members published in* Journal of Applied Psychology *or* Personnel Psychology

	Journal of Applied Psychology	*Personnel Psychology*
Travor C. Brown	–	1
Kenneth G. Brown	9	2
Thomas G. Cummings	1	–
Jonathon Halbesleben	6	–
Maura Sheehan	–	1
Marcus M. Stewart	1	1
Jon M. Werner	2	1
TOTALS:	17	6

Two additional outlets for I-O psychology research are *Human Performance* and the *International Review of I-O Psychology*. A search of all articles published in *Human Performance* from 2005 to 2014 produced 22 articles where "training" showed up within the article, though in only seven of these articles was training a "subject term." From 240 total articles, this is 9.2% of all articles where training is mentioned, yet only 2.9% where it was a key term. This latter figure is lower than that found by Cascio and Aguinis (2008) for articles on training published in either PP or the JAP.

Turning to the *International Review of I-O Psychology*, a similar search was conducted from 2005 to 2014 (in 2013, this review was folded into the *Journal of Organizational Behavior* as a special annual issue). Of 77 total articles published in this period, only three (3.9%) focused narrowly on training topics, that is, Annett and Stanton (2006, task analysis), Baldwin, Ford, and Blume (2009, training transfer), and Burke, Holman, and Birdi (2006, safety training). However, at least 13 more are relevant, especially when viewed from the broader lens of HRD (see Table 22.5). These articles add an additional 16.9% of all *International Review* articles in the past decade with coverage of training and HRD-related topics. Overall, then, more than 20% of the articles in the last 10 years of the *International Review* are relevant to HRD. This includes articles on organizational learning (Argote & Todorova, 2007), age and learning (Beier, 2008), e-learning (Brown, Charlier, & Pierotti, 2012), socialization (Ashforth, Sluss, & Harrison, 2007), coaching (Grant et al., 2010), career development (Gubler, Arnold, & Coombs, 2014), leadership development (Avolio & Chan, 2008), diversity management (Avery & McKay, 2010), and cost-benefit analysis (Cascio, 2007).

These topics are relevant to HRD (Swanson & Holton, 2009; Werner & DeSimone, 2012). Despite this, a journal search for the years 2005–2014 (conducted in June 2015) found no citations to articles published in the *International Review of I-O Psychology* in any article published in the four AHRD journals (HRDQ, HRDR, HRDI, and ADHR). Some articles published in these AHRD journals included citations from industrial psychology in general, but none cited

Table 22.5 *Training and HRD articles in the* International Review of Industrial and Organizational Psychology, *2005–2014, by Year*

Annett & Stanton (2006). Task analysis.

Burke, Holman, & Birdi (2006). A walk on the safe side: The implications of learning theory for developing effective safety and health training.

Argote & Todorova (2007). Organizational learning.

Ashforth, Sluss, & Harrison (2007). Socialization in organizational contexts.

Cascio (2007). The costs – and benefits – of human resources.

Dewe & Cooper (2007). Coping research and measurement in the context of work related stress.

Major & Cleveland (2007). Strategies for reducing work-family conflict: Applying research and best practices from industrial and organizational psychology.

Arnold & Cohen (2008). The psychology of careers in industrial and organizational settings: A critical but appreciative analysis.

Avolio & Chan (2008). The dawning of a new era for genuine leadership development.

Beier (2008). Age and learning in organizations.

Baldwin, Ford, & Blume (2009). Transfer of training 1988–2008: An updated review and agenda for future research.

Avery & McKay (2010). Doing diversity right: An empirically based approach to effective diversity management.

Grant et al. (2010). The state of play in coaching today: A comprehensive review of the field.

Brown, Charlier, & Pierotti (2012). e-Learning at work: Contributions of past research and suggestions for the future.

Gubler, Arnold, & Coombs (2014). Reassessing the protean career concept: Empirical findings, conceptual components, and measurement.

Lyons & Kuron (2014). Generational differences in the workplace: A review of the evidence and directions for future research.

---

the *International Review*. An important source of relevant information is not getting disseminated outside of I-O circles.

A study of topics covered in *Human Resource Development Quarterly* from 2005 to 2014 is revealing. Using an outline adapted from Table 22.1, Table 22.6 displays the major topics addressed in these 261 articles (percentages do not add up to 100%). The greatest number of articles (including editorials) addressed issues concerning defining HRD, theory building, and establishing boundaries for HRD in relation to other fields of study. This category included 45 articles, or 17.2% of all articles published. This is consistent with the frequent calls to address these issues (Hatcher, 2006; Hamlin & Stewart, 2011; Wang et al., 2015).

The next most studied topics in HRDQ in the past decade were employee attitudes pertaining to HRD (13.0%), career development (10.0%), trainee motivation (8.4%), teams (7.7%), training transfer (6.9%), organization development and change (6.9%), diversity (6.5%), leadership development (5.7%), coaching (5.4%), feedback (5.4%), and trainee personality characteristics (5.0%). An additional 5% of articles presented scale validation evidence for HRD-relevant constructs. Two articles dealt specifically with needs assessment (Bell & Ford,

Table 22.6 *Major topics and count in HRDQ from 2005 to 2014 (N = 261)*

A. Definitions, theory, boundaries of HRD as a field of study (n = 45 articles)
B. Strategic HRD (n = 8)
C. Needs assessment (n = 2)
  • Job competencies (n = 11)
D. Design Issues
  • Training transfer (n = 18)
  • Individual differences (n =5)
  • Motivation (n = 22)
  • Attitudes (n = 34)
  • Personality (n = 13)
E. Delivery Issues
  1. Approaches
  • E.g., Job aids, teaching styles, e-learning, corporate universities, outsourcing of training (n = 5)
  • Informal learning (n = 12)
  2. Topics
  • Basic job skills (n = 9)
  • Socialization (n = 3)
  • Sales/customer service training (n = 10)
  • Teams (n = 20)
  • Coaching (n = 14)
  • Feedback (n = 14)
  • Career development (n = 26)
  • Health/stress (n = 10)
  • Work engagement (n = 10)
  • Management/leadership development (n = 15)
  • Organization development and change (n = 18)
  • Global/cross-cultural training (n = 4)
  • Diversity (n = 17)
F. Evaluation Issues (n = 22)
  • Methodology/design (n = 9)
  • Scale validation (n = 13)
G. Connecting HRD research and practice (n = 18), e.g., "research-practice gap"

2007; Dachner et al., 2013), though an additional 11 articles addressed the topic of job competencies. Only one article dealt specifically with training evaluation models (Holton & Naquin, 2005), and three others measured trainee utility perceptions (Bell & Ford, 2007; Holladay & Quiñones, 2005; Madera, Steele, & Beier, 2011). Table 22.6 reveals both the breadth of topics covered in HRDQ over the past decade, as well as the high degree of overlap with topics covered in past *Annual Review of Psychology* articles on this subject.

Looking at the two I-O psychology journals, from 2005 to 2014, the JAP published 1,011 total articles, and 186 mentioned the word *training*. A comparison of topics addressed in these 186 JAP articles can be found in Table 22.7. In Table 22.7, comparisons are also given for training-related articles in PP, as

Table 22.7 *Major topics and count in JAP, PP, and HRDQ, 2005–2014*

	JAP (N = 186)		P.Psych. (N = 46)		HRDQ articles (N = 261)	
	Percent	Count	Percent	Count	Percent	Count
Definitions, theory development	0.0%	n = 0	0.0%	n = 0	17.2%	n = 45
Strategic training/HRD	2.7%	n = 5	6.5%	n = 3	3.1%	n = 8
Needs assessment	16.0%	n = 30	6.5%	n = 3	0.8%	n = 2
Competencies	2.7%	n = 5	6.5%	n = 3	4.2%	n = 11
Design Issues						
Training transfer	5.3%	n = 10	0.0%	n = 0	6.9%	n = 18
Individual differences	3.2%	n = 6	0.0%	n = 0	1.9%	n = 5
Motivation	10.1%	n = 19	8.8%	n = 4	8.4%	n = 22
Attitudes	18.6%	n = 35	8.8%	n = 4	13.0%	n = 34
Personality	19.2%	n = 36	10.7%	n = 5	5.0%	n = 13
Delivery approaches						
e.g., e-learning, corporate universities	1.1%	n = 2	4.3%	n = 2	1.9%	n = 5
Informal learning	0.0%	n = 0	0.0%	n = 0	4.6%	n = 12
Delivery topics						
Basic job skills	0.5%	n = 1	0.0%	n = 0	3.4%	n = 9
Socialization	0.5%	n = 1	0.0%	n = 0	1.1%	n = 3
Sales/customer service training	7.4%	n = 14	0.0%	n = 0	3.8%	n = 10
Teams	19.2%	n = 36	0.0%	n = 0	7.7%	n = 20
Coaching	3.2%	n = 6	4.3%	n = 2	5.4%	n = 14
Feedback	2.7%	n = 5	6.5%	n = 3	5.4%	n = 14
Career development	1.6%	n = 3	21.7%	n = 10	10.0%	n = 26
Health/stress	6.4%	n = 12	0.0%	n = 0	3.8%	n = 10
Work engagement	3.7%	n = 7	2.1%	n = 1	3.8%	n = 10
Management/leadership development	23.4%	n = 44	43.5%	n = 20	5.7%	n = 15
Organization development	0.5%	n = 1	2.1%	n = 1	6.9%	n = 18
Global/cross-cultural training	1.6%	n = 3	4.3%	n = 2	1.5%	n = 4
Diversity	4.8%	n = 9	23.9%	n = 11	6.5%	n = 17
Evaluation issues	14.4%	n = 27	67.4%	n = 31	8.4%	n = 22
Connecting training research and practice	0.5%	n = 1	0.0%	n = 0	6.9%	n = 18

well as the information from Table 22.6 concerning HRDQ. During this 10-year period, PP published 295 articles, of which 46 mentioned training. Looking first at the percentages, t-tests demonstrate the following:

- articles in HRDQ are more likely to address theory and definitional issues than articles in either JAP or PP (p < .01)
- articles in both JAP and PP more likely to address needs assessment than articles in HRDQ (p < .05)
- articles in both JAP and PP more likely to address evaluation than articles in HRDQ (p < .001)
- articles in JAP are more likely to address the topic of personality than articles in HRDQ (p < .001)
- articles in JAP are more likely to address teams than articles in HRDQ (p < .01)
- articles in PP are more likely to address career development than articles in HRDQ (p < .05); while articles in HRDQ are more likely to address career development than articles in JAP (p < .001)
- articles in both JAP and PP are more likely to address management/leadership development than articles in HRDQ (p < .001)
- articles in PP are more likely to address diversity/legal issues than articles in HRDQ (p < .001)

Shifting to a count of articles, rather than percentages, Figure 22.1 compares selected topics from Table 22.7 for the JAP and HRDQ. This shows graphically the strong emphasis in HRDQ on four topics, that is, theory and definitional issues, career development, organization development, and informal learning, with a corresponding lack of coverage of these same topics in JAP during this period. Figure 22.1 depicts the very strong focus in JAP on assessment, with almost no coverage of this topic in HRDQ. The top of the graph depicts the stronger focus on leadership, personality and teams in JAP than in HRDQ. Both journals have many articles pertaining to attitudes, and a similar (though lesser) number of articles on evaluation and motivation. Finally, HRDQ had somewhat more articles on training transfer, diversity, and coaching than did JAP.

From the material presented in the preceding text, I-O and HRD research on training do appear to be "parallel universes" that only sometimes intersect (e.g., Kraiger, 2014). This is so, despite the many common research interests that can be seen in the preceding discussion. The final section makes a call for joint research and implementation in the future.

Forward: Moving Toward What Future?

The need for training efforts that "move the needle" has never been greater. Two factors contributing to this are: (1) the skills gap, that is, the gap between applicant and worker skills and present work demands (Kochan, Finegold, & Osterman, 2012; Leubsdorf, 2014), and (2) the increasing

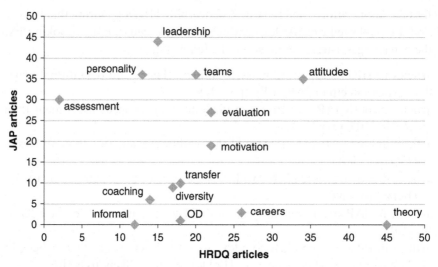

Figure 22.1. *Plot of selected topic comparisons for JAP and HRDQ, by article count.*

globalization of work (e.g., Hardy & Tolhurst, 2014; Rynes, 2012). Training and development should to be addressed from a strong research base, and in fact, there has been meaningful progress in advancing the "science of training" (Salas & Cannon-Bowers, 2001; Salas et al., 2012). Nevertheless, a different kind of gap is also evident, namely that between research and practice. This gap has been noted by authors from HRD (Hutchins & Burke, 2007; Keefer & Yap, 2007; Salas & Kosarzycki, 2003; Short, 2006), I-O psychology (Cascio, 2008; Rynes, 2012; Salas et al., 1999), and management (Ireland, 2012; Rynes, Giluk, & Brown, 2007; Tsui, 2013). Rynes (2012), for example, opined as follows: "The more I have tried to be an industrial and organizational (I/O) psychologist, the less I have been able to be of practical value to the organizations with and for whom I have worked" (409). The challenges of connecting the "science of training" with real-world implementation have been noted frequently since Campbell's (1971) strong words. In my review of topics addressed in HRDQ in the past decade, research-to-practice issues were highlighted in no less than 18 articles. This is the same count as was found for training transfer and organization development and change (see Table 22.5).

A shift that began in the 1980s was the migration of many I-O psychologists into schools of business. Aguinis et al. (2014) surveyed SIOP Fellows, and they provided evidence "that I-O psychologists affiliated with business schools currently constitute a majority of editorial board members and authors of articles published in Journal of Applied Psychology and Personnel Psychology" (284). Aquinis et al. (2014) made many bold predictions concerning future trends for I-O psychology, especially in terms of its relationship to business schools and the future of I-O psychology graduate programs (see also Cushenbery & Gabriel, 2014).

In the United States, the total number of bachelor's degrees awarded in 1980 was 929,417 (U.S. Census Bureau, 2012). In 2009, that number had climbed to 1,601,368, for an overall 30-year increase of 72.3%. Similarly, bachelor's degrees in business increased from 186,264 in 1980 to 347,985 in 2009, for an increase of 86.8%. However, for education, bachelor's degrees in education dropped from 118,038 in 1980 to 101,708 in 2009 (a decrease of 13.8%). Of the 27 categories used to track bachelor's degrees, the only other category with a net decrease from 1980 to 2009 was "physical sciences and science technologies," which decreased from 23,407 in 1980 to 22,466 in 2009 (a 4% decrease; U.S. Census Bureau, 2012).

Is it possible that by moving to business schools, I-O psychologists have assured the continued growth of their field? There will always be a need for schools of education, yet the numbers presented above demonstrate that bachelor's enrollment in education programs has declined in the past 30 years. As the AHRD has been most closely tied to faculty in schools of education, this has implications for the future of HRD as well. As noted previously, recent numbers are declining in terms of AHRD members, despite a sizable proportion of graduate student members.

Outside of North America, many HRD scholars are affiliated with business schools. Additionally, there are now more business school faculty on AHRD boards and publishing in AHRD journals. One potential bridge between I-O psychology and HRD is the AOM. AOM currently has more than 18,000 members. AOM has 25 divisions and interest groups covering a wide range of management topics. In 2015, the Human Resources Division has 3,281 members, and the Management Education and Development Division has 1,782 members, and both are natural connecting points for those interested in training and development (Morgeson & Lepak, 2015; MED, 2014). SIOP, AHRD, and AOM members could create and present symposia on jointly relevant topics at Academy of Management conferences. Another simple step would be for more researchers to attend and present their research at conferences for their "nonprimary" affiliations, e.g., SIOP members at AHRD conferences, or vice versa. Research awards that required collaboration across disciplines could spur integrated research efforts, for example, SHRM offers the Michael R. Losey Excellence in Human Resource Research Award every year; instead of focusing on a particular HRM researcher, SHRM could require future award winners to conduct collaborative research with the $50,000 award (SHRM, 2015). Similarly, research grants and other incentives could be structured to require interdisciplinary efforts.

In addition to fostering greater connections across the related professional associations, greater connections can be made by researchers across research topics. Tables 22.5 and 22.6, in particular, depict many research interests that are shared by I-O psychologists, HRD and management researchers. Learning is a central focus of each area, and topics such as leadership, teams, diversity, and ways to make more meaningful connections between research and practice would all benefit from broad-based research projects.

Conclusion

I-O psychology has strongly emphasized rigorous measurement and evaluation. Historically, the I-O focus concerning training and development has been narrow, that is, frequent emphasis on topics such as needs assessment, training transfer, and evaluation. An image this evokes is of individuals wearing tie-dye shirts with the logo "Evaluation is groovy!" This 1960s- and 1970s-style focus on rigor and evaluation is necessary, but has also led to questions such as this: "Why don't organizations pay attention to (and use) findings from the science of training?" (Salas & Kosarzycki, 2003).

In contrast, HRD as a field of study, with stronger roots in education, has focused more on vocational learning, continuing professional development, adult learning, and diversity. At the present time, HRD research seems broader than that published by I-O psychologists – at least as appearing in JAP and PP (Cascio & Aguinis, 2008). With this greater breadth, however, HRD scholars have often challenged the field to increase the rigor of HRD research (Jacobs, 2009; Reio, 2009; Russ-Eft et al., 2014). It should be noted that the interplay of rigor versus relevance in practice has been noted in psychology, HRD, and management (Cascio, 2008; Short, 2006; Tsui, 2013). Pertaining to training, rigorous evaluation methods often don't get used in practice (Salas et al., 2012).

Without question, strong theory-to-practice articles are commonly published in I-O psychology journals (e.g., Dierdorff, Surface, & Brown, 2010; Stanhope, Pond, & Surface, 2013), and strong methodological articles are routinely published in AHRD-affiliated journals (e.g., Brown, McCracken, & Hillier, 2013; Cook & Glass, 2014). However, to advance the science of training and evidence-based practices, stronger connections need to be made across disciplines. Greater collaboration and integration is necessary in the study of training and development across I-O psychology, HRD, and management (Aguinis & Kraiger, 2009). There also need to be more connections made with organizations such as ATD and SHRM (Rynes, 2012). Training researchers should seek out relevant theories and research across disciplinary backgrounds and traditional boundaries (e.g., Sadler-Smith's, 2014, use of design science to advance HRD). Scholars should make greater use of "bridge" journals, that is, journals that seek to be relevant and engaging for both researchers and practitioners. This would include journals such as *Human Resource Management* and *Advances in Developing Human Resources* to promote research-based practices. Scholars should seek disseminate their research across disciplines and journals, including JAP, PP, the AHRD-affiliated journals, the *European Journal of Training and Development*, as well as outlets such as *Human Performance*, *International Review of Industrial and Organizational Psychology*, and *Industrial and Organizational Psychology*.

Training and development is too important to be addressed by fragmented efforts stuck within academic silos. Paraphrasing Ronald Reagan, those in I-O and HRD need to tear down any "walls" holding back training research, including any self-imposed walls of simply not attending to or following related research outside one's "own" discipline. Innovation and research-based application are needed (Soken & Barnes, 2014). Let's do this together, including I-O, HRD, and management (Gubbins & Rousseau, 2015; Rynes, Rousseau, & Barends, 2014).

References

About AHRD. 2015. The AHRD vision. http://www.ahrd.org/?about_ahrd_2 (accessed June 18, 2015).

About ATD. 2015. Association for Talent Development. http://www.astd.org/About (accessed June 12, 2015).

Aguinis, H., and Kraiger, K. 2009. Benefits of training and development for individuals and teams, organizations, and society. *Annual Review of Psychology* 60: 451–474.

Aguinis, H., Bradley, K. J., and Brodersen, A. 2014. Industrial-organizational psychologists in business schools: Brain drain or eye opener? *Industrial and Organizational Psychology* 7(3): 284–303.

American Psychological Association. 2015. *Journal of Applied Psychology*. http://www.apa.org/pubs/journals/apl (accessed June 15, 2015).

Annett, J., and Stanton, N. 2006. Task analysis. *International Review of Industrial and Organizational Psychology* 21: 45–78.

Announcement of New 2015 SIOP Fellows. 2015. SIOP. http://www.siop.org/fellows/2015Fellows.aspx (accessed June 1, 2015).

Argote, L., and Todorova, G. 2007. Organizational learning. *International Review of Industrial and Organizational Psychology* 22: 193–234.

Arneson, J., Rothwell, W., and Naughton, J. 2013. Training and development competencies redefined to create competitive advantage. *T&D* 67(1): 42–47.

Arnold, J., and Cohen, L. 2008. The psychology of careers in industrial and organizational settings: A critical but appreciative analysis. *International Review of Industrial and Organizational Psychology* 23: 1–44.

Ashforth, B. E., Sluss, D. M., and Harrison, S. H. 2007. Socialization in organizational contexts. *International Review of Industrial and Organizational Psychology* 22: 1–70.

ATD. 2014. *2014 Annual Report*. Alexandria, VA: ATD.

Avery, D. R., and McKay, P. F. 2010. Doing diversity right: An empirically based approach to effective diversity management. *International Review of Industrial and Organizational Psychology* 25: 221–252.

Avolio, B. J., and Chan, A. 2008. The dawning of a new era for genuine leadership development. *International Review of Industrial and Organizational Psychology* 23: 197–238.

Baldwin, T. T., Ford, J. K., and Blume, B. D. 2009. Transfer of training 1988–2008: An updated review and agenda for future research. *International Review of Industrial and Organizational Psychology* 24: 41–70.

Beier, M. E. 2008. Age and learning in organizations. *International Review of Industrial and Organizational Psychology* 23: 83–105.

Bell, B. S. 2015. Personal communication, editor, *Personnel Psychology*, June 17.

Bell, B. S., and Ford, J. K. 2007. Reactions to skill assessment: The forgotten factor in explaining motivation to learn. *Human Resource Development Quarterly* 18(1): 33–62.

Benjamin, L. T., Jr. 1997. A history of Division 14 (The Society for Industrial and Organizational Psychology). In D. A. Dewsbury, ed. *Unification through Division: Histories of the Divisions of the American Psychological Association, Vol. II*, Washington, DC: APA.

Billett, S. 2014. Technical and vocational learning. In R. F. Poell, T. S. Rocco, and G. L. Roth, eds., *The Routledge Companion to Human Resource Development*, 30–39. London: Routledge.

Brown, K. G., Charlier, S. D. and Pierotti, A. 2012. e-Learning at work: Contributions of past research and suggestions for the future. *International Review of Industrial and Organizational Psychology* 27: 89–114.

Brown, T. C., McCracken, M., and Hillier, T. L. 2013. Using evidence-based practices to enhance transfer of training: Assessing the effectiveness of goal setting and behavioural observation scales. *Human Resource Development International* 16(4): 374–389.

Burke, M. J., Holman, D., and Birdi, K. 2006. A walk on the safe side: The implications of learning theory for developing effective safety and health training. *International Review of Industrial and Organizational Psychology* 21: 1–44.

Campbell, J. P. 1971. Personnel training and development. *Annual Review of Psychology* 22: 565–602.

Cascio, W. F. 2007. The costs – and benefits – of human resources. *International Review of Industrial and Organizational Psychology* 22: 71–109.

Cascio, W. F. 2008. To prosper, organizational psychology should … bridge application and scholarship. *Journal of Organizational Behavior* 29: 455–468.

Cascio, W. F., and Aguinis, H. 2008. Research in industrial and organizational psychology from 1963 to 2007: Changes, choices, and trends. *Journal of Applied Psychology* 93(5): 1062–1081.

Collings, D. G. 2014. Toward mature talent management: Beyond shareholder value. *Human Resource Development Quarterly* 25(3): 301–319.

Communities of Practice. 2015. ATD. https://www.td.org/Communities-of-Practice (accessed June 2, 2015).

Cook, A., and Glass, C. 2014. Do diversity reputation signals increase share value? *Human Resource Development Quarterly* 25(4): 471–491.

Cortina, J. 2014. About us: President's message. SIOP. http://www.siop.org/siophoshin.aspx (accessed October 6, 2014).

Cushenbery, L. D., and Gabriel, A. S. 2014. Reappraising the brain drain: Collaboration as a catalyst for innovation in industrial–organizational research. *Industrial and Organizational Psychology* 7: 347–351.

Dachner, A. M., Saxton, B. M., Noe, R. A., and Keeton, K. E. 2013. To infinity and beyond: Using a narrative approach to identify training needs for unknown and dynamic situations. *Human Resource Development Quarterly* 24(2): 239–267.

Daley, B. J., and Cervero, R. M. 2014. Continuing professional education, development, and learning. In R. F. Poell, T. S. Rocco, and G. L. Roth, eds., *Routledge Companion to Human Resource Development*, 40–49. London: Routledge.

Davis, P., Naughton, J., and Rothwell, W. J. 2004. New roles and competencies for the profession. *T&D* 58(4): 26–36.

Dewe, P., and Cooper, C. L. 2007. Coping research and measurement in the context of work related stress. *International Review of Industrial and Organizational Psychology* 22: 141–192.

Dierdorff, E. C., Surface, E. A., and Brown, K. G. 2010. Frame-of-reference training effectiveness: Effects of goal orientation and self-efficacy on affective,
cognitive, skill-based, and transfer outcomes. *Journal of Applied Psychology*
95(6): 1181–1191.

Dinero, D. 2005. *Training Within Industry: The Foundation of Lean.* Portland, OR:
Productivity Press.

Dooley, L. M., 2004. AHRD and ASTD: Competitors or collaborators? *Human Resource
Development Quarterly* 15(4): 359–361.

Ellinger, A. D. 2014. Celebrating 25 years of HRD scholarship: Happy silver anniversary Human Resource Development Quarterly! *Human Resource Development
Quarterly* 25(1): 1–3.

Farr, J. L. 1997. Organized I/O psychology: Past, present, future. SIOP Presidential
Address, April 11, St. Louis. http://www.siop.org/tip/backissues/tipjul97/Farr
.aspx (accessed June 12, 2015).

Ford, J. K., ed. 2014. *Improving Training Effectiveness in Work Organizations.* East
Sussex, UK: Psychology Press.

Goldstein, I. L. 1974. *Training: Program Development and Evaluation.* Monterey,
CA: Brooks/Cole.

Goldstein, I. L. 1980. Training in work organizations. *Annual Review of Psychology* 31:
229–272.

Goldstein, I. L., and Ford, K. 2002. *Training in Organizations: Needs Assessment,
Development, and Evaluation*, 4th ed. Boston: Wadsworth.

Gosser, K., and Cumberland, D. 2014. Employee and customer satisfaction in the restaurant industry: Research-driven interventions. http://c.ymcdn.com/sites/ahrd
.site-ym.com/resource/resmgr/Docs/scholarlyawardwinner2014.pdf   (accessed
June 2, 2015).

Grant, A. M., Passmore, J., Cavanagh, M. J., and Parker, H. M. 2010. The state of play
in coaching today: A comprehensive review of the field. *International Review of
Industrial and Organizational Psychology* 25: 125–167.

Gubbins, C., and Rousseau, D. M. 2015. Embracing translational HRD research for
evidence-based management: Let's talk about how to bridge the research–
practice gap. *Human Resource Development Quarterly* 26(2): 109–125.

Gubler, M., Arnold, J., and Coombs, C. 2014. Reassessing the protean career concept:
Empirical findings, conceptual components, and measurement. *Journal of
Organizational Behavior* S35: S23-S40.

Hamlin, B., and Stewart, J. 2011. What is HRD? A definitional review and synthesis of
the HRD domain. *Journal of European Industrial Training* 35(3): 199–220.

Hardy, C., and Tolhurst, D. 2014. Epistemological beliefs and cultural diversity matters
in management education and learning: A critical review and future directions.
Academy of Management Learning and Education 13(2): 265–289.

Hatcher, T. 2006. An editor's challenge to human resource development. *Human Resource
Development Quarterly* 17(1): 1–4.

Heller, F. A., and Clark, A. W. 1976. Personnel and human resources development.
Annual Review of Psychology 27: 405–435.

Holladay, C. L., and Quiñones, M. A. 2005. Reactions to diversity training: An international comparison. *Human Resource Development Quarterly* 16(4): 529–545.

Holton III, E. F., and Naquin, S. 2005. A critical analysis of HRD evaluation models
from a decision-making perspective. *Human Resource Development Quarterly*
16(2): 257–280.

HRDQ. 2015. HRDQ board meeting minutes, February 21.

Hutchins, H. M., and Burke, L. A. 2007. Identifying trainers' knowledge of training transfer research findings – closing the gap between research and practice. *International Journal of Training and Development* 11(4): 236–264.

Illeris, K. 2014. Adult learning. In R. F. Poell, T. S. Rocco, and G. L. Roth, eds., *Routledge Companion to Human Resource Development*, 21–29. London: Routledge.

Ireland, R. D. 2012. Management research and managerial practice: A complex and controversial relationship. *Academy of Management Learning and Education* 11(2): 263–271.

Jacobs, R. 2016. President's report to the membership, 2015. http://c.ymcdn.com/sites/ahrd.site-ym.com/resource/resmgr/Docs/2015-AHRD-Pres-Report.pdf (accessed June 1, 2015).

Jacobs, R. L. 2009. What to research? *Human Resource Development Quarterly* 20(1): 11–13.

Keefer, J., and Yap, R. 2007. Is HRD research making a difference in practice? *Human Resource Development Quarterly* 18(4): 449–455.

Kessels, J. 2014. Andragogy. In R. F. Poell, T. S. Rocco, and G. L. Roth, eds., *Routledge Companion to Human Resource Development*, 13–20. London: Routledge.

Kirkpatrick, D. 1959. Techniques for evaluating training programs. *Journal of the American Society for Training and Development* 13(11): 3–9.

Kochan, T., Finegold, D., and Osterman, P. 2012. Who can fix the "middle-skills" gap? *Harvard Business Review* 90(12): 81–90.

Koppes, L. L. n.d. A brief history of the Society for Industrial and Organizational Psychology, Inc., A Division of the APA. SIOP. http://www.siop.org/History/historynew.aspx (accessed June 12, 2014).

Koppes, L. L. 1997. Preserving the history of APA Division 14/SIOP. *The Industrial-Organizational Psychologist* 34(3): 37–39.

Kozlowski, S. W. J., and Salas, E., eds. 2009. *Learning, Training, and Development in Organizations*. New York: Routledge Academic.

Kraiger, K. 2014. Looking back and looking forward: Trends in training and development research. *Human Resource Development Quarterly* 25(4): 401–408.

Kraiger, K., ed. 2002. *Creating, Implementing, and Managing Effective Training and Development*. San Francisco: Jossey-Bass.

Latham, G. P. 1988. Human resource training and development. *Annual Review of Psychology* 39: 545–582.

Lee, M. 2014. The history, status, and future of HRD. In R. F. Poell, T. S. Rocco, and G. L. Roth, eds., *Routledge Companion to Human Resource Development*, 3–12. London: Routledge.

Leubsdorf, B. 2014. U.S. news: White House sets sights on skills gap in workforce. *Wall Street Journal*, July 23, A2.

Levy, P. E. 2009. *Industrial Organizational Psychology: Understanding the Workplace*, 3rd ed. New York: Worth.

Lyons, S., and Kuron, L. 2014. Generational differences in the workplace: A review of the evidence and directions for future research. *Journal of Organizational Behavior* S35: 139–157.

Madera, J. M., Steele, S. T., and Beier, M. 2011. The temporal effect of training utility perceptions on adopting a trained method: The role of perceived organizational support. *Human Resource Development Quarterly* 22(1): 69–86.

Major, D. A., and Cleveland, J. N. 2007. Strategies for reducing work-family conflict: Applying research and best practices from industrial and organizational psychology. *International Review of Industrial and Organizational Psychology* 22: 111–140.

McLagan, P. A. 1989. Models for HRD practice. *Training and Development Journal* 41(9): 49–59.

MED. 2014. Spring/Summer 2014 newsletter. http://division.aomonline.org/med/ (accessed October 27, 2014).

Morgeson, F. P., and Lepak, D. 2015. Five-year review (2010–2014) of the Academy of Management Human Resources Division. http://www.hrdiv.org/wp-content/uploads/2014/07/HR-Division-5-Year-Report-Final.pdf (accessed June 2, 2015).

Nadler, L. 1970. *Developing Human Resources*. Houston: Gulf Publishing.

Noe, R. A. 2013. *Employee Training and Development*, 6th ed. Burr Ridge, IL: McGraw-Hill/Irwin.

Outstanding HRD Scholar Award. 2015. Academy of Human Resource Development. http://www.ahrd.org/?outstanding_award (accessed June 12, 2015).

Personnel Psychology. 2015. http://onlinelibrary.wiley.com/journal/10.1111/(ISSN)1744-6570 (accessed June 15, 2015).

Poell, R. F., Rocco, T. S., and Roth, G. L., eds. 2014. *The Routledge Companion to Human Resource Development*. London: Routledge.

Reio, T. G. 2009. Contributing to the emergent research method conversation. *Human Resource Development Quarterly* 20(2): 143–146.

Richard A. Swanson Research Excellence Award. 2015. AHRD. http://www.ahrd.org/general/custom.asp?page=richard_a_swanson (accessed June 2, 2015).

Russ-Eft, D., Watkins, K. E., Marsick, V. J., Jacobs, R. L., and McLean, G. N. 2014. What do the next 25 years hold for HRD research in areas of our interest? *Human Resource Development Quarterly* 25(1): 5–27.

Rynes, S. L. 2012. The research-practice gap in I/O psychology and related fields: Challenges and potential solutions. In S. W. J. Kozlowski ed., *Oxford University Handbook of Organizational Psychology*, 1: 409–453. New York: Oxford University Press.

Rynes, S. L., Giluk, T. L., and Brown, K. G. 2007. The very separate worlds of academic and practitioner periodicals in human resource management: Implications for evidence-based management. *Academy of Management Journal* 50(5): 987–1008.

Rynes, S. L., Rousseau, D. M., and Barends, E. 2014. From the guest editors: Change the world: Teach evidence-based practice! *Academy of Management Learning and Education* 13(3): 305–321.

Sadler-Smith, E. 2014. HRD research and design science: Recasting interventions as artefacts. *Human Resource Development International* 17(2): 129–144.

Salas, E., and Cannon-Bowers, J. A. 2001. The science of training: A decade of progress. *Annual Review of Psychology* 52: 471–499.

Salas, E., and Kosarzycki, M. P. 2003. Why don't organizations pay attention to (and use) findings from the science of training? *Human Resource Development Quarterly* 14(4): 487–491.

Salas, E., Cannon-Bowers, J. A., Rhodenizer, L., and Bowers, C. A. 1999. Training in organizations: Myths, misconceptions, and mistaken assumptions. *Research in Personnel and Human Resources Management* 17: 123–162.

Salas, E., Tannenbaum, S. I., Kraiger, K., and Smith-Jentsch, K. A. 2012. The science of training and development in organizations: What matters in practice. *Psychological Science* 13(2): 74–101.

Schmitt, N., and Ford, J. K. 2014. Frederick R. Wickert (1912–2013). *American Psychologist* 69(3): 304.

Short, D. C. 2006. Closing the gap between research and practice in HRD. *Human Resource Development Quarterly* 17(3): 343–350.

SHRM. 2015. Michael R. Losey Excellence in Human Resource Research Award. http://www.shrm.org/about/awards/pages/loseyaward.aspx (accessed June 19, 2015).

Silzer, R., and Parson, C. 2013. Trends in SIOP membership, graduate education, and member satisfaction. *TIP: The Industrial-Organizational Psychologist* 50(4): 135–149.

SIOP Fellows. 2014. Society for Industrial and Organizational Psychology. http://www.siop.org/siop_fellows.aspx (accessed October 8, 2014).

SIOP Membership Services. 2015. Personal communication, June 2.

Soken, N. H., and Barnes, K B. 2014. What kills innovation? Your role as a leader in supporting an innovative culture. *Industrial and Commercial Training* 46(1): 7–15.

Stanhope, D. S., Pond III, S. B., and Surface, E. A. 2013. Core self-evaluations and training effectiveness: Prediction through motivational intervening mechanisms. *Journal of Applied Psychology* 98(5): 820–831.

Swanson, R. A., and Holton, E. F., III 2009. *Foundations of Human Resource Development*, 2nd ed. San Francisco: Berrett-Koehler.

Tannenbaum, S. I., and Yukl, G. 1992. Training and development in work organizations. *Annual Review of Psychology* 43: 399–441.

Tsui, A. S. 2013. Making research engaged: Implications for HRD scholarship. *Human Resource Development Quarterly* 24(2): 137–143.

U.S. Census Bureau, Statistical Abstract of the United States. 2012. Education: Higher education: Degrees. Table 302, p. 190. Bachelor's degrees earned by field: 1980–2009. https://www.census.gov/compendia/statab/2012/tables/12s0302.pdf (accessed June 12, 2015).

Wang, G. G., Sun, J. Y., Werner, J. M., Gilley, J. W., and Gilley, A. 2015. Re-conceptualizing the definition of HRD: A gateway to new research frontiers. Paper presented at the 2015 *Academy of Human Resource Development International Conference*, St. Louis, MS.

Werner, J. M. 2014. Human resource management and HRD: Connecting the dots, or ships passing in the night? In R. F. Poell, T. S. Rocco, and G. L. Roth, eds. *Routledge Companion to Human Resource Development*, 89–98. London: Routledge.

Werner, J. M. 2017. *Human Resource Development/Talent Development*, 7th ed. Mason, OH: Cengage.

Werner, J. M., and DeSimone, R. L. 2012. *Human Resource Development*, 6th ed. Mason, OH: Cengage.

Wexley, K. N. 1984. Personnel training. *Annual Review of Psychology* 35: 519–551.

Wexley, K. N., and Latham, G. P. 1981. *Developing and Training Human Resources in Organizations*. Glenview, IL: Scott, Foresman.

Wexley, K. N., and Latham, G. P. 2001. *Developing and Training Human Resources in Organizations*, 3rd ed. Glenview, IL: Scott, Foresman.

Wood, J. 2015. Personal communication, editorial assistant, *Journal of Applied Psychology*, June 17.

23 Strategic Training and Development and Their Role in Shaping Competitive Advantage

Lynn A. McFarland and Robert E. Ployhart

There is little question that human capital is one of the most important resources for competitive advantage. Perhaps this is because, more than any other resource, human resources have the potential to differentiate an organization from competitors (Nyberg et al., 2014). The modern economy is volatile, uncertain, complex, and ambiguous (Bigley & Roberts, 2001). Firm success is increasingly based on innovation, information, service, and teamwork (Ployhart & Hale, 2014). Hence, human resources are vital to organizational success for many firms, and must be a central component of any organizational strategy.

These changes place human resource professionals right in the center of organizational strategy; a place they may be unfamiliar with and potentially even uncomfortable. But human resource professionals should not shy away from their central role in developing and implementing organizational strategy. This is arguably the opportunity human resource managers have been waiting for; to be recognized as having a strong impact on organizational success and demonstrate the strategic value of human resource.

Training and development practices should be among the most powerful approaches human resource managers have to shape the quality of human capital resources – and by extension, strategic competitive advantage. The question is, *how does this occur?* Most research in strategic human resource management has focused on linking training and development practices to firm-level financial outcomes (Huselid, 1995; Jiang et al., 2012). This research is obviously important but does not pose or answer the question about how this occurs (Becker & Huselid, 2006). Answering this "how" question requires a multilevel and multidisciplinary approach that integrates the large literature on training and development in the "micro" literatures of industrial/organizational (I/O) psychology, human resource, and organizational behavior (OB).

This chapter will review the strategic importance of training and development in shaping human capital resources and contributing to competitive advantage. We first review the current landscape that requires training and development to play a central role in the implementation of organizational strategy. Second, we elaborate on the idea of building strategic human capital through training and development and the ways in which training and development can help generate competitive advantage. Third, we will provide strategies to help ensure that training and development efforts are aligned with strategic objectives to increase the likelihood that these interventions help the organization achieve a competitive advantage. Finally, we conclude with a discussion of directions for future research and practice.

The Importance of Training and Development in Strategy

Recruitment and selection are the first steps in the process of creating human resources that align with organizational strategy. Organizations can and should design recruitment materials and initiatives to attract appropriate individuals to organizational roles and use selection processes that will most effectively allow them to hire the appropriate individuals to implement the organization's strategy (Dubey & Gunasekaran, 2015; Ployhart, 2015; Ployhart, 2006; Simon et al., 2013). However, recruitment and selection can only accomplish so much. The landscape in which organizations must function is rapidly changing (Bigley & Roberts, 2001). Specifically, there are several demographic and environmental shifts that make it difficult to simply acquire the desired talent through recruitment and selection. These changes include baby boomer retirements and an increasing mismatch in education/skill versus employer needs. The result is a greater need for strategically oriented training and development efforts.

Increase in Retirements and Lack of Labor Participation

First, a defining characteristic of the baby-boomer generation is the sheer number of individuals in this generation. Baby boomers are aging and as they age, they are inevitably going to retire or pass away, leaving their former jobs to be filled (Carnevale, 2005). This results in organizations within all industries losing many of their most experienced employees; a disproportionate number of whom are organizational leaders. These departures leave a gaping hole for organizations to fill (Bluestone & Melnik, 2010; Venneberg & Eversole, 2010). Unfortunately, the generation poised to inherit many roles once held by these baby boomers, are too few to actually fill those positions. Not only are they simply lower in number (i.e., the birthrates declined after the baby boomers), but these younger groups are slightly less likely to be looking for employment than their baby-boomer counterparts (largely due to higher disability rates and the pursuing of higher education; Fujita, 2014). Therefore, this is simply a problem of having too few individuals entering a system from which too many are leaving.

Increase in Skills Gap

The second issue that compounds this generational talent shortage is the lack of individuals with the skills needed by organizations. There is a skills gap such that the types of skills organizations need to implement strategic objectives are not the skills being taught by those educating the incoming workforce (Atkinson, 1990; Capelli, 1995; Carnevale, Smith, & Strohl, 2010; Mckensey Global Institute, 2012). Therefore, we currently have a situation in which there are too few individuals available to fill important organizational roles and even those that are potential candidates for those roles typically do not possess the skills necessary to help organizations achieve their goals.

Thus, the burden lies on training and development to mold those who do not quite meet organizational needs but have the potential to do so, in such a manner that the organization gains a competitive advantage. One organization has gone so far as to coin the term *Teachable Fit* (ManPowerGroup, 2010) to refer to the fact that organizations cannot rely on the talent pool to provide the types of employees needed; they must hire employees that can be molded to fit the needs of the organization. Certainly, some skills are more difficult to teach than others and some characteristics may be a requirement of a job. For example, certain personality traits may be considered "a must" or a certain level of intelligence may be required. By contrast, things like written and oral communication skills can be taught if incoming employees do not have those skills. The key would be to identify individuals that have the proper basic personality traits and skills required for a particular job and then train the individuals to develop the skills they lack. In other words, organizations should not hire for the job, but hire individuals with the potential to be trained for the job.

The challenge of training employees because they are not immediately qualified may seem like a tremendous burden. However, this situation offers opportunity for organizations. Because training and development efforts will be required to get these employees prepared, organizations can use this effort to immediately begin ensuring the employees are not only trained on the necessary content, but ensure that the training is also aligned with organizational strategic objectives. Moreover, training can be used to further align the individual employee with those organizational objectives. In this way, alignment can be embedded in the on-boarding and training process. The current situation both requires and allows us to define fit broadly so as to include a whole array of concepts relevant to having strategically aligned human capital; thereby thrusting training and development into the vital role of developing strategic human capital.

We are certainly not the first to advocate that training and development be used to help organizations achieve strategic objectives (e.g., Kozlowski et al., 2000; Martocchio & Baldwin, 1997; Olian et al., 1998; Robinson & Robinson, 1989). However, despite the growing awareness that the two should be linked, little is explicitly stated about how to do so in the literature. In the next two sections, we will elaborate on the idea of building strategic human capital through training and development and the ways in which training and development can help generate competitive advantage; and then the best process for ensuring training and development are aligned with strategic objectives.

Competitive Advantage, Performance, and Strategic Resources

Organizational strategy is fundamentally concerned with making choices: where will a firm compete, how will it compete, and which resources will it leverage to create a competitive advantage (Barney, 1991; Porter, 1980)? Strategy explains why a firm exists and how it differentiates itself from competitors (and for most firms, how it makes money). A primary goal of strategy is to create a competitive advantage that is reasonably enduring and sustainable. Competitive advantage can be loosely defined in terms of a firm generating above-normal (or supranormal) economic returns, relative to competitors (Peteraf & Barney, 2003). That is, firms that achieve competitive advantage generate excessive returns relative to their inputs or what a competitor is able to achieve with similar inputs. Thus, strategy is about finding a sustainable way to differentiate the firm to achieve supranormal economic outcomes. Competitive advantage is always defined in reference to competitors, and thus is heavily influenced by factor markets and competitive environments (Barney, 1986; Campbell, Coff, & Kryscynski, 2012).

Competitive advantage is not the same as organizational performance (Barney & Wright, 1998; Ployhart et al., 2014). Organizational performance generally refers to the effectiveness by which a firm achieves key outcomes. These outcomes are most frequently market based (e.g., customer satisfaction), financial (sales), or accounting based (earnings before interest and taxes; Richard et al., 2009). Organizational performance can further be decomposed into external and internal performance. External performance is affected by factors both inside and outside the firm (e.g., profit, sales, earnings before interest, and taxes). Internal performance is affected by factors primarily inside the firm (e.g., worker productivity).

Organizational performance is related to competitive advantage, as a firm that performs poorly will have difficulty differentiating itself from competitors to achieve supranormal profits. But high performance is itself an insufficient condition for competitive advantage. Most firms compete based on performance and seek to maintain parity with competitors (Barney & Wright, 1998). A competitive parity exists when a firm is performing similarly, perhaps even better, then competitors, but is generating "normal" economic outcomes. However, when a firm performs very poorly, it can create a competitive disadvantage. Distinctions between competitive advantage, performance, parity, and disadvantage can be found in Barney and Wright (1998), Ployhart (2012), and Ployhart et al. (2014).

The reason it is important to understand these different types of organizational outcomes is because they are the targets around which strategy is based (Porter, 1980). Ployhart and Hale (2014) developed a functionalist view of strategy to summarize this process. A firm starts by developing a strategy to achieve competitive advantage through differentiation. This strategy then points to relevant external, and then internal, performance metrics that operationalize the strategy. From the identification of these metrics, it now becomes possible to develop a talent strategy that reinforces the firm's organizational strategy.

Talent Strategy and Strategic Human Capital Resources

A talent strategy explains how a firm will use its talent to implement the firm's strategy. A talent strategy determines how various organizational and human resource principles, policies, practices, and products (Posthuma et al., 2013) relate to implementing the firm's differentiation strategy. A talent strategy makes difficult decisions: Which employee groups and employees are critical and which play a more supporting role? Which human resource practices should be favored over others? How does a firm compete based on talent? Many equate talent strategy with workforce planning, but they are very different (Martin, 2014). Talent strategy is about making uncomfortable, difficult choices to achieve competitive advantage using talent. Planning is the slightly more comforting activity of determining how one will implement the talent strategy.

A talent strategy should start from the metrics emphasized by a firm's organizational strategy, and translate those metrics into resources that can influence those performance metrics. *Resources* are capacities for action that can be leveraged or accessed by the firm to influence performance outcomes and competitive advantage (Barney, 1991; Kraaijenbrink, Spender, & Groen, 2010; Wernerfelt, 1984). *Human capital resources* are "individual or unit-level capacities based on individual knowledge skills, abilities, and other characteristics (KSAOs) that are accessible for unit-relevant purposes," and *strategic human capital resources* are those that contribute to competitive advantage (Ployhart et al., 2014: 376).

A major reason strategy scholars have focused on human capital resources underlying competitive advantage is because they contain a number of unique characteristics that differentiate the firm in a manner that is difficult or costly for competitors to imitate (Barney & Wright, 1998; Coff, 1997). Because work is increasingly knowledge, team based, and service based, the unique characteristics of human capital resources are *valuable*. Having the right types of human capital resources, in the needed quantity, is *rare*. Human capital resources are also difficult or costly to imitate (*inimitability*), as building them is based on path-dependent processes that are causally ambiguous and socially complex. Finally, such resources may also be difficult or costly to substitute (nonsubstitutability).

Recent strategic management research has begun to examine how firms can build capabilities to manage resource portfolios or bundles. For example, Sirmon, Hitt, and Ireland (2007) present a framework of resource orchestration. They identify three broad sets of processes needed for structuring the resource portfolio. These processes can be mapped onto human capital resources and human resource. *Acquiring* processes relate to recruitment and selection activities intended to bring new human capital into the firm. *Accumulating* processes involve the internal development of resources, primarily through training and development activities. *Divesting* processes relate to compensation and performance management practices, and relate to retention and turnover. Thus, management's role is to create capabilities for structuring, bundling, and leveraging these resources to create a competitive advantage through talent strategy and organizational strategy.

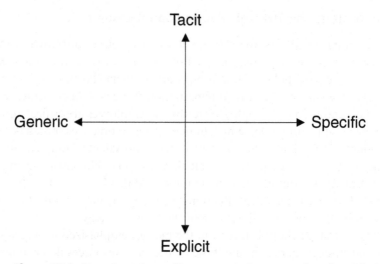

Figure 23.1. *Broad typology of human capital resources based on Ployhart and Moliterno (2011).*

Types of Human Capital Resources

The focus on human capital resources is therefore the gateway through which training and development activities, as well as micro human resource, OB, and I/O psychology, relate to competitive advantage (Ployhart & Hale, 2014). Human capital resources play a central role in the development of a talent strategy. However, there are different types of human capital resources. Figure 23.1 presents a broad typology of different types of human capital resources that is loosely based on a framework presented by Ployhart and Moliterno (2011). The first dimension is whether the resource is generic or specific. Generic human capital resources can be applied to different firms and contexts (e.g., cognitive ability), while specific human capital resources can only be applied to a specific firm or context (e.g., knowledge of a firm's managers and politics). The second dimension is whether the resource is explicit or tacit. Explicit resources may be codified and can be taught or learned through activities such as lectures or reading. Tacit resources are those that can more easily be learned by experience and are nearly impossible to codify or explain.

Each of these different types of human capital resources may exist at different organizational levels: individual, team, business unit (e.g., departments, stores), and firm. Human capital resources that exist at levels higher than the individual are not usually the simple aggregation of individual resources. Rather, through a process of resource emergence, higher-level resources will usually be similar but not identical to lower-level resources (Ployhart & Moliterno, 2011). Resource emergence occurs when lower-level KSAOs are transformed into a distinct, higher-level resource as a result of task demands requiring coordination, collaboration, and interaction (Kozlowski & Klein, 2000). Generally speaking, the greater the amount of interaction required among lower levels, the greater the distinctiveness of the higher-level resource. Thus, the antecedents and consequences will usually differ across levels, even when the higher-level resource is based on the combination of lower-level resources (e.g., firm-level cognitive resources are aggregations of lower-level cognitive ability).

The prevailing notion has been that human capital resources that are specific and/or tacit are expected to more strongly generate competitive advantage (Nyberg et al., 2014). The reason is because these types of resources are more valuable, rare, difficult to imitate, and hard to substitute (Barney, 1991). These arguments are based on human capital theory from economics (Becker, 1964).

However, recent research has challenged these prior assumptions and generated several new perspectives explaining how human capital resources can generate competitive advantage (Ployhart et al., 2014). First, there are many different types of human capital resources that reflect the KSAOs from which they originated. For example, there may exist cognitive and noncognitive human capital resources that may each individually, and in combination, contribute to competitive advantage (notice that both types of resources are generic). Second, even generic or explicit resources may underlie competitive advantage when they are based on aggregations of people or involve close coordination, because the process of aggregation is firm specific (Ployhart & Moliterno, 2011; Ployhart et al., 2014). For example, a firm-level human capital resource may be based on the emergence of many individuals, as a consequence of task demands that require great coordination. This resource cannot easily be duplicated by a competitor because it is based on collaborations among individuals. Further, if an employee leaves then the relationships, transactive memory, and shared knowledge must be rebuilt with a new employee – all of which take time. Hence, the specificity of human capital resources is nearly guaranteed when it is based on the aggregations of individuals.

With this understanding of competitive advantage, organizational performance, and human capital resources, it is finally possible to appreciate how and why training and development might influence firm performance and competitive advantage. It will be argued that training and development do not generate competitive advantage because they improve firm performance (although that is a noble goal), but rather because they shape the nature of human capital resources that can be leveraged to differentiate the firm.

Building Strategic Human Capital through Training and Development

There is already considerable evidence demonstrating that training and development generally accomplish the intended purpose to increase individual performance (Aguinis & Kraiger, 2003; Arthur et al., 2003; Lent & Hill, 2006; Satterfield & Hughes, 2007). Further, training and development have also been shown to affect antecedents of performance such as tacit knowledge, declarative knowledge, innovation, self-efficacy, and adaption to multi-cultural settings (Barber, 2004)

Beyond individual-level effects, some research has shown that training and development interventions have effects at both the unit and organizational levels as well. Two large-scale reviews and meta-analyses demonstrate effects of training and development on firm-level outcomes, but the effect sizes are quite variable (Nguyen, Truong, & Buyens, 2010; Tharenou, Saks, & Moore, 2007). In general, training and development can have reasonably strong influences on performance outcomes internal to the firm (e.g., productivity (Zwick, 2006). The effects become weaker as one extends the outcomes to external performance (e.g., financial performance). There have now been studies linking firm differences in training and development to unit-level employee commitment and competence, customer satisfaction, innovation (self-reported), and firm internal and external performance (Hatch & Dyer, 2004; Kim & Ployhart, 2014; Ployhart, Van Iddekinge, & MacKenzie, 2011; Sung & Choi, 2014; Van Iddekinge et al., 2009). While some research supports more universal relationships between firm-level training and development and outcomes (Tharenou et al., 2007), other studies find these relationships moderated by broader economic conditions (Kim & Ployhart, 2014).

Despite the great amount of research devoted to demonstrating the links between training and development efforts and performance and outcomes at both the individual and unit levels, little research has empirically demonstrated that alignment between organizational strategic objectives in the training and development process is related to outcomes (see Tharenou et al., 2007; for a few notable exceptions). This limited support should not be perceived as evidence that such a link fails to exist. Rather, we believe the failure to show such relationships lies with the fact that: (1) few organizations explicitly consider strategy in their training and development efforts and (2) most research is single level rather than multilevel.

Figure 23.2 addresses these concerns by illustrating how training and development contribute to competitive advantage through shaping the nature of human capital resource emergence. First, as based on a wealth of individual-level research, it is known that different training and development methods and practices will influence the creation of KSAOs. We noted earlier how these KSAOs may differ in terms of general and specific KSAOs (see Figure 23.1). While training may primarily lead to the creation of explicit knowledge, it is possible to build tacit knowledge through methods such as on-the-job training, apprenticeships, job shadowing, mentoring, and role plays. Thus, different training and development methods will lead to different types of KSAOs. These individual KSAOs, in turn, are the elements that are combined through a process of human capital resource emergence to become unit-level human capital resources (Ployhart & Moliterno, 2011).

As described in the prior section, different types of human capital resources will influence internal performance, external performance, and potentially competitive advantage. In general, tacit human capital resources should be more

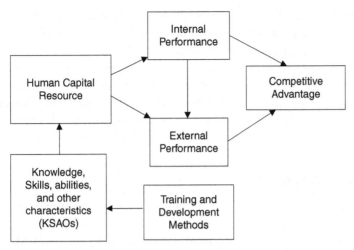

Figure 23.2. *Model predicting strategic human capital.*

closely linked to performance outcomes and competitive advantage (Hitt et al., 2001). However, in contrast to human capital theory predictions, both generic and specific human capital resources may underlie competitive advantage when they exist at the unit level through a process of resource emergence (i.e., aggregation) and are bundled with other resources (Ployhart et al., 2014).

What is perhaps most noteworthy about Figure 23.2 is that it recognizes the inherent multilevel/cross-level nature of strategic training and development. The review by Tharenou et al. (2007) clearly indicates there is essentially no empirical cross-level research on training and development (see also Kozlowski et al., 2001). The theoretical explanation for why training and development methods influence firm performance is because they influence the content and emergence of human capital resources, and it is the human capital resources that influence performance and competitive advantage. Hence, in contrast to most prior research, the effect of training and development on firm performance is not direct but rather mediated and cross-level.

A Process for Leveraging Training and Development for Competitive Advantage

For training and development to create strategic human capital, and thus create a competitive advantage, one must first ensure that training and development are aligned with business strategy (Kraiger & Ford, 2006; Tannenbaum, 2002). Several steps can be taken to make sure training and development efforts are aligned with the organization's strategic plan. In fact, research has shown that training and development efforts that are aligned with strategic objectives are more likely to result in learning transferring to the job (Carnevale, Gainer, & Viller, 1990; Cassner-Lotto & Associates, 1988). Given this, there is considerable discussion in the literature regarding the best ways to ensure alignment (Kraiger

& Culbertson, 2013; Kraiger & Ford, 2006). But to really ensure training and development are aligned with organizational objectives we need to push these efforts beyond the needs assessment stage.

We propose that strategic objectives should be considered at all stages and checks should be in place to ensure that alignment is on track. Therefore, we will go through the major stages of the traditional training design process and note ways alignment between strategy and training and development may be achieved. We begin this discussion with the needs assessment.

Assessing Training Needs

As noted by others, to ensure that training and development interventions are aligned with organizational strategy the training design, subject matter, and training medium must all be considered (Brown & Gerhardt, 2002). Most major training and development models include needs assessment as the first step (Goldstein, 1993).

Several aspects of the needs assessment lend themselves to the consideration of organizational strategy, which will help ensure training and development efforts are aligned (Noe, Clarke, & Klein, 2014; Reed & Vakola, 2006). In fact, most descriptions of needs assessment suggest that the first step should include an organization analysis (Kraiger & Culbertson, 2013; Noe, 2014). It is advised that the organization analysis explicitly consider the strategic goals of the organization when designing a training and development program (Noe, 2012). The thinking is that, before one can develop a training and development program to meet the needs of an organization, the organization's strategy must first be considered to ensure that any program that is implemented is consistent with the strategy and helps the organization achieve the targeted goals. The organization analysis typically involves interviewing high-ranking organizational members to ensure the strategy is understood and how the training and development program might fit within the context of that strategy.

A second task during the needs assessment is to gather a list of tasks and competencies required for the job (Kraiger & Culbertson, 2013; Noe, 2012). This step will involve interviewing key stakeholders and asking them about the types of characteristics their employees require to do the job well. However, it is important to ask these same stakeholders what KSAOs their employees need to contribute to the organizational strategy by contributing to a strong organizational competitive advantage. In other words, it is important to work backward. We must begin with a discussion of what employee characteristics are likely to lead to the ability to do the job well, but also the characteristics that will help the organization gain a competitive advantage. This distinction is similar to one made in the organizational fit literature (Kristof-Brown, Zimmerman, & Johnson 2005; Maden & Kabasakal, 2014). There has been much discussion about the difference between individuals that are a good fit for a job, versus individuals that are a good fit for an organization (O'Reilly, Chatman, & Caldwell 1991). Some individuals may be technically qualified for a particular role or job, but not have the characteristics necessary to help the organization achieve its strategy. For example, imagine a software developer that is exceedingly qualified to do programing required for jobs at both Google and IBM. However, the software developer is not comfortable being innovative and prefers a structured work environment. This software developer would arguably not be a good fit with Google. The individual is probably less likely to contribute to Google's organizational strategy than other equally qualified employees that may be a better fit for the innovative and unstructured environment of Google.

This same issue must be considered when we are in the midst of a needs assessment. If we want to be sure that training and development efforts help the organization achieve organizational strategy by training employees not just on the KSAOs they require for the job tasks they will engage in, but to best serve the organization and help it achieve objectives, we must explicitly consider those characteristics needed to achieve the higher-level organizational goals. An example might be training cleaning staff at a high-end hotel on service. This hotel may have the strategic goal of being the top in customer satisfaction among their competitors. Even with only limited customer contact, the cleaning staff's knowledge and commitment to service may alter how they interact with other staff in ways that support better overall customer satisfaction; potentially leading to a competitive advantage for the organization.

The tasks and competencies important for both the job and the organization should be reviewed by key organizational stakeholders that are aware and supportive of the organizational strategy, to ensure an adequate list is developed. These stakeholders should specifically be asked if they believe the tasks and competencies identified will help achieve the organization's strategy and lead to competitive advantage. Depending on the outcome of this evaluation, the tasks and competencies can be edited accordingly.

Another important step in the needs assessment that presents an opportunity to consider organizational strategy is the person analysis. The purpose of this analysis is to determine if the employees in the roles (under consideration for the training and development effort) really require training, and if so, what type of training might help address any deficiencies found. For example, during the person analysis it is important to determine if the lack of performance is due to external circumstances that have nothing to do with the employees. For instance, perhaps employees do not have the equipment they need to perform the job as it should be performed. If that is the case, training is not the issue and instead the organization should devote resources toward getting the equipment necessary to get the employees to perform well. Further, it may not be a lack of skill with the job but an issue of the employees not understanding how their job fits within the larger context of the organization's strategy. If this is the case, the employees do not need training on the skills required for the job, they may simply need training about how their role fits within the organization. Thus, the training will need to focus on educating employees about the organization's strategy as opposed to skills.

There is a good deal of research that can help organizations communicate their strategy to employees (Andrews et al., 2012). The first step is to ensure the organization's strategy is clear and direct enough to be easily digested by employees at all levels of the organization and this requires that the strategic plan be clear, attainable, and realistic (Ayers, 2015; Rajasekar, 2013). However, even with a clear and realistic strategic plan an organization may still need to demonstrate how an employee's actions can lead to their contribution to the strategic plan. In other words, it is helpful to operationalize the definitions for them so it is easier to see how their performance links to organizational success.

Some have suggested that organizations go so far as to create a "value map" that can help translate organizational strategy (Dickinson & Puleo, 2008; MacLean, 2005). This can be done in several ways. As an example, one might use a question and answer format. Provide a document that includes frequently asked questions (FAQ) about the organization's strategic plan. For example, it might include answers to questions such as: How does our organization define success? What outcomes will we examine to determine if we have been successful? How does your role contribute to organizational success? The bottom line is that when employees understand how their roles relate to organizational success, they are more likely to engage in those behaviors. It is also important that employees know you will be linking their rewards to the types of behaviors that will contribute to a competitive advantage. This will further highlight the organizational strategy and demonstrate the organization's commitment to the objectives.

Ensuring Transfer of Training

There already exists a large literature that provides excellent advice for how to ensure training transfers to the job (Broad & Newstrom, 1992; Haung, Ford, & Ryan, 2016; Noe, 2012). Whether we are trying to transfer job skills to the job or skills specific to the organization's strategic alignment, the same advice should hold true. However, we need to be careful that we do not just focus our attention on transferring the basic skills required for the job. We must be equally vigilant about ensuring that those skills that are deemed most relevant for generating a competitive advantage are also transferred back to the workplace. The transfer literature provides many useful strategies to accomplish this goal. For example, managers should be told of the importance of the newly learned skills and strongly encourage employees to demonstrate them in the workplace. Employees should even be rewarded for engaging in those behaviors. Trainees who believe that initiatives are supported by the organization and that the organization will follow up to ensure they learned what was expected, are more likely to transfer what they learned (Baldwin & Magjuka, 1991). Organizations should be sure to invest in posttraining interventions like booster training, follow-up meetings with supervisors, and mentoring and coaching, when transfer is critical to both job and organizational outcomes. Interventions that foster more rich communication are likely critical for ensuring the transfer of tacit knowledge.

There are already excellent sources to aid researchers and professionals to determine if the work environment supports transfer (e.g., Tannenbaum, 1997) and we do not see any reason why these same strategies would not work when strategic content is the focus.

Selecting Training Methods

The training methods selected should allow for the instruction of the material needed to be taught (Noe, 2012). For instance, research suggests that explicit knowledge may be easily conveyed through lecture or online instruction. However, tacit knowledge can rarely be easily conveyed using these approaches. Tacit knowledge usually requires more hand-on approaches such as role plays, business games, on-the-job training, work assignments (with performance support), or action learning. As noted previously, tacit knowledge is thought to make a stronger contribution to competitive advantage. Therefore, these latter methods may be more likely to yield desirable outcomes as far as human capital is concerned.

Evaluation

The fact that evaluation is typically listed as the last step in the training and development process should not be taken to mean that an evaluation plan should be a final consideration. In fact, the evaluation plan should be considered early in the training and development design process. Further, evaluation of the training program does not occur only when the training and development program is complete. Evaluations of the effectiveness of completed interventions should occur. These types of evaluations, that occur after the intervention has implemented, are referred to as summative evaluations. However, as noted by Brown and Gerhardt (2002), formative evaluations are also vitally important. Formative evaluations are done during the design phase of training and developments interventions. This may involve having stakeholders evaluate training goals before the intervention is designed. Or, it may involve a pilot test of the intervention on a group of subject matter experts prior to full implementation, so that changes might be made before the intervention is finalized.

With respect to aligning interventions with organizational strategic objectives, it seems formative evaluations are more crucial than summative evaluations. After all, once an intervention has been implemented it is too late to change it to ensure the efforts adequately reflect the organization's objectives. Using formative evaluations will allow one to alter the invention before it is implemented to ensure alignment occurs. However, the literature has little to say regarding how to use formative evaluation to achieve alignment. Brown and Gerhardt (2002) offer excellent advice for how to best use formative evaluation for optimum results. The key is to ensure, throughout the training and development design process, that the intervention adequately reflects the organization's goals.

A crucial step to ensure this is to constantly check-in with organizational stakeholders and get their opinions to ensure the interventions adequately reflect the strategic objectives of the organization.

Reevaluate

An important issue to consider is the fast rate of change in the environments in which organizations operate. For an organization to thrive, it must adapt to these changing conditions and this will inevitably result in changes in strategic objectives (Tannenbaum, 2002). The implications for training and development are clear. These interventions must adapt along with the strategic directions of the organization. Training or development programs should not be put in place and expected to fit the organization's needs for years to come. Instead, these programs must be evaluated routinely to ensure they are still aligned with the needs of the organization. Routine reevaluation requires that need assessments are not something done and then discarded. They must constantly be updated. To ensure training and development interventions adapt to these changes Tannenbaum (2002) suggests that organizations should ask themselves regularly: How have our goals changed? What are the key KSAOs needed for talent to help meet those new goals? Are our current training and development initiatives targeting those KSAOs?

Directions for Future Research

While our current literature offers many insights into how one might proceed to ensure that training and development initiatives contribute to competitive advantage, we have much to learn about how strategy and training might best be linked. We are just beginning to understand the profound impact an alignment of strategy and training and development may have on competitive advantage. We outline some specific areas we think need immediately research.

The first thing we should examine is the impact of culture on our current understanding of this literature. Almost all the literature on training and development is based on Western samples (Noe, Clarke, & Klein, 2014). Like other areas in organizations, the training and development function operates on a global scale. Therefore, we need to go beyond examining these issues with just a Western perspective, but consider that the strategies we have used all these years may not yield similar results when we apply them in other cultures. For example, in some cultures, certain stakeholders may not offer useful information or may even provide information that can decrease the alignment between interventions and organizational strategy. Further, while in some cultures it may be useful to include customers in the process of securing alignment, this approach may not be as effective in other cultures. We simply do not know enough about alignment, let alone how different sources and strategies to ensure alignment may translate to other cultures. This should be the focus of research efforts.

Second, many advocate that alignment efforts should focus on key or strategic roles (Becker & Huselid, 2006). However, there does not seem to be research that has actually empirically examined if this is the best course of action. Perhaps it would be best for organizational strategy to be embedded in the training and development process for all roles. Certainly, it is easier to embed strategic objectives within the context of training for some types of knowledge or competencies versus others. For example, it is easier to see how strategic objectives may best be considered when developing a training program for high-level leaders. But, it may be equally important to ensure even those operating within the most basic levels of the organization are aware of and share the organizational objectives. It may not seem important to include organizational strategic objectives into a training program for custodians within Boeing offices, for instance, but just imagine what might be accomplished if, even at these levels in the organization, the organizational objectives are known and shared among all employees. An explicit focus on only individuals in the strategic core creates equity problems that may inhibit knowledge sharing and teamwork; while training the broader employee population about organizational strategy and how they can contribute to it may increase cohesiveness and knowledge sharing. The potential benefits of embedding the organization's strategic objectives in all training and development programs can be great, while risks seem minimal. It will be important for future research to examine the effects of alignment between organizational strategy and training and development efforts for key roles versus more generic roles within the organization. It may be that the generic roles benefit more when the training efforts are aligned with strategy as compared to when the same approach is used for key roles. It will also be important to identify precisely how such training may lead to positive outcomes at each level. For example, connecting training to organization objectives may help create a sense of meaning and purpose that motivates learners to perform at their best for the organization. It may have the added benefit of encouraging trainees to learn and transfer what they have learned. That information would be useful to have and could help develop best practices.

Third, there are questions about how to explain alignment during training initiatives, when training is the means through which strategy is being communicated. For example, is it better to include a discussion, in the training program, explicitly about what the organization's strategic objectives are and how they relate to the person's role, or should we include strategic objectives even when we consider the content of training and development? For example, perhaps in all aspects of the training we should be demonstrating how a task fits within the larger context of an organization's strategy. In this way, the strategic objectives are both explicitly stated and implicitly conveyed throughout training and development efforts. Or, is it not worth the time and effort to weave strategy into training and development because the outcomes are not substantial enough?

Fourth, how does one best align training with other human resource functions and practices to achieve a firm's strategy? We know that firms that use bundles of high-performance work practices outperform those that do not (e.g., Jiang et al., 2012), but we know very little about how such practices should be internally aligned to achieve different strategic outcomes. For example, should a firm in a highly volatile industry emphasize more rigorous selection over training? An emphasis on selection contributes to developing higher-quality generic human capital resources, which enable greater firm flexibility. What combination of investments in selection versus training "pay off" most and is this combination dependent on industry type? Alternatively, perhaps the firm should focus more on training generic competencies and using compensation as a means to retain the desired talent. Clearly a firm that has poorly aligned human resource practices should suffer a competitive disadvantage, but do firms with more aligned human resource practices outperform those with practices less well-aligned?

Finally, research needs to better understand how to convey the business value of training and development. We believe such efforts will be more persuasive when the story is told from a strategic management perspective than when it is told from a human resource perspective. This means doing more than showing that a training group demonstrated higher individual performance than a nontraining group; it means linking the outcomes of training to firm financial performance. For example, how did the training enable the firm to differentiate itself from competitors? How did the training contribute to implementing the firm's strategy? How might training be used to prepare a firm for a new strategic initiative? We believe the place to start this research is by studying human capital resources, because these resources are the consequence of training that is most directly linked to competitive advantage.

Conclusion

It has always been assumed that training is important for firm performance. However, the theory and evidence linking training to firm-level outcomes remains rather sparse. Most prior research is also focused primarily on operational goals and performance, rather than differentiating the firm from competitors in a manner that builds firm strategy to create a competitive advantage (Ployhart & Hale, 2014). Training should be closely aligned with a firm's strategy if it will prove valuable for competitive advantage. Yet, for firms that compete primarily using talent, training should also help drive the firm's strategy. Much more scholarly work needs to be conducted linking the concepts and theories from strategic management to the concepts and theories of training and development. We believe a focus on human capital resources provides the critical conceptual linkage needed to stimulate such research, and hope this chapter provides a vision for achieving it.

References

Aguinis, H., and Kraiger, K. 2009. Benefits of training and development for individuals and teams, organizations, and society. *Annual Review of Psychology* 60(1): 451–474.

Andrews, R. Boyne, G. A., Meier, K. J., O'Toole, L. J., and Walker, R. M. 2012. Vertical strategic alignment and public service performance. *Public Administration* 90(1): 77–98.

Arthur, W. J., Bennett, W. J., and Edens, P. S. 2003. Effectiveness of training in organizations: A meta-analysis of design and evaluation features. *Journal of Applied Psychology* 88(2): 234–245.

Atkinson, Richard C. 1990. Supply and demand for scientists and engineers: A national crisis in the making. *Science* 248(4954): 425–432.

Ayers, R. S. 2015. Aligning individual and organizational performance: Goal alignment in federal government agency performance appraisal programs. *Public Personnel Management* 44(2): 169–191.

Baldwin, T. T., and Magjuka, R. J. 1991. Organizational training and signals of importance: Linking pre-training perceptions to intentions to transfer. *Human Resource Development Quarterly* 2: 25–36.

Barber, J. 2004. Skill upgrading within informal training: lessons from the Indian auto mechanic. *International Journal of Training & Development* 8(2): 128–139.

Barney, J. B. 1991. Firm resources and sustained competitive advantage. *Journal of Management* 17: 99–120.

Barney, J. B. 1986. Types of competition and the theory of strategy: Toward an integrative framework. *Academy of Management Review* 11(4): 791–800.

Barney, J. B., and Wright, P. M. 1998. On becoming a strategic partner: The role of human resources in gaining competitive advantage. *Human Resource Management* 37: 31–46.

Becker, B. E., and Huselid, M. A. 2006. Strategic human resources management: Where do we go from here? *Journal of Management* 32: 898–925.

Becker, G. S. 1964. *Human Capital.* New York: Columbia University Press.

Bigley, G. A., and Roberts, K. H. 2001. The incident command system: High reliability organizing for complex and volatile task environments. *Academy of Management Journal* 44(6): 1281–1299.

Bluestone, B., and Melnik, M. 2010. *After the recovery: Help needed.* http://www.encore.org/files/research/JobsBluestonePaper3-5-10.pdf (accessed May 21, 2017).

Broad, M. L., and Newstrom, J. W. 1992. Transfer of training: Action-packed strategies to ensure high payoff from training investments. *ERIC*, EBSCO*host* (accessed May 21, 2017).

Brown, K. G., & Gerhardt, M. W. 2002. Formative evaluation: An integrative practice model and case study. *Personnel Psychology* 55(4): 951–983.

Campbell, B. A., Coff, R., and Kryscynski, D. 2012. Rethinking sustained competitive advantage from human capital. *Academy of Management Review* 37: 376–395.

Cappelli, P. 1995. Rethinking the "skills gap." *California Management Review* 37(4): 108–24.

Carnevale, Anthony. 2005. The coming labor and skills shortage. *Training and Development* 59(1): 37–41.

Carnevale, A. P., Smith, N., and Strohl, J. 2010. *Help wanted: Projections of jobs and education requirements through 2018.* Washington, DC: Center on Education and the Workforce, Georgetown University.

Carnevale, A. P., Gainer, L. J., and Villet, J. 1990. *Training in America: The Organization and Strategic Role of Training*. San Francisco: Jossey-Bass.

Cassner-Lotto, J., and Associates. 1988. *Successful Training Strategies*. San Francisco: Jossey-Bass.

Coff, R. W. 1997. Human assets and management dilemmas: Coping with hazards on the road to resource-based theory. *Academy of Management Review* 22: 374–402.

Dickinson, G., and Puleo, M. 2008. Chronic misalignment. *Deloitte Review* 2: 37–49.

Dubey, R., and Gunasekaran, A. 2015. Shortage of sustainable supply chain talent: An industrial training framework. *Industrial and Commercial Training* 47(2): 86–94.

Fujita, S. 2014. *On the causes of declines in the labor force participation rate*. Philadelphia, PA: Federal Reserve Bank of Philadelphia.

Goldstein, I. L. 1993. *Training in Organizations*, 3rd ed. Pacific Grove, CA: Brooks/Cole.

Hatch, N. W., and Dyer, J. H. (2004). Human capital and learning as a source of sustainable competitive advantage. *Strategic Management Journal* 25(12): 1155–1178.

Hitt, M. A., Biermant, L., Shimizu, K., and Kochhar, R. 2001. Direct and moderating effects of human capital on strategy and performance in professional service firms: A resource-based perspective. *Academy of Management Journal* 44(1): 13–28.

Huang, J. L., Ford, J. K., and Ryan, A. M. 2016. Ignored no more: Within-person variability enables better understanding of training transfer. *Personnel Psychology* 70(3): 557–596.

Huselid, M. A. 1995. The impact of human resource management practices on turnover, productivity, and corporate financial performance. *Academy of Management Journal* 38: 635–672.

Jiang, K., Lepak, D. P., Hu, J., and Baer, J. 2012. How does human resource management influence organizational outcomes? A meta-analytic investigation of the mediating mechanisms. *Academy of Management Journal* 6: 1264–1294.

Kim, Y., and Ployhart, R. E. 2014. The effects of staffing and training on firm productivity and profit growth before, during, and after the Great Recession. *Journal of Applied Psychology* 99: 361–389.

Kozlowski, S. W. J., Brown, K. G., Weissbein, D. A., Cannon-Bowers, J. A., and Salas, E. (2000). A multilevel approach to training effectiveness: Enhancing horizontal and vertical transfer. In K. J. Klein, S. J. Kozlowski, K. J. Klein, S. J. Kozlowski, eds., *Multilevel Theory, Research, and Methods in Organizations: Foundations, Extensions, and New Directions*, 157–210. San Francisco, CA: Jossey-Bass.

Kozlowski, S. W. J., Gully, S. M., Brown, K. G., Salas, E., Smith, E. M., and Nason, E. R. 2001. Effects of training goals and goal orientation traits on multidimensional training outcomes and performance adaptability. *Organizational Behavior & Human Decision Processes* 85(1): 1–31.

Kozlowski, S. W. J., and Klein, K. J. 2000. A multilevel approach to theory and research in organizations: Contextual, temporal, and emergent processes. In K. J. Klein, and S. W. J. Kozlowski, eds., *Multilevel Theory, Research, and Methods in Organizations: Foundations, Extensions, and New Directions*, 3–90. San Francisco, CA: Jossey-Bass.

Kraaijenbrink, J., Spender, J.C., and Groen, A. J. 2010. The resource-based view: A review and assessment of its critiques. *Journal of Management* 36: 349–372.

Kraiger, K., and Culbertson, S. S. 2013. Understanding and facilitating learning: Advancements in training and development. In N. W. Schmitt, S. Highhouse,

I. B. Weiner, N. W. Schmitt, S. Highhouse, and I. B. Weiner, eds., *Handbook of Psychology: Industrial and Organizational Psychology,* 2nd ed., 12: 244–261. Hoboken, NJ: John Wiley & Sons Inc.

Kraiger, K., and Ford, J. K. 2006. The expanding role of workplace training: Themes and trends influencing training research and practice. L. L. Koppers, ed., *Historical Perspectives in Industrial and Organizational Psychology,* 281–309. Mahwah, NJ: Erlbaum.

Kristof-Brown, A. L., Zimmerman, R. D., and Johnson, E. C. 2005. Consequences of individuals' fit at work: A meta-analysis of person–job, person–organization, person–group, and person–supervisor fit. *Personnel Psychology* 58: 281–342.

Hill, C. E., and Lent, R. W. 2006. A narrative and meta-analytic review of helping skills training: Time to revive a dormant area of inquiry. *Psychotherapy: Theory, Research, Practice, Training* 43(2): 154–172.

MacLean, R. 2005. Map your value proposition: Strategy maps can reveal how EHS contributes to the business. *Environmental Protection* 16(6): 12–14.

Maden, Ceyda, and Hayat Kabasakal. 2014. The simultaneous effects of fit with organizations, jobs and supervisors on major employee outcomes in Turkish banks: Does organizational support matter? *The International Journal of Human Resource Management* 25(3): 341–366.

ManPowerGroup. 2010. Teachable Fit: A new approach for easing the talent mismatch. http://us.manpower.com/us/en/multimedia/fresh-perspective-hardest-jobs-to-fill.pdf (accessed May 21, 2017).

Martin, R. L. 2014. The big lie of strategic planning. *Harvard Business Review*, January/February.

Martocchio, J. J., and Baldwin, T. J. 1997. The evolution of strategic organizational training: New objectives and research agenda. In G. R. Ferris, ed., *Research in Personnel and Human Resources Management* 15: 1–46. Greenwich, Conn. and London.

McKinsey Global Institute. 2012. The world at work: Jobs, pay and skills for 3.5 billion people. http://www.mckinsey.com/insights/employment_and_growth/the_world_ at work (accessed May 21, 2017).

Nguyen, T. N., Truong, Q., and Buyens, D. 2010. The relationship between training and firm performance: A literature review. *Research & Practice In Human Resource Management* 18(1): 36–45.

Noe, R. 2012. *Employee Training and Development,* 6th ed. New York: McGraw-Hill Higher Education.

Noe, R. A., Clarke, A. M., and Klein, H. J. 2014. Learning in the twenty-first-century workplace. *Annual Review of Organizational Psychology and Organizational Behavior* 1: 245–275.

Nyberg, A. J., Moliterno, T. P., Hale, D., and Lepak, D. P. 2014. Resource-based perspectives on unit-level human capital: A review and integration. *Journal of Management* 40: 316–346.

Olian, J. D., Durham, C. C., Kristof, A. L., Brown, K. G., Pierce, R. M., and Kunder, L. 1998. Designing management training and development for competitive advantage: Lessons from the best. *Human Resource Planning* 21(1): 20–31.

O'Reilly, C. A., III, Chatman, J., and Caldwell, D. F. 1991. People and organizational culture: A profile comparison approach to assessing person–organization fit. *Academy of Management Journal* 34: 487–516.

Peteraf, M. A., and Barney, J. B. 2003. Unraveling the resource-based tangle. *Managerial and Decision Economics* 24: 309–323.

Ployhart, R. E. 2015. Strategic organizational behavior (STROBE): The missing voice in the strategic human capital conversation. *Academy of Management Perspectives* 29(3): 342–356.

Ployhart, R. E. 2012. Personnel selection and the competitive advantage of firms. In G. P. Hodgkinson, and J. K. Ford, eds., *International Review of Industrial and Organizational Psychology,* 27: 153–195. Wiley-Blackwell.

Ployhart, R. E., and Hale, D. 2014. The fascinating psychological microfoundations of strategy and competitive advantage. *Annual Review of Organizational Psychology and Organizational Behavior* 1: 145–172.

Ployhart, R. E., and Moliterno, T. P. 2011. Emergence of the human capital resource: A multilevel model. *Academy of Management Review* 36: 127–150.

Ployhart, R. E., Van Iddekinge, C. H. and MacKenzie, W. 2011. Acquiring and developing human capital for sustained competitive advantage: The interconnectedness of generic and specific human capital resources. *Academy of Management Journal* 54: 353–368.

Ployhart, R. E., Nyberg, A. J., Reilly, G., and Maltarich, M. A. 2014. Human capital is dead: Long live human capital resources! *Journal of Management* 40: 371–398.

Porter, M. E. 1980. *Competitive Strategy: Techniques for Analyzing Industries and Competitors.* New York: The Free Press.

Posthuma, R. A., Campion, M. C., Masimova, M., and Campion, M. A. 2013. A high performance work practices taxonomy: Integrating the literature and directing future research. *Journal of Management* 39: 1184–1220.

Rajasekar, J. 2013. A comparative analysis of mission statement content and readability. *Journal of Management Policy and Practice* 14(6): 131–147.

Reed, J., and Vakola, M. 2006. What role can a training needs analysis play in organisational change? *Journal of Organizational Change Management* 19: 393–407.

Richard, P. J., Devinney, T. M., Yip, G. S., and Johnson, G. 2009. Measuring organizational performance: Towards methodological best practice. *Journal of Management* 35: 718–804.

Robinson, D. G., and Robinson, J. 1989. Training for impact. *Training & Development Journal* 43(8): 34.

Satterfield, J., and Hughes, E. 2007. Emotion skills training for medical students: A systematic review. *Medical Education* 41(10): 935–941.

Simon, M. A., Gunia, B., Martin, E. J., Foucar, C. E., Kundu, T., Ragas, D. M., and Emanuel, L. L. 2013. Path toward economic resilience for family caregivers: Mitigating household deprivation and the health care talent shortage at the same time. *The Gerontologist* 53(5): 861–873.

Sirmon, D. G., Hitt, M. A., and Ireland, R. D. 2007. Managing firm resources in dynamic environments to create value: Looking inside the black box. *Academy of Management Review* 32: 273–292.

Sung, S. Y., and Choi, J. N. 2014. Do organizations spend wisely on employees? Effects of training and development investments on learning and innovation in organizations. *Journal of Organizational Behavior* 35(3): 393–412.

Tannenbaum, S. I. 1997. Enhancing continuous learning: Diagnostic findings from multiple companies. *Human Resource Management* 36: 437–452.

Tannenbaum, S. I. 2002. A strategic view of organizational training and learning. In K. Kraiger, ed., *Creating, Implementing, and Managing Effective Training and Development,* 10–52. San Francisco: Jossey-Bass.

Tharenou, P., Saks, A. M., and Moore, C. 2007. A review and critique of research on training and organizational-level outcomes. *Human Resource Management Review* 17(3): 251–273.

Van Iddekinge, C. H., Ferris, G. R., Perrewé, P. L., Blass, F. R., Perryman, A. A., and Heetderks, T. D. 2009. Effects of selection and training on unit-level performance over time: A latent growth modeling approach. *Journal of Applied Psychology* 94(4): 829–843.

Venneberg, D. L., and Eversole, B. W. 2010. *The Boomer Retirement Time Bomb: How Companies Can Avoid the Fallout from the Coming Skills Shortage.* Santa Barbara, CA: Praeger.

Wernerfelt, B. 1984. A resource-based view of the firm. *Strategic Management Journal* 5: 171–180.

Zwick, T. 2006. The impact of training intensity on establishment productivity. *Industrial Relations: A Journal of Economy and Society* 45: 26–46.

24 Hospitality Training Research

A Review and Implications for Future Research

J. Bruce Tracey

Research in the training and development domain has evolved considerably over the past two decades. During this time, scholars have examined a wide array of design- and delivery-related features that may influence the effectiveness and utility of many types of training initiatives (Aguinis & Kraiger, 2009; Arthur et al., 2003). There has also been growing emphasis on various individual differences and contextual factors outside the immediate learning context that may influence the effectiveness of various informal and formal training programs (e.g., Noe, Clarke, & Klein, 2014). The collective body of work has added substantive insights to our knowledge about the training process, and provides a fairly concrete and prescriptive means for providing a positive learning experience and bringing value to the organization (Brown & Sitzmann, 2011).

Another noteworthy trend has been an increase in research that focuses on training and development in hospitality organizations (Tracey, 2014). This emphasis stems from the growing commercial significance of this industry segment, which currently employs more than 14 million people in the United States,[1] and is supported by more than 200 higher education programs to meet the learning and development needs of this important and burgeoning sector. On the surface, there is a substantial degree of overlap in the topics that have been published in hospitality-specific research outlets compared to most discipline-based outlets that do not have an industry focus. Indeed, hospitality scholars have examined similar content areas (e.g., new employee programs, diversity, leadership) and design features (e.g., use of technology-enabled solutions, on-the-job approaches), as well as numerous individual (e.g., pretraining attitudes) and situational variables (e.g., climate for training), and the results are quite consistent with those that have been reported in the general management and industrial-organizational psychology literatures. However, a close inspection of some of the hospitality-specific studies suggests that there may be features associated with labor-intensive, service-focused settings that may dictate, at least to some extent, the use and utility of training policies and practices that have been found to be effective in other settings. For example, delivering consistent and high-quality customer service is a priority for hospitality firms. As such, some hospitality scholars have examined the use and utility of customer service data for establishing training needs and assessing training outcomes (e.g., Butcher, Sparks, & McColl-Kennedy, 2009; Wirtz, Tambyah, & Mattila, 2010). These types of studies are quite compelling because they provide a basis for extending our thinking about effective training policies and practices, as well as examining possible boundary conditions associated with the models and explanations that have been presented and tested to date.

The purpose of the chapter is to present a review of the training research that has been published over the past 20 years in hospitality-specific research outlets, and then discuss the implications in light of the trends and themes associated the training research that has appeared in general management and applied psychology journals (which will hereafter be referred to as the "general training literature"). The chapter will be divided into two main sections. The first section will present a discussion and analysis of the hospitality-specific training studies that have been published. The second section will offer a thematic comparison of the hospitality-specific findings with those that have been presented in the general training literature, identifying areas of overlap and uniqueness, and the implications for future research. To facilitate this analysis, and following the review procedures utilized by Burke and Hutchins (2007), a taxonomy of topics was developed as a basis for examining the respective literatures.

Given that the volume of hospitality-specific training research is comparatively small, the organizing framework was based on general themes that were addressed in recent reviews of the general training literature (e.g., Aguinis & Kraiger, 2009; Brown & Sitzmann, 2011; Noe, Clark, & Klein, 2014). Specifically, the following topics were used as the organizing and analytic framework for this review: (1) needs assessment and pretraining preparation (which includes research that examines specific content areas/topics, individual characteristics, and the work environment); (2) training design and delivery (including learning processes); (3) transfer of training; and (4) training evaluation. This framework was then used to address the following key questions:

- What topics demonstrated the strongest and most consistent results in the hospitality-specific training literature?
- What are the key similarities and differences in the results from hospitality-specific studies compared to those that have been published in the general training literature?
- What are the implications for future training and development research?

The articles targeted for this review were generated from a systematic search of three comprehensive databases. Hospitality and Tourism Complete was utilized initially to identify hospitality-specific training studies. Then, two additional databases – ABI/INFORM and Business Source Complete – were utilized to identify any additional hospitality-specific studies that may not be included in the Hospitality and Tourism Complete database.[2] A 20-year time frame was specified, and an extensive list of keywords were used to identify relevant articles. For example, terms such as *employee learning*, *trainee learning*, *training and learning*, *learning process*, *informal learning*, and related terms were used to identify studies that examined factors that may influence knowledge and skill acquisition. Only peer-reviewed studies were considered. In addition, review articles were eliminated, as well as articles that focused on topics other than training and development but discussed the implications of the findings for employee training and development. The search generated 112 hospitality-specific articles over the focal period. These articles were then organized into the categories that were included in the framework noted previously.

Findings from the Hospitality Training Literature

Needs Assessment and Individual Characteristics

As noted in Table 24.1, about 40% of the hospitality-specific training studies that were published during the focal period addressed questions related to needs assessment and individual characteristics. This category also included studies that examined hospitality-specific content that stem from training needs.

Several studies within this thematic domain addressed topics that are particularly relevant for service-intensive settings. Not surprisingly, one theme centered on the use and utility of data about customer service. For example, Butcher, Sparks, and McColl-Kennedy (2009) identified several organizational activities that may be incorporated into the needs assessment process and influence the design, implementation, and effectiveness of training programs that focus on developing customer service knowledge and skills, such as the use of "best practices" benchmarking and third-party/external "mystery shoppers" to assess service quality. In a related study, Wirtz, Tambyah, and Mattila (2010) examined factors that may influence the extent to which feedback from customer-contact employees about service quality may complement similar feedback gathered directly from customers. The authors found that feedback valence (positive vs. negative) and the intended use of the feedback information (developmental vs. evaluative) moderated the relationship between employee perceptions about trust in their company's leadership and their intentions to report customer feedback for establishing learning priorities. For example, in higher-trust contexts, customer-contact employees were more willing to report negative customer service feedback when the intended use of the information was for evaluative purposes. Thus, employees need to feel comfortable and confident that information sharing – particularly that which is negative – will be utilized in constructive and appropriate manner. These and related studies (e.g., Beck, Lalopa, & Hall, 2003; Magnini & Honeycutt, 2005; Ross, 2006) provide insights about the nature and scope of information about customer service that can be utilized to identify and refine training needs.

The second major theme associated with hospitality-specific research on training needs assessment focused on the roles and relevance of individual differences, particularly characteristics associated with demographic and cultural diversity – key attributes of the hospitality industry workforce. For example, Reynolds, Rahman, and Bradetich (2014) examined perceptions about the value of diversity training among a sample of hotel managers. The results showed

Table 24.1 *Hospitality-specific training articles published since 1995*

Topic	Number	Percentage of Total	Articles by Year
Needs Assessment and Individual Differences	45	40%	2011–present: 13 2006–2010: 16 2001–2005: 11 1995–2000: 2
Design and Delivery	43	38%	2011–present: 15 2006–2010: 12 2001–2005: 12 1995–2000: 4
Transfer of Training	6	5%	2011–present: 4 2006–2010: 2 2001–2005: 0 1995–2000: 0
Training Evaluation	18	16%	2011–present: 4 2006–2010: 6 2001–2005: 4 1995–2000: 4
Overall	112	100%	2011–present: 36 2006–2010: 36 2001–2005: 27 1995–2000: 10

that perceptions of value were high when accompanied with positive perceptions about corporate support for diversity initiatives, as well as positive perceptions about the benefits of diversity training for key stakeholders, including self, peers, and subordinates. Similar findings were reported in Masadeh's (2013) study of Jordanian hotel managers. In addition to perceptions of value, Wei-Tang, Martin, and Yeh (2002) examined the cross-cultural learning needs among a sample of expatriate hotel managers in the Taiwan lodging market. These results generated a profile of job competencies – such as sensitivity, adaptability, tolerance, resourcefulness, and self-confidence – that can be used as a guide for addressing learning needs in many types of culturally diverse work settings, as well as in situations when the work context may be new or novel. Thus, a specific development plan can be designed and implemented by using an individual's profile as a guide. The balance of studies in this domain examined a wide array individual characteristics that are context-specific – from attitudes about wine service training (Gultek, Dodd, & Guydosh, 2006) to management perceptions about training for part-time employees (Sobaih, 2011). The findings provide important insights about individual differences that may be particularly important to effective training design, implementation, and transfer across a variety of hospitality settings.

Training Design and Facilitation

Another 38% (43 articles) of the hospitality-specific training articles published within the past two decades have examined topics associated with design and facilitation. Several of these studies focused on learning processes. For example, Lam (2011) conducted a qualitative study that examined the informal learning efforts among a sample of frontline employees in the casino segment. The results suggested that factors such as empathy and emotional regulation may play an important role in acquiring customer relationship skills from on-the-job experiences. Similar findings were reported by Lundberg and Mossberg (2008) in their study on informal learning associated with "critical service encounters" among a sample of frontline food service employees. In addition, Salazar et al. (2005) found that employee satisfaction and motivation were significantly related to learning outcomes associated with a food-safety program. These studies highlight the relative importance of individual affect for learning in hospitality settings, as well as the benefits of less formal learning and development activities.

The majority of design-related training studies (43, 38%) examined the use of various instructional methods and delivery systems. One popular topic is e-learning and web-based training strategies. For example, Singh, Kim, and Feinstein (2011) found that a substantial number of multiunit restaurant companies (40% of those surveyed) use the Internet for training purposes. Similar findings were reported by Lema and Agrusa (2009) regarding the use of the Internet training for employees in the casino industry. In terms of Zakrzewski, Sammons, and Feinstein (2005) examined the efficacy of using digitized video and illustrated audio for acquiring procedural knowledge. In this quasi-experimental study, the subjects (undergraduate students) were randomly assigned to one of two conditions. One group viewed a video that showed how to perform a "Bishop Hat" napkin fold in 14 steps. The other group viewed an illustrated audio version of the video which presented images of all 14 steps. The participants were allowed to view the respective videos as many times as they wanted, and then complete the 14-step process. The results showed support for both methods, and there were no significant differences across the two groups in the measures procedural knowledge, assessed as the rate of video replay and the time it took the participants to complete the task.

The remaining design-focused studies have examined other learning-related strategies, such as the importance of social support for on-the-job training (e.g., Magnini, 2009; Zhang, Cai, & Wei-hua, 2002), job rotation (e.g., Lanier, Jackson, & Lanier, 2010), and cross-functional training (e.g., Chen & Tseng, 2012). And finally, one study that focused on both design and the transfer of training (which will be discussed in the next section) examined the role of design features that extended beyond the immediate learning context. Tews and Tracey (2008; 2009) investigated the impact of two posttraining interventions for enhancing the effectiveness of a formal training program on interpersonal skills for a sample of restaurant managers. The results demonstrated support for two on-the-job initiatives, a self-coaching supplement in which trainees used a guide to reflect, set goals, and develop action plans for maximizing the benefits of their learning experiences, and an upward feedback supplement in which trainees received feedback about the trainees' strengths and areas needing improvement. The results from this study have implications not only for training design, they are also relevant for promoting effective training transfer.

Transfer of Training

In comparison to other topics, hospitality training scholars have given scant attention to the transfer of training. The six studies (5%) that examined this topic have either confirmed the findings that have been established in the general training literature, or have offered modest extensions from previous efforts. For example, Frash et al. (2010) showed that several factors associated with trainee characteristics (e.g., trainees' motivation to transfer), training design (e.g., perceptions regarding the extent to which the focal training program included "activities and exercises that clearly demonstrated how to apply new knowledge and skills on the job": 408), and the work environment (e.g., manager support) were all significantly related to a behavioral measure of transfer among a sample of hotel employees who received training to use a new management information system. On a more granular level, Zhao and Namasivayam (2009) presented evidence that posttraining self-efficacy mediated the relationship between learning and posttraining transfer intentions. Similarly, Ballesteros and De Saá (2012) showed that several characteristics associated with the work environment, including perceptions about the unit's learning culture, supervisor support, and opportunities to use training, were significantly related to self-reported measures of learning and transfer among a sample of restaurant managers in Spain. So, although far from definitive, it appears that there are a considerable number of individual and work-related factors that influence the extent to which individual apply their newly acquired knowledge and skills on the job. And as discussed in more detail in the following text, the nature and relevance these factors will certainly benefit from additional inquiry.

Training Evaluation

Just more than 15% (18 articles) of the hospitality-specific training studies (18 articles) focused on training evaluation, the majority of which examined the impact of formal training programs on a variety of individual and unit-level outcomes. Several studies demonstrated a positive impact of training on individual assessments of job satisfaction and turnover intentions (e.g., Chiang, Back, & Canter, 2005; Costen & Salazar, 2011), as well as aggregate measures of satisfaction and actual turnover rates (e.g., Choi & Dickson, 2010). Additionally, Frash et al. (2008) presented findings that support hierarchical relationships among trainee reactions, learning, and transfer. And finally, Úbeda-García et al. (2013) found that a firm's overall training policy (e.g., offering continuous development programs) was significantly related to both objective and subjective measures of firm performance among a sample of hotels in Spain. In particular, the regular implementation of a training needs assessment was shown to have a significant impact on the hotels' earnings before interest and taxes after controlling for price point, number of employees, and related factors.

The remaining hospitality studies that evaluated training have considered the impact of factors outside the training context that may influence various training outcomes. For example, using data from a medium-sized multiunit restaurant company, Tracey and Tews (2004) found significant relationships among aggregate perceptions of service climate, training climate, and employee service capabilities, and level-four indices such as unit-level indicators of employee turnover and sales growth. Similar findings were reported by Tracey and Cardenas (1996). And as noted previously, the results from these studies clearly complement those discussed in the previous section, as many of the same individual and contextual factors may influence the application of newly acquired knowledge and skills to the job (i.e., training transfer), as well as the extent to which individuals are adequately prepared for learning and development activities (Aguinis & Kraiger, 2009).

Comparison of the Hospitality-Specific and General Training Literatures

Key Similarities

As noted in the introduction of this chapter, there is substantial overlap in the topics and findings that have been published in the hospitality-specific and general training literatures. In the needs assessment and pretraining preparation domain, the findings from industry-focused studies that considered the use and utility of customer service data for identifying training needs reinforce the conclusions reported by Fowlkes et al. (2000) and Morgeson and Campion (1997) who showed that using more experienced subject matter experts can improve the comprehensiveness and accuracy of the needs assessment process, though it should be noted that previous research has demonstrated concerns in recall with more experienced individuals (Richman & Quiñones, 1996). And while not all customers can be considered experts on customer service, it is likely feedback back from customers can be integrated with that from other sources (e.g., supervisor and self-assessments) to enhance the accuracy and comprehensiveness of the training need assessment process. In addition, the hospitality-specific studies that have examined the roles and influence of individual differences are consistent with those that have addressed similar topics in general training literature. For example, the importance of perceptions about diversity were supported by Rynes and Rosen's (1995) study, which showed that perceptions about top management support for diversity, diversity incentives for managers, and the use of a "broad, inclusionary definition of diversity," and similar variables, were positively related to the adoption of diversity training and perceptions of diversity training success. Similarly, several studies have examined the nature and influence of various context-specific individual attitudes, motivation, knowledge, and skills that may influence a myriad of learning and training outcomes – from human resource professionals' perceptions of interviewer training (e.g., Camp et al., 2011) to multimedia self-efficacy (e.g., Christoph, Schoenfeld, & Tansky, 1998).

Regarding research that has examined the learning process, the hospitality-specific studies that have demonstrated the importance of affective (e.g., Lam, 2011) and motivational factors (e.g., Salazar et al., 2005) support the findings from similar studies that have been published in the general training literature. For example, Warr and Bunce (1995) reported a significant negative relationship between learning task anxiety and an assessment of learning among a sample of managers who participated in an "open-learning" program that was designed to offer trainees greater discretion in their efforts to acquire new knowledge and skills. Bell and Kozlowski (2008) extended these findings and showed that trainees who received an emotion-control strategy approach to learning a complex computer simulation reported significant lower anxiety than those who did not participate in the focal strategy. Similarly, a number of studies have reported significant relationships between pretraining self-efficacy and motivation and posttraining measures of learning (e.g., Chiaburu & Marinova, 2005; Colquitt, LePine, & Noe, 2000; Facteau et al., 1995; Tracey et al., 2001), among other important training outcomes.

In terms of design-specific considerations, there are two primary areas of overlap in the hospitality-specific and general training literatures. The first is the growing focus on technology-based solutions. As noted previously, a few hospitality-specific studies have focused on the use (e.g., Singh et al., 2011) and utility (e.g., Zakrzewski et al., 2005) of e-learning platforms. These results augment those reported in studies that have examined various individual factors, particularly motivational constructs (e.g., Brown, Charlier, & Pierotti, 2012), that may influence the effectiveness of various web- and computer-based instructional delivery systems (e.g., Brown et al., 2012; Sitzmann et al., 2006; Sitzmann, 2011). The second area of overlap is the growing interest in informal approaches to learning and training. The hospitality-specific studies that have examined factors such as social support for on-the-job learning (e.g., Magnini, 2009) extend findings from studies in the general training literature that have demonstrated significant relationships between various individual differences (e.g., personal learning orientation; Choi & Jacobs, 2011) and work-related characteristics (e.g., work pressure; Doornbos, Simons, & Denessen, 2008) and informal learning outcomes (Noe, Tews, & Marand, 2013; Noe et al., 2014). These results are particularly noteworthy in light of the lack of structure that is assigned to training in many hospitality organizations (Sobaih, 2011).

Although the number of hospitality-specific studies that have examined transfer of training topic is small, the findings are consistent with those that have been reported in the general training literature. For example, the results from Frash et al.'s (2010) study on the roles of individual and work-related characteristics on transfer outcomes are clearly aligned with the results reported in Blume et al.'s (2010) meta-analysis. Both studies showed that individual characteristics such as motivation and work-related characteristics such as perceptions about supportiveness of the work environment were among the strongest predictors of training transfer. And as noted previously, similar findings were reported in the hospitality-specific studies by Zhao and Namasivayam (2009) and Ballesteros and De Saá (2012).

And finally, in terms of training evaluation, the hospitality-specific studies that considered the impact of various training initiatives emphasize Aguinis and Kraiger's (2009) call to continue documenting the benefits of training. And while none of the industry-related studies considered new evaluation methods or models, the results lend indirect support for some of the frameworks that promote a broad and comprehensive approach to evaluation. For example, the study by Frash et al. (2008) supports the decision-based assessment model offered by Kraiger (2002) by demonstrating links between specific evaluation results and a broad array of functional and strategic decisions – from providing feedback about learning progress to trainees, to promoting future training and development activities. Similarly, the work by Tracey and his colleagues (e.g., Tracey and Cardenas, 1996; Tracey and Tews, 2004) supports several features that are embedded in Holton's (2005) evaluation model, which incorporates a wide array of individual, work, and organizational factors that may explain the utility of many formal and informal learning and development initiatives.

Key Differences

There are two primary difference in articles published in the hospitality-specific and general training literatures. The first difference is in the emphasis given to the various areas of focus, or research themes. Within the hospitality-specific literature, the majority of scholarly attention was given to two themes: needs assessment and individual differences (which includes studies that examined specific training topics) and design and delivery. Moreover, the attention was evenly split: 40% (n = 45) and 38% (n = 43), respectively. In contrast, Werner (2017, this volume) noted that of the 261 articles published in *Human Resource Development Quarterly* from 2005 to 2014, only 4.9% (n = 13) focused on needs assessment and individual differences (i.e., job competencies). However, the value jumps to 70% (n = 183) if articles that also addressed specific training topics (which are derived, in theory, from training needs) are included. So, while there is a high degree of overlap in the areas of focus that have been addressed in hospitality-specific training studies and those in the general training literature, it appears that some of the research themes may have greater priority for hospitality settings compared to nonhospitality settings – a finding that further reinforces the importance of considering the context in which training will be used.

The second primary difference is the way in which the research has been framed. The studies that have been published in the general training literature typically emphasize both the practical and conceptual implications of the focal research. Many papers begin with a discussion regarding the importance of training in work organizations, and then present a review of the extant research and a framework or set of propositions that are intended to build on and extend the current body of knowledge. In contrast, most of the hospitality-specific training research offers a reasonably strong practical grounding, but the conceptual foundation of many studies rarely extends beyond that which has been examined in previous research (both hospitality-specific and general training studies). Indeed, a great deal of emphasis is given to applied concerns (e.g., the importance of training for enhancing frontline employee service capabilities and performance, which in turn may influence a wide array of customer outcomes), but the models and frameworks that have been used as a basis for examining the focal relationships are typically those that have been tested and supported in prior studies.

While the conceptual advances from many of the hospitality training studies cited in the preceding text have been fairly modest and primarily reflect generalization efforts, as discussed in more detail in the following text, it may be worthwhile to consider the core and/or unique components associated with hospitality settings. As noted previously, doing so may generate insights regarding the relative importance of various work-related and individual factors, and articulate some of the primary contingencies that may influence the impact use and utility of training.

Implications for Future Research

In light of the similarities and key difference noted previously, there are several implications for future training research. First, the findings from hospitality-specific studies suggest that additional consideration should be given to contextual factors that may influence the roles and relevance of various training processes and outcomes. For hospitality organizations, one of the most important strategic and operational priorities is to design and execute business processes that create value for customers. One of the more compelling frameworks, depicted in Figure 24.1, for describing how hospitality and other service-intensive firms create value for customers and achieve superior performance is the service-profit chain (SPC). Based on an integrative framework derived from several academic fields, including marketing, human resource management, and operations management, the SPC framework posits that employee capabilities, satisfaction, and productivity will have a direct influence on customer perceptions of service quality, which in turn will affect financial performance (Heskett, Sasser, & Schlesinger 1997). There is some fairly compelling empirical support for the proposed relationships. For example, Schlesinger and Zornitsky (1992) found significant relationships among employee service capabilities, employee satisfaction, and customer satisfaction. Similarly, Salanova, Agut, and Peiro (2005) showed that a firm's service climate had a positive impact on employee service performance, which in turn was significantly related to a measure of

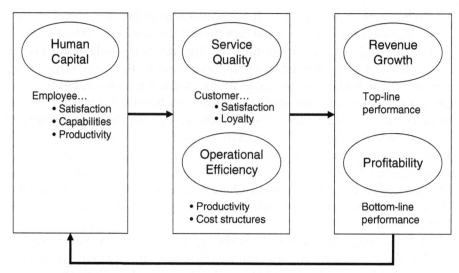

Figure 24.1. *The service-profit chain.*

customer loyalty. And there is fairly robust support for the links between customer satisfaction, loyalty, and firm financial performance (e.g., Anderson, Fornell, & Lehmann 1994; Bernhardt, Donthu, & Kennett 2000).

In light of the strong support for the SPC framework and the contextual importance of customer service for hospitality settings, one avenue for future training research is to consider the ways in which information from customers (and other important external stakeholders) can be used for assessing learning needs, developing employee service capabilities, and evaluating the success of training efforts. As noted in the preceding text, several hospitality studies have examined the utility of using customer data for needs assessment purposes (e.g., Beck et al., 2003; Butcher et al., 2009; Magnini and Honeycutt, 2005; Ross, 2006; Wirtz et al., 2010). Additional consideration should be given to the types of customer data that may be used. For example, in addition to general perceptions about satisfaction and loyalty, it may be beneficial to examine more specific types of customer feedback, especially that which associated with the behaviors that are demonstrated by frontline employees during service interactions (e.g., the extent to which employees respond quickly and effectively to complaints, demonstrate cooperative behaviors with other frontline service staff when responding to requests). Moreover, there is evidence that customer-generated feedback from some online sources may be biased and lack credibility (e.g., Cox et al., 2009; O'Mahony & Smyth, 2010). In addition, research has shown that positive customer feedback may be viewed and interpreted differently than negative customer feedback (e.g., Torres et al., 2015). As such, the weight and relevance of different sources and types of customer-generated feedback for both needs assessment and evaluation purposes should be targets of future research, particularly because many types of training programs that are conducted in hospitality settings are designed to have a direct or indirect impact on customers.

Moreover, it would be helpful to examine the utility of alternative methods for assessing customer service performance. For example, in addition to customer satisfaction surveys, many hospitality companies hire "mystery shoppers" to conduct independent assessments of the service experience and provide feedback regarding the extent to which the focal service standards have been met. It would be useful to know if and how this type of information can be utilized as data sources for assessing training needs.

Another consideration for future research is to examine the relative importance of individual differences and task characteristics that are most relevant in customer-centric settings. As noted previously, there is evidence that empathy and emotional regulation may play a key role in learning customer service skills (e.g., Lam, 2011). In addition, a strong team orientation and behaviors that foster a climate that is adaptive and responsive to change have been shown to be particularly important in hospitality settings (e.g., Testa & Sipe, 2012). Going forward, it would useful to compare the influence of factors such as empathy and emotional regulation with general mental ability, conscientiousness, and other individual differences (e.g., positive psychology; Saks and Gruman, 2017, this volume) that may influence the learning process – and especially learning outcomes that are critical in service settings, such as the ability to anticipate guest needs or respond quickly to customer requests. Similarly, it would be helpful to compare the roles and impact of perceptions about the general service climate (e.g., Schneider, White, & Paul, 1998) in relation to perceptions about the training climate on pretraining preparation and posttraining transfer, as the former may have more salience and impact in hospitality settings. Moreover, this suggestion reinforces that framework advanced by Kozlowski and his colleagues (e.g., Kozlowski et al., 2000) that suggests that some types of climate may be more conducive to promoting training preparation and transfer than others. Investigating these and related relationships reflects an important part of the theory building process (Aguinis and Gottfredson, 2010) and has the potential to offer needed specificity regarding what variables influence training effectiveness across different settings.

Another salient feature of many hospitality environments that has substantial implications for training is high employee turnover (Hinkin and Tracey, 2010), which consistently ranks among the highest across all major industries in the United States.[3] However, despite this significant challenge, many of the "top" hospitality companies – which enjoy lower-than-average turnover rates, among other positive performance outcomes (Hinkin and Tracey, 2010) – have developed and implemented some fairly comprehensive training programs for new employees (Tracey et al., 2015). Unfortunately, the relative efficacy of the various program components has yet to be determined. For example, each of the 31 companies in Tracey et al.'s study placed a great deal of emphasis on informal learning. In light of the benefits that can be generated from this approach (e.g., Tannenbaum et al., 2010), it would be helpful to examine the differential impact of informal compared to more formal learning methods, especially for developing effective customer service knowledge and skills, as well as for promoting higher employee engagement and commitment (and ultimately, reducing turnover). For example, a field experiment similar to that reported in Tews and Tracey (2008) could be conducted in which both formal and informal training methods are used – separately, as well as in combination – to facilitate new employee training. A comprehensive evaluation could then be used to identify the relative impact of the approaches (or combination) on various outcomes during and after the program, including intermediate and longer-term employee commitment and retention. Similarly, error management training strategies (e.g., Keith & Frese, 2008), which focus on identifying and preventing service problems before they arise (as well as resolving problems that do occur) may be particularly effective for not only ensuring service consistency, but may also reduce the need for service recovery efforts, which may mitigate job stressors and other negative consequences, including employee turnover (e.g., Kao et al., 2014; Kim & Jogaratnam, 2010; Vanderpool & Way, 2013). Again, the type and source of customer information should be considered in the development and implementation of error management programs, as well as the balance between formal and informal instructional methods. Further investigation of these and related design options may offer insights regarding the broader (i.e., beyond knowledge and skill acquisition) and potentially unexpected consequences (e.g., greater engagement and retention) that result from implementing an appropriate blend of instructional methods.

And finally, in light of the rather dynamic and many times unpredictable nature of hospitality settings, it may be useful to integrate some of the emerging research on human resource flexibility as a means for advancing our conceptual understanding about contingencies that may influence training decisions. For example, two key dimensions of flexible human resource systems include resource flexibility and coordination flexibility in human resource practices (Way et al., 2015; Wright and Snell, 1998). In terms of training, resource flexibility may be evident "if the context and procedures enable employees to learn broad skills and knowledge that can be used to perform a variety of alternative work activities" (Way et al., 2015: 3). Under this condition, the organization's existing (and typically varied) learning opportunities can be leveraged to develop employees who can be deployed for a wide range of needs and purposes (e.g., cross-functional job assignments). Alternatively, "coordination flexibility in HR practices would include the development and implementation of training programs that address new or emerging skill demands" (Way et al., 2015: 3–4). In this situation, training and development experiences would be more focused and designed to facilitate specialized knowledge and skills. Thus, the design and implementation features associated with more broadly based development programs, such as general customer service skills that can be utilized in a wide array of contexts and functions, may be quite distinct in terms of design and implementation when compared to programs that are more narrow and address specialized needs, such as anticipating the technology support that can be offered to a guest who is making inquiries about reserving space for a business meeting. However, it should be emphasized that an organization's human resource flexibility may be one of several contingencies that should be considered when designing and implementing any effective training program and broader learning and development system.

Conclusion

The emerging training research that has focused on hospitality settings highlights the importance of the context in which training is applied. And while a substantive amount of attention has been given to the roles and relevance of work-related factors, the priority that is placed on customer service signals the need for additional attention on various strategic and operational contingencies that influence needs assessment, design, and evaluation decisions. The training research that has been conducted in hospitality settings points to some new opportunities for enhancing our understanding about several major training decisions, such as the use of customer service data in the training needs assessment process, and the differential utility of informal learning methods for acquiring both generalizable and context-specific knowledge and skills.

As Noe et al. (2014) recently emphasized, there are a number of "facilitating factors" embedded in many organizational contexts that may influence training in a number of ways, from perceptions about work-family climate that may influence an individual's discretionary learning efforts, to social networks and emotions that may play a direct role in learning and skill acquisition. The importance of customer service may be among the contingencies that have wide-ranging influence on training processes, and efforts to learn more about these and related contextual factors can help clarify the conditions for effective training and development.

Notes

1 Bureau of Labor Statistics, Industry at a glance, http://www.bls.gov/IAG/TGS/iag70 .htm (accessed July 25, 2016).
2 It should be noted that there is a substantive degree of overlap among these databases. ABI/INFORM and Business Source Complete have access to many of the journals that are listed in the Hospitality & Tourism Complete database. However, as would be expected, the latter includes many more industry-specific journals than those included in ABI/INFORM and Business Source Complete.
3 Bureau of Labor Statistics, Economic news release, http://www.bls.gov/news.release/ jolts.nr0.htm (accessed July 27, 2016).

References

Aguinis, H., and Gottfredson, R. K. 2010. Best-practice recommendations for estimating interaction effects using moderating multiple regression. *Journal of Organizational Behavior* 31: 776–786.

Aguinis H., and Kraiger K. 2009. Benefits of training and development for individuals, teams, organizations, and society. *Annual Review of Psychology* 60: 451–74.

Anderson, E. W., Fornell, C., and Lehmann, D. R. 1994. Customer satisfaction, market share and profitability: Findings from Sweden. *Journal of Marketing* 58: 53–66.

Arthur, W. J., Bennett, W. J., Edens, P., Bell, S. T. 2003. Effectiveness of training in organizations: A meta-analysis of design and evaluation features. *Journal of Applied Psychology* 88: 234–245.

Ballesteros, J. L., and De Saá, P. 2012. The influence of organisational context on training success in the restaurant industry. *Service Industries Journal* 32: 1265–1282.

Beck, J., Lalopa, J., and Hall, J. 2003. Insuring quality service: Training mystery shoppers. *Journal of Human Resources in Hospitality and Tourism* 2: 41–57.

Bell, B. S., and Kozlowski, S. W. J. 2008. Active learning: Effects of core training design elements on self-regulatory processes, learning, and adaptability. *Journal of Applied Psychology* 93: 296–316.

Bernhardt, K., Donthu, N., and Kennett, P. 2000. The relationship among customer satisfaction, employee satisfaction, and profitability: A longitudinal analysis. *Journal of Business Research* 47: 161–172.

Blume, B. D., Ford, J. K., Baldwin, T. T., and Huang, J. L. 2010 Transfer of training: A meta-analytic review. *Journal of Management* 36: 1065–1105.

Brown K. G., and Sitzmann T. 2011. Training and employee development for improved performance. In S. Zedeck, ed., *APA Handbook of Industrial and Organizational Psychology*, 2: 469–503. Washington, DC: American Psychological Association.

Brown, K. G., Charlier, S. D., and Pierotti, A. 2012. E-learning at work: Contributions of past research and suggestions for the future. *International Review of Industrial and Organizational Psychology* 27: 89–114.

Burke, L. A., and Hutchins, H. M. 2007. Training transfer: An integrative review. *Human Resource Development Review* 6: 263–296.

Butcher, K., Sparks, B., and McColl-Kennedy, J. 2009. Predictors of customer service training in hospitality firms. *International Journal of Hospitality Management* 28: 389–396.

Camp, R. R., Schulz, E., Vielhaber, M. W., and Wagner-Marsh, F. 2011. Human resource professionals' perceptions of interviewer training. *Journal of Managerial Issues* 23: 250–268.

Chen, L-C., and Tseng, C-Y. 2012. Benefits of cross-functional training: Three departments of hotel line supervisors in Taiwan. *Journal of Hospitality and Tourism Management* 19: 1–8.

Chiaburu, D. S. and Marinova, S. V. 2005. What predicts skill transfer? An exploratory study of goal orientation, training self-efficacy, and organizational supports. *International Journal of Training and Development* 9: 110–123.

Chiang, C-F., Back, K-J., and Canter, D. D. 2005. The impact of employee training on job satisfaction and intention to stay in the hotel industry. *Journal of Human Resources in Hospitality & Tourism* 4: 99–118.

Choi, W., and Jacobs, R. L. 2011. Influence of formal learning, personal learning orientation, and supportive learning environment on informal learning. *Human Resource Development Quarterly* 22: 239–257.

Choi, Y., and Dickson, D. R. 2010. A case study into the benefits of management training programs: Impacts on hotel employee turnover and satisfaction level. *Journal of Human Resources in Hospitality and Tourism* 9: 103–116.

Christoph, R. T., Schoenfeld, Jr., G. A., and Tansky, J. W. 1998. Overcoming barriers to training utilizing technology: The influence of self-efficacy factors on multimedia-based training receptiveness. *Human Resource Development Quarterly* 9: 25–38.

Colquitt, J. A., LePine, J. A., and Noe, R. A. 2000. Toward an integrative theory of training motivation: A meta-analytic path analysis of 20 years of research. *Journal of Applied Psychology* 85: 678–707.

Costen, W. M. and Salazar, J. 2011. The impact of training and development on employee job satisfaction, loyalty, and intent to stay in the lodging industry. *Journal of Human Resources in Hospitality and Tourism* 10: 273–284.

Cox, C., Burgess, S., Sellitto, C., and Buultjens, J. 2009. The roles of user-generated content in tourists' travel planning behavior. *Journal of Hospitality Marketing and Management* 18: 743–764.

Doornbos, A. J., Simons, R. J., and Denessen, E. 2008. Relations between characteristics of workplace practices and types of informal work-related learning: A survey study among Dutch police. *Human Resource Development Quarterly* 19: 129–151.

Facteau, J. D., Dobbins, G. H., Russell, J. E. A., Ladd, R. T., and Kudisch, J. D. 1995. The influence of general perceptions of the training environment on pretraining motivation and perceived training transfer. *Journal of Management* 21: 1–25.

Fowlkes, J. E., Salas, E., Baker, D. P., Cannon-Bowers, J. A., and Stout, R. J. 2000. The utility of event-based knowledge elicitation. *Human Factors* 42: 24–35.

Frash, R., Antun, J. Kline, S., and Almanza, B. 2010. Like it! Learn it! Use it? *Cornell Hospitality Quarterly* 51: 398–414.

Frash, R., Kline, S., Almanza, B., and Antun, J. 2008. Support for a multi-level evaluation framework in hospitality training. *Journal of Human Resources in Hospitality* 7: 197–218.

Gultek, M. M., Dodd, T. H., and Guydosh, R.M. 2006. Attitudes towards wine-service training and its influence on restaurant wine sales. *International Journal of Hospitality Management* 25: 432–446.

Heskett, J. L., Sasser, Jr., W. E., and Schlesinger, L. A. 1997. *The Service Profit Chain.* New York: The Free Press.

Hinkin, T. R., and Tracey, J. B. 2010 What makes it so great? An analysis of HR practices among Fortune's best companies in the hospitality and service segments. *Cornell Hospitality Quarterly* 51: 158–170.

Holton, E. F., III 2005. Holton's evaluation model: New evidence and construct elaborations. *Advances in Developing Human Resources* 7: 37–54.

Kao, F-H., Cheng, B-S., Kuo, C-C., and Huang, M-P. 2014. Stressors, withdrawal, and sabotage in frontline employees: The moderating effects of caring and service climates. *Journal of Occupational & Organizational Psychology* 87: 755–780.

Keith, N., and Frese, M. 2008. Effectiveness of error management training: A meta-analysis. *Journal of Applied Psychology* 93: 59–69.

Kim, K., and Jogaratnam, G. 2010. Effects of individual and organizational factors on job satisfaction and intent to stay in the hotel industry. *Journal of Human Resources in Hospitality and Tourism* 9: 318–339.

Kozlowski, S. W. J., Brown, K. G., Weissbein, D. A., Cannon-Bowers, J., and Salas, E. 2000. A multi-level perspective on training effectiveness: Enhancing horizontal and vertical transfer. In K. J. Klein and S. W. J. Kozlowski, eds., *Multilevel*

Theory, Research, and Methods in Organizations, 157–210. San Francisco: Jossey-Bass.

Kraiger, K. 2002. Decision-based evaluation. In K. Kraiger ed., *Creating, Implementing, and Maintaining Effective Training and Development: State-of-the-Art Lessons for Practice*, 331–375. San Francisco: Jossey-Bass.

Lam, C. S. 2011. Frontline employees' informal learning and customer relationship skills in Macao casinos: An empirical study. *UNLV Gaming Research and Review Journal* 15: 35–57.

Lanier, D., Jackson, F. H., and Lanier, R. 2010. Job rotation as a leadership development tool. *Consortium Journal of Hospitality and Tourism* 14: 21–25.

Lema, J. D., and Agrusa, J. 2009. Relationship of WWW usage and employee learning in the casino industry. *International Journal of Hospitality Management* 28: 18–25.

Lundberg, C., and Mossberg, L. 2008. Learning by sharing: Waiters' and bartenders' experiences of service encounters. *Journal of Foodservice* 19: 44–52.

Magnini, V., and Honeycutt Jr., E. D. 2005. Face recognition and name recall: Training implications for the hospitality industry. *Cornell Hotel and Restaurant Administration Quarterly* 46: 69–78.

Magnini, V. P. 2009. An exploratory investigation of the real-time training modes used by hotel expatriates. *International Journal of Hospitality Management* 28: 513–518.

Masadeh, M. 2013. Perspectives on foreign training: Middle managers in Jordan's international hotel chains. *European Journal of Tourism Research* 6: 20–35.

Morgeson, F. P., and Campion, M. A. 1997. Social and cognitive sources of potential inaccuracy in job analysis. *Journal of Applied Psychology* 82: 627–655.

Noe, R. A., Clarke, A. D. M., and Klein, H. J. 2014. Learning in the twenty-first century workplace. *Annual Review of Organizational Psychology and Organizational Behavior* 1: 1–31.

Noe, R. A., Tews, M. J., and Marand, A. D. 2013. Individual differences and informal learning in the workplace. *Journal of Vocational Behavior* 83: 327–335.

O'Mahony, M., and Smyth, B. 2010. A classification-based view recommender. *Knowledge-Based Systems* 23: 323–329.

Reynolds, D., Rahman, I., and Bradetich, S. 2014. Hotel managers' perceptions of the value of diversity training: An empirical investigation. *International Journal of Contemporary Hospitality Management* 26: 426–446.

Richman, W. L., and Quiñones, M. A. 1996. Task frequency rating accuracy: The effect of task engagement and experience. *Journal of Applied Psychology* 81: 512–524.

Ross, G. F. 2006. Ethical, career, organizational, and service values as predictors of hospitality traineeship interest. *Tourism Culture and Communication* 6: 121–136.

Rynes, S., and Rosen, B. 1995. A field survey of factors affecting the adoption and perceived success of diversity training. *Personnel Psychology* 48: 247–270.

Saks, A. M. and Gruman, J. A. 2017. Implications of positive psychology for learning and training. In K. G. Brown, ed., *The Handbook of Workplace Training and Employee Development*. New York: Cambridge University Press.

Salanova, M., Agut, S., and Peiro, J. M. 2005. Linking organizational resources and work engagement to employee performance and customer loyalty: The mediation of service climate. *Journal of Applied Psychology* 90: 1217–1227.

Salazar, J., Ashraf, H-R., Tcheng, M., and Antun, J. 2005. Food service employee satisfaction and motivation and the relationship with learning food safety. *Journal of Culinary Science and Technology* 4: 93–108.

Schlesinger, L. A., and Zornitsky, J. 1991. Job satisfaction, service capability, and customer satisfaction: An examination of linkages and management implications. *Human Resource Planning* 14: 141–149.

Schnieder, B., White, S. S., and Paul, M. C. 1998. Linking service climate and customer perceptions of service quality: Test of a causal model. *Journal of Applied Psychology* 83: 150–163.

Singh, D., Kim, Y-S., and Feinstein, A. H. 2011. Internet utilization as a medium for training employees in multi-unit restaurants. *Journal of Foodservice Business Research* 14: 122–145.

Sitzmann, T. 2011. A meta-analytic examination of the instructional effectiveness of computer-based simulation games. *Personnel Psychology* 64: 489–528.

Sitzmann, T., Kraiger, K., Stewart, D. and Wisher, R. 2006. The comparative effectiveness of web-based and classroom instruction: A meta-analysis. *Personnel Psychology* 59: 623–664.

Sobaih, A. E. E. 2011. Half job-half training? Management perceptions of part-time employee training in the hospitality industry. *Journal of Human Resources in Hospitality and Tourism* 10: 400–420.

Tannenbaum, S. I., Beard, R., McNall, L. A., and Salas, E. 2010. Informal learning and development in organizations. In S. W. J. Kozlowski and E. Salas, eds., *Learning, Training, and Development in Organizations*, 303–332. New York: Routledge.

Testa, M. R., and Sipe, L. 2012. Service-leadership competencies for hospitality and tourism management. *International Journal of Hospitality Management* 31: 648.658.

Tews, M. J., and Tracey, J. B. 2008. An empirical examination of interventions for enhancing the effectiveness of interpersonal skills training. *Personnel Psychology* 61: 375–401.

Tews, M. J., and Tracey, J. B. 2009. Helping managers help themselves. *Cornell Hospitality Quarterly* 50: 245–257.

Torres, E. N., Adler, H., Behnke, C., Miao, L., and Lehto, X. 2015. The use of consumer-generated feedback in the hotel industry: Current practices and their effects on quality. *International Journal of Hospitality Tourism and Administration* 16: 224–250.

Tracey, J. B. 2014. A review of human resources management research: The past 10 years and implications for moving forward. *International Journal of Contemporary Hospitality Management* 26: 679–705.

Tracey, J. B. and Cardenas, C. G. 1996. Training effectiveness: An empirical examination of factors outside the training context. *Hospitality Research Journal* 20: 113–123.

Tracey, J. B., and Tews, M. J. 2004. An empirical investigation of the relationships among climate, capabilities, and unit performance. *Journal of Hospitality and Tourism Research* 28: 298–312.

Tracey, J. B., Hinkin, T. R., Tannenbaum, S. I., and Mathieu, J. E. 2001. The influence of individual characteristics and the work environment on varying levels of training outcomes. *Human Resource Development Quarterly* 12: 5–23.

Tracey, J. B., Hinkin, T. R., Tran, T. L. B., Emigh, T., Kingra, M., Taylor, J., and Thorek, D. 2015. A field study of new employee training programs: Industry practices and strategic insights. *Cornell Hospitality Quarterly* 56: 345–354.

Úbeda-García, M., Marco-Lajara, B., Sabater-Sempere, V., and Garcia-Lillo, F. 2013. Does training influence organisational performance? Analysis of the Spanish hotel sector. *European Journal of Training & Development* 37: 380–413.

Vanderpool, C., and Way, S. A. 2013. Investigating work-family balance, job anxiety, and turnover intentions as predictors of health care and senior services customer-contact employee voluntary turnover. *Cornell Hospitality Quarterly* 54: 149–160.

Warr, P., and Bunce, D. 1995. Trainee characteristics and the outcomes of open learning. *Personnel Psychology* 48: 347–375.

Way, S. A., Tracey, J. B., Fay, C. H., Wright, P., Snell, S.A., Chang, S., and Gong, Y. 2015. Validation of a multi-dimensional HR flexibility measure. *Journal of Management* 41: 1098–1131.

Werner, J. 2017. Training from the perspective of human resource development and industrial and organizational psychology: Common past, parallel paths – Going where? In K. G. Brown, ed., *The Handbook of Workplace Training and Employee Development*. New York: Cambridge University Press.

Wei-Tang, T. H., Martin, L., and Yeh, Y. R. 2002. Cross-cultural impact and learning needs for expatriate hotel employees in Taiwan lodging industry. *Journal of Human Resources in Hospitality and Tourism* 1: 31–46.

Wirtz, J., Tambyah, S. K., and Mattila, A. S. 2010. Organizational learning from customer feedback received by service employees. *Journal of Service Management* 21: 363–387.

Wright, P. M., and Snell, S. A. 1998. Toward a unifying framework for exploring fit and flexibility in strategic human resource management. *Academy of Management Review* 23: 756–772.

Zakrzewski, C. S., Sammons, G., and Feinstein, H. 2005. A new approach to CAI: Online applications for procedural based activities. *Journal of Hospitality and Tourism Education* 17: 47–54.

Zhang, L. Cai, L. A., and Liu, W-L. 2002. On-job training: A critical human resources challenge in China's hotel industry. *Journal of Human Resources in Hospitality and Tourism* 1: 91–101.

Zhao, X., and Namasivayam, K. 2009. Posttraining self-efficacy, job involvement, and training effectiveness in the hospitality industry. *Journal of Human Resources in Hospitality and Tourism* 8: 137–152.

25 Informal Learning

Saul Carliner

On the one hand, informal learning – that is, learning in which learners establish their own objectives and determine for themselves when they have completed it (Driscoll & Carliner, 2005) and that often occurs incidentally as part of another activity and unconsciously (Marsick & Watkins, 2015; Wihak & Hall, 2011) – has underlaid human development since the beginning of time, long before people formalized instructional processes with tutors, schools, and universities (Sleight, 1993).

On the other hand, since the 2000s, the trade press on training and human resources has treated the topic as a contemporary one. Several recent developments have generated this renewed interest. The first is technology. Since it was first piloted in the 1960s, computer-based training (now called e-learning) has touted individualization as one of its advantages (Clark & Mayer, 2016). Learners take online courses individually, and the computer can tailor responses to an individual's needs. Since the rise of online information (Redish, 2012) in the 1980s and 1990s and the World Wide Web in the 1990s and 2000s, the concept of instruction has expanded from material within an instructional program to material more widely available online, and from material proposed by the system to material actively sought by learners (Driscoll & Carliner, 2005). Gery (1991; 1995; 2002) or suggested by a particular application of online learning and information called an electronic performance support system (EPSS), which provide workers with the assistance they need online and within the context of a particular job task. Assistance can take the form of instruction, information, online guidance in performing a task, chat with an expert, access to knowledge bases, and having the system perform a task for the worker (Gery, 1991). Some see EPSSs as a natural application for mobile devices (mobile learning [called m-learning] is described in Wasserman and Fisher, 2017, this volume); in fact, many popular apps for smart phones feature characteristics of EPSSs.

A second development that has fueled interest in informal learning is an increasing emphasis in higher education on preparation for the workplace. Professional education programs like medicine and other licensed health care professions have long featured clinical education programs, practicums that provide students with the opportunity to apply classroom lessons in real work settings under the close supervision of experienced professionals (Ribeiro, 2015). The concept has been expanded to a variety of other disciplines through programs like internships and cooperative education.

A third development that has fueled interest in informal learning is conditions within the field of training. Expenditures on training, as measured in inflation-adjusted dollars per worker have dropped over the past 25 years, a trend that has accelerated since the 2000s (Carliner & Bakir, 2010; Lavis; 2011) and some organizations are relying on informal learning to fill the void (Lavis, 2011). In addition to the economic influences on the rise informal learning, it is also a response to trainers' increasing disenchantment with classroom learning (Cross, 2011). Interest in promoting transfer of training from the classroom to practice has also grown among trainers, who see informal learning an additional means of facilitating transfer. In addition, wide promotion of 70:20:10, a proposition about the extent to which informal learning should occur (70:20:10 Forum, n.d.; Lombardo & Eichinger, 2000), has further fueled interest among trainers.

This chapter explores informal learning, focusing on its role in training and development. It first defines informal learning in general as well as the specific context of the workplace. Then it describes the forms informal learning takes and the processes of informal learning. The chapter closes by suggesting challenges and opportunities for conducting research on informal learning.

What Is Informal Learning?

As noted earlier, informal learning refers to learning in which workers establish their own objectives and determine for themselves when they have completed it. Jay Cross, whose 2007 book, *Informal Learning: Rediscovering the Natural Pathways That Inspire Innovation and Performance,* brought the concept into wide consciousness among the training and development community, adds that:

> Informal learning is the unofficial, unscheduled, impromptu way most of us learn to do our jobs. Informal learning is like riding a bicycle: the rider chooses the destination and the route. The cyclist can take a detour at a moment's notice to admire the scenery or help a fellow rider. (Cross, n.d.)

Carliner (2012) refers to this as *true* informal learning.

True informal learning contrasts with three related types of learning that typically occur outside of formal educational settings. The first is *nonformal* learning, which refers to events, such as lectures, exercise classes, and demonstrations, whose goals are as much social and physical as they are intellectual, but involve learning. The second type of learning related to informal learning is *incidental* learning: the knowledge and skills acquired unintentionally in situations not formally intended to provide instruction; learning is an unanticipated by-product of the experience. The learning might occur through conversations with co-workers or through on-the-job experiences. In some cases, the learning offers the benefits of deeper knowledge of a subject and an expanded base of skills. In other cases, the lessons learned might actually pose a problem because the learner might have drawn incorrect conclusions from these experiences and no process exists for verifying and correcting the knowledge acquired. The third type of learning related to informal learning is *self-directed* learning, which refers to "any increase in knowledge, skill, accomplishment, or personal development that an individual selects and brings about by his or her own efforts using any method in any circumstances at any time" (Gibbons, 2002: 2). Typically, learners work with an instructor or similar coach to plan the program of study that is outlined in a learning contract, a formal agreement that provides some form of acknowledgment for completing the program. Some people refer to this as intentional informal learning (Schulz & Rosznagel, 2010).

Although technically distinct from one another in the research literature, many people do not distinguish among nonformal, incidental, and self-directed learning in the workplace nor do they consider their distinction from informal learning. In the vernacular, people treat the four as a single concept.

Furthermore, nonformal, incidental, self-directed, and *true* informal learning happen on their own schedules and usually without verifying that workers learned material in a way that is consistent with practice in the workplace. That creates a problem because most workplaces have prescribed protocols for performing many processes and expect workers to follow them. In addition, practical issues, such as a lack of time or the inability to find enough learners to fill a class, force workers to learn these protocols and related concepts outside of formally scheduled training programs. In these instances, many employers facilitate informal learning by providing resources like on-the-job training, reference materials, and access to expertise so workers. By doing so, however, informal learning in the workplace often has characteristics of formal learning and therefore differs from *true* informal learning. In response, British researchers Janice Malcolm, Phil Hodkinson, and Helen Colley (2003) proposed a definition of informal learning tailored to the context of the workplace. Their definition acknowledges the formal characteristics of some informal learning. It specifically proposes that informal learning involves shared control over the:

- Process of learning, which focuses on whether the employer or worker has control over the process. The more the employer controls the process, the more formal it is.
- Location of learning, which can occur in a place intended for learning (such as a meeting room) or not (such as the water cooler). Learning that occurs in a place intended for learning tends to be more formal.
- Purpose of learning, which refers to whether learning is a primary or secondary goal of the activity. When learning is a primary goal, the more formal it is.
- Content of learning, which refers to whether the material is abstract and conceptual or technical and practical. The more abstract and conceptual the material, the longer term its application and the more formal the learning.

Wihak and Hall (2011) added a fifth characteristic: consciousness, which refers to the extent to which workers are aware they learned something. The more conscious the worker that learning occurred, the more formal the learning. Carliner

(2012) adapted these concepts to provide a definition of informal learning tailored for the workplace context:

> Situations in which some combination of the process, location, purpose, and content of instruction are determined by the worker, who may or may not be conscious that an instructional event occurred. (5)

Furthermore, the extent to which workers determine the process, location, purpose, and content of instruction, and are aware that instruction occurred, can vary widely among situations that are labeled as informal learning.

What Forms Does Informal Learning Take?

Livingston (2015), Wihak and Hall (2011), Hughes and Campbell (2009), and Livingstone and Scholtz (2006) identify several types of activities that facilitate informal learning in work-related contexts, ranging from formal lunch-and-learn sessions to the learning that occurs when performing tasks alongside another worker. Eraut (2007) suggests a three-part framework for classifying these activities: (1) work processes with learning as a by-product; (2) learning activities or processes embedded in work activities; and (3) learning processes at or near the workplace. The next several sections explore each of these categories.

Work Processes with Learning as a By-Product

The first category of activities that facilitate informal learning in work-related contexts are ones in which the learning occurs in situ: that is, while performing a work task, receiving feedback from a colleague, solving an immediate work-related problem, and persisting with a work-related challenge until stumbling onto something that works. In these instances, learning is a by-product of the work process. Table 25.1 lists common work processes that facilitate informal learning as a by-product (Carliner, 2012; Colley, Hodkinson, & Malcolm, 2003; Eraut, 2007; Wihak et al., 2008).

Learning Activities or Processes Embedded in Work Activities

The second category of activities identified by Eraut (2007) and that facilitate informal learning in work-related contexts is formal learning activities that occur in the workplace and self-directed learning processes that are embedded in work, such as conducting research for a project. Table 25.2 lists examples of formal learning activities and processes that occur in the workplace and that facilitate informal learning.

Learning Processes at or Near Workplace Processes

The third category of activities that facilitate informal learning in work-related contexts is learning processes at or near a workplace. The activities range from

Table 25.1 *Work processes with learning as a by-product*

Work Process	Description
Work assignments and projects	An undertaking performed as a job requirement and through which workers learn. Workers feel that work assignments and projects offer some of the most significant learning opportunities because they let workers immediately apply skills and knowledge and see the results (Laiken et al., 2008). Others value work assignments and projects because they provide workers with the opportunity to develop new skills or try ones that they learned in the past that would atrophy without use.
Developmental assignments	Either ongoing job tasks or temporary job placements that let workers stretch their knowledge and skills in ways they have not experienced before, and that usually involve greater visibility and responsibility than they have had before. Examples include adding budgetary responsibility to the job of an individual contributor or a placement as an administrative assistant to a senior executive to gain a new perspective on the organization.
Independent research and study	An effort by a worker to investigate a topic and develop expertise in it. Sometimes, the employer initiates the project by asking a worker to investigate a particular issue. Sometimes, the worker initiates the project, usually studying in depth about a topic of personal interest.
Trial and error	Workers attempting to apply skills and knowledge on the job and adjusting those skills and knowledge in response to the extent to which the result succeeds or not. Typically trial and error involves: (1) attempting to do something, (2) partially or completely failing in that effort, (3) determining why the effort partially or completely failed, (4) figuring out how to address the problem, (5) trying out the correction, and (6) determining whether the correction worked (and if it did not, repeating the process until the worker lands on a change that does work). Trial and error is one part (admittedly extreme) of the process of practicing skills and developing fluency with them. Fluency refers to the speed and ease with which workers perform a given task. The more frequently workers perform a task successfully, the faster they do so and the more comfort they feel. Workers develop fluency with job tasks through repeated performance and ongoing success.
Meetings	An event in which two more people interact at the same time for a particular purpose. Different types of meetings have different purposes: A status meeting provides people who work together with an opportunity to tell one another how their work is progressing; a working meeting brings together people for the purpose of completing part or all a particular task; announcement meeting, which brings together people for informing them about a particular piece of news, such as a new policy or product, or a change in personnel; and an annual meeting, which brings together stakeholders in an organization to provide them with a report on events of the past year, report vital statistics about the organization, and outline plans for the coming year. Meetings can be small and loosely structured or large and formally structured, and can occur face to face or virtually online.

(cont.)

Table 25.1 (*cont.*)

Work Process	Description
Documentation	The formal policies, processes, procedures, product descriptions, product plans, reports, and similar materials describing the operations of the organization. These sources are often a primary tool that workers use to informally learn about their jobs and job-related tasks.
Knowledge bases	The less formal counterpart to documentation. These include project files, responses to help line calls, transcripts of ongoing discussions and similar materials that workers can search for insights into applying the formal policies, processes, and procedures in the documentation. Some of the materials in knowledge bases are informal notes; some of the materials are more structured tips, suggestions, and lessons learned.
Advertising and similar brief messages	Short (30 seconds to 5 minutes) messages that: (1) build awareness about an issue to generate interest in a subsequent formal training program; (2) provide support for retention of knowledge taught in a formal training program through brief knowledge recall questions and reminder messages; (3) provide guidance in applying concepts taught in a formal training program through brief reminders and tips; and (4) help develop new skills, one small step at a time (called *microtraining* and *microlearning*).

semi- to formally structured activities, such as job shadowing, visiting other sites, and preparing for a qualification, like a certification. Table 25.3 lists examples of learning processes at or near workplaces that facilitate informal learning.

What Issues Should Training Professionals Consider Regarding Informal Learning?

This section describes suggests characteristics of informal learning that have emerged in the literature and should be considered when attempting to promote, facilitate, and recognize it in the workplace. Some of the literature suggests theoretical frameworks from which to consider informal learning. Some suggests characteristics of the informal learning process. Some of the literature suggests the supports needed for successful informal learning in the workplace. And some of the literature addresses challenges in evaluating informal learning. After a brief discussion of the challenges of conducting research on informal learning, the following sections summarize the findings.

The Challenges of Conducting Research on Informal Learning

Unlike much-researched formal learning, only a limited body of empirical research exists on informal learning in the peer-reviewed literature on training, adult education, educational technology, industrial and organizational

Table 25.2 *Learning activities or processes embedded in work activities*

Activity	Description
On-the-job training (OJT)	A structured program that workers follow to develop skills and knowledge needed to perform one or more aspects of their work assignments. On-the-job training usually involves a formal presentation of content – sometimes delivered orally or read by the worker, a demonstration of skills, and the opportunity to practice skills and receive feedback from a more experienced colleague.
Giving and receiving feedback	Feedback refers to reactions to an individual's performance in job and work-related tasks, identifying the aspects of the task the worker performed effectively and those on which the worker did not perform effectively and, when feasible, offering suggestions for resolving problem with performance (Tesmer, 1993). Learning occurs on both sides of the feedback discussion.
Performance support	Defined earlier in this chapter and which provides workers with the assistance they need online and within the context of a particular job task (Gery, 1991).
Coaching	Formal efforts to provide workers with feedback on their performance of a particular task or job and, if needed, suggestions on how to improve performance. Coaching relationships typically involve two parties: workers, who perform a job or task and coaches, who provide the feedback and suggestions (International Coach Federation, n.d.).
Mentoring	A relationship between a *mentor* – someone with experience who "provides advice, guidance, support, and feedback" (Driscoll and Carliner, 2005: 188) – and a *protégé,* someone who wants to learn from the experience of the mentor. Mentoring relationships "facilitate personal and professional growth, and … foster career development" (Driscoll & Carliner, 188). Mentoring contrasts with coaching in that mentoring is often provided outside of the context of a job, is intended for the personal development of the protégé, and has no formal agenda unless the protégé suggests one. In contrast, coaching is usually provided within the context of a particular job with the intention of improving performance in that job.
Communities of practice	Groups of people share a characteristic and discuss opportunities, challenges, and feelings related to their shared experiences. Communities can meet in person or online (or a combination of the two). Examples include professional associations, clubs, chambers of commerce, and affinity groups (people who share a common demographic characteristic, such as a women's, Latino, or LGBTQ affinity group). Some meet in person, some interact online, and some interact both in person and online. Topics of discussion typically emerge from the common interest of the group (Wenger, 2000). Social media like Facebook and LinkedIn facilitate the formation and operations of these communities.

(cont.)

Table 25.2 (*cont.*)

Activity	Description
Networks	The complex web of people with whom a worker interacts. In the past, networks primarily consisted of people with whom people had a face-to-face work or social relationship. With the rise of social media, these networks also include people with whom a person has only had online contact (Poell et al., 2000).
Gaming simulations	Activities that let workers interact with a model of a particular environment (the simulation) and see the consequences of their choices (the gaming component). Depending on the nature of the simulation, workers often receive feedback on their participation. Augmented reality, a technology that enhances the realism of the simulation experience, is discussed in another chapter in this handbook.
Case studies	Structured reports about past work experiences. A complete case study describes the problem or challenge faced; requirements for a solution; selection and development of a solution; subsequent results with the solution; and lessons learned from the experience. Case studies can come from within the organization or from outside sources, and address successful and unsuccessful efforts. Under ideal circumstances, workers would read and discuss case studies with others. In informal learning, however, workers typically find case studies and determine for themselves how to transfer the knowledge to their jobs.

psychology, and vocational and career development. Perhaps part of the reason for this situation is a natural tendency to focus on formal learning, which is the primary job task of training and development groups (Carliner & Bernard, 2011; Carliner & Price, 2015).

Perhaps part of the reason for this situation is the difficulty of studying informal learning (Carliner, 2012). Because informal learning usually happens outside of formally scheduled events and often occurs unconsciously, this phenomenon does not easily lend itself to experimental research. Other quantitative methods pose challenges, too. Survey research, for example, typically relies on after-the-fact, self-reported data, which has its own reliability issues. Web analytics, an emerging area of interest for education researchers, can provide accurate information about how frequently and how long individual online resources were used, but those numbers only track activities and behaviors; they do not assess results, much less learning. For example, a web page might have appeared on a workers' screen for four hours, but that worker might have been distracted with a problem for 3 hours and 55 minutes of that time. Or a knowledge base might have had 500 visits, but 417 of those visits were from members of the team that developed the knowledge base rather than users for whom they developed it.

Table 25.3 *Learning processes at or near workplace processes*

Process	Description
Formal courses	As ironic as this might sound, the courses that have been formally scheduled and have formal learning objectives and, perhaps, a formal assessment of learning, can also serve as informal learning experiences, especially when the learner initiates the enrollment. The courses are often ones that are not sponsored by the employer. Rather, they are probably offered professional and trade associations or take the form of continuing education programs offered by public schools, colleges, and universities; and courses offered by museums, arts associations, and other community organizations. Some of these courses are one-time events; others are part of larger certificate or degree programs. Informal learners might not have an interest in the certificate or degree but take these courses because they address a developmental need.
Tutorials and guided tours	Formal instructional programs that workers at their own initiative for as long as they find value in the formal programs. Tutorials are formally structured lessons and usually include presentation of material, demonstration of skills, practice of skills with feedback, and an assessment of skills. Guided tours are brief presentations of topics or demonstrations of the skill, but do not provide opportunities for practice, feedback, or assessment.
Lunch and Learns	An event of 90 minutes or less that occurs over a meal (typically lunch, hence the name) and that addresses technical or developmental content. Lunch and Learns typically occur within a particular workplace and, often, within a particular department. Although Lunch and Learn sessions rarely have formal learning objectives, successful events usually have a tight focus on a single topic and keep the presentation short (Wihak et al., 2008).
Seminars, symposia, conferences, and webinars	Special types of meetings intended that let participants explore one or more topics with a facilitator. In many instances, organizations sponsor these events to update the knowledge and skills of current staff members or business partners (such as suppliers and customers). Organizations like these events because they are often shorter than a full training course (such as a seminar or webinar), or let participants tailor an agenda to their own needs and interests (such as a conference), or let participants consider a topic in-depth (such as a seminar).

As a result, most of the in-depth research on informal learning emerges from qualitative studies (Carliner, 2012). Some of those studies are observational and require a long period to conduct. They yield rich, thick data. But the number of participants is small and the data challenging to synthesize. Other qualitative studies primarily rely on after-the-fact interviews, which pose similar challenges to self-reported data. Furthermore, although transferrable, results of qualitative studies are not generalizable.

Two particular challenges have arisen when studying informal learning. One pertains to pinning down the competencies acquired informally. Carliner (2012) and Livingstone (2001) note that part of this challenge arises from the fact that informal learners establish their own criteria for choosing what to learn and determining its successful completion. The tools upon which researchers traditionally rely to specify and measure learning – formal learning objectives and criterion-referenced assessments and follow-up evaluations – are philosophically and intellectually inconsistent with the learner-driven approach of informal learning. Furthermore, because learning is self-defined in informal learning, researchers primarily rely on self-report data for identifying what workers learned and the extent to which they mastered those competencies.

To avoid solely relying on self-report data, Eraut (2000) suggests using observations. But he also notes the limits of observation: Because much informal learning is tacit, observations alone fail to elicit it. To address this limitation, Eraut recommends that researchers present their observations to participants and, in the resulting conversations, Eraut has observed that participants mention events that the researchers had not witnessed and that also resulted in tacit learning (Eraut, 2000). Marsick and Watkins (2011) also note that eliciting such tacit learning from participants remains an ongoing challenge.

Livingstone (2001) raised the second challenge facing research in informal learning: that "very little cumulative development of understanding of the phenomenon of informal learning [has occurred] to date. Researchers keep rediscovering portions of informal learning anew with little effort to date to replicate earlier discoveries" (Livingstone, 2001:18).

If the research on informal learning in the workplace is limited, research in other fields can help inform understanding of the phenomenon. For example, research in museum visitor studies (such as Berry, Carbone, & Haeckel, 2002; Meyer & Schwager, 2007) and the usability of web-based marketing communication (such as Nielsen, ongoing) and suggests characteristics of material that attracts learners to it and how they pay attention to it. Research on user experience design and visitor studies (such as Falk & Dierking, 2000; 2012; Nielsen, ongoing) provides insights into the ease and success with which people find material, the extent of time spent with it, and the accuracy and longevity of learning it. The fields of museum visitor studies (such as Falk & Dierking, 2002; 2012), prior learning and assessment (Spencer, 2008) and web analytics (such as Chen, Chiang, & Storey, 2012; Zikopoulos & Eaton, 2011) also suggest ways to approach the evaluation of informal learning.

The following sections interweave the findings from research in training and continuing education and these other disciplines.

Guiding Frameworks for Informal Learning

Three general frameworks are typically mentioned to guide inquiry into informal learning. The best known among practicing professionals and researchers is 70:20:10, a proposition that has its roots in the work of Allen Tough (1978) and was further developed by Lombardo and Eichinger (2000) from the Center for Creative Leadership. This framework posits that 10% of job-related learning occurs through formal instruction, 20% through coaching, and the remaining 70% through learning in the context of the job (Rabin, 2014; 70:20:10 Forum, 2013). This framework is popular in professional circles, buoyed by broad coverage, such as that offered by the UK-based Chartered Institute for Personnel and Development, which has actively promoted the concept to its members. The primary appeal of 70:20:10 is intuitive; it seems to reflect the way that people learn on the job. But researchers note that 70:20:10 has never been validated empirically (De Bruykere, Kirschner, & Hulshof, 2015). Furthermore, the little empirical research that has been conducted on the extent of informal learning in the workplace has either solely focused on the extent of material learned formally and informally (such as Hall and Cotsman, 2015) or the extent of participation of adults in informal learning activities for work- and non-work related activities (such as Livingston, Hart & Davie, 1997; 1999).

Marsick and Watkins (1990; 2001) propose an alternative framework that is grounded in the empirical evidence: the triggers framework. This framework posits that "triggers" in the workplace spark both conscious and unconscious learning. When they first proposed the triggers framework, Marsick and Watkins saw formal and informal learning as separate from one another. Dale and Bell (1999) agreed, advising against solely relying on either formal or informal learning. By 2009, after further evidence of informal learning was added to the literature, Marsick (2009) concluded that formal and informal learning are actually interrelated. One of the most powerful ways this interrelationship is experienced is in the transfer of learning, in which a concept or process taught in the classroom and that learners might perceive as abstract or vague becomes increasingly concrete and relevant through application on the job and feedback on the performance (Burke & Hutchins, 2007). Informal learning can also fill intentional and unanticipated gaps left by formal training. For example, Millar (2008) describes a situation in which some enterprising fast food workers who, having learned about the importance of efficiency in the restaurant where they worked, decided to increase production from the 10 hamburgers they were instructed to make per hour to 12. But the business owner specifically limited production to 10 as a result of anticipated sales and food safety concerns, two topics overlooked by the training and not considered by the workers. This example also identifies one of the primary challenges of informal learning; workers learn their own lessons that might conflict with the best interests of the employer.

Expanding on the relationship between formal and informal learning in the triggers framework, Carliner (2012) proposed a framework that anticipates the types of incidents that would trigger learning: events related to the phase in the life cycle of a job. The general issues that trigger a need to learn and the nature of that learning (formal or informal), are often tied to the tenure of a worker in a particular job. For example, early in a worker's tenure in a position, socializing into the job triggers informal learning (Eraut, 2007). Later in a worker's tenure in a position, becoming more effective and efficient in a job and keeping up with changes to technology and the industry – most of which are incremental – also trigger informal learning. This also suggests why studies tracking participation in formal training (such as Bélanger & Robitaille, 2008) often show lower participation by experienced workers and studies of participation in informal learning show higher levels of participation among more experienced workers (such as Livingstone, 2001).

The common thread running through these frameworks is their focus on the broader process of learning rather than the successful achievement of learning objectives and outcomes, which tends to dominate research on formal learning. Perhaps that difference in focus might reflect a need among researchers to get a handle on what informal learning is and why people engage in it – another thread that underlies all three of the frameworks presented – before studying the cognitive processes underlying it.

Admittedly, some informal learning focuses on developing specific skills needed to perform a task immediately or offers a self-directed approach to training that would, under other circumstances, occur formally through a course (such as structured on-the-job training). Such training emphasizes skills rooted in the psychomotor and cognitive domains of knowledge. But proponents of informal learning argue that its greatest benefit is in the affective domain: developing, perceptions, feelings, and attitudes (Cross, 2007). Such development focuses on the personal and social construction of knowledge and understanding, usually in ways that do not lend themselves to the specification of observable and measurable objectives nor assessment with criterion-referenced assessments (Marsick & Watkins, 2011; Poell et al., 2000) but are central to development for the job all the same. Consider, cooperative education, internships, and apprenticeships, which help students transfer knowledge and skills acquired in the classroom to the job under the supervision of experienced professionals. More than just strengthening technical skills learned in formal courses and other structured learning programs and seeing their application in real-world settings, cooperative education, internships, and apprenticeships help learners develop professional judgment, strengthen their self-efficacy for the job, and help learners start to construct their professional identities (Eraut, 2007; Ribeiro, 2015). Such application learning, self-efficacy building, and identity formation continues on the job, sometimes consciously, often unconsciously.

What Research Suggests about the Informal Learning

Although the extensiveness of research-based insights into informal learning do not match those of formal learning, the research has illuminated many aspects of it. The next several sections summarize some of the key findings, including extent of participation in informal learning, the nature of knowledge developed informally, facilitators of informal learning, and evaluation of informal learning.

Extent of Participation in Informal Learning
The earliest research on informal learning primarily focused on documenting the extent of the phenomenon and the nature of the study undertaken. Between

the 1960s and 2000s, several studies conducted in different countries explored the extent to which adults participated in informal learning, both for work and personal reasons. The research generally found that more than half of all adults participate in some type of intentional learning and some studies found that as many as 90% of all adults participate (Beinart & Smith, 1998; Livingstone, Hart, & Davie, 1997; 1999; NALL, 1998; Penland, 1977; Tough, 1971; 1978), although some studies did find participation rates below 50% (Blomqvist, Niemi, & Ruuskanen, 1998; Statistics Canada 1997 [as reported in Livingstone, 2001]). Researchers noted that participation levels are similar across all adults, regardless of educational attainment and socioeconomic status (Livingstone, 2011). That research also found that two thirds of that intentional learning occurred outside of institutionalized adult education programs and courses.

Tough (1971; 1978) called these intentional learning efforts "adult learning projects" and documented them in case studies. His case study research suggests that 98% of all adults participate in these "projects." Because of the large proportion of projects that occurred outside of an institution, later researchers suggested that adult education is an iceberg (Brookfield, 1981), with formal learning only addressing a small proportion of this type of education (the tip of the iceberg, that is).

In terms of the amount of learning in which individuals engage, Tough (1978) reported that the typical adult engages in five adult learning projects per year. Other research has tried to quantify the number of hours spent on informal learning. All but one study has found that adults spend hundreds of hours per year on their projects, from a low of 20+ hours per year (Blomqvist, Niemi, & Ruuskanen, 1998) to a high of 750 hours (Livingstone, Hart, & Davie, 1999; NALL, 1998), and most suggesting between 300 and 500 hours per year (Beinart & Smith, 1998; Livingstone, Hart, & Davie, 1997; Penland, 1977). As a point of contrast, employers provide workers with an average of 31.5 hours of formal training per year (Miller, 2014).

The extent to which workers learn informally on the job ranges between 40% to 60%. In its biannual survey of learning and development in Canada, the Conference Board of Canada found that the percentage was 42% in 2006 (Hughes & Grant, 2007) and 56% in 2008 (Hughes & Campbell, 2009). In its 2014 survey, 55% of organizations reported further increases in informal learning (Hall & Cotsman, 2015).

Nature of Knowledge and Skills Developed Informally
Because these studies all explored adult education, they describe the combined effort invested in learning for work and personal goals. In the Canadian context, Livingstone (2001) identified four major categories of adult informal learning: employment (or work)-related learning; household work-related learning, community volunteer work-related learning, and other general interest learning.

According to Livingstone (2001), the most common topics for employment-related informal learning included keeping up with new or general knowledge in a field (71% of adults participated), new job tasks (63%), problem solving and communications (63%), employment-related computer learning (61%), occupational health and safety (55%), and other new technologies and equipment (52%).

Within these subject areas, informal learning seems best suited for imparting tacit knowledge (Eraut, 2007; Livingstone, 2001). Eraut (2007) notes that action in most professional contexts is characterized by a combination of routinized actions that often require little thought and actions that fall outside the routine that require decision making. Much of the informal learning on the job prepares workers to perform these routines fluently and helps workers develop the intuition needed to handle non-routine actions. Livingstone (2001) adds that formal learning works best for pre-established knowledge bases that have been explicitly recorded while informal learning works best for situational knowledge.

Within these subject areas, however, researchers seem to agree that explicit knowledge is more effectively and efficiently taught formally and tacit knowledge informally (Eraut, 2000; 2007; Livingstone, 2001). In fact, Carliner (2012) notes that the "learning" of explicit information often attributed to informal learning is not learning at all; it is merely information sharing. Workers acquire the information to complete an immediate job task without any expectation retaining the information, much less the developing a new skill.

About the acquisition of tacit knowledge, Eraut notes, "Much professional work deals with complex situations that require the use of complex knowledge that defies simple forms of representation. These problems do not challenge only researchers, they also have a huge influence on early career learning" (2007: 404). Eraut identified three types of tacit knowledge: Tacit understanding of people and situations, routine actions, and the implicit rules that underlie intuitive decision making within the context of the job. Livingstone (2001) amplifies this framework, suggesting that situational knowledge is best taught informally, while preestablished and explicitly recorded knowledge is best taught formally.

Facilitators of Informal Learning

Although the research has not generated a list of proven relationships from gold standard research, the research has shed light on several practices that facilitate informal learning in the workplace.

One is effective self-study skills. Livingstone (2001) noted, many adults do not know which competencies they need to develop and, as a result, spend a lot of time learning without much to show for it. Sitzmann et al. (2010) added that, even in formal learning, many learners do not have strong self-assessment skills. Some researchers have responded by developing self-assessment tools for learning (such as Leigh & Watkins, 2005). Downing (2007) noted the specific importance of teaching skills for searching for content; many workers use an incomplete set of keywords and act on one of the first results from a search, without assessing the appropriateness of those results.

A second facilitator of informal learning in the workplace is management "permission" to learn on work time. Although much work-related informal learning occurs subconsciously, much also happens intentionally. Workers need to learn a practice a new skill and might make errors in the process; other workers need to search for instructions or information to perform tasks. But many workplaces explicitly or implicitly discourage such learning and frown on errors. In some cases, pressure to respond to the largest number of calls in the least amount of time prevents workers from properly learning (Downing, 2007). In other cases, workers feel guilty about learning on work time, feeling it is unproductive use of their time (Westbrook & Veale, 2001).

A third facilitator of informal learning in the workplace is the actual job assignment. Eraut (2007) found that some work assignments inherently promote more learning than others, based on the responsibilities and tasks faced by workers. Specific factors of the work assignment that affect learning include the allocation of and structuring of work, the nature of the encounters that people have in their jobs, the relationships that exist in the job, and the performance expectations of the worker, including the extent to which the worker participates in establishing these expectations.

Materials prepared for learning and other purposes are the fourth facilitator of informal learning in the workplace. Examples of these materials include policies and procedures, product specifications, project files, knowledge bases, and videos. Dale and Bell (1999) observed that many workers use these materials for learning. Carliner (2012) adds the importance of subscribing to specialized sources of external information, too, to support informal learning efforts. Examples of specialized sources of information include databases of articles and private research reporting services.

A study of learning mid-career by Eraut (2000) identified a fifth facilitator of informal learning in the workplace: confidence. He notes that confidence:

> arose from successfully meeting *challenges* in one's work, while the confidence to take on such challenges depended on the extent to which learners felt *supported* in that endeavour by colleagues, either while doing the job or as back up when working independently. Thus there is a triangular relationship between challenge, support and confidence. (Eraut, 2007: 417)

This issue of confidence in informal learning parallels the concept of self-efficacy in formal learning (Bandura, 1994).

Coaching and feedback is a sixth facilitator of informal learning in the workplace. Downing (2007) and Livingstone (2001) report that, without feedback to the contrary, workers assume that they correctly mastered the material they learning informally. Eraut (2007) notes that the lack of feedback affects workers' motivation and confidence to learn. One of the factors affecting feedback quality results from the fact that informal learning often occurs privately and its results are usually applied out of sight of others. As a result, the person evaluating the learning might not have sufficient awareness to provide useful feedback.

A seventh facilitator of informal learning in the workplace is line management. Eraut (2007) and Ellinger and Bostrom (1999) both suggest that line managers play a significant role in coaching informal learning. Ellinger and Bostrom (1999) suggest specific management behaviors that promote learning. Eraut

(2007) notes that managers have a responsibility for making sure that feedback is provided to workers, though he adds that important that managers need to share feedback responsibilities with other members of their staffs.

An eighth facilitator of informal learning in the workplace is senior management. When senior leaders of an organization formally acknowledge the informal learning efforts of their workers and discuss their own informal learning, they explicitly model this type of learning and provide permission to learn on work time and encouragement for doing so (Dale and Bell, 1999).

Evaluation of Informal Learning

Trainers are conditioned to evaluate programs using Kirkpatrick's four-level evaluation framework (Arthur et al., 2003). But the Kirkpatrick framework was designed for formal learning and makes certain assumptions that do not apply to informal learning: that learning happens through discretely scheduled events designed around learning objectives that are formally stated in observable and measurable terms. More fundamentally, the underlying purpose for conducting evaluation according to the Kirkpatrick model does not apply to informal learning: to determine the extent to which a program developed by an organization to meet a particular performance objective has been well-received by workers, has achieved the intended performance objective, and has warranted the investment (Carliner, 2012).

Evaluation of informal learning serves two key purposes: identifying what individuals have learned informally and which resources workers use to learn informally (Carliner, 2012). Identifying what individuals have learned informally serves two purposes. The first is making sure that learners have not misunderstood or misapplied knowledge, which could eventually lead to problems in the workplace. This can be assessed through observations in the workplace accompanied or conversations between workers and managers or coaches to "surface" the learning (Marsick & Watkins, 2011), both accompanied with corrective feedback and coaching if needed. In addition, self-assessments can help workers determine for themselves the extent to which they have acquired skills and knowledge.

The second purpose of evaluating what workers have learned informally is formally recognizing the additional capabilities they have acquired with promotions, new positions, and salary increases. Certification – the validation of competence by a third party (Hale, 2011) – offers an independent means of performing this type of evaluation and providing recognition.

Identifying which resources workers use to learn informally serves two purposes. One is to determine sources of influence on workers. Trainers can assess this overtly by directly asking workers on employee surveys which sources they use to learn informally and who influences them the most in the workplace. But this is self-reported data after the fact and might not provide a complete picture of influences on workers. So, trainers might use web analytics to also get a sense of which materials workers use.

In addition to data on overall use of individual resources, trainers might also look for patterns of use, such as whether people in a particular department or division rely more on certain sources than those in other departments and divisions; whether workers access resources (and therefore learning) on work or personal time; and spikes in use of particular resources (which might indicate some external event that drove workers to learn informally which trainers, in turn, might investigate further).

In addition, trainers might specifically track use of materials for which the organization pays a subscription or developed with its own resources, to determine the extent to which actual use matches anticipated use, and investigate why differences might exist.

Research Opportunities for Informal Learning

One benefit of the limited research on informal learning in the past is that it provides many opportunities for future research. Perhaps the most urgent need is the development and validation of theory around how people learn informally and its relationship to formal learning. This need is urgent because the 70:20:10 proposition is gaining wide recognition and some people – including training directors and academics – believe that this is also a funding formula: that is, organizations should only use 10% of their learning funds for formal learning and spend 70% on informal learning (Catanach, 2013). Such beliefs do not reflect the cost structures of formal and informal learning. Moreover, with training spending already on the decline (Carliner & Bakir, 2010; Hall & Cotsman, 2015), organizations adopting 70:20:10 as a funding formula might exacerbate skills challenges about which many employers also complain (Cappelli, 2012). This belief has practical consequences for organizations and their workers.

Such research needs to address the following specific issues: how workers choose the subjects for which they initiate learning; how frequently they initiate learning and what means they use to accomplish it; how learners determine when they have achieved a learning goal; how workers validate their own knowledge; which types of knowledge, skills, and attitudes workers acquire through incidental learning; the extent to which incidental learning corroborates and contradicts institutionally sanctioned learning; and the role of values in informal learning.

Additional research opportunities exist for exploring the impact of various organizational supports on learning, such as the impacts of rewards and punishments for learning on work time; the impact of organizational policies and culture on the willingness of workers to learn informally on personal time; and the impact of modeling of informal learning by leaders of an organization on the extent of informal learning in which the rank-and-file participates.

Some future research work is methodological: determining how to reliably track what workers have learned informally and the amount of time they spend doing so. Most studies rely on self-reported data (such as Grant Wofford, Ellinger, & Watkins, 2013; Hall & Cotsman, 2015; Livingstone, 2001). Observational data would be helpful but because informal learning typically happens incidentally and without a formal schedule, conducting observational research requires extensive resources and would generate substantial quantities of data, posing significant challenges for data analysis. The new Experience API (Tin Can) – a means of tracking what people are using for the purpose of learning and the extent people are using it – could collect data with minimal human involvement, but like most web analytics, requires a closer look to determine its validity and representativeness.

But perhaps the initial methodological work is in the area of definitions. Because informal learning in the workplace refers to programs like on-the-job training and internships that are often formally structured and organized but happen outside of a classroom, worker-initiated learning such as mastering certain capabilities of software, and incidental learning, such as confronting a management challenge, the informal learning studied by one researcher might substantially differ from the informal learning studied by another. Standardizing terminology around informal learning might permit researchers to more easily describe phenomena and, in turn, address some of the methodological issues identified in the previous paragraph.

Conclusion

Although humans have relied on informal learning throughout our history, this type of learning has generated new interest as employers reduce spending on training, as jobs become increasingly flexible and specialized, and as technology facilitates the broad exchange of knowledge, within and outside of organizations and job categories.

This new attention to informal learning encourages employers to facilitate it and reward workers who engage in it with increased responsibility, promotions, and salary increases. But because trainers still lack a complete understanding of informal learning compared with formal learning and its impact on the work environment, trainers should be cautious when promoting it in their workplaces.

References

70:20:10 Forum. n.d. *The 70:20:10 Framework.* https://www.702010forum.com/about-702010-framework (accessed April 11, 2016).

Arthur Jr., W., Bennett Jr., W., Edens, P. S., and Bell, S. T. 2008. Effectiveness of training in organizations: A meta-analysis of design and evaluation features. *Journal of Applied psychology* 88(2): 234.

Bandura, A. 1994. *Self-Efficacy.* New York: John Wiley and Sons.

Beinhart, S., and Smith, P. 1998. *Research Report No. 49: National Adult Learning Survey 1997*. Sudbury, UK Department for Education and Employment.

Bélanger, P., and Robitaille, M. 2008. *A Portrait of Work-Related Learning in Quebec*. Ottawa, ON: Canadian Council on Learning, Work and Learning Knowledge Centre.

Berry, L. L., Carbone, L. P., and Haeckel, S. H. 2002. Managing the total customer experience. *MIT Sloan Management Review* 43(3): 85.

Blomqvist, I., Niemi, H. and Ruuskanen, T. 1998. *Participation in Adult Education and Training in Finland 1995*. Helsinki: Statistics Finland.

Brockett, R., and Hiemstra, R. 1991. *Self-Direction in Adult Education: Perspectives on Theory, Research and Practice*. New York: Routledge.

Brookfield, S. 1981. The adult education learning iceberg. *Adult Education (UK)* 54(2): 110–118.

Brown, K. G., Charlier, S. D., and Pierotti, A. 2012. e-Learning in work organizations: Contributions of past research and suggestions for the future. In G. P. Hodgkinson and J. K. Ford, eds., *International Review of Industrial and Organizational Psychology*, 27: 89–114. Chichester, UK: John Wiley and Sons.

Burke, L. A. and Hutchins, H. M. 2007. Training transfer: An integrative literature review. *Human Resource Development Review* 6(3): 263–296.

Cappelli, P. 2012. *Why Good People Can't Get Jobs: The Skills Gap and What Companies Can Do About It*. Philadelphia: Wharton Digital Press.

Carliner, S. 2012. *Informal Learning Basics*. Alexandria, VA: ASTD Press.

Carliner, S., and Bakir, I. 2010. Trends in spending on training: an analysis of the 1982 through 2008 training annual industry reports. *Performance Improvement Quarterly* 23(3): 77–105.

Carliner, S., and Bernard, C. 2011. An integrative review of literature on the perceptions of HRD. *Proceedings of the 2011 Academy of Human Resource Development Research Conference in the Americas*. St Paul, MN: Academy of Human Resource Development.

Carliner, S., and Price, D. W. 2015. What's in a name? Training matters, *Training* July/August: 56–58.

Catanach, J. 2013. *Case study of an award-winning program: Best deployment of a hosted LMS*. Sydney: LearnX Australia.

Clark, R. C., and Mayer, R. E. 2016. *E-learning and the Science of Instruction: Proven Guidelines for Consumers and Designers of Multimedia Learning*. New York: John Wiley and Sons.

Colley, H., Hodkinson, P., and Malcolm, J. 2003. *Informality and Formality in Learning: A Report for the Learning and Skills Research Centre*. London: Learning and Skills Research Centre.

Cross, J. n.d. What is informal learning? *Informal Learning Blog*, http://www.informl.com/the-informal-learning-page (accessed September 30, 2015).

Cross, J. 2007. *Informal Learning: Rediscovering the Natural Pathways that Inspire Innovation and Performance*. San Francisco: Pfeiffer.

Cross, J. 2011. *Informal Learning: Rediscovering the Natural Pathways That Inspire Innovation and Performance*. New York: John Wiley and Sons.

Csikzentmihalyi, M., and Hermanson, K. 1995. Intrinsic motivation in museums: What makes visitors want to learn? *Museum News* 74(3): 35–37 and 59–62.

Dale, M., and Bell, J. 1999. *Informal Learning in the Workplace*. London: Department for Education and Employment.

De Bruyckere, P., Kirschner, P. A., and Hulshof, C. D. 2015. *Urban Myths about Learning and Education*. London: Academic Press.

Downing, J. 2007. Using customer contact centers to measure the effectiveness of online help systems. *Technical Communication* 54(2): 201–209.

Driscoll, M., and Carliner, S. 2005. *Advanced Web-Based Training Strategies: Unlocking Instructionally Sound Online Learning*. New York: John Wiley and Sons.

Ellinger, A. D., and Bostrom, R. P. 1999. Managerial coaching behaviors in learning organizations. *Journal of Management Development* 18(9): 752–771.

Eraut, M. 2000. Non-formal learning and tacit knowledge in professional work. *British Journal of Educational Psychology* 70(1): 113–136.

Eraut, M. 2007. Learning from other people in the workplace. *Oxford Review of Education* 33(4): 403–422.

Falk, J. H., and Dierking, L. 2000. *Learning from Museums: Visitor Experiences and the Making of Meaning*. Walnut Creek, CA: AltaMira Press.

Falk, J. H., and Dierking, L. D. 2012. *Museum Experience Revisited*. New York: Taylor & Francis.

Gery, G. 1991. *Electronic Performance Support Systems*. Tolland, MA: Gery Performance Press.

Gery, G. 1995. Attributes and behaviors of performance-centered systems. *Performance Improvement Quarterly* 8(1): 47–93.

Gery, G. 2002. Task support, reference, instruction, or collaboration? Factors in determining electronic learning and support options. *Technical Communication* 49(4): 420–427.

Gibbons, M. 2002. *The Self-Directed Learning Handbook*. San Francisco: Jossey-Bass.

Grant Wofford, M., Ellinger, A. D., and Watkins, K. E. 2013. Learning on the fly: Exploring the informal learning process of aviation instructors. *Journal of Workplace Learning* 25(2): 79–97.

Hale, J. 2011. *Performance-based Certification: How to Design a Valid, Defensible, Cost-effective Program*. New York: John Wiley & Sons.

Hall, C., and Cotsman, S. 2015. *2015 Learning and Development Outlook*. Ottawa, ON: Conference Board of Canada.

Hughes, P. D., and Campbell, A. 2009. *Learning and Development Outlook 2009: Learning in Tough Times*. Ottawa, ON: The Conference Board of Canada

Hughes, P. D., and Grant, M. 2007. *2007 Learning and Development Outlook*. Ottawa, ON: Conference Board of Canada.

International Coach Federation. n.d. What is professional coaching, Coaching FAQs. https://www.coachfederation.org/need/landing.cfm?ItemNumber=978&navItemNumber=567 (accessed August 23, 2016).

Laiken, M., Edge, K., Friedman, S., and West, K. 2008. Formalizing the informal: From informal to organizational learning in the post-industrial workplace. In K. Church et al., eds., *Learning through Community: Exploring Participatory Practices*, 187–204. Dordrecht, The Netherlands: Springer.

Lavis, C. 2011. *Learning and Development Outlook 2011: Are Organizations Ready for Learning 2.0*. Ottawa, ON: Conference Board of Canada.

Leigh, D., and Watkins, R. 2005. E-learner success: Validating a self-assessment of learner readiness for online training. In S. Carliner and B. Sugrue, eds., *Proceedings of the 2005 ASTD Research-to-Practice Conference-in-a-Conference*. Alexandria, VA: ASTD Press.

Livingstone, D. 2010. *The Relationship between Workers' Practical Knowledge and Their Job Requirements: Findings of the 1998, 2004 and 2010 National Surveys of Work and Lifelong Learning*. Canadian Society for Training and Development Conference. Toronto, November 17.

Livingstone, D. W. 2001. *NALL Working Paper #21: Adults' Informal Learning: Definitions, Findings, Gaps, and Future Research*. Toronto: Ontario Institute for Studies in Education.

Livingstone, D. W. 2015. *Lifelong Learning in Paid and Unpaid Work: Survey and Case Study Findings*. New York: Routledge.

Livingstone, D. W., and Scholtz, A. 2006. *Work and lifelong learning in Canada: Basic findings of the 2004 WALL survey*. Toronto: Centre for the Study of Education and Work, and the Ontario Institute for Studies in Education at the University of Toronto.

Livingstone, D. W., Hart, D., and Davie, L. E. 1997. *Public Attitudes Toward Education in Ontario 1996: Eleventh OISE/UT Survey*. Toronto: University of Toronto Press.

Livingstone, D. W., Hart, D., and Davie, L. E. 1999. *Public Attitudes Toward Education in Ontario 1998: Twelfth OISE/UT Survey*. Toronto: University of Toronto Press.

Lombardo, M. M., and Eichinger, R. W. 2000. *The Career Architect Development Planner*. Minneapolis, MN: Lominger Inc.

Malcolm, J., Hodkinson, P., and Colley, H. 2003. *Informality and Formality in Learning: A Report for the Learning and Skills Research Centre*. London: Learning and Skills Research Centre.

Marsick, V. J. 2009. Toward a unifying framework to support informal learning theory, research and practice. *Journal of Workplace Learning* 21(4): 265–275.

Marsick, V. J., and Watkins, K. 1990. *Informal and Incidental Learning in the Workplace*. London: Routledge.

Marsick, V. J., and Watkins, K. E. 2001. Informal and incidental learning. In S. B. Merriam, ed., *The New Update on Adult Learning Theory*. San Francisco: Jossey-Bass.

Marsick, V. J., and Watkins, K. 2011. Pursuing research in organizations that is useful to practice. Academy of Human Resource Development Research Conference in the Americas, Schaumberg, Illinois.

Marsick, V. J., and Watkins, K. 2015. *Informal and Incidental Learning in the Workplace (Routledge Revivals)*. New York: Routledge.

Meyer, C., and Schwager, A. 2007. Understanding customer experience. *Harvard Business Review*, February.

Millar, R. 2008. *Plenary: Informal learning in the workplace*. Third annual symposium of the Work and Learning Knowledge Centre. Work and Learning Knowledge Centre of the Canadian Council on Learning. Ottawa, ON.

Miller, L. 2014. *2014 ASTD State of the Industry Report*. Alexandria, VA: ASTD Press.

NALL. 1998. *Lifelong Learning Profiles: General summary of findings from the first Canadian survey of informal learning*. http://www.nall.ca. (accessed May 12, 2017).

Nielsen, J. 2016. AlertBox. https://www.nngroup.com/articles/author/jakob-nielsen (accessed September 21, 2016).

Penland, P. 1977. *Self-Planned Learning in America*. Pittsburgh, PA: University of Pittsburgh.

Poell, R., Chivers, G. E., Van Der Krogt, F. J. and Wildemeersc, D. A. 2000. Learning-network theory: Organizing the dynamic relationships between learning and work. *Management Learning* 31(1): 25–49.

Rabin, R. 2014. *Blended Learning for Leadership: The CCL Approach*. Greensboro, NC: Center for Creative Leadership. http://insights.ccl.org/wp-content/uploads/2015/04/BlendedLearningLeadership.pdf (accessed September 21, 2016).

Ribeiro, O. 2015. Becoming a clinical educator: An exploration of what clinical educators do and how they prepare to teach in a healthcare setting. PhD thesis, Montreal, QC: Concordia University.

Redish, J. 2012. *Letting Go of the Words: Writing Web Content That Works*. Burlington, MA: Morgan Kaufmann.

Schulz, M., and Rosznagel, C. S. 2010. Informal workplace learning: An exploration of age differences in learning competence. *Learning and Instruction* 20(5): 383–399.

Sitzmann, T., Ely, K., Brown, K. G., and Bauer, K. N. 2010. Self-assessment of knowledge: A cognitive learning or affective measure? *Academy of Management Learning and Education* 9(2): 169–191.

Sleight, D. 1993. A developmental history of training in the United States and Europe. https://msu.edu/~sleightd/trainhst.html (accessed August 23, 2016).

Spencer, B. 2008. Have we got an adult education model for PLAR? Online Proceedings of the Canadian Association for the Study of Adult Education (CASAE). http://auspace.athabascau.ca/handle/2149/1794 (accessed May 12, 2017).

Statistics Canada. 1997. *Adult Education and Training in Canada: Report of the 1994 Adult Education and Training Survey*. Ottawa, ON: Statistics Canada.

Tessmer, M. 1993. *Planning and Conducting Formative Evaluations: Improving the Quality of Education and Training*. New York: Psychology Press.

Tough, A. 1971. *The Adult's Learning Projects*. Toronto, ON: OISE Press.

Tough, A. 1978. Major learning efforts: Recent research and future directions. *Adult Education Quarterly* 28(4): 250–263.

Wasserman, M. E., and Fisher, S. L. 2017. One (lesson) for the road? What we know (and don't know) about mobile learning. In K. G. Brown, ed., *The Handbook of Workplace Training and Employee Development*. New York: Cambridge University Press.

Wenger, E. 2000. *Communities of Practice: Learning, Meaning, and Identity*. Cambridge: Cambridge University Press.

Westbrook, T. S., and Veale, J. R. 2001. Work-related learning as a core value: An Iowa perspective. *Human Resource Development Quarterly* 12(3): 301–317.

Wihak, C., and Hall, G. 2011. *Work-Related Informal Learning: Research and Practice in the Canadian Context*. Ottawa, ON: Canadian Council on Learning.

Wihak, C., Hall, G., Bratton, J., Warkentin, L., Wihak, L. and MacPherson, S. 2008. *Work-Related Informal Learning: Research and Practice in the Canadian Context*. Ottawa, ON: Work and Learning Knowledge Centre of the Canadian Centre for Learning.

Zikopoulos, P., and Eaton, C. 2011. *Understanding Big Data: Analytics for Enterprise Class Hadoop and Streaming Data*. New York: McGraw-Hill.

26 An Operations Management Perspective on Employee Training and Workforce Planning

Barrett W. Thomas, Mike Hewitt, and Scott E. Grasman

All organizations seek a workforce that meets the needs of their current customers and yet can meet the (perhaps different) needs of their customers in the future. A flexible workforce plays a key role in meeting both these needs. In the near term, a flexible workforce enables an organization to accommodate the day-to-day fluctuations in demands for its current products or services. In the longer term, a flexible workforce enables an organization to meet market demands for new products or services. However, a challenge for any organization is that building a flexible workforce, which is typically done through on-the-job or off-the-job training activities, often reduces their capabilities in the short term. Thus, an organization must balance a desire for a flexible workforce against these near-term sacrifices.

In this chapter, we review how the field of operations management (OM) approaches this challenge. OM is the "management of the systems or processes that create goods and/or provide services" (Stevenson, 2015: 4). Here, we are particularly interested in the management of the workforce such that specific processes produce their desired outputs. In particular we are interested in workforce planning, or, how organizations assign tasks to individuals in their workforce. And we will examine these processes from two perspectives: (1) meeting customer demands for products or services in the near term, and, (2) building a flexible workforce. We note that decisions relating to hiring and retention also impact workforce flexibility and organizational capacity. However, in this chapter, we focus on the management of an existing workforce.

One of the key challenges companies face in meeting customer demands in the near term is uncertainty both in terms of demand and supply. Uncertain demand comes from not knowing how much and in some cases exactly what customers will want. Uncertainty in supply is the result of many factors including absence, illness, and a skill mix mismatched to demand. As an example, the U.S. Bureau of Labor Statistics reports that 2.9% of the workforce was absent on any given day in 2015 (U.S. Bureau of Labor Statistics, 2016). It is well known from the study of queues, or waiting lines, that organizations can hedge against these uncertainties by adding capacity above and beyond the fore-casted or expected level of demand (Cachon & Terweisch, 2012). Examples of such capacity include floaters (permanent members of the workforce trained in multiple skills), temporary labor, and individuals working overtime (Qin, Nembhard, & Barnes, 2015). While such capacity can enable an organization to handle uncertainties in both supply and demand it is also costly, particularly as it often remains idle.

Another solution is to pool capacity, or, to group resources together so that a task may be performed by any resource in the group as opposed to one spe-cific, preassigned resource. We experience pooling when we wait in a single line at a bank and proceed from the front of the line to the first available teller. In such a system, we never wait in line unless all the tellers are busy. Conversely, we experience the drawbacks of a nonpooled queueing system when we choose the "wrong" checkout line at a grocery store that has one checkout line for each cashier. In such cases, one may have to wait for the cashier in the chosen line to become free when there is a cashier in another line that is available.

In manufacturing pooling occurs when a worker is trained in multiple skills and can switch jobs to where the worker is needed most. For example, at Marlin Steel, a Baltimore-based manufacturer of customer metal forms, workers are trained to work at multiple different manufacturing cells. This way, if there is little work at say the wire basket cell, then workers from that cell can be moved to laser cutting or sheet metal production to accommodate greater demand on those cells (Marlin Steel, 2015).

Multiskilled workers are often referred to as being cross-trained. While cross-training is common, it is often not possible to train every worker on every pos-sible task. Often, cross-training is costly (both in terms of dollars or time). Further, because organizations have limited budgets (both in time and money) for training, cross-training an individual on multiple tasks may mean that they are less proficient at a task they perform than if they had specialized on it.

Thus, there is a large volume of academic literature devoted to determining how many and which individuals should be cross-trained when cross-training all individuals is not desirable or feasible. For example, Hopp, Tekin, and Van Oyen (2004) identify three "levels" of decisions that must be made when implement-ing a flexible or cross-trained workforce: (1) Should there be any cross-training? (2) If workers are to be cross-trained, what workers should be cross-trained and in what skills? (3) Given a cross-trained workforce, what workers should do what jobs?

An active research area in OM is to answer these questions posed by Hopp et al. (2004) in different settings and under different assumptions. To answer this question, OM employs mathematical optimization. Mathematical optimization is the formulation of a decision-making process as a mathematical problem whose solution indicates the optimal set of actions.

In this chapter we first discuss the state of research. In reviewing the state of research, we particularly focus on optimization models for workforce planning and on research in cross-training and workforce flexibility. We conclude by discussing the gaps in the research and what these suggest for the need for interdisciplinary research.

State of Research

In this section, we discuss the state of research in workforce planning. As discussed previously, this review focuses on the use of existing workforce capacity to create a flexible workforce. We provide a basic overview of cross-training and its literature. A detailed review can be found in Qin et al. (2015). Hopp and Van Oyen (2004) offer additional insight through their framework for assessing both production and service environments in terms of their suitability for cross-training.

Background

We first review two concepts that are often seen and referred to in the workforce planning literature: (1) *configuration* and (2) *skill pattern*. Configuration refers to the number of tasks on which each employee should be trained and partially answers the second question posed by Hopp et al. (2004). Skill pattern then refers to the skills that should be grouped together for cross-training. Skill pattern answers another part of the second question posed by Hopp et al. (2004). As such, much of the existing research in workforce planning seeks to answer one (or more) of the following questions: (1) What should the configuration be? (2) What skill patterns should an organization employ? (3) What skill pattern should be assigned to each employee? (4) Given a cross-trained workforce, what worker should do each job?

Configuration

In general, answering the configuration question is straightforward: train workers on only one task, train all workers on all tasks, or train workers on some tasks. However, the first option offers no flexibility and the second is expensive (due both to the direct costs of training and wages and the indirect costs of lost efficiency and quality) and most likely infeasible except for all but the simplest operations. Fortunately, Jordan and Graves (1995) show that it is effective to cross-train workers in only two skills, if the tasks are "chained" together, a concept known as two-skill chaining. In two-skill chaining, employees are cross-trained on just two skills, and each employee has overlapping skills with just one other employee (see Figure 26.1 for an example). Though Hopp et al. (2004), Bokhorst and Gaalman (2009) and others later show that matching the configuration to the detailed system needs can provide benefits, Jordan and Graves (1995) show that two-skill chaining offers almost all of the benefits of a fully cross-trained workforce.

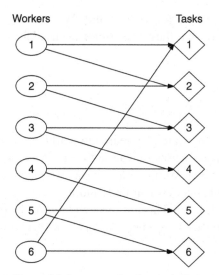

Figure 26.1. *Example of two-skill chaining for six workers and six tasks.*

Skill Pattern and Allocation

Given a configuration, it is then necessary to determine which skills should be grouped together for cross-training (called the "skill pattern" by Hopp & Van Oyen [2004]) and which workers should be assigned to which skill patterns (called the "allocation" by Hopp & Van Oyen [2004]). These two questions are often answered by mathematical optimization. Mathematical optimization involves modeling processes and systems using mathematical equations. These models are then used within optimization frameworks to optimize system performance.

For example, consider a situation in which a company wishes to allocate two workers to four tasks over the course of four time periods such that periods might represent hours of a working day. To model this situation, we include a variable x_{ijt} to represent whether worker i does task j in period t. In this case, $i = 1, 2, j = 1, 2$, and $t = 1, 2, 3, 4$. Assume that the workers have different productivities on each task. To account for these productivities, we introduce the parameters p_{ij} to represent the productivity of worker i on job j. The output of the tasks earns different amounts of profit when sold. We represent the profit for each sold unit of product j as π^j. For the purposes of the example, assume that everything produced is sold. The objective is to maximize profit.

Figure 26.2 depicts the mathematical programming formulation. Equation (1) specifies that the objective is to maximize profit. Equation (2) requires that each worker do no more than one job in each period. Finally, Equation (3) restricts the variable x_{ijt} to taking on values of only 0 or 1. In the problem specified in the preceding text, the skill patterns are treated as a given. Because what skills are grouped together and which workers are assigned to those skill patterns might depend on the characteristics of the workforce in question, however, the answers to the two questions are interdependent. Further, the development of skill patterns often results from the learning-by-doing that results

$$\text{maximize} \sum_{i=1}^{2} \sum_{j=1}^{4} \sum_{t=1}^{4} \pi_j p_{ij} x_{ijt} \tag{1}$$

subject to

$$\sum_{j=1}^{4} x_{ijt} \leq 1, \qquad \forall \, i = 1,2, \, t = 1,\ldots, 4, \tag{2}$$

$$x_{ijt} \text{ binary} \qquad \forall_1 = i = 1,2, j = 1,2, t = 1,\ldots, 4, \tag{3}$$

Figure 26.2. *Mathematical programming formulation for workforce allocation.*

from doing allocated work. Despite a history of results demonstrating differences in individual worker performance (Hunter, Schmidt, & Judiesch, 1990) and its impact on production (Buzacott, 2002; Chen, Thomas, & Hewitt, 2015; Nembhard & Shafer, 2008; Shafer, Nembhard, & Uzumeri, 2001), much of the literature ignores both workforce heterogeneity and learning by doing.

As an example, Agnihothri, Mishra, and Simmons (2003) consider the case of field service technicians who have two possible task types: electrical and mechanical. The paper seeks to determine which workers will be cross-trained and which will not. Because workers are undifferentiated, the question reduces to determining the number of workers who are trained only on the individual tasks and the number who are cross-trained. As an additional example, Zhu and Sherali (2009) consider a workforce in which employees have different skillsets and each month new employees are hired and the work allocated among different locations given the skillsets available in the locations. Like Agnihothri et al. (2003), the choice in Zhu and Sherali (2009) is really one of how many of a particular skill pattern are needed.

An examination of Agnihothri et al. (2003) and Zhu and Sherali (2009) raises an additional complication. Each problem is set in a different production setting. Results are not necessarily generalizable as different settings require different decisions. For example, consider a workforce planning problem in which we are seeking to determine which of m serial production jobs (see the example in Figure 26.3a) each member of a workforce of size n less than m workers should do in each of T periods to maximize production. A similar problem is that of assigning n workers to m stations of two parallel production lines (see the example in Figure 26.3b). Even if the objective (e.g., maximizing production) in both cases is the same, the models and solutions to the problems are not necessarily compatible.

With the challenges of problem setting in mind, we return to the questions of skill pattern and allocation. As noted earlier, these two decisions are in reality integrated decisions. Just as there is a stream of research that considers the skill pattern question independently, there is also literature that discusses allocation independently. This literature takes the skill pattern as a given. It is neither chosen nor developed. Thus, there are some number workers with each skill pattern,

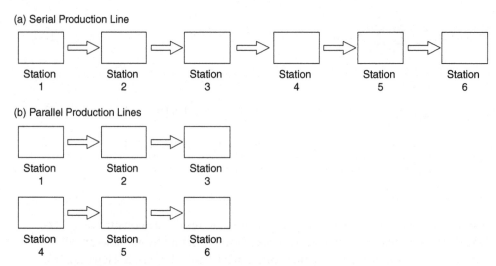

Figure 26.3. *Example of two different production processes.*

and the optimization problem is to allocate the workers to the existing work. For example, Kovacs et al. (2011) consider the problem of the scheduling and routing of differently skilled technicians to service jobs. The problem is challenging because not every technician is qualified to do every job. Similar examples of technician scheduling can be found in the literature (Cordeau et al., 2010; Eitzen, Panton, & Mills, 2004; Firat & Hurkens, 2011). Attia, Duquenne, and Le-Lann (2014), Campbell and Diaby (2002), Ahn, Righter, and Shanthikumar (2005), Heimerl and Kolisch (2009), and Campbell (2010) among others discuss the allocation of cross-trained workers in a service setting. Sabar, Montreuil, and Frayret (2012), Huang et al. (2009), McDonald et al. (2009), and Winch, Cai, and Vairaktarakis (2007) offer examples in manufacturing.

State of the Art

Given that much of the extant literature treats skill pattern and allocation choices independently, the question arises as to why. In the situations, such as those considered by Zhu and Sherali (2009) and Kovacs et al. (2011), the models and resulting solutions are meant to cover very short time frames. In such short time frames, it is impossible to observe learning and to develop a cross-trained workforce. Yet, as noted earlier, Shafer et al. (2001), Gans et al. (2010), and Chen et al. (2015) show that ignoring such learning even over the course of a month can lead to not only to an underestimation of capacity, but also very different work assignment policies.

Further, cross-training requires that a worker either be trained offline, in which case the employee is not available for current production needs, or the employee learns by doing, in which case the employee is at least initially not as effective as a more experienced employee or makes a mistake that costs the company directly (rework) or indirectly (poor satisfaction and reduced customer loyalty).

$$y = K \left[1 - e^{-(x + p)/r} \right]$$

Figure 26.4. *Three parameter exponential learning curve.*

Either way, capacity suffers. Certainly, there are times when demand may be such that the firm can spare the capacity. Yet, given today's lean workforces, particularly in the United States, the more likely case is that the firm incurs an overtime cost to make up lost capacity or even lost sales if the capacity cannot be recuperated. Uzumeri and Nembhard (1998) noted as far back as 1998 that the increasing pace of new process, product, and service introductions means that workers are spending more of their time on the steep part of the learning curve. Thus, the process of cross-training is a continuous one.

The challenge is that integrating these decisions tests the limits of existing mathematical optimization methods. The greatest challenge comes from incorporating individual changes in productivity that result from experience on the job. These individual changes are often described in the literature by a mathematical function called a *learning curve*. As an example, consider the three-parameter exponential learning curve first proposed by Bevis, Finniear, and Towill (1970), depicted in Figure 26.4.

In the equation, the parameter K defines the asymptotic production rate, or the maximum possible rate of production. The curve captures prior experience in parameter p, and the parameter r is learning rate. Then y is the resulting productivity given x units of experience. In the case of this three-parameter exponential learning curve, the learning rate represents the time needed to reach 63% of the asymptote's production rate.

Research on how people learn though experience has a long history in the literature. The first learning curve seems to have been introduced by Wright (1936). Dar-El (2000) provides review of learning and forgetting models developed before 2000. Reviews of more recent work can be found in Jaber and Sikström (2004) and Anzanello and Fogliatto (2011). We note that, in this chapter, we focus on models of individual rather than organizational learning. For a discussion of learning at the organization level, see Bailey (1989), Lapre, Mukherjee, and Van Wassenhove (2000), and Pisano et al. (2001).

In recent years, improving data collection capabilities have led to the development of more sophisticated learning functions. For instance, Nembhard and Uzumeri (2000a) introduces a three-parameter hyperbolic function, and Nembhard and Uzumeri (2000b) extends the function to include forgetting. Until recently, such models would have been theoretical as it was almost impossible to collect enough data for parameter estimation. Nembhard (2001) examine several models of forgetting and identify those with robust performance. Shafer et al. (2001) introduce a model that accounts for the recency of a task.

The learning curves proposed in the literature have a similar shape as the learning curve presented Figure 26.4. Notably, as demonstrated graphically in Figure 26.5, learning curves are curves and not lines. Curves pose particular challenges in optimization problems, particularly when the curve defines a

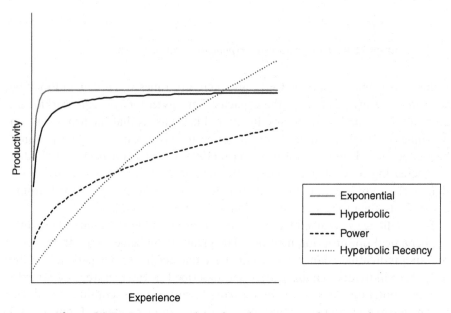

Figure 26.5. *Common models of productivity as a function of experience.*

constraint. Thus, while several authors have incorporated models of learning or of learning and forgetting into optimization models for workforce management covering a variety of different applications, a common theme is the challenge in solving large-sized instances. The success of exact solution approaches has been particularly limited.

As an example, Nembhard and Norman (2007) uses general purpose solver and is limited to problems with only 2 workers, 4 tasks, and 10 time periods. One way around the challenges of nonlinear learning curves is to use mathematical techniques to prove that the optimal solution has a certain structure. Looking back at the optimization problem posed in earlier for an example of optimal structure, is that there exists an optimal solution such that each worker works a single task for all four periods. In the literature, Armbruster, Gel, and Murakami (2007) identify how to optimally allocate workers in a production system known as a bucket brigade. Nembhard and Bentefouet (2012) study a variant of the serial production line problem. By exploiting particular mathematical structure, the authors solve instances with up to 96 workers, 96 tasks, and 246 periods, a very large problem by the standards of many that are found in the literature. However, the results do not generalize. Similarly, focusing on a production setting known as a flow line, Bentefouet and Nembhard (2013) are able to prove the optimal work assignments for two workers and two tasks. While such results can be useful for developing "rules of thumb" and offer general insight into production strategies, these particularly also do not generalize.

Given the limits of structural results, another stream of research relies on approximations of the learning curve. While such approximations can make the mathematical optimization problems easier to solve, they come with a loss of

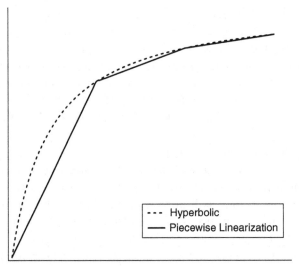

Figure 26.6. *Example of a piecewise-linear approximation of a learning curve.*

model fidelity. As examples, Corominas, Olivella, and Pastor (2010), Olivella, Corominas, and Pastor (2013), and Sayin and Karabati (2007) use what are called piece-wise linear approximations of the learning curves (see the example in Figure 26.6). While these approximations transform the problems from nonlinear (curves) to linear and thus allow the application of powerful commercial solver technologies, there are two downsides. Notably, piecewise-linear approximations of learning curves underestimate the actual productivity. This downside can be lessened by adding more segments. For example, instead of approximating the curve with three lines as in Figure 26.6, the curve could be approximated with six lines. However, more segments increase the problem size and make them more difficult to solve. Other methods of approximation and problem settings differing from those just discussed can be found in Nembhard and Bentefouet (2012) and Gutjahr et al. (2008).

An alternative to approximating the learning and forgetting curves is to use heuristic methods. As the name implies, heuristic methods do not return provably optimal solutions, but often produce very good solutions to a problem. Using the optimization problem posed earlier, an example heuristic might be a rule that greedily assigns Worker 1 to the task on which he or she is most productive and then assigns Worker 2 to the task on which he or she is most productive, excluding the task assigned to Worker 1. The advantage of heuristics is that they often do not require any approximation of the learning curve. Further, heuristic techniques have a history of finding acceptable solutions to problems whose solutions can be described as a sequence of actions. Solutions to the skill pattern/allocation problems can be described in such ways.

Several heuristic approaches to task assignment with learning can be found in the literature. Nembhard (2001) introduces rule-based heuristics for assigning heterogeneous learners to production runs of varying lengths on a serial production line. As an example of such heuristics, one rule is to assign faster learners to shorter production runs and slower learners to longer runs. Nembhard (2001) demonstrates the value of the heuristics by demonstrating that they lead to better outcomes than the application of random worker assignments. Examples of other heuristic approaches applied to a variety of settings are given in Kim and Nembhard (2010), Nembhard and Bentefouet (2014), and Yan and Wang (2011).

Given the challenges in exactly solving problems that include learning curves, the literature is sparse. Heimerl and Kolisch (2010) consider the assignment of project work to employees who learn by doing. An interesting feature of the work is that the authors include skill targets. In theory, these targets force the organization to meet the current needs of its customers, but also help position the organization so that it has the skills to meet the needs of its customers in the future. Like Nembhard and Norman (2007) discussed earlier, however, Heimerl and Kolisch (2010) solve a problem with 4 workers, 6 tasks, and 10 periods.

Recently, Hewitt et al. (2015) showed that the nonlinearity of learning curves could be made linear, also known as linearizing, though the use of additional variables and constraints. Using this technique, the authors solved exactly problems with 20 workers, 40 tasks, and 40 periods. Such problems are significantly larger than other problems in the literature that have been solved exactly. Hewitt et al. (2015) also use their technique in conjunction with a heuristic to greatly reduce the computation time required to find solutions without sacrificing solution quality.

Research Opportunities

While the review of the literature demonstrates that there are significant methodological challenges in solving skill pattern and allocation problems, there are also research gaps that impact model fidelity. As discussed, there has been a significant amount of research that presents quantitative models of human learning as a function of experience and elapsed time. However, there are many other aspects of human performance that are not currently quantified in the way that the relationship between learning and experience are. In this section, we will talk particularly about the relationship between experience and quality. Further, this chapter has not yet discussed "induced" learning, actions that management can take to help employees learn and improve productivity, in contrast to "autonomous" learning or learning due to experience.

The Impact of Experience on Quality

In the OM literature, quality refers to how closely the product or service conforms to specifications. Quality plays an important role in OM because a product or service that does not meet specifications, or is defective, must often be "reworked" or scrapped. In other cases, there are generally material and labor costs associated with the defective product or service. Just as importantly, the production of a defective product or service means that capacity was used on an output that could not be used to satisfy customer demand. Further, there has long been a recognized link between learning, quality, and productivity (Deming, 1982; Fine, 1986).

Yet, despite the important of quality and the known existence of the link between quality and experience, most of the work in the literature ignores connections between experience and quality. Consider the case of the relationship between quality and productivity. Using data presented in Badiru (1995), Jaber and Bonney (2003) shows that productivity for reworking defective items increases with experience and that quality declines as workers forget what they have learned due to repeated interruptions to a production process. Using the original learning curve presented in Wright (1936) and the results in Jaber and Bonney (2003), Jaber and Guiffrida (2004) presents a combined learning curve function that accounts for learning from the rework of defective items and determines the amount of time needed to produce good items given that defects will occur. However, the derivation is analytical and not empirically validated. Jaber and Givi (2014) extends Jaber and Guiffrida (2004) to include forgetting, but again presents an analytical derivation combining previous curves and does not empirically validate the curves.

Neither Jaber and Guiffrida (2004) nor Jaber and Givi (2014) capture the possibility that workers might produce fewer defects as they learn. Some work has captured the concept by acknowledging that workers learn from the quality improvement that comes with a line stop, often referred to as *jidoka* in the Toyota Production System (see Womack and Jones [2003] for more on the Toyota Production System). The basic idea is that when defects begin to appear in the product, the production line is stopped, the source of the defect is identified and corrected, and the production process is restarted. Focusing on quality and learning at the organization level, Lapre et al. (2000) shows that waste reduces over time due to organizational learning and that the reduction follows the form of a "learning" curve. Unfortunately, it is not clear if or how these findings would apply at the individual level, the level of interest in this chapter. Using data gathered from an experiment done with operators controlling remote robotic arms, Bukchin, Luquer, and Shtub (2002) demonstrate that reductions in the defect rate can be fit to learning curve models, in particularly one resembling the original from Wright (1936). Jaber (2006) incorporates the results of Bukchin et al. (2002) to capture quality improvements used to determine the size of production runs.

While Lapre et al. (2000) and Bukchin et al. (2002) offer strong evidence for the impact of increased experience on increased quality, the research is nowhere near as developed as that for the link between experience and productivity. Of note, it is not clear if the effect is the same for manufacturing-like process and more service- or knowledge-based process. All are prone to errors, and more research is needed.

Induced Learning and Other Managerial Effects on Productivity

The most noticeably missing research is related to the impact of training on future performance and learning. Notably, there is a lack of analytical models to describe such learning and its effects on productivity. For instance, Wirojanagud et al. (2007) and Fowler, Wirojanagud, and Gel (2008) model workers with differing general cognitive abilities having different costs and different resulting productivities from training on a particular skills. However, the differences are specified as parameters rather than in a functional form as is seen with learning curves. In addition, there is no indication of how training impact future learning. Perhaps most famously, Judd (1908) shows that the children who underwent training learned faster than the group that did not undergo training. The experiment was replicated with BB guns replacing darts by Hendrickson and Schroeder (1941). In more modern literature, Dar- El (2000) discusses the improvement in learning rate due to training in a manufacturing context, and Bianco et al. (2010) suggest that such an effect exists between fellowship and nonfellowship trained surgeons. Further, there is evidence that the productivity gains due to training depend on the structure of the training (Greeno, Smith, & Sternberg, 1993; Kaminsky & Sloutsky, 2011; Son & Goldstone, 2009). Does the structure of the training impact future learning is well?

In addition to training, managers also control with whom a worker works, and it well known that one learns from one's co-workers (Lim & Johnson, 2002; Salomon & Globerson, 1987). To capture the impact of this transfer, Nembhard and Bentefouet (2015) introduces a straightforward modification of the learning curve of Mazur and Hastie (1978) to account for learning by transfer in a serial production line. We note that, in this case, "transfer" is not used in the context of how effective training is, the context in which it is used in Blume et al. (2010), for example. To modify the learning curve, Nembhard and Bentefouet (2015) adds a transfer factor to account for the experience of a worker's co-workers and the worker's ability to learn through transfer such experience. While Nembhard and Bentefouet (2015) attempt to fill an important gap in our understanding of learning, there is no empirical justification for the model.

In addition to its impact on learning, management impacts performance in other ways. There is evidence that workers change how they work as their workload increases. Tan and Netessine (2014) show that restaurant servers switch from seeking to maximize sales to maximizing speed as their work volume increases. Similarly, Batt and Terwiesch (2012) show that doctors adjust their behavior to improve throughput times as their workload increases. Interestingly, Brown et al. (2005) show the opposite for call center workers. Brown et al. (2005) find that service times increase with workload, though they determine that the relationship is not causal. Rather, periods of higher demand coincide with a customer mix with higher mean service times.

Levy (1965) suggests that greater supervision on a first shift led to greater productivity over time for a first shift team than for a second shift team. A related effect is found by Pierce, Snow, and Mcafee (in press) who show that the increased use of information technology to monitor employees increases productivity. At the same time, Sze (1984) find that call center workers face "shift fatigue," a slowdown in performance over the course of their working hours.

Relatedly, Kuntz, Mennicken, and Scholtes (2014) show medical workers become more error prone as their workload increases. With increasing workloads, Powell, Savin, and Savva (2012) show that hospital reimbursements fall because doctors are less diligent in their paperwork. Detert et al. (2007) demonstrate that restaurant food loss decreases with increase managerial oversight. Aral, Brynholfsson, and Van Alstyne (2012) showed that multitasking across multiple projects increased the productivity of IT workers. The reason for the increase is that, when the worker is waiting for the completion of a task on a project on which the worker is not directly working, the availability of another project absorbs the workers idle time. In contrast, KC (2014) showed an inverted U-shaped curve for physicians in an emergency department. Productivity initially increases with workload, but then begins to decline after a certain point. KC (2014) speculates that the difference between their finding and that of Aral et al. (2012) is because that IT workers' projects have a long time horizon whereas physicians in an emergency department are working multiple patients across a short time horizon. As a result, as the workload increases past a certain point, physicians experience cognitive overload (Allport, Styles, & Hsieh, 1994; Speier, Valacich, & Vessey, 1999), diminishing performance. As with the previously cited literature, both Aral et al. (2012) and KC (2014) introduce regression equations to determine their results. Such equations have many independent variables, making it challenging to fit them for individual workers.

The cited work indicates that many factors affect productivity. To provide managers with better insight, these factors need to be incorporated into optimization models. However, while all the cited work uses regression-based models to qualify their conclusions, the models were not necessarily developed with the purpose of prediction. Simply, work still needs to be done to develop equations that provide an accurate measure of performance given the factors affecting productivity. Nonetheless, they offer a starting place for the development of predictive models of human performance.

Conclusions

The review in this chapter demonstrates that the OM literature is beginning to connect the how with the what of workforce flexibility. Recent work recognizes that configuration, skill patterns, and allocation need to be integrated decisions. Configurations and skill patterns are the result of the ways in which management allocates its heterogeneous and learning workforce.

In the discussion of the OM literature, the key to integrating configuration, skill patterns, and allocation is the availability of models, like the discussed learning curves, that quantify how productivity is impacted by experience and other factors as well as mathematical optimization techniques that can handle the challenges of these models. The first step is the development of the quantitative models of human behavior. The forms of these models need to be known before optimization techniques can be developed to solve them. More data is the key to developing such models.

Fortunately, we live in a "big data" world. The cost of collecting, storing, and analyzing data is falling rapidly. Already a large dataset derived from the call center of U.S. Bank (Donin et al., 2006) has led to a stream of research on workforce planning in call centers (Arlotto, Chick, & Gans, 2014; Gans & Zhou, 2002; Gans, Koole, & Mandelbaum, 2003; Gans et al. 2010). Most importantly, data is increasingly playing a role in human resources decisions. Notably, companies are gathering more data than ever before about employees before hiring them. In 2015, 23% of companies report requiring skills tests of prospective hires, up from 16% five years ago (Zumbrun, 2015). While such tests are being blamed longer hiring process (Zumbrun, 2015), they are evidence that companies find value in the time and expense of the data that they are gathering.

At the moment, the "datafication" of human resources (Bersin, 2013) is focused on hiring, retention, compensation, and performance evaluation (Bersin, 2013; Block, 2015; Lohr, 2013; Peck, 2013). However, there is no doubt that the data used in these areas will be integrated and augmented with employee-level data operational data. This data will be the data that helps overcome the challenges discussed in this chapter.

References

Agnihothri, S. R., Mishra, A. K., and Simmons, D. E. 2003. Workforce cross-training decisions in field service systems with two job types. *Journal of the Operational Research Society* 54(4):410–418.

Ahn, H.-S., Righter, R., and Shanthikumar, J. G. 2005. Staffing decisions for heterogeneous workers with turnover. *Mathematical Methods of Operations Research* 62(3):499–514.

Allport, A., Styles, E. A., and Hsieh, S. 1994. Shifting intentional set: Exploring the dynamic control of tasks. In C. Umilta and M. Moscovitch, eds., *Attention and Performance XV: Conscious and Unconscious Information Processing*, 421–452. Cambridge, MA: MIT Press.

Anzanello, M. J., and Fogliatto, F. S. 2011. Learning curve models and applications: Literature review and research directions. *International Journal of Industrial Ergonomics* 41(5): 573–583.

Aral, S., Brynjolfsson, E., and Van Alstyne, M. 2012. Information, technology, and information worker productivity. *Information Systems Research* 23(3-part-2): 849–867.

Arlotto, A., Chick, S. E., and Gans, N. 2014. Optimal hiring and retention policies for heterogenous workers who learn. *Management Science* 60(1): 110–129.

Armbruster, D., Gel, E. S., and Murakami, J. 2007. Bucket brigades with worker learning. *European Journal of Operational Research* 176(1):264–274.

Attia, E.-A., Duquenne, P., and Le-Lann, J.-M. 2014. Considering skills evolutions in multi-skilled workforce allocation with flexible working hours. *International Journal of Production Research* 52(15): 4548–4573.

Badiru, A. B. 1995. Multivariate analysis of the effect of learning and forgetting on product quality. *The International Journal of Production Research* 33(3):777–794.

Bailey, C. D. 1989. Forgetting and the learning curve: A laboratory study. *Management Science* 35(3):340–352.

Batt, R. J., and Terwiesch, C. 2012. Doctors under load: An empirical study of service time as a function of census. https://opimweb.wharton.upenn.edu/files/?whdmsaction=public:main.file\&fileID=5133.

Bentefouet, F., and Nembhard, D. A. 2013. Optimal flow-line conditions with worker variability. *International Journal of Production Economics* 141(2):675–684.

Bersin, J. 2013. The datafication of human resources. Forbes.com, July 19.

Bevis, F., Finniear, C., and Towill, D. 1970. Prediction of operator performance during learning of repetitive tasks. *International Journal of Production Research* 8(4):293–305.

Bianco, F. J., Cronin, A. M., Klein, E. A., Pontes, E. E., Scardino, P. T., and Vickers, A. J. 2010. Fellowship training as a modifier of the surgical learning curve. *Academic Medicine: Journal of the Association of American Medical Colleges* 85(5):863–868.

Block, L. 2015. *Work Rules!* New York: Twelve.

Blume, B. D., Ford, J. K., Baldwin, T. T., and Huang, J. L. 2010. Transfer of training: A meta-analytic review. *Journal of Management* 36(4):1065–1105.

Bokhorst, J., and Gaalman, G. 2009. Cross-training workers in dual resource constrained systems with heterogeneous processing times. *International Journal of Production Research* 47(22): 6333–6356.

Brown, L., Gans, N., Mandelbaum, A., Sakov, A., Shen, H., Zeltyn, S., and Zhao, S. 2005. Statistical analysis of a telephone call center. *Journal of the American Statistical Association* 100(469): 36–50.

Bukchin, J., Luquer, R., and Shtub, A. 2002. Learning in tele-operations. *IIE Transactions* 34(3):245–252.

Buzacott, J. 2002. The impact of worker differences on production system output. *International Journal of Production Economics* 78(1):37–44.

Cachon, G., and Terwiesch, C. 2012. *Matching Supply with Demand*, 3rd ed. New York: McGraw-Hill Education.

Campbell, G. M. 2010. A two-stage stochastic program for scheduling and allocating cross-trained workers. *Journal of the Operational Research Society* 62(6): 1038–1047.

Campbell, G. M., and Diaby, M. 2002. Development and evaluation of an assignment heuristic for allocating cross-trained workers. *European Journal of Operational Research* 138(1): 9–20.

Chen, X., Thomas, B. W., and Hewitt, M. 2015. The technician routing problem with experience-based service times. http://myweb.uiowa.edu/bthoa/iowa/Research.html (accessed August 17, 2017).

Cordeau, J.-F., Laporte, G., Pasin, F., and Ropke, S. 2010. Scheduling technicians and tasks in a telecommunications company. *Journal of Scheduling* 13(4): 393–409.

Corominas, A., Olivella, J., and Pastor, R. 2010. A model for the assignment of a set of tasks when work performance depends on experience of all tasks involved. *International Journal of Production Economics* 126(2): 335–340.

Dar-El, E. M. 2000. *Human Learning: From Learning Curves to Learning Organizations.* Boston, MA: Kluwer Academic Publishers.

Deming, W. E. 1982. *Quality, Productivity, and Competitive Position.* Boston, MA: Massachusetts Institute of Technology, Center for Advanced Engineering Study.

Detert, J. R., Treviño, L. K., Burris, E. R., and Andiappan, M. 2007. Managerial modes of influence and counterproductivity in organizations: A longitudinal business-unit-level investigation. *Journal of Applied Psychology* 92(4): 993–1005.

Donin, O., Feigin, P. D., Mandelbaum, A., Zeltyn, S., Trofimov, V., Ishay, E., Khudiakov, P., and Nadjharov, E. 2006. *DataMOCCA: DATA model for call center analysis. Technical report 4.1.*, Tel Aviv, Israel: Industrial Engineering and Management, Technion University.

Eitzen, G., Panton, D., and Mills, G. 2004. Multi-skilled workforce optimisation. *Annals of Operations Research* 127(1–4): 359–372.

Fine, C. H. 1986. Quality improvement and learning in production systems. *Management Science* 10: 1301–1315.

Firat, M., and Hurkens, C. A. J. 2011. An improved MIP-based approach for a multi-skill workforce scheduling problem. *Journal of Scheduling* 15: 363–380.

Fowler, J., Wirojanagud, P., and Gel, E. 2008. Heuristics for workforce planning with worker differences. *European Journal of Operational Research* 190(3): 724–740.

Gans, N., and Zhou, Y.-P. 2002. Managing learning and turnover in employee staffing. *Operations Research* 50(6): 991–1006.

Gans, N., Koole, G., and Mandelbaum, A. 2003. Commissioned paper: Telephone call centers: Tutorial, review, and research prospects. *Manufacturing and Service Operations Management* 5(2): 79–141.

Gans, N., Liu, N., Mandelbaum, A., Shen, H., and Han Ye. 2010. Service times in call centers: Agent heterogeneity and learning with some. In J. O. Berger, T. T. Cai, and I. M. Johnstone, eds., *Borrowing Strength: Theory Powering Applications – A Festschrift for Lawrence D. Brown*, 6: 99–123. Beachwood, OH: Institute of Mathematical Statistics.

Greeno, J. G., Smith, D. R., and Sternberg, R. J. 1993. Transfer of situated transfer of situated learning. In D. K. Detterman and R. J. Sternberg, eds., *Transfer on Trial: Intelligence, Cognition, and Instruction*, 99–167. New York: Ablex.

Gutjahr, W. J., Katzensteiner, S., Reiter, P., Stummer, C., and Denk, M. 2008. Competence-driven project portfolio selection, scheduling and staff assignment. *Central European Journal of Operations Research* 16(3): 281–306.

Heimerl, C., and Kolisch, R. 2009. Scheduling and staffing multiple projects with a multi-skilled workforce. *OR Spectrum* 32(2): 343–368.

Heimerl, C., and Kolisch, R. 2010. Work assignment to and qualification of multi-skilled human resources under knowledge depreciation and company skill level targets. *International Journal of Production Research* 48(13): 3759–3781.

Hendrickson, G., and Schroeder, W. B. 1941. Transfer of training in learning to hit a submerged target. *Journal of Educational Psychology* 32(3): 205–213.

Hewitt, M., Chacosky, A., Grasman, S., and Thomas, B. W. 2015. Integer programming techniques for solving non-linear workforce planning models with learning. *European Journal of Operational Research* 242(3): 942–950.

Hopp, W., and Van Oyen, M P. 2004. Agile workforce evaluation: A framework for cross-training and coordination. *IIE Transactions* 36(10): 919–940.

Hopp, W. J., Tekin, E., and Van Oyen, M. P. 2004. Benefits of skill chaining in serial production lines with cross-trained workers. *Management Science* 50(1): 83–98.

Huang, H.-C., Lee, L.-H., Song, H., and Thomas Eck, B. 2009. SimMan – A simulation model for workforce capacity planning. *Computers and Operations Research* 36(8): 2490–2497.

Hunter, J. E., Schmidt, F. L., and Judiesch, M. K. 1990. Individual differences in output variability as a function of job complexity. *Journal of Applied Psychology* 75(1): 28–42.

Jaber, M. Y. 2006. Lot sizing for an imperfect production process with quality corrective interruptions and improvements, and reduction in setups. *Computers and Industrial Engineering* 51(4): 781–790.

Jaber, M. Y., and Bonney, M. 2003. Lot sizing with learning and forgetting in set-ups and in product quality. *International Journal of Production Economics* 83: 95–111.

Jaber, M. Y., and Givi, Z. S. 2014. Imperfect production process with learning and forgetting effects. *Computational Management Science* 12(1): 129–152.

Jaber, M. Y., and Guiffrida, A. L. 2004. Learning curves for processes generating defects requiring reworks. *European Journal of Operational Research* 159(3): 663–672.

Jaber, M. Y., and Sikström, S. 2004. A numerical comparison of three potential learning and forgetting models. *International Journal of Production Economics* 92(3): 281–294.

Jordan, W. C., and Graves, S. C. 1995. Principles on the benefits of manufacturing process flexibility. *Management Science* 41(February): 577–594.

Judd, C. H. 1908. The relation of special training to general intelligence. *Educational Review* 36: 28–42.

Kaminsky, J. A., and Sloutsky, V. M. 2011. Representation and transfer of abstract mathematical concepts. In V. F. Reyna, ed., *The Adolescent Brain: Learning, Reasoning, and Decision Making*, 67–93. Washington, DC: American Psychological Association.

KC, D. S. 2014. Does multitasking improve performance? Evidence from the emergency department. *Manufacturing and Service Operations Management* 16(2): 168–183.

Kim, S., and Nembhard, D. A. 2010. Cross-trained staffing levels with heterogeneous learning/ forgetting. *IEEE Transactions on Engineering Management* 57(4): 560–574.

Kovacs, A. A., Parragh, S. N., Doerner, K. F., and Hartl, R. F. 2011. Adaptive large neighborhood search for service technician routing and scheduling problems. *Journal of Scheduling* 15 (5): 579–600.

Kuntz, L., Mennicken, R., and Scholtes, S. 2014. Stress on the ward: Evidence of safety tipping points in hospitals. *Management Science* 61(4): 754–771.

Lapre, A. S., Mukherjee, and Van Wassenhove, L. N. 2000. Behind the learning curve: Linking learning activities to waste reduction. *Management Science* 46(5): 597–611.

Levy, F. K. 1965. Adaptation in the production process. *Management Science* 11(6): B136–B154.

Lim, D. H., and Johnson, S. D. 2002. Trainee perceptions of factors that influence learning transfer. *International Journal of Training and Development* 6(1): 36–48.

Lohr, S. 2013. Big data, trying to build better workers. *The New York Times*, BU4.

Marlin Steel. 2015. How cross-training drives employee engagement in manufacturing jobs. https://www.marlinwire.com/blog/ how-cross-training-drives-employee-engagement-in-manufacturing-jobs (accessed September 30, 2015).

Mazur, J. E., and Hastie, R. 1978. Learning as accumulation: A reexamination of the learning curve. *Psychological Bulletin* 85(6): 1256–1274.

McDonald, T., Ellis, K. P., Van Aken, E. M., and Koelling, C. P. 2009. Development and application of a worker assignment model to evaluate a lean manufacturing cell. *International Journal of Production Research* 47(9): 2427–2447.

Nembhard, D., and Uzumeri, M. 2000a. An individual-based description of learning within an organization. *IEEE Transactions on Engineering Management* 47(3): 370–378.

Nembhard, D., and Uzumeri, M. V. 2000b. Experiential learning and forgetting for manual and cognitive tasks. *International Journal of Industrial Ergonomics* 25(4): 315–326.

Nembhard, D. A. 2001. Heuristic approach for assigning workers to tasks based on individual learning rates. *International Journal of Production Research* 39(9): 1955–1968.

Nembhard, D. A., and Bentefouet, F. 2012. Parallel system scheduling with general worker learning and forgetting. *International Journal of Production Economics* 139(2): 533–542.

Nembhard, D. A., and Bentefouet, F. 2014. Selection policies for a multifunctional workforce. *International Journal of Production Research* 52(16): 4785–4802.

Nembhard, D. A., and Bentefouet, F. 2015. Selection, grouping, and assignment policies with learning-by-doing and knowledge transfer. *Computers and Industrial Engineering* 79: 175–187.

Nembhard, D. A., and Norman, B. A. 2007. Cross training in production systems with human learning and forgetting. In D. A. Nembhard, ed., *Workforce Cross Training*, 111–129. Boca Raton, FL: CRC Press.

Nembhard, D. A., and Shafer, S. M. 2008. The effects of workforce heterogeneity on productivity in an experiential learning environment. *International Journal of Production Research* 46(14): 3909–3929.

Olivella, J., Corominas, A., and Pastor, R. 2013. Task assignment considering cross-training goals and due dates. *International Journal of Production Research* 51(3): 37–41.

Peck, D. 2013. They're Watching You at Work. *The Atlantic* (December): 72–82, 84 .

Pierce, L., Snow, D., and Mcafee, A. 2015. Cleaning house: The impact of information technology monitoring on employee theft and productivity. *Management Science* 61(10): 2299–2319.

Pisano, G. P., Bohmer, R. M., and Edmondson, A. C. 2001. Organizational differences in rates of learning: Evidence from the adoption of minimally invasive cardiac surgery. *Management Science* 47(6): 752–768.

Powell, A., Savin, S., and Savva, N. 2012. Physician workload and hospital reimbursement: Overworked physicians generate less revenue per patient. *Manufacturing and Service Operations Management* 14(4): 512–528.

Qin, R., Nembhard, D. A., and Barnes II, W. L. 2015. Workforce flexibility in operations management. *Surveys in Operations Research and Management Science* 20(1): 19–33.

Sabar, M., Montreuil, B., and Frayret, J. M. 2012. An agent-based algorithm for personnel shift-scheduling and rescheduling in flexible assembly lines. *Journal of Intelligent Manufacturing* 23(6): 2623–2634.

Salomon, G., and Globerson, T. 1987. Skill may not be enough: The role of mindfulness in learning and transfer. *International Journal of Educational Research* 11(6): 623–637.

Sayin, S., and Karabati, S. 2007. Assigning cross-trained workers to departments: A two-stage optimization model to maximize utility and skill improvement. *European Journal of Operational Research* 176(3): 1643–1658.

Shafer, S. M., Nembhard, D. A., and Uzumeri, M. V. 2001. The effects worker learning, forgetting, and heterogeneity on assembly line productivity. *Management Science* 47(12): 1639–1653.

Son, J. Y., and R. L. Goldstone, J. Y. 2009. Contextualization in perspective. *Cognition and Instruction* 27: 51–89.

Speier, C., Valacich, J. S., and Vessey, I. 1999. The influence of task interruption onindividual decision making: An information overload perspective. *Decision Sciences* 30(2): 337–360.

Stevenson, W. J. 2015. *Operations Management*, 12th ed. New York: McGraw-Hill.

Sze, D. Y. 1984. OR practice – A queueing model for telephone operator staffing. *Operations Research* 32(2): 229–249.

Tan, T. F., and Netessine, S. 2014. When does the devil make work? An empirical study of the impact of workload on worker productivity. *Management Science* 60(6): 1574–1593.

U.S. Bureau of Labor Statistics. 2016. Labor force statistics from the current population survey. http://www.bls.gov/cps/cpsaat47.htm (accessed September 30, 2016).

Uzumeri, M., and Nembhard, D. A. 1998. A population of learners: A new way to measure organizational learning. *Journal of Operations Management* 16(5): 515–528.

Winch, J. K., Cai, X., and Vairaktarakis, G. L. 2007. Cyclic job scheduling in paced assembly lines with cross-trained workers. *International Journal of Production Research* 45(4): 803–828.

Wirojanagud, P., Gel, E. S., Fowler, J. W., and Cardy, R. 2007. Modelling inherent worker differences for workforce planning. *International Journal of Production Research* 45 (3): 525–553.

Womack, J. P., and Jones, D. T. 2003. *Lean Thinking*. New York: Free Press.

Wright, T. P. 1936. Factors affecting the cost of airplanes. *Journal of Aeronautical Sciences* 3(4): 122–128.

Yan, J.-h., and Wang, Z.-m. 2011. GA based algorithm for staff scheduling considering learning-forgetting effect. 2011 IEEE 18th International Conference on Industrial Engineering and Engineering Management: 122–126.

Zhu, G., and Sherali, H. 2009. Two-stage workforce planning under demand fluctuations and uncertainty. *Journal of the Operational Research Society* 60(1): 94–103.

Zumbrun, J. 2015. Behind lingering job listings. *The Wall Street Journal*, June 19 A3.

27 Workplace Training from the Sociological Perspective

David B. Bills and Herman van de Werfhorst

More than 20 years ago, sociologists David Knoke and Arne Kalleberg observed that a "comprehensive theory of job training in U.S. organizations does not exist" (Knoke & Kalleberg, 1994: 537). Since that time, American sociologists have produced an impressive body of research on workplace training. Still, Knoke and Kalleberg's claim that this research lacks coherence remains a fair characterization of the literature.

Unlike American sociologists, whose concerns with skill acquisition, career mobility, and status attainment have only occasionally extended to job training (Bills, 2003; Bills & Hodson, 2007), European sociologists have produced a robust and cumulative body of research and theory on workplace training. Part of the discrepancy in the research interests of American and Continental sociology is simply because workplace training is embedded in corporate and social welfare institutions to a far greater degree in much of Europe than it is in the United States.

In this chapter, we will first discuss the sociology of workplace training in the United States. We will isolate what is distinctive about a sociological approach to training, as opposed to the much larger body of literature produced by labor economists. Virtually all economic analyses of workplace training are based on Human Capital Theory (HCT), which holds that both employers and workers invest in training because it enhances the skills that employers require and reward. Most sociologists and a growing number of economists are skeptical of those versions of HCT that fail to take into account such sociological factors as social networks, discrimination, and the differential power of labor market participants (Acemoglu & Pischke, 1999; Wolf, 2002). In the following sections, we will discuss how sociological research on training differs in the United States and in Europe. In the final section, we will present a few exemplary sociological studies of workplace training, largely as a way to indicate promising directions for research.

Workplace training is an enormously diverse and often ambiguous concept. Many analysts of training have bemoaned the difficulties of devising valid and reliable definitions and measurements of various kinds of training (Bills & Hodson, 2007; Moodie, 2002; Nilsson, 2010). Rather than trying to settle definitional issues here, we follow the broad definition adopted by the European Centre for the Development of Vocational Training: "All structured activities that aim to provide people with knowledge, skills and competencies necessary to perform a job or set of jobs, whether or not they lead to a formal qualification" (CEDEFOP, 2008: 8).

Workplace Training in the United States

By all accounts, the system of worker training and skill acquisition in the United States is loosely coordinated. The United States has never developed a centralized plan or set of policies or institutions at the national level capable of motivating the provision of training across occupational, industrial, or regional boundaries. There is little centralized integration of strategies, evaluation, or implementation of training. National training policy in the United States primarily consists of the aggregated but loosely integrated set of state policies, which vary widely in coverage and funding. To the extent that there is a thematic emphasis across the United States, there is some focus on "second chance" training programs, that is, programs that focus on labor market participants whose earlier educational or training investments are inadequate to the demands of employers for job skills (Bloom, 2010). Here too, commitment to such programs varies from state to state.

This lack of coordination and direction occurs despite the fact that almost all labor market participants – employers, workers, policy makers, and researchers – routinely endorse training as a solution to problems on both the demand side (unemployment) and the supply side (skill shortages). There is no lack of national, regional, and state-level blueprints for economic and workforce development adducing the logic of worker training to improve international competitiveness in an increasingly globalized labor market. While the economic returns to at least some types of training programs are unclear or not readily demonstrated, belief in the efficacy of training is widespread. Despite this faith, the American system of training remains fragmented and by many accounts undersized relative to the skill demands of a highly developed and diversified economy. Efforts to bring some semblance of order to the American system of workforce development have been generally unsuccessful. Even relatively ambitious legislation intended to broaden the scope and efficacy of training to encompass such diverse groups as adult workers, youth, migrants, and dislocated workers (such as the New Workforce Investment Act [1998] and the School to Work Opportunities Act [1994]) have persistently fallen short of producing a seamless web of skill acquisition.

As we describe in more detail in the following text, the lack of direction and coordination that characterizes the American system contrasts with much of the industrialized world. Empirical studies of Vocational Education and Training systems (or VETs) have demonstrated a variety of models that nations use to develop worker skills. The paradigmatic case is the German "dual system" of skill acquisition. Under the German model, employers rely on a dual system that combines general but at least partly occupation-specific education offered in vocational schools with apprenticeship training located in actual workplaces.

Employers provide training in broad and presumably portable or transferable skills, with the understanding that regulations are in place to protect them from the poaching that might occur in a less administered labor market. The dual system spans a wide range of large and small firms across many industrial sectors. Monitoring and oversight are important features of the dual system.

The German model is widely regarded as a successful system of skill acquisition, but in some senses the German system works differently in theory than in practice. Many have questioned the continuing viability of the model given the increasing pressures of changing skill demands, the shift from manufacturing to service industries, and rising unemployment (Hoeckel & Schwartz, 2010; Protsch & Solga, 2016). While certainly showing resilience for some time, the ability of the system to continue to adapt to new technologies and markets will be an important issue over the coming decades.

Apprenticeships, a staple of skill acquisition in many nations, have never thrived in the United States. American apprenticeships serve primarily to upgrade training for already employed adults, rather than as an entry into a field (as they still are in much of the world). We typically think of apprenticeships as characteristic of blue-collar trade occupations, but they predate that in the United States. The knowledge bases of many professions were once passed along through apprenticeships before they moved into university settings. Law, for instance, was once learned largely through apprentice-type relationships (Jardine, 2012).

Over time, the training functions of industrial and craft apprenticeships migrated to vocational high schools, which at one time were quite common in the United States. The growth and development of vocational high schools was not a case of these schools usurping the training function previously carried out by apprenticeships. In fact, apprenticeship as a form of industrial training was in substantial decline well before the growth of mass public secondary schooling in the United States (Jacoby, 1991). High schools assumed the training role largely because employers were no longer willing to do so.

Community colleges have come to be the chief providers of skills to much of the American workforce (beyond those acquired in high school and those acquired on the job). Even with recent enrollment declines after decades of growth, an increasing share of training is taking place in the country's vast and diverse community college system, which consists of some 1,200 institutions (Bailey, Jaggars, & Jenkins, 2015). Both the stated mission and the actual activity of community colleges have shifted more than once since these institutions began more than a century ago. Originally envisioned as academically oriented "junior colleges," community colleges have moved uneasily between the roles of preparing students to transfer to four-year colleges and universities, the provision of vocational training, personal development coursework, remedial instruction, and to an increasing extent, economic development (Dougherty & Bakia, 2000).

The community college system is a vast and complex one. Community colleges vary greatly in the efforts they expend on training. Dougherty (2003) has demonstrated that the level of involvement that community colleges have in the provision of training is conditioned by their place in the local ecology of employers, other providers, and public support, and concludes that "while most community colleges offer employee training, some offer a lot and many only a little" (Dougherty, 2003: 83).

A relatively new and rapidly growing presence on the postsecondary landscape is the for-profit college. While these institutions are only now beginning to receive sustained scholarly attention, research reported by the independent nonprofit Institute for College Access and Success has highlighted the distributional effects of for-profits at both the individual and social levels. The for-profit sector receives the largest share of its revenues from taxpayer funded student aid, and attracts about one-quarter of all federal financial aid awarded to college students. For-profits allot far larger shares of expenditures to marketing, advertising, and recruiting relative to instruction than do other postsecondary institutions. Despite their consumer message of flexibility, opportunity, and responsiveness to student need, students drop out of for-profits at rates far beyond those of students in other educational sectors, often leaving them with heavy debt (with greatly elevated default rates) and no marketable credentials (Lang & Weinstein, 2012). The regulation of for-profit educational institutions will likely be a major public policy issue in the near future.

In addition to for-profit institutions, employers and workers can now seek specialized skills and training through a range of institutions and settings that includes, among others, corporate universities and other industry-based centers, company certification, state-supported customized labor training, and largely unregulated and diffuse web-based instruction. To these we can add technical institutes, area vocational schools, proprietary schools, shorter-term job training programs, and firm-based training paid for in part by public funds. Much of the expansion in the training sector has come from outside of the traditional K–12 and postsecondary systems.

Who Participates in Job Training?

Assessing the determinants of participation in workplace training is more complex than it might first appear to be. Specifically, who *gets* training and who *provides* training are different though related questions. The former question focuses on the individual-level characteristics of the recipients of training. Most studies of racial, gender, or other disparities in participation in training would fall into this category. In contrast, the latter question is more concerned with how different employers and organizations offer opportunities or support for episodes of training. Knoke and Kalleberg (1994) are more in the "who provides" category. They use the National Organizations Survey (a representative sample of U.S. work organizations, first collected in 1991 and repeated several times since then) to show that "[h]igh levels of formalization and extensive internal labor markets are especially associated with greater job-training efforts" (1994: 544). While researchers have not always been clear about whether employers or workers are the primary initiators of training, we will not dwell on that distinction here, but will instead examine inequalities in access to and participation in training more generally.

While the United States invests proportionately less in the training of its workforce than do many comparable nations (and is often, in fact, alleged to underinvest in training, see McDuffie & Kochan, 1995), the sheer volume of worker training is enormous. In 2011, American private sector firms with at least 100 employees spent some 60 billion dollars on training. This figure does not include the substantial amount of training provided by smaller firms. Estimates from such sources as the Bureau of Labor Statistics and the American Society for Training and Development have put expenditures in training as anywhere from less than 2% of payroll to as much as 10%. The latter estimate includes indirect and opportunity costs, and if one includes the costs of "learning tools and technologies," as the training industry does, the figure becomes significantly higher yet. Even among young adults, who receive less training than mid-career workers, training is common. About 5% of high school graduates who do not go on to college do enter training programs. A smaller but still significant number of young people who leave college without a degree do the same.

Exactly how much money and time employers are willing to invest in training rises and falls with the business cycle (Felstead & Jewson, 2014). Whatever verbal commitments employers may make about the importance of upgrading the skills of their workforces, training budgets are typically quite vulnerable to recessionary economic conditions.

Opportunities to participate in job training are unequally allocated. In a recent review of the literature on inequalities in access to training, Bills and Hodson (2007: 261) concluded that "[m]ore educated workers participate more often than less educated workers, whites get more training than do African-Americans or Hispanics, and workers in their prime working years get more training than either older or younger workers. Workers in higher status occupations and those in larger firms are more likely to receive training than workers in more marginal positions and those with smaller employers."

With some important but not necessarily predictable or systematic exceptions, the patterns through much of the world broadly parallel those of the United States. O'Connell and Byrne (2012: 285) cogently summarized this body of research as showing that "current allocation principles are in inverse relation to need, and training is more likely to exacerbate rather than mitigate existing labour market inequalities." We say more about this in the following text.

Taken collectively, this pattern of participation in workplace training demonstrates the "Matthew Effect" (Merton, 1973) or its closely related concept, "cumulative advantage" (DiPrete & Eirich, 2006). Named for the biblical "parable of the talents," in which those with early advantages (or disadvantages) receive still greater rewards (or penalties) largely because of their early leads, the application of the Matthew Effect demonstrates the tendency of skilled, experienced, and occupationally well-placed workers to command a disproportionate share of available training, despite the arguably greater need of less advantaged workers. Schindler, Weiss, and Hubert (2011) argue that the tendency of employers to invest in the skills of the already highly skilled may make sense from an economic logic, although the effect of this is likely to increase the gap between organizational haves and have-nots. We develop this argument more fully in a later section.

Empirical knowledge about gender differences in access to and participation in training is surprisingly tentative. Bills and Hodson (2007) observed that in the United States, while women may receive more training than do men, less of this training is associated with high expected wage returns than is the case for men. Scholars from outside the United States have reported positive, negative, and mixed effects of gender on participation in training. Two generalizations on gender differences in training seem secure. First, there are substantial differences across societies in the extent to which women participate on a par with men in training efforts. Second, more rigorous studies with a fuller range of controls often detect a sex gap in training (to the detriment of women) that may be missed in less well-specified models (Dieckhoff & Steiber, 2011; Gronland, 2012; Knoke & Ishio, 1998).

Does Job Training Pay?

There is an enormous literature on the economic returns to training. While there have been significant sociological contributions to this body of research, economists have by far accounted for the largest share of this work. To a great degree, the econometric models estimated by economists and sociologists are essentially the same. The assumptions underlying these models and the behavioral interpretations made of the parameter estimates, however, are typically quite different. Thus, we will not review the economics literature in any depth, but refer the reader instead to some exemplary reviews of the economics of training (e.g., Nilsson, 2010). We will instead provide a general overview of the sociological literature.

Determining the value of training requires resolving several conceptual and methodological issues. First, analysts need to determine whether the beneficiaries of training are workers, employers, or a broader public (e.g., states, regions, or nations). Ideally, of course, all parties would benefit, but there is no a priori reason to expect all to benefit equally (or at all) from training. Second, issues of nonrandom selection into both occupations (which have different likelihoods of providing avenues to training) and training programs come into play in the evaluation of training programs. Researchers have become increasingly aware that some part of the apparent effect of training may be due to the characteristics of those who participate in various kinds of training programs. Third, there are many kinds of training that are provided for many different reasons, and there is little reason to think that these are equally effective, particularly when the goals of training are often quite different. Fourth, training is an inherently longitudinal enterprise. While excellent panel data with information on training are now readily available, many earlier analyses of training relied on cross-sectional data, making any imputation of cause and effect suspect.

The general conclusion from the research on the returns to training seems clear – most training is of some value most of the time and under most conditions. Workers are better off when their skills have been enhanced, and their employers are better off with more skilled employees. As with all generalizations, this one has its caveats. The conditions under which this is true, and how true it is, are complicated.

If we think of the effectiveness of training as the extent to which it leads to higher pay, more job security, and other valued employment outcomes, then training is of the most value to those who are already in relatively skilled employment. As Holzer (2013) has observed, "Evaluation evidence shows that training programs linked to employers and good-paying jobs are often cost-effective." Workers with a solid base of skill and experience on which to build are more able to translate training into increased chances of promotion and wage gains than are less skilled and less experienced workers. In contrast, training works less well for those without jobs at all. In general, training helps people do their jobs better and be rewarded for this, but it is less successful at putting people into jobs. Not surprisingly, training even less often leads people into what would generally be regarded as "good" jobs. The experience of training programs for the unemployed is mixed but not terribly positive. This is the case both for new labor market entrants trying to negotiate the school to work transition, and for those who already have some labor force experience.

An interesting study by Heinrich et al. (2013) estimated the impacts on the earnings and employment of program participants of the two primary adult workforce support and training programs under the U.S. Workforce Investment Act (WIA). One of these programs was directed at workers who had been dislocated from their jobs, while the other was aimed at adult workers who already held jobs. In both cases programs participants showed measurable gains. These gains were, however, significantly smaller for the Dislocated Worker Assistance program participants than for WIA Adult Employment and Training Activities participants, who typically came in with poor work histories. Andersson et al. (2013) reported a similar finding, although in their study the wage and employment effects for dislocated workers were basically insignificant.

Does training pay off at the company level? The empirical evidence is that under most conditions, employers too benefit from providing training to their workers. Training leads to productivity growth at the firm level. The positive relationship between training and firm-level productivity does not, however, hold across the board. Nilsson (2010) reported that "training on average has positive economic effects. However, these effects are not universal. Training does not automatically increase productivity and increasing productivity does not necessarily translate into increased profitability" (256). Nilsson also found that the training that does increase productivity of firms is more likely to be designed for more high-level skills and employees such as managers or other white-collar workers rather than vocational training. Further, the benefits to employers seem to be especially strong when training is combined with investments in technology (Boothby, Dufour, & Tang, 2010) or when accompanied by "high performance" policies and practices (O'Connell & Byrne, 2012).

Nilsson (2010) and others (Bassi et al., 2000; Finegold & Levine, 1997) have observed, often with some consternation, that the whole infrastructure of workplace training is typically rather opaque to employers. Very few companies actually measure the productivity results of the training they provide, and very few really have clear conceptions of either the costs or the benefits of their investments in training. The finding that employer knowledge of the impact of training is so flawed and piecemeal challenges the claim of HCT (Becker, 1964) that employer behavior is primarily rational and instrumental, leaving the door open for a conception of training that sees it as more socially embedded in organizational life. As we discuss in more detail in the final section of this essay, the importance of training often goes beyond its instrumental role in enhancing skills and by extension company productivity.

Summary

As the previous sections showed, enrollment in training is highly stratified by earlier forms of skills and credentials. Workers with higher-level qualifications and those with higher-level skills are more likely to enroll in formal training programs than workers with lower-level credentials or lower levels of cognitive skill or ability. This suggests a "complementarity" of education, skills, and training, rather than a "substitution" that would emerge if training were mainly offered to lower-skilled workers to compensate for a lack of competences. If those with higher-level qualifications are afforded the opportunity to further advance their careers, then at least part of the growing inequalities across the life course between higher and lower educated workers may be explained by differences in training incidence and effects. These "Matthew Effects," discussed previously, emerge when earlier advantages are translated into further advantage across the life course (DiPrete & Eirich, 2006).

There are various explanations for this complementarity effect. These explanations include more efficient learning among more highly educated workers, their supposedly higher "taste" for career improvement, and an interest of employers in retaining highly skilled workers to avoid loss of specialized skill. These factors may also explain why employers are not only willing to pay for highly specialized training that would only benefit their own organization (or industry), but also for more general training programs, such as those designed to improve the self-realization of professional workers, or to acquire general management skills (Acemoglu & Pischke, 1999). The standard human capital model of general and specific skills does not adequately explain such training enrollment patterns.

Workplace Training across Countries

In this section, we examine whether there are cross-national differences in training enrollment and training effects on career outcomes. Following the complementarity-substitution dichotomy, we first ask who participates in training to determine whether the Matthew Effect is universal. That is, we review research to determine whether the pattern of complementarity of earlier skill acquisition and further training is found across many Western countries. Is it true that the better educated are the ones who are enrolled in further training everywhere? This perspective examines the existence of complementarity versus substitution at the *individual level*.

Second, we are interested in the complementarity-substitution dichotomy at the *country level*. Is it true that organizations try to compensate for a lack of specific skills generated in the educational institutions in their society? If more training emerges in countries with educational systems that are weakly connected to the labor market, we can speak of a form of substitution, or compensation, for an initial lack of skills by means of adult training. If, by contrast, training enrollment is higher in societies with educational systems that can be characterized by a strong connection between education and the labor market, the already superior education-based skills acquired in such systems translate in further skill advantage of these economies. An association between initial education quality and training enrollment at the country level could then point to "Matthew Effects" where inequality is more strongly accumulating in some countries than in others.

Third, we discuss the economic returns to training in comparative perspective. Does training pay off everywhere to the same extent?

Who Participates in Job Training?

Training participation is widespread in many countries. Data from the 2007 Adult Education Survey shows that, across 26 European countries, 6.3% of adults participated in some form of formal training, and 16.9% in any form of informal training in the 12 months prior to the survey (Blossfeld et al., 2014). Based on the European Union Labor Force Survey 2003, but restricted to the labor force instead of all adults, O'Connell and Jungblut (2008) report higher incidences, with informal training participation varying between 46% in Denmark and 6% in Italy. Yet higher participation rates are reported in the recent international Adult Skill Survey of 2012, with participation rates among adults in a given year varying between 65% in Scandinavian countries, 59% in the United States, and 25% in Italy (OECD, 2014).

Certainly, some of these large differences in rates of participation across societies are due to vastly different conceptualizations and measurements of training. Still, there are some common patterns in the cross-national differences in training participation. Participation in training (both formal and informal) is highest in the Scandinavian countries, intermediate in Western Europe, and lowest in Southern, Central, and Eastern Europe (Bassanini et al., 2005; Blossfeld et al., 2014; Roosmaa & Saar, 2010).

Moreover, participation in training is on the rise. O'Connell and Jungblut (2008) show that, between 1993 and 1999, the percentage of firms that offered some form of training rose from 52% to 64% across 133 European countries. In some countries, the provision of training is almost universal from the organizational perspective, with 91% of Swedish firms offering training.

The rise of training throughout Europe fits with an increased focus on lifelong learning in educational and economic policy. Green (2002: 624) sees a cross-national convergence of the policy discourse on lifelong learning, with a strong emphasis on "choice, diversification, flexibility and decentralization." Analyzing documents written under the auspices of UNESCO, Biesta (2006) notes that training and lifelong learning are increasingly framed from the perspective of economic productivity instead of personal fulfillment. According to critics of the lifelong learning agenda, a mantra is emerging in advanced economies, particularly in Europe, that emphasizes that more training is necessary for the (rapidly changing) economy. Training is, according to the proponents of lifelong learning, a prerequisite for the adaptation of the stock of human capital to the needs imposed by rapidly changing technology. From a sociological perspective such mantras (or "myths") could emerge even if there is no evidence that the economy benefits from such decentralized and diversified forms of skill acquisition (Meyer & Rowan, 1977; Wolf, 2002).

Turning from overall participation rates to societal-level *inequalities* in participation by skill or education level, the complementarity between education and training is widespread. Even in the most "training-egalitarian" countries, the odds of being enrolled in training are twice as high for college graduates as they are for high school graduates. In the most unequal countries the odds ratio rises to around eight in favor of college graduates (Roosmaa & Saar, 2010; cf. O'Connell & Jungblut, 2008). Overall participation rates are pretty similar between men and women in European countries, but when labor market variables are added women have lower participation rates than men (Dieckhoff & Steiber, 2011). This study also showed that the education gradient in training participation is similar between men and women.

Despite the consistent pattern of complementarity, inequalities by education level seem to be smaller in countries with higher overall participation rates (O'Connell & Jungblut, 2008; Roosmaa & Saar, 2010). This pattern is, however, mainly because high-participation countries are all very egalitarian in terms of access of different education groups. Among low-participating countries there is much more variability in the inequality in participation, with low levels of inequalities in the Czech Republic, the Netherlands, and Hungary, and much higher levels of inequality in the Baltic States (Roosmaa & Saar, 2010).

Clearly overall participation rates do not provide sufficient insight into cross-national patterns of inequality. Therefore, we now turn to an exploration of contextual influences on training incidence and inequalities by education/skill groups.

Who Participates in Job Training (across Countries)?

An important source for cross-national variation in training enrollment stems from the educational system. One important empirical regularity is that training enrollment is on average lower in countries with a stronger VET sector (Bosch & Charest, 2008; Brunello, 2004; O'Connell & Jungblut, 2008). This pattern points to a substitutive effect of training systems that "repair" the failure in the provision of work-relevant skills in the initial education system. Studies in political economy have emphasized that there are two equilibria for skills provision, and the emergence of one equilibrium versus the other depends on broader institutional and coordination arrangements (Busemeyer & Trampusch, 2012; Estevez-Abe et al., 2001; Iversen & Soskice, 2001). A specific-skill equilibrium emerges in coordinated market economies often found in continental Europe, where employers' organizations, trade unions, and the state coordinate employment relations in institutions placed at some distance to the market. Such coordination institutions make it possible to develop "joint deals" covering specific skill provision in the educational system in the interest of employers, and employment protection in the interest of employees. Workers are willing to invest in specific skills in the VET system, thereby restricting the pool of jobs for which they would be well-educated, but only if employers offer employment protection in return.

In liberal market economies, by contrast, employment relations are more directly affected by market functioning. In these societies, typically found in Anglo-Saxon countries, VET systems are only weakly developed, as workers are not interested in restricting their employment opportunities if there is weak protection in the labor market. The consequence of this general skill model is that employers have to provide training to get a skilled workforce. Empirical research has shown that strong VET systems, in particular in combination with strong employment protection legislation, are associated with lower youth unemployment rates, thereby smoothing the transition from school to work (Breen, 2005). So, liberal market economies not only face the challenge to provide training to workers, but also must incorporate school leavers into employment. Clearly that last challenge is more difficult to repair with increased training provision on the job, as employers are not offering training to people who are not working for them. Blossfeld et al. (2014) report that training enrollment is further enhanced in countries with adult education policies, but also by more general measures of education such as education expenditure.

The size and strength of the VET system is not only related to average levels of training participation, but also to lower inequalities in participation by educational attainment (Brunello, 2004; Busemeyer & Trampusch, 2012). One could see this pattern as another piece of evidence for a substitutive effect of VET institutions, as it is not the highest educated who are offered training. Inequalities in training participation between education groups are particularly high in Southern Europe, especially in formal employer sponsored forms (Blossfeld et al., 2014). Importantly, studies have highlighted that educational gradients in training participation may be primarily understood through differences in organizational or occupational characteristics (O'Connell & Byrne, 2012; Schindler et al., 2011). Skills would then mostly have indirect effects on training participation through the placement in training-rich organizations and occupations. To the extent that this is the case, also cross-national patterns may be explained by cross-national differences in the strength of school-work linkages, but we are not aware of any evidence in that direction. Also, the finding that training incidence is larger in countries with higher participation rates in higher education (Bassanini et al., 2005) can potentially be explained by the occupational structure.

Recent evidence suggests that VET systems do a much better job in smoothing the transition from school to work than in keeping older workers in employment. Hanushek, Woessmann, and Zhang (2011) argue that VET systems are associated with smooth transitions in the beginning of the career, but those same systems strongly stratify the likelihood of being employed after age 50. Older workers with vocational qualifications are much more likely to be out of employment than older workers with general education. If this pattern is true, which has yet to be confirmed with longitudinal data, it suggests that training in the mid- to late career is essential in systems with strong vocational education. Wolbers (2005) showed with European data that older workers in vocational systems are more likely to be enrolled in training than older workers in general education systems.

Does Job Training Pay?

From a human capital perspective one would expect that training helps further careers, and should thus be related to higher wages and faster career progression across countries. Comparative work suggests, however, that the returns to training are far from consistent. A three-country comparison showed that training reduced the odds of unemployment, and increased the odds of finding employment, only in Germany and not in Denmark and the United Kingdom (Dieckhoff, 2007). Career improvement (finding a higher-level job) was associated with training in Germany and Denmark, but not in the United Kingdom. Furthermore, a multination comparison showed that the wage returns to formal training (i.e., leading to a certificate) were zero once earlier educational attainment and skills were controlled (Triventi & Barone, 2014). Returns to nonformal training (without a certificate) was positive in most countries, however.

Thus, despite the strong evidence of an association between the strength of the VET system and (inequalities in) training enrollment, there is much weaker evidence for cross-national differences in effects of training on career outcomes.

Summary and Future Research

Together this suggests that there is complementarity between prior skills and participation in training within countries, and substitution between countries. That is, within countries we see that the best educated *individuals* are typically enrolled in training more often than workers with less education, while *countries* seem to be able to compensate a lack of work-specific skills generated in initial education. This is understandable given that the explanations for complementarity (within countries) reflect efficiency in the eyes of employers (leading to larger inequalities *within* countries); while the substitution between countries can be explained by the same logic of efficiency, but now potentially leading to lower inequalities *between* countries.

Future research could more explicitly spell out the within- and between-country inequality effects of training. Such a research agenda could build upon research questions on the Matthew Effects generated within systems, and substitution effects across countries, in relation to returns to training. Importantly, the within- and between-country inequality effects could emerge even if the returns to training were invariant between countries and individuals.

Other Sociological Research on Workplace Training

In this final section, we discuss a few contributions to the sociology of workplace training that go beyond the traditional concerns with participation in and outcomes of job training. We believe that these topics merit greater attention and open up important areas for further research.

The Lived Experiences of Trainees and Employers

A few sociologists have been less concerned with the utilitarian or economic value of workplace training and have focused instead on the ways in which training is embedded in the social, political, and cultural life of organizations. Ethnographer Charles Darrah (actually an anthropologist rather than a sociologist) argued that organizational training must be seen more broadly than merely as instrumental activity conducted within the walls of a firm. Darrah held that training may impart useful skills, but could play a key role in day to day organizational life. His case study of the pseudonymous "Kramden Computers" delineated how different parties to training (e.g., production workers, trainers, support staff trainers, production floor management) derived different things (e.g., power, status, autonomy) from their involvement in company training. In the company that Darrah studied, control over training exposed shifting power differentials among organizational actors. Employees in Kramden Computers showed great ingenuity in using their control of the training function to enhance their standing in the company hierarchy.

Case studies by sociologists Ducey, Gautney, and Wetzel (2003), Boyle and Boguslaw (2003), and Paap (2003) have likewise dug beneath the surface of econometric models of workplace training to provide rich insights into how training is implicated in the distribution of power, identity, and status in organizations. Ducey et al. (2003), for instance, focused not on training outcomes, but rather on "the political and economic context that produced this [communication skills training] course and how the instructor, curriculum, and participated enacted and transformed it" (2007: 49). Such careful studies at the level of the workplace can do much to provide a fuller sociological understanding of the complexity of workplace training.

The Failure of Diversity Training

An impressive program of research by sociologists Alexandra Kalev, Frank Dobbin, and their colleagues has asked why the substantial amounts of money that corporations have spent on diversity training has done so little to change the attitudes and behaviors of the employees who have undergone the training (Dobbin, Kim, & Kalev, 2011; Kalev, Dobbin, & Kelly, 2006). After a careful analysis of a range of empirical data, they conclude that the ways in which many organizations have gone about implementing diversity training are in themselves responsible for the limited success, or even outright failure, of this training. Specifically, the fact that diversity training is typically mandatory, with an implicit assumption of discriminatory bias on the part of those being trained, often leads participants to reject the training. The authors show that diversity training may backfire when corporations fail to pay attention to the motivations and beliefs of its recipients.

We would welcome research that examines how managers frame, package, and deliver training to workers and how this presentation is interpreted and lived by workers. Such research would be an exceptional opportunity for sociologists to draw on the insights of scholars of other disciplines who have written extensively on diversity training. Scholarship well represented by the series of papers assembled by Bell and Kravitz in *Academy of Management Learning and Education* (2008), for example, have been neglected by sociologists, despite their obvious relevance to the concerns raised by Kalev, Dobbin, and others.

Should We Make or Should We Buy?

Organizational researchers, particularly specialists in strategic management, have long recognized that firms have to make choices between acquiring resources from outside of their own boundaries, or producing these resources themselves. Sociologists have begun to apply this distinction between the decision of whether to outsource or "grow one's own" to the study of workplace training. Knoke and Janowiec-Kurle (1999) used the National Organizations Survey (described in the preceding text) to identify several organizational and individual characteristics that were associated with the strategies that employers used to assemble a skilled workforce. An interesting study of Korean employers by Chang (2003) found significant effects of organizational factors on employer decisions between making and buying skilled workers, although these fit no obvious patterns.

Bellman et al. (2014; also Bellman & Janik, 2007) show that the "make or buy" decision between hiring from the outside and training provided within can be a complex one, often involving far more than a simple dichotomous option. They found that German employers had to decide between five hiring alternatives: new trainees, external unskilled staff, external skilled staff with initial vocational education, technicians and master craftsmen, and external staff with higher education. Among their most important findings were that companies with low turnover, high employee retention, and a reliance on firm-specific skills were especially likely to "make" their own employees. Technological and market factors were less important determinants of how employers assembled more or less skilled labor forces.

This sort of careful attention to the contingencies faced by organizational decision makers opens up a promising avenue for sociological research on workplace training. Particularly in the emerging American employment environment of shrinking training budgets and an increased focus on hiring from the outside rather than promoting from within, we need to know more about what it is that employers value about training and how they go about allocating the resources to implement it.

Conclusion

Workplace training is a critical aspect of skill development at the level of individual workers, specific organizations, regions, and national economies. The sociology of workplace training has elucidated the determinants of who participates in training programs and episodes, what sorts of employers are most likely to provide training, and the outcomes of training for both workers and their employers. Much of this research is based on quantitative panel data and sophisticated statistical modeling. Other sociological research, relying more on organizational case studies and qualitative methodologies, has delineated the micro- and meso-level processes in which training is embedded in the work setting. We argue for more research using both designs, and encourage sociologists to work toward a more coherent and comprehensive theoretical and conceptual grounding of workplace training.

References

Acemoglu, D., and Pischke, J. 1999. Beyond Becker: Training in imperfect labour markets. *The Economic Journal* 109(453): F112–F142.

Andersson, F., Holzer, H. J., Lane, J. I., Rosenblum, D., and Smith, J. 2013. Does federally-funded job training work? Nonexperimental estimates of WIA training impacts using longitudinal data on workers and firms. Working Paper 19446. Cambridge MA: National Bureau of Economic Research.

Bailey, T., Jaggars, S., and Jenkins, D. 2015. *Redesigning America's Community Colleges: A Clearer Path to Student Success*. Cambridge, MA: Harvard University Press.

Bassanini, A., Booth, A. L., Brunello, G., De Paola, M., and Leuven, E. 2005. Workplace training in Europe (SSRN Scholarly Paper No. ID 756405). Rochester, NY: Social Science Research Network.

Bell, M. P., and Kravitz, D. A. 2008. From the guest co-editors: What do we know and need to learn about diversity education and training? *Academy of Management Learning & Education* 7: 301–308.

Bellmann, L., Grunau, P., Troltsch, K., and Walden, G. 2014. Make or buy: Train in-company or recruit from the labour market? *Empirical Research in Vocational Education and Training* 6(9).

Bellmann, L., and Janik, F. 2007. To recruit skilled workers or to train one's own? Vocational training in the face of uncertainty as to the rate of retention of trainees on completion of training. *Zeitschrift für ArbeitsmarktForschung - Journal for Labour Market Research, Institut für Arbeitsmarkt- und Berufsforschung (IAB), Nürnberg [Institute for Employment Research, Nuremberg, Germany]* 40(2/3): 205–220.

Biesta, G. 2006. What's the point of lifelong learning if lifelong learning has no point? On the democratic deficit of policies for lifelong learning. *European Educational Research Journal* 5(3–4): 169–180.

Bills, D. B., ed. 2003. *The Sociology of Job Training. Research in the Sociology of Work* 12. Elsevier Publishing.

Bills, D. B., and Randy Hodson. 2007. Worker training: A review, critique, and extension. *Research in Social Stratification and Mobility* 25: 258–272.

Bloom, D. 2010. Programs and policies to assist high school dropouts in the transition to adulthood. *The Future of Children* 20: 89–108.

Blossfeld, H., Kilpi-Jakonen, E., Vono de Vilhena, D., and Buchholz, S., eds. 2014. *Adult Learning in Modern Societies: An International Comparison from a Life-Course Perspective.* Cheltenham, UK: Edward Elgar.

Boothby, D., Dufour, A., and Tang, J. 2010. Technology adoption, training and productivity performance. *Research Policy* 39: 650–661.

Bosch, G., and Charest, J. 2008. Vocational training and the labour market in liberal and coordinated economies. *Industrial Relations Journal* 39(5): 428–447.

Boyle, M. E., and Boguslaw, J. 2003. Job training as business and community development: Reframing theory and practice. In D. Bills, ed., *The Sociology of Job Training, Research in the Sociology of Work* 12: 103–137. Boston, MA: Elsevier/JAI Press.

Breen, R. 2005. Explaining cross-national variation in youth unemployment: Market and institutional factors. *European Sociological Review* 21(2): 125–134.

Brunello, G. 2004. Labour market institutions and the complementarity between education and training in Europe. In D. Checchi and C. Lucifora, eds., *Education, Training and Labour Market Outcomes in Europe*, 188–210. Basingstoke: Palgrave MacMillan.

Busemeyer, M. R. and Trampusch, C., eds. 2012. *The Political Economy of Collective Skill Formation.* Oxford University Press.

CEDEFOP 2008. *Terminology of Europeaneducation and training policy. A selection of 100 key terms. Director.* European Centre for the Development of Vocational Training. Luxembourg: Office for Official Publications of the European Communities.

Chang, W. 2003. Hiring and training in Korean establishments: Do employers substitute making for buying? In D. Bills, ed., *The Sociology of Job Training, Research in the Sociology of Work* 12: 31–48. Boston, MA: Elsevier/JAI Press.

Dieckhoff, M. 2007. Does it work? The effect of continuing training on labour market outcomes: A comparative study of Germany, Denmark, and the United Kingdom. *European Sociological Review* 23(3): 295–308.

Dieckhoff, M., and Steiber, N. 2011. A re-assessment of common theoretical approaches to explain gender differences in continuing training participation. *British Journal of Industrial Relations* 49: s135–s157.

DiPrete, T. A., and Eirich. G. M. 2006. Cumulative advantage as a mechanism for inequality: A review of theoretical and empirical developments. *Annual Review of Sociology* 32: 271–297.

Dobbin, F., Kim, S., and Kalev. A. 2011. You can't always get what you need: Why diverse firms adopt diversity programs. *American Sociological Review* 76: 386–411.

Dougherty, K. 2003. The uneven distribution of employee training by community colleges: Description and explanation. *Annals of the American Academy of Political and Social Science* 586: 62–91.

Dougherty, K., and Bakia, M. 2000. Community colleges and contract training: Content, origins, and impacts. *Teachers College Record* 102 (1): 197–243.

Ducey, A. M., Gautney, H., and Wetzel, D. 2003. Regulating affective labor: Communication skills training in the health care industry. In D. Bills, ed., *The Sociology of Job Training, Research in the Sociology of Work* 12: 49–72. Boston, MA: Elsevier/JAI Press.

Estevez-Abe, M., Iversen, T., and Soskice, D. 2001. Social protection and the formation of skills: A reinterpretation of the welfare state. In P.A. Hall and D. Soskice, eds., *Varieties of Capitalism: The Institutional Foundations of Comparative Advantage*, 145–183. Oxford, UK: Oxford University Press.

Felstead, A., and Jewson, N. 2014. 'Training floors' and 'training ceilings': Metonyms for understanding training trends. *Journal of Vocational Education & Training* 66(3): 296–310.

Finegold, D., and Levine, D. L. 1997. Institutional incentives for employer training. *Journal of Education and Work* 10(2): 109–127.

Green, A. 2002. The many faces of lifelong learning: Recent education policy trends in Europe. *Journal of Education Policy* 17(6): 611–626.

Hanushek, E. A., Woessmann, L., and Zhang, L. 2011. General education, vocational education, and labor-market outcomes over the life-cycle. *National Bureau of Economic Research*. Retrieved April 10, 2013.

Heinrich, C. J., Mueser, P. R., Troske, K. R., Jeon, K., and Kahvecioglu, D. C. 2013. Do public employment and training programs work? *IZA Journal of Labor Economics* 2: 1–23.

Hoeckel, K., and Schwartz, R. 2010. *Learning for Jobs: OECD Reviews of Vocational Education and Training: Germany*. Paris, France: Office of Economic Cooperation and Development.

Holzer, H. J. 2013. *Good Workers for Good Jobs: Improving Education and Workforce Systems in the US*. Institute for Research on Poverty Discussion Paper No. 1404-13. Madison, WI: University of Wisconsin-Madison.

Iversen, T., and Soskice, D. 2001. An asset theory of social policy preferences. *The American Political Science Review* 95(4): 875–893.

Jacoby, D. 1991. The transformation of industrial apprenticeship in the United States. *Journal of Economic History* 52(4): 887–910.

Jardine, R. 2012. A brief history of legal education in America: From apprenticeships and back again? *The Docket* (October): 1–3.

Kalev, A., Dobbin, F., and Kelly, E. 2006. Best practices or best guesses? Assessing the efficacy of corporate affirmative action and diversity policies. *American Sociological Review* 71: 589–617.

Knoke, D., and Ishio, Y. 1998. The gender gap in company job training. *Work and Occupations* 25: 141–167.

Knoke, D., and Janowiec-Kurle, L. 1999. Make or buy? The externalization of company job training. *Research in the Sociology of Organizations* 16: 85–106.

Knoke, D., and Kalleberg, A. L. 1994. Job training in U.S. organizations. *American Sociological Review* 59: 537–546.

Lang, K., and Weinstein, R. 2012. Evaluating student outcomes at for-profit colleges. Working Paper 18201. Cambridge, MA: National Bureau of Economic Research.

McDuffie, J. P., and Kochan, T. A. 1995. Do U.S. firms invest less in human resources? Training in the world auto industry. *Industrial Relations* 34: 147–168.

Merton, R. K. 1973. The Matthew effect in science. In N. W. Storer, ed., *The Sociology of Science*, 439–459. Chicago, IL: University Chicago Press.

Meyer, J. W., and Rowan, B. 1977. Institutionalized organizations: Formal structure as myth and ceremony. *American Journal of Sociology* 83(2): 340–363.

Moodie, G. 2002. Identifying vocational education and training. *Journal of Vocational Education and Training* 54(2): 249–266.

Nilsson, A. 2010. Vocational education and training – an engine for economic growth and a vehicle for social inclusion? *International Journal of Training and Development* 14(4): 251–272.

O'Connell, P. J., and Byrne, D. 2012. The determinants and effects of training at work: Bringing the workplace back in. *European Sociological Review* 28(3): 283–300.

O'Connell, P., and Jungblut, J. 2008. What do we know about training at work? In K.U. Mayer and H. Solga, eds., *Skill Formation: Interdisciplinary and Cross-National Perspectives*, 109–125. New York, NY: Cambridge University Press.

OECD. 2014. *Education at a Glance 2014*. Paris, France: Organization for Economic Cooperation and Development.

Paap, K. 2003. Voluntarily put themselves in harm's way: The "bait and switch" of safety training in the construction industry. In D. Bills, ed., The Sociology of Job Training, Research in the Sociology of Work 12: 197–227. Boston, MA: Elsevier/JAI Press.

Protsch, P., and Solga, H. 2016. The social stratification of the German VET system. *Journal of Education and Work* 29: 637–661.

Roosmaa, E., and Saar, E. 2010. Participating in non-formal learning: patterns of inequality in EU-15 and the new EU-8 member countries. *Journal of Education and Work* 23: 179–206.

Schindler, S., Weiss, F., and Hubert, T. 2011. Explaining the class gap in training: the role of employment relations and job characteristics. International Journal of Lifelong Education 30(2): 213–232.

Triventi, M., and Barone, C. 2014. Returns to adult learning in comparative perspective. In H-P. Blossfeld, E. Kilpi-Jakonen, D. Vono de Vilhena, and S. Buchholz, eds., *Adult Learning in Modern Societies. An International Comparison from a Life-Course Perspective*, 56–76. Cheltenham, UK: Edward Elgar.

Wolbers, M. H. J. 2005. Initial and further education: Substitutes or complements? Differences in continuing education and training over the life-course of European workers. *International Review of Education* 51(5–6): 459–478.

Wolf, A. 2002. *Does Education Matter? Myths about Education and Economic Growth*. London: Penguin.

Index

Academy of Human Resource Development
(AHRD), 524, 527–30, 537
Academy of Management (AOM), 537
adaptive performance, 75–92
  anticipated vs. unforeseen circumstances
    closed vs. open skills, 89
    cognitive ability, 78–81
    environment, 88
    maximum vs. typical measurement
      contexts, 89–90
    motivational traits, 82–84
    personality, 81–82
    proximal states, 84
    training design, 84–87
  attitudinal training, 91–92
  conceptual relation to transfer, 76–78
  definition, 76
  post-training intervention, 91
adaptive thinking training, 243–44
after-action reviews, 245–46
American Psychological Association, 523
American Society for Training Directors
  (ASTD). *See* Association for Talent
  Development (ATD)
Association for Talent Development (ATD),
  522, 523
attention, 30–32, 159
augmented reality (AR), 278–89, 299, 308
  accelerated learning, 286–87
  definition, 278–80
  embedded training, 281
  feedback, 281–82
  human–machine system interaction, 287–88
  medical uses, 282–86
  social interaction, 288–89
  tunneling effect, 285
automation, 1

behavioral change, 12–13
behavioral modeling training, 444, 458, 459,
  460
Brunswik Symmetry, 129
business school teaching, 495–514
  balancing roles, 507–12

competing commitments, 511
  mindfulness, 510–11
  positivity, 510
class size, 505–06
class time, 506
cultural context, 504
facilities, 505
'guide' role, 497–98
institutional context, 505, 511–12
lectures, 496–97
program culture, 505
quality, 514
relevance to professional trainers, 512–13
'ringmaster' role, 499, 501–02, 503–04, 508
'rockstar' role, 498–99, 501, 502, 503, 508
'sage' role, 498
student knowledge, 506–07
student openness, 506

Cattell-Horn-Carroll theory of ability, 125
codifiability of knowledge, 46
cognitive ability, 123–42, 442, 445
  aptitude-by-treatment interaction, 134–35,
    140, 141–42
  crystallized intelligence, 126, 133
  demographic differences, 177–78
  domain knowledge, 126–27, 130–31, 133,
    138–39
  executive control, 133–34
  fluid intelligence, 125–26, 130–31
  general vs. specific ability, 127–30, 133, 138
  group performance, 136
  historical overview, 124–25
  teamwork, 135–38, 140
  training technologies, 140–41
cognitive frame-changing, 242–43
cognitive load, 235, 331
  extraneous load, 20, 21–22, 23
  germane load, 20, 22
  intrinsic load, 20
communication training, 391
competitive advantage, 41, 42–43, 44, 48, 55,
  481, 545, 546, 547, 548, 549, 550, 551,
  552–53, 556, 557, 558, 560

Lightning Source UK Ltd.
Milton Keynes UK
UKOW05n0321031217
313779UK00014B/290/P